SAGE was founded in 1965 by Sara Miller McCune to support the dissemination of usable knowledge by publishing innovative and high-quality research and teaching content. Today, we publish over 900 journals, including those of more than 400 learned societies, more than 800 new books per year, and a growing range of library products including archives, data, case studies, reports, and video. SAGE remains majority-owned by our founder, and after Sara's lifetime will become owned by a charitable trust that secures our continued independence.

Los Angeles | London | New Delhi | Singapore | Washington DC | Melbourne

WOMEN and WORK in PRECOLONIAL INDIA

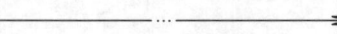

WOMEN and WORK in PRECOLONIAL INDIA

A Reader

Edited by
VIJAYA RAMASWAMY

SAGE

Los Angeles | London | New Delhi
Singapore | Washington DC | Melbourne

First published in 2016 by

SAGE Publications India Pvt Ltd
B1/I-1 Mohan Cooperative Industrial Area
Mathura Road, New Delhi 110 044, India
www.sagepub.in

SAGE Publications Inc
2455 Teller Road
Thousand Oaks, California 91320, USA

SAGE Publications Ltd
1 Oliver's Yard, 55 City Road
London EC1Y 1SP, United Kingdom

SAGE Publications Asia-Pacific Pte Ltd
3 Church Street
#10-04 Samsung Hub
Singapore 049483

Published by Vivek Mehra for SAGE Publications India Pvt Ltd, typeset in 10.5/12.5 pt Times New Roman by Zaza Eunice, Hosur, Tamil Nadu, India, and printed at Chaman Enterprises, New Delhi.

Library of Congress Cataloging-in-Publication Data Available

ISBN: 978-93-515-0741-3 (PB)

SAGE Team: Shambhu Sahu, Sanghamitra Patowary, Megha Dabral and Ritu Chopra

This is for
My Sisters:
Lalita, Tara and Padmini
'We had joy, we had fun,
we had seasons in the sun'
and
For Geeta, Raji and Jaya
My Sisters by Marriage
for the love and acceptance I have received.

Contents

Foreword by Aparna Basu xi
Preface xiii
Acknowledgements xv
Introduction xvii
Vijaya Ramaswamy

Section I: Women and the Household: Canonical Prescriptions and Their Feminist Critique 1

Chapter 1: The Daily Duties of Women 3
Julia Leslie

Chapter 2: Position and Status of Women in the Upaniṣads 9
T. R. Sharma

Chapter 3: Woman in the Household 13
M. A. Indra

Chapter 4: Economic Rights of Ancient Indian Women 22
Sukumari Bhattacharji

Chapter 5: Dynamics of Women's Work in the Śāstric Sources: Household and Beyond 37
Kavita Gaur

Chapter 6: Tracking Economic Transitions: Tamil Women from Tribe to Caste and Changing Production Roles 49
Vijaya Ramaswamy

Chapter 7: The Question of Women's 'Agency': Women, Work and Domesticity in Early Textual Traditions 65
Jaya Tyagi

Section II: Women and Work in Early Textual Traditions 89

Chapter 8: The Woman Worker 91
I. B. Horner

Chapter 9: Of Dasas and Karmakaras: Servile Labour in Ancient India 98
Uma Chakravarti

Chapter 10: Women and Work in Kautilīya's Arthaśāstra 120
Upasana Dhankhar

Section III: Women and Economic Resources: Women's Property Rights 135

Chapter 11: Proprietary Rights during Coverture 137
Anant Sadashiv Altekar

Chapter 12: Proprietary Rights: Inheritance and Partition 150
Anant Sadashiv Altekar

Chapter 13: The Legal Status of Women: Their Right of Inheritance 177
M. A. Indra

Chapter 14: Property Rights of Women in Ancient India 185
N. N. Bhattacharyya

Chapter 15: Turmeric Land: Women's Property Rights in Tamil Society since Early Medieval Times 195
Kanakalatha Mukund

Chapter 16: Property Rights of Women in Medieval Andhra 209
A. Padma

Section IV: Contextualising Women's Work in the Public Domain 215

Chapter 17: State of the Field: Perspectives on Women and Work in Early South India 217
Vijaya Ramaswamy

Chapter 18: Women's Professions in Medieval Andhra 243
A. Padma

Chapter 19: Temple Women and Work in Medieval Kēraḷam 259
Anna Varghese

Chapter 20: Gender, Caste and Labour: Ideological and Material Structure of Widowhood 277
Uma Chakravarti

Chapter 21: Work and Gender in Mughal India 310
Shireen Moosvi

Section V: Devaradiya: Hand-maidens of God or Sex-workers? 327

Chapter 22: Courtesans 329
Vatsyayana Mallanaga

Chapter 23: Temple Women as Temple Servants 352
Leslie Orr

Chapter 24: In the Business of Kama: Prostitution in Classical Sanskrit Literature from the Seventh to the Thirteenth Centuries 392
Shalini Shah

Chapter 25: Prostitution in Ancient India 418
Sukumari Bhattacharji

About the Editor and Contributors 443

Foreword

It is with some hesitation that I write this Foreword. Firstly, because I am not a scholar of ancient and medieval India with which this volume is largely concerned and secondly, because I am not a labour historian. I agreed to write at the insistence of Professor Vijaya Ramaswamy for whose scholarship and dedication to her work, I have the greatest admiration and respect. She asked me perhaps because I have worked extensively in the area of women's history, but of colonial and contemporary India.

The majority of women in every country and in all ages have usually been workers. Their participation as workers has always been necessary for social and economic development. In all societies, they are usually involved in household activities such as child rearing, cooking, cleaning, fetching water and fuel and care of the elderly and sick. This kind of work is not recognised as work but as a woman's duty. Women have worked outside the home as well, especially in the domain of craft work and labour. Women's participation as workers in the public sphere increased in Europe and Great Britain after World Wars I and II when men were fighting and women had to work in factories and offices.

In India, with women's participation in the freedom struggle and growing women's education and awareness, women started emerging out of the kitchen and began to take their place alongside men as supplementary breadwinners. Today, women can be seen as doctors, lawyers, journalists, architects, in the media and in almost every profession. However, as wage earners or self-employed entrepreneurs, they continue to be responsible for their domestic duties. Thus, women bear a double burden, unless they are affluent and can afford domestic help. They have to balance their jobs with looking after the children and other housework. Therefore, women suffer from a sense of guilt about their inability to do adequate justice to either their jobs or their duty as homemakers.

The 1980s and 1990s were the decades of great creativity in Indian labour history. Study of labour moved from trade unions to a study of workers themselves. The growing interest in labour history led to the first conference devoted to Indian labour history at the International Institute of Social History in Amsterdam in 1995 and the founding of the Association of Indian Labour Historians in the following year. The dynamism of the intellectual horizons of Indian labour history in that period is captured in the work of three labour historians—Raj Chandavarkar, Dipesh Chakravarti and Chitra Joshi.

In the majority of labour histories, however, till a few decades ago, the presence of women in the domestic or public domain as workers was missing. Their contribution to the household income or the overall economy was absent. Women were represented either as good wives or prostitutes. In more recent times, we have had feminist historians such as Samita Sen, Tanika Sarkar, Chitra Joshi, Bina Agarwal, Jayati Sen, Devaki Jain, Radha Kumar and others who have focused on women's labour.

Women's work when outside the home was sporadic, ill-paid and mostly in the unorganised sector. Even today, 94 per cent of Indian women work in the unorganised sector. Men were regarded as producers, as breadwinners and women as consumers. Men performed work outside the house which was more hazardous, since it was believed that outside work required physical strength. Men's work was considered to be the opposite of women's work.

This volume is a scholarly study of women's unrecorded presence in the household economy as well in the wider production process. It covers a vast historical span and links the theme of woman and work from ancient to late medieval India. It stops at the beginning of colonial rule in Indian history, as feminist economic historians have worked on this theme.

This anthology is perhaps the first of its kind in mapping ways of looking at women and work in precolonial India through essays by distinguished scholars drawing on a variety of sources such as the Upanishads, Arthashastra and other epigraphical records as well as literary works and canonical texts. It deals with themes such as changing production role of Tamil women from tribe to caste, women's property rights in ancient and medieval India, devadasis and prostitution in precolonial India and various other issues.

The volume provides a panoramic survey of women and work in precolonial India. The authors have salvaged available data on women's paid and unpaid, visible and invisible in order to highlight their contribution work to the economy.

It is a path-breaking book and should be of great interest not only to labour historians, but also to all students of history. I would like to congratulate Professor Vijaya Ramaswamy for her very informative and scholarly Introduction and for bringing out this much needed volume.

Aparna Basu
Formerly Professor of History
University of Delhi

Preface

My mother Sethu Ramaswamy worked all her life and passed away at the ripe old age of 88 in 2012, cooking for the family till the last. In her autobiography *Bride at Ten, Mother at Fifteen* (2003, 2010 and 2013), she wrote that her whole life seemed to consist of endless meals cooked and waiting to be cooked. Yet, she had never been a 'working woman' in the accepted definition of the term. The hours spent in stitching clothes for us because my parents could not afford to buy ready-made garments (expensive in the 1950s) and the time she spent in tutoring us after finishing her household chores made it seem as if her day consisted of more than 24 hours.

As an economic historian with feminist ideas, I realised how very little the work of such 'house wives' was reflected in our social histories. There were, however, instances of 'working women' such as spinsters (women who spun yarn for a living), housemaids and prostitutes in ancient records, literary texts and inscriptions. I began salvaging evidences of women and work from the historical sources available for ancient and medieval India. In the process, I came across the writings of feminist historians like Uma Chakravarti who had made pioneering studies in this area. In more recent times, a number of scholars have begun to seriously engage with the historical material on women and work. Many of these figure in this volume. Courses on 'Women and Work' have also been introduced in the curriculum of women's studies across the country.

It is in this immediate context that this volume was born. This reader addresses the needs of students and scholars who have become participants in the process of 'salvaging' the history of women and work from the grey regions and inner recess of Indian social history where they have been partially but dimly visible.

Since its inception, academic activism within the Indian women's movements has been seen as social activism, and it is hoped that this volume will also be seen as a small but sure step along the long road to redressing gender imbalances in this country.

Vijaya Ramaswamy

Acknowledgements

I am extremely grateful to the following publishers/authors who have allowed the essays to be reprinted in this reader:

Oxford University Press for allowing me to reproduce a brief section from Julia Leslie's book.

The Department of Ancient History and Archaeology, Banaras Hindu University to reproduce the essays from the late R. P. Tripathi edited volume, published by the department. The essays reprinted here in this reader are by late N. N. Bhattacharya and T. R. Sharma.

Indira Chandrasekhar, publisher of Tulika Books, and Uma Chakravarti for their permission to reproduce sections from *Everyday Lives, Everyday Histories: Beyond the Kings and Brahmanas of Ancient India* (2006).

Sudhir Kakkar and Wendy O'Flaherty for extending their permission to publish a chapter from their translation of Vatsyayana's text *Kamasutra.*

Harbans Mukhia of the *Medieval History Journal* and Shalini Shah for extending their permission to reproduce the article 'In the Business of Kama: Prostitution in the Classical Sanskrit Literature from the Seventh to the Thirteenth Centuries'.

Tanika Sarkar for her gracious permission to reproduce two essays on 'Economic Rights of Ancient Indian Women' and 'Prostitution in Ancient India' from her late mother Sukumari Bhattacharji's celebrated book *Women and Society in Ancient India.*

The management of *Economic and Political Weekly* and Kanakalatha Mukund for granting permission to reproduce the essay 'Turmeric Land: Women's Property Rights in Tamil Society since Early Medieval Times'.

Leslie Orr for her ready consent for the reprinting of sections of her chapter 'Temple Women as Temple Servants' from her book *Donors, Devotees and Daughters of God: Temple Women in Medieval Tamilnadu.*

I am also deeply grateful to Professor Shireen Moosvi for giving her consent to reprint her article 'Work and Gender in Mughal India'.

I am grateful to A. Padma for her kind consent to reprint her essays—'Women's Property Rights in Medieval Andhra' and 'Women's Professions in Medieval Andhra' for the present reader.

I would like to specially acknowledge Jaya Tyagi, Kavita Gaur, Anna Varghese and Upasana Dhankar for specifically writing essays for this reader.

I recall with gratitude and reverence I. Horner and M. A. Indra for their remarkable essays written in the early decades of the last century which have been reproduced here for the benefit of young scholars.

I am in debt to Motilal Banarsidass Publishers for permitting the reprint of two chapters from A. S. Altekar's pioneering study *The Position of Women in Hindu Civilization from Prehistoric Times to the Present Day* published in the 1930s, at a nominal fee. I would like to warmly thank Mr B. N. Verma of the Primus Publishing House for negotiating this consent.

My grateful thanks to the SAGE Publications team for making this volume available to our students. Their gracious cooperation has made putting together of this reader a pleasure for me.

Introduction*

VIJAYA RAMASWAMY

Women live like bats and owls, labour like beasts and die like worms...

Margaret, the Duchess of Newcastle, England, circa 1660 CE[1]

In a majority of labour histories till a few decades ago, the presence of women either in the domestic or in the public domain as workers, contributing to the household income or the overall economy, was conspicuous by its absence. Women's work within the household was seen as their 'duty' rather than as 'work', while their work outside the household was sporadic, ill-paid and not part of the formal sector of 'wage-earning' labour. Enforced invisibility or distorted visibility within patriarchal spaces can only be contested through a rigorous study of women's unrecorded presence in the household economy as well as in the broader domain of production. This book is an effort to understand the 'being' and 'doing' of women, to map the interweaving of women and work over a vast historical span of time, beginning with women's writings on the theme of women and work, and going on to historically plot women's agency in labour processes.

Women, as a biological and social category, have been on the margins of history for centuries and the correlation between women and work is its most neglected segment. Women's labour, by and large being considered informal, was neither recognised nor recorded, not just by men but perhaps also by women themselves. History passed them by. To quote Virginia Woolf in her celebrated classic *A Room of One's Own*:

> I saw a very ancient lady crossing the street... And if one asked her, longing to pin down the moment with date and season, what she was doing on the fifth of April, 1868, or the second of November, 1875, she would look vague and say that she could remember nothing. For all the dinners were

* I am extremely grateful to the anonymous reviewer for her invaluable comments which have helped me to revamp this introduction as well as re-organise the text for the benefit of the scholars who would seek to use it.

[1] Quoted in Virginia Woolf, *A Room of One's Own* (London: Hogarth Press, 1974[1929]), 93.

> cooked, the plates and cups washed; the children sent to school and gone into the world. Nothing remains of it. All has vanished. No biography or history has a word to say about it.[2]

Feminist historians have already written much about the absence of women from histories. What is even more offensive to women's sensibilities is their limited and, therefore, distorted inclusion in historical spaces. Women were invariably represented in terms of bi-polarities—either as good wives or as prostitutes, either as pious 'private' women or seductive 'public' women. The presence of women, either in the domestic or in the public domain as workers, contributing to the household income or the overall economy, is conspicuous by its absence within the patriarchal register.

In a thought-provoking article on 'Folklore, Anthropology and Social History', E. P. Thompson talks about the neglect of women's history by historians due to their preoccupations with 'becoming', a process in which 'women are rarely seen as prime agents in political, military or even economic life'.[3] On the other hand, he points out:

> If we are concerned with 'being' then, the exclusion of women would reduce history to futility. We cannot understand the agrarian system of small cultivators without examining inheritance practices, dowry and the familial development cycle.... The economy can only be understood within the context of a society textured in these kinds of ways. The 'public' life arises out of the dense determinations of the 'domestic' life.[4]

To Thompson's statement, I am further adding that the 'domestic' is not distinct and separate from the public. The 'housewifisation' of much of women's labour is a major cause of this dichotomous thinking.

If the problem is seen as vexatious in terms of mapping the history of women and work in colonial India, it is doubly so in the case of precolonial India where women's presence was recorded only in certain normative/stereo-typical ways, leaving out for the most part of their historically marginalised but socially significant contribution to the economy both within the household and outside it, in the public domain of labour. This collection of essays takes the theme of women and work in India from ancient times up to the late-medieval period but stops on the threshold of colonialism except where the authors have found it necessary to provide inter-connections between the precolonial and colonial phases in the perspective of the changing facets of women's work. This anthology stops at the precolonial period because the subsequent period has been, fortunately, covered comparatively better by feminist economic historians.

SITUATING THE THEME OF WOMEN AND WORK IN WESTERN AND INDIAN HISTORIOGRAPHY

In this section, I propose to look at some select contributions to the historiographical trope on women and work, commencing from the pre-historic period, covering the whole of ancient

[2] Woolf, *A Room of One's Own*, 134.

[3] E. P. Thompson, 'Folklore, Anthropology and Social History', *The Indian Historical Review* III, no. 2 (1977).

[4] Thompson, 'Folklore, Anthropology and Social History'.

India up to the eighth century, and concluding with essays focusing on the medieval world of women and work. Since women and work in the colonial period are, technically, out of the frame of the present book, the discussions around this period essentially involve the ways in which scholars of colonial India have studied various ramifications of mapping, quantifying and computing women's work/labour in different economic domains. These insights are relevant since they have been used by the scholars of ancient India and medieval India to understand women and work in the precolonial milieu.

In this chapter, I have plotted out, at some length, the course taken by Western (in the present European context) historiography on women and work. The purpose of such an exercise is not to suggest close parallels in terms of women's work cultures between two very divergent spatial tropes, traditionally described as the 'occident and the orient' and located in entirely different eco-geographical and cultural zones. Rather, in the absence of similar historiographical traditions in the precolonial Indian context, this extensive exercise forays into Western studies on women and work, and is intended to suggest potential areas of analysis and possible methodologies one could employ in explorations into women and work in the Indian context.

The present anthology is perhaps the first of its kind in mapping ways of looking at women and work in precolonial India, through scholarly essays that draw on different kinds of sources, ranging from epigraphical records to literary works and canonical texts. While many of the essays have been reproduced here with the permission of the publisher/authors who are vested with the copyright, quite a few essays have been presented specifically for this book. Since both the scholarly works and historical evidence in the Indian context are few and far between, this chapter seeks to intersperse the history of women and work in the European context with the evidence presented in these essays in the present anthology on similar or related themes.

WOMEN HUNTERS AND WARRIORS: EVIDENCE FROM ARCHAEOLOGY AND LITERARY TEXTS

Archaeologists are struggling to gender work from the sparse evidence available during pre-historical and early historical periods. An intrepid explorer of this area was Margaret Ehrenberg.[5] In 1989, in her book, *Women in Pre-history*, she discussed the importance of women in Palaeolithic and Mesolithic foraging societies[6] in which women not only hunted small animals but gathered plant food such as fruits, nuts, leaves and roots, bulbs and undomesticated wild crops like millets. Since women gathered nearly 80 per cent of the food, Ehrenberg calls them 'major food providers'.[7]

It is noteworthy that women hunters were also a familiar part of the earlier economies on the Indian canvas and the Sangam texts refer to Valli, the consort of the deity of the hilly tracts 'Marudam' as a 'skilled hunter'. This role of women also finds its sculptural

[5] Ehrenberg, *Women in Pre-history*: Oklahoma Classical Cultural Series (University of Oklahoma Press, 1989).
[6] Ibid., 50–62.
[7] Ibid., 52.

representations from around the eighth century, as for instance a sculpture in the temple built by a Pandian king at Vallimalai in North Arcot district of Tamil Nadu. Adrienne Mayor in her book, *The Amazons: Lives and Legends of Warrior Women across the Ancient World*, has interesting information on women hunters and warriors drawing upon sources as varied as the *Mahabharata*, the Puranas and sculptural depictions. There is some information on women warriors and hunters in the *Agni Purana* which describes their proficiency in fencing and archery. Female hunters with bows are depicted in the Bharhut reliefs of the third century BCE from north-eastern India. Full breasted bow women (Svaghni) appear in ancient and medieval carvings on temples at Palitana (north-western India) and in the temple at Bhatkal in Karnataka.[8] Anil K. Tyagi's book, *Women Workers in Ancient India*, makes some references to women who took to hunting.[9]

THE BEGINNINGS OF FARMING AND WOMEN IN AGRICULTURE

Farming became well established in Southwest Asia by 6000 BCE and a little later in South Asia. Ehrenberg points out: 'The discovery of farming techniques has usually been assumed to have been made by men, but it is in fact very much more likely to have been made by women'.[10] The irrefutable logic in this argument lies in the fact that it is women who through their 'gathering' activities first became acquainted with crops that could be domesticated.

My essay in this anthology attempts a brief overview of women in the farming sector in early Tamizhaham (also spelt Tamilaham) roughly defined as the age of the Sangam—the third century BCE to the third century CE—parallel to the megalithic period in Peninsular archaeology. The movement from tribe to caste got reflected in the peasantisation of many tribal groups, referred to in the Sangam texts and in subsequent Tamil inscriptions as '*kudi*'. It appears that, while women played a predominant role in hoe-cultivation, the 'over-determination' of farming characterised by the *Marudam tinai* (arable ecozone) in comparison to the other ecozones such as *Mullai tinai* (pastoral ecozone) and *Kurinji tinai* (forest ecozone) changed gender equations in the agricultural domain. Over a period of 400 years, from the late-Sangam age (third century onwards) to beginnings of state formation under the Pallava and Chola rulers, the Peninsular region witnessed major developments such as the royal donations of Brahmadeya lands to non-cultivating Brahmins and lands to military chiefs under the Chola dynasty. These developments resulted in socio-economic stratification in the agrarian sector, consisting of *kudi* (cultivator-tenants), *kadaisiyar* (land-less agricultural labour) and the rent extracting Brahmin landlords. Inevitably, Brahmanisation also meant the beginnings of patriarchy with women losing their right to handle the plough, although many of the other back-breaking activities in the agricultural sector ranging from

[8] Adrienne Mayor, *The Amazons: Lives and Legends of Warrior Women across the Ancient World* (Princeton, NJ: Princeton University, 2014), 408–09.
[9] Anil K. Tyagi, *Women Workers in Ancient India* (New Delhi: Radha Publications, 1994), 34, 116 and 123.
[10] Ibid., 77.

seeding, transplanting, weeding, irrigating to harvesting were still being handled by women (Ramaswamy, Chapter 6 of this book). These tasks, however, reinforced the patriarchal subordination of women, rather than endowing them with either any significant income or power within the economic domain. The technological transition from hoe to plough agriculture has been recorded as one of the important markers in changing the gender balance within the agricultural domain in the context of traditional Asian (and African) economies, although there are other variables as well, such as changing the societal structure due to Brahmanisation and the beginnings of temple urbanism in both northern and southern India.

This is a major plank of the arguments raised by Ester Boserup in her discursive analysis of *Women's Role in Economic Development*.[11] To quote from Boserup[12]:

> The main farming instrument in those regions, the plough, is used by men helped by draught animals, and only the hand operations—or some of them—are left for women to perform.... The land is prepared for sowing by men using draught animals, and this thorough land preparation leaves little need for weeding the crop, which is usually the women's task. Therefore women contribute mainly to harvest work and to the care of domestic animals.... Sometimes such women perform only purely domestic duties, living in seclusion within their own homes and appearing in the village street only under the protection of the veil, a phenomenon associated with plough culture, and seemingly unknown in regions of shifting cultivation where women do most of the agricultural toil.

At the same time, Boserup made up certain dichotomous categories such as the association of men with cash crops and women with subsistence crops, male dominance deriving from plough agriculture in contra-distinction to women's dominant agency in hoe agriculture and their subsequent marginalisation with the change in technology from hoe to plough.[13] Some of these observations are only partially true and certainly cannot be seen as dichotomous categories. Many of Boserup's observations have been set aside by later-day scholars.[14]

One of the sharpest critiques of Boserup's study on women and work is the observation that, although her work is centred around colonised 'developing' countries such as India, she predominantly uses Western frames of reference. The result of such an approach being 'constructed in poverty, elaborated on negation, African women became passive objects

[11] Ester Boserup, *Woman's Role in Economic Development* (London: Earthscan, Sterling, 2007[1970]), 12–14 of the section 'The Plough, the Veil and the Labourer'.

[12] Ibid., 13–15.

[13] Ibid., 47 ff. For the impact of the technological shift from hoe to plough on the gendering of agricultural labour, see section 'The Plough, the Veil and the Labourer' in Chapter 1 on 'Male and Female Farming Systems', pp. 12–23.

[14] Contrary to her impression that women's participation in labour will decrease in the capitalist set-up, historians have been able to identify what they have called 'feminization of labour' in the age of capitalism and colonialism. This meant increased use of 'cheap' female labour within the rural economic sector on the one hand, and the feminization of even the male work force on the other. As a "fallout of the changing nature of employment where irregular conditions, once thought to be the hallmark of women's 'secondary' employment, have become widespread for both sexes", men also became part of the informal, unorganized sectors of labour (pre-dominantly identified with 'working women') under certain conditions. For a very interesting discussion on 'feminization of labour' read 'Introduction: Boserup Revisited' by the editors Nazneen Kanji, Su Fei Tan and Camilla Toulmin in the 2007 edition of Ibid., ix–xi.

of study, to be poked, prodded and stripped of any redeeming quality and dignity'.[15] Since this criticism would also apply to her analysis of the Asian women, the applicability of her conceptual categories to the Indian historical situation becomes fraught with some tension. Her study is, nevertheless, invaluable because it was one of the pioneering works that sought to look at the Asian and African contexts of women's labour in the agricultural sector.

WOMEN IN THE POTTERY SECTOR IN THE PRE-HISTORIC AND EARLY-HISTORIC PERIODS

Ehrenberg refers to the seminal contribution of women to the linear pottery culture which flourished in Central Europe and South America between 5500 and 4800 BCE.[16] It is worth comparing her statement in the European context with the arguments raised by Indian scholars on craft work.[17] Women in Peninsular India are visible through the Tamil Sangam literature, making pottery and weaving basket in the economy of the Sangam age (circa 300 BCE and 300 CE), a perspective that has been discussed by me in a chapter in this anthology. The presence of women potters was ubiquitous and one of the famous women poets of the Sangam period was Veni Kuyattiyar, and literally 'the potter woman called Veni'.

I would also like to draw attention here to the recent archaeological excavations at Indor Khera (not too far from the famous Harappan site Hatranji Kheda) near Bulandshahr in Uttar Pradesh. The site has yielded both pottery and evidence of potters' dwellings. Archaeologists Supriya Varma and Jaya Menon have studied pottery production within potters' households on the basis of archaeological evidence from Indor Khera.[18] However, they are unable to draw definitive conclusions about women potters from their evidence. Supriya Varma tells me that while it is clear that pottery production involved the whole household, it is not possible to make out the precise gender division of labour. While women would obviously have been involved in kneading the clay and painting the pots, it appears that the potter's wheel may have been wielded exclusively by men although one cannot say this with certainty.[19]

MAPPING WOMEN AND WORK IN THE MEDIEVAL WORLD

How did women perceive the nature of their work within the framework of the many societies present in the medieval European world? Here I would like to examine a few books–the

[15] Julie McCune, 'Problematic Aspects of Ester Boserup's Woman's Role in Economic Development', from the internet site www.africaresource.com, Friday, 16th June 2006, Essays and Discussions.

[16] Ehrenberg, *Women in Pre-history*, 90–91.

[17] Vijaya Ramaswamy, 'The Kudi in Early Tamilaham and Tamil Women from Tribe to Caste' in *From Tribe to Caste*, ed. Dev Nathan (Shimla: Indian Institute of Advanced Study, 1997), 223–46.

[18] Varma and Menon in Kumkum Roy, ed., *Looking Within Looking Without: Exploring Households in the Subcontinent Through Time* (New Delhi: Primus Books, 2015), 19–48.

[19] Conversation with Supriya Varma, Associate Professor, Centre for Historical Studies, Jawaharlal Nehru University, on the possibility of gendering pottery production at Indor Khera, 5th May 2015, Jawaharlal Nehru University, New Delhi.

medieval text *The Treasure of the City of Ladies or the Book of the Three Virtues* written by Christine De Pisan in 1404;[20] and modern works such as Judith Bennet's book *Ale, Beer and Brewsters*[21] and Eileen Power's incisive study of *Medieval Women*[22] which has a major chapter on women and work in medieval Europe. Unfortunately, there are no comparable studies in the Indian context. Quite a few of the essays that have endeavoured to tackle this theme find space in this anthology including the three essays by me, A. Padma and Shireen Moosvi (Chapters 16, 18 and 21, respectively).

In the context of medieval Europe, the effort to record women's histories in the spheres of work and labour had begun way back in the fourteenth century. Christine de Pisan (1365–1430) was a rare presence in medieval Italy—a woman who was a professional writer. She was a renowned poet and the author of a biography of Charles V of France, whose patronage her family had enjoyed. *The Treasure of the City of Ladies* was, however, her most significant work from a gender perspective. Her representation of medieval European women has substantial sections on women's actual and potential contribution to the economy, both within their households and beyond it. Her focus is, however, primarily on the upper class/royal households and not on the common working women. She states that the princess should discuss and supervise the financial health of the state and hold periodic meetings with administrators and revenue collectors. She should try to ensure that there is no unjust tax burden on the poor. She should also similarly maintain a tight supervisory control over the finances of the royal household. Here the work of upper class women is seen primarily as one of regulating the distribution of resources especially food.[23] Of greater interest are her sections on the wives of merchants, artisans and servant maids. She also has a section on the trade of prostitution.

In the section 'Of Wives of Merchants', Pisan points out the affluent lifestyles of the merchants' wives in commercial towns such as Genoa, Venice, Florence, Lucca and Avignon, referring primarily to the merchant wives of the cities along the Mediterranean coast. Pisan makes the point repeatedly that their wealth was obtained not through wholesale trade but through petty retail trade. After deprecating their aping the manner and sartorial habits of the women of noble birth, she concludes by telling the wives of tradesmen: 'If you rich women want to be saved… see that in your business dealings you do not deal fraudulently or deceitfully with your neighbours'.[24] The wives of artisans are advised by Pisan to thoroughly learn the crafts practised by their husbands so that they can continue the business even in the absence of their husbands.[25] Pisan makes the very interesting distinction between the craft groups such as goldsmiths, embroiderers, armourers and tapestry makers who benefit from growing demand and live in cities, on the one hand, and poor crafts families such as

[20] Christine De Pisan, *The Treasure of the City of Ladies or the Book of the Three Virtues*, trans. Sarah Lawson (Penguin Books, Chaucer Press, Suffolk, England, 1985[1404]).

[21] Judith Bennet, *Ale, Beer and Brewsters* (London: Oxford University Press, 1999).

[22] Eileen Power, *Medieval Women*: Cambridge University Series, ed. by M. M. Postan (Cambridge: CUP, 1997).

[23] Pisan, *The Treasure of the City of Ladies*, 76–77.

[24] Ibid., 156.

[25] Ibid., 167–68.

the shoemakers and masons who lead a less comfortable yet socially secure life, on the other hand.[26]

This unique text authored by Pisan has no parallel in the medieval Indian situation. However, the fifteenth century Telugu text *Kreedabhiramamu* of Vinukonda Vallabharayadu, which borders on the erotic, does refer to working women like Teliki (oil mongers) women, Medara (basket makers) women, etc. In fact, the text states that Medara women were so poor that they sometimes took to the profession of prostitution in order to raise their families (Ramaswamy, Chapter 17 of this book). The *Kreedabhiramamu* also refers to small eateries/inns owned by women where a meal cost merely one *ruka*.

A major production sector where women have registered their presence is in the domain of liquor brewing which was usually done at home by women to supplement the family income. Women's work in the sector for the production and sale of liquor is brought out in Judith Bennet's *Ale, Beer and Brewsters*,[27] which looks at the location of the Brewster in the seventeenth century English economy and society. Women at this time were part of the workforce engaged in low-skill jobs, such as ale brewing, which were also poorly paid. Like spinsters, who spun for their living, in the absence of a spouse to support them, the female brewster was also usually unmarried, although married women from low-income families did join the profession. Ale brewing required limited capital and simple equipment and women could work from their homes. However, in the course of the fifteenth century, as ale became transformed into beer, rendering it more profitable, control over its production increasingly passed into the hands of men. Bennet also looks at the late-medieval literature to show that ale-women/wives were seen as cunning cheats whose religion was also suspect since 'they consorted with Jews'. A classic example of such negative portrayals of the brewster was to be found in John Skelton's poem *The Tunning of Eleanour Rummyng*, written in 1517. The obvious logic to this negative portrayal was the male takeover of breweries and the need to eliminate competition from the well-entrenched female brewsters who fought to stay in business despite their lack of capital and other resources.

If one were to compare the European situation with the Indian one, it is noteworthy that, even as early as the Sangam period in South India (300 BCE to 300 CE), the Sangam texts state that women were in charge of brewing of liquor in their homes and their daily door-to-door sale. Women distilled strong liquor from rice soaked in water for several days till it ferments (similar to the Japanese *Saaki*) and also from fruits (see Ramaswamy, Chapters 6 and 17). Shireen Moosvi in her essay on work and gender in the Mughal Empire, a part of the present anthology, refers to the employment of women belonging to the liquor distilling castes by the Mughal emperors. Women were employed to serve liquor in the court and it can be presumed that these women were also involved in the production of home-brewed liquor. Women also served as wine servers in taverns. Moosvi points out that there is an interesting pictorial representation in the *Miftåul Fuzala* of a tavern where women are serving wine and eatables and also entertaining the guests by singing with musical instruments. Women's involvement in liquor distilling and sale in the precolonial Indian context continued till such time as it became big business at which juncture men took over the liquor industry.

---

[26] Ibid., 167.

[27] Bennet, *Ale, Beer and Brewsters*.

Eileen Power, who lectured and wrote extensively on medieval women in the European social milieu, provided a fascinating range of women as doers—whether it was in farming or crafts, whether as social workers, nuns or educationists. Her essays were published posthumously by her colleague M. M. Postan under the title *Medieval Women*.[28] Here, I shall only take up for a brief review the third chapter of her book titled *The Working Woman in Town and Country*. After a brief allusion to women's work within the home and its importance in adding up to the economic life of nations, Power goes on to discuss women's presence in the medieval labour market, hiring out their skills. For married women, working meant the supplementing to a meagre family income. Even guilds, which technically debarred women from entering a trade, recognised women's participation in household craft production. In 1372, when articles were drawn up for the leather workers and pouch makers of London and for dyers serving these trades, wives of dyers of leather were sworn together with their husbands to do their calling.[29] Power writes:

> …the wife of a craftsman almost always worked as her husband's assistant in his trade, or if not, she often eked out the family income by some such bye industry as brewing and spinning; sometimes she even practiced a separate trade as a *femme sole*.[30]

References to Women craftspersons in the medieval Indian context are few and far between. In an article in which I had surveyed the history of crafts and craftspersons in medieval Peninsular India, I had attempted to look at the gender division of labour within crafts.[31] Women in most cases worked in an ancillary capacity in the crafts sector and were involved with etching, ornamenting and polishing work but rarely with primary production. There were, however, two notable exceptions both from Dharwar pertaining to the eleventh century and twelfth century, respectively. One from Gadag inscribed under the image of Uma Mahesvara says that Revakabbarasi, the wife of Vavanarasa, made the sculpture.[32] The other from Kalkeri says that Saraswati Gandidasi Malloja made the image of Suryadeva.[33] In the first case, the female sculptor is essentially defined in terms of her marital relationship, whereas in the second, only the name of the father is given which was the usual practice in all the inscriptions.[34] The mention of just two women out of nearly 80 inscriptions relating to craftsmen's names shows that the exception may prove the rule. However, it does suggest that women might have sometimes taken to crafts out of economic necessity. In the present anthology, Shalini Shah's essay on prostitution draws our attention to an extremely interesting reference in the Jayamangala, a ninth century commentary on the *Kamasutra* written by Yasodhara. In his ninefold classification of prostitutes, she includes the *silpakarika* who

---

[28] Power, *Medieval Women*, 7–8.
[29] Ibid., 55.
[30] Ibid., 53.
[31] Ramaswamy (2004).
[32] *Annual Report of Epigraphy*, 464, Southern Circle (Madras: Govt. of Tamil Nadu, 1961–62).
[33] Ibid., 109 of 1949–50.
[34] Vijaya Ramaswamy, 'Vishwakarma Craftsmen in Early Medieval Peninsular India', *Journal of the Economic and Social History of the Orient* 47, no. 4 (n.d.): 548–582.

were female artisans. Yasodhara describes them as wives of dyers and weavers (Chapter 23) who also practised the trade besides taking to prostitution.

Power provides the very interesting statistics for medieval Europe that the population of women was higher than that of men—in 1383, in Frankfurt, it was 1100 women to a 1000 men; in 1449, in Nuremberg, it was 1207 women to 1000 men and in Basel, in 1454, women outnumbered men with a ratio of 1246:1000.[35] This meant that there were many unmarried women. While the high born entered nunneries, the others hired out their services. Spinsters and destitute women had to take on some occupation for their survival. It is believed that the term spinster for an unmarried woman came from the compulsion of her single status which forced her to take to spinning as her livelihood for her mere survival.

The evidence from India moves in tandem with the evidence presented by Power. Spinning was women's work in the Indian plains, whereas in the hills men would spin on a wooden spindle. In the Sangam literature, spinsters were described as *alir pendir* (woman without a husband) or as *parutti pendir* (the cotton women). The medieval Indian literature is also replete with instances of women spinning, either to supplement the family income or if they were unmarried women or widows, for sheer survival.[36] The *Palnattu Viracharitra* of Srinatha, written in the fifteenth century, states that, while men worked in the fields, women spun thread at home.[37] A few essays in this collection look at women spinsters (and weavers as in the case of Dhankar's essay) in the handloom industry (see Dhankar, Ramaswamy and Shireen Moosvi in Chapters 10, 17 and 21, respectively).

Power points out that, in medieval Europe, it was customary for widows to carry on their husband's trade. Men used to mention in their wills that their apprentices should serve out their term with their widows, and they also used to will their tools and implements of their craft to their wives.[38] Power gives the detailed business career of an English widow named Rose de Burford in the fourteenth century. A medieval trade record called 'The Hundred Rolls' of 1274 mentions, among great wool merchants, the widows of London like Isabella Buckerel who 'make great trade in wool'. Widows in the Indian context entering the trade of their husbands was quite rare, although not completely absent. Among the Gudigara caste of itinerant goldsmiths in the Karnataka region, it was customary for the widow to carry on her husband's trade. An extremely significant theoretical exploration by Uma Chakravarti in the present collection is titled 'Gender, Caste and Labour: Ideological and Material Structure of Widowhood'. The connection between work and widowhood is also drawn in the essays by Sukumari Bhattacharji (Chapter 25). The historical fact of widows taking to prostitution out of sheer economic compulsion is figured in quite a few of the essays in this anthology under the section on prostitution as profession.

[35] Power (1999), 55.
[36] Vijaya Ramaswamy, *Textiles and Weavers in South India*, 2nd edn. (Delhi: OUP, 2006).
[37] Ibid.
[38] Power (1999), 55–56.

WERE THERE GUILDS OF WORKING WOMEN?

In the context of medieval Europe, it has been argued that women were not, and possibly could not, be organised into guilds because of their involvement in multiple crafts usually at an informal level. A woman could spin at home, brew ale and also go out to work in the textile industry, thereby making a tidy income. Women were major participants in the tasks of shearing the lamb and all processes connected with the textile industry which included combing and carding of wool, spinning and weaving. They also made bread and ran small inns most successfully. They also retailed all kinds of products from salt to butter, cheese and flour. A medieval text *Mirour de l'Omme* writes that women were sharper than men as retailers and did not let go off a single coin.[39] There was considerable male opposition to the competition offered by women in trade and business reflected in the many laws that were framed to confine and limit women's participation in economic enterprises.[40] It is logical that male artisans and businessmen should be opposed to the very idea of women organising themselves into guilds.

The medieval text *Piers Plowman* refers to Rose the Regrater who did weaving and supervised spinning (probably by employing women spinners), brewed ale at home and did retail (huckster) business:

> My wife was a weaver and woollen cloth made
> She spake to the spinners to spinnen it out
> ...I bought her barley malt, she brew it to sell
> ...Rose the Regrater (retainer) was her right name
> She hath holden huckster all her life time.[41]

Daryl M. Hafter's work *Women at Work in Industrial France* is significant for its insights into the formation of women's guilds.[42] Her two outstanding chapters, 'The Use of Gender in Economic Life' and 'Guildswomen and Ouvrieres', situate the position of women in early modern economy and the ambivalent attitude towards women's guilds. In 1750, the guild of female linen-drapers of Le Havre consisting of 69 women put in a request to the parliament at Rouen to allow them to join the all-male guild of 88 merchants so that they could benefit from the trade in cotton and woollen textiles since their own trade was limited to linen goods. Their request was turned down.[43] Men feared women's competition and tried to exclude them from capital, other resources as well as a place in their well-organised guilds. However, guildswomen enjoyed certain special privileges and powers which their less for-

---

[39] Ibid., 68.
[40] Ibid., 60.
[41] William Langland, *The Vision of William Concerning Piers the Plowman* ed. W. W. Skeat (Oxford, 1886), 51; vide Ibid., 62.
[42] Daryl M. Hafter, *Women at Work in Industrial France* (State College, PA: The Pennsylvania State University, 2007).
[43] Ibid., 51.

tunate 'working' sisters, did not have. To quote Hafter, 'Guildswomen are a quintessential example of privileged women in a man's world.'[44]

It is noteworthy in the medieval Indian context that the only group of working women to band themselves into an organisation—Sani Munnoouru—were the dancing girls or prostitutes. Around the fourteenth century, this corporate organisation from the Andhra region, which was a part of the Vijayanagar empire, also enjoyed the privilege of being a part of the temple trustees in areas such as Simhachalam (Vishakhapatnam district) and Pedakallepalli (Krishna district) in the present-day Andhra.[45]

WOMEN IN MENIAL AND MISCELLANEOUS SERVICES: MAIDS, WET-NURSES AND MOURNERS

There are scattered references to women labourers and menials, especially women slaves, in many Hindu canonical texts as well as Buddhist sources. Clarisse Bader, who was among the earliest women scholars to write about Indian women, uses some of this information in her book written in French as far back as 1867. Its English translation was done by Mary E. R. Martin around 1880. She gives the example of the Brahmanical women who 'laboured' in collecting *kusa* grass and the *soma* plant for Vedic sacrifices.[46] While the work by the Brahmin women would be regarded as a part of their ritual duties rather than as labour, there is also reference to *dasis* or menial women who gathered firewood and cut reeds for basketry. In Buddhist texts and to some extent in administrative tracts like Kautilya's *Arthashastra* there is reference to women's labour. Uma Chakravarti has looked at the Buddhist evidence on *dasis* and *karmakaras* in Ancient Indian society and her short but insightful piece on the *Agrihinis* forms a part of the present anthology (Chapter 9). The reference to women's labour in the *Arthashastra* has been looked at in the present volume by Upasana Dhankar (Chapter 10).

Sometimes the status of the *paricharika* or maid servant was almost synonymous with that of the *dasi* or slave. She is literally and figuratively turned into a commodity in the Buddhist saying of Visaka, *ithi bhandanam uttamam*,[47] which would translate as 'this is a high quality commodity'. The story of Jabala in the *Chandogya Upanishad* provides a case in point where so many men sexually exploit the *paricharika* that she cannot say who the father of her child is. A book which seeks to put together some of this evidence is Anil K. Tyagi's *Women Workers in Ancient India*.[48] Tyagi devotes much space to the *paricharika* or *karmakari*. The terms can indicate both the domestic servant as well as female slaves called *dasis*. He points out that perhaps slaves were expensive and so free labour might have been preferred by the employers.[49] The servant was supposed to do the sweeping and swabbing,

---

[44] Ibid., 60.

[45] Ramaswamy (2010), 69.

[46] Uma Chakaravarti reads Clarisse Bader against the grain in her article, 'Whatever Happened to the Vedic Dasi?' in *Recasting Women: Essays in Colonial History*, ed. Kumkum Sangari and Sudesh Vaid (New Delhi: Kali for Women, 1989), 44–45.

[47] vide Bimla Churn Law, *Women in Buddhist Literature* (Varanasi: Indological Book House, 1981), 37.

[48] Tyagi, *Women Workers in Ancient India*. Unfortunately, it was not possible to include any chapter from Anil Tyagi's book in the present anthology because the copyright clearances could not be obtained from the publishers.

[49] Ibid., 69.

bathe/message the master or mistress, apply scents, wash their feet, fetch water from the well or the river, clean the rice and wash the dishes. Buddhist literature also contains references to women hawkers, oil and liquor sellers. The text *Boghasamharapeta*, in fact, says that four women hawkers were caught cheating by using false weights.[50] Scattered references to women in Jain societies pertain particularly to the lower castes of women including wet nurses, attendants, messengers and the inevitable courtesan.[51]

My essay (Chapter 17) refers to the employment of women as wet-nurses. In the Sangam literature these women are referred to as *chevili thai* or 'foster women'. For the medieval period, Moosvi's essay (Chapter 21) deals with the employment of slave women in various menial capacities. It is, however, noteworthy that the wet-nurses of the Mughal kings cannot be described as ill-used or powerless since wet-maids like Maham Anaga enjoyed the king's confidence and played an active role in court politics.

Construction work was another work domain where women worked for very low wages. An unusual essay on the theme of women and labour was Stephen Blake's 'Contributors to the Urban Landscape: Women Builders in Safavid Isfahan and Mughal Shahjahanabad'.[52] In my essay on women and work in early India which provides a bird's-eye view of women in different occupations from the ancient to the medieval period, I have referred to a thirteenth century inscription from Tiruvamattur in which there is reference to both men and women being engaged in construction work with the clear injunction that women workers were to be paid as wage (*kooli*) just half of what was paid to their male counterparts (Chapter 17).

Before I close this section, I would like to refer to the professional option women found as paid mourners in any house where a death had occurred. In fact, a thirteenth century inscription from the Pudukkottai state records that when death occurred in any household, the *Valaichchi* women (low caste/untouchables) put a cloth over their heads and mourned the dead with loud wails.[53] The singing of these lamentation songs constituted a special repertoire since songs meant for young wives dying in child birth would be very different from the songs on the death of the master of the household or the almost celebratory tone of the dirges sung at the death of elderly persons. Cleaning of the death-polluted house the next day with cow dung was also their job. They were paid for both. Professional mourning as women's work has no parallel in Western societies to the best of my knowledge and has, therefore, escaped the critical gaze of Western feminist scholars.

WOMEN IN THE HOUSEHOLD

Kitchen as Woman's Place: Kitchen as Woman's Space

What does the kitchen signify for women as their work space and equally their personal and social place? If one were to bring together the notion of 'kitchen work' and 'kitchen space', it is important to understand ways in which intimate places have been experienced

[50] B. C. Law cited in Ibid., 63.

[51] K. C. Jain, *Bodh aur Jain Sahitya me Nari Jeevan* (1967) vide fn 1 of Ibid., 28.

[52] Gavin R. G. Hambley, ed., *Women in Medieval Islamic World: Power, Patronage and Piety* (New York: St. Martin's Press, 1998).

[53] Inscriptions of the Pudukkottai State, No. 601.

and understood. A pioneering attempt in this direction was Gaston Bachelard's *The Poetics of Space*.[54] Out of the house (especially the kitchen) spin 'worlds within worlds' what Bachelard describes as 'personal cosmoses'. Although Bachelard's book does not explore the tantalising possibilities of kitchen spaces, his broad perceptions can be extended to a gendered landscaping of the interior of the household. Here, in the kitchen, women created dishes, controlled and directed the pecking order, deftly handled finances to manage household requirements including food provisions and contested the intrusion of other women into their kitchen space. The contestations typically involved the mother-in-law and daughter-in-law or the 'co-wives'/wife and mistress.

Women's Work and Women's Role Within the Household

Manusmriti,[55] an ancient canonical text has been dated between the second century BCE and the second century CE. The *Manusmriti* can be seen as a text illustrating the nature of the work that was assigned to women within the household in traditional societies. This obviously involves her work within the household. According to Manu, a woman's main duties were oriented towards taking care of her husband, children and the extended family as nurturer and provider.[56] In addition, she had to perform the physical tasks of drawing water from the well, churning, husking, winnowing and other such 'homely' tasks.[57] Manu interestingly, also credits her with a head for finance. She had to manage the everyday running of the household and balance the family budget.[58] As the controller of her husband's earnings she was in charge of domestic finances and was the paymaster. *Manusmriti* points out that collecting and spending money was in the hands of the housewife[59] because she was expected to exercise frugality. The *Grihyasutras* also detail the kind of work women could do within the household both in the ritual and in the social sphere. This anthology has a major section on situating women and work within the space of the household as well as beyond it. The essays by Jaya Tyagi (Chapter 7) and Kavita Gaur (Chapter 5) specifically look at canonical texts to explore women's agency and spaces within the household. Both these essays have been written specifically for this volume and both seek to re-open traditional texts in order to look at women's work within the household and beyond it by factoring in women's agency.

---

[54] Gaston Bachelard. *The Poetics of Space: The Classic Look at How We Experience Intimate Places*, tr. Maria Jolas from French (MA: Beacon Press, 1964). (French original in 1958.)

[55] Patrick Olivelle, ed., *Manusmriti* as *Manu's Code of Law: A Critical Edition And Translation of the Manava-Dharmasastra*, with Editorial Assistance of Suman Olivelle (New Delhi: Oxford University Press, 2006), chapter IX, verses 10–12. See also Narayan Ram Acharya Kavitirtha, ed., *Manusmriti* (commentary by Kulluka), 10th edition (Bombay: Nirmaya Press, 1946), IX: 10–12.

[56] Olivelle, *Manusmriti*, Chapter IX, verse 27, 751.

[57] Ibid., verses 10–11, 748.

[58] The assumption that the wife is expected to handle the domestic expenses occurs in quite a few of the verses from the *Manusmriti*. For example verse 150 in Chapter V says 'she should be alert in the handling of household matters and tight fisted (literally, since the expression used is *amukta hastaya*) in dealing with household expenditure (p. 588).

[59] Ibid., Chapter IX, verse 10, 748. The exact line is 'arthasya sangrahe cha enam vyaye'.

The *Manusmriti* is only an entry point to the nature of women and work in the context of Peninsular India. While it gives an indication of canonical thinking on the prescriptive role of women, the contextual variations in the case of South India make it necessary to understand the historical trajectories in the Sangam age (roughly datable from 300 BCE to 300 CE as with the *Manusmriti*) in terms of the Peninsular problematic rather than the Indo-Gangetic. The Sangam Tamil texts of the early Christian era talk about the household and the duties of the housewife as the qualities expected of an *illal* or *manaivi*. The very nomenclature used for a married woman in Tamil firmly locates her within interior spaces. The term *illaval* (also called *illa kizhathi* and *illal*) for the wife is derived from the term *illam*[60] for a house. The synonymous term *manaivi* is derived from the term *manai*[61] meaning 'house', again referring to the 'house-wife'. An even more evocative term is *aham*[62] which indicates interiority (for example as in 'aham' poetry like *Ahananuru*) as well as, specifically, the house-site. The word for wife which is derived from *aham* is *ahamudaiyal* literally meaning 'she who is the mistress of the home'.

The *karpiyal* of the *Tolkappiyam* deals entirely with the prescriptive role for women. As with the *Manusmriti*, this normative text from the Sangam era, roughly contemporaneous with the *Manusmriti*, also stresses on chastity, the qualities of mothering and nurturing.

Cooking, feeding, cleaning, etc., have been defined as the 'unwaged' labour of the housewife. The Sangam text *Maduraikanchi*[63] states that *illara magalir*, literally meaning 'housewives', should wake up at dawn and sweep their homes. The *Nedunelvaadai* instructs them to light iron lamps with wicks soaked in clarified butter.[64] They should also commence their household chores at the crack of dawn. The housewife's space and the woman's place have been perceived traditionally by feminist scholarship as a reflection of patriarchal oppression and the undervaluation of the woman's household labour.

Feminist debates in recent times have, however, opened up fresh ways of perceiving 'domestic space'. In her management of her domestic space, a woman does not merely assert her agency but also achieves control and power. The hermeneutic analysis of the terms used for the 'housewife' in the Tamil language opens up some very interesting lines of discussion on the nature of power exercised by the housewife and her agency and control over the domestic space. The potential power implied in the Tamil terms for housewife ties up this discussion with the more general debate on the household space. The recent debates among feminist scholars explore the notion of the domestic space of the housewife as an empowering space. Anthropologist Felicia I. Ekejiiuba, writing in the context of West African society, states:

---

60 E. V. Anantharaman, ed. *Kalittogai*, with commentary by Nachchinarkiniyar (Madras: Saiva Siddhanta Kazhagam, 1967/1925), verse: 110:12 and 94:15; U. V. Swaminathaiyyar, ed., *Kurunthogai* (Madras: Kapir Achukootam, 1962/1972), verse: 8; and A. Narayanaswami, ed., *Natrinai Nanuru* (Madras: Saiva Siddhanta Kazhagam, 1962/1967), verse: 295.

61 Swaminathaiyyar, *Kurunthogai*, verse: 181.

62 Ibid., verse: 371–74.

63 *Maduraikanchi*, verse: 664 vide Vidyanandan, 1954, 254.

64 *Nedunelvaadai*: 42, Ibid.

> The concept of the household as it is currently applied, is itself part of a subtle ideological transformation which has facilitated the assertion of colonial power, nationally, and male power domestically. The concept clouds the true pattern of gender interaction and power relations, portraying the impression of men as sole providers and of female dependence and passivity, as opposed to their active participation in socio-economic processes.[65]

In contrast to the notion of 'housewifization' and the passivity of the housewife, Ekejiuba offers the concept of a 'female-directed hearth-hold' as an empowering space for women. The hearth-hold centres on the hearth or stove where a woman is responsible for food security.[66] This relates specially to the agricultural domain where the woman controls and probably directs the 'sharing of the grain heap' within the 'domestic' space.

Essays on gendering the household and situating the nature of women and work within the household (as well as beyond it) form an important section of this anthology. The lead piece is an extract from a chapter of Julia Leslie's book *The Perfect Wife*, which deals with women's household duties delineated as 'sthri dharma' in the *Sthridharmapaddhati*, reproduced here with permission from the Oxford University Press. Apart from the essays by Jaya Tyagi and Kavita Gaur, written specifically for this volume, this section also reproduces an essay by T. R. Sharma based on canonical sources from a seminar organised by the Late Professor Tripathi in Banaras Hindu University. The editor is grateful to the Department of Archaeology and Ancient Indian History of Banaras Hindu University for granting permission to reproduce this brief but useful article presented at this seminar.

Women's property rights have been given a special place in this analogy because of the close connection between women's financial need and economic security, which often is the cause of their joining the workforce. While an extremely useful essay by Sukumari Bhattacharji situates the economic rights of women in ancient times, the essays by Altekar, Indra and Bhattacharya (Chapters 11–12, 13 and 14, respectively) look at the canonical positions on women's property. Kanakalatha Mukund (Chapter 15) looks at the historical course of the *Manjakani* (also called *sthri dhana*) rights in the region of South India. I am grateful to the Department of Archaeology and Ancient Indian History and Culture of Banaras Hindu University for granting permission to include the Late N. N. Bhattacharya's piece on women's property rights.

MOVING BEYOND THE HOUSEHOLD: PROBLEMATISING THE DEVARADIYAR

Prostitution is the only domain that was recognised as 'women's work domain' from the earliest times. This is reflected in all early textual and literary traditions from the *Manusmriti* and Vatsyayana's *Kamasutra* (dated between 400 BCE and 200 CE) to political and literary

---

65 Felicia Ekejiuba, 'Down to Fundamentals: Women-Centred Hearthholds in Rural West Africa', in *Women Wielding the Hoe*, ed. Deborah Fahy Bryceson (Oxford: Oxford University Press, 1995), 50.

66 Ibid., 47–61.

texts like the *Arthashastra* and plays such as Shudraka's *Mrichakatika*, written around the second century BCE, which revolves around the prostitute Vasantsena. Beginning with an extract from the *Kamasutra*, the present anthology looks at the economic and social ramifications of prostitution in early India through essays by Sukmari Bhattacharji and Shalini Shah for the ancient period, while A. Padma's essay focuses on the Andhra region for the medieval period.

In the historiography of the Mughal period, it is predominantly the courtesans or prostitutes that have attracted the attention of scholars of Mughal history with some notable exceptions like Shireen Moosvi who has mapped women's work in other spheres as well.

While prostitution as a profession situates women within the public work space, some historians have chosen to conflate the categories of Devaradiyar, ranging from temple menials to professional dancers and wealthy and influential temple trustees. The Devaradiyar are located not in the public domain but within the sacred precincts of the temple, and branded as sacred prostitutes, a term that is as inaccurate as it is misleading. Two essays in this anthology look much more critically at the role–functions of temple women, thereby complicating the neat connection that had been drawn between the Devaradiyar and prostitution. Leslie Orr looks at the Devaradiyar of the Chola period in terms of the multiplicity of their functions, as temple-servants, dancers, musicians and even temple trustees (Chapter 23). Prostitution does not figure in this trope. The issue is raised more sharply by Anna Varghese in her essay which is titled 'Temple women and work in Medieval Keralam', moving the discussion beyond prostitution as the work (and sole work) of the Devaradiyar. This essay is, therefore, placed under the Section 'Contextualizing Women's Work in the Public Domain' (Chapter 19) rather than in the last section which historically situates prostitution as women's work.

CONCLUDING REFLECTIONS

In recent years, gyno-critical studies of everyday life, re-evaluating women's work and the process of housewifization, have become a major area of research within the postcolonial discourse. The challenge lies in steering clear of all abstracted textual forms which feed directly into the requirements of either capitalism or bureaucratic power and control. Such efforts in the context of Indian history must, perforce, remain very tentative. This book which seeks to place before scholars a panoramic survey of women and work in history in precolonial India covering the period from the ancient to the late-medieval period, should be seen as initial steps towards a much more ambitious feminist enterprise. The primary endeavour has been to salvage available data on women's work both paid and unpaid, both visible and less-visible, in order to highlight women's contribution to the work domain and indicate directions of movement and change in women's work/labour history.

BIBLIOGRAPHY

Original Texts (in Sanskrit, Tamil, Kannada or Telugu)

Tamil Works:

Sangam Texts

(The Sangam texts referred to in this introduction can be dated roughly between third century BCE and third century CE)
Ahananuru ed. with commentary by Venkataswami Nattar N. M. and R. Venkatachalam Pillai (Madras: Saiva Siddhanta Kazhagam, 1943).
U. V. Swaminathaiyyar and S. Kalyana Sundaranar, ed., *Aingurunuru* (Madras: Kapir Achchukootam, 1957).
Malaippadukadam from the *Pattupattu*, Anthology, ed. U. V. Swaminathaiyyar (Madras: Kapir Achukootam, 1965).
Perumppanatruppadai in *Pattupattu*, Anthology, ed. U. V. Swaminathaiyyar (Madras: Kapir Achukootam, 1965).
U. V. Swaminathaiyyar (ed.), *Perunkadai* (Madras: Publishers not known, 1924).
Porunaratruppadai in the *Pattupattu* Anthology, ed. U. V. Swaminathayyar (Madras: publishers not known, 1937).
U. V. Swaminathayyar, ed., *Purananuru* (Madras: Kapir Achukootam, 1963).
V. R. Ramachandra Dikshitar, ed., *Silappadikaram* of Ilango Adigal (a Post-Sangam text) (New York: New York University Press, 1954 [originally published in 1939]).

Sanskrit Texts

Arthashastra of Kautilya (third century to second century CE) ed. and trans. in three parts by R. P. Kangle (Bombay: University of Bombay, 1965).
Manasollasa (12th century Sanskrit text) of Somesvara III, ed. Shrigondekar (Baroda: 1939), verses: 1817–18.

Medieval Texts in Tamil, Telugu, Persian and French

Kreedabhiramamu of Vinukonda Vallabharaya ed. and transl. Rao, Velcheru Narayana and David Shulman under the title, *Kreedabhiramamu: A lover's guide to Warangal* (New Delhi: Permanent Black, 2002).
Kreedabhiramamu of Vinukonda Vallabharaya, ed. Veturi Prabhakara Sastry (Muktiyala/Hyderabad: Manimanjari, 1960).
A. S. Usha, ed., *Futuhat-us-Salatin*, trans. Agha Mehdi Hasan, 3 volumes (Aligarh: Aligarh Muslim University, 1976–77).

Epigraphical Records (inscriptions on rocks and copper plates)

K. R. Srinivasa Aiyar, ed. and trans., *Inscriptions of the Pudukkottai State* (Pudukkottai: Pudukkottai State Press, 1941–46 [originally published in 1929 by the Sri Brihadamba State Press of Pudukkottai]).
South Indian Inscriptions (Madras: Govt. of Tamil Nadu, 1890 onwards).
S. Subramanya Sastri and V. Viraraghavacharya, eds., *Tirumalai-Tirupati Devasthanam Inscriptions*, 6 vols. (Madras: 1931–38).
T. N. Subramanian, ed., *South Indian Temple Inscriptions* (Madras: Madras University, 1957).

Secondary Works in English (also includes works translated from other languages into English)

Clarisse Bader, *Women in Ancient India: Moral and Literary Studies*, trans. Mary E. R. Martin, reprinted under the Chowkhamba Sanskrit Series, vol. 44 (Varanasi: Chowkhamba Publishers, 1964 [originally published in French in 1867 and the English translation in 1925)].

Alice Clark, *The Working Life of Women in the Seventeenth Century* (London: Routledge, 1919).

Stephen Blake, 'Contributors to the Urban Landscape: Women Builders in Safavid Isfahan and Mughal Shahjahanabad', in *Women in Medieval Islamic World: Power, Patronage and Piety*, ed. Gavin. R. G. Hambley (New York: St. Martin's Press, 1998).

Uma Chakravarti, *Everyday Lives, Everyday Histories: Beyond the Kings and Brahmanas of 'Ancient' India* (New Delhi: Tulika Books, 2006).

B. Hemlatha, *Life in Medieval Northern Andhra* (New Delhi: Navrang Publishers, 1991).

Olwen Hufton, 'A History of Women in the West', in *Renaissance and Enlightenment Paradoxes*, ed. Natalie Zemon Davis and Arlette Farge, General Editors Georges Duby and Michelle Perrot, volume III (Cambridge, MA and London: The Belknap Press of Harvard University Press, 1993), 15–45.

J. K. Kamat, *Social Life in Medieval Karnataka* (New Delhi: Abhinav Publications, 1980).

Vijaya Ramaswamy, 'Women and the "Domestic" in Tamil Folk Songs', *Man in India* 74, no. 1 (1994): 21–37 and reprinted in Kumkum Sangari and Uma Chakravarti, eds., *From Myths to Markets: Essays on Gender* (Shimla: Manohar and the Indian Institute of Advanced Study, 1999), 39–55 and 41–42.

Vijaya Ramaswamy, 'Women and Farm Work in Tamil Folk Songs', *Social Scientist* 21, nos. 9–11 (1993, September–November): 113–29.

Vijaya Ramaswamy, 'Aspects of Women and Work in Early South India', *Indian Economic and Social History Review*, no. 23 (1989): 81–99.

Wilhelm Rau, *Weben und Flechten in Vedischen Indien* (in German) (Weisbaden: University of Wiesbaden, 1970).

Aloka Parashar Sen, ed., 'Temple girls and the Land Grant Economy', in *Social and Economic History of Early Deccan: Some Interpretations* (New Delhi: Manohar, 1993), 240–77.

Women and the Household: Canonical Prescriptions and Their Feminist Critique

Section I

Chapter 1 The Daily Duties of Women*

(*strīṇām āhnikam*; Sdhp. 2v. 5–21 r.3)

JULIA LESLIE

'Now the daily duties of women are examined.'[1]

The daily practice of the orthodox Hindu householder (male) is an important topic of *dharmaśāstra*, described in detail in numerous *smṛtis*, *purāṇas* and digests (e.g. Gaut.1.5, 1.9; Āp.II.1.l–II.4.9; Yājñ.1.96–127; Mārk.P.29–30,34; Kūrm.P.II.18–19; Sm.C.I.p.88–232; Sm.A. p.18–48; etc.). For of all the *āśramas*—Vedic student (*brahmacarya*), householder (*gṛhastha*), forest hermit (*vānaprastha*), and renouncer or ascetic (*saṃnyāsin*, *yati*, etc.)—that of householder is repeatedly described as the best.

The *āśrama* theory, examined in detail by Olivelle (1974; 1978; 1984), involves a gradual progression through three main stages of development. In the first, only the householder state receives wholehearted recommendation. The second encourages the notion of a choice between four separate and permanent states (*vikalpa*, 'alternative'). The third regards the four *āśramas* as a continuous series of temporary states (*samuccaya*, 'together'; i.e., in sequence in one lifetime). In all three versions of the theory, however, the householder state is held to be the best.

The earliest exposition of the *āśrama* theory is presented by Gautama and Baudhāyana. (For an analysis of the corrupt text into 'Proto-' and 'Deutero-Baudhāyana', see Olivelle 1984.) Gautama notes the idea of a choice in the form of a *pūrvapakṣa* (*āśramavikalpam*; Gaut.I.3.1–2), without approval. For, in Gautama's view, the householder is quite literally the source (*yoni*) of the other three: only he produces children (*aprajanatvād itareṣām*, Gaut. 1.3.3; cf. Rāgh. on Manu VI.87; Baudh.11.6.11.27). Moreover, the order of householder is the one explicitly enjoined (*pratyakṣ-avidhānād*; Gaut. 1I.4.35) in all the Vedas, *dharmaśāstras*, *itihāsas* and *purāṇas* (Har. on Gaut.I.4.35). Baudhāyana even denies that there is a choice. The notion of four alternative paths is dismissed as a misunderstanding (Baudh.II.6.11.9) or the invention of a demon (Baudh.II.6.11.28). Baudhāyana stresses the ımportance of

---

* Reproduced with permission from the publisher from Julia Leslie, *The Perfect Wife: The Orthodox Hindu Woman According to the 'Stridharmapaddhati' of Tryambakayajvan*, Oxford University Press, Delhi (1989), pp. 44–50.

[1] *tatra Strīṇām āhnikam nirūpyate //sdhp. 2 v. 5*

family life; the payment of the three debts (to the seers by study, to the gods by sacrifice, to the ancestors by sons); and thus the urgent need to produce children (Baudh.II.6.11.33–4).

The next stage in the development of the *āśrama* theory is shown in the views of Āpastamba and Vasiṣṭha. The four orders are now seen to be equally valid in the sense that one may attain liberation through any one of them (Āp.II.9.21.1–2), but they are still mutually exclusive and permanent. (It is important to distinguish here between studentship as a temporary first stage and perpetual studentship as a permanent state of celibacy; cf. Olivelle 1984: 85.) Nonetheless, Āpastamba devotes a large number of *sūtras* to proving that the householder state is superior to any of the celibate alternatives (Āp.II.9.23.3 ff.).

The third stage may be found in Manu, Yājñavalkya and the later *smṛtis*. The *āśramas* are now no longer alternative states but successive stages, each leading to the next in a steady progression towards liberation (Manu IV.1, VI.33). But still the householder stage is best (Manu III.77–8, VI.89–90). This remarkably persistent eulogy of the householder underlines the fact that all *dharmaśāstrins* are, of course, householders themselves.

In order to fulfil his significant part in the scheme of things, the householder must observe a clearly defined timetable of ritual and quasi-ritual activities, all included under the general heading of *gṛhasthadharma*, the ordained rites and duties of the householder.

The day is sometimes divided into two (*pūrvāhṇa*, 'before noon', and *aparāhṇa*, 'afternoon'); or three (*prātaḥsavana*, 'morning' *mādhyandinasavana*, 'midday', and *tṛtīyasavana*, 'evening', corresponding to the three pressings of *soma*); or five (*prātaḥ* or *udaya*, 'dawn', *saṃgava*, 'morning', i.e., when the cows are collected for milking, *mādhyandina* or *madhyāhna*, 'midday', *aparāhna*, 'after-noon', *and sāyam*, *sāyāhna* or *astagamana*, 'evening'). Most commonly, however, the division is into four parts (*pūrvāhna*, *madhyāhna, aparāhṇa, sāyāhna*), further subdivided into eight: that is, sixteen divisions covering the twenty-four hours of day and night (e.g., Daksa II.4–5; Kaut. I. 19; Kāty. quoted by Apar. on Yājñ.II.i; and even Vidyārṇava's twentieth-century presentation of the *āhnika* rules, 1979:1). The normal unit of calculation is thus one and a half hours.

With regard to the different *varṇas*, no specific *āhnika* rules are laid down for the *vaiśya* or *śūdra.* These men would presumably adjust the *āhnika* rules prescribed for brahmin householders to suit themselves. The *āhniḳa* rules for a king are given in detail in Kaut. I.19 (of. also Manu VII. 145–7, 151–4, 216–26; Yājñ. I.327–33). In the first part of the day (6.00–7.30 a.m.), the king should attend to matters of defence, income and expenditure; in the second (7.30–9.00 a.m.), he should consider the affairs of the people; in the third (9.00–10.30 a.m.), he should bathe, eat and study the Veda; in the fourth (10.30–12.00 noon), he should receive revenue and assign tasks; in the fifth (12.00–1.30 p.m.), he should consult his ministers and consider the secret information brought by spies; in the sixth (1.30–3.00 p.m.), he may amuse himself; in the seventh (3.00–4.30 p.m.), he should review his army; in the eighth (4.30–6.00 p.m.), he should confer with his commander-in-chief. At the end of the day, he should perform the evening *saṃdhyā* (V.9–17). In the first part of the night (6.00–7.30 p.m.), he should consult his secret agents; in the second (7.30–9.00 p.m.), he should bathe, eat and study; in the third (9.00–10.30 p.m.), he should enter his bedchamber; in the fourth and fifth (10.30 p.m.–1.30 a.m.), he should sleep; in the sixth (1.30–3.00 a.m.), he should wake and contemplate the *śāstra* (i.e. of politics) and the duties of the coming day; in the seventh (3.00–4.30 a.m.), he should meet with his councillors and send out secret agents; and in the eighth (4.30–6.00 a.m.), he should receive blessings from his priests, see his doctor, chief cook and astrologer, perform the appropriate rituals, and go to court (v. 18–24). Alternatively, as Kautilya adds (thereby undermining the entire system), the king may divide his days and nights as he needs (v. 25).

Although Tryambaka probably intended his treatise for the edification of the women at court (who were presumably of largely *kṣatriya* families), the *āhnika* rules it prescribes for women have little in common with the rulings given above for their king. It is thus more appropriate to compare Tryambaka's rulings for women with those prescribed for brahmin householders.

Daksa, for example, also divides the day into eight parts (II.4–5). For practical purposes, the day's timetable begins in the last division of the night (i.e. 4.30–6.00 a.m.) when a man should wake, perform the necessary ablutions and the *ācamana* ritual, clean his teeth, bathe, and observe the twilight rituals (*saṃdhyā*). In the first division of the day (6.00–7.30 a.m.), he should worship his special deity and pay homage to his teacher. In the second (7.30–9.00 a.m.), he should study the Veda. In the third (9.00–10.30 a.m.), he should work for the maintenance of his family, following only those professions permitted to his *varṇa*. In the fourth (10.30–12.00 noon), he should bathe and perform the midday *saṃdhyā*. In the fifth (12.00–1.30 p.m.), he should perform the five great sacrifices (*pañca mahāyajñāh*): to *brahman* (*brahmayajña*, by the study or recitation of the Veda), to the gods (*devayajña*, by ritual offerings into the fire), to the ancestors (*pitṛyajña*, by the ritual of *tarpaṇa*), to all beings (*bhūtayajña*, by *bali* offerings), and to men (*manuṣ-yayajasña*, by offering hospitality to guests). These five observances absolve the householder of the five types of sin committed every day in the home (of. Manu III.68–71; Vis.Sm.59.19–20 etc.). In the fifth part of the day, the householder should also take his main (midday) meal. In the sixth and seventh (1.30–4.30 p.m.), he should study secular literature (epics, *purāṇa* and so on). In the eighth (4.30–6.00 p.m.), he may receive or visit friends and perform the evening *saṃdhyā* rituals. From 6.00 p.m. until 9.00 p.m., he should attend to the duties omitted during the day and spend time with his family. From 9.00 p.m. until 4.30 a.m., he may take rest (Dakṣa II; Vidyārṇava 1979: 1–2).

Let us compare these typical basic divisions with the daily timetable prescribed for women by Tryambaka. The first point to notice is that Tryambaka divides the night (and presumably the day as well) into six parts instead of the usual eight (Sdhp.2v.8). This ruling is not specific to women, for the quotation cited is addressed to the householder 'together with his wife' (*patnyā saha*). For Tryambaka then, the unit of calculation is two hours instead of one and a half. However, since Tryambaka rarely specifies the exact times or periods during which a particular duty should be performed, Figure 1.1 contains a rough timetable demonstrating the parallels between a woman's day as he describes it and that of a (brahmin) man as described in *smṛti* literature in general.

A large proportion of the *āhnika* rulings cover activities to be carried out in the last division of night. In addition to most of the duties prescribed for men, a woman must also prepare the day's quota of rice or millet, sweep the house and smear it with cow-dung, perform the ritual of threshold worship, and attend to the cows. When her husband performs the morning fire sacrifice, she assists him. At dawn, she makes an offering to the sun. In the morning, while her husband studies the Veda and works at his profession, she attends to her household duties. At midday, when he performs, the five great sacrifices, she assists him. When he eats, she serves him, eating what he leaves. After the meal, while he studies the epics and *purāṇas*, she clears away the meal, washes, sweeps and cleans. In the evening, while he is visiting friends, she is still doing housework, for the food for the evening meal must be prepared afresh. At the evening sacrifice, she assists him again. Her final *āhnika* duties concern going to bed and sexual intercourse. Several of these duties are beautifully illustrated in two palm-leaf manuscripts in the British Library collection: milking the cows, cooking, serving food to her husband, tending her children, nursing an infant, massaging her husband's feet as he lies in bed, eating the remains of his meal, and a variety of postures for sexual intercourse (British Library: OR. 11689, OR. 11612; cf. Lostly 1980: 14–45; cf. Gaur 1980: 23–5). The paintings depicting children and the wife's involvement with them draw our attention to a curious omission in the *Strīdharmapaddhati*; while Tryambaka assumes that the good wife will produce sons, he not only shows no further interest in them, but makes no allowance for them in her day.

Topics discussed in relation to women	*Equivalent topics for men*
Before dawn	
1. waking	waking
2. housework (grinding grain etc.)	
3. ablutions	ablutions
At dawn	
1. fire worship	fire sacrifice
2. offering water to the sun	*saṃdhyā* ritual worship of special deity
Topics discussed in relation to women	*Equivalent topics for men*
Day	
1. paying respect to elders	homage to teacher
2. housework	Vedic study work for maintenance of family
3. midday rituals: *devapūjā* *vaiśvadevapūjā* *atithipūjā*	bath and *saṃdhyā* *pañca mahāyajñāḥ* (i.e., Vedic recitation to *brahman*; sacrifice to the gods; *tarpana* for the ancestors; *bali* offerings for all beings; *atithipūjā*)
4. meal time duties: serving at meals, *bali* offering, clearing away, housework, etc.	midday meal study of epics, *purāṇa*, visiting friends, etc.
Evening	
1. fire worship, etc.	evening *samdhyā*
2. going to bed and intercourse	

Figure 1.1 Parallel Timetable for Women and Men

Tryambaka also specifies no time when a woman may simply rest. Indeed, he lists 'sleeping in the daytime' among the six things that corrupt women and which they should therefore avoid (see section IV, p. 275, note 6). Since it is assumed that a woman has no education, it is less surprising that she is not advised to study. Judging by Tryambaka's prohibitions on 'roaming around' and spending time in other people's homes (section IV, p. 275, note 6), we would not expect her to be allowed to visit friends, certainly not on her own. Taken at face value, then, a woman should always be busy about her work. The traditional pattern of an Indian day, however, suggests that the hot period after the midday meal might well be given to rest. It is at this time that women might be encouraged to listen to readings from the epics or *purāṇas*, or even from a work such as the *Strīdharmapaddhati* (Introduction, pp. 22–23 and 232–23).

Before embarking on a discussion of each ruling, it may be instructive to consider at the outset what types of rullngs these may be. The crucial question is how each ruling relates to its equivalent for men. The answer takes the form of four quite distinct categories.

First, there are those rulings which, according to Tryambaka, are exactly the same for women as for men. These include the rulings concerning what one may or may not see first thing in the morning (*darśanīyāny adarśanīyāni ca*; section IIA, pp. 54–57), urinating and defecating (*mūtrapurīṣotsargah*, section IIA, pp. 69–71), and cleaning the teeth (*dantadhāvanam*; section IIA, pp. 78–82). This group of rulings clearly requires the operation of the *ūha* of gender (see section I, pp. 40–43).

Secondly, there are those rulings which are the same in principle for women as for men, but different in detail. For example, the rules on purification (*śaucam*) are applicable to men and women except that for women the colour of the earth used and the number of lumps required is different (section IIA, pp. 71–72). The rule concerning sipping (*ācamanam*) and bathing (*snānam*) also fall into this category. When a twice-born man sips, the water must touch his heart, throat or palate; when a woman sips, it need only touch her mouth (section IIA, pp. 75–77). A man performs his ritual bath with mantras, a woman without (section IIA, p. 83). Generally speaking, however, both rituals are applicable to women as well as men. Similarly, both men and women must wake early, but the wife should wake before her husband (section IIA, p. 52). Both must eat but the wife should serve her husband and eat only what he leaves (section IIC, pp. 221–27). This is a large group of rulings and the implications are interesting. I shall deal with each in its place.

The third category, a very important one, consists of those rulings in which the wife assists her husband in his ritual obligations (*pativratabhāginī*). In the early morning meditation (*devatādhyānam*), for example, the man must meditate 'with his wife' (section IIA, pp. 52–54). In the fire sacrifice (*agniśuśrūṣā*), although the wife has little to do, she must be present for the ritual to bear fruit (section IIB, pp. 132–41). In the ceremony of paying homage and hospitality to guests (*atithipūjā*), the wife must prepare the food and serve the guest on her husband's behalf (section IIC, pp. 210–14). These rulings indicate the role and status of the wife in the joint ritual duties enjoined upon the married couple. I shall deal with this in some detail in the section on serving the sacred fire (*agniśuśrūṣā*) (section IIB, pp. 107–15).

Finally, there are the duties peculiar to women. These are predominantly rulings concerning housework, such as grinding grain (section IIA, pp. 58–9), cleaning the house (p. 59), smearing it with cow-dung (pp. 59–63), clearing away way after the meal (section IIC, pp.

229–33), and so on. As is clear from the parallel timetable, these duties are to be performed when the husband is studying religious literature or working for the family maintenance. They are thus both part of a woman's religious path and her contribution to the family. The parallel with the man's religious duties becomes more apparent in the context of Manu's dictum on marriage for women a wife serving her husband is like a student serving his teacher; and her household duties are equivalent to her husband's performance of the fire sacrifice (Manu II.67; see Section I, p. 35, note 16). Looked at from this point of view, household tasks become part of the powerful *vrata* or religious observance of the wife. Hence the high tone in which these apparently mundane tasks are described.

Chapter 2 Position and Status of Women in the Upaniṣads*

T. R. SHARMA

The Upaniṣads are the repository of ancient philosophical discussions as visualised by the Āryans. The Āryans being very much impressed by the phenomena of the nature right from the time of the Ṛgveda had started interpreting the nature in a philosophical manner. This tradition got fully matured in the times of the Upaniṣads. The vast majority of the philosophical analysis, as depicted in the Upaniṣads, points at this maturity of the early Āryans. A careful reading of the Upaniṣadic literature shows that the whole gamut of this philosophical analysis was not in isolation with regard to man and woman taken together representing the whole universe. We can very well form an imaginative picture of the position and status of women from the speculative thinking of the seers of the Upaniṣads, whose prime concern was to establish the supremacy of the Ātman doctrine. It may be pointed out here that it is not an easy task to extract exact information from the Upaniṣads which are more metaphysical in nature than social.

Among the major Upaniṣads it is the Bṛhadāraṇyakopaniṣad, according to which, woman is an essential and integral part of man's personality, and he becomes complete with the company of a woman only. This Upanisad tries to emphasise that husband and wife are like the two parts of sky. The whole of the firmament is visualised as two parts of the sky in the Bṛhadāraṇyakopaniṣad (1.4.3)[1] in the form of husband and wife. It is stated in this connection that one part is incomplete without the other. This clearly shows that women played an important role in the society and she provided a sense of completeness. It is partinent here to examine the comments of Śaṅkara[2] who observes that half of the sky in the form of man is empty without the woman, and man becomes complete with the company of woman by

* Reproduced with permission from L.K. Tripathi (ed.) *Position and Status of Women in Ancient India*, Seminar Papers, Vol. I. Published by Department of Ancient Indian History Culture and Archaeology, Banaras Hindu University, Varanasi–221005 (1988), pp. 41–46.

1 *Tasmād ayamākāśaḥ strīyā pūryate.*

2 *Yasmāt ayaṁ pūruṣārdh ākāśaḥ striyārdhaśūnyaḥ punar udvahanāt tasmāt pūryate striyārdhena.* Śaṅkara on BU., 1.4.3, Gorakhpur, Saṁvat, 2029.

marrying her. This passage very vividly points out that man's personality is incomplete without the partnership of woman and his personality is developed into a complete one by marrying her.[3]

The Upaniṣads generally follow the tradition of the Saṁhitās in holding the woman in high esteem. From the early times the woman is supposed to look after the household affairs of the family. The Bṛhadāraṇyakopaniṣad (4.5.1) speaks of Yājñavalkya having two wives, namely Maitreyī and Kātyāyanī. Out of these two, Maitreyī is more popularly known as Bhrhmavādinī for her philosophical bent of mind. It is mentioned in this Upaniṣad that ordinarily the woman folk was mainly interested in the household affairs, and such women were known as Strīprajñā. This word (Strīprajñā) has been explained by Śaṅkara as those women is have the intellect concerned (only) with the household affairs.[4] Kātyāyanī was this type of a lady, whereas the other one, that is, Maitreyī, being not much interested in the household affairs, was popularly known as Brahmavādinī or Brahmavadanaśiiā. That is the reason why Yājñavalkya chose Maitreyī for philosophical discussion leaving aside Kātyāyanī.[5] Incidentally this passage is indicative of the fact that polygamy was prevalent in the times of the Upaniṣads.

Like modern times, the woman was considered as a biological necessity for the birth of a son in the Upaniṣads. It was thus the duty of the woman to take care of the semen deposited in her by the husband and she was very much protected by the husband in this process.[6]

Woman has been rightly associated with Kāma in the Bṛhadāraṇyakopaniṣad (3.9.11). Śaṅkara[7] in this connection observes that the association of a man with a woman in love is a spiritual union and woman is its chief deity. This passage indirectly reflects the ancient Indian tradition of considering Kāma (love) as part of the spiritual discipline of a man.[8] The Bṛhadāraṇyakopaniṣad (6.4.6)[9] compares woman with wealth and praises her by saying that she is the best form of wealth (Lakṣmī) among the whole of the womanfolk in the world. Woman was not considered as a mere means of enjoyment in the times of the early Upaniṣads. It is noteworthy that how ancient seers of the Upaniṣads had tried to give a religious feeling to the mundane act of sleeping with a woman. In the Chāndogyopaniṣad (2.13.1)[10] the act of sleeping

---

[3] Cf. (i) *Ardho ha vā eṣa ātmano yaj jāyā. Tasmāt yāvaj jāyāṁ na vindate naiva tāvat prajāyate'sarvo hi tāvad bhavati*. ŚB., 5.2.1.10.
(ii) *Ardho ha vā eṣa ātmano yat patnī*. TS., 6.1.8.5.
(iii) *Tasmāt puruṣo jāyāṁ vittvā kṛtstaram ivātmānaṁ manyate*. AA., 1.2.5.

[4] *Strīprajñā-striyāṁ yā ucitā sā strīprajñā-saiva yasyāḥprajñā gṛhaprayojanānveṣāṇalakṣaṇā sā strīprajñā tasmin kāle āsit Kāty āyānī.* śaṅkara on BU., 4.5.1.

[5] *Athaivaṁ sati ha kila yājñavalkyo' nyat Pūrvasmād gārhastha-lakṣaṇāt vṛttāt pārivrājyalakṣaṇāṁvṛttam upakariṣyann upācikīrṣuḥ san. Ibid.*

[6] (i) AU., 2.1, Gorakhpur, Saṁvat 2029.
(ii) *Ibid*., 2.2.
(iii) *Ibid*., 2.3.

[7] *Ya evāyaṁ Kāmamayaḥ puruṣo' dhyātmamapi kāmamaya eva. Tasya kā devateti striya iti hovāca; strīto hi kāmasya dīptirjāyate.* *Śaṅkara* on BU., 3.9.11.

[8] For a similar idea, see BU., 4.1.6 and 4.3.13.

[9] (i) Śrī ha *vā eṣā strīṇām.*
(ii) Cf. *Strīyāś ca śriyaś ca* geheṣu *na viśeṣo' sti kaścana.*
MSm, 9.29.

[10] *Ṣtriyā saha śete sa udgīthaḥ.*

with a woman has been described as Udgītha. The sight of a woman was always considered to be auspicious in the times of the Upaniṣads. The Chāndogyopaniṣad (5.2.7-8) while speaking of a ritual known as Mantha states that if a man sees a woman then he should think that his ritual has become prosperous.[11] It is further stated in this Upaniṣad, in relation to the works associated with the fulfilments of desires, that if a man sees a woman even in a dream then he should think that there is prosperity or fulfilment of the objects of the actions being performed.[12]

Women enjoyed a very respectable position in the times of the Principal Upaniṣads—this fact is very well borne-out by the above analysis. There is another class of the Upaniṣads known as Sectarian or minor Upaniṣads. These Upaniṣads are many and varied in nature. They are popularly known as Sectarian for they eulogise the main deity of a particular sect. Some of them are designated as Vaiṣṇava, some as Śaiva, and some as Śākta Upaniṣads; among them Viṣṇu, Śiva and Śakti are respectively elevated to the position of the supreme God. From the study of these Sectarian Upaniṣads it can be said that the old bias against the woman of the Vedic times and of the Manusmṛti has greatly influenced some of their Vaiṣṇava Upaniṣads. It is well known that the Śūdra and the woman are debarred from the Vedic studies in the Smṛtis. It is very important to note that this bias against women regarding Vedic studies is nowhere reflected in the principal Upaniṣads. A somewhat plausible explanation for this bias against the women is offered by Altekar who observes:

> It must be pointed out that exclusion of woman from Vedic studies and sacrifices was not due to any deliberate plan to lower their status. Custodians of the Vedic lore honestly believed that no one should be allowed to recite and use the Vedic mantras who had not studied them properly. Women found it impossible to devote the necessary time for this purpose on account of their early marriage. It is therefore, but fair they should not be allowed to invite on themselves and their relatives those dreadful calamities, which were honestly believed to result from an incorrect recitation of Vedic stanzas. The desire was not to humiliate woman but rather to save them from dire consequences.[13]

Among the Vaiṣṇava Upaniṣads, the Nṛsiṁhatāpinyupaniṣad (Pūrva)[14] (1.7) declares that the preceptors do not desire to give Sāvitrī Praṇava, Yajus and Lakṣmī to the women and the Śūdras. Furthermore, this Upaniṣad makes the general statement that whosoever knows the 32 lettered Sāman mantra, such as a man, obtains immortality.[15] According to this Upaniṣad, if a Śūdra or a woman per chance knows Sāvitri, Lakṣmī, Yajus and Praṇava, he or she goes down dead.[16] There is a clear-cut direction for a preceptor not to give any

---

[11] *Sa yadi strīyaṁ paśyet samṛddhaṁ karmeti vidyāt.*
Ch U., 5.2.7.

[12] (i) *Yadā karmasu kāmyeṣu strīyaṁ svapneṣu paśyati samṛddhiṁ tatra jāniyāt.* *Ibid.* 5.2.8.
(ii) Śaṅkara interprets prosperity as the fulfilment of the objects of actions.
Cf. *Yadā karmasu kāmyeṣu kāmārtheṣu strīyaṁ svap neṣu svapnadarśaneṣu svapnakāleṣu vā paśyati samrddhiṁ tatra jānīyāt. Karmaṇāṃ phalaniṣpattir bhaviṣyatīti jāniyād ityarthaḥ.*
Śaṅkara on Ch:. U., 5.2.8.

[13] Altekar, A. S., *PWHC,* Delhi, 1962, pp. 205–6.

[14] *Sāvitriṁ praṇavaṁ yajurlakṣmīṁ strīśūdrāya necchanti.* p. 180.

[15] *Dvātriṁśad akṣaraṁ sāma jāniyād yo jānīte so' mṛtattvaṁ ca gacchati. Nṛsiṁhapūrvatāpinyupaniṣad,* 1.7, Adyar, 1953, p 180.

[16] *Sāvitriṁ lakṣmīṁ yajuḥ praṇavaṁ yadi jānīyāt strī śūdra sa mṛto' dhogacchati.: Ibid.*, 1.7, p. 180

of these four to a Śūdra or a woman.[17] If a preceptor gives any one of them, he also goes down dead along with him or her.[18] The commentator Upaniṣadbrahmayogin observes in the commentary thereon that if a woman or a Śūdra happens to know the Sāvitrī etc. through some other means, she and the Śūdra go down dead just by its knowledge.[19] The worst type of Narakas are recommended for a preceptor who gives such a knowledge to either a Śūdra or to a woman, according to the commentator Upaniṣadbrahmayogin.[20]

As we have seen above, the sectarian Upaniṣads, particularly the Vaiṣṇava Upaniṣads do not recommend the Vedic studies for women in general. There is another Vaiṣṇava Upaniṣad known as Kṛṣṇopaniṣad which compares women with the hymns of the Ṛgveda. This also states that they are of the form of Brahman.[21] This comparison of women with Brahman clearly indicates two diametrically opposed positions, as enjoyed by the women in the times of these Upaniṣads. On the one hand they were despised to the extent of being denied the knowledge of Sāvitrī, Praṇava, Yajus and Lakṣmī and on the other hand they were held in high esteem because they are described as of the form of Brahman.[22] A possible explanation for such a situation in the times of the sectarian Upaniṣads can be offered by saying that on the one side these Upaniṣads were holding women in high esteem and on the other side they were greatly influenced by the popularity of the Smṛti literature, which had just preceded these Upaniṣads, wherein the law-givers had debarred the Śūdras and the women from the Vedic studies. From the study of these sectarian Upaniṣads and more so the Vaiṣṇava Upaniṣads it appears that they were greatly influenced by this social bias against the women particularly in the field of education.

In the above lines a brief survey has been made with regard to the position and status of women in the Upaniṣadic age. This survey has also included for this purpose the sectarian Upaniṣads. After a careful study of the principal Upaniṣads it can be said that women in general enjoyed a very respectful position in the society. There were mainly two types of women in the society, that is, one type of women devoted themselves to the higher learning and the other type of women was mainly engaged in the household affairs. The personality of a man was supposed to be incomplete without woman. His personality was completed by marrying a woman. It goes without saying that woman was praised as the best form of Lakṣmī (wealth) among the whole of the feminine world. Influenced by the Smṛti literature the sectarian Upaniṣads in general and the Vaiṣṅava Upaniṣads in particular developed a particular bias against the women. These Vaiṣṇava Upaniṣads did not allow women to be given the knowledge of Sāvitrī, Praṇava, Yajus and Lakṣmī. The Upaniṣads held women in general in high esteem.

---

[17] Cf. *Bhāryā putraś ca dāsaś ca traya evādhanāḥ smṛtāḥ/*
Yatte samadhigacchanti yasya te tasya taddhanam//
MSm. 8.416.

[18] *Tasmāt sarvadā nācaṣṭe yadyācaṣṭe sa ācāryas tenaiva sa mṛto' dho gacchati. Ibid.*

[19] *Sāvitryādikaṁ strīśūdraJātiḥ upāyāntareṇa yadi jāniyāt vedanamātreṇa sa mṛto' dho gacchati*. Upaniṣadbrahmayogin on *Ibid*., 1.7, p. 180.

[20] *Yadyācaṣṭe tadā strīśūdraguruḥ so' yam apakīrtibhāk vyādhyādināmṛtaḥ kumbhīpākādinarakajātam anubhūya tataḥ śūkarādiyoniṁ sthāvarabhāvaṁ vā gacchati. Ibid.*

[21] *Brahmarūpā ṛcaḥ strīyaḥ* Kṛṣṇopaniṣad, 13, Adyar, 1953, p. 24.

[22] Cf. *Tā vai striyaḥ brahmarūpā eva bhavantītyarthaḥ*.
Upaniṣadbrahmayogin on *Ibid*., 13, p. 27.

Chapter 3 Woman in the Household*

M. A. INDRA

The home, in ancient India, was a perfectly human institution. It was a living organism, every part of which was vital and fully conscious of the other part. Its unity and solidarity was unique; no incidental wave of disintegration or disruption could ever disturb it. For ages, this wonderful institution exercised a very healthy influence over all aspects of national and corporate life. In this pattern of vitality and unity, woman filled, by no means a place of insignificance. Here in this sphere at least, she enjoyed abundance of honour, affection and sympathy.

In the Rigvedic time, we find the home well- established, with the father as patriarch, possessing complete control over the household, where the centre was primarily the woman—the very embodiment of that great moral and spiritual force, that ultimately worked itself out in the creation and development of modern civilised society.

It was the renowned sage Vishvamitra, who realised the moral and the spiritual force of woman, thousands of years ago, and ecstatically declared, '*Fayedastam*', that is, the wife is the home (3-53-4)' and nobody has spoken a greater truth since those remarkable and memorable words were uttered.

The wife was verily the home[1] and woman the main spring of those human activities that uplifted the race from its savage condition. The ancient Aryans never looked upon woman as the cause of human downfall-as she was later supposed to be. On the other hand, the important part that she played in advancing human civilisation was fully appreciated and recognised.

The very creation of the universe was ascribed by the Aryans, to the union of Prakriti and Purusha 'nature beneath and will or Power above' (X-129-5). Woman is Prakriti and man is Purusha and union of these two has created the home and made the world what it is to-day.

* Previously published in *The Status of Women in Ancient India*. Motilal Banarsidass Publishers (1955). pp. 22–40.

[1] Shatapatha XII—8—2—6. According to the Shatapatha Brahman, the proper place for woman is the home. Therefore they should be respected in all matters of the household. (गृहा: वै पत्न्यै प्रतिष्ठा:)

Thus, wife was regarded an indispensable member of the family without whom the consummation of human life was not possible. It was generally made imperative on all for the proper discharge of their duties-spiritual and earthly-to marry and to have progeny. The necessity of a female partner was so great that the scriptures allowed man to remarry at once after the death of his wife; else he could not perform any religious rite.

According to ancient ideals, the wife is the half of man and hence as long as he does not obtain her, so long is he not regenerated, for so long is he incomplete.[2] This idea has been well-preserved even so late as in the Epic literature which clearly lays down that a man's half is his wife; therefore she is called *Ardhangini.* The wife is her husband's best of friends. The wife is the source of *dharma artha* and *Kama.* The wife is the source of salvation.'[3] Again, 'those that have wives can perform religious acts; those that have led domestic lives, those that have; wives, can be happy and those that have wives can achieve good fortune'.[4]

The Mahabharata does not indulge in any exaggeration when it goes to the extent of saying that 'the sweet-speeched wives are their husbands' friends on the occasion of joy. They are as fathers on occasions of religious acts. They are as mothers in hours of illness and woe'.[5] Indeed in the domestic life, woman used to be supreme. In regulating activities in the home, her word was to be final. Immediately after her marriage, she is instructed to 'go to the house to be a mistress there'.[6] She is further asked to bear full sway over her husband's father, mother, brothers and sisters.[7] She is again and again addressed as the queen of the house, who rules over all the members of the family as ocean rules over all the rivers of the world.[8] In another verse of the Rigveda she, after being blessed with happiness and prosperity, is asked to look after the affairs of the house and to guard its interests, as sedulously as possible.[9]

From the preceding references, it is abundantly plain that in the Vedic India, women occupied a very proud position in the household. They were not merely slaves of their lords, as they decidedly became in the later ages. To them were entrusted the heavy responsibilities and duties of maintaining good order in the family. All the component parts of the house owed their systematic working to the central authority—the wife, who never failed to make her presence felt. In fact, she was the very axis on which the wheel of household-life in ancient India turned.[10]

If we compare the above position of an Indian woman with that of her sister in the ancient history of any western country, we have every reason to keep our heads erect with just pride about the comparative loftiness of our hoary civilisation.

---

[2] Shatapatha Brahman, V—2—1—10.
[3] Mahabharata, Adiparva, 74—40.
[4] Mahabharata, Adiparva, 74—42.
[5] Mahabharata, Adi Parva, 74—43.
[6] Rigveda, X—85—26.
[7] *Ibid*, X—85—46.
[8] Atharva, XIV—1—43.
[9] Rigveda, X—85—27.
[10] The words Pati (master) and Patni (mistress) used in the Rigveda, signify the equality of position of husband and wife in the household.

Under the laws of Rome, the son and the wife were classed, not as a person, but as a thing in the family of *pater familias* over whom the latter exercised absolute jurisdiction of life and death.

If the wife was seduced by another, the action maintainable against the seducer was not that of adultery, but one for theft. As both the son and the daughter occupied the position of a chattel, they could not marry without their parents' consent.

A Roman marriage differed from a Hindu marriage in that the contracting parties in the one case were the husband and wife, While the husband and wife play no part at all in a Hindu marriage, Which is arranged for them by their parents.

In Greece, the wife looked after and performed other menial offices; in Rome, the wife was somewhat free from those obligations, but still her position was not that of a mistress. The position of the Hindu wife in the household was certainly more that of a *domina* than that of a dependant.

We may again quote here at some length the passages from the Mahabharata which will conclusively elucidate the point that the place of women in the household was that of honour and respect and that as wives they enjoyed not only the rights of equality, but even the privilege of superiority: 'Her father and brothers and father-in-law and husband's brothers should show her every respect and adore her with ornaments, if they be desirous of reaping benefit, for such conduct on their part always produces considerable happiness and advantage.'[11]

'If the wife does not like her husband or fails to please him from such dislike or absence of joy, the husband can never have children for increasing his family.'[12]

'Women O King, should always be adored and treated with honour. There the very gods are said to be propitiated, where women are treated with respect.'[13] 'Those houses which are cursed by women meet with destruction and ruin, as if scorched by some Atharvan rites. Such houses lose their splendour. Their growth and prosperity ceases.'[14]

'By respecting women, man is sure to acquire the fruition of all his objects.'[15]

The inference that in the household women were treated with honour and due consideration, is also supported by those two erudite scholars—Macdonell and Keith. As per the distinguished professors,

> [The poetical ideal of the family] was undoubtedly hight (Rv. VIII-31-5, 6) and we have no reason to doubt that it was often fulfilled. Moreover, the wife on her marriage was at once given an honoured position in the house, she is emphatically mistress of her husband's house, exercising authority over her father-in-law, her husband's brother and his unmarried sisters. No doubt, the case contemplated is one, in which the eldest son of a family has become the head, owing to the decrepitude of the parents, his wife then taking the place of the mistress of the joint family, while the brothers and sisters are still unmarried. It is not inconsistent with the great stress elsewhere (Rv. VIII-6-24) laid on the respect due to a father-in-law, who then is probably regarded as still in possession of his faculties

[11] Mahabharata, Anushasan Parva XVI—3.
[12] *Ibid*. XVI—4.
[13] Mahabharata Anushasan Parva XVI—5.
[14] *Ibid*. XVI—6.
[15] *Ibid*. XVI—7.

and controls,the house, while his son continues to live with him. The respect would no doubt equally apply if the son had set up a separate home of his own.[16]

Now a few words may also be said about the duties and responsibilities which a wife in the household generally used to perform. A rough idea of her daily programme, can be formed from a few passages in the Rigveda which will throw as well an interesting side-light on the status allotted to the fair sex.

A woman in ancient India was regarded as an excellent housewife, who rose early with the dawn and roused all from sleep and sent the servants about their respective business,[17] She at once applied herself to the performance of her household duties-dusting, sweeping, and washing the floor that admitted of washing and cleansing the cooking pots and utensils. She bathed early and offered jointly with her husband the morning oblations to the sacred household-fire, the Lord of the house. Another oblation was offered in the midday and a third in the evening.

Her first and foremost duty was to keep the sacred flames alive. As soon as the cows were milked and milk brought home in pails, she stirred it over the fire churned some of it for butter and proceeded to prepare the meals of the day. The young daughters took charge of the little ones and duly fed and nursed them. After midday meal she attended to her toilet, dressed herself and the children neatly.[18] Often she had male and female servants under her, whom she employed in their respective duties and treated kindly.[19]

She also looked after the cows and other domestic animals and supervised the work entrusted to her.[20] Occasionally, accompanied by other women, she rambled about and climbed the hills to pluck flowers.[21] She was dutiful to her husband's parents affectionate to her husband's brothers and sisters, and devotedly attached to her lord, who was never slow in reciprocating her sentiments.[22]

The conception of an ideal housewife is still more advanced in the Epic literature. But we have every reason to believe that this conception was hardly translated Into actual practice and it does not in any way reflect the real conditions, prevailing in those ages However, we feel persuaded to record it, only to give a faint idea of the existing beliefs and notions, obout ideal womanhood.

---

[16] Vedic Index, I—pp. 485–6.

In 'Vedic religion' Professor Macdonell also writes (pp. 158):

'The normal household had one husband and one wife on a level of equality; at the hearth which was the altar of sacrifice and even sometimes composed the hymns'.

[17] Rigveda, I—124—4.

[18] Rigveda, I—123—11.

[19] *Ibid.* X—85—43.

[20] *Ibid.* X—85—44.

[21] *Ibid.* 15—6—2.

[22] Rigveda, X—85—46.

Thus in the Anushasan Parva[23] of the great Epic:

> Gifted with a good disposition, endued with sweet speech, sweet conduct and sweet features and always looking at the face of her husband and deriving as much joy from it as she does from looking at the face of her child that chaste woman who regulates deeds by observing the prescribed restraints-comes to be considered as truly righteous in her conduct. Listening to the duties of married life and performing all those sacred duties, that woman who considers virtue as the foremost of all the objects of pursuits, who observes the same vows which are observed by her husband, who adorned with chastity looks upon her husband as a god, who waits upon and serves him as if he were a god, who surrenders her own will completely to that of her husband's—who is cheerful, who observes excellent vows, who is gifted with good features and whose heart is completely devoted to her husband, so much so that she never thinks even of any other man, is considered as truly righteous in conduct. That wife who, even when addressed harshly and looked upon with angry eyes by her husband, appears cheerful to him, is said to be truly devoted to her husband. She who does not cast her eyes upon the moon or the sun or a tree that has a masculine name, who is worshipped by her husband and who is gifted with beautiful features, is considered to be truly righteous lady. The woman who treats her husband with the affection which one shows towards her child, even when he happens tn be poor or diseased or weak or worn-out with the toil of travelling, is considered to be as truly righteous in her conduct.

Shukracharya,[24] a post-epic authority on the subject, records the real conditions and describes the duties that a woman in the household was to perform. Thus, she was required to rise earlier than her husband and after performing toilet she changed her night dress. Then she smeared the floor of the house with cow-dung and cleansed the vessels of the daily sacrifice and the kitchen. The utensils were washed with hot water. After having done these minor things, she daily bowed before her father-in-law and mother-in-law and then put on the clothes which were given by her husband or father or other relations. She was further required to follow her husband like the shadow of a tree and always be at his command like a slave. She was to take meals when her husband had taken them. She was to spend the whole day in considering matters entirely related to the house and was particularly to be attentive to the needs and desires of her lord—always subordinating her own comforts and convenience to his.

The above uncharitable remarks about women in the Sanskrit literature have led many an English scholar to believe that the status occupied by women was far from honourable. Says Dr Barnett in his 'Antiquities of India' (pp. 109), 'Women *per se,* however did not rank high in the eyes of the law which laid down as a principle that a woman is for all her life in tutelage, first to her father, then to her husband and lastly to her son. A wife who bore only daughters or no children at all could be superseded by her husband marrying another woman, who then took precedence of her. Even under the most favourable conditions the nuptial bed was not one of roses for the wife. She was expected to show her devotion to her husband by the most humble and minute services, preparing all the meals of the household, eating the food left by her husband and sons, washing the kitchen vessels, smearing the floors with burnt cow-dung aud respectfully embracing her lord's feet at bed time'.

---

[23] Mahabharata, Anushasan Parva, CXLVI.

[24] Shukhra, IV—4, 6, 7, 14.

The foregoing strong views expressed by the learned doctor are perhaps an over-statement, but by no means, without some foundation. In fact, they are substantially true. Manu—the highest authority on social matters—concedes to women only a place of dependence in the household. According to him, a woman must be kept in subordination, day and night, by the males of the family.[25] Not only a girl or a young woman but even an aged one is not to do anything independently even in her own house[26]. For, it is again emphasised, that a woman's father protects in childhood, her husband protects her in youth and her sons protect her in old age, she is never fit for independence.[27] (Na stri swatantryam arhati)

In household affairs she is so much subservient to her husband that her very individuality is submerged in that of her lord's. A wife has been compared to a river and a husband to an ocean[27]. After reaching the latter the former completely loses its separate entity. The qualities of a wife are said to be identical with those of the husband. She falls or rises with the fall or rise of her male associate. It is said that Akshamala, a woman of the lowest birth, being united to Vasishtha and Sarangi being united to Mandapala became worthy of honour.[28] Thus they attained eminence in the work by the respective good qualities of their husbands.

For guarding and controlling women, an interesting expedient has been devised by Manu that 'the husband should employ his wife in the collection and expenditure of wealth, in keeping everything clean, in the fulfilment of religious duties, in the preparation of his food and looking after the household utensils'.[29]

The idea of the subordination of woman in the household is supported by Yajnavalkya also, who lays down that a woman should never be separated from her male protectors.[30] The Mahabharata echoes the same sentiments in the Anushasan Parva, by observing that 'a woman, at no period of her life, is free'.[31] Again the great Epic gives expression to its profound belief in the subservience of women by saying that, 'Manu, on the eve of his departure from the world, made over women to the care and protection of men, for they are weak and that they fall an easy prey to evils.'[32] Shukra generally holds women to be false

---

[25] Manu, IX—2 2. *Ibid*, V—147.

[26] Manu, IX—3 and V—148. Also Narada writes 'Through independence woman goes to ruin, though she be born in a noble family. Therefore the lord of creatures ordained dependence on them' (XIII—30). See Baudhayana II—2—3, 4 5 and II—2—4—2 also Vasishtha V 1, 2. A woman is not independent; the males are her masters—including father, husband and Sons.

The perpetual tutelage is however explained by some as nothing more than a control or supervision over the morals of women, by those versed in the sacred scriptures and who are by reason of such training supposed to possess virtue and selfcontrol. Thus a woman during the several guardianships at different periods of her life is restrained from the doing of something –*Akarya karanat*–as Mitakshara puts it, and not that there is any restraint on her in respect of the observance of what is commanded by the Shastras. ('Position of Women', pp. 41. by Dr. Dwarka Nath.) See also Manu, IX 6, 7.

[27] Manu, IX—32.

[28] *Ibid.*, IX—24.

[29] Manu, IX—11.

[30] Yajnavalkya, III—86.

[31] Mahabharata, Anushasan Parva, XLVI—14—7.

[32] *Ibid.*, XLVI—14—2.

When Bhishma is asked by bewailing Draupadi as to the right of her husband Yudhishthira to pawn her in the game of dice, when he himself was no longer a free man, having been lost to Shakuni, the royal sage is faced with

and treacherous. He instructs a husband never to trust his wife in a matter of dispute without testing her words by his own direct observation.[33] However, these remarks of Shukra are insignificant in comparison with the greatly objectionable remarks about the female sex which disfigure some of the chapters of the Anushasan Parva.

The subject is introduced in this way. The great sage Narada, in order to gain an insight into female nature approaches courtezan Panch Shura, who after pretending reluctance to besmirch the fair fame of her own sex, lets herself go with a venge ance and her delineation as explained by the gloss of the commentator Nilakantha is so obscene in some parts, that it is impossible to quote it. Suffice it to say that it rivals the most depraved methods of sensuality practised in the last days of the Roman Empire or in some of the modern countries of the West.[34]

Lest we console ourselves with the thought that nothing better could be expected of a hardened sinner like Pancha Shura, in the next chapter, Yudhishthira is made to say very uncomplimentary things about the female sex and his considered opinion is that 'their virtue is a mere tradition'. This is confirmed in the following chapter by no less a personage than Bhishma himself, who observes that women were virtuous in ages long past, and tells the story of Ruchi-the wife of the sage Deva Sharma-who was long pursued by the god Indra with foul designs, but without success, thanks to the vigilant care of the sage's pupil, 'who did not hesitate to cast the previous record of this lustful god in his teeth much to his discomfiture and did his best to save her from being licked up by the King of the gods as mischievous dog licks up the butter deposited at the sacrifice'.[35]

However, Bhishma in the end is charitable enough to say that both kinds of women, virtuous and unchaste, are to be found in the world and then follow some verses full of dignified respect for the gentle sex-which are more in consonance with the spotless character of the great hero, who had led the pure life of celibacy in order that the sons of his step-mother might not be deprived of the throne.

'This mighty earth', pronounces the great royal sage, is upheld by the great virtue of chaste women—the mothers of the people. They should be respected, adorned and protected—the gods delight to dwell where they are treated with respect; and where they are disregarded, all

anigmatic bewilderment and hesitatingly concedes to Yudhishthira the right of pawning Draupadi in as much as she being his wife was perpetually subordinate to him even after be had been vanquished. A fully packed house of ministers, preceptors, sages and law-givers also gave its tacit consent to Bhishma's utterance and witnessed the molestation, of an Aryan lady, who but for the divine miracle, stood completely senseless at the imbecility of her elders and resigned herself to the justice of her Lord. Needless to say that man's injustice to woman was indemnified by the merciful God in His strange manner.

[33] Shukra, III—163.

[34] 'Throughout her life,'says a woman writer discussing the position of her sex in the days of Rome's supremacy, 'a woman was supposed to remain absolutely under the power of father, husband or guardian and to do nothing without their consent. In ancient times this authority was so great that the father and husband could after calling a family-council put the woman to death without public trial. The reason that women were so subjected to guardianship was on account of unsteadiness of their character, wickedness of their sex and their ignorance of the legal matters'.

Eugene Hecker 'A short history of woman's rights with special reference to England and U.S.A.', pp. 2.

[35] Mahabharata, Anushasans Parva Ch. 46.

religious observances come to naught. Prosperity is synonymous with women; a house which is accursed of women does not shine, nor increases in prosperity, but loses all loveliness. But the above excellent remarks are followed by the enunciation of the old Roman doctrine which relegates woman to a perpetual state of tutelage.[36] This doctrine, it will be observed, has been, at first, expounded in Manu, where the good and bad points of the gentler sex are described in detail. And it is clear from the perusal of other Dharma Shastras as well, that in the post-epic ages, the place allotted to women in the household was that of subordination and her voice, though supreme in ordinary domestic affairs, was of secondary importance in matters, vitally affecting the whole family. The reason for the dependence and subservience is mentioned by Asahya, a commentator on the Narada Smriti, who observes that the Lord of creatures has ordained women to be dependants, because they have no right to study the Shastras and consequently lack the knowledge to discriminate between right and wrong and between Dharma and Adharma, since such discrimination is derived only from the study of the Shastras. Thus we can understand that in the early Vedic age when women could be initiated in the sacred lore, their position was not one of subordination and their rights were equal to those of men; but with the withdrawal of that right, their general status suffered. Really the incompetency of women to study the Vedic lore reduced them to the inferior status of Shudras, who also were debarred from performing any sacrificial act. This is also the reason why in numerous metrical texts of the Smritis and Epics, Stri and Shudra are generally classed together in one category.[37]

There is one thing more to which we should like to refer here in the end, that the Hindu Law was most one-sided and unfair towards women regarding conjugal fidelity. Even in this delicate matter women were left cruelly alone and in a state of utter helplessness. While no faithfulness was required on the part of a husband who could keep openly as many concubines as he liked, without any detriment to his marital rights, the slightest unfaithfulness on the part of a wife was severely punished. Says Manu, 'Though unobservant of approved usage or enamoured of another woman or devoid of good qualities, yet a husband must certainly, be revered as a god by a virtuous wife.'[38]

But the slightest unfaithfulness could deprive a woman of her conjugal rights, including the right of maintenance. A husband however depraved, decrepit and destitute, was to be worshipped by women as a god; but a wife on the least pretext could be put to severe social ostracism, though not actually forsaken. The common sense as well as the sense of fair-play requires that the rules of constancy and faithfulness—if they were held to be good—ought to have been held uniformly good on either side. It is simply adding insult to injury, to render the already weaker sex still more incapacitated in the eyes of law, and thus make it absolutely dependent on and subservient to the sterner sex.

It is these unjust and inhuman rules that seem to have made the lot of women unbearable. The subordination of women in the household appears to have gone to such proportions as

---

[36] Mahabharata, Anushasana parva, Ch. 46.

[37] Institutes of Narada by Dr Jolly, pp. 186.

Another reason for woman's subjection to man is that a woman has to perpetuate the race; so she has to be protected in every way from the sordid struggles of the world and not to be exposed to physical and economic strain.

[38] Manu, V—154 also Gautama, XVIII—2, 3.

to allow husbands to have complete mastery over their persons and even to permit their sale. These indications in some Dharmashastras which go to prove the fact that at certain stages of the Indian civilisation, women could be bought and and sold like ordinary movable and immovable property. Says Narada in Chapter 12, verse 53 of his Dharmashastra,

'The issue of these women, *who have been purchased for a price*, belongs to the begetter, but when nothing has been paid for a woman, his off-spriug belong to her legitimate husband.'

The Asura form of marriage among the ancient Hindus was nothing but a sale of the daughter by the father. According to the Mahabharata, the practice of sale and purchase of daughter has been known to human beings for a long time. But it goes to the credit of the royal sage Bhismha that he disapproves of the practice by laying down that 'no one should bestow his daughter upon any person by sale. A wife should never be purchased. Nor should a father sell his daughter.'

Manu also is not uncharitable in this respect. He unequivocally denounces the usage of giving daughter for a price. 'Even a Shudra', says he,

> ought not to take a nuptial fee when he gives away his daughter, for he who takes a fee, sells his daughter covering the transaction by another name. Neither ancients nor moderns who were good men have done such a deed. Nor have we heard in former creation of such a thing as the covert sale of a daughter for a fixed price, called a nuptial fee. Therefore no father who knows the law must take even the smallest gratuity for his daughter; for a man who through avarice takes a gratuity is seller of his off-spring.[39]

Baudhayana's protest also against the sale of a daughter is vehement. He declares that 'a female who has been purchased for money is not a wife; she cannot assist at secrifices offered to the gods or the manes'. He ordains heavy punishment for fathers who sell their daughters for a fee.[40]

Notwithstanding the above sympathetic observations made by Manu, we have every reason to believe that his general attitude towards women was one of respectful distrust and reverent disbelief.[41] He, most certainly, treated them as caged birds in the household and regarded them as unworthy of sharing the serious responsibilities of man. In his opinion, women were ornaments of the house, who were to be kept safe and-looked after with utmost care and vigilance. The only duties that they had to discharge were confined to the four-walls of the house. Even in this limited sphere woman was not an absolute mistress as she certainly was in the Vedic times, but a mere dependant always subordinate to the male members of the family. This is what was the position of woman in the household.

---

[39] Manu, IX—100.

[40] Bandhayana, I—11—21—2.

[41] Manu, III—51.

Chapter 4 Economic Rights of Ancient Indian Women*

SUKUMARI BHATTACHARJI

The Vedas (especially, the *Rig Veda Saṃhitā*) are generally silent about the economic conditions of women in that period. Although some data may be gleaned occasionally for the economic position of men, their profession and their prosperity, very little is known about the women. We know that Vedic women carded and possibly spun wool, fetched water and tended cattle but we do not know whether they earned anything other than the bare maintenance for these services. Undoubtedly women looked after household duties; the kitchen and the nursery were in their charge, but then as now, these services were not measured in economic terms and, therefore, no payment was made. The maid had no separate identity, this she acquired, after a fashion, only at marriage. The *Brāhmaṇas* categorically call a son a blessing, a girl child a curse; so except affectionate parents, others would look upon the daughter as a nuisance, to put it mildly, on sufferance at home until she is given away at marriage.

Atri in a late *Saṃhitā*, however, says that a maiden had a share in her father's, brother's or ancestral property.[1] This property she was free to sell, mortgage or hold as her own. Obviously, we are now thinking of the kulapā kanyā, the 'amāju' or 'amājurā', the old maid. In literature, we do not see her except as a virtuous 'brahmacārinī', the 'Sāṃkrtyāyani' or the 'Paṇḍitakauśikī', the spiritual descendants of the Upanisadic 'brahmavādinī' to whom possessing, selling or mortgaging property had not the least of significance. Possibly there were other old maids who were neither learned nor given to meditation, who needed money to live on and perhaps to live well and independently. It may be that in exceptional circumstances they could own property. But even Atri does not mention the right to donate property. We shall come to this later.

'A maiden who is bought or sold should never be taken as a wife.'[2] This proves that maidens could be bought or sold.

* Reproduced with permission from Tanika Sarkar. Previously published in Sukumari Bhattacharji's *Women and Society in Ancient India*. Basumati Corporation Limited. Calcutta (1994), pp. 42–61.

In dire circumstances by the consent of both the parents, say some scriptures. The son begotten on a wife bought as a girl was debarred from performing the obscquial rites for the father. For the sake of marriage a virgin's respectability, that is, social viability as a virgin could not be tarnished at will. He, who does so out of spite, had to pay a fine of 225 panas:[3] so her social prestige had an economic value. He who gives a girl with some defects, suppressing them, to the groom has to pay a fine of 96 paṇa.[4]

'A twice-born who knows his wife's friend (presumably a virgin)...should perform an ordinary penance and give away a milch cow.'[5]

Manu lays down that Brahmin brothers should separately give a quarter of their shares (in parental property) to an unmarried sister. Failing to do so brings doom upon them.[6] Gautama says that unmarried daughters not well settled in life shall inherit the property of the mother's deceased husband.[7] There is a controversy about whether the dowry of the unmarried daughter should be provided by the brothers *before* or *after* the mother's death. But Baudhāyana and long before him the Taittirīya *Samhita* around the eighth century BC says 'strīyo nirindriya adāyādīh'.[8] That is, women in general (and sisters in particular) are not entitled to a share of the family property.[9]

When the betrothed of a maiden dies, she belongs to her father alone. If a maiden is carried away forcibly and not married by the abductor she may be lawfully married to another.[10] 'A newly married daughter-in-law, an unmarried daughter, a sick female inmate, an *enciente*—these the householder may feed before feeding his guests.'[11] Girls were sometimes given some instructions, though the Vedic lore was denied to them; the *Bharadvāja Gṛhya Sutra*[12] names four inducements for marrying a girl—wealth, beauty, intelligence and family. For intelligence the *Mānava Gṛhya Sūtra* substitutes the world 'vidyā', learning. The *Bṛhadāraṇyaka Upaniṣad* lays down a rite for obtaining a learned daughter.[13] Such texts explain the appearance of Gārgī, Sulabhā and other learned women. But although grammarians lay down rules for framing feminine forms for women who were teachers on their own[14] yet we have no way of knowing whether they could earn by teaching. Possibly not, but exceptionally may be. Only a very late tantric text says, 'a householder should instruct the daughter equally as his sons.'[15]

In some of the eight forms of marriages it was the bride's father who paid the groom's party; only in the 'Āsura' form of marriage payment was made by the groom's parents. In the 'Āsura' form of marriage the bridegroom pays money to her father *and* to the bride herself, out of the promptings of his own desire.[16] In the 'Brāhma', 'Daiva' and 'Ārṣa' forms the bride's father has to give wealth, ornaments, a pair of oxen or other gifts according to his ability. In the 'Brāhma' marriage, a well-attired and be-jewelled girl was given, in the 'Ārṣa' the bride was given after an ox and a cow or two oxen and two cows were given to the groom.[17] Apparently, the current social distaste for the practice is expressed in the name 'Āsura'. But at marriage, when wealth changed hands, it was the bride or her parents who benefited from it. What is known as 'strīdhana', the bride's wealth, could be of three kinds: 'pana', with which the bride was purchased; 'yautaka', gifts given to the girl at marriage by her relations and friends and 'saudāyika', gifts given to the bride or to the couple either at her or at his place by the respective friends and relations. Yājñavalkya[18] says: what has been given to a woman by the friends, mother, the husband, or brothers, or is received by her at the nuptial fire, or presented to *her on her husband's marriage with another wife* is 'strīdhana'.

What has been given to her by her kindred (i.e., persons related through her mother or father) as well as her fee or gratuity or what has been presented to her after marriage by her husband or her father's family is also 'strīdhana'.[19] Clearly society at one time disapproved of the bride's father accepting money from the groom; Manu says[20] that an erudite father should not take any bride price 'kanyāśulka', for, by taking a dowry (kanyāśulka) out of greed, he (the girl's father) becomes the seller of his offspring…Even the acceptance of a pair of cows and bullocks (by the father of the bride from the bridegroom) is designated as a dowry by certain authorities. (The acceptance of a dowry be it costly, or be it of insignificant value constitute the sale of a girl.) We notice that while the practice of paying dowry to the groom is present in palpable or incipient forms, there is no text forbidding the groom's father accepting it, no one calls the transaction a 'sale' which in reality it was.

'This injunction against 'kanyāśulka' signifies a radical swing to 'varapana', an inevitable sign of Sanskritisation during the Kushana age when the earliest version of Manusaṃhitā was composed. Modern dowry is entirely the product of the forces let loose by British rule'.[21] 'Dowry is characterised by asymmetry, uncertainty and unpredictability.'[22] Dowry for the groom is a sign of hypergamy 'rampant in castes with continuous hierarchy; dowry mainly at the upper levels, and bride price mainly at the lower levels, and both dowry and bride price among status-seeking middle ranking families.'[23]

Whether it is dowry or bride price—it indicates affluence in society but much more so in 'dowry' than in 'bride price'. But this reluctance to accept bride price presumably signifies many social changes; apart from affluence which enabled the bride's family to pay a dowry, it may signify the cessation of large-scale warfare numerically reducing the male population, a desire for hypergamy, social climbing through wealth and, in the final analysis, it may have been based on some notion of potlatch whereby the bride's father realised that what he spent as dowry would be realised back at his son's wedding. And it definitely signifies the social demotion of women, for, when a man marries and thus saves a girl from the ignominy of maidenhood, her father had to pay him a price for this good office. A desire for ostentation and display was also there. Manu, who along with the *Bhagavadgītā and Vātsyāyana* was a formidable influence in society in the early centuries AD, calls the tune for the next two millennia. He enunciates the different forms of marriage, in the first three of which it was the bride's father who pays money, gives gifts to the groom; only in the 'Asura' form is the reverse true. Its pejorative name 'Asura' may hark back to its origin from the Dravida countries where it was widespread until a couple of centuries ago.

But 'Kanyāśulka' had been imbibed as a custom prevalent from the later Vedic age. We hear: 'Indra, you are a greater donor than a partially fit son-in-law or brother-in-law.'[24] So, defective grooms compensated with money. An effort to reconcile dowry with 'kanyāśulka' is found in the *Āpastamba Dharmasūtra* (II: 6 : 13 :10 :11) which says 'there is no selling or buying of the issue. At marriage a hundred great charioteer' fighters should be given and then they should be returned to the giver; there 'buying' is merely a word of praise; the relationship is based on religion.' Kautilya says, 'For mlecchas the sale of daughters was not condemned.'[25] Yājñavalkya very rationally says that neither son nor daughter could be sold.[26]

The *Mitākṣarā* gloss on the passage says that 'though one cannot sell one's wife or daughter, one is their owner'. We remember that Śunahśepha, a son, could be sold by the father, but there are also instances of sale of daughters.

Dowry has been explained as the cost of the bride's maintenance. This theory holds no water, because she contributes to the household work and produces, with luck, an heir to the family wealth. It has also been said to be the 'dakṣiṇā' of the 'kanyādana'. This also is fallacious because frequently the so-called 'dakṣiṇā' is out of all proportion to the 'dāna', the woman, a social non-entity. Esther Boserup says that after the withdrawal of women from the outdoor productive labour force, dowry come in is a compensation because men had to be hired in their place [27] There may be an element of historical truth in it.

Dowry is not 'strīdhana' because it was given at the instance of the groom's father. 'Peninsular India', says M. N. Srinivas, 'was the bride-price area including among the Brahmins; from there it spread to the north through a hankering for hypergamy, for social climbing'.[28]

Now, the dowry paid by the bride's father was given to the groom and his father, hence it did not constitute any part of 'strīdhana', the wife had no say on its use or misuse. If the would-be bride dies after 'kanyāśulka' has been paid by the groom, he takes back what he had paid.[29] A late text by Aparārka categorically says that 'the 'saudāyika' was under the full control of the wife'; she could sell or give even immovable properly. She could keep it intact; neither the husband nor her sons or her (or his) brothers could take it or give it away; the woman had complete control over it. But what was given to her by friends and relations at the time of wedding at her parent's place was definitely 'yautaka', a form of 'strīdhana' and what was given to the couple at her or his place at/after wedding was 'saudāyika' and the bride was entitled to at least half of it. Manu also says: 'To a woman whose husband marries a second wife, let him give an equal sum as a compensation for the supersession, provided no strīdhana has been bestowed on her but if she has been allotted, let him allot half'.[30] But 'on the death of a son-less 'putrikā' the husband shall unhesitatingly take the entire estate left by her.'[31] Viṣṇu, however, says that the property of a son-less person goes to the wife, then to daughters, and then to the brothers and the brothers' sons.[32]

In these texts we find local, regional and temporal variations of customs and attitudes. Some authors took a more humane stand than others. But the general picture is bleak and uncharitable for the wives. What the husband gave to her at his subsequent marriage was entirely hers. Nārada says that the husband had to give one-third of his property to the first wife at his second marriage. And this she was free to handle at her will. At least theoretically. Yājñavalkya[33] says that the husband has no right to touch the 'strīdhana' except during a famine, a necessary religious purpose, at times of disease or during his imprisonment. Although the extenuating circumstances all sound quite innocuous, they actually provide plenty of loopholes for interpretation suitable to the husband. At another place Yājñavalkya says, 'A husband is not liable to make good the property of his wife taken by him in a famine, or for the performance of a duty, or during illness or under restraint'.[34] In yet another text he says: 'The separate properly of a childless woman, married according to Brāhma 'Daiva' 'Arṣa' or 'Prājāpatya' (modes) goes to her husband' So society just could not visualise or tolerate a woman handling her own personal property. And Vaśiṣṭha defines it quite clearly: 'What has been given to her on her husband's next marriage, what was given to her by kindred (as 'saudāyika' or 'yautaka') and her 'sulka' or what was given to her after marriage is the woman's property, her 'strīdhana'.[35] Manu says that the mother's dowry is the portion of her daughter, and the daughter's son shall take the entire estate of a son-less man.[36]

But, then, Manu says[37]: 'Friends or relations of a woman, who out of folly or avarice live upon the property *belonging to her*, or the wicked ones who deprive her of the enjoyment of her *own belongings* such as cloth, etc., go to hell.' Now, first, theoretically her personal belongings could include much beyond mere 'cloth, etc.', for it could be something, as the text says, which 'friends and relations could live upon out of avarice.' A very early text, the *Maitrāyaṇī Saṃhitā*, a later Vedic text of approximately the eighth century BC says: 'Relations of a woman who live by selling carts, clothes, and gold ornaments which are her 'strīdhana' commit a sin and suffer a worse fate in the next world.'[38] So 'clothes, etc.', was a mere eye-wash; the in-laws sometimes—possibly more often than not—shamelessly lived upon the wealth she brought with her. Thus, even a rich father's daughter—as her 'strīdhana' amply testify—had no real security at her in-laws' place. Debarred from academic training and, therefore, from a lucrative vocation, helpless, in a hopeless, minority among an overwhelming majority of avaricious in-laws she had no real way of protecting what was her very own, let alone enjoy it. Therefore, such things happened, the author is neither making empty conjectures nor putting ideas into innocent heads. And one wonders how far the fear of going to hell or a worse fate in the next life deterred, those who lived upon the poor girl's 'strīdhana'. Enjoying unearned property is in most cases quite alluring. Devala, however, maintains that 'kanyāśulka' and the profits from usury are the woman's personal possession, the husband has no control over it. Jaimini also says that women do hold certain kinds of property. But Kātyāyana says that what wealth a woman earns through crafts or what is given by other in love, the husband is the proprietor of all that. What remains is 'strīdhana'.[39] Clearly, not much would remain, for, this text brings her earnings and her gifts under her husband's control. It is difficult to imagine any other kind of 'strīdhana'.

What is the wife's role in administering the household funds and property? Āpastamba says: 'The couple administered the family wealth.'[40] Even the philosophical text *Pūrvamīmāṃsā* says that 'the couple owns the property jointly'.[41] We remember the Indo-European root of the Sanskrit word 'dampatī': it comes from domos + pati, the lords of the house, and who was it? The couple. Clearly both Āpastamba and the *Pūrvamīmāṃsā* hark back to the original meaning of the words.

'When the husband leaves his home on a business trip he must go after making provisions for the wife's maintenance.'[42] 'If during his absence the wife drinks or attends public dances she should be fined six 'kṛṣṇalas.'[43] But a woman is not bound[44] to repay the debt contracted by her husband or sons. The, debt contracted by the wives of milkmen, wine sellers, actors, washer men and hunters should be liquidated by the husbands, for, their livelihood depends upon them, that is, upon the earnings of their wives. A debt which she has promised to repay, that which she has contracted along with her husband and what she had taken herself must be repaid by the woman; nothing else a woman is bound to repay. 'The taker of a debtor's wife has to repay her husband's debt.'[45] The very question, of repayment of debts presupposes a woman's financial ability to pay. But in such cases the payment was made from the common household funds, and when she had no access to it, presumably from her 'strīdhana'. At the back of this notion is the assumption that a woman should not, and therefore cannot, possess wealth. Medhātithi[46] says that whatever a woman earns is the husband's, Ā says that 'some predecessors think that ornaments belong to wife and also such wealth as came from her agnates'.[47] There seems to be a controversy regarding the bride's ownership of even her ornaments, about those she brought from her parents' place! Baudhāyana says, 'The daughter inherits her mother's, jewellery and whatever else is customary.'[48] Manu sets an upper limit for 'strīdhana'—up to 2000 panas.[49] But land and houses do not constitute 'strīdhana', say these authors, presumably because they cannot be removed to her in-law's place. Jaimini agrees that women do and can own certain types of property. Manu says that the sources of 'strīdhana' are six: at marriage, during the bridal procession, gifts given out of love; from brothers and from parents. Kātyayāna adds an interesting rider: 'what she earns through crafts, and what she is given out love is under the husband's control the rest is 'strīdhana'.'[50] It is a cruel realisation that what she earns herself is not her own. 'Yautaka' technically means, what is given to the couple (yutaka) when they are seated together.[51] 'A wicked spendthrift wife has no right over her 'strīdhana'.'[52] It was not very difficult for wicked avaricious in-laws to prove that a wife is a spendthrift and thus snatch away from her what legally belonged to her. 'Strīdhana' promised by the husband has to be paid to the wife.'[53]

The payment of 'kanyāśulka' laid a burden on the wife, because she and everybody else regarded her as a bought commodity. 'This', says the ancient text, the *Mailrāaṇī Saṃhitā*, 'is acting false, when a woman bought by her husband commits adultery with others'. But we should remember that when the dowry system came into vogue the groom never regarded himself as a purchased commodity although he was that in a much truer sense than the bought wife, because 'kanyāśulka' had always been a mere nothing compared to dowry which is a status symbol, besides being an unfair and unashamed extortion.

Manu says,

> Wives cannot be kept by force; it is by the application of the following expedients that they can be kept under control. They should be employed in storing and spending money (i.e., looking after the family economy), in maintaining the cleanliness of their persons and of the house, the beddings, wearing apparels, household furniture. Imprisoned in the house and guarded by their male relations, (bad) women are still not sufficiently protected.[54]

So, one of the measures for keeping the wife under control, so necessary as a guarantee of a legitimate heir, was to engage her in household work of various kinds which were never translated into monetary terms, so that she was always made to feel that she was a financial burden to the family.

Once the woman lost her husband, society began to look upon her as a financial menace and liability. In an agricultural society where the joint family was the unit, the threat of segmenting the cultivable land owned by the family was very real. This could happen if at the husband's death the land came to the widow, she remarried and her new husband was to be given her share of the land. Both ideas must have been repugnant to the other brothers. Later Vedic lawmakers, except one or two, laid down that the widow should be burned alive with the corpse of her husband. Or if she was allowed to live at all, the law-givers made her life a living death with a thousand pinpricks in her daily existence to remind her that she had no economic shelter.

Yājñavalkya says that 'a woman having no husband should be taken care of by the father, mother, son, brother, mother-in-law, father-in-law; otherwise she will be an object of censure.'[55] In the list of her guardians all except the last two are members of her own family who were expected to take her into their custody and be her financial provider. Āpastamba, Manu and Nārada agree that the widow of a son-less husband cannot inherit, Gautama, however, says that she is an heir with her 'sapiṇḍas' and 'sagotras'.[56] Elsewhere, Yājnāvalkya lays down that a sonless man's widow is his first heir;[57] in this he is joined by Viṣṇu and Kātyayāna. If a woman's husband is not heard of for eight or ten years she may remarry.[58] If the husband leaves a separate individual property and a son or sons, the widow is entitled only to maintenance. Manu is ambivalent regarding 'niyoga'—another man begetting a son on the widow, he condemns it.[59] Widows, and for that matter, women in general, cannot adopt a child by themselves, because they cannot pronounce the necessary Vedic mantras. So they could not by themselves adopt a child on whom they could lean financially.

One of the seven fates Narada visualises for a widow is for her to be purchased by a foreigner.[60] Remarriage, which is technically enjoined upon her by Parashara makes her a 'punarbhu' who forfeits her rights to her husband's property. She could also be given to a stranger by her elders and she had no say in the matter, but even then she had to forego the right to her husband's property. We may recall that because in the area controlled by the Dayabhaga rules, widows did inherit the husband's property, which they could not do in the areas under Mitākṣarā; between 1815 and 1818, total 2,366 widows were burned in Bengal, of which 1,845 were from Calcutta alone. A widow has been a pitiable creature even in the *Rgvedic* times or we would not have a prayer for non-widowhood. But the epics and even Manu do not condemn them to death, Kunti and Gāndharī and the three queens of Daśaratha, widows in Buddhist and Jain literature lived and lived respectably. Among the lower ranks, before the unfortunate contamination of Sanskritisation reached them, there was no widow burning, it caught on with Sanskritisation. Literature does not give us instances of the widows of the so-called lower ranks.

The economic problem of widows was considerably complicated by polygamy and by the social 'weightage given to the mother of a male child. Widows with daughters only or childless widows suffered economically and generally had to fall back on their parents or brothers. At their in-laws' places they were looked down upon as an imposed liability. Besides, a man with wives from different castes left his affairs in a further tangle where authors of the *Smṛtis* differed with each other regarding the fate of the widows; some upheld the widow's claim to maintenance, others to bare subsistence. Sometimes there are discrepancy between scriptures and practices recorded in literature. Gautama[61] says 'the estates of a childless person go to his wife'. Yet in the *Abhijñānaśakuntal*,[62] we hear that when such a case was reported to Dusyanta, he says that the scriptures say that these estates will be forfeited by the crown. He possibly had a different authority or mere local customs to guide him.

Divorce was not accepted in the Western sense of the term. Although there are scriptural texts which lay down that even a hostile wife could not be forsaken. But if there is mutual hatred, the couple can separate.

> If a husband wishes separation, because of some change for the worse in a wife, he should return what he had taken from her. If a wife desires freedom because of a similar change in the husband then he should not give her what he had taken from her. In religious weddings there is no divorce.[63]

Clearly the text reluctantly grants both parties the rights to separate on the ground of hatred, but while the man's initiative to separate is respected, the woman is punished financially, because on separation she loses her 'strīdhana'.

Rape, a common feature in all societies, is treated somewhat leniently. Yājñavalkya says[64] that a man pays 10 paṇas for raping a maidservant. If he rapes a female religious mendicant he pays 24 paṇas.[65] The first question that strīkes us about the master raping the maid was how was she to force the man to pay? Who would believe her, who would take her side? While a female mendicant's words have more credibility and it is likely that she would get paid if she insisted, but the whole proposition sounds somewhat unreal.

Literature gives us umpteen instances where the rapist goes scot-free. Besides, laws and customs were so lenient to the upper caste men that women of the so-called lower castes were easily available without any payment. Hence the text was not expected to act as a deterrent. The abject position of women in society rendered her eminently vulnerable to man's lust, and such men acted with impunity with the connivance of the law-givers and with social sanction.

Unchaste wives were punished with horrendous cruelty; the *Dharmasūtra* texts on such punishment reads like passages from sadist authors. Other texts lay down:

> One should deprive an unchaste wife of all her rights, make her live poorly, taking only 'one morsel of food. She should always be chidden, and should lie on the ground but she should live in her husband's house (so that she might withdraw from her sinful courses).[66]

Now, the question is: what happens when she mends her ways? Does she then get a full meal and the right to his bed? 'If a husband renounces a wife who carries out his command, is skilful in work, has given birth to heroic sons, such a wife should be given one-third of (her husband's) properly and maintenance.'[67] What makes the wife's life lack economic and social security is that even a flawless wife could be dismissed with only one-third of the husband's property. Not only did society have a double standard for men and woman, but it is difficult to see the wife who falls out of her husband's favour getting even her legal claim in full. 'A false wife should be kept imprisoned in a room on an allowance of daily sustenance. A wife violating the duties of chastity undergoes penance; she should be kept under guard and given food.'[68] An adulterous woman should be deprived of her authority (over servants, etc.), made to wear dirty clothes, given a bare minimum of food, for subsistence. If she conceives from the other man, she should be driven away.[69] Vaśīṣṭha says:[70] 'Wives of the three upper castes committing adultery with sūdras should be driven away. If the wife tries to kill the husband or the instructor (guru), she should be driven away.'[71] Gautama lays down that 'if a wife of the three upper castes commits adultery with a man of a lower caste she should be devoured by dogs.'[72]

On the other hand, Āpastamba[73] and Baudhāyana[74] both lay down that a son should always serve the mother without speaking to her, even if she becomes outcaste for some grievous sin.

An outcaste father may be abandoned, presumably because he could fend for himself, and he controlled the family funds, but the son should never abandon his mother even if she is fallen.

There are inherent contradictions between the texts stipulating harsh punishments for the unchaste wife, and the essential, but basic and minimal humanity of the son not abandoning his mother. Literature presents a totally different picture; 'fallen' wives are cursed, punished, abandoned and even killed (*cf* Sītā, Ahalyā and Reṇukās).

Prostitution in India is known from the Vedic times. The many synonyms possibly signify many grades or classes, the highest of them was the 'gaṇikā' who was trained in the various arts at the state's expense; her charges were also the highest. Buddhist texts say that Sālāvatī at Rajagṛha charged a hundred kārṣāpanas per night and Amrapali's fees led to a dispute between Rajagrha and Vaisali. The play *Mṛcchakatika* tells us of a client sending a thousand gold coins for her favour; the story of Ardhakāśī is well known. The 'gaṇikā' lived in a palace, sumptuously, had many servants, maids, procurers, Vitas, Pīṭhamardas, male attendants, and musicians at her service. Kauṭilya says that the 'gaṇikā' was paid a monthly salary from the royal treasury and the 'pratigaṇikā', her substitute, got half of this sum. 'Possibly the 'gaṇika's' palace, entourage and establishment were state property with life interest.'[75] This means that the '*ganikā*' did not only not possess it but could neither sell, nor mortgage nor donate it. This rule holds for those who belonged to an establishment; but there were others, beside the avaruddhās, that is, women kept temporarily by men who provided for them, who ran an establishment singly. We may conjecture that what these women earned became part of their own possessions, after paying obligatory taxes to the state.

The court paid the courtesans an annual salary of between 1,000 and 2,000 paṇas. Anyone who wished to redeem a courtesan and make a free woman of her, or marry her paid the state redemption money of 24,000 paṇas. This was a considerable sum of money, but then her salary also was high. One of the reasons why the state undertook to bear the courtesān's education was that the king and his nobles often summoned young and pretty courtesāns to entertain them. Another reason was that the superintendent of the courtesans, the 'gaṇikādhyakṣa' was frequently employed to extort politically relevant information which the 'gaṇikās' would skilfully make their customers divulge to them.

But 'gaṇikās' were often quite rich on their own; in most cities the best of them were known as 'nagarśobhinīs', that is, decorations to the cities, and could attract wealthy customers. In the *Dhammapada* commentary we hear of Sālāvatī's daughter Sirimā earning 1,000 paṇas every night. A rūpājīva who was socially and accomplishment-wise inferior to a 'gaṇika', and who usually lived with wine- or meat-sellers, etc., earned only a fee of 48 panas. If a man forcibly assaulted a 'gaṇikā's daughter he had to pay a fine of 54 paṇas, also a fine of 16 times her mother's fees, possibly a kind of hush-money used at the time of her marriage. A 'pumścalī', in the bottom rung of the hierarchy had no fixed fees, Kauṭilya says that old and retired prostitutes should be employed as cooks, store-keepers, cotton-wool, and flax spinners and in certain other manual jobs. They could also be employed as matrons, 'matṛkas', in brothels or be trainers of courtesans and earn something. But the pension promised by Kauṭilya in the *Arthāśastra* was something that had very little guarantee for these otherwise helpless women: A prostitute was obliged to inform the brothel-keeper about her income and expenditure.[76]

The 'devadāsīs' or temple prostitutes were paid in grain as some others employed by the states also were. The devadāsīs' income is nowhere stated clearly nor were their duties specified. Their ranks swelled from the pious wish of rich patrons who desired to earn merit for the next world by buying girls for the temples. No courtesan whether in the brothel or in the temple enjoyed security of the person; the *Gautama Dharmasūtra* categorically states that 'the murder of a prostitute is no crime'.[77]

We have seen that in general, women were not allowed to earn or possess property. The *Śatapatha Brāhmana*, an early text, presumably of the eighth-seventh centuries BC say's that the wife had no property rights, nor had she any right over her own body (IV 4: 2:13). Quite early, around the seventh century BC the *Śatapatha Brāhmana* gives a ritual justification of this. In a rite the sacrificial butter was beaten with a stick, 'so should a husband beat his wife so that she had no right over her body or over any property.'[78] Yet we have evidence of women donors in society. Not only queens but a female Jain disciple of the venerable Jayasena, or the female Jain convert of Sīhamitra, the female pupil of Sathisiha, the female pupil of Puṣyamitra, etc.,[79] Dharmasomā, the wife of a caravan-leader, or Kocchā, a female lay disciple of ascetics, gave various kinds of gifts to the pious Jain brethren and the temples. The *Bṛahatkalpabhāṣyasutra* mentions the gift of a grove by courtesan Āmrāpalī. Ānāthapiṇḍada's daughter fed Buddha and thousands of his disciples. We also hear of gifts by courtesans and other Buddhist women who donated monasteries, 'caityas' 'viharas', groves, bridges, wells, ponds and money. In the fifth century AD Chandragupta II's daughter queen Prabhavatī gave rich gifts. In the Bhaumaka dynasty in Orissa is listed six queens out of a total of seventeen monarchs. Diddā Khemā in the Rājatarangiṇi ruled as a regent and later as a monarch. In the same book queens Chuddā and Damarī led armirs in battle. Doubtless, these queens wielded economic power also. But most of these are late evidences, post-Tantric, after a time of widespread deification of the woman as a goddess. No wonder, queens, were looked up to as exercising a kind of extra-human potency as agents, like the kings. They, too, had been revered all through history;[80] then so was the queen who handled wealth on her own authority and power.

Now the question that strikes us is: if women did not possess any money how could they make such expensive gifts. One answer is that rich 'gaṇikās' who ran their own establishments owned the wealth they earned after paying the state tax. A sense of moral guilt often prompted them to spend substantial portions of their wealth in pious enterprises. Secondly, not everyone in society obeyed the rules laid down by the scriptures verbatim, some women did possess their 'strīdhana', which if they came from royal or noble or merchant families, could be quite substantial and often they found themselves in a position to silence slander or censure, because money talks. So they could and did make gifts. Thirdly, parallel laws with different sanctions co-existed, especially, in matriarchal regions, Fourthly, not all gifts recorded as donations from women, saints, wives, widows or courtesans are to be taken literally, quite often some devotee or disciples made donations in the name of pious, powerful or famous women. Also some generous husbands would encourage such pious expenditure although Āpastamba says that 'when the husband is away from home, the wife may make the usual expenditure; that shall not be counted as theft.'[81] The clear corollary is that if she undertakes some unusual expenses, she should be regarded as stealing the husband's money! Yet society provided enough loopholes through which in exceptional circumstances women could donate or spend what was their own.

We hear of Sparta of the 4th, 3rd centuries BC that 'Nearly two-fifths of the whole country belongs to women, because there are many heiresses and because of giving large dowries.'[82] In Athens if a dowry was given, the law did require that it should be returned if the marriage came to an end.[83] Under Roman law 'Brides could be purchased'.[84] If the husband put her away for any other reason (than adultery) he had to give her one half of his property,[85] the reminder being forfeited to the goddess Ceres, the 'peculium' which they might use as if it were their own, though technically it belonged to the pater.'[86] 'The Voconian law provided that a person in the first class in the census, the wealthiest, could not appoint a woman heir',[87] In Crete, 'A daughter could be given her portion without waiting for her father's death.' The son-less father's property came to the daughter known as 'patroiukhos' (or 'epikleros')[88]. Thus we see that except the Voconian law prescribing for the wealthiest section of society, at places under different laws, women could and did inherit property in Greece and Rome.

Under the Gortyn law 'A married female slave could herself possess property for the divorce regulations state that she may take her movables (presumably personal property) and small livestock.'[89] Thus even the slave under the generous Gortyn law could possess property. But the general picture is dismal even in Greece and Rome compared to their men's right of possession and use of property, although compared to India the laws were more liberal. Control over women's property by men is part of a paradigm of an all-round control over her, ordained by the state through its religious instructor.

> The state in order to be a control of the means of reproducing human beings and in order to submit these means to the interests of the economic system which happens to be in force at the time, has been obliged to extend its control and subjugation to that of her own body. She has, therefore, lost the real ownership of her own body.[90]

We remember how the Brāhmaṇa injunction of beating sacrificial butter with a stick gives a ritual justification: 'thus beaten the wife loses control over her own body and property.' The juxtaposition of body and property is significant; the body also is a part of the property.

We must remember Draupadī's question to Duhsasana when she was being dragged to the court for public insult. She asked him, 'Did King Yudhiṣṭhira stake and lose himself in the gamble before he lost me?' The question is extremely pertinent: she insinuates that if Yudhiṣṭhira had lost himself first then he had no right to stake Draupadī. In other words, she admits tacitly that if he had staked her as a free agent then she was really under the hold of the Kauravas, that is, she is virtually a possession of her husband who could pawn her. Long before, the gambler in the Ṛgveda laments that he had pawned his wife. So, the wife was treated as the husband's possession. Devayānī was part of Sarmiṣṭhā's dowry; but Yayāti who married Sarmiṣṭha enjoyed Devayānī slyly and begot Anu, Puru and Druhyu in her. So, just as the inanimate parts of the dowry could be misappropriated by the husband, so could the human entourage which accompanied the bride.

That women could be used as commodity is proved by the story of Mādhavī. When Gālava, unable to procure fees for his preceptor, asked king Yayāti for a donation, the latter pleaded a depleted treasury. But he offered Gālava an option: the king's pretty young maiden daughter could be borrowed and lent out to kings for a year until the latter had a son by her and in gratitude offered Gālava some money. Gālava lent her to three kings, in succession for a year each, until he raised enough money to pay his fees for the preceptor. Neither Yayāti, nor Gālaya nor the four kings found this method foul or heinous; and the preceptor accepted the fees, presumably cheerfully. Only Mādhavī expressed her profound disgust at the whole affair by firmly declining to marry. She had been used as a lucrative chattel and her innermost soul revolted at this. She undertook penance.

Analysing the deprivation of ancient Indian women from earning, possessing or disbursing money, from selling, pawning, mortgaging and donating money or other kinds of property, we find several reasons. After the Aryans had conquered the major portion of northern Indian land-tract, they had a supply of inexpensive slaves. Before, women of the family assisted their menfolk in outdoor economic activities and were thus a recognised part of the productive system. They enjoyed a modicum of human dignity as breadwinners or breadwinners' assistants. But with a large force of slaves at the Aryans' beck and call, women did not have to participate in the strenuous outdoor work. By then the surplus in production and trade both inland and overseas, accumulated in the hands of a privileged few in a class-divided society. From the Brāhmana literature onwards, we have mention of conspicuous consumption by a handful of families belonging to the upper stratum of society.

Then, the anxiety to leave the property to the legitimate heir led to strīcter confinement of women in the inner apartments and greater vigilance by the males. Besides, this way by keeping indoors, the women preserved the delicacy of their appearance, most welcome to the male owners of property. Then, it became clear that women, most of whom were virtually illiterate, skilled only in the domestic chores, were economically a burden to their husbands and this facilitated the process of their being looked upon as chattels. In the second century BC Vātsyāyana openly says about women twice in two different contexts—about the maiden and about the prostitute—that they should dress up richly and attractively 'because women are a commodity'.[91]

Now if women themselves are looked upon as commodity, as possession or property, one does not expect them to enjoy any freedom to handle property or wealth. Society was afriad to treat them as human individuals.

Women's contribution to housework was never measured in terms of money, hence although many of them did a lot of household chores, they were treated as economically dependent on men for food, clothes, shelter and other necessities of life. Even being engaged in productive work is not enough, she is still treated as a liability and is expected to be subordinate to the father, brother, husband or son. When she has cash and real property that she can handle at will, only then is her economic identity recognised. It is the legal sanction, plus a conscious freedom to spend, save or do what she likes with her wealth that gives her the recognition of a woman of substance. The 'strīdhana' or 'saudāyikā' or 'yautaka' was theoretically entirely her own; but the consciousness shared by society and the woman herself' that she was a 'bharyā' or 'bhāraṇīya', that is, to be fed and therefore in bond under the husband and in-laws for her maintenance, like the 'bhṛītya', servant, facilitated the plunder of the 'strīdhana' by the in-laws. Only the very rich women, like queens whose wealth was augmented by political power had real control over their money. Or the courtesan who 'earned' her own money, paid tax and sometimes was really so rich that the king and merchants had to take cognizance of her power was occasionally free to wield power in society through their money. Besides, rich donors are everywhere respected and money carries no taint to greedy donneés. Pious works launder the taint in money everywhere and at all times.

But apart from these exceptions, the ordinary maids, housewives, or widows were quite under the thumb of the men of their families, because their labour at home, however heavy, was not regarded as productive; their sole worth lay in their reproductive role. But even there, they were seen as 'the field', the harvest belonged to the seed-owner. For long centuries, society slowly but surely removed from under the women's feet the bottom board of self-confidence by depriving her of education and by assigning such a mindless role to them within the house, that their general intelligence was curbed and men proclaimed that the women neither need money nor could be trusted with it.

NOTES

1. VV 380.
2. Ibid.
3. *Manu*, VIII
4. *Manu*, VIII: 244.
5. *Saṃvarta* 162.
6. *Gautama:* IX, 118.
7. *Gautama:* XXIX, 11.
8. V: 5 : 8 : 2.
9. Nirindriyā adāyādāśca striyo iti matah. Adāyādā bhaginyeti.
10. Vaśiṣṭha XV.
11. *Visnu* LXVII : 30.
12. I: 11.
13. VI: 4: 17
14. 'Ācaryā and upādhyāyā'.
15. *Mahānirvāṇatantra* VIII: 35, 47.
16. *Manu* III: 317.
17. *Manu* II X : 29.
18. *DS* II.
19. *Yāj* II: 145, 147.
20. III: 51.
21. M N Srinivas 1989, *The Cohesive Role of Sanskritisation,* OUP, p. 102.
22. Ibid., p. 16.
23. Ibid., p. 121, FN 5.

24. *RV* I: 109: 2.
25. III: 73.
26. II: 175.
27. *Women's Role in Economie Development*, George Allen and Unwin, 1970.
28. Srinivas, op cit, 1989, p. 100.
29. *Yajñavalkya DS* II: 146.
30. III: 52.
31. *Vyāsa DS* IV: 30.
32. *Viṣṇu DS* VIII: 4, 5.
33. V: 95.
34. II: 151
35. XV: 11: 18.
36. IX: 131.
37. III: 52.
38. *MS*: 1: 11.
39. V: 904.
40. II: 6: 13: 17–18.
41. VI: 1: 17–21.
42. *Manu* IX: 74.
43. Ibid.
44. To repay the debt.
45. *Saṃhitā II*: 49–52.
46. On *Manu* VIII : 416.
47. *DS* II: 6: 14: 9.
48. *DS* II: 2 : 49.
49. VIII: 416; also *Kātyāyana DS* 902.
50. 904.
51. *Kātyāyana DS* 905, 907, 911.
52. *Kātyāyana DS*, op cit, 914.
53. *Kātyāyana DS*, op cit, 916.
54. *Manu* IX: 10, 11.
55. I: 86.
56. XVIII: 19.
57. II: 135.
58. *Nārada DS* Strīpurusau Section VV 98–101.
59. IX: 64-8.
60. V: 45.
61. *DS* XXIX: 9.
62. Act V.
63. Kautilya: *Arthaśāstia: Dharmasthīya* III: 16.
64. *Arthaśāstra Dharmasthīya* II, II: 294.
65. *Arthaśāstra Dharmasthīya* II, op cit, 296.
66. *Yājñavalkya DS* I: 70.
67. *Yājñavalkya DS*, op cit, I: 76.
68. *Gautama DS* XXIII last verse.
69. *Yājñavalkya DS* I: 70, 72.
70. *DS* XXI: 12.

71. *DS* XXI, op cit, 10.
72. XXIII: 24.
73. *DS* I : 10: 28, 29.
74. *DS* II: 2: 48.
75. Moti Chandra: *The World of Courtesans*, Vikash, 1973, p. 48.
76. See my article, 'Prostitution in Ancient India' in *Social Scientist*, No. 165, February, 1987, included in this collection.
77. XXII :2.
78. IV: 4: 3: 13.
79. *Epigraphia Indica*, Vol. IV, p. 199.
80. cf 'aṣṭanām lokapālānām mātrābhirnimito nrpah'.
81. II: 6: 20.
82. *Civilisation of the Ancient Mediterranean: Greece and Rome*, Vol. I, p. 594.
83. *Civilisation of…*, op cit, 596.
84. P. 613.
85. The individual property of' women and slaves.
86. P. 614.
87. P. 620.
88. P. 592.
89. Sarah B Pomeroy: *Goddess, Whores, Wives and Slaves,* New York, 1975, p. 41.
90. Nawal El Saadawi: *The Hidden Face of Eve*, Zed Press, 1980, p. 63
91. II: 1: 13; IV: I: 1.

Chapter 5

Dynamics of Women's Work in the Śāstric Sources: Household and Beyond

KAVITA GAUR

In the context of the representation of women in early historic period, historians often throw light upon the economic roles of women through specific angles/perspectives. The notion of 'women workers'[1] is confined to certain categories such as hired labourers, prostitutes, wet nurses, espionage, domestic servants, singers, and dancers, who are explicitly identified as women earning their livelihood.[2] On the other hand, the familial roles of women are valorised; and their domestic labour is never translated into economic terms.[3] The interface between social and economic status of women is succinctly described in this statement: 'women whose social status was legitimate, did not have equivalent legitimate access to an independent economic status, whereas women whose socio-sexual status are ambivalent at best, were more easily recognised as independent actors.'[4]

The interplay of women, work and class has been studied by historians. With respect to engagement of women in economic processes, it has been argued that women of rural classes participate actively in economic activities along with their men while women in urban societies are less likely seen to be involved in economic roles.[5] The representation of women in a rural–urban scenario is conceptualised in another work where author suggests

---

[1] A. K. Tyagi, *Women Workers in Ancient India* (New Delhi: Radha Publications, 1994).

[2] By women workers, Tyagi meant women engaged in productive activities such as agricultural and craft activities; weaving, dyeing and washing professions; occupations such as nurses, espionage, maid servants; women slaves; singing, dancing and prostitution (Tyagi, *Women Workers*, 3). The author also points out that the idea of exploitation appears to be linked with the working class women in the context of early India.

[3] Sukumari Bhattacharji, *Women and Society in Ancient India* (Calcutta: Basumati Corporations, 1994), 50. Bhattacharji argued that wives are supposed to undertake household duties of various kinds but it is not translated into monetary terms. And above this, wives are regarded as the financial burden of the family.

[4] See Kumkum Roy, ed., *Women in Early Indian Societies* (New Delhi: Manohar Publishers, 1999).

[5] See Vijaya Ramaswamy, 'Aspects of Women and Work in Early South India', *Indian Economy and Social History Review* 26, no. 1 (1989): 81–89.

that women have limited control over economic processes either in rural or urban areas.[6] While commenting upon the relation of gender, labour and class, Chakravarti argued that women of lower classes, despite having relative economic independence, were not regarded as equivalent to men.[7] Till now scholars have mainly confined themselves to viewing the relation of women and work in specific paradigms. This chapter seeks to examine the layers in which women engage with work activities within and beyond the household sphere.[8]

This chapter inquires into the dynamic engagement of household women in varied range of domestic and economic activities. It points out the distinction noticed in the *śāstras* with regard to women undertaking economic activities through the household and women's engagement in economic activities outside the household. It draws attention to upper class wives who, though located in household sphere, contribute to wider economic processes through domestic space and are identified as 'government employees'. It also brings forth the categories of upper class women being engaged in undertaking varied range of productive activities within the domain of the household. The nature and extent of economic activities are studied in detail. It also analyses the provisions related to livelihood being outlined for women of the household in situations of the absence of men. Further, it also assesses the notion of working women being frequently tied or associated with the profession of sex-workers or a degraded class in normative texts.

This chapter is based on three principle *śāstras* in the Brahmanical framework, namely the *Arthaśāstra* assigned to Kauṭilya, the *Manusmṛti* ascribed to Manu and the *Kāmasūtra* ascribed to Vātsyāyana. Each text is supposed to be compiled over a period ranging from 200 to 500 years or more.[9] The date and origin of these texts remain a complex and debatable issue amongst historians. However, the *Arthaśāstra* is generally placed between the fourth/third century BCE to the second century CE;[10] the *Manusmṛti* is located between the second century BCE to the second/third century CE;[11] and the *Kāmasūtra* is supposed to be placed around the end of the third century CE.[12] Hence, these texts belong to an almost contemporary period ranging from fourth century BCE to the third century CE, therefore, being used for this chapter.

---

[6] See Chitrarekha Gupta, '"Rural-Urban Dichotomy" in the Concept and Status of Women', in *Position and Status of Women in Ancient India*, ed. L. K. Tripathi (Varanasi: Benaras Hindu University, 1988), 188–96.

[7] See Uma Chakravarti, 'Gender, Caste, and Labour: The Material and Ideological Structure of Widowhood', *Economic and Political Weekly* 30, no. 36 (1995): 248–56.

[8] This chapter is a part of an unpublished PhD thesis: Kavita Gaur, 'Understanding the Household: Norms and Everyday Lives in Textual Traditions (c. 3rd century BCE to 5th century CE)' (unpublished PhD thesis, Jawaharlal Nehru University, 2014).

[9] See Kumkum Roy, 'The King's Household: Structure/Space in the Śāstric Tradition', *Economic and Political Weekly* XXVII, nos. 43–44(1992), 55–60.

[10] R. P. Kangle, *Kautiliya Arthaśāstra*, Part I (Delhi: Motilal Banarsidass, 2003), 98–106.

[11] Patrick Olivelle (tr.), *Dharmasūtra Parallels* (Delhi: Motilal Banarsidass, 2005), 18–25.

[12] H. C. Chakladar, *Social Life in Ancient India: Studies in Vātsyāyana's Kāmasūtra* (Delhi: Bhartiya Publisihing House, 1976), 11–35.

I

Here, an attempt to examine the representation of the women of the household in economic and domestic activities and their contribution to domestic resources is being made. One also needs to point out here that some women may have been engaged in economic activities within the household, while others may have been engaged in activities outside the household and providing support to their households. Besides, there are certain domestic activities, though not defined in economic terms, yet increase the resources of the household.

The *Arthaśāstra* appears to engage women of the household in spinning; and they are supposed to perform activities within the household. The state makes provision for female slaves who are supposed to supply raw-materials to these women at home. This is evident in the statement:

> And those women who do not stir out, those living separately, widows, crippled women or maidens, who wish to earn their living, should be given work by sending his own female slaves to them with a (view to) support (them). Or, if they come themselves to the yarn house, he should cause an interchange of goods and wages to be made early at dawn. The lamp (should be there) only for the inspection of the yarn. For looking at the face of the woman or conversing with her on another matter, the lowest fine for violence (shall be imposed), for delay in the payment of wages, the middle fine, also for payment of wages for work not done. (AS II.23.11–14)[13]

Possibly, these women such as *aniṣkāsiṇyah* would have belonged to the upper castes; as the text mentions that they do not come out of the household. The kind of restrictions outlined in interactions with these women is indicative of the fact that they may have belonged to the upper caste. Interestingly, the provision regarding the wages (*vetana*) of these women is also an issue of discussion in the text. The state appears to be vigilant in outlining the issue of the wages of wives. Interestingly, this provides us an instance where productive activities are undertaken within the household whose economic value (payment) has been recognised.

Another significant aspect noted here is that the above injunction includes different types of women such as widows, crippled women, maidens, and mentions that it includes women who were living separately and wished to earn their living. It needs to be pointed out here that this economic role is assigned to women who are old and needed a livelihood for their maintenance. Or it could be said that this provision is specifically to provide maintenance to elderly women members of the household. Interestingly, the inclusion of the maiden along with other categories of secluded and elderly women suggests that the text may be indicating the presence of unmarried women in the household. The employment of these maidens suggests that they may have been able to earn their livelihood through these means, and they were able to maintain themselves in the natal household.

Another instance in the *Arthaśāstra* reiterates the notion of wives being regarded as generators of resources through making provision for their employment in spinning. This is evident in the statement:

---

[13] AS stands for the *Arthaśāstra*.

> He should get yarn spun out of wool, bark-fibres, cotton, silk cotton, hemp and flax through widows, crippled women, maidens, women who have left their homes and women paying off their fine by personal labour, through the mother of the courtesan, through old female slaves of the king and through female slaves of temples whose service of the gods has ceased. (AS II.23.2)

It could be noted here that women who had left home (*pravrajitā*) or were performing labour to pay their debts (*daṇḍa pratikāriṇībhī*) are talked about in the statement.

The above discussion suggests that some women may have performed work within the household and some women may have opted to undertake work in the place of production. It could also be suggested that the state appears to have provided employment to both types of women. The state appears to have encouraged these women of the household to work harder by giving gifts to them on festive days. This is noticed in the statement: 'After finding out the amount of yarn, he should favour them with oil and myrobalan unguents. And on festive days, they should be made to work by honouring (them) and making gifts' (AS II.23.4–5). Interestingly, the role of wives in assisting their husbands (*kuṭuṃbināh*) on the manufacture of white liquor on festive occasions for medicinal purposes is outlined in the text. This is evident in the statement: 'Women and children should make a search for (ingredients used in) in liquor and ferments' (AS II.25.38). Here, the manufacturing of liquor appears to be more of a domestic activity instead of an economic activity as they are permitted to produce for particular purposes. And, the division of labour between husband and wives is noticeable.

There are certain instances in the *Arthaśāstra* where the involvement of wives in economic transactions is not clearly mentioned. However, the indications of their earning capacity are observed in the text. For instance, wives in certain communities appear to have generated resources for the sake of the household. The earning capacity of wives is reflected in the responsibility for debt assigned to them. This is noticed in the statement: 'And the wife (shall not be held liable) for the debt incurred by their husband, if she has not assented to it, except in the case of cowherds and farmers tilling for half the produce' (AS III.11.23). This implies that wives of cowherds (*gopālaka*) and farmers (*ardhasītikebhyah*) were liable for the debt incurred by their husbands. The relationship between husband and wives in certain communities appear to be in stark contrast to the conventional household. The provision of sharing the responsibility for debt in lower communities is also indicative of the rights and responsibilities of both man and woman to earn a livelihood. The notion of the debt-paying capacity indicates that wives would have generated resources.

The wives, presumably belonging to lower communities such as *naṭas*, *nartakas*, etc., are recognised as tax-payers in the *Arthaśāstra*. This is indicated in the statement: 'Their musical instruments, when coming from foreign lands, shall be charged a fee per show of five *paṇas*' (AS II.27.26). Wives of *naṭas*, *nartakas*, etc., were also supposed to pay a special fee on performing in specific cases. The levying of taxes means the charge (of the state) upon the property or income of the individual; it presumes that the individual is earning income or generating revenue resources. Hence, it appears that wives of these communities could be regarded as generating resources for their households. The role of wives in procreative activities contributed to further production processes; however, it is not emphasized much in the text. It could be argued here that wives would have played a role in both productive and reproductive processes related to households.

In the *Manusmṛti*, the text does not recognise the role of women of upper classes as generating resources or participating in productive activities. In an instance, the text includes men who live upon the livelihood undertaken by their wives as committing a secondary sin (*upapātaka*) which leads to loss of caste (MS XI.64). The term *stryajīvo abhicāro* is mentioned here which means wives obtaining a livelihood through transgressive activities (*vyabhicāro*). However, the text does not clearly mention what constitutes transgressive activities.

The *Manusmṛti* also provides an insight into the household of lower communities where wives are envisioned as earning wealth or providing subsistence, hence contributing to the generation of resources in the household. This is evident in the following statement: 'The above rule does not apply to wives of travelling performers or to wives who earn a living of their own, for such men get their women to attach themselves to men and, concealing themselves, get them to have sexual liaisons' (MS[14] VIII.362).

It has been mentioned in the context of outlining the sexual crimes of women of twice-born men where the definition of adultery and its punishments have been laid out. Within this background, the text mentioned that sexual liaison is seen as a form of livelihood in lower communities; hence, exceptions were made to the norms defined earlier in the text. The above statement also indicates two or three features related to the household of lower communities. Wives of lower ranks were expected to earn a livelihood for their families through sex work. Interestingly, the authority was vested with their husband, and hierarchical relations within the household were not altered despite the earning of their wives. The husbands were expected to conceal their identity probably due to the low status associated with the profession of their wives.

Interestingly, the *Kāmasūtra* speaks of a diverse range of productive activities undertaken by wives within the household and without payment. In the situation of the presence of the husband as well, the engagement of wives in various domestic and productive activities is discussed in the *Kāmasūtra*. The role of wives in the generation and supervision of a diverse range of resources is highlighted in contrast to the role of the householder. This is evident in the statement: 'In well-weeded plots of ground she sees to the planting of beds of herbs and green vegetables, and clumps of sugarcane, and patches of cumin seeds and caraway, mustard seed, parsley, soy-beans, and bay-trees' (KS IV.1.6). 'And in the orchard she makes charming plots of open ground and has a well dug, or a pool or a pond, in the middle of it' (KS IV.1.7–8).

Here, the wife is represented as sowing various fruits, vegetables and edible plants, such as radishes, arrowroot, ginger, wormwood, mangoes, melons, cucumber, eggplants, pumpkins, squashes, round yams, trumpet-flowers, horse-eye beans, sesame, etc. (KS IV.1.29). The productive activities seem to have been undertaken within the domain of the household. The text does not explicitly clarify whether these productive activities are undertaken to meet the requirements of the household or are used commercially as well.

Wives were also expected to undertake weaving and spinning within the household. This is apparent in the statement: 'She spins threads from cotton balls and then weaves clothes with those threads' (KS[15] IV.1.33). Their role in the supervision of agricultural and pastoral activities within the household is also mentioned in the text. It states: 'She sees to the tilling

[14] MS stands for the *Manusmṛti*.

[15] KS stands for the *Kāmasūtra*.

of the fields, the care of the cattle, and the upkeep of the carriages. She looks after the rams, cocks, quails, parrots, pheasants, cuckoos, peacocks, monkeys, and deer' (KS IV.1.33). This suggests that her responsibility was not to be confined to the boundaries of the household but her supervision of agricultural fields is also highlighted.

The term '*grāmīṇa yoṣitā*' is used for women (presumably wives) belonging to rural classes in the section on other men's wives. They are mostly represented as engaged in activities related to agriculture and pastoral work such as doing chores, filling granaries, working in the field, purchasing cotton, wool, flax, linen and bark, spinning thread, and buying, selling and exchanging goods (KS V.5.6). The possibility of their belonging to lower classes cannot be denied either. At the same time, this provides an insight into the generative activities undertaken by wives of lower communities for the sake of the subsistence of their households.

II

This section discusses the control, organisation, management and utilisation of the collective resources of the household by wives. The *Arthaśāstra* does not talk much about the domestic duties or their control over household resources.

As expected, in the *Manusmṛti*, the role of women of twice-born men participating in economic activities does not find any mention. With respect to domestic activities, the text states that serving the husband and taking care of the house is viewed as equivalent to consecratory rites for women (MS II.67). The domestic duties of the householder are discussed elaborately in the text in the context of ritual activities outlined for him. It is beyond doubt that in the preparation of various offerings, the assistance of the wife would have been primary. But the text does not mention it, probably to undermine the significance of the bride in an ideal household; the text merely mentions the responsibilities of wives.

The domestic duties of wives have been precisely summed up in the following injunction. The text says: 'he should employ her in the collection and the disbursement of his wealth, in cleaning, in meritorious activity, in cooking food and in looking after household goods' (MS IX.11). However, one should treat the above statement with a degree of caution as it is intended for the purpose of confining wives within the realm of the household. It has also been noticed that the husband is represented as commanding and employing her (*niyojayet*) in these activities. The role of wives in various aspects such as ritual, economic, cooking and household requirements (*pāriṇāhya*)[16] has been acknowledged as 'assistance' in the text.

The participatory role of wives in the distributive function and management of resources could be noticed in the fact that they are expected to look after the collection of wealth and expenses, and cooking and taking care of the household (MS IX.11). There is a mention of

[16] The term *pāriṇāhya* initially referred to the goods that a bride used to bring with her after the marriage. The term could be said to be associated with the term *pariṇaya* which means leading the bride round the fire and the goods which were brought by her after marriage termed as household goods. See Patrick Olivelle (tr.), *Manu's Code of Law: A Critical Edition and Translation of the Mānava Dharmaśāstra* (New Delhi: Oxford University Press, 2007), 323.

the performance of elaborate ritual activities for the householder on an everyday basis. Wives would have played a crucial role in the preparation of offerings or making arrangements for providing hospitality to various social categories. But here the active role of wives is neither mentioned nor expected of this text. Wives are also expected to be economical in consumption. This is evident in the following statement: 'she should be always cheerful, clever at housework, careful in keeping the utensils clean and frugal in her expenditures' (MS V.150).

The interaction of wives with other social categories seems to be restricted. The role of wives of twice-born men in the management and allocation of resources is not explicitly mentioned in the text. Their occasional participation in such processes is suggested in the following statement: 'Mendicants, bards, men consecrated for sacrifice and the artisans may converse with women, unless they have been explicitly banned' (MS VIII.360). As the household is regarded as the source for providing almsfood to the mendicant student, the role of wives in distribution may be assumed.

The optimum utilisation and management of resources are supposed to rest on wives in the *Kāmasūtra*. This is evident in the following statement:

> She makes butter from the milk left over from meals, and also from sesame oil and molasses; she oversees the grinding and pounding when the rice is boiled, she makes use, afterwards, of the water, the froth, the husks, the uncooked kernels, and the coals. (KS IV.1.33)

The management and supervision of resources of the household by wives is further elaborated in the subsequent statement: 'She increases capital and decreases expenditures as much as possible, by authorising buying and selling to be accomplished by incorruptible servants carrying out orders' (KS IV.1.46). The command over servants in the household is supposed to have vested in wives. They were the ones who were expected to know the wages and maintenance of servants (*bhṛtya*) in the household (KS IV.1.33). Wives were conceived as directing the limits and norms for each servant (*bhṛtyajananīyam*) and honouring them on festival days (KS IV.1.41).

Regarding control over resources of the household, the text states that wives are supposed to manage the finances of the household on behalf of their husband. The wife is expected to keep a track of the income and expenditure of the household by supervising the stock and use of pots of wines and liquor, and the transactions related to household goods (KS IV.1.35). She is represented as undertaking purchases when the prices are reasonable. This is evident in the statement: 'When the price is right, at the right time, she buys household goods made of clay, bamboo, wood, leather, and iron' (KS IV.1.27). She is also permitted to speak to her husband regarding financial matters which is evident, for instance, in the statement: 'If he has spent too much or spent the wrong amount, she tells him in private' (KS IV.1.14). This implies that wives had autonomy in the utilisation of resources, in other words, in organising the financial affairs of the household.

The control over distribution of resources of the household is also conceived to have being enjoyed by wives. The wife is represented as keeping an account of the annual income and undertaking expenditure accordingly (KS IV.1.32). The text states: 'She collects the man's discarded, worn-out clothes, both many coloured and pure white, and gives them as favours to servants who have done good work, and as gifts that bestow honour, or she uses them for something else' (KS IV.1.34).

This implies that wife is represented as the one deciding on the disposal of items, its recipients and utilisation.

Though the control over disposal of resources is supposed to be undertaken by wives, they are expected to disclose everything to their husband (KS IV.1.40–41). The involvement of wives in transactions is acknowledged; and wives are responsible for organising productive activities related to the sowing of various fruits and vegetables. The acquisition and management of resources for the sake of the household is underlined in the text. In other words, to maintain the availability of all the required household goods, she is supposed to keep the stock of household items. It states: 'She lays in a stock of salt and oil as well as hard-to-get perfumes, spices, and medicines, and keeps them hidden within the house' (KS IV.1.28). It should be pointed out that wives are not represented in a participatory role in various tasks mentioned above whereas their active role in supervision and management of resources within the household is emphasized in the *Kāmasūtra*.

It could be suggested here that wives were expected to play a key role in household activities, agricultural activities and pastoral services. Surprisingly, wives of the urban area seem to be regarded as having control over a diverse range of resources within the household and were provided with the right to manage and organise the expenditure according to the budget.

III

In the brahmanical theoretical construct, the householder is generally presumed to be the generator as well as the upholder of the household. And, the householder is regarded as being responsible for making provision for sons and wives before leaving the household. There are instances where women are assigned roles to maintain the household in the absence of the householder in the *śāstras*. This section addresses the conditions outlined for the women in the absence of the householder.

However, the notion of 'absence' of the householder, in the texts, differs. For instance, the *Arthaśāstra* mentions that the *brāhmaṇa* (householder) may have gone abroad for the purpose of study or may have become a wandering monk (AS III.4.28, 37).[17] On the other hand, the *Manusmṛti* mentions that the householder may have gone abroad for business (MS IX.74), for learning or fame for six years or for pleasure for three years (MS IX.76). The notion of absence in both these texts seems to be the physical absence of the householder for some objectives. However, in the case of the *Kāmasūtra*, there is no discussion on the absence of the *nāgaraka*. In other words, the text does not define the reason of absence of the urban man; it only talks about the provisions with regard to the wives' behaviour in the absence of the *nāgaraka*.

Maintenance is an act of providing means of subsistence to the family members in the absence of the householder. According to Agnes, the term 'maintenance' signifies a notion of dependency and reduces the wife to a subordinate position and does not award recognition to

[17] This also implies that the householder, even at this stage, would have diverged from their household obligations.

her as an equal partner in marriage.[18] Here an attempt has been made to examine the notion of maintenance outlined for the householder in the three *śāstras* and to explore the flow of resources in the household in the absence of the presumed head of the family.

In the *Arthaśāstra* the provision of maintenance (*bharmaṇya*)[19] to wives by their husband is defined in two ways. The text states that if the maintenance is supposed to be fixed and to be paid at regular intervals, the husband is supposed to pay in instalments (AS III.3.4). In case the maintenance is not fixed and paid after a certain time, then he is expected to provide food and clothing according to the status of the dependents (AS III.3.3). The provision of maintenance is also applied in the context of providing the wife with a bride-price (*śulka*), woman's property (*strīdhana*) and compensation (*adhivedanikā*) for supersession (AS III.3.5).[20] This implies that the maintenance is provided to wives out of the resources which are their own, that is, *strīdhana*, in case of separation. The text reiterates that the husband is permitted to remarry if he provides compensation and a suitable maintenance (*vṛtti*) to the previous wife (AS III.2.41). However, the text states: 'If the (wife) is staying in her father-in-law's family or has become separated, the husband is not to be sued' (AS III.3.6). This means that if the wife, though superseded, stays in the *śvaśurakula,* she is not expected to be provided maintenance. Or, if 'she lives separately', the husband is not supposed to make provision for her.[21] The possibility of the wife being provided a share of the property beforehand or earning livelihood could have been the reason for the absence of maintenance in the latter case. The above passage also suggests that the concept of maintenance is not defined in explicit terms; the concept of maintenance does not carry additional resources from the side of the husband. Rather, it is the *strīdhana* which is considered as a form of maintenance and supposed to be provided to wives.

The *Arthaśāstra* outlines the conditions of providing maintenance to wives. Another instance indicates the situation where the husband would have gone abroad without providing for her and is supposed to be liable for the loan undertaken by the wife in his absence (AS III.11.24). Here, the legal entity of the wife is visible and the role of undertaking transactions on behalf of the husband in the latter's absence could be pointed out. In the context of renouncing the household, the text states that if the husband renounces without making provisions (*aprativídhāya*) for sons and wife, the lowest fine for violence shall be levied upon the householder (AS II.1.29). Interestingly,

---

[18] Agnes Flavia, 'Conjugality, Property, Morality, and Maintenance', in *Handbook of Gender*, ed. Raka Ray (New Delhi: OUP, 2012), 58.

[19] The term *bharmaṇya* is defined as the allowance given for maintenance of a wife separated from the husband. The term *grāsacchaādanam* is the usual expression for maintenance given to a person. See R. P. Kangle (tr.), *Kautiliya Arthaśāstra*, Part II (Delhi: Motilal Banarsidass, 1972/2003b), 201.

[20] Supersession means replacing the wife with the other one. In the *Arthaśāstra*, the wife may be replaced if she does not bear offspring or bears only daughters (AS III.2.38). In order to obtain a son, another wife is supposed to be brought in the household (AS III.2.39). See Kangle (2003b, 199).

[21] Rangarajan has interpreted the verse as: if she is financially independent, she is not provided for maintenance (L. N. Rangarajan (tr.), *Kautiliya: The Arthashastra* [New Delhi: Penguin Group, 1992], 374). Kangle has appropriately translated if the wife has separated herself as the term *vibhaktāyām* is mentioned in the Sanskrit text. See R. P. Kangle, *Kautiliya Arthaśāstra*, Part I (Delhi: Motilal Banarsidass, 1965/2003), 100.

the maintenance of the wife (*strīvṛtti*) does not come under the purview of the state's responsibility (AS III.5.28).

In one of the instances, women whose husbands have gone abroad (*proṣita*) are included amongst women who wish to maintain themselves, and they are supposed to be employed by the superintendent of yarns in spinning (AS II.23.11). This indicates that in order to support her household, the women could be employed under the state for spinning. This provision could have been in situations where the husband may not have provided for the wife or household members.

Alternatively, the text directed the wife to utilise her maintenance, which is part of her *strīdhana*, to look after the extended family of her son and daughter-in-law (AS III.2.16). This is supposed to be undertaken in the absence of any provision by the husband who has gone abroad. Wives are also expected to be kept under the kinsmen of the conjugal household for a period of four or eight years in the absence of any provision by the husband (AS III.4.26). Afterwards, wives are supposed to be released by the kinsmen (AS III.4.27). Probably, the wife could have been permitted to stay at her natal household. The text also states that when the household has fallen to critical times or the prosperity of the household has faded with the absence of the head of the household and the wife is released by the relatives, women are supposed to remarry for the sake of their livelihood (AS III.4.30). This may imply that wives are not preferred to be engaged in economic activities to meet their household requirements in the absence of the owner; instead, they are obliged to remarry to secure the means of subsistence.

Interestingly, the *Manusmṛti* critically states that if the householder with means (*śakta*) gives to others (*parajane dātā*) instead of providing subsistence to his own people (*svajane dukhajīvini*), this is declared as fake law (*dharmapratirūpakah*). This is evident in the statement: 'When a man of means gives to outsiders while his own people live in misery that is counterfeit Law, dripping with honey but poisonous to taste' (MS XI.9). The householder also warned that he will suffer in his life and after death if he did not make provision for dependents. The text says: 'If a man does anything for his welfare after death to the detriment of his dependents, it will make him unhappy both when he is alive and after his death' (MS XI.10).

The *Manusmṛti* also lays down the provision of the maintenance of the wife in the absence of the husband but not with the same zeal as mentioned in the *Arthaśāstra*. The text states that any woman will deviate from the righteous path if starved for livelihood (*avṛttikarṣitā*) in the absence of the husband (MS IX.74). In the absence of such provision, wives are expected to maintain themselves by engaging in craft activities. This is noted in the text as follows: 'If he provides for her before going away, she should live a life of restraint; but if he leaves without providing for her, she may maintain herself by engaging in respectable crafts' (MS IX.75). The text emphasises upon the fact of living a restricted life for wives in case they are provided for.

The text does not clearly mention the 'respectable crafts' (*śilpae agarhitaye*) which are supposed to be undertaken by wives. However, craft activities, in the *Manusmṛti*, are represented as being reserved for the *śūdra varṇa* and associated with the notion of 'serving the twice-born men' (MS X.100). It could be suggested here that wives could be regarded as generators of resources in the absence of the husband through employment in craft activities. Their employment in a specific activity suggests the underlying role assigned to wives, in the absence of the husband, in the text. Hence, they are not visualised as making any significant contribution in productive activities.

Similarly, the text mentions the period for which wives should wait for their husbands who have gone abroad. This is as follows: 'A wife should wait for eight years when her husband has gone away for a purpose specified by Law, for six years when he has gone for learning or fame, and for three years when he has gone for pleasure' (MS IX.76). Surprisingly, the text does not deal with the issue of what the wife has to do after the lapse of this period of waiting. The text is completely silent about the issue of maintenance of wives in such a situation. On the other hand, the *Arthaśāstra* provides for the remarriage of women for maintaining themselves. No such provision is noticed in the *Manusmṛti*. Probably, the text is against the issue of remarriage of women, and therefore has not dealt with this issue.[22]

In contrast to the *Arthaśāstra* and the *Manusmṛti*, the *Kāmasūtra* does not recognise the role of the conventional householder as the preserver of the household. In other words, expectedly, the role of the *nāgaraka* as the maintainer of the household is not at all recognised in the *Kāmasūtra*. On the other hand, all major household responsibilities are supposed to be managed by wives in the presence as well as absence of the husband. At times when husbands are away on a journey, wives are expected to manage the household (*gṛhānvekṣet*) (KS IV.1.44). However, in this text, the husband is not represented as making provision for his wives in his absence. Instead, wives are represented as carrying out their usual and daily tasks (*nityaṃ naimittikā*) along with the mission to accomplish the work (*karmaṇā samāpane*) begun by their husbands. This is evident in the statement: 'She spends the usual amount on undertakings for daily tasks and special occasions. She also sets her mind on accomplishing those undertakings that he has begun' (KS IV.1.44). This also implies that wives are recommended to manage and organise the finances of the household in the absence of husbands. It has been observed here that the *Kāmasūtra* is totally indifferent to the presence and absence of the urban householder.

Interestingly, the text also addresses a similar issue in relation to the daughters of a king and ministers of the state. It states that in case of separation from their husband, the daughter of a king and ministers of the state (*rājaputrī, mahāmātrasutā*) were permitted to make their living on the basis of the 64 fine arts (KS I.3.20). The 64 arts include weaving, garland making, wood-working, carpentry, architecture, metallurgy and cultivation of athletic skills which indicates various economic avenues related to craft activities for these women in the absence of their husbands (KS I.3.15). It needs to be emphasised here that livelihood opportunities are recognised for women of upper classes in this text.

In contrast to the *Arthaśāstra*, the *Manusmṛti* is more emphatic about the responsibility of the householder towards his dependents. Both texts seem to have a different logic for dealing with this issue; the *Arthaśāstra* prefers remarriage while the *Manusmṛti* prefers occupation rather than remarriage. The *Manusmṛti* suggests that the lack of livelihood leads women to deviate from the righteous path; hence, the avenue of livelihood is permitted. On examining the *Kāmasūtra*, one observes that the text is not addressing households in misery. Another interesting observation in the *Kāmasūtra* is that though wives are expected

---

22 The *Manusmṛti* states that after the death of the husband, the wife is expected to eat flowers, roots and fruits and is prohibited to mention the name of the other man. She is expected to live a celibate life until her death (MS V.157–158). See Olivelle (2007, 146).

to wear religious symbols and perform vows and worship in the absence of the householder, which suggests that ritual dependency is outlined for wives, economic dependency is not mentioned in the text.

This chapter attempts to highlight the dynamics of household women and work in varied spheres. The instances of unmarried old women being engaged in economic activities is also noticed in the *Arthaśāstra*. The *Arthaśāstra* mentions the involvement of different categories of women of the household in economic activities whereas the *Manusmṛti* permits wives to be engaged in productive activities under certain conditions. On the other hand, the *Kāmasūtra* discusses the role of wives as generators of resources within the domain of the household. Specifically, in the *Arthaśāstra*, the notion of women working from within and beyond the domain of the household is acknowledged. However, the *Manusmṛti* does not mention the spatial context of work of the household women while the *Kāmasūtra* explicitly mentions the range of work being performed by wives within and outside the domain of the household. The diverse range of commodities to be grown in the household of the *nāgaraka* indicates the possibility of commercial transactions but the text does not mention it. It also highlights the households of the lowest communities where wives are regarded as undertaking work to maintain their households, even as hierarchical relations within such households is seen as being upheld in the *Manusmṛti*.

IV

Another issue which could be emphasised in the text is that wives of lower communities are treated and stereotyped as 'sexual servants' or performing similar activities as of *veśyās*. Is it because they are moving out of the households to provide subsistence to their family? Or is it because their husband, that is, actors, dancers, singers, musicians, story-tellers, bards, rope-dancers, showmen and wandering minstrels are supposed to be employed within the institution associated with the courtesans. Possibly, these are lower communities which are the necessary adjuncts to the institution of courtesans; therefore, wives of these men may have been conceived or treated similar to *veśyās* in the text. Even the *dāsis* who are supposed to learn the arts of courtesans are prescribed for one who lives by stage (AS 2.27.28).

Similarly, in the *Kāmasūtra*, the inclusion of *Paricārīkā*, *Naṭī* and *Śilpakārikā* as categories of courtesans indicates that the category of working women of lower classes are labelled as 'sex-workers'. They are basically the wives of occupational categories. They seemed to have been incorporated in the framework of 'sexual labour' only and, therefore, may have been termed as courtesans in the *Kāmasūtra*. However, the categories of *Kulaṭa*, *Svairiṇī* and *Prakāśavinaṣṭā* are basically the wives who broke away from their household to fulfil their desires. Their description suggests that they may have been termed as courtesans because they posed threat to their conventional role. It is interesting to note that some category of wives are employed as courtesans with the label of 'wives' while others are identified as 'courtesans' due to the fact of either being employed in work activities or because they are wives of lower working classes.

Chapter 6 Tracking Economic Transitions: Tamil Women from Tribe to Caste and Changing Production Roles*

VIJAYA RAMASWAMY

This essay is aimed at situating women and work in the Tamil region in terms of indigenous structures and concepts linked to the broader question of tribe to caste transition. Since this will be primarily a study from below based on Tamil sources, any resemblance to any of the existing models or paradigms will be, by and large, accidental. The term Kudi has been used here since it is historically specific and is a generic term meaning 'inhabitant'. In locating the place of gender in any societal transformation, some of the significant variables would be the role of women in production; social status of women especially in the context of notions of female sexuality, marriage and widowhood; and women in religion. This study will concentrate only on the core area of work and will study the role of women in production and overall economy in the context of tribe to caste transitions and societal transformation in early Tamil Nadu known as the Sangam age.

TAMIL SOURCES AND DATING PROBLEMS

This study will be based on the extremely rich data on the culture of the Tamils available in Sangam literature. The classical Sangam age goes back roughly to the third century BCE and forward into the second/third century CE Sangam literature can be divided into three major categories, each consisting of collections of poetic anthologies—*Ettutogai, Pattupattu and the Pandinen Kilkanakku. Ettutogai* comprises the following eight anthologies: *Narrinai; Kurunthogai; Aingurunuru; Padirrupattu; Paripadal; Kalittogai; Ahnanuru (Aham); Purananuru (Puram).* The second major collection, *Pattupattu* comprises the following ten: *Tirumurugatrupadai; Porunarartruppadai; Siruppanartruppadai;*

* This essay draws upon my previously published article 'The Kudi in Early Tamilaham and the Tamil Women from Tribe to Caste' in Dev Nathan (ed.) *From Tribe to Caste*. Published by Indian Institute of Advanced Study. Shimla. pp. 223–246. The essay is, however, only concerned with tracking the changes in women's work as a result of the transition from tribe to caste.

Perumpanartruppadai; Mullaipattu; Maduraikkanchi; Nedunalvadai; Kurinjipattu; Pattinappalai; Malaipadukadam. The last category consists of the 18 works known as *Pandinen Kilkanakku.* These are by and large didactic in nature and characterised by the prominent presence of Jain and Buddhist theology and ethics. The most celebrated ethical text from the last category is the *Tirukkural,* which among other things can be treated as a catechism of patriarchy and its author Tiruvalluvar is believed to have been a Jain. The authors of the didactic texts *Naladiyar* and *Palamoli Nanuru* (four hundred proverbs) were also Jains. As a part of the same collection, Kapilar, said to have been a Brahmin, wrote *Inna Narpatu,* literally, 164 maxims enumerating the things to be avoided in one's life.

Sangam literature gets its name from a college or Sangam of Tamil poets who flourished under the patronage of the Pandyan kings of Madurai. The literature is divided into three phases-the beginning (mudal Sangam), the middle (idai Sangam) and the end (Kadai Sangam). A chronological classification of this literature is crucial to an understanding of the processes, which brought about societal transformation whether in terms of tribe to caste, in terms of the emergence of patriarchy or changes in religion and the Dravidian world-view. The chronological categorisation of the plethora of Sangam texts is however, fraught with difficulties. Dates for the *Tokappiyam*, a detailed work on Tamil grammar and poetics, range from the pre-Panini dating assigned to it by the celebrated Tamil scholar Maraimalai Adigal and following him E. S. Varadaraja Iyer (1948: XIII) who give 450 BCE as a rough date, to P.T. Srinivasa Iyengar (1930: 70) who prefers the date first or second century CE. At the end of the spectrum is George Hart who is inclined to date it to the fifth century CE (1976: 41). The range of dates for the *Tirukkural* is no less, stretching from the pre-Christian era (Dikshitar: 1930: 135–9) to the sixth-eighth century (Srinivasa Iyengar: 1930: 584). Another major problem is that even within a particular anthology such as the *Puram Nanuru* (henceforth *Puram*) there could be later interpolations. Again, even the *Ettutogai* group which is generally taken to be the earliest one, contains texts like the *Kalittogai* and the *Paripadal* which have been dated to the fifth century CE.

Given all these problems of dating and chronology, Tamil scholars are now looking at this literature in terms not only of its language and style but also the social context in an effort to contextualise it. One of the most recent efforts in the direction is that of Sundara Rajan (*The Socio-Economic structure of the Tamil Country: 1991*). Although this work does not attempt a chronological classification of Sangam literature, it is a positive contribution in the understanding of societal transformation. In the present paper a chronological categorisation of Sangam literature is attempted on the understanding that such a division is vital to study any society in transition. Keeping in view as many variables as possible—Sanskritisation of language and customs, changes in the religious pantheon and ritual, changes in the peasant economy and beginnings of urbanisation, emergence of patriarchy and state formation—the literature of the Sangam age can be divided into three historical blocks.

THE HISTORICAL BLOCKS IN EARLY TAMILAHAM

Early Tamilaham was divided into different regions on the basis of terrain and ecology. The logic of change and development in these eco-zones was also different. The Kudi of each zone followed different subsistence patterns and therefore the forces of caste stratification, Brahmanisation and socio-economic transformation operated in different ways in each zone and among the various kinds of Kudi. The transition from tribe to caste, which theme informs the logic of the three historical blocks, is most true of the peasant societies, especially in the Marudam region, The hilly and coastal regions of Tamilaham do not subscribe to the transition pattern outlined in these historical blocks. These blocks, however, are important in that they represent the mainstream changes in Tamil society and the Kudi of the other regions have to be seen in terms of their differential response of these changes.

Ettutogai seems to belong to the period from the fourth-third century BCE to the early Christian era. The primary preoccupations were *aham* dealing with the 'domestic', the interior, themes of love and *puram*, which dealt with the public, the exterior, themes of war. The *aham* and *puram* themes form a part of all the five tinais or eco-zones into which the Tamil landscape was divided by the Sangam writers. In this phase *Kalavu* or pre-marital courtship seems to have been the norm and elopement was fairly common. Marriage ritual involved only the tali made of tiger's nails, which the hunter gave his beloved. Marriage involved no ritual around the sacred fire, which is so central to Vedic Brahmanism. Women usually exercised full initiative over the choice of a husband. They were also co-sharers and equal partners with men in all economic activities. It appears likely that the earlier parts of the *Tolkappiyam* (the Tamil grammatical work comparable to Panini's *Ashtadhyayi*) were written in this phase. The settings for the *Ettutoqai* poems were rural. The existence of metallurgy and metal crafts is proved by the material artifacts found in archaeological megalithic sites- Kannattur and Kanchipuram (Chingleput district); Tirukkampuliyur and Alagiri (Tiruchchirapalli district); Arikkemedu in Pondicherry and Adichachanallur (Tirunelveli district). The nature of gender division is the metal crafts is not quite clear. On the basis of the evidence of the world-view of the early Tamils gathered from their material culture and its literary expression, Thani Nayagam (1970: 6) makes the interesting observation: 'The only fact which is clear is that most, if not al of the Tamil-speaking groups were originally matrilineal and even, in some cases matrilocal'.

The *Pattupattu* group of anthologies seems to have the characteristic of a society in transition and may be said to represent the second of the historical blocks. Mayon, the shepherd god of the Mullai region, is very clearly identified with the Sanskritic-Brahmanical god Vishnu. The *Mullaipattu* likens clouds to 'Mal who holds in his large hands the discus and conch, in whose breast resides Lakshmi and who rose up after the water was poured (by Mahabali) into his hand'. All these constitute references to the *dashavatara* (ten incarnations) of Vishnu. This phase witnessed the gradual transition to the Vedic-Brahmanical form of marriage and therefore gradual control over the sexual freedom of women. There are increasing references to Brahmanical practices. The *Kalittogai* which technically belongs to the earlier Ettutogai group but can be placed in this phase in terms of its style and content, uses a Sanskritic simile when it says: 'my breath comes out in gasps like the smoke of the yajnas performed by the Brahamanas learned in the Vedas' (Kalittigai I: 35, II: 22-56 vide Srinivas Iyengar: 1989: 570).

The fifth to seventh centuries can be said to constitute the third historical block by when the agrarian tracts had been more or less transformed into caste societies with an overarching patriarchal framework. The concepts of purity and pollution were used against both women and the social groups, which were now becoming identified as untouchables.

The entire *Kilkanakku* texts as well as the epics—*Silappadikaram, Manimekalai, Neelakesi* and others—are described as post-Sangam texts. Many of the epics of this period were written mostly by the Buddhists and Jains. The *Kilkanakku* texts like the *Tirukkural* were didactic and prescriptive in nature emphasising patriarchal values. The plurality of voices which is heard in the early Sangam texts is absent in the historical phase after the third century CE. Our of the early Sangam anthologies while there are at least 154 poems among the 2,381 which carry the signatures of women, there are no women writers either in the *Kilkanakku* or the post-Sangam epics. In this phase patriarchy seems to have become steadily dominant. This trend is most clearly perceived in the *Naladiyar* and the *Tirukkural* which deal with the three purusharthas or objectives of life: *dharma* or righteous living, *artha* or material wealth and *kama* or love/desire.

These texts increasingly describe the values of a caste based society, essentially in the agrarian tracts but gradually spreading to other regions. The obsession with the Brahmanical elite male concepts of purity and pollution were reflected in the attitudes towards both women and lower castes. *Naladiyar* warning against female beauty comments that women were merely 'a pack of bones, nerves, blood, marrow and skin'. (Naladiyar: 46 vide Sundara Rajan: 1991:155). Menstruating women began to be considered polluting. In one of the later poems in the *puram* which could belong to the third century or later, a menstruous woman is called '*kalamtodamagal'* that is 'one who cannot touch the plough (Puram: 299 vide Hanumanthan: 1979:32). From being partners of men in the 'domestic' and public' spheres women become snares and temptations. At the same time negative attitudes towards life's pleasures came to be emphasised in the doctrines of Buddhism and Jainism and were reflected in the epic *Manimekalai*. The attitudes highlighted in these tended to reinforce the Brahmanical image of women as potentially dangerous who had to be controlled. In the overarching patriarchal structure which came to dominate Tamilaham by the sixth-seventh century CE, women (of all social classes) and the men of the lower castes/class were marginalised and dominated.

These three historical blocks of early Tamilaham based on Sangam literature are not there in absolute terms. Due, perhaps, to interpolations or the inherent chronological uncertainties a text from the first phase could reflect the characteristics of the second or third phase. Secondly, the poems of the puram dated from a very early to a fairly late (fourth century CE) period. But in broad terms it is possible to discuss the theme of women from tribe to caste especially in peasant societies in terms of these three historical blocks.

THE KUDI OF THE FIVE TINAIS

The eco-system and the societal structure of the early Tamils were based on five categories or eco-types called *Tinai* enumerated in the *Tolkappiyam.* Each region was inhabited by occupational groups called 'Kudi'. The term 'Kudi' meaning 'Inhabitants' seems preferable to the term 'tribe' since not all inhabitants of the various eco-zones could be described as tribal in character. Each *tinai* was presided over by a deity and named after a characteristic flower or tree.

Kurinji: Kurinji stands for the mountain region. Kurinji was a flower grown in this region and the deity was Murugan or Seyon, 'the red one', also meaning 'the beautiful one', the god of war. This name in the later phase gets translated into the Sanskritic tradition as Kartikeya, the son of Siva and the commander-in-chief of gods. The Kudi are referred to as Kavanar. These later on come to be called 'Urali' literally 'nomads' and are listed as a scheduled tribe in the Census of India,1951 (and the subsequent ones) and also in the Mandal Commission report (Mandal, 1991). However the 1961 census clarifies that while the Urali is a scheduled tribe in the Tamil region, they are in the scheduled caste list in Kerala (Ramamurthy and Rajan: 1961). The Kudi who specialised in hunting were the Eyinar and the Vettuvar. The Kuravar are another social group referred to in Sangam sources. Their womenfolk were called Kuratti or Kuramagal and these women were know for their skill in foretelling the future and their medicinal knowledge. Thurston citing the 1901 census lists the Kurava as a tribe and equates them with the Korcha (name specific to the ceded districts) and the Yerukala of Andhra. Thurston describes the Kuravan and Kuratti as thieving gypsies (Thurston: 1909: III: 438). The Mandal Report also lists the 'Malai Kuravan' as a scheduled tribe (Mandal: 1991: 47).

It is noteworthy that the Kurava do not figure merely as hunters but primarily as hill side agriculturists. They grew food crops like beans, seasamum, panicum, rye and a particular variety of rice called *chamai* which is said to have grown 'in a bamboo filled with small leaves' (*Puram: 120: 1–14*). Cultivation was heavily dependent on rain irrigation (*Puram: 168:5–6; 129:1*). The Kuravar also grew sweet potatoes and ground nuts, which constituted an important part of their diet (*Puram 109: 3–8*). Extraction of honey was another major preoccupation of the Kurinji region. Both men and women were equally involved in both agriculture and honey extraction. In fact the *Puram* verse quoted above, after describing rice cultivation, says that they could also get things which did not involve use of the plough and then describe honey extraction, etc.

Early Sangam literature also contains references to the Kurava as petty chieftains. The poetess Ilaveyiniyar, herself a Kuratti, composed a poem in praise of Erakkon describing him a great Kurava chieftain (*Puram: 157: 1–8 vide Hanumanthan: 1979: 128*). What is of special significance is that the Kuravas had a matriarchal system.

Mullai: One of the pioneering writers on the Sangam age assumes that there was an evolutionary process by which the ancient Kudi of the Tamil country moved into the Mullai or pastoral region. He states: 'When human beings multiplied in the Kurinji region and available food supply began to shrink, they migrated to the next region, the Mullai or forest land… Cattle breed fast, especially in the Mullai and hence arose the institution of private property' (Srinivasa Iyengar: 1989: 9). This evolutionist view is however difficult to prove in terms of the south Indian evidence where right from the period of the *Tolkappiyam* the five *tinais* seem to have more or less co-existed. Moreover, agriculture was practised not only in Marudam which is the river valley eco-zone but also in Kurinji, the hilly tract and in Mullai the pastoral tract. Nor is there evidence to indicate that only shifting cultivation was practised in Kurinji and Mullai. On the contrary the plough seems to have been in use.

The *Mullai tinai* or eco-zone represented the pastoral region with deep forestation. The presiding deity was called Mayon, 'the dark one', and the shepherd god who in the Sanskritic version is Gopala or Krishna, a manifestation of Vishnu. The Kudi inhabiting this region were the Ayar, Kovalar, Idaiyar and Eiyanar. The feminine equivalents were Aaichchiyar, Kovicchiyar and Idaichchiyar. The economy of the region was predominantly based on cattle rearing and dairy farming. Women played a crucial role in the pastoral economy. Besides dairy farming, various kinds of pulses and staple foods like rye were grown in the Mullai tract. A poem from the Puram is descriptive of the economy of Mullai:

> The reapers of pulses eat the food made by husking and cooking the ragi grains and also the sour porridge cooked by the Iyaimagal; (shepherdess) by boiling in white curds the velai leaves which grow in the evening by the street full of the droppings of cattle. (Puram: 215: 1–5 vide Srinivas Iyengar: 1989: 269)

It has been argued that the institution of kingship may have originated in the Mullai region. The joint family system arose because pasture lands, parcelled out into tiny bits, would become too small to maintain a flock. The patriarchal head of a large family may have gradually assumed the status of a king. The support for such an argument is found in the Tamil language where one of the early terms for king, 'kon', also means a herdsman and that for a queen, Aachchi, means a shepherdess (Srinivasa Iyenagr: 1989: 10). Thurston in his report on the south Indian castes and tribes tends to treat the Ayar as being synonymous with the Idaiyar or the kon (the full name may be kolayar). Interestingly in common Tamil parlance now-a-days these terms are treated as purely occupational categories rather than as caste or tribal names. The pastoral groups who came to be known at some historical point of time as Kurumbas, figure as scheduled tribes in the census reports (cr 1961: I: pt.V-A:XXII) and in the Mandal Report (1991: 47). The references to Kurumbas in Sangam literature are in the sense of petty cheiftains. For instance the poetess Auvaiyar praises Neduman Anji as one who conquered the many forts of the Kurumbas (Puram: 97: 1–4). Another verse also from the *Puram* describes the proclamation of war by a Kurumba cheiftain (293: 1–2). The evidence indicates that as pastoralism lost its importance with the beginnings of feudalism and large scale land ownership on Tamilaham, roughly from the seventh century (Pallava period) onwards, the pastoral groups lost their social status. They failed to enter the caste system even at the lower levels or perhaps opted to remain out of it. It is also likely that some of them took to agriculture wholetime and become absorbed into the peasant society of the agricultural tract.

Neydal: Neydal referred to the coastal region, the characteristic flower being possibly a variety of the water lily and the presiding deity Varuna, the rain god. Fishing and manufacture of salt seem to have been the mainstay of the economy of the Neydal. The Kudi who lived by fishing are referred to as Paradavar, Valaignar, Nulayar, Timilar and Panar. The salt extractors were known as Umanar and the women as Umanatti. Paddy was also cultivated in the Neydal region. In lines which accurately describe the economy of this *tinai* the Puram says: The great Ulavar (farmers) who reap the paddy in the heat of the sun, jump on to the waves of the clear sea; the Paradavar (fisherfolk) who own strongly built boats, drink the hot liquor and dance the Kuravai dance with their womenfolk (Puram: 24: 1–16 vide Srinivasa Iyengar: 1989: 260).

The term Umanar as a social category is not to be found in any of the census reports. The Paradavar or Paravar are however mentioned as a caste group who must have earlier enjoyed a lot of power in society (Thurston: 1909: VI: 141). In a mythological work called *Valaiveesu Puranam*, the Paravar claim to be connected to the royal line of the Kurus through the legendary matasyagandhi, the mother of sage Vyasa and the queen of king Shantanu with whom the Hindu epic *Mahabharata* begins. This is of source an obvious attempt at Sanskritisation. Sangam evidence shows that the Paravas must have been independent rulers who were conquered by the Cholas and Pandyas. The Sangam poet Unpoti Pasumkutayar praises the Chola king called Ilanche Chenni as one who defeated the southern Paradavar and Mankuti Marutanar, another Sangam poet, praises the Pandian King Nedunchelian as 'a lion in the battle against Paradavar' (*Puram*: 378 and *Maduraikkanchi*: 96: 97 vide Hanumanthan: 1979: 127). The Paravas do not seem to have reconciled themselves to their inferior status within the Hindu caste framework because in the British colonial era a large number of converts to Christianity came from the Parava or fishermen community (Oddie: 1991: tables on 248–50).

Marudam: The Marudam *tinai* was located in the river valleys and constituted the settled agricultural tract. Marudam was typified by a red flower of the same name and overseen by Vendan who as Indra emerged in the Sanskritic pantheon as the king of the gods. As with the Mullai region, the Marudam must also have been open to the influences of an emergent patriarchy. The concept of family with the man as the patriarch developed alongside notions of land ownership. Sangam literature in dealing with the Marudam region (as also to some extent the Mullai), deals with a proliferation of specialised occupational groups. The development of economic and social stratification is most clearly to be perceived in the Marudam. It is noteworthy that the king in ancient times was also called Vendan, the name of the patron deity of the agricultural tract.

Despite the close relationship between peasant societies and patriarchy, it is not possible to postulate a one-to-one equation between plough agriculture and patriarchy or between swidden cultivation and matriarchy. South Indian evidence indicates that it was settled agriculture which prevailed in Kurinji, Mullai and other *tinais* although it might have been mostly in the nature of a one-crop cycle. Women in these regions were co-sharers with men in the economic sphere. The situation in Marudam seems no different because women are crucial to all agricultural activities. They may not have handled the plough although the farmer's wife is called Ulatti, literally 'one who plough'. The sheer weight of the plough may have made it difficult for the woman to handle it. Nevertheless planting seeds, guarding crops, husking paddy and pounding grain have been exclusively women's occupations since Sangam times. Both genders were equal participant in irrigational activities and the *temmangu* genre of Tamil folk songs appears to be centred around this joint economic activity. Harvesting was again a joint activity of men and women.

Ritually also women were crucial to all agricultural activities. Goddess Korravai who was the deity of the Palai region was worshipped in all the five eco-zones. The reproductive woman was both potentially auspicious and dangerous since she could create and destroy human lives and it is in this sense that the worship of Korravai, both in the battlefield and the cultivable field, should be seen. The origin of Korravai worship lay in the adoration of the mother goddess as a symbol of fertility. In fact the ancient custom of plucking the heads of corn and offering them to the mother goddess as a ritual sacrifice and then consuming them, marks the beginning of his worship (Kailasapathy: 1966: 66–84). However, with Sanskritisation and Brahmanisation, Korravai is transformed into Durga Paramesvari and it is noteworthy that in south India worship of Durga in her ritual aspect of Sri Vidya is an exclusively male domain and women are kept severely out. It is therefore possible to argue, on the basis of the evidence of the Marudam region, that there is no logical nexus between settled peasant agriculture and patriarchy. The fall in the social and ritual status of women in stratified peasant societies is to be looked at in terms of the emergence of the Brahmadeyas and the process of Sanskritisation.

The dominant Kudi in the Marudam region were obviously the agriculturists. The term used for a farmer is 'Ulavan' literally 'one who ploughs' and 'Ulatti' is its feminine form. (Tolkappiyam: Porul Adikaram: 20). The same text also states that plough cultivation is the only means of livelihood for the 'Velan madar'. The term Vellalar itself occurs in the Sangam anthology called *Paripadal*, which falls under *Ettutogai*. However, it is very important to note that *Paripadal* itself although it falls under *Ettutogai* is definitely a later work (Hanumanthan: 1979: 123). So this term which denotes landownership (vel=soil and alar=owner/controller) does not occur before the third century CE. The term used in *Paripadal* for plough is *er*. There is an alternative explanation to the origin of the term Vellalar. Srinivasa Iyengar says that the term was actually derived from 'Vellam' meaning 'flood' and the Vellalar specialised in channelising flood waters from irrigation (Srinivasa Iyengar: 1989: 13). Another term for a farmer in the Sangam age is Karalar. Since kar in Tamil means clouds, this term has been interpreted as 'those who channelise rain water for irrigation' (Srinivasa Iyengar: 1989: 13). Sangam literature has quite a few reference to sluices, wells and tanks, the most striking being a verse from the *Puram* which refers to a Valai fish which gets caught in the swift current of water flowing from the tank into the channel and sluices and finally ends up on the slushy cultivated field (*Puram*: 209: 1–12).

In the period after the seventh century, with the growing system of land grants under the Pallavas and Cholas, the Vellalas emerged as the dominant caste in large parts of Tamilaham. In conjunction with the Brahmins, they became the main upholders of patriarchy and a stratified caste society. The term 'Ulavar' in course of time no longer denoted any specific community but became a generic term for a farmer.

All the other Kudi mentioned in the Marudam region like the Kuyavan (potter), the Kollan (blacksmith) and Vannan (washermen) constitute the lowest rungs of caste society.

Palai: The fifth division, Palai, had no land type of its own and hence it has been accepted as a secondary division. It refers to the arid waste lands and the name is derived from the prevalence of a tree called 'Palai' (most probably a variety of cactus), the tendrils and branches of which do not fade through the summer or winter. The Maravas and the Eiynar constitute the most important Kudi of this region. The Maravas whose name is derived from the word 'maram' meaning heroism, are representative of the highly militant spirit of the early Tamils whose *Puram* poetry is mostly preoccupied with wars and cattle raids. The Maravas figure in Sangam literature as petty cheiftains. The *Narrinai* (33: 1–7) says that the Maravas with the arrow fixed to their bow "watch intently the lonely and fearsome road. "Thurston describing the Maravas as a tribe, says that along with the Kallar, they must have constituted one of the earlist tribes in south India (Thurston: 1901: V: 22). Alongwith the Maravar, the Mallar and the Mazhavar seem to have constituted the martial classes of early Tamilaham. The *Paditrupattu* in the *Ettutogai* collection contains the comment that the Maravas relished wars and wore anklets to the battlefield (*Paditrapattu*: 22: 20, 28: 3–4 vide Hanumanthan: 1979: 125). It also says of them that they never retreated from the battlefield nor did they sleep in the military camps (*Paditrupattu*: 57: 1; 58: 4; *Narrinai*: 18; 5–6 vide Hanumanthan 1979: 9).

P.T. Srinivasa Iyengar opines that the Maravas had been matriarchal in early times (1989: 9). However Thurston, in describing the Maravas from various sources including an anthropological field survey, clearly describes them as patriarchal (Thruston: 1909: V: 22–48). Some sects of the Maravas practice non-Hindu customs like burial of the dead and also re-marriage of widows (Thurston: 1909: V: 40–41). However the majority of the Maravas have gone through a process of Brahmanical acculturation as a result of which they have also taken to cremating the dead and follow the patriarchal pattern with respect to women. The Maravas however found no acceptance in the hierarchical caste based societies and consequently their frustrated militancy turned them into anti-social elements. The Maravas and Kallar, who mainly inhabit the dry zones of Ramanathapuram and Pudukottai, acquired ill repute as thieves and robbers perhaps from the early medieval times. Even today the term 'Kallar' is used in Tamil as a generic term for robbers. It seems most probable that with the spread of stratified peasant society and Sankritisation, the Maravas and Kallar became economically marginalised and had to use their proficiency in arms to take to robbery as a means of livelihood. An administrative report from Tirunelveli (a major Marava region) dated march 1899, estimates that the Maravas formed just 10 per cent of the population but committed 70 per cent of the docoities in the district (Thurston: 1909: V: 28). Some Maravas, however, continued to retain their status of petty chieftains right into the twentieth century. The Sethupathis of Ramanathapuram, who offered such stiff resistance to British colonial rule, were Maravas.

WOMEN IN THE ECONOMY OF TAMILAHAM

Early Sangam literature is, by and large, a description of the countryside and the rural economy. Here women seem to have been co-sharers with men both in domestic and public spheres. More than 60 per cent of the agricultural operations were in the hands of women. However, with the growth of townships, women's share in the economy went down since women were peripheral in the context of both commerce and crafts. The late-Sangam and post-Sangam literature has extensive descriptions of townships and ports. It is noteworthy that it is also this phase of literature which describes a social structure that is both Brahmanical and patriarchal. Texts like *Maduraikkanchi* and *Silappadikaram* seem to describe a traditional patriarchal situation.

The Sangam texts, despite their primary preoccupations with *aham* and *puram,* incidentally throw light on the economy and participation of women in it.

The two primary concerns of the Neydal or coastal region were fishing and manufacture of salt. Women played an important role in both activities. The salt producers were known as Umanar and their wives as Umanatti. The *Narrinai* comments that the occupation of the Umanar being in the nature of itinerant trade, they moved around a lot (138: 1–3). The *Aham Nanuru* (henceforth *Aham*) says that from the movement of their vast caravans it would appear as if an entire village is moving. Salt producers were known as Alavar and the place of salt extraction as *alam*. The *Peumpanartruppadai* describes how the husband and wife extracted salt and heaped it on the sea shore. It was loaded into a cart and hawked from door to door and from village to village. The text describes that it was the woman who drove the bullock cart loaded with salt. She had an additional pair of bullocks to be harnessed in case the ones pulling the cart got tired. They hunted animals on the way and ate this meat. Besides salt, the Umanar also appear to have sold pepper bags, which were also loaded in the cart. Jars of pickles hung beneath the cart (*Perumpanartuppadai*: 50–65). Young girls and women also carried headloads of salt and sold them from door to door. The *aham* says that beautiful Neydal women used to exchange rock salt for paddy from peasant women (*Aham*: 140: 3–8). The Umanar women are said to have walked with their bracelets tinkling and loudly proclaimed that they would barter salt for grain (Aham: 390: 8–9). This obviously means that they went into the agricultural tracts of Marudam, Kurinji and Mullai to sell their salt (*Kurunthogai*: 269: 5).

In the same Neydal region while both women and men did the fishing, it was only the women who sold the fish and bartered them for grain and pulses from the agricultural region. Timilar, Panar, Valaignar and Paradavar were fisherfolk constituting the Kudi of Neydal. A verse from the *Aham* says that the Timilar women sold fish which their menfolk had caught (Aham: 320: 1–4) but there are also references to women themselves catching fish. Another verse, also from the *Aham*, describes how a Panar woman would capture the Varal fish (considered a delicacy) with the help of thin ropes bound to a stick (*Aham*: 216: 1–2 vide Sasivalli: 1989: 293). The *Aham* further describes how the Panamagal or fisherwomen would sit in street corners and sell their fish (*Aham*: 126). Young fisher girls watched over the fish drying in the sun and these were then preserved by the women who cut them up and salted them (*Narrinai*: 63: 1–2; 45: 6–7). The fish was then bartered for paddy. The *Aingurunuru* says that the Valaiyar sold the *Varal* fish and got year old white rice in exchange (*Aingurunuru*: 46: 1–3 and 48. Also *Puram*: 343: 1). Apparently pearl diving was also one of the occupations of the coastal region. The *Aham* refers to young fisher girl (Panamagal) who refused to exchange her fish for paddy but instead chose to trade them for big pearls (*Aham*: 126: 7–12). Apparently pearls were then not so expensive that they would become a luxury item.

The manufacture and sale of toddy was predominantly in the hands of women and this occupation was common to all the eco-zones. In fact the women of almost all communities (with the exceptions of the Brahmins) were themselves hard drinkers. The coastal women are also said to have processed and sold toddy made from palmyra juice or from rice. The Valaiyar fisherfolk are said to have been highly skilled in preparing liquor, with equal gender participation. The toddy prepared from the palmyra was known as *pennai*. The *Pattinappalai* says that the Paradavar (fisherfolk) of the Neydal (coastal region) first offered liquor to the gods and then drank it. Yet another reference in the *Siruppanartruppadai* from the same region, refers to the *Naulayarmagal* (fisherwomen) using the logs of a special tree called *akil* to prepare a sour liquor much relished by the paradavar (*Siruppanartruppadai*:

154–59 vide Saivalli: 1989: 299). Toddy was also prepared in the Kurinji region either from honey called *tekkal-teral* or from rice called *toppi*. In fact in early Sangam literature women are exclusively associated with the making of rice toddy (*Perumpanartruppadai*: 142 vide Ramaswamy: 1989: 91). The *Perumpanartruppadai* also describes the process by which housewives made toddy at home. First a kind of rice starch was prepared which was then allowed to ferment for the whole day. Finally impurities were drained from it (*Perumpanartruppadai*: 275–81). This liquor is referred to as *narumpili*. Toddy was also prepared from fruits, sugarcane and coconut. The *Puram* describes the Paradavar women as hard drinkers who consumed a liquor made out of palm, sugarcane and coconut juice (Puram 24: 1–16 vide Ramaswamy: 1989: 91) Sangam anthologies both from *Ettutogai* and *Pattupattu* show that women of both lower and upper strata consumed liquor freely (especially *Pattinappalai*: 108).

These texts also contain quite a few references to women hawkers selling toddy while the texts do not appear to contain corresponding references to male hawkers. The *Aham* says that the Ariyal girls sold toddy which they carried on their heads in pots (*Aham*: 157: 1–4). The toddy was usually exchanged for rice (*Perumpanartruppadai*: 214: 15). Thus both the manufacture and sale of liquor seem primarily to have been in the hands of women. It is only with the progressive influence of Brahmanisation that restrictions begin to be placed on women consuming liquor and they are also marginalised within the liquor making industry.

The extraction of fish oil in the Neydal region was again done primarily by women and the *Perumpanartruppadai* (214, 215 vide Subrahmanian: 1966: 232) says that both toddy and fish were exchanged for honey and edible roots (from the Kurinji region).

In the Mullai region, the economy was pastoral. Cattle breeding and grazing seem to have been men's occupations but dairy farming and the sale of dairy products was a sector of the Mullai economy in which women played a leading, possibly even a dominant part. The *Perumpanartruppadai* gives a detailed account of work of shepherdess. The shepherdesses of the ancient Tamilaham were known by such names as Aaichchiyar, Kovichchiyar, Idaichchiayr, etc. In a somewhat clumsy *simile* the rhythmic churning of the curds by the shepherdess is linkened to a tiger's roar (*Perumpanartruppadai* vide Ramaswamy: 1989:85). The process of setting curds by curdling the milk is itself used as a *simile* in the *Puram* which says, 'like the curd being squirted on to a pot of milk from the fingers of a tired shepherdess' (*Puram*: 276: 4–5). In the *Puram* it is stated that the curds were directly exchanged with farmers for foodgrains (*Puram*: 33: 1–6). However, the *Perumpanartruppadai* which is later text says that the shepherdess of the Mullai sells her buttermilk from door to door in the Kurinji region and with the money she gets, she buys foodgrains for her household (156-60 vide Ramaswamy: 1989:85). Although these two references constitute two bits of evidence in isolation, they could perhaps be treated as indicators of two different economic situations. The system of barter in the *Puram* is partially replaced by cash payment for products in the *Perumpanartruppadai*. Another reference from the text says that the shepherdess prepared ghee (clarified butter) and hawked it. She would not accept the gold, which was offered for it but gets a good milch buffalo, a good cow and another black cow in exchange for her products. This judicious investment (*mudal*) enables her to expand her business (*Perumpanartruppadai*: 164: 5 vide Ramaswamy 1989: 85). Perhaps these references in the *Perumpanartruppadai* are indicative of an economy in transition.

Besides hawking dairy products, the women of the Mullai region also sold meat. In the Pandya country the prosperous housewife exchanged paddy for the goat meat brought by the shepherdess (*Puram*: 33). In front of the thatched huts of the Kovalar, hides of skinned goats were spread on wooden cots to dry (*Puram*: 148: 154).

Women seem to have been seminal to the agrarian economy as well, whether the system was one of shifting cultivation involving the use of the hoe or one of settled plough cultivation. Weeding of plants and clearing the fields, seed planting, guarding of the crops, husking and winnowing of the paddy and pounding of the grain were all economic activities done entirely by women. Besides these tasks performed exclusively by women, they were co-sharers with men in the tasks of both irrigation and harvesting. The Eyirriyar women smoothened and weeded the fields with furrows, which had an iron tip, called *Kozhu* (*Perumpanartruppadai*: 90–97). The evidence of the Sangam literature regarding these specific agricultural functions of women is borne out by the genre of the folk songs, linked to each of these activities (Ramaswamy: 1993).

While mature women undertook the heavier tasks of weeding and planting, young unmarried girls were sent to the fields to keep a watch over the paddy, millets and other crops. This was also the time for romantic dalliance and courtship called *kalavu. Kalavu* was an accepted aspect of social life and the notions of female sexuality as something dangerous that had to be controlled by confining young girls to the home came in only with Brahmanism.

The husking and pounding of grain with a big pestle (*ulakkai*) by two women standing face to face is a recurrent theme in Sangam literature. The *Malaipadukadam* and the *Kurunthogai* both refer to the women singing as they pound the grain. These are sometimes referred to as Kuramagal and Kapilar's *Kurinjipattu* (a part of *Kalittigai*) deals with these grain-pounding songs. Alternatively these songs are also referred as *vallaipattu*, probably the term used for them in the Marudam region.

The farmer was called Ulavan and his wife as Ulttti, literally 'one who ploughs'. A poem from the *Nartrinai* describes their work in the fields. They wake up at dawn and have a hearty meal consisting of rice mixed with fish soup (the fish being got in barter from the Neydal). Then they and their wives go to the fields where the women plant in the wet clay. 'Thus the ploughmen who have yoked the buffalo are ploughing the field, have built up many stacks of paddy which looks like paddy hills' (*Nartrinai*: 60: 1–8 vide Srinivasa Iyengar: 1989: 179). This verse shows clearly a gendered division of labour. There is also no evidence in any Sangam text that women handled the plough. An explanation for this, perhaps somewhat simplistic, could be that the women did not handle the plough because it was too heavy and not because of any ritual taboo. It is not unlikely that the taboo on women touching the plough was a superimposition by Brahmanical patriarchy. This argument appears logical because the non-touching of the plough by women would otherwise have been reflected in an association of women with pollution. Evidence of female pollution however starts figuring in Sangam literature only at a later stage. The gender bias is also not visible although its undertones may have existed. Nevertheless it was in agricultural tracts of the Marudam that a combination of factors led to class differentiation, caste stratification and the emergence of a patriarchal structure.

GENDER FROM TRIBE TO CASTE

The river valleys were the first to develop a certain degree of economic stratification based on land ownership. The *Tolkappiyam* makes a striking distinction between those who subsist by ploughing their own lands (*uluthunbar*) and those who subsist by getting their lands ploughed by others (*uluvithunbar*). It is noteworthy that the sections of the *Tolkappiyam* dealing specifically with the economy are dated to the fifth century or even later. This is also roughly the period of the *Paripadal* where the term 'Vellalar' in the sense of a landowner is used for the first time. In the *Kurunthagai,* the poet speaks of 'oru eru Ulvan', literally 'a peasant with one ploughshare' (vide Subrahmanian: 1966: 221). This comment is possible only in the context of a differentiated society where you can have a small farmer with one plough and a big landowner using many ploughs. Within the Marudam region, over a period of time, the Vellalas emerged as superior agricultural castes while the Pallar formed into low-caste agriculturists or landless labourers. Probably the term in the *Puram* called 'kadaisiyar' literally 'the last in society' pertains to the Pallar and they are in fact returned as a sub-caste of the Pallar in the 1901 census (Thurston: 1909: VII: 303–10). The Mandal Report basing itself on the previous census returns (1961: vol. I, pt. V-A: XX) lists both the Pallar and the Kadaiyar as scheduled castes (Mandal: 1991: 26).

Sangam society consisted of various types of craftsmen and social groups like the Pulaiya who dealt with rituals concerning birth and death. There are scattered references in Sangam literature to potters (Kuyavar), blacksmiths (Kollar) and carpenters (tachchar). Auvaiyar uses the metaphor of a carpenter who could fashion eight chariots in a day! (*Puram*: 87). The Pulaiyar, Panar, Velar and Totiyar attended on occasions of death and performed acts like the lighting of the cremation fire and offering worship to the memorial stones in which the spirit of the dead person was believed to reside. The Pulatti and the Panatti were as closely associated with death. In fact by the medieval times, the Valaichiyar (fisherwomen) began to act as professional mourners. (Inscription of the Pudukottai State: 601 vide Ramaswamy 1989: 95).

Clearly then, Sangam society was stratified in terms of occupational differences but there were no caste hierarchies. The word 'jati' itself is absent in the Sangam literature and it occurs only once in the sense of a bio-physical category and not in the sense of caste (*Tolkappiyam: Marabiyal*: 42). The south Indian evidence strongly suggests that the varna system and the hierarchical division of society into castes, were both superimposition of Vedic Brahmanism on the south. Even though the Pulaiyar may have been regarded as low born in the context of their association with death, neither the concept of pollution nor of untouchability was attached to them during the Sangam age. There seems to have been free inter-mixing and interdining among the various social groups called 'Kudi' and Auvaryar's celebrated poems testify to the fact that the Panar and their female counterparts the Viraliayar, who were nomadic bards, freely shared liquor and meat with the Sangam cheiftains. Thus there was economic differentiation in early Sangam society but not class differentiation. These Panar along with other economically dependent groups would be termed 'low caste' within the Brahmanical discourse.

The gradual but powerful penetration of Vedic Brahmanism along with Buddhism and Jainism, is clearly visible in the post Sangam era. Their influence gets reflected in the didactic *Kilkanakku* literature. *Naladiyar,* a Jain text roughly datable to the fourth century CE or later, refers to the Paratavar (fisherfolk of the Neydal or coastal region) as Kadaiyar. *Naladiyar* being a Jain text must have considered the oil pressers as destroyers of thousands of oil seeds and hence 'impure' and 'low born' (Hanumanthan: 1976:140). The word 'jati' in the sense of caste also occurs in its present connotation in another Jain *Kilkanakku* text-*Palamoli Nanuru* (four hundred proverbs), which like most of the other didactic texts, belongs to the period from the fourth to the sixth centuries. The *Achcharakkovai* glorifies the value system of the Vedic Brahmansim. The notions of purity and pollution-that the brahmin is pure and the Pulaiya impure (and therefore untouchable) because of what they do, is also encountered for the first time in the *Achcharakkovai.*

The seventh century in Tamilaham witnessed the beginning of the system of land grants to Brahmins called *Brahmadeya.* Starting with the Pallavas of Kanchipuram, this system spread fairly rapidly into the Chola and Pandya countries. The land grant system to Brahmins gradually led to the formation of a quasi-fedual structure in Tamilaham. The Brahmadeyas were linked to state formation in these regions. The Chola, Pandya and Pallava started a new phase of massive temple building activity and the granting of fertile tracts to temples as Devamanya and to Brahmins as Brahmadeya, both quite often tax free (*irraiyili*). The Brahman grantees very often formed an alliance with the dominant agricultural group the Vellalar, together controlling not only the agricultural surplus but also the products of crafts labour and even merchandise in the form of commercial tolls.

The concepts of control and subordinates lie at the root of a system that has non-cultivating proprietors like the Brahmins. Production in such a situation is possible only through force and/or prescriptive codes like 'service' and 'loyalty', which the feudal landlords expected in implicit measure from the peasants and their other dependants.

The male head of the household exemplified the same fedual system and became the patriarch of the family. The peasant woman despite her position as co-sharer in agricultural operations, became socially and ritually inferior and subordinate to the male. At the societal level, the Kudi, engaged in essential but socially inferior occupations like the Pallar and the Pulaiyar, became ritually and socially distanced from the Brahmins and the Vellalas. These then formed the rung below even the Shudra *varna* and became untouchables. It is only in the early medieval period that the terms like Paraiya and Chandala come to be used for these social groups. In brief, in the course of the sixth-seventh centuries and continuing well into the medieval period, women and lower social group who were seminal to production became socially marginalised while the Brahmins who were peripheral to production became the nucleus of the society.

The transformation of the Kudi of Kurinji and Neydal regions like the Kuravar or the Maravar either into the socially outcast tribes or the lowest entrants into the Shudra category in the caste hierarchy partly came about as a result of state formation in Tamilaham. The Chola conquest over the Kuravs or the extension of the Panadya territory into the Ramanathapuram-Pudukottai regions through the conquest and displacement of the Maravas, led to the loss of independence and status for these groups. The Kuravas have, either deliberately or by the force of circumstances, failed to integrate into the caste society at any level. The Maravas are to this day widely feared as a thieving tribe and are an ostracised group in the Tirunelveli region, what was perhaps the *Palai tinai* of the Sangam age. Interestingly although they were themselves marginalised in the entire process of Brahmanisation, the Maravas have adopted the patriarchal values of the Brahmans, and copied faithfully their marriage practices.

TAMIL WOMEN IN THE URBAN SETTING

Gender and caste differentiations are even more pronounced in the urban centres of early Tamilaham. There is a plethora of town and city description in the epics—*Silappadikaram* and the *Manikekalai*. Thus, even in terms of locale there is a vast difference between the rural landscape which forms the setting for the early Sangam poetry and the urban landscape which provides the backdrop of the epics and much of *Kilkanakku* literature.

The monsoon of the Arabian sea was discovered by Hippalos in the middle of the first century CE providing impetus to the trade between India, the Mediterranean and West Asia. At the same time, maritime movements from Kalinga along the Bay of Bengal led to the entry of Buddhism and Jainism into south India. Beginning from Andhra, the hetrodox faiths spread rapidly into the Tamil area. The Jains are even today, in the south India as well as in north, predominantly traders. The Jain and Buddhist texts and epics of the period deal with wealthy monasteries located in urban centre and trade entrepots. The entire story of *Silapppadikaram* primarily moves between two cities-Kaveripumpattinam of the Cholas and Mudurai of the Pandyas. However trade and craft activities in these towns were predominantly male occupations and women were peripheral to the urban economy. It was inevitable that men who played a dominant role in the economy should establish their dominance over women.

There was, at the same time, a search for patronage from the kings and merchants on the part of the monasteries of the heterodox faiths. Combined with the anxiety not to lose their social base to Vedic Brahmanism, the dependence on patronage came to carrode what had been the most significant contribution of the heteodox faiths. Their egalitarian ideology and rejection of ritual superiority had led to the entry of both low castes and women in large numbers into Buddhism and Jainism. These faiths also managed to win the support of the Kalabra tribal kings who dominated south Indian polity from the fourth to sixth centuries. As nomadic rulers with no ritual authority the Kalabras patronised the hetrodox, anti-Hindu, Anti-Brahmin faiths.

By the sixth to seventh centuries, Buddhism and Jainism had moved very close to Vedic Brahmanism in their ideas of patriarchy and caste dominance. Both heterodox monasteries and Hindu *mutts* were heavily funded by grants from kings, nobles, merchants and other wealthy sections of society. Economic dependence on the dominant groups of a caste ridden society led to acceptance and reinforcement of patriarchal values in religion and society.

It is therefore possible to conclude that due to a variety of internal and external factors, women's role and status in economy and society fell sharply during the course of the mainstream transformation of Tamil society from tribe to caste. Even where communities such as Maravas retained their identity, they adopted the patriarchal framework. However, in the peripheral eco-zones as in hilly tracts, in contrast to the core agricultural regions, the establishment of a caste stratified society was much more inchoate. As a consequence, gender differentiation among the groups or Kudi inhabiting these areas was also proportionately less accented.

REFERENCES

Aham Nanuru (Aham), ed. Somasundaranar, P.V., Madras, 1974.

Aingurunuru, ed. Swaminathaiyyar, U.V. and Kalyana Sundarayyar, S., Madras, 1944.

Dikshitar, Ramachandra, *V.R. Studies in Tamil Literature and History*, Luzac and Co. London, 1930.

Hart, George L., 'Ancient Tamil Literature: Its Scholarly Past and Future' in Stein Burton *Essays on South India*, Vikas Publishing House, New Delhi, 1976.

Hanumanthan, K.R. *Untouchability—a historical study*, Koodal Publishers, Madurai, 1976.

Iyengar, Srinivasa, P.T., *History of Tamils*, Asian Educational Services, New Delhi, 1989 (I[st] edition 1930).

Kailasapathy, K., *Tamizhar Vazhvum Vazhipadum*, Makkal Veliyeedu (Peoples' Press), Madras, 1966.

Kurunthogai ed. Swaminathaiyyar, U.V., Madras, 1937.

Mandal Commission Report of the Backward Classes Commission, *Reservations for Backward Classes*, 1980, Akalank Publications, 1991.

Narrinai, ed. Narayanaswami, A., Madras, 1952.

Oddie, Geoffrey, A., *Hindu and Christian in South-East India*, London Studies on South Asia, A., No. 6, University of London, 1991.

Perumpanaruppadai, in *Pattupattu*, ed. Swaminathaiyyar, U.V., Madras, 1931.

Puram Nanuru (Puram), ed. Swaminathaiyyar, U.V., Madras, 1935.

A.S. Ramamurthy and C.T. Rajan, *Thandan/Uraly, Scheduled Castes of Tamil Nadu*, V.I.No.10, Monograph series, Census of India, 1961.

Ramaswamy, Vijaya, 'Aspects of Women and Work in Early South India', *Indian Economic and Social History Review*, Vol. XXVI, No. I, Jan–Mar, 1989.

Sasivalli, V.C., *Pandai Tamizhar Tozhilgal*, International Institute of Tamil Studies, Madras, 1989.

Subrahmanian, T.N., *Sangam Polity*, Asian Publishing House, Bombay, 1966.

Sundararjan, S, *Ancient Tamil Country-Its Social and Economic Structure*, Navrang, New Delhi, 1991.

Thaninayagam, X.S., *Tamil Culture and Civilization*, Asia Publishing House, Bombay, 1970.

Thurston, Edgar, *Castes and Tribes of South India*, 7 vols., Reprint, Cosmos, New Delhi, 1975, (I[st] edition, Government Press, Madras, 1909).

Tolkappiyam (*Poruladhikaram*), Vol. I, Pt. I and Vol. II, Pt. II, ed. Varadaraja Iyer, E.S. Annamalai University, Tamil Series, No. 9, Annamalai Nagar, 1948.

Chapter 7

The Question of Women's 'Agency': Women, Work and Domesticity in Early Textual Traditions

JAYA TYAGI

Women have never been a homogenous category. Different categories of women have dealt with issues related to garnering of and management of resources for individual, familial, kin and societal needs even while constantly dealing with sociopolitical systems and patriarchal mindsets in different ways. One cannot envisage any society where women may have been passive participants in social processes. They have been engaged in myriad activities relating to production and reproduction of economic, social, cultural, physical and human resources while constantly negotiating for access to some of these resources and also for decision making, for enhancing their role and stature in society. Women have always been pushing at the boundaries of their existence, even while these boundaries are being constantly redefined and demarcated by political and religious ideologues.

In ancient societies, we know that women's contributions and their active engagement in production and reproduction activities would have been there, yet they are not easy to retrieve because of the nature of the sources which have been compiled and written for varied purposes. When we refer to the agency of women,[1] we need to re-examine the manner in which we look at agency itself as women have different histories when compared to men, their agency and the societal impact of that agency are also different. Patriarchal ideologies are diverse and varied and just as there are multiple ideologies, there are varied negotiations and resistances to them. Generally, we associate agency with resistance and ability to control situations in a manner which will be conducive to improved conditions; however, in the case of women (and other marginal categories) the question of agency is complicated as our sources do not record women's individual or collective responses, and we have to deduce

[1] In feminist literature, agency has been variously described in different ways—the exercise of agency (Jolly 1998, 1), 'free agency' (Manderson 1990, 30), 'an active agency' (Haggis 1998, 85), 'praxis and agency' (Misciagno 1997, xxii), instrumental agency (Molyneux 1998, 79 cited in Lynn Parker, *The Agency of Women in Asia 3* [Singapore: Marshall Cavendish International Private Ltd., 2005], 3). There is also 'negative agency' women struggle to find a voice, sometimes take drastic measures (Gayatri Spivak, 'Can the Subaltern Speak? Revised edition', in *Can the Subaltern Speak? Reflections on the History of an Idea*, ed. Rosalind C. Morris [New York: Columbia University Press, 2010], 21–80).

how women would have participated, contested or complied within society. Sometimes women participate willingly, at other times they resist in their own way, at still other times they are not cognizant of the manner in which they are being deprived of decision making and resource generation. Individual reactions of women to systems of control and domination must have been there, yet they are rarely preserved in history, sometimes deliberately so. It is powerful groups and their voices that have got recorded and been retained in patriarchal traditions for social, political and ideological reasons. The penchant for focusing on larger socio-political power structures by social historians is what makes the marginal groups (including women) slip through the enormous gaps in historical studies—thus, the need for historical 'retrieval' and to look at sources in a manner where we also explore what they seek to hide and the agendas that they attempt to put forth and why they chose to do so.

We also have to acknowledge the fact that in constrained circumstances women may not be able to exercise their agency in the manner that they want to, or articulate it. Compliance with social norms as well as resistances to them is all part of the choices women have to make constantly, sometimes in a conscious and deliberate manner and at other times unconsciously. Resistances are also varied and can be radical but may also be nuanced and subtle. Thus, when attempting to retrieve instances where women can be termed as 'social actors', or as persons in their own right,[2] we have to acknowledge the possibility of 'negative agency' or 'limited agency' and realize that within the limits and constraints that women face, they try to constantly negotiate and work towards contributing in different ways.[3] An aspect of agency that we need to focus on is that it is not only restricted to resistance, but it also compels existing patriarchal ideologies to reformulate their strategies.[4] Agency may not always lead to empowerment or change in situation; sometimes it triggers off changes in strategies of domination.

Ideology plays a crucial role in creating dominant power structures, and how women seek to negotiate within these power structures is critical.[5] Jonathan Freedman has shown how dominance is a set of ideas or practices usually favourable to a particular minority within a society who appear to hold sway over the whole of that society and who act to reproduce this same condition. This section tends to be 'hegemonic, pervasive, exclusionary and conservative'.[6] Thus, textual traditions tend to project male-centric notions and represent women in a particular manner. However, these representations can be studied to retrieve

---

[2] Strathern (1988, 70) cited in Parker (*The Agency of Women in Asia*).

[3] Scholars have shown how women have to cope and strategize according to differing constraining patriarchal systems. Some of these may be construed as 'bargains with patriarchy'; others have shown how sometimes the 'path of least resistance' may be deliberately taken by women as a basic survival strategy.

[4] Foucault has shown how 'where there is power, there is resistance'. He has also shown how 'this resistance is never in a position of exteriority in relation to power'.

[5] Cultural hegemonies in society exist as co-opting groups participate in overall systems because of ideological compulsions. Clifford Geertz has explained how ideologies map problematic social realities—they 'render otherwise incomprehensible social situations meaningful', and are 'matrices for the creation of a collective conscience'. See Clifford Geertz, *The Interpretation of Cultures: Selected Essays* (New York: Basic Books Inc, 1973).

[6] Jonathan Freedman, 'Culture, Identity and World Process', in *Domination and Resistance*, ed. M. Rowlands, C. Tilley and D. Miller (London: Unwin Hyman, 1989), 63.

the manner in which women would have constantly negotiated with societal norms and traditions even while being an integral part of the society. We now understand that in order to unravel the deeply embedded and intertwined networks of patriarchy in normative, religious ideologies, we need to tackle our sources in a more comprehensive manner. There is a need to review early traditions according to the 3R's, emphasized upon by feminist scholars. These are, 're-reading, re-conceiving and reconstructing'.[7] In the early Indian context, there are multiple overlapping spaces in the diverse sources and traditions, especially in relation to their attitudes towards women.

When dealing with issues related to women, work and property, the question of agency becomes even more contentious as domestic work has not been properly acknowledged or quantified as contributing towards societal growth. Ancient textual traditions show a remarkable predilection for overemphasizing women's reproductive roles, usually at the cost of their overall contributions in social and economic production. Even while dwelling upon women's bodies as reproductive vessels, textual traditions seek to ignore and not give due cognisance to women in domestic or reproduction activities. In spite of all these limitations, textual traditions can still be used as sources to derive information on women and work, primarily through re-reading and 'deconstructing' them to read the text, context as well as the subtext in these traditions. The anxieties of the texts, the silences and oblique references give us information on the manner in which women would have made considerable contributions through their active engagement in society.

Representations of women usually do not reveal how women were actually living, nor do they deal with issues related to their daily existence. But they do show us the *perceptions* related to women and can help us trace the manner in which ideologies evolved. There is need to have a more comprehensive view of how gendered attitudes are reflected in normative and theological traditions, giving them legitimacy and sacralising them, and how the ideas then flow into social, political and cultural spaces. The representation of women that we find in texts and women's responses to these have also been subject to constant evolution and change. It is from these representations that we can gauge the role that women have played in the domestic sphere.

HOUSEHOLDS IN TEXTUAL TRADITIONS

The study of households is essential for understanding any society as personal and political spaces are intertwined and reinforce each other. The role of all members of the family, especially women and children, working in the interest of the family in pre-industrial societies has only now begun to get attention. Studies have revealed the economic and social contribution of women and girls, which had earlier been ignored in historical analyses. Studies have shown how the participation of women in the labour market was strongly related to the traditional values of 'family economy' that included daughters. The task of

[7] June O'Connor, 'Rereading, Reconceiving and Reconstructing Tradition: Feminist Research in Religion', *Women's Studies: An Interdisciplinary Journal* 17 (1989, June): 101–23.

how production is managed (and gendered) in the family has been taken up by Scoot and Tilly who have brought attention to the role of women in the family economy in the context of the nineteenth century Europe.[8] Thus, the importance of the domestic organization of production needs to be understood and questions need to be raised about how, as Scott and Tilly say, 'family organization and relationships are determined by a household's labour needs and subsistence requirements'. Tilly refers to the family as a 'mediating unit' between the individual worker and the economic system and it is increasingly being realized that the decision making power of the household brings traditions, values and interests of its own that impact all of society.

In the context of ancient societies, Elise Boulding has shown how women have contributed to household production in agricultural societies. She refers to the fact that 'the household unit in society through the First Millenium C.E. was responsible for about 90 percent of the total production of city states and empires'. Household production, according to her, can be defined as 'what is produced inside and adjacent to the home, including courtyard and kitchen garden, family workshop and farm fields'.[9] Wilk and Rathje have shown how households are the level at which social groups articulate directly with economic and ecological processes; therefore, they are at a level at which adaptation can be directly studied. 'They reflect changes taking place at the social and economic level. At different stages of cultural evolution, in different kinds of environments and in different social strata, households perform different functions and therefore differ in size, organization and development cycle.'[10]

The study of domesticity and the representation of households in texts lead us towards a greater understanding of how texts seek to represent the role of women in the domestic space and whether these are accurate depictions. The projection of the household as an area for production, consumption, distribution and 'pooling' of resources and the participation of women in production and sharing experiences regarding food, cooking and eating can be seen in varied texts like the *Gṛhyasūtras* (henceforth, GSs), the *Maṇusmṛiti* (MS) and the *Matsymahāpurāṇa* (MMP). It is relevant to study these texts as they tell us about normative ideology and the role that was envisaged for women in formulating decisions, negotiation and co-ordinating the management of resources.

Women's participation in domestic spaces requires a fairly complex treatment as they have been presented in textual traditions in a considerably complex manner. The traditions also tell us how women seek to use their domestic status to create sociopolitical spaces for themselves. References to domestic observances and praxis can be used as sources which lead us into the mind of those who formulate normative conceptualizations and reflect socio-cultural attitudes and their anxieties towards women. In order to understand these traditions, one has to not only trace how normative constructs have evolved but also the way in which women have responded to them. In this quest, as we have seen, the role of ideological conceptualizations in revealing some of the complexities relating to the house-

[8] Jean W. Scott and Lousie A. Tilly, 'Women's Work and the Family in Nineteenth century Europe', *Comparative Studies in History* 17 (1975): 36–64.

[9] Elise Boulding, *The Underside of History* (California: West View Press, 1976), 9.

[10] R. R. Wilk and W. L. Rathje, ed., 'Archaeology of the Household', *Americal Behavioural Scientist* 25, no. 6 (July–August 1982), 611–725.

hold is considerable. Women are represented as domesticated, devout wives, prostitutes or as goddesses. However, in each of these 'categories' of representation we get a glimmer of the potential or real agency of women. We also see how ideologically, each of these categories have to be placed or 'evaluated' on the value-laden scale of propriety, auspiciousness and progenitiveness. Women have to constantly 'prove their worth' on all these levels to justify their existence. One of the main reasons for this approach towards women, the need to clearly define (and regulate) their ritual, social and cultural roles is the anxiety related to women's bodies and the need to control their reproductivity. The representation of women, mainly in relation to fertility, seems to have been a conscious and deliberate one and also discriminatory as both men and women are involved in reproduction.

When retrieving material on how the household was envisaged in early Indian traditions, we have to first explore the instances when the household, familial issues and social relationships are discussed and what is the intention and purpose behind the authors discussing the household at that particular juncture. Early texts are not exactly devoted towards an explanation of the structure and nature of productive and social relationships. Analysis of the context in which the households are discussed tells us about how conceptualization of what the household should be like and how it should exist was crucial and always in the minds of the different authors of different textual genres in ancient India.

The need to define the household and relations within it was determined by the need to organize labour towards household work and it was also related to property concerns. Perceptions on the organization of labour have a direct bearing on our understanding of the role of the household. In the modern context, Leela Dube has shown how the question of women's labour has been ignored and, if tackled, taken to 'the arena of the family, myths of motherhood and the devaluation of housework'.[11] Susan Viswanathan has shown how 'the housewife is the transformation of the creative energies of the women in to one systematic type of labourer'—one who is primarily concerned with reproduction, the birth of new members of the labour force and their sustenance.[12]

If we try to analyse early households and work-related and property issues within them historically, then we see that in the Rigveda (RV), although the texts reveal a patriarchal society and there is an attempt to delineate different categories of work reflecting a tripartite society divided into brahmanas, rājanya and vaiśya, the division is a male-centric one. Men are differentiated on the basis of occupations and status-based hierarchies, while women's identities and work-related activities are juxtaposed with men; they are not mentioned separately as it is understood that they will support the males in whatever activities they perform. *Jana*, *viś*, *kula*, *grāma* and *gṛha* are terms which are used in a generic manner. The reference to *daṁpati*, the dual conjugal unit, seems to imply that they were an economic and social unit performing production as well as reproduction activities. There is no real understanding of individual property as such and that is why both individual men and women are not associated with it. The RV reflects a social order in which production was limited and

[11] Leela Dube, 'Gender Biases and Social Sciences', in *Women in Indian History: Social, Economic, Political and Cultural Perspectives*, ed. Kiran Pawar (Patiala: Vision and Venture, 1996), 5.
[12] Susan Viswanathan, 'From Housewifization to Androgyny', *India International Quarterly* (Winter, 1996): 177.

although there are terms used for wealth, this related to cattle, gold, chariots and *dāsas*, not landed wealth or property. There is not much reference to the use of paid workers or slaves in agriculture or craft production, which shows that household production was the norm.

In the later Vedic texts, the Brahmana texts and other texts, the overwhelming association of women with reproductive activities was because of the key role they played in production as well as in producing potential producers. Claude Meillasoux has shown that agricultural societies function on the basis of group cohesiveness and continuity; they evolve households which secure food and seed from previous production cycles. In these societies older men gain control over food, knowledge and women. Women and children become valuable sources of labour and hence the control of reproduction predates property.[13]

Absence of private ownership of landed property meant that the question of inheritance could not have signified much for men and women. Scholars have shown how in the RV, the term *putrikā* meant a child of the family and not a brotherless daughter, the legal heir to her father's property, as it came to mean in later texts. Thus, one sees that social segregation was not deep rooted in RV. Status categories did exist but not class or *varna* categories and although gender categories existed, the differentiation was not so deep-rooted as they were not associated with proprietary, status and *varna* differentiation.[14] *Vārya* and *bhāga* in RV are terms for division, but not of land as it was not a form of property, and agriculture was practised along with animal husbandry. Land was subject to joint or corporate holding, so there was no question of individual ownership of land. Individual possession is referred to in later parts of RV; even women seem to be entitled to have a share of cattle wealth as a marriage gift, as is suggested in the 'wedding hymn' RV X.85.13–38. Sāyaṇa explains the term *vahatu* as 'cow and other gifts given for pleasing the girl'. *Śatapatha Brāhmaṇa* IV.4.2.3 states, 'women own neither themselves nor an inheritancer'. Yāska in his Nirukta II.4 says that women are not entitled to partition and inheritance. But because of parallel traditions, women's proprietary rights could not be totally ignored; *pāriṇāhya* used in the *Taittiriya Saṁhitā* VI.2.1.1 indicates the authority of the wife on family resources.[15] Yāska also states 'some hold that daughters do not inherit'.[16] Brahmanical theorists, while denying women's right to inherit their father's or husband's property, could not ignore women totally as their contributions with regard to labour and reproductivity was considerable; thus, some notions of wealth are associated with women. *Baudhayana DS*, II.2.3.46 does concede the right to movable property in the form of *strīdhana*.

The emergence of private property as a category of wealth and the gendering of property rights are not isolated; they are related to social divisions. The laying down of norms related to conjugality, marriage, inheritance was an attempt to regulate production, reproduction and social order. One needs to interrogate why normative texts such as the GSs, the MS and the MMP feel the need to demarcate the role of the household and its members so categorically. It is because they understand the significance of the social and economic role of the

---

13 Meillasoux, cited in Gerda Lerner, *The Creation of Patriarchy* (New York: Oxford University Press, 1986), 36–61.
14 Vijay Nath, 'Women as Property and their Right to Inherit Property', *Indian Historical Review* 20 nos 1–2 (1993): 2.
15 The term recurs in Jaimini's *Pūrvamīmāmsāsūtra* VI.10.10, and *Manu* IX.11.
16 Yāska's *Nirukta*, 53; Nath ('Women as Property', 9).

household in production and reproduction activities. The intervention of ideologues into the domestic space is so that they can control it, ideologically mould it and tap it as a potential source of revenue and wealth. Within these texts too there are enormous variations—while the early GSs are still chiselling out and laying down the structure of the household and the role of the householder as the *grhapati*, the MS is more concerned with the individual duties, the status and property rights of different categories of household members and the MMP with the propriety related to household members. Let us turn to these texts to see what they reveal about the household as a centre for work and production activities.

HOUSEHOLD PRODUCTION IN THE EARLY GṚHYASŪTRAS (800 TO 400 BCE)[17]

Studies on gender in ancient India reveal that by the sixth century BCE a framework is deeply entrenched which shows the need for regulating work and production activities through maintenance of *varna* and gender hierarchies. The fact that texts like the GSs contain rituals highlighting the role of the *grhapati* is significant. The son and wife are crucial members, the son more than the wife; thus, defining and identifying the role of the household vis-à-vis the kin. The emphasis on the son and wife shows the anxiety related to production, property and labour but also reveals the need for keeping the demarcations between proprietorial rights and labour activities separated. Thus, while the GS rituals emphasize the presence of the wife, which shows that she is integral for the household to function as a working unit, her role as the producer of progeny is emphasized more than the work she performs. While the *grhapati* was projected as the sacral head of the family, the roles of these individual members were not so chiselled out, as the *grhapati* was projected as the controller of resources and manager of labour; clearly, the *grha* could not exist without him.

We are able to recognize the critical role of the wife in the anxiety with which texts mention how the choice of the wife as an accomplished one, one who is *sarvalakṣanasampanna*, is critical for the household. While the household is treated as a sacral space, the *grhapati* being attributed with a divine and cosmic role with his ritual activities, it is clear from the rituals related to production and reproduction activities that it is these two functions that were the primary functions of the household. While having progeny, especially sons, is stressed upon as a sacral activity of the household, there is a growing understanding that the household is to be projected as a viable producing unit, to be tapped for its resource and labour potential and in ways in which women would be contributing significantly.

The manner in which the GSs refer to the *grha*, it seems that a preliminary requirement for setting up the household is marriage; the householder is usually mentioned along with his wife—*gṛhapatīh patnī ca*.[18] The references to the rituals of the household as *pākayajña*, which some interpret as 'to cook, bake' and some as 'small, uncomplicated, feeble, weak',

[17] For details on the household and rituals of the households in the GSs, see Jaya Tyagi, *Engendering the Early Household: Brahmanical Precepts in the Early Grhyasutras* (New Delhi: Orient Longman Publishers, 2008).
[18] *Pāraskara* GS II.9.14.

seem to show an attempt amongst the authors of the GS to delineate the domestic space as separate from the public space. The rituals associated with the householder show that there is an attempt to keep him ritually connected in all the seasons, throughout the year, from morning to evening. This shows that the household was a centre of activities, which were critical to the sustenance of society. Thus, morning and evening oblations, the *agnihotra* were conducted along with appeasement of the *visvedevas*, the ancestors, through rites like the *aṣṭakās*, the full moon sacrifice, *darśapūrṇamāsa*; the seasonal rites—the winter solstice rite, *pratyavarohaṇa*; the seasonal ones like the *mārgaśīrṣa*, *śrāvaṇa*, and solar ones like the *agrahāyaṇa* (ascent of sun). The rites were all associated with offering of food items. The *Pāraskara* GS III.3.1–2 refers to how integral the offering of food is to rites like the *aṣṭakās*. It included offering of food items, such as rice, boiled rice, sesamum seeds, rice-milk, cakes, and animal sacrifice accompanied with the feeding of brahmanas.

That the household members were jointly responsible for the various activities of the household can be seen from the manner in which the *Āśvslāyana* GS refers to how the household fire should be maintained by the householder or his wife, son, daughter or pupil.[19] The mention of the daughter along with the wife and other male members of the family shows that they contributed towards the household activities. The *Gobhila* GS states that the householder should perform all the *balis* himself, but then goes on to state that the wife should perform the evening *balis* and he must offer the morning ones.[20] There were special occasions when the wife could perform the *bali* rites. *Pāraskara* GS states that she performs it outside the house for appeasing malevolent deities who harm offspring, and then feed the brahmanas.[21] The *Gobhila* GS also mentions that in the absence of the householder, the wife should perform the *darśapūrṇamāsa* rite while also stating that if they like, his wife may offer the morning and evening oblations over the domestic fire, for his wife is his house, *gṛhāh patnau*, and that fire is the domestic fire.[22] However, there are conflicting statements, for example, the *Āpastamba* GS III.8.3 states that a sacrifice performed by a wife of one who has not received the *upanayana* initiation is rejected.[23] This shows that there was an ideological pressure on women too to marry those who had undergone initiation rites. Here, we see how although the wife would have been integral to the production and reproduction activities of the household, her sacral role was strictly restricted because of her gender and rites like the upanayana demarcated gender distinctions within the household as young boys would be initiated but not young girls.

That the wife was involved in household work like cooking can be seen from references in the *Gobhila* GS to the fact that once the wife has made the morning and evening meal, the *gṛhapati* makes her announce that the food is ready.[24] It seems that the GSs make an attempt to delineate work and performance of labour (of women and other male members) from the management of food and household resources, which was to be controlled by the

---

[19] *Aśvalāyana* GS 1.9.1–7.
[20] *Gobhila* GS I.4.15.
[21] *Pāraskara* GS I.12.4, 5.
[22] *Gobhila* GS I.4.17–19; I.3.15
[23] *Āpastamba* GS III.8.3.
[24] *Gobhila* GS I.3.16.

householder. That food items were an essential aspect of the household's resources can be seen in the concern with relation to food and its availability. The ritual of *annaprāśana* mentioned in *Āśvslāyana Gṛhyasūtra* (AGS) I.16.1, *Śaṇkhāyana Gṛhyasūtra* (SGS) I.27.1, and *Pāraskara Gṛhyasūtra* (PGS) I.19.1 refers to all types of food items including goat's flesh, partridge flesh, fish, boiled rice with ghee, curds and honey. Verses invoking Annapati, the lord of food, to 'give food without pain to the body' and to give strength, *śuṣmiṇa*, energy, *ūrjā*. Further, the child's leftovers were supposed to be finished off by the mother at this rite, showing the significance of the mother's role in child rearing. The significance of the mother in child rearing is reiterated in the *caula* rite, the first time when the child's hair is cut. After cutting, according to the *Gobhila Gṛhyasūtra* (GGS) II.9.17, the hair with its ends turned eastward is to be given to the mother with *śamī* leaves; the mother is supposed to bury it in cow dung. The proper disposal of the hair is significant; it should not fall in hands of someone who can harm the child and the mother is the most reliable choice and the dung would shield the hair as well as enhance the strength and virility of the child. The texts recommend that all these rites are to be conducted for girls too, but without the chanting of mantras. This shows that there was segregation in the household on the basis of who had access to Vedic learning, and women of the household, even though contributing in a significant way, were kept apart from Vedic chants.

In spite of attempts in the texts to underline the *gṛhapati's* control over household resources, that the wife is critical in the dispensation of food and other resources can be seen in the references to rituals like the *upanayana*, wherein once a boy is initiated as a *brahmacārin*, he is expected to lead a life of frugal discipline, living off begging of alms and the first alms that he begs for are from his mother. However, even though we get ample evidence that women were performing actively in household work, their role is sought to be marginalized through rituals like the *upanayana*. The fact that the rite of passage was to be conducted on male children meant that boys were expected to undertake formal training for their future contributions as active producers after the *upanayana*, under a guru or a trainer. The segregation of children on the basis of gender in the household shows that the texts seek to ignore the value of the labour of young girls and women while trying to tap the labour potential of young boys. The implication is that the girls were expected to learn informally from other women in the household; the value of such informal networks of transferring knowledge and skills is barely recognized, except in a revealing statement in the *Āpastamba* GS where it is clearly stated that 'one should learn from women (*strī*) what ceremonies (are required by custom)'.[25] The symbolic imagery of the *upanayana*—when a person becomes *dvija*, literally twice born—seems to imply that this second ritual birth was more important than the impure earlier one from his mother's womb and, thus, this second birth under the aegis of the brahmana was essential. The issue of re-birth and womb imagery in initiation rites has been studied by Kaelber, while vivid womb imagery were represented in the Atharvaveda (AV) and the Brahmanas; this is not so in the GSs, where the womb imagery changes to one of 'difficult passage'. According to Kaelber, in the GSs there is an 'anti womb' imagery. Kaelber does not link this to changing perceptions with

[25] *Āpastamba* GS I.2.15.

regard to women; it seems that the contributions of women in terms of productivity and regenrativeness were being appropriated by brahmana priests.[26]

Women were actively engaged in cooking, maintenance of the household and contributing towards the household resources as it is clear that the household was being projected in the GSs as a centre for production, distribution and consumption of resources. Even reproduction was critical for societal production and this is represented as a sacral activity in these texts. The elaborate manner in which production activities like agriculture and cattle rearing are mentioned in the GSs, the references to the household as a centre for the distribution and transmission of resources, management of food and also dispensation of resources within the community show that these texts attempt to project the role of the household as a viable unit for production. Women were an integral part of the household, although from the GSs it seems that while they were contributing actively with relation to providing labour for the production activities, decision making and proprietary roles were ideally to be carried out by the males. However, in reality, in an individual day-to-day capacity, women must have been actively involved in decision making, in adding to the income and value of the household as there are various references that can be made relating to the manner in which women contributed to the household. Thus, the texts seem to seek to control and limit the role of women and this could be because of the anxiety related to women's potential agency.

There are ample references to the varied activities that the household carried out; these include production, distribution and transmission of resources. Distribution can be further divided into pooling and distribution within the households and exchange among households. The texts refer to how rites that ensure that resources are channelized in a way that is beneficial for the *grha* are undertaken through various channels, *dāna* and *dakṣina* to brahmanas, alms to *brahmacārins*, hospitality rites and through rituals which involve participation of the community.

The role of the household in providing benefaction is constantly maintained in the GSs—the *Śaṇkhāyana* GS recommends giving of food to a *śrotiya* and a *brahmacārin*.[27] Food is also to be offered to a woman under the household protection, *sauvāsinī*, to pregnant women, *garbhiṇī*, to boys, *kumāra*, and to old people, *sthāvira*. Food is to be thrown for dogs and for various animals. The mention of such a list shows that there was need to ideologically motivate the household members to part with food, both cooked and uncooked, for the purpose of providing sustenance to members who were not involved directly in the household work. The *Śaṇkhāyana* GS explains the procedures for extending hospitality to guests.[28] The need to perform seasonal sacrifices shows that attempts were made to ensure that different tasks related to agricultural activities such as food production, cattle rearing and associated tasks were in tandem with the changing seasons through carefully conducted rituals in which the householder and his wife participated.

[26] W. O. Kaelber, 'The Dramatic Element in Brahmanic Initiation: Symbols of Death, Danger and Difficult Passage', *History of Religions* 18 (1978): 54.

[27] *Śaṇkhāyana* GS II.14.19–22.

[28] *Śaṇkhāyana* GS II.17.4.

The rituals of the household in the GSs revolve around everyday events. Hunger is a state that has to be averted; thus, the *Gobhila* GS states that one who performs a rite without fasting becomes powerless, hunger attacks him, he does not gain favour amongst the people and his offspring will be perverse.[29] The *Āśvslāyana* GS refers to the manner in which agricultural activities were performed, in which women participated actively.[30] Growing of cereals was one of the primary activities of the GSs household and, thus, the *Āśvslāyana* GS claims that one can move into a new house only when it is provided with seed for growing of crops. The *Pāraskara* GS refers to the need for ploughing a field, *kṣetra*, properly.[31] The other term used is *urvarā*. The text mentions the need for a clean spot that has been ploughed with the *phāla*, under an auspicious *nakṣatra*.[32] The *Pāraskara* GS states that oblations of curds, rice grains, perfumes and fried grains are to be made to Indra, Parjanya, Udālākaśyapa, Svātikārī, Sītā and Anumati and then the bullocks are to be offered honey and ghee.[33] Brahmanas are to be fed during this occasion. Most *gṛhya* rites involve elaborate food preparation and cooking. The *Gobhila* GS IV.4.27 refers to the *halābhiyoga*, the setting into motion of the plough where the sacrifice is to be conducted according to the *sthālipāka* ritual.[34] The term means literally 'cooking in the pot' and is one of the *pākayajña* rites. *Pākayajña* means 'sacrifice with cooked offerings' and denotes domestic rites as compared to the *haviryajña* that denotes the formal *śrauta* rites. *Sitāyajña* was a rite conducted for protecting the crops. The reference to different types of soil for tilling and those involved in tilling shows the significance of such agricultural activities. *Kṛṣīvala* was the tiller of soil, *kṣetra*, the field.

References to the different techniques employed in cooking and the different kinds of foods available show how the domestic space was envisaged as one which produced enough, not only to sustain the needs of the members of the household but also of other categories. Terms for food and cereals like *akṣata dhāna*, which was used for roasted cereal, usually barley, show how production of cereals was an important aspect of the household. The above-mentioned *annaprāśana* rite for celebrating the first feeding of cereals to a child was done by the father. *Sattū*, flour of cereal, which was roasted and ground, was used. Different types of cooked food were offered to the brahmanas—*apūp*, rice cakes; *caru* was rice boiled with barley; *odana*, boiled rice; *payasa*, boiled rice with milk. Dairy products were mixed with ghee—*pṛṣātaka* was a mixture of curds and ghee, *sarpi* was some form of clarified butter, *dahi*, curds, were also offered. Vegetables, *śāka*, were part of the diet. *Madhu*, honey, was used as a sweetener and *madhuparka* was a mixture of honey, curds and milk, offered to special guests. *Mudga* were a kind of beans. Terms that were used for cooking utensils used in rituals included: *darvī*, a spoon; *juhū*, a ladle; *śruva* was another kind of sacrificial ladle. The use of the winnowing basket, *śūrpa*, and grind stones, *dṛṣad*, *ullūkhanna,* mortar and pestle in rituals shows elaborate food preparation procedures involving chaffing, winnowing,

---

[29] *Gobhila* GS I.6.2, 3.

[30] *Āśvslāyana* GS II.10.2.

[31] *Pāraskara* GS II.17.6.

[32] For further details, see Tyagi (*Engendering the Early Household*, 259–63).

[33] *Pāraskara* GS II.13.1–8.

[34] *Gobhila* GS IV.4.27.

grinding and pounding of grain. The upkeep of animals as a household activity is indicated in the myriad references to animals—*dharuṇam mātre* referred to a calf and the mother cow, *aja* was the goat and *ajinam*, the skin of the goat was used in households; *aśva* (the horse) is referred to frequently and these animals seem to have been looked after with care.

DOMESTICITY IN THE MS

In later texts like the epics and the MS, there is recognition of the need for households to consolidate their acquisitions and channelize their wealth towards clearly defined and worthy causes—for the authors there is need for capturing this wealth. The texts hint at competing claims for the household's resources. The MS, Buddhist and Jaina texts and also literary works seem to have tried to capture the patronage of wealthy and elite households by referring to them, laying out the manner in which inheritance and property is to be drawn out and, thus, redefining notions of household linkages, kinship and domesticity. There is also careful delineation of property as the basic function of the household is projected as one of maintaining its proprietary interests. Is it a wonder that the *grhapati* of Buddhist texts is a synonym for one who has extensive proprietary interests, one who employs *karmakāras* and gives patronage to the *sangha* and also the king?

Marriage-augmented resources as well as kin gained from marriage became critical in allowing households to become custodians of wealth. The competition for power and resources meant that your own brothers and cousins were competitors and to garner support against them, affinal ties had to be made strategically and significantly. Thus, marriage and ties emerging from marriage were crucial and in the epics it is not surprising that princesses of strong kingdoms are passionately coveted. These princesses were critical in fulfilling the grand designs of their kinsmen for power and domination.

The household is crucial in the MS; the need to clearly regulate the dharma of the householder and his wife is underlined. The male protagonist is prioritized but also reined in and controlled through an elaborate discussion of *patidharma*. It is interesting that the duties and role of the householder are defined; there seems to be a conscious effort towards a moral and ethical code for men in the domestic space too, albeit not as stringent as the one for women. And of course, *patidharma* was only part of the many roles that a man could aspire to—*rājyadharma* and other ways of dealing with his intellect and power are also defined, whereas for women, her only dharma according to the MS was *patnidharma*. *Patnidharma* is reinforced over and above the reproductive role of the wife (which has already been established in texts like the GSs). The MS is essentially prescriptive, meant for the brahmana, and makes a tremendous effort to maintain exclusivity for them. The prescribed norms are aimed at a small, exclusive audience, with the expectation of transmission of these values through brahmanas and *kṣatriyas* who would serve as role models. The text aims at indirect percolation of values and norms and is also highly elitist and keeps the privileges of the elite strictly defined, making little attempt to include other categories. In fact, there is a conscious attempt to emphasize on maintenance of the *varna* order and prohibit intermingling, *varṇasaṁkara*.

The MS not only shows the chain of command in the domestic sphere but also clearly defines women's role in the domestic space; somehow the onus of maintaining harmony within the household is on the women. The MS extends its area of intervention in the domestic space by not only focussing on her domestic duties but also elaborating on the expected congenial behaviour from women. Thus, MS 5.150 states—'She should be always cheerful, clever at housework, careful in keeping the utensils clean, and frugal in her expenditures'.[35]

The husband is expected to use her services optimally. Thus, MS 9.11 states—'He should employ her in the collection and disbursement of his wealth, in cleaning, in meritorious activity, in cooking food, and in looking after the household goods'.[36] In an attempt to build upon the work ethos the MS 10.13 refers to the things that corrupt women. Drinking, associating with bad people, living away from the husband, travel, sleep and staying in the house of others are the six things that corrupt women.[37]

One of the reasons why familial relationships get attention in early texts is because of the need to define property rights. In fact, one of the main roles of the elite households of textual traditions seems to be proprietary, the need to protect and care for property and clearly delineate the channel of succession for coveted property. This is one of the areas in which the household and its members are mentioned, because of the need to limit or to clearly define household member's stake in property. As individual property becomes important, the right of inheritance of progeny was underlined. In fact, it is proprietary interests which make the texts emphasize on progeny rather than kinsmen or brothers. This is carried forward in the *Purāṇas* when we see lineages being drawn out on the basis of progeny and brothers' lineages being split as separate, parallel, disconnected ones.

The need for managing and controlling household work and labour meant that women and other household members were treated as property, and this is underlined in the exclusive proprietary rites of the householder and the husband over the other members of the family.[38] The treatment of women and children and even brothers as property, be it in the Vedic texts, Brāhmaṇas or the epics, has been explored by scholars. Even in the Mahabharata, closest kin such as wife and son were treated as alienable property. This gets replaced in later society; according to Vijay Nath and in Northern Black Polished Ware (NBPW) society and the Iron Age, the patriarch was no longer empowered to gift, pledge or sell any member of the family, be it the son or wife as per texts such as the *Āpastamba* DS and the *Yājñavalkyasmṛti*.[39] This may mean that elite households would be using the labour of categories other than immediate kinspersons, both men and women; *dāsas* and *karmakāras* would have contributed towards household production. The numerous references to the

[35] *sadā prahriṣṭayā bhāvyam grihakārye ca dakśayā/ susanskriopaskarayā vyaye cāmuktahastyā*. Patrick Olivelle, *Manu's Code of Law: A Critical Edition of the Mānava Dharmaśāstra* (Delhi: Oxford University Press, 2006; The University of Texas Centre for Asian Studies, 2005), 146, 588.

[36] *arthasya sangrahe chainām vyaye chaiv niyojayet/ śauche dharme~nnapaktyām cha pāriṇāhyasya chekśaṇe*

[37] *pānam durjansamsargah patyā ca viraho~Tanam/ svapno~nyagehavāsaśrcha nārīsadūṣṇāni ṣaṭ*

[38] Vijay Nath refers to how two facts are emphasized in any assessment on property related to women of the household, one that they were regarded as chattel and the second, their limited competence to own property. See Nath ('Women as Property', 1).

[39] *Āpastamba* DS II.6.13.1, 1 *Yājñavālkya smṛti* II.125.

substitute of 'stand in' *dāsīs* in the epics shows how women were used for menial labour as well as sexual activities, their reproductivity tapped for progeny. Property and wealth, at least theoretically, remained with the head of the household who had claim to the wealth of all the individual members of the household.[40]

This is complex as we see that the position of household members was not static, and there were significant variations in their status. In brahmanical tradition, household relationships and some cognisance to women's property begins to be discussed with regard to right to inheritance in an effort to keep property within the family and keep it from falling in the hands of 'others'. This becomes a much debated issue in śāstric traditions and one can try to understand the dichotomy between the contentious position of women in the household and their seemingly continually expanding proprietary rights as women of the household, as some scholars have pointed out. It seems that women were being acknowledged as having the potential to own and manage landed properties, as there was a need to emphasize that they could do so only in the absence of male heirs. The anxiety related to hierarchically differentiating wives on the basis of *varṇa* and sons on the basis of their mothers in the MS seems to indicate the volatility in polygynous households, the potential agency of the co-wives, the competing claims for resources and decision making in the same and hence, the need to keep the women in control.

The control over household members is conceded by Manu who not only wants control of the husband over wife but also maintains that a wife cannot be released from her husband either by sale or by repudiation;[41] and that a wife cannot be treated like a chattel as she is obtained from the gods, she is not received like cattle and gold in the market. Yet, the MS also makes contradictory statements, saying they were part of the war booty.[42] When the ownership of progeny is discussed, women are equated to the field or livestock; ownership of the field determines ownership of the harvest, irrespective of who 'plants the seed'. There are many sections in the MS which show the manner in which women were treated as property, to be owned, alienated, bought, sold and even mortgaged. Vijay Nath also shows that the husband's proprietary right over wife becomes crucial, seen in the status of the *kṣetraja* son; thus, the MS regards a wife as husband's property in which if a stranger sows in another's field, the fruit belongs to the owner of the land.[43]

---

[40] Nath ('Women as Property', 7) shows that women are bracketed with property on two occasions—when the need to protect property is emphasized, and where property is described as yielding prestige and status, as R. S. Sharma also states. He points out that the institutions of private property and family centring around the wife were the chief reasons for the origin of the state and the main motive for social action. Women along with property became the chief source of conflict in society (R. S. Sharma, *Perspectives in Social and Economic History of Early India* [Delhi: Munshiram Manoharlal Publishers, 1983], 39–44).

[41] MS VIII.416.

[42] MS 7.96 states that, 'Whatever a man wins—chariot, horse, elephant, parasol, money, grain, livestock, women, all goods and base metal—all that belongs to him'. Similarly, in a section on false testimony related to land, women are equated with land; thus, MS 8.90 states that, 'False testimony concerning water, they say, is similar to that concerning land; the same is true of false testimony concerning the sexual enjoyment of women and concerning all gems, whether they are aquatic or lapidary' (Olivelle, *Manu's Code of Law*, 172).

[43] Nath ('Women as Property', 6).

The obsession of the texts with women indicates that women's significance emerged from the key role they played in production and producing producers. N. N. Bhattacharya shows how Dharmasūtras are openly in favour of patrilineal inheritance and proclaims that property should rather go to near or remote agnates, *sapiṇḍa* and *sakulya* relations, of the property holder rather than to daughters.[44] Āpastamba, Baudhāyana, Vasiṣṭha say that ornaments and wealth bestowed on her by her relations, both agnate and cognate, should be absolutely owned by her.[45] N. N. Bhattacharya also states that the *smṛtis* have distinct codification of the rules relating to ownership, inheritance and partition. Manu gives the first elaborate and 'systematic exposition' on these, and his approach seems to have been followed, 'with certain conservative and liberal reservations', by later law givers, Yājñavalkya, Nārada and Bṛhaspati in the Gupta period and Kātyāyana, Vyāsa and Parāśara in the post-Gupta period.[46]

Manu's work has contradictory principles when it comes to women and property; on the one hand, it allows women to become exclusive owners of such wealth that is gifted to them by the relations, *strīdhana*.[47] On the other hand, he emphasizes that property should be transmitted only through the male line and women have no right to inherit paternal property. The stress on patrilineal inheritance apart, Manu does attempt to take into account different laws that refer to women's right to inherit property. Ultimately, he works out a compromise; he does not mention that sisters have equal entitlement to patrimony as brothers but says that for marriage of sisters brothers should forego one-fourth of their own share in favour of sisters.[48] This means that Manu did not project daughters as the natural heirs of their fathers, but the father was at liberty to give wealth to daughter as gift—*pitṛdatta* and *anvādheya* categories of *strīdhana*. The preoccupation with property shows that the MS was referring to elite households. The anxiety with relation to women who were economically sound to be able to exercise agency can be seen.

Hierarchies were drawn out on the basis of who had access to property. Property was to divided amongst the sons on the basis of the seniority of birth and if the wives were from different *varṇas*, then on the seniority of the wives. MS 9.122–25 refer to the fact that if the first born is from a junior wife, he would be treated as the eldest and senior-most and then others would be ranked on the basis of the seniority of their mothers. However, if the wives were of the same rank, then they would be ranked according to their birth. This would put pressure on women to conceive and also points at acknowledgement of prevalence of polygamy.

Manu also refers to the *putrikā* or daughter's son functioning as an heir for a sonless father.[49] The mother's wealth would pass to the daughters, according to the MS. While

---

[44] N. N. Bhattacharya, 'Proprietary Rights of Women in Ancient India', in *Women in Early Indian Societies*, ed. Kumkum Roy (Delhi: Manohar, 2001), 118.

[45] *Āpastamba* II.6.14.19, *Baudhāyana* II.2.49, *Vasiṣṭha* XVII.48–9.

[46] Thus, Manu had a tremendous impact on later law givers, including Sankara who unconditionally says that in social matters Manu is final.

[47] MS IX.194.

[48] MS IX.118.

[49] MS IX.127. Nath ('Women as Property', 11) refers to the different occasions in the MS when gifts can be given to the daughter, over which she has right: *Adhyāgni*—before the nuptial fire; *Adhyāvahanika*—in the bridal procession;

earlier *dharmaśāstras* such as Baudhāyana, Āpastamba and Gautama mentioned only male *sapiṇḍa* as fit for inheriting, Manu referred to the right of the appointed daughter, *putrikā*. However, Manu uses the issue of property to further regulate women's behaviour. In one section, the MS refuses the right to property to one who marries on her own but also refers to the protection of women as a duty of the state and since this is mentioned along with property issues, it seems that the state was being enjoined to protect the proprietary rights of women who did not have kinsmen to protect them. Thus, the text states that a girl who chooses her husband on her own must not take with her any ornament coming from her father or mother or given by her brothers; if she takes them, it is theft.[50] The same protection (as that to a child who inherits an estate) must be extended to 'barren' women, women without sons or bereft of family, women devoted to their husbands, widows and women in distress. If their in-laws usurp their property while they are alive, a righteous king should discipline them with the punishment laid down for thieves.[51] The text seems to show that the mother also has a stake in property as long as she is alive—after the father and mother have passed on, the brothers should gather together and partition the paternal inheritance evenly, for they are incompetent while those two are alive.[52] The use of the dual, *jīvatoh*, shows that as long as either of the two is alive, they have a say in the property. It shows that both husband and wife were involved in the management of their property. This also shows that it is the brothers who gather; sisters do not have a role to play in the division. The fact that women were contributing through their work is clear from the limits placed on the acquisition of wealth by a girl which include wealth acquired through work done by her which belonged to husband, according to Manu.

As long as there were sons to inherit, property could be safely disposed of. The problem arose in the absence of a male heir. In the absence of the male heir, Manu deviates from the earlier dharma writers by stating clearly that the daughter is equal to the son and 'someone else' (*anyo*) cannot grab (*haret*) the property if she is there.[53] Further reinforcing a woman's access to some forms of property, unmarried daughters are given the mother's property and the status of the daughter's son is reinforced, not only as the heir to property, but also as one who has the ritual responsibility of performing the rites of oblation after death. The daughter's son is equated to the son's son as both daughter and son have come from the father's body. The stress on being directly related made the daughter's son's role significant and this was at the cost of other male relatives. However, if a son was born after the daughter's son was

---

Prītidatta—out of love; *Bhṛātṛmātṛpitṛprāptam*—received from brother, mother and father. These seem to include several occasions when gifts were given to the bride but these exclude gifts from others, except from close kinspersons.

[50] *alankāram nādadīta pitryam kanyā svayamvarā/ mātrikam bhrātridattam vā steyam syāddydi tam haret* MS VIII.27–28/MS IX.92.

[51] *vaśāputrāsu chaivam syātrakṣaṇam niṣkulāsu cha/ pativratāsu cha strīṣu vidhavāsvāturāsu cha// jīvantīnām tu tāsām ye tatdhreyuh svabāndhavāh/tā~chiṣyāchchauradaṇđen dhārmikah prithvīpatih* (Olivelle, *Manu's Code of Law*, 168, 663).

[52] *ūdhrvam pituśrcha matuśrcha sametya bhrātarah samam/ bhajeranpaitrikam rikthamanīshāste hi jīvatoh* MS 9.104.

[53] MS 9.127–30 deals with a man without a male issue in the following way. A man without a son should make his daughter a 'putrikā' in the following manner: 'The child this girl bears will be the one who performs my ancestral rites' (*aputro~nena vidhinā sutām kurvīta putrikām/ yadpatyam bhavedasyām tanmama syātsvadhākaram*).

appointed as the heir, then the property was to be divided amongst them equally, as the law of primogeniture did not apply (*jyeṣṭa*) to the daughter's son.[54] Further reducing the rights of other male relatives, the MS appoints the husband of the *putrikā* in the absence of a son from the daughter. MS 9.135, 136: If a *putrikā* somehow dies childless, the husband of the *putrikā* shall indeed take the property without hesitation.[55] When a daughter, whether she is appointed or not, bears a son by a man of equal status, by that son his maternal grandfather becomes a man who has a son's son, and the latter shall offer him the rice ball and inherit his property.[56]

Chapter 9 in the MS deals with the manner in which a woman's property is to be disposed of on her death which shows that there were instances when women had control over property—and in the maternal estate, the brothers and sisters seem to have equal rights. This estate, *mātrikam*, seems to be different from the *strīdhana* over which only daughters had rights. That mothers were managing their properties seems to be implied. However, when the MS elaborates subsequently on the gifts, they seem to be the same and, thus, there seems to be a confusion over this. Moreover, the last verse shows that women were not supposed to alienate paternal property and they had to consult their husbands on any issue related to property.[57] The MS states that, 'When their mother dies, all the uterine brothers and sisters would divide the maternal estate equally among themselves.'[58] If those sisters have any daughters, one should joyfully give them also, as is proper, something from their maternal grandmother's property.[59] Similarly, in a section on miscellaneous rules on inheritance, the text states that, 'The mother shall receive the inheritance of a childless son; and if the mother is also dead, the father's mother shall inherit that property.'[60] There also seems to

[54] Thus, MS 9.131–34 states that: Anything that is part of a mother's separate property becomes the share of her unmarried daughters; and the daughter's son shall take the entire property of a man without a son (*mātustu yautakam yatsyayāt kumārībhāga eva sah/ dauhitra eva cha haredaputrasyākhilam dhanam*).

[55] *aputrāyām mritāyām tu putrikāyām kathamchana/ dhanam tatputrkābhrtā haretaivāvichārayan*

[56] *akritā vā kritā vāpi yam vindetsadriśātsutam/ pautrī mātāmahastena daddyātpiṇḍam hareddhanam*

[57] Tradition presents six types of women's property: what a woman receives at the nuptial fire, what she receives when she is taken away, what she is given as a token of love, and what she receives from her brothers, mother and father (*adhyagnayadhyāvāhanikam dattam cha prītikarmaṇi/ bhrātṛmātṛpitṛprāptam ṣadivadham strīdhanam smritam*). What she receives subsequent to the marriage and what her husband gives her out of affection—upon her death that property goes to her children even if her husband is alive (*anyāvadheyam cha yaddattam patyā prīten jchaiva yat/ patyau jīvati vritāyāh prajāyāstaddhanam bhavet*). In a *brāhma*, Divine, Seer's, Gāndharva or Prājāpatya marriage, the property of a woman is awarded to her husband alone, if she dies childless (*brāhmadaivārṣagāndharvaprājāpat yeṣu yaddhanam/ atītāyāmprajasi bhartureva tadiṣyate*). In a demonic or subsequent form of marriage on the other hand, any property given to a woman is awarded to her mother and father, if she dies childless (*yatvasyāh sthāddhanam dattam vivāheṣvāsurādiṣu/atītāyāmaprajasi mātāpitrostadiṣyate*). Any property given somehow won to a woman by her father goes to the unmarried brahman daughter, or that daughter's offspring (*striyāstu yadbhvedvitam pitrā dattam kathamchana/ brāhmaṇī taddhretkanyā tadpatyasya vā bhavet*). Women must never alienate common property of the family, or even her own private property, without the consent of her husband (*na nirhāram striyah kuryuh kaṭumbādvahumadhyagāt/ svakādapi cha vitāddhi svasya bharturnājñayā*) (Olivelle, *Manu's Code of Law*, 200, 783).

[58] MS 9.192–200.

[59] *jananyām samsthithāyām tu samam sarve sahodarāh/ bhajeranmātrikam ṛktham bhaginyaśrcha sanābhayah yāstāsām sayurduhitarastāsāmapi yathāhartah/ mātāmahyā dhanātkinchit pradeyam prītipūryakam*

[60] MS 9.217: *anapatyasya putrasya mātā dāyamavāpruyāt/ mātaryapi cha vritāyām piturmātā hareddhanam*

be some attempt to protect the rights of a widow and to protect her from property grabbers, 'Any ornaments worn by a woman while her husband was alive shall not be partitioned by his heirs; if they do, they fall from their caste.'[61]

These developments can be related to developments in the institution of private property and the patriarchal family. The extension of agriculture in the NBPW phase increased the significance of landed property and accentuated joint hold of the family in land holdings. Trade, profit making and craft specialization provided wider avenues for individual enterprise. Money economy led to new forms of property, rendering the accumulation of wealth easier. Forms of property came to include land along with cattle, slaves, goods and objects and metal currency. There were two contradictory developments in this phase. Landed estates controlled jointly by family were treated strictly as part of patrilineal inheritance, in which an individual's right to ownership and alienation was generally disregarded, or circumscribed. Secondly, growth of individual enterprise and metal currency led to greater right and complete ownership over movable items of property which led to recognition of women's rights to some limited categories of property known as *strīdhana.* The meaning and scope of *strīdhana* expanded continually during the period of the *dharmashastric* traditions.

We find that different sources refer to the circumstances in which women may own property. Thus, Pali sources and votive inscriptions testify to women as religious beneficiaries on large scale; however, the urban base of this group is conspicuous according to feminist historians. There are earlier examples of women like Ambapali and Sama who had access to different types of wealth.[62] The role of women monastics in channelizing resources and patronage, working towards propagation and spread of cults like Buddhism, has not been given even prominence when we discuss women and work in Ancient India. These *bhikkunīs*, once they had entered the monastic establishments, seemed to have contributed to the spread and dispersal of the religious causes they espoused, channelizing both funds and followers for their cause, an aspect of Buddhism that is rarely given importance, even though there are many inscriptions that show women as patron. Dhammapāla's Paramatthadīpāni (fifth to sixth centuries CE) categorically refers to the role that *bhikkunīs* played in the spread of Buddhism. Women workers in the monasteries played an important role as conduits for tapping the resources of the households and directing them towards the *sangha.* In an earlier article on the Patimokkha rules of the Vinaya Pitaka, I have shown how the text refers to monastic dependency on women of the household for alms and food.[63] Lay women, from households, and the monastic women must have created networks that buttressed the spread of Buddhism.

---

[61] *patyau jīvati yah strībhiralankāro dhrito bhavet/ na tam bhajerandāyādā bhajamānāh patanti te*

[62] Nath ('Women as Property', 11).

[63] Vijay Tyagi, 'Organized Household Production and the Emergence of the Sangha', *Studies in History* XXIII, no. 2 (2007): 271–87.

WOMEN AS PATRONS IN THE PURĀṆAS

By the time of the *Purāṇas*, the urgency to include women and tap their potential, both as patrons and 'devout' propagators, seems to have been understood and indicates the potential agency of women as managers and dispensers of resources. Women were seeking spiritual salvation actively, performing ritual observances and giving patronage to sects and even though these were well within the confines of patriarchy, they seem to have negotiated for an enhanced social role by underlining and overemphasizing their religiosity. In negotiating for their roles, all categories of women tried to gain legitimacy for themselves by turning to ritual observances to show that they had a sacral role to play. They attempted to compete with each other in piety and performance of religious observances and devotion to the family and in the textual traditions the *pativratā* dharma was espoused by women with apparent fervour.[64]

The *Purāṇas* attempt to do this well within the confines of the 'domestic' realm and seek to merge the pious nun of the Buddhist traditions with the *pativratā* wife to come up with the ideal of the *suvratā-pativratā* devout wife. The standards of social, moral and ethical propriety are also reconstructed in these texts with women being projected as agents of change. Highly motivated, exemplary standards of religious observances are expected to be maintained by wives who are projected as the vanguard of sobriety and propriety, through *vratas* and ritual observances. The household, from being a sacral and divine centre for reproduction, production, socialization, also becomes a vehicle through which moral propriety and ideological propagation of particular value systems (in this case Puranic) are carried forward.

In the context of the *Purāṇas* it seems that the effort is to impinge on the consciousness of the audience who must have listened to reciters. The *sumangalā*, *pativratā* and *suvratā* wife is constantly projected in Puranic traditions so that the notion becomes impinged in the consciousness of the audience of the *Purāṇas*, a clear effort to promote and propagate this ideological role model.

The association of women and goddesses with wealth and fecundity in these traditions shows an understanding of their contribution to the economy. Julia Leslie has shown how Śrī is regarded as venerable; even the MS sees no difference between virtuous child bearing wives, *strīyāh* and goddesses of fortune, *Śrīyah*. The fact that the devout wife assumes the stature of a Goddess can be seen in the Mahābhārata wherein Śrī herself declares that she resides in women who are devoted to truth, attend to their housework, obey their husbands and behave with the appropriate decorum.[65] The relationship between land, women and goddesses, which is consistently drawn out in textual conceptualizations, shows the connections that were made between femininity and productivity. As land began to become scarce and venerated, representations of feminine form as fecund, associating it with productivity of land and also material wealth, became more common. Land was the source of wealth, but because of its value it could be alienated, sold, bought and mortgaged. Ownership of land

[64] For a detailed analysis of the role of women as patrons, see Jaya Tyagi, *Contestation and Compliance: Retrieving Women's Agency from Puranic Traditions* (New Delhi: Oxford University Press, 2014).

[65] Mahabharata.13.11.10 ff. (Julia Leslie, *Roles and Rituals for Hindu Women* [New Delhi: Motilal Banarsidass, 1992], 107–27).

becomes crucial and we have seen how in this scenario, proprietary rights evolve which allow women to inherit in the absence of immediate male heirs. Thus, instead of allowing coveted land to lapse to the state or to other male kinsmen, it was preferred that in the absence of the son, the daughter's son, the *putrikā* would get property. Along with the value of land, the growing demand for material goods, something that is elaborated in the references to *dāna*, show the value placed on such commodities.

An elaborate iconography develops around Goddess Lakṣmī, the source of all wealth; the references to gold, silver and other precious metals associated with her show this. In the *Matsyamahāpurāṇa* (MMP), the goddess is conceptualized as capital, a resource that has to be tapped, and this shows changing notions of wealth and how the cult of Lakṣmī gets promoted. Association of the feminine with wealth, prosperity and the need to control these for the use of men is indicated in rituals like the *Guḍadhenudānavidhi*[66] which involves the image of a cow and a calf to be made with raw sugar.

Women were playing an active role in the activities but they were clearly competing amongst themselves for resources. One of the reasons women may have felt the need to underline their piety while performing domestic roles is to deal with the advantages that elite men have in societies which encourage polygynous social practices for the upper echelons (the presence of which is amply reflected in the sources). Rich and powerful men took multiple wives and had many children while women would be constantly negotiating for status, space and resources in households with other women and children. The wives performed *vratas* to further highlight their agency in keeping the household prosperous and thriving, granting long lives to the men and keeping rival women at abeyance (which also draws attention to their lack of ability to use agency in any other way). Thus, women used ritual observances to underline their sacral status in the household, so that they could maintain their tenuous hold over the household in whatever way the men in the household allowed them to.

The circumstances of these early households were constrained and there was intense competition for attention, control over resources and even conjugal rights; women would compete amongst themselves for the control over the household and for capturing resources for their progeny. This reflects on the manner in which patriarchal societies operated: men (some, not all) had the power and resources to command different services from women—physical, laborious, emotional, spiritual and sexual. Women had to compete, not with men, as there was hardly any scope for that, but with other women for limited decision making roles, confined domestic spaces and for resources. In negotiating for their roles, all categories of women tried to gain legitimacy for themselves by turning to ritual observances to show that they had a sacral role to play, attempting to outdo each other in piety and performance of religious observances and devotion to the family.

It was not only the wives who underlined their steadfast *pativrata* qualities, temple women too were piously devoted to their ritual roles in the temple and the courtesan also had sacral rites seeking to legitimize her existence. One of the recurring motifs in the Puranic myths is that of devout, divine and sacred women who performed austerities and

[66] MMPL XXXII.

these women were from both *deva* and *daitya* categories. The device of ritual in myths is used for projecting the agency of women in various ways; by suggesting that divine women undertook them, the texts aim at a percolative effect, so that performance of austerities (accompanied with the mandatory *dāna*) becomes popular amongst the elite and propertied. One can say that the incorporation of women protagonists wielding power and influencing decision making, even if it is directed towards the advancement of their individual families, is historically significant. It seems that the author/s of the MMP were trying to project their anxieties by discussing these women who were able to wield power. The fact that they attribute it to the austerities they perform is a brahmanical device used in a retrospective manner to explain any power that does not emanate directly from them (it is not surprising that kings, powerful men, all gain power only through the conduct of rituals). In the texts, there are spaces where women are envisaged to have some degree of agency and this seems to hint at social acquaintance with women who could wield power and control. This is obviously in response to the society around them where the author/s were probably dealing with powerful women who were taking charge of social domains like the household and the community, if not public arenas like the state.

Another interesting aspect of these myths being represented in the MMP is the relative assertiveness of the *daitya*, *asura* women. Can one suggest that these women seem to have had a less controlled upbringing and could make more choices? In the conceptualizations of the authors then, were assertive women representing 'other' cultures where women had more say, had more access to resources and were (relatively) less under the control of patriarchal norms? Are these texts then trying to reach out towards such cultures, by including the concept of the austere *daitya* women who brought wondrous changes in their clans through their devout austerities? Are some of the images of these *daitya* women based on *actual* women, from disparate cultures, tribal (and migrant) populations and also from within the brahmanical communities who may have taken to alternative religious discourses like Buddhism, Jainism and other sects? It is tempting to imagine that the image of the powerful, devout and austere *daitya* women which the *Purāṇas* project is partly inspired from these women.[67]

Women's *vratas* in Puranic traditions include *vratas* meant for *veśyās*, prostitutes, which again shows how assimilative these *vratas* attempt to be. They also give some indication of the resources that *veśyās* had access to. The *puṇyastrīṇāmsadācāravrata* is one such reference.[68] The *vrata* shows how *brāhmaṇas* were not averse to tapping the resources of the prostitutes for themselves and encouraging them donate freely to *brāhmaṇas* while performing *vratas* for their salvation. The *vrata* involves giving not only material things to *brāhmaṇas* but also satisfying the sexual demands of the 'worthy *brāhmaṇa*' and also if he should so wish it,

---

[67] Marglin refers to the association of *daityas* with tribals in the specific context of Orissa. Connecting the myths that link tribals and the king in kinship relationship, she shows how in the origin of King Pṛthu, the birth of Pṛthu is accompanied with the birth of Niṣādas, and as O'Flaherty shows, the myth which explains the origin of kingship shows that Pṛthu was churned out of the body of the King Vena who was killed by the sages and while he was born out of his hands, the Niṣādas were born from his thighs ([O'Flaherty 1976, 321] cited in Fredrique Apffel Marglin, *Wives of the God King: The Rituals of the Devadāsis of Puri* [Delhi: Oxford University Press, 1985]). The myth is also included in the MMP and has been discussed in the 'Introduction' of this work.

[68] MMP LXX. For details regarding the *vrata* see Appendix XI.10.

then the demands of some other man whom he may recommend. These are the instructions to the *veśyās:* 'You should give away cows, land, grain and gold, according to your means in charity on the sacred day of worshipping the Devas or the ancestors.... You should act as per what the brāhmaṇas say.'

There are other legends connected to *veśyās'* magnanimity. The text refers to a legend relating to a *veśyā* named Līlāvatī who was devoted to Śiva and gave a mound of salt to her preceptor, along with trees of gold. It seems that salt was as valuable as gold. The gold trees were made by

> a skilled śūdra named Śauṇḍa, a gold smith by profession who lived in her house and made beautiful gold trees and images of Devas with faith and skill and did not charge anything for his labour as he thought that these were meant for *dharma kārya*—acts of religiosity. The wife of the goldsmith fixed those trees on the mount in an aesthetic manner.[69]

Līlāvatī, by virtue of her charity and her devotion to her guru, was liberated from her sins and went to the realm of Śiva, while the śūdra goldsmith and his wife were reborn as a king and queen.

The story reveals how women were conceptualized as patrons and employers. It also gives us a quaint tableau of the manner in which households functioned—the husband and wife as a production unit, being employed by the courtesan. The assimilative nature of the text can be seen from the manner in which all categories of people—śūdra, courtesans, the devout wife—are encouraged to work together towards performing religious acts. The benefits, as elaborated, include health, wealth and kingdom, *lokeṣvaparājitatvamārogya saubhāgyayutā ca lakṣmī*. The pressure to make donations to *brāhmaṇas* is sought to be sustained by mentioning that the benefits are cumulative and can allow a *śūdra* to be reborn as a king and also allow a *veśyā* to attain liberation.

The *Vibhūtidvādaśīvrata*[70] is another *vrata* in which the *vrata mahātmya* (efficacy, the benefits accruing from its performance) involves the legend of the largesse of a courtesan This also shows how women from different walks of life were conceptualized as patrons and how the benefits of their good deeds were supposed to lead to their own *mokṣa* as well as better lives in future births for others too. The agency of women, albeit through the performance of such rites, seems to be clearly indicated.[71] In this legend a famous courtesan Anamgavatī donates mounds of salt, a bedstead and other objects including the golden kalpa tree to her guru. The courtesan also offers 300 gold coins to the couple who were observing the *vrata* which they did not accept, being charged with *sattvaguṇa*. The courtesan, further pleased, ordered four kinds of delicious food to be brought for them to eat. They declined to eat and expressed delight in meeting her and wanted to keep the fast themselves. They were kept awake all night and in the morning the courtesan gave away mounds of salt and beddings and villages, garments, *kamaṇḍalu* and cows. She fed her friends, poor men, blind men, misers, kinsmen and also both of them. Owing to this devotion to Viṣṇu, the same couples

[69] MMP LXX.
[70] MMP XCIX, C.
[71] MMP C.

were born as the king and his wife while the courtesan became the rival of Ratī, the wife of Kāmadeva, called Prīti.

This shows the manner in which the texts seek to tap the resources that courtesans seem to have had access to in the ancient traditions. These included villages, cows, gold, garments and food. The texts contain exaggeration but still reveal the expectations of the brahmanas with respect to the courtesans and how some of them may have amassed wealth.

BIBLIOGRAPHY

G. Buhler, ed., *Āpastambiya Dharmasūtram* (Bombay: Bombay Sanskrit Series, 1932).
Chandrakanta. *Gobhilagṛhyasūtra* (Calcutta: Baptist Mission Press, 1908).
F. Knauer, *Mānava Gṛhyasūtra* (Batavia: M. J. Dresden, 1897).
S. R. Sehgal, *Śaṇkhāyana Gṛhyasūtra* (Delhi: Munshiram Manoharlal, 1960).
R. Shama Sastri, *Baudhāyana Gṛhyasūtra* (Mysore: Mysore Sanskrit Series, nos 32/55, 1920).
N. N. Sharma, ed., *Āśvalāyana Gṛhyasūtra* (Delhi: Eastern Book Linkers, 1976).
Adolf Friedrich Stenzler. *Pāraskara Gṛhyasūtra* (Leipzig: Kashi Sanskrit Series, 1876).
H. H. Wilson, ed. and trans., *Matsyamahāpurāṇam* (Delhi: Nag Publishers, 1983).

Women and Work in Early Textual Traditions

Section II

Chapter 8 The Woman Worker*

I. B. HORNER

Among the better classes in Buddhist Indian society, the great majority of women were supported by children, husband, or father. They did not do much, if any, work beyond their household tasks as mother, wife, or daughter. But among the poorer people the case was different, and there are various records which refer to self-supporting women who were engaged in a trade or a profession.

It is said, for example, that a certain woman was the keeper of a paddy-field; and she gathered and parched the heads of rice, doing the work herself.[1] Another is described as watching the cotton-fields,[2] where she used sometimes to spin fine thread from the clean cotton[3] in order to while away the time.

Women also appear to have been capable of functioning as keepers of the burning-grounds. Two references are made to the same woman, Kāḷī, who was engaged in this occupation,[4] although no mention is made of any wage she might have received. She evidently had at heart the welfare of those who came to meditate in the charnel-field, for she provided them with objects suitable for the contemplation of Impermanence.

A spirited description of a woman acrobat occurs in the Dhammapada Commentary.[5] Although it is the only reference to a woman who earned her livelihood by such arts, it is illuminating. For it is probable that some of the five hundred tumblers with whom she was, were also women. They used annually or twice a year to 'visit Rājagaha, and give performances for seven days before the King.... One day a certain female tumbler climbed a pole,

* Previously published in I. B. Horner's *Woman Under Primtive Buddhism*, Motilal Banarsidass Publishers. New Delhi (1989), pp. 83–94.

[1] Dhp. Cmy. on verse 118.

[2] Jātaka, 546.

[3] *Ibid.*

[4] Theragāthā Cmy. on cxxxvi.; Dhp. Cmy. on verses 7–8. This Kālī is not to be confused with the slave-woman of the same name mentioned below.

[5] Dhp. Cmy. on verse 348.

turned somersaults thereon, and balancing herself on the tip of the pole, danced and sang as she trod the air'. A son of a great merchant fell in love with her, but her father would not give his daughter for money, and suggested that the youth should travel about with them. The people delighted in these acrobatic performances, and 'stood on beds piled on beds' in order to obtain a good view. They tossed up gifts to the tumblers, who also earned 'much gold and money'.

Such were, perhaps, the more unusual ways in which women supported themselves. Far more numerous were domestic female slaves, born to this status of other domestic slaves, like Puṇṇā, in the household of Anāthapiṇḍika.[6] They formed part of the property of most wealthy householders. 'Wives and children, bondwomen and bondmen, goats and sheep, fowl and swine, elephants, cattle, horses and mares, together with gold and coins of silver':[7] all these ties the houseman is said to pursue with blind and avid appetite. But knowing that they are fetters and encumbrances, even the unconverted man, when speaking in praise of Gotama, might say: 'He refrains from accepting slave-women or slave-men'.[8] All these are thought to be subject to the round of rebirth, to decay and impurity, and also, with the exceptions of the inanimate gold and coins of silver, to disease, death and sorrow.

There is only one reference in canonical literature to a slave-woman who was maltreated.[9] She had tried her mistress's patience past bearing. Her name was Kāḷī, and she had endeavoured to find out whether the reputation her mistress, Videhikā, had for gentleness and mildness was true. She therefore got up later and later three mornings running. At first her mistress merely questioned her and frowned; the next *morning* she complained; and the third morning she struck Kāḷī on the head with a lynch-pin, and drew blood.

It nowhere appears that slave-women were over-worked. There were multitudes of them in the royal establishments, some of whom waited upon the queens, and performed such duties as daily buying flowers for them,[10] and looking after the jewels of the ladies in the royal harem.[11] In other households they pounded rice,[12] an arduous task, and helped with the cooking.

Three slave-women called Puṇṇā are mentioned: the one referred to above; one of whom it is said that the brahmin Pokkharasāti's heart and mind does not read the heart and mind of his domestic slave, Puṇṇikā,[13] meaning that not even a brahmin has omniscient powers; and another who is mentioned in the Milindapañha as one of the seven people who did 'acts of devotion which bare fruit even in this life'.[14] But she is the only one to be omitted from

[6] Therīgāthā Cmy. on lxv.
[7] Majjhima, i., *162*.
[8] Dialogues, i., p. *5*.
[9] Majjhima, i., *125–126*.
[10] Dhp. Cmy. on verses 21–23.
[11] Jātaka, 92.
[12] *Ibid.,* 45.
[13] Majjhima, ii., 201.
[14] Milindapañha, iv., I, 37.

the more detailed descriptions given later[15] of the merit-working acts done by these people. Doubtless she attained some blissful state, but was she freed from bondage in this life?

Slave-women could be emancipated, but only with the consent of their master. It is significant that in all recorded cases where such a step was taken, it was in order to enable the freed-woman to enter the Order,[16] for slaves were ineligible for ordination.[17]

Khujjuttarā,[18] a slave-woman of Queen Sāmāvatī, did not apparently become emancipated on her conversion to Buddhism. She reformed her conduct in so far as after the first time that she had heard Gotama preach she spent the whole of the eight pieces of money that the queen had given her for buying flowers, instead of spending only four and keeping the other four for herself. Being asked by the queen why she had brought back so many flowers on this particular day, she said that she had heard the discourse given by the Exalted One, and had acquired understanding of the Dhamma. She then preached it to the queen, who became a believer, and to all her women-attendants. They begged Khujjuttarā to be to them as a mother and a teacher, and to go to hear every discourse given by the Teacher, and then return and teach it to them. In this way she came to know the Tipiṭika by heart, and it is said that the Master assigned her pre-eminence among his female lay disciples, who were learned in the Scriptures and able to expound the Dhamma.

Besides slave-women some of the more prosperous householders had also in their retinues vast troupes of female musicians. Gotama himself, before he entered on the homeless way, is said to have been 'ministered to by bands of women musicians',[19] and it is recorded of Yasa the noble youth that 'in the palace for the rainy season, he lived during the four months (of that season), surrounded with female musicians, among whom no man was'.[20] The instruments played by such women included the flute, lute, tabor and drum.[21] In a passage in the Milindapañha the drum (*bheri*) is described as making a sound 'by the action or effort of a woman or a man'.[22] Seven kinds of musical instruments are alluded to in the Dialogues,[23] but they are not specified. Cymbals[24] were in vogue.

An almost necessary concomitant of music was dancing. Although the true ascetic should abstain from being a spectator at shows or fairs with nautch-dances (*nacca*), singing (*gīta*), and instrumental music (*vādita*),[25] this prohibition did not apply to the laity. Sound prompted sight to aid in dispelling the tedium of the days of torrential rains, and dancing-girls abetted

---

[15] *Ibid.,* iv., 8, 25.

[16] Therīgāthā Cmy. on lxv.; Dhp. Cmy. on 314.

[17] See below, p. 146.

[18] Dhp. Cmy. on verses 21–23.

[19] Majjhima, i., *504.*

[20] MV, i., *7, 1, 2*; *cf.* Dialogues, ii., *170.*

[21] *Ibid.*

[22] Milindapañha, iv., *6, 58.*

[23] Dialogues, ii., *183.*

[24] *Samma* and *tāḷa*, perhaps a gong, Dialogues, ii., *170.*

[25] Dialogues, i., *5, 7.*

in this work, performing as was their wont upon large woollen carpets,[26] sometimes singing themselves[27] and making music also.[28]

In order to show the highest honour to King Mahā-janaka, his subjects prepared a great festival, and when they were presenting their offerings 'a crowd of King's ministers sat on one side, on another a host of brahmins, on another the wealthy merchants and the like, and on another the most beautiful dancing-girls'.[29]

But they were not employed solely for entertainment: they were sometimes put to other uses. Queen Sīlavatī, the consort of Okkāka, had no child.[30] The people complained that the realm would perish, and counselled the king to send out a band of dancing-women of low degree into the streets. If no one of these, however, gave birth to a child he should then send a company of women of good standing, and finally a band of the highest rank. The expeditions were to receive religious sanction, but this was not so much to regularise the status of the nautch-girl, for she was already accepted as a necessity to the wealthy, as to insure a successful result. But when the king and the people knew that they were doomed to disappointment, the failure of the women to give birth to a child was attributed to their lack of merit and to their immorality: a Hindu rather than a Buddhist interpretation.

Thus women professional workers consisted largely of domestic-slaves, nautch-girls and women musicians. In addition to these, a large part of the female population who did not otherwise gain their livelihood, or who were not otherwise supported, were courtesans. They also were sometimes well versed in dancing, singing and lute-playing.[31] Although the extent of prostitution in ancient India is disputed, it had existed before the Buddhist days,[32] despite the importance given to marriage in the Vedic Age: but for some girls who were without protestors,[33] a life of prostitution was an obvious course to pursue. Their conduct was regretted by some members of the population. 'Aśvapati, the prince, boasts that his kingdom has no thief, churl or drunkard, none who neglect the sacrifice or the sacred lore, no adulterer or courtesan'.[34] In the Laws of Manu courtesans are portrayed as ceremonially unclean, and brahmins are enjoined never to eat food which has been offered by harlots,[35] for it is said to exclude from the (higher) worlds.[36] Further a king should know clever harlots to be a thorn in the side of his people,[37] should instigate them to commit offences, then bring them into his power[38] and punish them.[39]

---

[26] MV., v., *10*, 3.
[27] Jātaka, *529*.
[28] *Ibid., 132, 313.*
[29] *Ibid., 539.*
[30] *Ibid., 531.*
[31] MV., viii., 1, 3.
[32] C.H.I., vol. i., p. 97; Macdonell and Keith, *loc. cit.,* vol. i., p. 395; *cf.* vol. i., pp. 30, 147, 481; vol. ii., p. 496.
[33] C.H.I., vol. i., pp. 88–89.
[34] Keith, *Religion and Philosophy of the Vedas and Upanishads,* p. 585.
[35] Manu, iv., 209.
[36] *Ibid.,* 219.
[37] *Ibid.,* ix., 259, 260.
[38] *Ibid.,* ix., 261.
[39] *Ibid.,* ix., 262.

In spite of adverse public opinion and in spite of punishments, courtesans persisted into the Buddhist days, when they formed a far from negligible portion of the community, as is shown by the very ease with which they are used in similes.[40] Some, like Vimalā[41] and Sirimā,[42] appear to have been prostitutes because their mothers were. Yet among this class of women the birth-rate must have been somewhat low. Hence comparatively few girl-children would be born to enjoy their mother's favour,[43] for courtesans were fully aware, as Sālavatī phrased it, that 'men do not like a pregnant woman. If anyone should find out regarding me that the courtesan Sālavatī is pregnant, my whole position would be lost.'[44] There is no record that female infanticide was ever committed by a courtesan; but if sons were born to them they ran a certain risk of being murdered.[45] Sālavatī and the courtesan of Kosambi[46] and the courtesan of Rājagaha[47] all gave orders that their sons should be put into an old winnowing basket and cast away on the dust-heap. Sālavatī's was saved by the prince, Abhaya, and lived to become a famous physician. On the other hand, both Ambapālī and Abhaya's mother each had an almsman son.

Four courtesans, Vimalā, Abhaya's mother, called Padumavatī, Aḍḍhakāsī and Ambapālī, having been converted to Buddhism, entered the Order and attained to arahanship. To each of these, too, verses are attributed in the Therīgāthā. Of Vimalā[48] little other mention is made,[49] and none of Abhaya's mother:[50] she was the town-belle of Ujjenī, and her boy, Abhaya, was King Bimbisāra's son. On the other hand, Aḍḍhakāsī[51] is important, as in order to circumvent the difficulties of her ordination a relaxation in the discipline was granted.[52] And Ambapālī[53] became and remained famous as one of the most loyal and generous supporters of the Order.

This beautiful woman is said to have come into being spontaneously in the king's gardens at Vesālī at the foot of a mango tree; but really she was half-sister to Vāsiṭṭhī,[54] their mother coming of a clansman's family at Vesālī.[55] By her beauty, talents and desirability Ambapālī made this town ever more and more flourishing.[56] But as she grew older she seems to have come under the influence of her son, the Elder Vimala-Kondañña, and 'later on, out of faith

[40] Theragāthā, verse 939, *gaṇikā va vibhūsāyaṃ,* 'like courtesans do they parade their gear.'
[41] Therīgāthā, xxxix.
[42] Sutta Nipāta, Cmy., i., 144.
[43] See above, p. 20.
[44] MV., viii., I, *2–4.*
[45] The putting away of an illegitimate child is referred to in the Rig-Veda. Macdonell and Keith, *loc. cit.*, vol. i., p. 395.
[46] Dhp. Cmy. on verses *21–23.*
[47] MV., viii., *1, 4.*
[48] Therīgāthā, xxxix., *cf.* below, p. *184.*
[49] She occurs again Theragāthā, verses *1150–1157*, again being rebuked by Mahā-Moggāllana.
[50] Therīgāthā Cmy. on xxvi., see below, p. *185.*
[51] *Ibid.,* on xxii., see below, pp. *143, 184.*
[52] See below, p. *143.*
[53] Therīgāthā Cmy. on lxvi., see below, p. *185.*
[54] Therīgāthā Cmy. on li.
[55] Mrs. Rhys Davids, *Gotama the Man,* Londan, 1928, p. 149.
[56] MV., viii., 1, 1.

in the Master, she built a vihāra in her own gardens',[57] for she had become exceedingly rich. One day, having heard that Gotama was at Koṭigāma, she ordered a number of magnificent vehicles to be made ready,[58] and drove up to the place where he was preaching, finishing the journey on foot, owing to the impassability of the roads.[59] After he had taught and gladdened her with a religious discourse, she asked him and the fraternity of almsmen to take their meal at her house on the next day. He accepted, and although shortly afterwards he received an invitation for the same day from the princely family of the Licchavis, he refused them and kept his promise to Ambapālī; not so much because she was rich, for the Licchavis were rich also, but for the sake of keeping troth; or because, although there is no trace in the records that she was repenting or that he was blaming her, he may have felt that she was needing his advice at a crisis in her life more than they. Her disdain of the Licchavi men, her clients, as they drove up in their gorgeous chariots, also pointed to the change of heart which she was experiencing.

Soon after, when Gotama was at Ñālika, she offered her mango-grove 'to the fraternity of almsmen with the Buddha at its head'. He welcomed this donation graciously. It would be of great use to the Order and he could not have wished to rebuff one on the path of regeneration. She finally attained arahanship.[6]

Besides Ambapālī, other courtesans appear to have benefited the Order in various ways. It is said that at the assemblies of Sulasā the courtesan and of Sirimā the courtesan, eighty-four thousand people penetrated to a knowledge of the Dhamma.[60] Nothing is said to show why Sirimā was endowed with virtue. She appears to have been a malicious woman, who was asked by Uttarā, a female lay-disciple to act as concubine to her husband for a fortnight while she herself went away to hear the preaching. Sirimā became angry with Uttarā, and injured her. But Uttarā made her ask pardon from Gotama, and she confessed the evil she had done to Uttarā.[61] Sulasā's story appears in a Jātaka.[62] She lived in Benares and had heaps or courtesans in her train. One day, as she was watching from her window, she saw a robber who had been captured, and who was being led to the place of execution by royal command. She fell in love with him, and thought that if she could free him she would give up her bad life and live respectably with him. She managed to gain his freedom by sending a thousand pieces to the chief constable and then lived with him in delight and harmony. Later he wanted to rob her, but she threw him over a precipice.[63]

Further, a group of courtesans saved the life of a lay-disciple,[64] who was returning from listening to a discourse on the Dhamma. But for their intervention he would have been killed in mistake for the real thieves who had fled. Yet, having saved him, they neither mocked at him nor tried to seduce him.

---

57 Therīgāthā Cmy. on lxvi.
58 MV., vi., 30; Mhp., ii., §17.
59 Therīgāthā Cmy. on lxvi.
60 Milindapañha, vi., 4.
61 Dhp. Cmy. on verse 223.
62 Jātaka, 419.
63 Cf. the story of Bhaddā Kuṇḍalakesā, Therīgāthā Cmy. on xlvi.
64 Dhp. Cmy. on verse 165.

A courtesan who seems to have come under the spell of the Dhamma was Bindumatī.[65] In the time of Asoka, it is said that by an Act of Truth, that is by calling 'to mind the attributes of the Buddhas who almspeople, courtesans are never openly condemned in the literature, being regarded as more piteous and low than blameworthy. Hence, although they come towards the end of a long list of trades and professions given in the Milindapañha,[66] even so they were said to be capable, with brahmins and nobles, not merely of knowing that a certain new city was regular, faultless, perfect and pleasant, but also that 'Able indeed must that architect have been by whom this city was built'.

According to the outlook of their own times, it would be thought that a woman was a prostitute on account of the working out of her karma. It was partly because of the notion of karma that the profession was frankly permitted by the social code of the day, and was more openly recognised then than now. Prostitution was regarded as a condition to which a person was reborn as a desert for some offence which, as it was thought, had overtaken her in a previous existence. But she need not remain in this condition. By willing to change, by willing to strive against the stream, and to cultivate the upward mounting way[67] and to live well, a woman could become different, could grow,[68] and escape from the prison of sense-desires

REFERENCES

Dhp.cmy *Dhammadpada Commentary* of Buddhaghosha ed. Eugene Watson Burlingame in the *Proceedings of the American Academy of Arts and Sciences*, Vol. 45, No. 20 (Jun., 1910), pp. 467–550.

Jataka, The Stories from the Life of Buddha's Former Births, ed. E.B.Cowell and W.H.D.Rouse, 1895 and 1907, Cambridge University Press, Cambridge.

Therigatha Translated by Mrs. Rhys Davids as *Therigatha: Psalms of the Sisters,* published in 1909 (publishers not given).

Dialogues of the Buddha, Digha Nikaya, edited and translated from Pali by T.William Rhys Davids, Oxford University Press, H. Frowde, London, 1899.

Majjhima Nikaya Translated by Lord Chalmers, London, 1926.

Milinda Panha Questions of King Milinda translated by T.William Rhys Davids in 1890 (publisher not known but republished by Dover Publications, London in 1963.

Mahavagga of Vijaya Pitaka translated by T.William Rhys Davids and Oldenburg in Published in the *Sacred Books of the East,* volumes XIII and XVII in 1881 and 1882.

Mrs. Rhys Davids, *Gotama the Man,* London, 1928.

Samyutta Nikaya The Book of the Kindred Sayings, tr C. A. F. Rhys Davids & F. L. Woodward, 1917–30, 5 volumes, Pali Text Society, Bristol, UK.

[65] Milindapañha, iv., I, 47.

[66] Milindapañha, v., 4.

[67] Therīgāthā, verse 99.

[68] Saṃy. Nik., XXXVII., iii., 3, § 34.

Chapter 9

Of Dasas and Karmakaras: Servile Labour in Ancient India*

UMA CHAKRAVARTI

WOMEN IN SERVITUDE AND BONDAGE: THE *AGRIHINIS* OF ANCIENT INDIA

The earliest accessible literary references point to an extremely significant but relatively unrecognised fact: the capture of large numbers of women slaves by the Aryans from the subjugated dasa people. These references are doubly significant because men slaves are rare in the *Rgveda.*[1] Further, women slaves are frequently spoken of in the context of wealth, and are listed along with gold, cattle and other assets in the Later Vedic literature.[2] It appears reasonably certain from these references that there were more women slaves than men slaves in Vedic society, and that they were also considered more valuable. The *Aitareya Brahmana* states that 10,000 women slaves were gifted by the king of Anga to his chief priest along with cattle, wealth and gold.[3] One of the Rgvedic hymns mentions a gift of 50 dasis to a priest.[4] Another reference mentions ten chariots carrying abducted dasis, said to constitute a part of *dakshina.*[5] The *Chandogya Upanishad* lists female slaves along with cattle, horses, gold, fields and houses, to demonstrate the grandeur of their owners.[6] Particularly significant is the fact that in the early Vedic literature cattle and women slaves constitute the only forms of movable property, and are transferable, unlike land.[7]

The predominance of women slaves over men slaves and the value attached to them requires some explanation both from the point of view of the history of slavery and the study of women in history. Sharma has suggested that women were an important object for whom the wars between the Aryans and the dasas were fought.[8] He argues that women are highly valued in a tribal context since they are 'the producers of producers'.[9] It is possible that the

* Reproduced with permission from the author and the publisher, from *Everyday Lives, Everyday Histories: Beyond the Kings and Brahmanas of 'Ancient' India.* Tulika Books, New Delhi, 2006, pp. 86–100.

Aryans, whose numbers decreased during their long trek to India, required to replenish their stock, for which women would have been needed urgently. I suggest that women slaves, at least in the early stages of Indian history, not merely provided a source of cheap labour but also doubled up as reproducers and replenishers of a declining stock, and this explains their numerical preponderance over male slaves in the Vedic literature. The value attached to women slaves can be explained at least in part by their sexual and biological attributes, which added to their value as sources of labour, a characteristic they shared with men.

A significant point to note here is the association of brahmana priests with the possession of a large number of dasis.[10] The dasis are frequently stated to be objects of either dana or dakshina, and are handed to the chief priests by the king.[11] It is possible that the king represents the conqueror who has captured the dasis from the subjugated dasa people. The fact that the dasis are handed over to the Brahmana priests in such large numbers (running into thousands in one reference)[12] may signify a more fundamental process than would appear at first glance. If the dasis were functioning even partially as replenishers of the declining stock of the Aryans, then it would be necessary for them to go through a process of acculturation or aryanisation themselves: and the agency for this diffusion is likely to have been the priest. The association of Brahmanas with a large number of women survived into later times. The post-Vedic Buddhist literature frequently alludes to the association negatively when Brahmanas are attacked for leading a degenerate existence.[13]

Apart from their biological function, dasis are also likely to have contributed to domestic production centring round cattle in the predominantly pastoral Early Vedic society. Subsequently, when agriculture began to replace pastoralism, there are occasional references to dasis in the context of agriculture. The *Atharvaveda* refers to dasis being engaged in subsidiary agricultural operations.[14] However, the earlier predominance of dasis over dasas gradually began to give way with the emergence of a full-scale agricultural economy. Both dasis and dasas are now mentioned together, working within the household of the master as well as outside it. References to dasas and dasis working the land are usually of a general kind, and may represent family units that jointly worked the land in much the same way as teams of family labour in contemporary times. Occasionally dasis alone are mentioned, as for example the dasi who watched over her master's field in one of the *Jataka* stories,[15] but on the whole the dasis now begin to be closely associated with domestic labour. In fact all specific references to dasis in the Buddhist narrative literature are in the context of domestic service. Also, dasis predominate over dasas in domestic service and it is clear that the real burden of domestic labour fell upon them.

A pertinent reference in Buddhist literature distinguishes between the work of the dasis and the work of the wives within the household. Buddhaghosha describes the work of the slave girl (*dasi bhoga*) as working in the fields, removing filth, fetching water, and doing other menial and drudge jobs. Dasi bhoga is opposed to *sunisa bhoga*, which designates the work of the daughter-in-law.[16] It was this distinction in domestic service between dasis and the womenfolk of the family (which obviously had its own gradation, with the daughter-in-law only one step above the slave girls) that was invoked by one spirited daughter-in-law who refused to be cowed down by her father-in-law's authority, and protested to him that she was not a *kumbhadasi* (a slave girl who carried water).[17] The heavy burden of domestic labour was strongly resented by some women who then shifted the burden on to their slave women. This is clear from the example of a young wife of an old Brahmana in *Vessantara Jataka* who repeatedly pesters her husband to get her at least one dasi to take over the domestic chores.[18]

Among the most strenuous and burdensome tasks of domestic labour performed by the dasis was the drawing and fetching of water. The kumbhadasi is described as having to get up early in the morning in order to fetch water, which had often to be carried over vast distances.[19] It was considered particularly arduous because of the perennial nature of the task. Further, the sheer quantity of water required in a hot country such as India must have placed a heavy burden on the kumbhadasis. Husking rice was also considered to be a heavy task. One dasi is depicted as continuing to pound the rice till well after sunset. She collapses with exhaustion and attempts to revive herself by seeking a breath of fresh air.[20] The work of a dasi included cooking, making the beds, lighting the lamps, milking the cows and so on—in short, all the drudgery of domestic labour.[21] Even the Brahmana gurus made use of slave women to labour for them. One reference describes the young (and able-bodied) disciples of a Brahmana guru waking up the dasi early in the morning and asking her to prepare food for them.[22]

Some references in ancient literature suggest other functions for dasis apart from domestic service: as guards,[23] in the retinue of their well-to-do masters, as errand girls.[24] Sometimes hundreds of slave girls accompanied rich brides to their new homes as part of their dowry.[25] As early as the *Atharvaveda,* we get a reference to a dasi who accompanied her newly married mistress to her new home in order to entertain her there.[26] A special category of dasis were *dhatis*, or wet nurses. Chanana is not quite certain whether the dhatis were slave women, but from their general description it does not appear that they had much freedom.[27] The dhati dasis accompanied their mistresses to their new homes after marriage and lived with them for the rest of their lives.[28] Kautilya also refers to dasis among nurses and prescribes special rules for them.[29]Although the relationship between the nurse-mothers and their mistresses was often characterised by great intimacy, the work of the dhatis was regarded as unclean since their garments were invariably soiled with various kinds of unpleasant discharges.[30]

Considerably higher in terms of prestige were the *nataka itthis*, who were women in the harems of princes and monarchs. Although they did not have the status of wives, since they could be disposed of to others or even inherited,[31] they had a few years of comparative comfort. The dasis in the royal entourage did not have to labour physically, having merely to entertain their masters and generally please them. Although they were more privileged than other dasis because of their physical appeal, they were totally dependent upon their looks, which were necessarily of a temporary nature. The literature gives evidence of their later years when the distinction between them and other dasis virtually disappeared. Some of them became nursemaids and stayed on royal service. The ever-pragmatic *Arthashastra,* with its comprehensive rules concerning all available sources of labour, suggests that old *devadasis* and old dasis of the king should be employed usefully to cut wool, fibre, cotton and flax.[32] Since weaving was under state supervision, a large number of women were employed in state workshops: hence harem inmates who retired could simply be transferred to the state workshop. The work of carrying raw material of and from other women, who would not venture out of their houses themselves and who worked at home, also fell upon the ex-dasi inmates of the royal harem.[33] According to the *Arthashastra,* a prostitute slave (brothels were run by the state), once past the enjoyment stage, could be put to work in the store or the kitchen.[34] Some were employed in drinking houses as serving girls.[35] Others less fortunate might end up as wandering spies who pick up information and pass it on to the institute of espionage.[36] In their mature years, therefore, the women in the king's service lost some of their comforts and were reduced to the level of the rest of the labouring dasis.

It is fairly evident from numerous references in the *Jatakas* that the dasis were often subjected to threats and abuses from their masters. The slave girl Punika, for example, was required to fetch water all day long, from dawn right into the night.[37] This was an arduous job, especially in winter, but Punika had no respite because of the threats and abuses showered upon her. The fact that her master was a devoted Buddhist did not in any way alleviate her suffering. The threat of physical violence probably reduced the slave girls to a situation in which they were completely under the control of their masters. Buddhist literature frequently uses the expression 'meek as a hundred-piece slave girl',[38] which makes it evident that the dasis had been so completely suppressed that they became synonymous with meekness. Meekness alone, however, was no guarantee against violence. We have the example of a dasi who was beaten by her master for not handing over the wages she had earned by working for someone else.[39] This would suggest a practice similar to the one in Greece where slave owners, when not using the labour of their slaves themselves, would hire them out to others and collect the wages. Another heart-rending account is of a dasi called Rajjumala who had been badly abused from childhood. The mistress often catches hold of her hair, and slaps and kicks her. To escape this torture, the girl has her head shaved by the barber, but her mistress then ties her head with rope and beats her. Unable to bear the torture any further, Rajjumala escapes to the forest and attempts to commit suicide.[40]

Notwithstanding all the instances of physical violence against dasis that we have cited, by far the most vulnerable area of a slave girl's existence was the sexual abuse and sexual violence she could be subjected to. This was a special burden that slave women had to bear—not only did they labour like the dasas, but they were also exposed to sexual exploitation. The Buddhist literature gives an example of a slave girl who is forced to sleep with her master. When the mistress finds out about the incident, she cuts off the girl's nose in a fit of jealous rage.[41] The action is directed against the victim and not the violator, as is usual even today. There is evidence to suggest that sexual exploitation of a dasi did not constitute infringement of the law and that a master could act as he pleased in relation to a female slave. It was for the master to decide in what way he used or abused her servitude.

The fact that sexual exploitation of dasis was common is taken note of in the *Arthashawstra*, which attempts to contain the practice to a section of dasis. Kautilya ruled that no master should have pledged dasis (ahitaka) attending on him while he bathed.[42] The violation of a pledged dasi would cause the master to forfeit the value of the pledged amount.[43] Sexual violence against a pledged dasi who was a nursemaid or a cook in domestic service resulted in freeing her. The master was also liable to receive punishment.[44] If a master raped a dasi who was pledged to him and was under his protection, or helped another to do so, he was not only to forfeit the purchase value but also compensate her with money.[45] Similarly, the daughter of a pledged dasa or dasi who was violated by the master was to be compensated with jewellery and money as contribution towards her *sulka*, or nuptial fee.[46] Apart from this, he had to pay a fine to the ever-vigilant state. If the master produced children through his dasi, the dasi and the offspring would be freed.[47] The *Arthashastra* also provided for the protection and maintenance of the dasi during pregnancy.[48]

It is difficult to estimate the effect that Kautilya's injunctions may have had in reducing the sexual exploitation of dasi women, especially since their vulnerability was an outcome of their position: as women who were partially or completely under the control of their masters. Most significant is the distinction that Kautilya makes between the ordinary dasi and the ahitaka dasi, since almost all his injunctions apply to the latter—the bondswomen over whom the master had only partial control. This category, as we have earlier pointed out, was just beginning to emerge. The protective rules for ahitaka dasis were in keeping with the protection to the ahitakad asas in terms of the kind of work that could be allotted to them. They enjoyed immunity from impure work and from physical violence. For the older categories of dasis, over whom the master had absolute control and who could not look forward to possible redemption, there was no such protective legislation; it is reasonably clear that other categories of dasis continued to be sexually exploited, even legally. All that the *Arthashastra* seems to have succeeded in doing was to establish the superior control of the state over the masters. Since many of the offences were made punishable by imposing fines instead of imprisonment, the prevalence of sexual exploitation was utilised by the state to its advantage.

I will end this discussion on female slave labour in ancient India by pointing to another significant reference. According to Chinese accounts, in the sixth and seventh centuries there were no female slaves in India.[49] It is important to note that this implies that there were a few male slaves and that the situation was exactly the reverse of the position that we began this discussion with. At the beginning of the period, female slaves outnumbered male slaves. At the end of the period, there was a decline in the institution of slavery generally and the virtual disappearance of dasis in particular. What meaning can one derive from this? Is it possible that women slaves were now hardly required for their labour and that they were unnecessary for purposes of mass reproduction? The society and, in particular, the economy were relatively more stable in the sixth and seventh centuries than they had been in Early Vedic times, which may account for the comparative absence of dasis during this period. It is also possible that female slave labour was being replaced by visti, or forced labour, rendered by women in rural India. The *Kāmasutra*, for example, has an interesting reference which indicates that visti was imposed on the womenfolk by the headman of the village.[50] According to Vatsyayana, unpaid work of various kinds, such as filling up the headman's granaries, working on his fields, taking things to his house, cleaning or decorating his residence, and spinning the yarn of cotton, flax and hemp for his clothes, was rendered by the womenfolk of the village.[51] I have earlier argued that the burden of visti was usually shifted on to the poorest sections of the village, and there is no reason to think that it was otherwise for women. Further, while Vatsyayana's statement might suggest the reduced need for slave labour in early medieval times, the vulnerability of women to sexual exploitation survived even in visti. Vatsyayana concludes his statement on the performance of visti by women by pointing out that these are occasions when sexual intercourse may be had with such women.

A striking example of the exploitation of women in debt bondage is the statement made by Narada and Vishnu that women, like cattle, could be lent out to others.[52] Featuring in a list of items along with gold and grain, but especially associated with cattle, are women (men are missing from the list) who may not only be lent out but upon whom it is normal to levy interest. For both women and cattle the interest that is prescribed is the same: one issue.[53] This means that when a woman was borrowed and subsequently returned to the original owner, she would have to be returned along with one of the issues that she would have produced during the period of loan. If she has had more than one issue, the borrower would be entitled to keep the others. Even as a theoretical proposition this smacks of crass materialism and a peculiarly insensitive form of exploitation. Quite obviously, bondswomen were mere objects, and the notion of a family unit did not exist for them. Whatever was the form of extraction of labour from these women, the exploitation they suffered was unique to them.

PERCEPTIONS OF EXPLOITATION

Interesting facts about slavery and labour in ancient India can be gleaned from the existing literature, especially from the rich Buddhist narrative literature. The sources include material that, when pieced together, provides a perspective on exploitation—both of the exploiters and the exploited. The *Digha Nikaya* highlights the tremendous social distance that existed between one human being and, another with the king and the dasas representing the two extremes. What is more significant is that the dasa is depicted as being aware of his low status in relation to the king, even though both share the basic characteristics of being men. The dasa says to himself:

> Here is Ajatasattu, the King of Magadha. He is a man and so am I. But the king lives in full enjoyment of the five pleasures of the senses—a very god methinks—and here am I a slave, working for him, rising before him and retiring later to rest, keen to carry out his pleasure, anxious to make myself agreeable in deed and word, watching his very looks.[54]

The dasa clearly recognises the wide and unbridgeable gap between the king and the slave, representing as they do opposite ends of the social and political hierarchy.

The Buddhist texts also refer to an interesting case of a dasi's awareness of her skill, labour and meekness not only being taken for granted, but also leading to the mistaken notion that her mistress is a gentle-tempered woman. The dasi thinks to herself, 'Now, does my mistress have an inward ill temper that she does not show because I do my work so carefully?' She proceeds to test and expose the real temperament of the mistress by getting up late three mornings in succession. The mistress's temper begins to crack under the strain of her dasi's self-indulgent and unslave-like behaviour, and she begins to abuse and threaten her. On the third morning, when the dasi shows no signs of mending her. ways, the mistress says, 'Well now, Kali, why did you get up late today?' 'That's nothing, mistress', replies the dasi. Infuriated by this reply the mistress shouts, 'That's nothing indeed, bad slave', and, grabbing the bolt of a door, she physically assaults the dasi by giving her a vicious blow on the head. Kali, the slave woman, then shows her blood-spattered head to the neighbours[55] and effectively puts an end to the myth of the 'gentle temper' of her mistress.

The consciousness of exploitation and the consequent tension arising from it is apparent in another statement in the *Majjhima Nikaya*, where the master of some dasas complains to the Buddha that the dasas do one thing with their bodies, say another with their speech, but have something else in their minds.[56] Apparently, the masters are not unaware of the undercurrent of resentment that the dasas harbour because of their low position. One of them implicitly recognises[57] that the surplus controlled by him is produced through the labour of his dasa-karmakaras. Pali texts also indicate that the dasa-karmakaras often carried out orders under duress and fear of punishment.[58] The atmosphere of coercion and physical violence is graphically summed up in the *Mahabharata:* 'Men acquire [other] men as slaves, and by beating and otherwise subjugating them, make them work day and night. These people are not ignorant of the pain that is caused by beating and chains'.[59] The same passage has also been rendered as follows:

> Human beings, enslaved by human beings, are exploited by them;
> Tortured, shackled and incarcerated are forced to work day and night;
> Though they (who do this) themselves know the agony evoked by torture and chains.[60]

The perception of exploitation appears to have crystallised into an act of retaliation at least in one instance, described in the Pali sources. According to the *Vinaya Pitaka*, the dasa-karmakaras of the Sakyans violated the Sakyan womenfolk to wreak vengeance on them.[61] The significant aspect of this reference is that it was the dasa-karmakaras of one of the gana-sanghas who were responsible for this instance of retaliatory action. It has been argued elsewhere that this collective action was possible because of certain characteristics of the social organisation of gana-sanghas. Since the dasa-karmakaras worked on the land for joint masters and were themselves a group in relation to their masters, it was easier for them to take collective action against their masters. Group consciousness among the dasa-karmakaras was possible not only because they shared the same material interests, but also because they could translate this into a feeling of solidarity in opposition to their masters.

Given the evidence for the perception of exploitation, it would not be out of place to analyse the attitudes of the philosophers of ancient India towards the contemporary economic situation, especially towards servitude and exploitation. It has been suggested that some of the 'heterodox' (nonconformist) philosophers, particularly Gotama Buddha, were actually social philosophers,[62] and that they represented a more humanitarian and egalitarian approach to the lower sections of society.[63] The sixth century BC witnessed one of the major efforts by philosophers towards an understanding of human existence. I have earlier argued that the period was characterised by sharp economic and social inequalities, accompanied by a breakdown of familiar traditional institutions. Basham has pointed to a relationship between the breakdown of tribal units and the rise of the 'heterodox' philosophies;[64] but it should be emphasised that the breakdown of tribal units was also related to the emerging economic and social differentiation. It is against this background that the large-scale spread of philosophical speculation must be viewed.

Chattopadhyaya argues that the central concept of *dukkha* or sorrow in the teachings of the Buddha was a result of the transformation of concrete material suffering into a metaphysical principle of eternal suffering. He suggests that through this transformation the Buddha gave a completely subjective turn to the most oppressive problems of his age.[65] However, the Buddha also responded more directly to the changing environment by postulating a dialectical relationship with the new society. On the one hand, he rejected the emerging inegalitarian structure of society and created the institution of the *sangha*, where all men were equal regardless of their origin. The sangha, created as a parallel society, did not encourage private property and was based on the vanishing pre-class tribal societies of the past.[66] But, at the same time, the Buddha conceded the existence of both social and economic disparities in the world outside the sangha. The Buddhist attitude to economic disparity, and especially to poverty, is certainly more humane than that of the Brahmanical tradition. The ideal society envisaged by the Buddha was one in which the king had the responsibility for abolishing destitution. The ideal king was expected to ensure full employment for all sections of people in his kingdom. He was also advised to establish a perpetual grant to provide food for the hungry and money for the needy.[67] The Buddhist utopia clearly had no place for poverty and exploitation, but, unfortunately, the ideal society was a distant concept in the face of the existing reality.

The Buddha, therefore, had to come to grips with this harsh reality, which he attempted to temper with moderation. He banned, for example, his lay followers from living on an income derived from the slave trade.[68] The Buddha's awareness of the suffering inherent in servitude is evident in his statement that servitude (*dasyam*), debt, imprisonment, illness and a journey through the wilderness were the most painful miseries one could experience.[69] He exhorted his lay followers to treat their dasa-karmakaras with consideration—by assigning them work according to their capacity, by supplying them with food and wages, by tending them in sickness, by granting them leave occasionally, and by sharing delicacies with them. He concluded that if the masters followed this code, they would be rewarded with loyal workers who would rise before their masters, go to bed after them and serve them dutifully.[70]

The Buddha's exhortation to his lay followers regarding the ideal treatment to be meted out to the dasa-karmakaras also indicates the parameters within which he viewed the problem of exploitation, which could at best be tempered but not eradicated. More significant, the Buddha expressed his disapproval of dasa-karmakaras who were envious of their master's wealth.[71] Similarly, even though entry to the sangha was technically open to all, a later ruling closed its doors to debtors and runaway slaves. Further, slavery itself was rationalised to some extent by suggesting that a person was born a slave because of the *paapam* (bad deeds) committed in a previous birth.[72] This is not very different from Narada's belief that a person is born as a dasa in the creditor's house if he defaults on the repayment of a debt.[73]

A survey of the ideas of all the major thinkers of ancient India clearly reveals that not one of them recommended abolition of slavery. Even a humanitarian king like Ashoka did not use his power to legislate against slavery, though he expressed repentance for the sufferings of the Kalinga war and the capture of thousands of Kalingans. Both Ashoka and the Buddha did, however, exhort that the dasas and karmakaras be treated with moderation. This may be interpreted as an instinctive application of management techniques. Their exhortations appear to be directed more towards social harmony while ensuring maximum output of labour from the dasa-karmakaras. The thinkers of ancient India accepted hierarchical relations and the appropriation of surplus. The only differences among them related to the method of appropriation: the more humane suggested less cruel but more efficient techniques of appropriation which would not generate hostility and conflict. Simultaneously, the 'heterodox' philosophers offered relief from existing miseries in a future existence.

The Buddhists and the Jainas also offered immediate relief—in their sanghas, their parallel societies—although even this relief was denied to the debtor and the dasa.

A more direct relationship between slavery and philosophical thought has been suggested by D.P. Chattopadhyaya, who bases his argument on the life and teaching of Makkhali Gosala.[74] Makkhali Gosala, a contemporary of the Buddha and Mahavira, was one of six 'heterodox' philosophers of the sixth century BC. The central tenet of his Ajivika doctrine, which is also apparent in the ideas of at least two of the five other thinkers of that period, is belief in the principle of *niyati* (fate), and may be summed up in the slogan *n'atthi purisakare*, meaning 'human effort is ineffectual'.[75] The dominant theme of this philosophy is that of human ineffectuality in controlling or shaping one's destiny. It is important to relate these ideas to the significant episodes in Makkhali Gosala's life.

According to a Jaina source, Makkhali Gosala was born in the cowshed of a wealthy cattle owner while his parents were travelling and were unable to find accommodation in the main village. He was named after his birthplace—*gosala* or cattle shed.[76] A later Buddhist source corroborates the account of his birth in a cowshed, but it also states that Gosala was a slave. According to the Buddhist account, once Gosala the slave was carrying a pot of oil over a muddy patch, and he stumbled while walking and spilt the oil. Fearing the wrath of the master who was accompanying him, he attempted to flee but was caught by the master who grabbed the edge of his robe. Leaving his robe behind, Gosala escaped in a state of nudity and became a naked mendicant.[77] Thus Gosala was a runaway slave. An even more significant, though sketchy, reference to Makkhali Gosala is made in the *Mahabharata.* Manki (who is identified with Makkhali Gosala) purchases a couple of young bulls with the last of his resources after a series of failures in all his ventures. One day the bulls break loose and are accidentally killed. Manki thereupon utters a long chant on the power of destiny, and the advisability of desirelessness and inactivity. Basham associates the story with the leader of the Ajivika sect, and links his chant with the typical cry of the peasant impoverished by the failure of his crops or herds.[78] The common feature in all these stories is the uncertainty of material conditions and the feeling of inadequacy in being able to cope with them.

Additional information on Makkhali Gosala suggests that he spent some years as an associate of Mahavira but subsequently split with him, and that he died after a bout of illness.[79] This may be interpreted as a breakdown following a sense of complete disillusionment. Significantly, Purana Kassapa, whose teachings are similar to those of Makkhali Gosala and who is another contemporary of the Buddha, is also described as a runaway slave. His teaching career ended in humiliation, whereupon he committed suicide.[80] Purana Kassapa's teachings make no distinction between good and evil, or between murderers, plunderers and torturers, and others who give alms and perform 'meritorious' actions.[81] Taken together, the views of Purana Kassapa and Makkhali Gosala are characterised by a deep sense of futility, moral collapse and the powerlessness of human effort. These were probably an outcome of their own experiences and their perceptions of the world around them. The views are similar to the images used by bonded labourers of Bihar, who may be far removed in time but not in sentiment when they describe their situation as one in which they are surrounded by a limitless expanse of water with no sight of land anywhere.[82] The same is echoed in the song of the hali,[83] the bonded labourer of Gujarat, even today:

I go in darkness
I return in darkness
My whole life is full of darkness
There is no ray of light.

NOTES

1. Sharma, 'Conflict, Distribution and Differentiation', p. 3.
2. *Chandogya Upanishad,* XXIV.2.
3. *Aitareya Brahmana,* VIII.22.
4. *Rgveda,* VIII.56.3.
5. Ibid., X.86.5.
6. *Chandogya Upanishad*, XXIV.2
7. *Rgveda*, X.62, 10; Sharma, 'Conflict, Distribution and Differentiation', pp. 10–11.
8. Sharma, 'Conflict, Distribution and Differentiation', p. 3.
9. Ibid.
10. *Aitareya Brahmana,*VIII.22; *Brihadaranyaka Upanishad*, translated by Madhavanand, VI.2.7; *Mahabharata,* II.33.52; *Rgveda,* 1.158.5, 6.
11. Ibid.; Chanana, *Slavery in Ancient India,* p. 21.
12. *Aitareya Brahmana*, VIII.22.
13. *Sutta Nipata,* translated by Fausboll, p. 49.
14. *Atharvaveda,* XII.4.9.
15. *Jataka,* edited by Fausboll, I, p. 163.
16. *Vinaya Pitaka,*Vol. III, p. 135.
17. *Dhammapada Atthakatha,* Vol. I, p. 400; Chanana, *Slavery in Ancient India,* p. 160, note 108.
18. *Jataka,* edited by Fausboll, Vol. VI, p. 523.
19. *Dhammapada Atthakatha*, III, p. 157.
20. Ibid., p. 321.
21. *Majjhima Nikaya*, edited by Kashyap, Vol. I, p. 167.
22. *Jataka*, edited by Fausboll, p. 318.
23. Ibid., p. 290.
24. Ibid., p. 211.
25. Burlingame, *Buddhist Legends*, Vol. 29, Part II, p. 2.
26. *Atharvaveda*, VII.90.1.
27. Chanana, *Slavery in Ancient India*, p. 48.
28. Ibid.
29. *Arthashastra,* 3.13.11.
30. *Jataka,* edited by Fausboll, III, p. 309.
31. *Dhammapada Atthakatha,* III, p. 166; *Jataka,* edited by Fausboll, V, p. 278; *Jataka,* edited by Fausboll, V, p. 259.
32. *Arthashastra,* 2.23.2.
33. Ibid.
34. Ibid., 2.27.8.
35. Ibid., 2.25.15.
36. Ibid., 1.12.13.
37. *Jataka,* edited by Fausboll, III, p. 167.
38. Ibid., I, p. 299.
39. Ibid., I, p. 402.
40. Malalasekhara, *Dictionary of Pali Proper Names,* Vol. II, p. 706.

41. Burlingame, *Buddhist Legends*, Vol. 30, Part III, p. 194.
42. *Arthashastra*, 3.13.9.
43. Ibid., 3.13.11.
44. Ibid., 3.13.12.
45. Ibid.
46. Ibid., 4.12.26.
47. Ibid., 3.13.23.
48. Ibid., 3.13.20.
49. Jan Yun Hua, 'Hui Chao's Record on Kashmir', pp. 119–20.
50. *Kamasutra*, V.5.5.
51. Ibid.
52. Vishnu, VI.11–15; Narada, 1.106–07.
53. Ibid.
54. *Dialogues of the Buddha,* translated by Davids, Vol. I, p. 163.
55. *Majjhima Nikaya,* p. 163.
56. Ibid., Vol. II, p. 5.
57. *Samyutta Nikaya,* p. 91.
58. *Majjhima Nikaya, Middle Length Sayings,* Vol. II, p. 9.
59. *Mahabharata,* XII, 262.38.
60. Patil, *Dasa-Sudra Slavery,* p. 2.
61. *Vinaya Pitaka*, Vol. I, p. 241.
62. Ling, *The Buddha,* p. 142.
63. Ambedkar, *Buddha and His Dhamma; Dialogues of the Buddha,* Vol. I, pp. 96, 103.
64. Basham, *History and Doctrines of the Ajivikas,* p. 285.
65. Chattopadhyaya, *Lokayata*, pp. 500–02.
66. Ibid., p. 503.
67. *Digha Nikaya,* edited by Kashyap, Vol. II, pp. 56–57; *Dialogues of the Buddha,* Vol. I, pp. 115–16.
68. *Anguttara Nikaya,* edited by Morris and Hardy, Vol. II, p. 208.
69. *Dialogues of the Buddha,* Vol. I, p. 83.
70. *Digha Nikaya,* edited by Kashyap, Vol. II, p. 182.
71. *Anguttara Nikaya, Book of Gradual Sayings,* Vol. V, p. 27.
72. *Jataka*, edited by Fausboll, Vol. VI, p. 235.
73. *Dharmakosa*, Vol. I, Part 2, p. 695; Sharma, 'Usury in Medieval India', p. 74.
74. Chattopadhyaya, *Lokayata*, pp. 514–24.
75. Basham, *History and Doctrines of the Ajivikas*, p. 9.
76. *Bhagvati Sutra*, V; Basham, *History and Doctrines of the Ajivikas*, p. 35.
77. Basham, *History and Doctrines of the Ajivikas,* p. 37.
78. Ibid., p. 9.
79. Ibid., pp. 58–62.
80. Chattopadhyaya, *Lokayata*, pp. 513–14.
81. *Dialogues of the Buddha*, Vol. I, p. 70.
82. Personal communication from Dr A. Chakravarti based on fieldwork in Bihar.
83. Song of *hali*, bonded labourer of Gujarat, *Point of View*, Vol. VI, No. 52 (1978), p. 32.

WORKS CITED

Agrawala, V.S. (1953), *India as Known to Panini,* Lucknow: University of Lucknow.
Aitareya Brahmana (1879), edited by T. Aufrecht, Bonn: Marcus.
Alavi, Hamza (1981), 'Peasants and Revolution', in A.R. Desai (ed.), *Peasant Struggles in India,* Bombay: Oxford University Press.
Aloysius, G. (1998), *Religion as Emancipatory Identity: A Buddhist Movement among the Tamils under Colonialism,* Delhi: New Age.
Alsdorf, L. (1974), 'The Impious Brahman and the Pious Candala', in L. Cousins *et al.* (eds), *Buddhist Studies in Honour of J.B. Horner,* Holland: Reidel. Altekar, A.S. (1987), *The Position of Women in Hindu Civilization,* Delhi: Mocilal Banarsidass, reprint.
Ambedkar, B.R. (1957), *The Buddha and His Dhamma,* Bombay: Siddhartha Publications.
Amore, R.C. and Larry D. Shinn (1981), *Lustful Maidens and Ascetic Kings,* New York: Oxford University Press.
Anderson, Perry (1974), *Passages from Antiquity to Feudalism,* London: Verso.
Anguttara Nikaya (1885–90), in five volumes, edited by R. Morris and E. Hardy, London: Pali Text Society.
———. (1932), translated by F.L. Woodward and E.M. Hare as *The Book of Gradual Sayings,* Vol. V, London: Pali Text Society.
———. (1959), in four volumes, edited by Bhikkhu J. Kashyap, Nalanda Devanagari Pali Series, Bihar Government.
Anitha, S. *et al.* (1995), 'Interviews with Women', in Tanika Sarkar and Urvashi Butalia (eds), *Women and the Hindu Right: A Collection of Essays,* Delhi: Kali for Women.
Apastamba Dharmasutra (1975), translated by George Buhler, in *Sacred Laws of the Aryas,* Delhi: Motilal Banarsidass, reprint.
Apte, Hari Narayan (1961), *Pan Lakshyant Kon Gheto* (in Marathi), translated by Srinivas Kochar into Hindi as *Karm Dhyan Deta Hai,* New Delhi: Sahitya Akademi.
The Arthashastra. See *The Kautilya Arthashastra.*
Arudra (1992), *Sita Ram ki Kya Lagti Thi* (in Hindi), Delhi: People's Publishing House.
Ashtadhyayi of Panini (1962), in two volumes, edited and translated by S.C. Vasu, Delhi: Motilal Banarsidass.
Atharvaveda (1936), edited by Dr. Raghuvira, Lahore.
Arhava le, Parvatibai (1986), *Hindu Widow,* Delhi: Reliance, reprint. Bacchetta, Paola (1996), 'Hindu Nationalist Women as Ideologues: The Sangh, the Samiri and Differential Concepts of the Hindu Nation', in Kumari Jayawardena and Malathi de Alwis (eds), *Embodied Violence: Communalizing Women's Sexuality in South Asia,* Delhi: Kali for Women.
Bader, Clarisse (1925), *Women in Ancient India*, London: Longmans Green. Bagchi, Jashodhara (1985), 'Positivism and Nationalism: Womanhood and Crisis in Nationalist Fiction, Bankim Chandra's *Anandmath', Economic and Political Weekly,* Review of Women's Studies, Vol. 20, No. 43.
Bahmana Vagga, Dhamma pada (1881), translated by F. Max Mueller, *Sacred Books of the East,* Vol. X, Oxford: Clarendon Press.
Bailey, H.W. (1959), 'Iranian Arya and Daha', *Transactions of the Philological Society,* London, pp. 71–115.
Balagopal, K. (1993), 'Why Did December 6, 1992 Happen?', *Economic and Political Weekly,* Vol. 28, No. 17.
Ballhatchet, K.A. (1956), 'Some Aspects of Historical Writing on India by Christian Missionaries', paper presented at South Asia Seminar, School of Oriental and African Studies, London.
Barna, B.M. (1970), *Pre-Buddhist Indian Philosophy,* Delhi: Motilal Banarsidass, reprint.
Basham, A.L. (1971), *The Wonder that Was India,* Delhi: Rupa and Co.
———. (1981), *The History and Doctrine of the Ajivikas,* Delhi: Morilal Banarsidass, reprint.
Baudhayana Dharmasutra (1986), translated by George Buhler, in *Sacred Laws of the Aryas,* Vol. II, Delhi: Motilal Banarsidass, reprint.
Beck, Brenda (1969), 'Color and Heat in South Indian Ritual', *Man,* New Series.
———. (1986), 'Social Dyads in Indic Folktales', in Blackburn and Ramanujan (eds), *Another Harmony,* Delhi: Oxford University Press.
Benveniste, Emile (1973), *Indo-European Language and Society,* translated by E. Palmer, London: Faber and Faber.

Berg, C. (1951), *The Unconscious Symbolism of Hair,* London: Allen Unwin. Berlin, H. Ludders (1973), *A List of Brahmi Inscriptions,* Varanasi: Indological Book House.

Bhagavad Gita (1968), edited by S.K. Belvalkar, Poona: Bhandarkar Oriental Research Institute.

Bhagavata Purana (1905), Bombay.

Bhagvati Sutra (1918–21), Bombay.

Bharucha, Rustom (1994), 'On the Border of Fascism: Manufacture of Consent in Roja', Economic and Political Weekly, Vol. 29, No. 23, pp. 1389–95.

Bhattacharji, Sukumari (1994), *Women and Society in Ancient India,* Calcutta: Basumati Corporation.

———. (1999), 'Prostitution in Ancient India', in Kumkum Roy (ed.), *Women in Early Indian Societies,* Delhi: Manohar.

Bhattacharya, Santwana (1995), 'Retelling Epic Tales' (an interview with Nabaneeta Dev Sen), *Indian Express,* 16 July.

Biardeau, Madeleine (1969), 'Etudes de Mythologie Hindou: II', *Bulletin de!'Ecole Frmifaised 'Extreme-Orient,* Vol. 55, pp. 59–105.

———. (1981), 'The Salvation of the King in the Maha bharata', *Contributions to Indian Sociology,* Vol. 15, pp. 75–97.

Blackburn, Stuart H. and A.K. Ramanujan (eds) (1986), *Another Hannony: New Essays on the Folklore of India,* Delhi: Oxford University Press.

Blackstone, Kathryn R. (2000), *Womenin the Footsteps of the Buddha: Struggle for Liberation in the Therigatha,* Delhi: Motilal Banarsidass.

The Book of Discipline (1941), in five volumes, translated by LB. Horner, London: Luzac and Co.

Borthwick, Meredith (1984), *The Changing Role of Women in Bengal 1849–1905,* Princeton: Princeton University Press.

Bose, A.N. (1942), *Social and Rural Economy of North-East India,* in two volumes, Calcutta: University of Calcutta.

Bottomore, Tom *et al.* (1983), *A Dictionary of Marxist Thought,* Oxford: Basil Blackwell.

Bougie, Celestin (1971), *Essays on the Caste System,* Cambridge: Cambridge University Press.

Brihadaranyaka Upanishad (1881), translated by F. Max Mueller, in *The Upanishads,* Vol. XV, Oxford: Clarendon Press.

———. (1950), translated by Swami Madhavanand, Almora: Advaita Ashram.

Brihaspati Sutra (1941), edited by I.V. Rangaswami Aiyangar, Baroda: Oriental Institute.

Buike, Father Kami! (1996), *Ramkatha,* Allahabad: Indian Press.

Burke, Peter (1978), *Popular Culture in Early Modem Europe,* London: Temple Smith.

Burlingame, E.W. (1921), *Buddhist Legends,* Harvard Oriental Series, Vol. 29, Cambridge, MA: Harvard University Press.

Byres, T.J. (1986), 'The Agrarian Question and the Differentiation of the Peasantry', Foreword in Atiur Rahman, *Peasants and Classes: A Study in Differentiation in Bangladesh,* London: Zed Books.

The Cambridge Economic History of India (1982), Vol. I: *c. 1200–c. 1750,* edited by Tapan Raychaudhari and Irfan Habib; Vol. II: c. *1757–1970,* edited by Dharma Kumar, Cambridge: Cambridge University Press.

Chakraborty, Haripada (1973), *Asceticism in Ancient India,* Calcutta: Punti Pustak.

Chakravarthy, Venkatesh and M.S.S. Pandian (1994), 'More on *Roja',* *Economic and Political Weekly,* Vol. 29, No. 11, pp. 642–44.

Chakravarti, Uma (1981), 'The Rise of Buddhism as Experienced by Women', *Manushi,* No. 8.

———. (1983a), 'The Development of the Sita Myth: A Case Study of Women in Myth and Literature', *Samya Shakti,* Vol. 1, No. 1; also in this volume.

———. (1983b), 'Renouncer and Householder in Early Buddhism', *Social Analysis,* No. 13, pp. 70–83; also in this volume.

———. (1985a), 'The *Agrihinis* of AncientIndia', *Teaching Politics,* Vol. 11, No. 2.

———. (1985b), 'Of *Dasas* and *Karmakaras:* Servile Labour in Ancient India', in Ursa Patnaik and Manjari Dingwaney (eds), *Chains of Servitude: Band age! and Slavery in India,* Delhi: Orient Longman, pp. 35–75; also in this volume.

———. (1985c) 'Towards a Historical Sociology of Stratification in Ancient India', *Economic and Political Weekly,* Vol. 20, No. 9, 2 March, pp. 356–60; also in this volume.

Chakravarti, Uma (1986), 'The Social Philosophy of Buddhism', *Social Compass,* Vol. 23, Nos 2–3, pp. 199–221; also in this volume.
———. (1987), *The Social Dimensions of Early Buddhism,* Delhi: Oxford University Press.
———. (1989), 'Whatever Happened to the Vedic *Dasi?:* Orientalism, Nationalism and a Script for the Past', in Kumkum Sangari and Sudesh Vaid (eds), *Recasting Women: Essays in Colonial History,* Delhi: Kali for Women, pp. 27–87; also in this volume.
———. (1993a), 'Conceptualizing Brahmanical Patriarchy in Early India: Gender, Caste, Class and Stace', *Economic and Political Weekly,* Vol. 28, No. 14, 3 April, pp. 579–85; also in this volume.
———. (1993b), 'Social Pariahs and Domestic Drudges: Widowhood among Nineteenth-Century Poona Brahmanas', *Social Scientist,* Nos 244–46, September–November.
———. (1993c), 'Women, Men and Beasts', *Studies in History,* Vol. 9, No. 1, pp. 43–70; also in this volume.
———. (1995), 'Gender, Caste and Labour: The Material and Ideological Structure of Widowhood', *Economic and Political Weekly,* Vol. 30, No. 36; also in this volume.
———. (1996), 'In Search of the Peasant in Early India: Was the *Gahapati* a Peasant Producer?', in V.K. Thakur and Ashok Anshouman (eds), *Peasants in Indian History: Theoretical Issues and Structural Enquiries* (Essays in Memory of Professor R.K. Chaudhary), Patna: Janaki Prakashan, pp. 150–78; also in this volume.
———. (1998), *Rewriting History: The Life and Times of Pandita Ramabai,* New Delhi: Kali for Women.
———. (1999), 'Of Hegemonic Agendas and Contesting Voices: Towards Recovering a Sitayana', unpublished MS.
———. (2003), *Gendering Caste: Through a Feminist Lens,* Kolkata: Scree.
———. (2005), 'Re-inscribing the Past: Inserting Women into Indian History', in Kamala Ganesh and Usha Thakkar (eds), *Culture and the Making of Identity in Contemporary India,* Delhi: Sage.
———. (2005), 'Women's Histories in South Asia', in Prem Poddar and David Johnson (eds), *A Historical Companion to Postcolonial Thought in English,* New York: Columbia University Press.
Champakalakshmi, R. (1996), *Trade, Ideology and Urbanization: South India 300 BC to AD 300,* Delhi: Oxford University Press.
Chanana, D.R. (1963), *The Spread of Agriculture in Northern India,* Delhi: Suman Prakashana.
———. (1990), *Slavery in Ancient India,* Delhi: People's Publishing House, reprint.
Chandogya Upanishad (1930), edited by E. Senart, Paris: Les Belles Lettres.
Chandra, Pratap (1978), *Metaphysics of Perpetual Change: The Concept of Self in Early Buddhism,* Bombay: Somaiya Publications.
Chandra, Sudhir (1987), 'Lake of Palms: An Essay in Understanding Early Indian Nationalism without the Imperialist Discourse', paper presented at the seminar on Communication and Society, Nehru Memorial Museum and Library, Delhi.
Chartier, Roger (1982), 'Intellectual History or Socio-cultural History? The French Trajectories', in D. La Capra and S.L. Kaplan (eds), *Modern European Intellectual History,* New York.
Chattopadhyaya, B.D. (1990), *Aspects of Rural Settlements and Rural Society in Early Medieval India,* Calcutta: Centre for Studies in Social Sciences.
———. (1994), *The Making of Early Medieval India,* Delhi: Oxford University Press.
Chattopadhyaya, D.P. (1968), *Lokayata,* Delhi: People's Publishing House. Chattopadhyaya, Gautam (1965), *Awakening in Bengal: Early Nineteenth Century Selected Documents,* Calcutta: Progressive Publishers.
Chaudhuri, Nirad C. (1974), *Scholar Extraordinary: The Life of Rt. Hon. Friedrich Max Mueller* P.C., Delhi: Oxford University Press.
Chayanov, A.V. (1987), *The Theory of Peasant Economy,* Delhi: Oxford University Press.
Chowdhry, Prem (1994), *The Veiled Women: Shifting Gender Equations, Haryana 1880–1980,* Delhi: Oxford University Press.
Clark, T.W. (1961), 'The Role of Bankimchandra in the Development of Nationalism', in C.H. Philips (ed.), *Historians of India, Pakistan and Ceylon,* London: Oxford University Press.
Coburn, Thomas (1995), 'Sita Fights while Rama Swoons: A Shakta Version of the Ramayana', *Manushi,* No. 90.
Cohn, Bernard (1985), 'The Command of Language and the Language of Command', in Ranajit Guha (ed.), *Subaltern Studies IV,* Delhi: Oxford University Press.

Colebrooke, H.T. (1795), 'On the Duties of the Faithful Hindu Widow', *Asiatic Researches,* 4.
———. (1805), 'On the Vedas, or Sacred Writings of the Hindus', *Asiatic Researches,* 8.
Cone, Margaret and Richard F. Gombrich (1977), *The Perfect Generosity of Prince Vessantara,* Oxford: Oxford University Press.
Coomaraswamy, Ananda (1916), *Buddha and the Gospel of Buddhism,* New York: Harper Torchbooks.
Cullavagga (1956), edited by Bhikkhu J. Kashyap, Nalanda Devanagari Pali Series, Bihar Government.
———. (1958), in *Vinaya Pitaka,* Nalanda: Pali Publication Board.
Cunningham, J.D. (1849), *History of the Silihs,* London: John Murray.
Dandekar, R.N. (ed.) (1990), *The Mahabharata Revisited,* Delhi: Sahitya Akademi.
Das, Arvind (1988), 'Electronic Religiosity: Meaning of Goswami Ramanand Sagar', *Times of India,* 5 August.
Das, R.M. (1962), *Women in Manu and His Seven Commentators,* Varanasi: Indological Book House.
Das, Veena (1976), 'Indian Women: Work, Power and Status', in B.R. Nanda (ed.), *Indian Women from Purdah to Modernity,* Delhi: Vikas, pp. 129–45.
———. (1977), *Structure and Cognition: Aspects of Hindu Caste and Ritual,* Delhi: Oxford University Press.
———. (1981), 'Kama in the Scheme of Purusarthas', *Contributions to Indian Sociology,* New Series, Nos 1–2.
Dasgupta, Madhusraba (2000), 'Usable Women: The Tales of Amba and Madhvi', in Mandakranta Bose (ed.), *Faces of the Feminine in Ancient, Medieval and Modern India,* Delhi: Oxford University Press.
Davids, T.W. Rhys (1970), *Buddhist India,* Delhi: Indological Book House, reprint.
———. (1972), *History of Indian Buddhism,* Allahabad: Rachana Prakashan, reprint.
Davis, Natalie Z. (1975), *Society and Culture in Early Modern France,* Stanford: Stanford University Press.
Dehejia, Vidya (1988), *Slaves of the Lord,* Delhi: Munshiram Manoharlal.
Deshpande, C.R. (1978), *Transmission of the Mahabharata Tradition,* Shimla: Indian Institute of Advanced Study.
Dev Sen, Nabaneeta (1997), 'Rewriting the Ramayana: Chandrabati and Molla', in Geeti Sen (ed.), *Crossing Boundaries,* Delhi: Orient Longman, pp. 163–77.
Dhammapada Atthakatha (1906), Vol. I, edited by H.C. Normann, London: Pali Text Society.
Dhaniya Sutta, Sutta Nipata, Khuddaka Nikaya (1959), Vol. I, edited by Bhikkhu J. Kashyap, Nalanda Devanagari Pali Series, Bihar Government.
Dhannakosa, Vol. I, edited by Laxman Shastri Joshi, Wai.
The Dialogues of the Buddha (1973), *Digha Nikaya,* in three volumes, translated by T.W. Rhys Davids, Delhi: Motilal Banarsidass.
Digha Nikaya (1958), in three volumes, edited by Bhikkhu J. Kashyap, Nalanda Pali Devanagari Series, Bihar Government.
———. (1976), edited by E. Carpentier, London: Pali Text Society.
Doniger, Wendy and Brian Smith (1991), *The Laws of Manu,* Delhi: Penguin Books.
Drekmeier, Charles (1962), *Kingship and Community in Early India,* Stanford: California University Press.
Duff, Grant (1826), *History of the Marathas,* London: Longmans Green.
Dumont, Louis (1972), *Homo Hierarcbicus,* London: Paladin.
———. (1976), 'World Renunciation in Indian Religions', *Contributions to Indian Sociology,* Vol. 4.
Dutt, R.C. (1888), *A History of Civilization in Ancient India,* Delhi: Vishal.
———. (1943), *Pratap Singh: The Last of the Rajputs,* Allahabad: Kitabistan.
Dutt, 5. (1924), *Early Buddhist Monachism,* London: Kegan Paul.
Epigra phica Indica (1970), edited by Jas Burgess, IX, No. 5, 45, 1.29, Delhi: Motilal Banarasidass, reprint.
Erndl, Kathryn M. (1991), 'The Mutilation of Surpanakha', in Paula Richman (ed.), *Many Ramayanas: The Diversity of a Narrative Tradition in South Asia,* Delhi: Oxford University Press.
Feer, M.L. (1963), *A Study of the Jatakas,* Calcutta: Susil Gupta.
Femia, Joseph V. (1987), *Gramsci's Political Thought: Hegemony, Consciousness, and the Revolutionary Process,* Oxford: Clarendon Press.
Fick, R. (1920), *The Social Organization of North-east India in Buddha's Time,* Calcutta: University of Calcutta.

Finley, M.I. (1964), 'Between Slavery and Freedom', *Comparative Studies in Society and History,* Vol. 6; republished in *Economy and Society in Ancient Greece,* Harmondsworth: Penguin Books, 1983.
Fiske, Adele M. (1976), 'Buddhism in India today', in Heinrich Dumoulin and John C. Maraldo (eds), *Buddhism in the Modern World,* London: Collier Macmillan.
Fuller, C.J. and Penny Logan (1985), 'The Navaratri Festival in Madurai', *Bulletin of the School of Oriental and African Studies,* Vol. 47, Part I.
Ganesh, Kamala (1985), 'Women's Seclusion and the Structure of Caste', paper presented at the Asian Regional Conference on 'Women and the House hold', Delhi.
Gautama Dharmasutra (1975), translated by George Buhler, in *Sacred Laws of the Aryas,* Vol. I, Delhi: Motilal Banarsidass.
Ghose, J.C. (1885), *The English Works of Raja Rammoham Roy,* Calcutta: Oriental.
Ginzburg, Carlo (1980), *The Cheese and the Worms,* London: Routledge and Kegan Paul.
Gokhale, B.G. (1968), 'Dhamma as a Political Concept', *Journal of Indian History,* Vol. 46, Part II.
Guha, R. (1963), *A Rule of Property for Bengal: An Essay on the Idea of Permanent Settlement,* Paris and The Hague: Mouton.
———. (ed.) (1981), *Subaltern Studies: Writings on South Asian History and Society,* Vol. I, Delhi: Oxford University Press.
———. (1987), 'Chandra's Death', in R. Guha (ed.), *Subaltern Studies V,* Delhi: Oxford University Press.
Gupta, Dipankar (1981), '"Caste", Infrastructure and Superstructure', *Economic and Political Weekly,* Vol. 16, No. 51.
Habib, Irfan (1982), 'The Peasant in Indian History', Presidential Address to the 43rd session of the Indian History Congress held at Kurukshetra; republished in *Essays in Indian History: Towards a Marxist Perspective,* Delhi: Tulika, 1995.
———. (1995), *Essays in Indian History: Towards a Marxist Perspective,* Delhi: Tulika Books.
Hansen, Kathryn (1988), 'The *Virangana* in North Indian History: Myth and Popular Culture', *Economic and Political Weekly,* Vol. 23, No. 18, pp. WS 25–33.
Hardy, Friedhelm (1983), *Viraha Bhakti: The Early History of Krsna Devotion in South India,* Delhi: Oxford University Press.
Harper, Edward B. (1969), 'Fear and the Status of Women', *Southwestern Journal of Anthropology,* Vol. 25.
Hart, George (1973), 'Woman and the Sacred in Ancient Tamil Nadu', *Journal of Asian Studies,* Vol. 32, No. 2, February, pp. 233–50.
Hatalkar, V.G. (1973), 'M.G. Ranade', in S.P. Sen (ed.), *Historians and Historiography in Modern India,* Calcutta: Institute of Historical Studies.
Heesterman, J.C. (1964), 'Brahmin, Ritual and Renouncer', *Wiener Zeitschrift uuml die Kunde Sud-und Ostasiens,* Vol. 8, pp. 1–31.
———. (1981), 'Householder and Wanderer', *Contributions to Indian Sociology,* Vol. 15, pp. 251–71.
Heimsath, Charles (1964), *Indian Nationalism and Hindu Social Reform,* Princeton: Princeton University Press.
Herrenschmidt, Olivier (2004), 'Ambedkar and the Hindu Social Order', in Surendra Jondhale and Johannes Beltz (eds), *Reconstructing the World: B.R. Ambedkar and Buddhism in India,* Delhi: Oxford University Press, pp. 42–43.
Hershman, Paul (1974), 'Hair, Sex and Dirt', *Man,* New Series, Vol. 9, No. 2. Hiltebeitel, Alf (1981), 'Draupadi's Hair', *Pumshartha,* Vol. 5, pp. 179–214.
Hilton, Rodney (1973), *Bond Men Made Free: Medieval Peasant Movements and the English Rising of 1381,* London: Methuen.
Hobsbawm, Eric (1983), 'Introduction: Inventing Traditions', in Eric Hobsbawm and Terence Ranger (eds), *The Invention of Tradition,* Cambridge: Cambridge University Press.
Hocart, A.M. (1950), *Caste: A Comparative Study,* London: Methuen.
Horner, LB. (1975), *Women under Primitive Buddhism,* Delhi: Motilal Banarsidass, reprint.
Huilgol, Glynn (1979), 'The Sanctification of Sita', *Women's Sociological Bulletin,* Vol. 1, No. 3.
Hultzsch, E. (1969), Vol. I, *Corpus Inscriptionum Indicarum,* Delhi: Indological Book House.
lnamdar, Radhabai *et al.* (1911), *Position of Widows,* typescript, Eur. MS D 356, India Office Library.

Jain, J.C. (1947), *Life in Ancient India as Depicted in the Jain Canon,* New Book Company.
Jain, P.C. (1971), *Labour in Ancient India,* Delhi: Sterling.
Jaini, P.S. (1970), '*Shramanas:* Their Conflict with Brahmanical Society', in J.W. Elder (ed.), *Chapters in Indian Civilization,* Dubuque, Iowa: Kendall Hunt.
———. (1991), *Gender and Salvation: Jaina Debates on the Spiritual Liberation of Women,* Berkeley: University of California Press.
Jamison, Stephanie (1999), *Sacrificed Wife, Sacrificer's Wife,* New York: Oxford University Press.
Jan Yun Hua (1962), 'Hui Chao's Record on Kashmir', *Kashmir Research Bi Annual,* 2.
The Jataka (1957), edited by E.B. Cowell, translated by R. Chalmers *et al.,* London: Pali Text Society.
Jataka (1964), in six volumes, edited by V. Fausboll, London: Pali Text Society.
Jha, V.V. (1974), 'From Tribe to Untouchable: The Case of the Nishadas', in R.S. Sharma and V.V. Jha (eds), *Indian Society: Historical Probings,* Delhi: People's Publishing House.
Jones, Kenneth (1976), *Alya Dharma: Hindu Consciousness in 19th Century Punjab,* Delhi: Manohar.
Jones, William (1807), 'On the Chronology of the Hindus', in Lord Teignmouth (ed.), *The Works of William Jones,* London: John Stockdale, Piccadilly and John Walkes.
Jordens, J.T.F. (1978), *Dayananda Saraswati: His Life and Ideas,* Delhi: Oxford University Press.
Kakar, Sudhir (1978), *The Inner World,* Delhi: Oxford University Press.
Kamasutra (1929), edited by Damodar Shastri, Banaras: Chowkhamba Sanskrit Series Office.
Kane, P.V. (1941), *History of the Dharmashastras,* Vol. II, Part I, Poona: Bhandarkar Oriental Research Institute.
Karve, Irawati (1974), *Yuganta: The End of an Epoch,* Delhi: Sangam Books. Kaul, Shonaleeka (2005), *The City in Early India: A Study of Literary Perceptions,* Ph.D. thesis, Jawaharlal Nehru University, Delhi.
The Kautilya Arthashastra (1986), in three volumes: Part I, text critically edited by R.P. Kangle; Part. II, translation by R.P. Kangle; and Part III: A Study, by R.P. Kangle, Delhi: Motilal Banarsidass.
Kaviraj, Sudipta (1987), 'The Myth of Infinity: The Construction of the Figure of Krishna in *Krishnacarita',* Occasional Papers, Nehru Memorial Museum and Library, Delhi.
Kolenda, Pauline (1987), 'Widowhood among "Untouchable" Chuhras', in *Regional Differences in Family Structures in India,* Jaipur: Rawat Press.
Kopf, David (1969), *British Orientalism and the Bengal Renaissance,* Calcutta: Firma K.L. Mukhopadhyaya.
Kosambi, D.D. (1957), *Exasperating Essays: Exercises in the Dialectical Method,* Pune: Mudra Press.
———. (1962), *Myth and Reality: Studies in the Formation of Indian Culture,* Bombay: Popular Prakashan.
———. (1975a), *The Culture and Civilization of Ancient India,* Delhi: Vikas, reprint.
———. (1975b), *An Introduction to the Study of Indian History,* Bombay: Popular Prakashan, reprint.
Latyayana Srautasutra (1872), edited by Anandachandra Vedantaragesa, Calcutta.
Leach, E.R. (1958), 'Magical *Hair*', *Journal of the Royal Anthropological Institute of Great Britain and Ireland,* Vol. 88, pp. 147–64.
Lerner, Gerda (1986), *The Creation of Patriarchy,* New York: Oxford University Press.
Leslie, Julia (1989), *The Perfect Wife: The Orthodox Hindu Woman according to the Stridharmapaddhati of Tryambakayajvan,* Delhi: Oxford University Press.
Ling, Trevor (1976), *The Buddha,* Middlesex: Penguin Books.
Ludden, David (1989), *Peasant History in South India,* Delhi: Oxford University Press.
Macdonell, A.A. and A.B. Keith (1912), *Vedic Index of Names and Subjects,* London, published for the Government of India.
Mackay, E. (1948), *Early Indus Civilization,* London: Luzac and Co.
Mahabharata (1933–39), critical edition by V.S. Sukhtankar *et al.,* Poona: Bhandarkar Oriental Research Institute.
Mahabhashya of Patanjali. See *Vyakarana Mahabhashya of Patanjali.*
Mahavagga (1956), edited by Bhikkhu J. Kashyap, Nalanda Devanagari Pali Series, Bihar Government.
———. (1958), in *Vinaya Pitaka,* Nalanda: Pali Publication Board.
———. (1974), translated by T.W. Rhys Davids and H. Oldenberg as *Vinaya Texts,* Part I, *Sacred Books of the East,* Vol. XIII, Delhi: Motilal Banarsidass, reprint.

Maitra, Prita (1991), 'Master of the Game', *Sunday,* 22 October–2 November, pp. 44–53.
Majjhima Nilwya (1958), in three volumes, edited by Mahapandita Rahula Sankritayan and P.V. Bapat, Nalanda Devanaga ri Pali Series, Bihar Government.
Majjhima Nilwya (1958), in three volumes, Nalanda: Pali Publication Board.
———. (1976), translated by LB. Horner as *The Middle Length Sayings,* London: Pali Text Society
Majumdar, R.C. (1961), 'Nationalist Historians', in C.H. Philips (ed.), *Historians of India, Pakistan and Ceylon,* London: Oxford University Press.
Malalasekhara, G.P. (1960), *Dictionary of Pali Prnper Names,* in two volumes, London: Pali Text Society.
Mallik, A.R. (1961), 'Modern Historical Writing in Bengali', in C.H. Philips (ed.), *Historians of India, Pakistan and Ceylon,* London: Oxford University Press.
Mani, Lara (1986), 'Production of an Official Discourse on Sati in Early Nineteenth Century Bengal', *Economic and Political Weekly,* Review of Women's Studies, Vol. 26, No. 17.
Manu Dharmashastra (1984), translated by George Buhler as *The Laws of Manu, Sacred Books of the East,* Vol. XXV, Delhi: Motilal Banarsidass, reprint.
Marshall, J. (1931), *Mohenjodaro and the Indus Civilization,* Vol. I, London: A. Probsthain.
Masud, Iqbal (1992), 'Images of Dominance', *Indian Express,* 16 August.
Matilal, B.I. (ed.) (1993), *Moral Dilemmas in the Mahabharata,* Shimla: Indian Institute of Advanced Study.
Max Mueller, F. (1859), *A History of Sanskrit Literature,* London: Longmans Green.
———. (1892), *India: What It Can Teach Us,* London: Longmans Green.
Max Mueller, Georgina (1902), *Life and Letters of F. Max Mueller,* London: Longmans Green.
Medick, Hans and David Warren Sabean (1984), *Interest and Emotion: Essays on the Study of Family and Kinship,* Cambridge: Cambridge University Press.
Mehta, Ratilal (1939), *Pre-Buddhist India,* Bombay: Examiner Press.
Meenakshi, K. (1986), 'Old Inda-Aryan to Middle Indo-Aryan', in Sabyasachi
Bhattacharya and Romila Thapar (eds), *Situating Indian History,* Delhi: Oxford University Press.
Menon, Dilip (1993), 'The Moral Community of the Teyyattam: Popular Culture in Late Colonial Malabar', *Studies in History,* Vol. 9, No. 2, pp. 187–219.
Milindapanha (1962), edited by V. Trenckner, London: Pali Text Society.
———. (1964), translated by I.B. Horner as *Questions of King Menander,* Vol. I, London: Luzac and Co.
Mill, James (1840), *The History of British India,* with notes by H.H. Wilson, fifth edition, London: James Madden.
Morgan, L.H. (1958), *Ancient Society,* Calcutta, reprint.
Mukherjte, Prabhati (1988), *Beyond the Four Varnas: The Untouchables in India,* Delhi: Motilal Banarsidass.
Murcott, Susan (1991), *The First Buddhist Women: Translations and Commentary on the Therigatha,* Berkeley: Parallel Press.
Murshid, Ghulam (1983), *Reluctant Debutante,* Rajshahi: Rajshahi University.
Murri G.S. and A.S.K. Aiyangar (1950), *Edicts of Asoka,* Madras.
Nandy, Ashis (1983), *The Intimate Enemy: Loss and Recovery of the Self under Colonialism,* Delhi: Oxford University Press.
Naradasmrlti (1889), translated by J. Jolly in *The Mlnor Law-Books, Sacred Books of the East,* Vol. XXXI, Oxford: Clarendon Press.
Nehru, Jawaharlal (1982), *The Discovery of India,* Delhi: Oxford University Press.
Neufeldt, Ronald W. (1980), *Max Mueller and the Rigveda: A Study of its Role in His Work and Thought,* Calcutta: Minerva.
Neumayer, E. (1983), *Prehistoric Indian Rock Paintings,* Delhi: Oxford University Press.
Nidana Katha (1973), translated by T.W. Rhys Davids as *Buddhist Birth Stories,* Delhi: Indological Book House.
Niranjana, Tejaswini (1994), 'Integrating Whose Nation? Tourists and Terrorists in *Roja*', *Economic and Political Weekly,* Vol. 29, No. 3, pp. 79–82.
Obeyesekere, Gananath (1981), *Medusa's Hair: An Essay in Personal Symbols and Religious Experience,* Chicago: University of Chicago Press.

O'Flaherty, Wendy D. (1976), *The Origins of Evil in Hindu Mythology,* Berkeley: University of California Press.
———. (1985), *Tales of Sex and Violence,* Delhi: Motilal Banarsidass.
———. (1999), *Splitting the Difference: Gender and Myth in Ancient Greece and India,* Chicago: University of Chicago Press.
Oldenberg, H. (1882), *The Buddha: His Life, His Doctrine, His Order,* London: Williams and Norgate
Oldenberg, H. (1920), 'On the History of the Indian Caste System', *Indian Antiquary,* Vol. XLIX.
Olivelle, P. (1976), 'A Definition of World Renunciation', *Wiener Zeitschrift fiir die Kunde Sudund Ostasiens,* Vol. 20, pp. 75–83.
Pacittiya (1940), translated by L.B. Horner as *The Book of Discipline,* Oxford University Press.
———. (1958), Vol. I, *Vinaya Pitaka,* edited by Bhikkhu J. Kashyap, Nalanda Devanagari Pali Series, Bihar Government.
Padma Purana (1950), edited by Ravisenacharya, translated by Daulat Ramji, Delhi: Veer Sena Mandali.
Pande, G.C. (1974), *Studies in the Origins of Buddhism,* Delhi: Motilal Banarsidass.
Pandita Ramabai (1887), *The High Caste Hindu Woman,* published by Pandita Ramabai, Philadelphia.
Parajika (1958), in *Vinaya Pitaka,* edited by Bhikkhu J. Kashyap, Nalanda: Pali Publication Board.
Parasher, Aloka (1991), *The Mlecchas in Early India,* Delhi: Munshiram Manoharlal.
Patil, S. (1982), *Dasa-Sudra Slavery: Studies in the Origins of Indian Slavery,* Delhi: Allied Publishers.
Patterson, Orlando (1982), *Slavery and Social Death: A Comparative Study,* Cambridge, MA: Harvard University Press.
People's Union for Democratic Rights (PUDR) (1983), *Inside the Family,* Delhi.
Philips, C.H. (1961), 'James Mill, Mountstuart Elphinstone and the History of India', in C.H. Philips (ed.), *Historians*
Piggott, S. (1948), *Pre-historic India,* Harmondsworth: Penguin Books.
Pillai, J.M. Somasundaram (1959), *Two Thousand Years of Tamil Literature,* Madras: The South India Saiva Siddhanta Works Publishing Society.
———. (1968), *A History of Tamil Literature with Texts and Translations,* Annamalainagar, published by the author.
Poddar, Arvind (1976), *Renaissance in Bengal: Search for Identity,* Shimla: Indian Institute of Advanced Study.
Pollock, Sheldon (1993), 'Ramayana and the Political Imagination in India', *Journal of Asian Studies,* Vol. 52, No. 2, May.
Prasad, Jaishankar (1974), *Dhruvaswamini,* Allahabad: Leader Press.
Pushp, P.N. (1980), 'Ramayana in Kashmiri Literature and Folklore', in V. Raghavan (ed.), *Ramayana Tradition in Asia,* Delhi: Sahitya Akademi, pp. 534–45.
Raghavan, V. (ed.) (1980), *The Ramayana Tradition in Asia,* Delhi: Sahitya Akademi.
The Raghuvamsa of Kalidasa (1985), translated by C.R. Devadhar, Delhi: Motilal Banarsidass.
Rai, G.K. (1976), 'Forced Labour in Ancient and Early Medieval India', *The Indian Historical Review,* Vol. 3, No. 1, pp. 16–42.
Ramanujan, A.I.C (1985), *Poems of Love and War,* Delhi: Oxford University Press.
———. (1985), *Speaking of Siva,* Harmondsworth: Penguin Books.
———. (1991), 'Three Hundred Ramayanas: Five Examples and Three Thoughts on Translation', in Paula Richman (ed.), *Many Ramayanas: The Diversity of a Narrative Tradition in South Asia,* Delhi: Oxford University Press, pp. 22–49.
Ramaswamy, Vijaya (1989), 'Aspects of Women and Work in Early South India', *Indian Economic and Social History Review,* Vol. 26, No. 1, pp. 81–99.
———. (1996), *Divinity and Deviance: Women in Virasaivism,* Delhi: Oxford University Press.
———. (1997), *Walking Naked: Society, Spirituality in South India,* Shimla: Indian Institute of Advanced Study.
The Ramayana of Valmiki (1957), Vol. II, translated by H.P. Shashi, London: Shanti Sadan.
———. (1958), edited by S. Kuppuswami Sastrigal *et al.,* Madras.
———. (1976), translated by Makhan Lal Sen, Delhi: Munshiram Manoharlal.
The Ramayana of Vabniki: An Epic of Ancient India (1986), Vol. II, *Ayodhyakanda,* edited by Sheldon Pollock, Princeton: Princeton University Press.
Rao, Velucheri Narayana (1991), 'A Ramayana of Their Own: Women's Oral Tradition in Telugu', in Paula Richman (ed.), *Many Ramayanas: The Diversity of a Narrative Tradition in South Asia,* Delhi: Oxford University Press, pp. 114–36.

Ramagar, Shercen (1991), *Enquiries into the Political Organization of the Harappan State,* Pune: Ravish Publishers.
Raychaudhari, H.C. (1972), *Political History of Ancient India,* Calcutta: University of Calcutta.
Reddy, Snehalata (1973), *Sita;* republished in *The Other Side,* September 1985.
Rgveda (1971), edited by R.T.H. Griffith, Varanasi: Chowkhamba Sanskrit Series Office.
Richman, Paula (ed.) (1991), *Many Ramayanas: The Diversity of a Narrative Tradition in South Asia,* Delhi: Oxford University Press.
Riseew, Carla and Rajni Palriwala (1997), *Shifting Circles of Support,* Delhi: Sage.
Robinson, E.J. (1957), *Tamil Wisdom: Traditions Concerning Hindu Sages and Selections from Their Writing,* Madras; reprint, Delhi: Asian Educational Services, 2001.
Rosselli, John (1980), 'The Self-Image of Effeteness: Physical Education and Nationalism in 19th century Bengal', *Past and Present,* Vol. 86.
Rowbotham, Sheila (1976), *Hidden History: Rediscovering Women in History from the 17th Century to the Present,* New York: Vintage Books.
Roy, Kumkum (1987), 'Women in Early India', unpublished typescript.
———. (1992), 'The King's Household: Structure/Space in the Sastric Tradition', *Economic and Political Weekly,* Vol. 27, Nos. 43-44, pp. WS55–60; reprinted in Kumkum Sangari and Uma Chakravarti (eds), *From Myths to Markets: Essays on Gender,* Shimla: Indian Institute of Advanced Study and Delhi: Manohar, 1999.
———. (1994), *The Emergence of Monarchy in Early India 800–400 BC,* Delhi: Oxford University Press.
———. (1998), 'Unravelling the Kamasutra,' in Mary E. John and Janaki Nair (eds), *A Question of Silence?: Sexual Economies of Modern India,* Delhi: Kali For Women.
———. (2002), 'Goddesses in the Rgveda: An Investigation', in Nilima Chitgopekar (ed.), *Invoking Goddesses: Gender Politics in Indian Religion,* Delhi: Shakti.
———. (2003), 'Of *Theras* and *Theris:* Visions of Liberation in the Early Buddhist Tradition', in Vijaya Ramaswamy (ed.), *Re-searching Indian Women,* Delhi: Manohar.
———. (2005), 'Recent Writings on Gender Relations in Early India', in Kirit Shah (ed.), *History and Gender: Some Explorations, Jaipur:* Rawat Press.
Ryan, Bryce (1953), *Castes in Modern Ceylon,* New Jersey: Rutgers University Press.
Sadharma Pundarika (1953), edited by Nalinaksha Dutta, Calcutta: Asiatic Society.
Samyutta Nikaya (1952), translated by F.L. Woodward and C.A.F. Rhys Davids as *The Book of Kindred Sayings,* in five volumes, London: Pali Text Society.
———. (1959), in four volumes, edited by Bhikkhu J. Kashyap, Nalanda Devanagari Pali Series, Bihar Government.
Sangari, Kumkum (1999), 'Consent, Agency and Rhetorics of Incitement', in *Politics of the Possible: Essays on Gender; History, Narratives, Colonial English,* Delhi: Tulika Books, pp. 364–409.
Sarkar, S.C. (1958), 'Derozio and Young Bengal', in A.C. Gupta (ed.), *Studies in Bengal Renaissance,* Jadavpur: National Council of Education Bengal.
Selwyn, Tom (1979), 'Images of Reproduction: An Analysis of a Hindu Marriage Ceremony', *Man,* Vol. 14, No. 4, December
Sangari, Kumkum and Uma Chakravarti (eds) (1999), *From Myths to Markets: Essays in Gender,* Shimla: Indian Institute of Advanced Study and Delhi: Manohar.
Sankalia, H.D. (1967–68), 'Archaeology and the Ramayana', *Puratattva,* Vol. 1.
Saraswati, Dayananda (1915), *Satyarth Prakash,* translated by Chiranjiva Bharadvaja, Agra: Arya Pratinidhi Sabha.
Sarkar, Jadunath (1928), *India through the Ages;* reprint, Calcutta: Orient Longman, 1979.
Sarkar, S.C. (1958), 'Derozio and Young Bengal', in- A.C. Gupta (ed.), *Studies in Bengal Renaissance,* Jadavpur: National Council of Education Bengal.
Selwyn, Tom (1979), 'Images of Reproduction: An Analysis of a Hindu Marriage Ceremony', *Man,* Vol. 14, No. 4, December.
Sen, Sukumar (1977), *The Origin and Development of the Rama Legend,* Calcutta: Rupa and Co.
Sen, Sunil (1961), 'Romesh Chandra Dutt', in C.H. Philips (ed.), *Historians of India, Pakistan and Ceylon,* London: Oxford University Press.
Senivaratne, Sudarshan (1978), 'The Mauryan State' in H.J.M. Claessen and P. Skalnik (eds), *The Early State,* The Hague.

Shanin, Teodor (1972), 'Chayanov's Message: Illuminations, Miscomprehensions, and the Contemporary "Development Theory"', in A.V. Chayanov, *The Theory of Peasant Economy and the Awkward Class: Political Sociology of Peasantry in a Developing Society, Russia 1910–25,* London: Oxford University Press.
Shanin, Teodor (ed.) (1971), *Peasants and Peasant Societies,* Harmondsworth: Penguin Books.
Sharma, R. (1971), *A Socio-Political Study of the Valmiki Ramayana,* Delhi: Motilal Banarsidass.
Sharma, R.S. (1958), *Sudras in Ancient India: A Social History of the Lower Order Down to circa AD 600,* Delhi: Motilal Banarsidass; second revised edition, 1980.
———. (1965), 'Usury in Early Medieval India (AD 400–1200)', *Comparative Studies in Society and History,* Vol. 3, No. 1.
———. (1965), *Indian Feudalism,* Delhi: Macmillan.
———. (1977), 'Conflict, Distribution and Differentiation in RgVedic Society', *The Indian Historical Review,* Vol. 4, No. 1.
———. (1983a), *Material Cultureand Social Formations in Ancient India,* Delhi: Macmillan.
———. (1983b), *Perspectives in Social and Economic History of Early India,* Delhi: Munshiram Manoharlal.
Shastri, Shakuntala Rao (1959), *Women in the Sacred Laws,* Bombay: Bharatiya Vidya Bhawan.
Shatapatha Brahmana (1964), edited by A. Weber, Varanasi: Chowkhamba Publishers.
Singh, Pankaj K. and Jaidev (1999), 'Decentering a Patriarchal Myth', in Kumkum Sangari and Uma Chakravarti (eds), *From Myths to Markets: Essays in Gender,* Shimla: Indian Institute of Advanced Study and Delhi: Manohar.
Sinha, Mrinalini (1986), 'Colonial Politics and the Ideal of Masculinity', paper presented at the Third National Conference of Women's Studies, Indian Association of Women's Studies, Chandigarh.
———. (1995), *Colonial Masculinity: The 'Manly' Englishman and the Effeminate Bengali in the Late Nineteenth Century,* Manchester: Manchester University Press.
'The Sita Who Refused the Fire Ordeal,' (1981), *Manushi,* Vol. 8.
Mrs Speier (1856), *Life in Ancient India;* reprinted as *Phases of Indian Civilization,* Delhi: Cosmo.
Spivak, Gayatri Chakravorty (1987), 'A Literary Representation of the Subaltern: Mahasweta Devi's "Stanadayani"', in R. Guha (ed.), *Subaltern Studies V,* Delhi: Oxford University Press.
Stein, Burton (1980), *Peasant State and Society in Medieval South India,* Delhi: Oxford University Press.
Stephens, Julie (1992), 'Feminist Fictions: A Critique of the Category "Non-Western Woman" in Feminist Writings on India', in R. Guha (ed.), *Subaltern Studies VI,* Delhi: Oxford University Press.
Stokes, E.G. (1961), 'The Administrators and Historical Writing on India', in C.H. Philips (ed.), *Historians of India, Pakistan and Ceylon,* London: Oxford University Press.
Sukhtankar, V.S. (1957), *On the Meaning of the Mahabharata,* Bombay: The Asiatic Society of Bombay.
Sutherland, Sally (1992), 'Seduction, Counter Seduction and Sexual Role Models: Bedroom Politics and the Indian Epics', *Journal of Indian Philosophy,* Vol. 19, pp. 53–61.
———. (1996), 'The Political and Social Ramifications of the Construction of Gender in the Valmiki *Ramayana*', paper presented at the Ramayana Conference, University of Hyderabad.
Sutra Kritanga (1895), translated by Hermann Jacobi, *in jaina Sutras,* Vol. II, *Sacred Books of the East,* IX.V, Oxford: Clarendon Press.
Sutta Nipata (1958), *Khuddaka Nikaya,* Nalanda: Pali Publication Board.
———. (1977), translated by V. Fausboll, *Sacred Books of the East,* Vol. XI, Part II, Delhi: Motilal Banarsidass.
Sutta Pitaka (1958), comprising the *Digha Nikaya* (three volumes), the *Majjhima Nikaya* (three volumes), the *Samyutta Nikaya* (four volumes) and the *Anguttara Nikaya* (four volumes), Nalanda: Pali Publication Board.
Syed, A.J. (ed.) (1985), *D.D. Kosambi on History and Society: Problems of Interpretation,* Bombay: University of Bombay.
Talbot, Cynthia (1995), 'Rudraina-devi, the Female King: Gender and Political Authority in Medieval India', in David Shulman (ed.), *Syllables of Sky: Studies in South Indian Civilization,* Delhi: Oxford University Press.
Tambiah, S.J. (1970), *Buddhism and the Spirit Cults of North-East Thailand,* Cambridge: Cambridge University Press.
Thapar, Romila (1978a), 'Dana and Dakshina', in *Ancient Indian Social History: Some Interpretations,* Delhi: Orient Longman.
———. (1978b), *Exile and Kingdom: Some Thoughts on the Ramayana,* Bangalore: Mythic Society.

Thapar, Romila. (1978c), 'Renunciation: The Making of a Counter Culture?', in *Ancient Indian Social History: Some Interpretations,* Delhi: Orient Longman.
———. (1981), 'The Householder and the Renouncer in the Brahmanical and Buddhist Traditions', *Contributions to Indian Sociology,* Vol. 15.
———. (1983), *From Lineage to State,* Delhi: Oxford University Press.
Thapar, Romila (1990), *A History of India,* Vol. I, London: Penguin Books.
———. (1999), *Sakuntala: Texts, Readings, Histories,* Delhi: Kali for Women.
Theragatha, Khuddaka Nikaya (1958), edited by Bhikkhu J. Kashyap, Nalanda: Pali Publication Board.
Therigatha (1948), translated by C.A.F. Rhys Davids as *Psalms of the Sisters,* London: Pali Text Society.
Thorner, Daniel (1971), 'Peasant Economy as a Category in Economic History', in T. Shanin (ed.), *Peasants and Peasant Societies,* Harmondsworth: Penguin Books.
———. (1972), 'Chayanov's Concept of Peasant Economy', in A.V. Chayanov, *The Theory of Peasant Economy and the Awkward Class: Political Sociology of Peasantry in a Developing Society, Russia 1910–25,* London: Oxford University Press.
Threatened Existence: A Feminist Analysis of the Genocide in Gujarat (2003), International Initiative for Justice in Gujarat, December.
Tod, James (1920), *Annals and Antiquities of Rajasthan, 1829–1830,* edited by William Crooke, London: Oxford University Press.
Tripathi, R.S. (1937), *History of Ancient India,* Delhi: Motilal Banarsidass. Tyagi, Jaya (2001), *Women in the Grihyasutras,* unpublished Ph.D. thesis, University of Delhi.
Uberoi, J.P.S. (1969), 'The Five Symbols of Sikhism', in Darshan Singh Maini (ed.), *Sikhism,* Patiala: Punjabi University.
Uberoi, Patricia (ed.) (1994), *Family, Kinship and Marriage in India,* Delhi: Oxford University Press.
The Uttararamacharita of Bhavabhuti (1993), edited by M.R. Kale, Delhi: Motilal Banarsidass.
Vasan, S.S. (1953), *Avvaiyar* (film).
Vasishtha Dharmasutra (1975), translated by George Buhler, in *Sacred Laws of the Aryas,* Vol. II, Delhi: Motilal Banarsidass.
Vasudevan, Geeta (1981), *Women in the Ramayana,* unpublished M. Phil. paper, Jawaharlal Nehru University, Delhi.
Vinaya. Pitaka (1879–93), edited by H. Oldenberg, London: Pali Text Society.
———. (1958), Volumes I–IV:Vol. I, *Parajika;* Vol. II, *Pacittiya;* Vol. III, *Mahavagga*; Vol. IV, *Cullavagga,* Nalanda: Pali Publication Board.
Vinaya Texts (1881), edited by T.W. Rhys Davids and H. Oldenberg, Oxford: Clarendon Press.
Vishnttsmriti (1880), translated by J. Jolly as *The Institutes of Vishnu, Sacred Books of the East,* Vol. VII, Oxford: Clarendon Press.
Vivekananda, Swami (1958), *Complete Works,* Vol. II, Calcutta: Advaita Ashrama.
Voigt, Johannes H. (1967), *F.M. Max Mueller: The Man and His Ideas,* Calcutta: Firma K.L. Mukhopadhyaya.
Vriji, K.J. (1952), *Ancient History of Saurashtra,* Bombay.
Vyakarana Mahabhashya of Patanjali (1892), edited by Franz L. Kielhorn, Vol. I, Bombay: Central Book Depot.
Wagle, N.N. (1966), *Society at the Time of the Buddha,* Bombay: Popular Prakashan.
Warder, A.K. (1956), 'On the Relationship between Buddhism and Other Con temporary Systems', *Bulletin of the School of Oriental and African Studies,* Vol. 18.
———. (1970), *Indian Buddhism,* Delhi: Motilal Banarsidass.
Weber, Max (1960), *The Religion of India,* New York: The Free Press.
Wheeler, R.M. (1953), *The Indus Civilization,* Cambridge: Cambridge University Press.
Yajnava lkyasmritisamvat (1986), Banaras: Chowkhamba Sanskrit Series Office.
Yalman, Nur (1963), 'On the Purity of Women in the Castes of Ceylon and Malabar', *Journal of the Royal Anthropological Institute of Great Britain and Ireland,* Vol. 93, pp. 25–28.
Zinn, Howard (1999), *A People's History of the United States,* New York: Harper Collins.

Chapter 10

Women and Work in Kautilīya's Arthaśāstra

UPASANA DHANKHAR

INTRODUCTION

Society and state for the purposes of establishing and propagating themselves may assign different status and roles to women. Though the human existence has variations but a few patterns are idealized, propagated and suggested through different mechanisms to reproduce the socio-economic and political order. Though the socio-economic and political structures generally replicate each other, yet the requirements of each one can give rise to variations that may affect each other. For example, a study of the *dharmasastric* literature shows that a brahmanic-patriarchal society confines women to the households and defines them with reference to men. On the other hand, the *Arthaśāstra* tradition concerned primarily with governance and economics, looks upon women as an economic resource and mentions about women engaged in various kind of economic activities as well as state services.

The *Arthaśāstra* claims to be a codification of the 'many treatises on the science of politics as have been composed by ancient teachers for the acquisition and protection of earth' (KA, I.1.10. Evidently, the treatise is concerned with gaining and maintaining the territorial authority. However, maintenance of this authority is referred to in terms of *pālana*, that is, sustenance and management. For the said purposes, the *Arthaśāstra* gives not only a detailed administrative structure but also elaborate instructions for formulation of various policies and utilization of various resources. Everyone and everything that falls within the domain of the ruler is looked upon as a resource for the cause of the state.

Women in this text are no different from other animate or inanimate resources that can be utilized for the purposes of the state. They are yet another asset that can help in maintenance of the state authority and ensuring its smooth functioning. They have both productive and reproductive potential which can be subordinated to the interests of the state. Since the political power is the overriding motive, the *Arthaśāstra* often overlooks the questions of morality in the face of material interests. 'Material wellbeing alone is supreme,' says Kauṭilya (KA I.7.6). Further, it insists that 'spiritual good and sensual pleasures depend on material well-being' (KA I.7.7). Thus, it is important to remember that the roles assigned to women in this text were those which the state wanted them to play for its very own needs. How far these roles were taken up, under what conditions and with how much willingness are matters of conjecture. Following study is an attempt to draw some tenable inferences in this regard.

Since the provisions of the *Arthaśāstra* are largely concerned with the structure and functions of the state, it is perhaps important to have a look at the nature of state this text seeks to establish. It is important to note that the state besides being a power structure is also a facilitator of the activities. Its authority can help promote or demote various possible activities. Evidently, just the way a society determines the features of the polity, the influence of the state can have determining impact on various social actors and institutions.

ARTHAŚĀSTRA AS THE SOURCE

Before we make a survey of the women as mentioned in the *Arthaśāstra*, it is advisable to mark a few overriding concerns of the text that can shed light on the nature of state and society envisaged in the text, for these concerns have a bearing upon the depiction of women as well.

Firstly, as stated earlier the motive of the *Arthaśāstra* is to channelize all resources towards the ends of the state. Maximum utilization of the resources for the said purpose, being the primary objective of the text, necessitates the various kinds of penalties, guarantees and promises which can help in attaining this objective. Unmistakably, the roles and functions mentioned for women in the text were those that were regulated in the interest of the state, and in order to make these so-called jobs for women more acceptable, the state proclaims that it would ensure that these roles were given sanction as well as a sense of security. Thus, the mentioned provisions cannot be taken at face value. The gap between the theory and the practice needs to be carefully examined by corroboration of provisions of the text with other sources. The state here is a powerful entity and its influence seems to reach the individual members of the family as well.

Secondly, it is important to remember that the text is meant for the knowledge of a limited few. The princes, their advisors and a few other people of importance were possibly the people who had access to this knowledge apart from the teachers/political scientists. The motive of all these people was to safeguard the state and their own interests therein. The functions they envisaged for women were meant to fulfil the interests of the ruling class; therefore, the protective provisions or privileges (if any) given to women need to be interpreted in the light of these concerns. The roles assigned to them must have been extremely well deliberated in this long tradition and there is a need to understand the different aspects with due caution. All the same the male domination is conspicuous, so much so that 'unruly' women were punished by the state and had to pay fines, the money for which was earned by working for the state enterprises.

Thirdly, though the text deals largely with political and economic matters, it is by no means silent on the domestic life and social order. The negotiation between polity and society, for the purposes of maintenance of politico-economic order and protection of vested interests, needs to be carefully scrutinized. How different layers of social structure were sought to be adjusted for the benefit of the privileged classes in particular and men in general is a testimony to the attempts at curtailment of liberties of women as well as an acknowledgement of the voices of dissent.

It is important to note that both the *dharmasastras* and the *Arthaśāstra* primarily voice the concerns and opinions of the men in power and authority. This power and authority might have been derived from political, economic, social or ritual status. There is little hope of tracing the ideas and opinions of women in these texts. Thus, wherever possible we need to discover their voices through astute observation of commissioning of some activities and omission of the others.

Assessing the economic roles of women in the *Arthaśāstra* requires a thorough study of the various roles in which women are mentioned in the text, as well as the roles and matters on which the text is silent. Further, individual mentions need to be grouped and regrouped to understand the economic role and position of women in general. Enlisting the references to various activities, they are mentioned in provisions relating to them is only half the work done, for we need to understand the deliberations behind all that has been allowed to find space in the provisions of this text.

Women are by no means a homogeneous class/category. The *Arthaśāstra* gives us information on women who were engaged in economic activities of various kinds. They formed a part of both the skilled and the unskilled workforce. They were into professional as well as non-professional employment. Some of their vocations were related to their gender, while the others were not. There were female state employees as well as independently working women. Similarly, some of them were engaged in activities which though not dependent on their biological constitution are nonetheless categorized as women's domain, for example, domestic chores. Some of them were actual state employees, while some others were in contractual relations with the state. This grouping and regrouping of activities mentioned shall help us to understand their place in the economic sphere as a whole.

REPRESENTATIONS OF WOMEN AND WORK IN THE *ARTHAŚĀSTRA*

We can perhaps begin by mentioning a few roles that women performed and thereafter start putting them into various categories to understand the implications. However, it is important to remember beforehand that even within these categories there were variations, many of which are mentioned within the text under perusal. Various terms mentioned for women in the *Arthaśāstra* give us the idea of their possible economic roles and status; some of the important mentions are *silpavati*, *aniskasini*, *dasi*, *vidhava*, *kanyaka*, *nyangah*, *prositas*, *vrddha-rajadasibhi*, *devadasi*, *matrka*, *rupajiva*, *ardhasitikas*, *ganika*, *pratiganika*, *pumscali*, *bandhaki*, *vesya*, *svairini*, *pravarjita*, *dandapratikarini*, *dhatri*, *paricarika*, *upacarika*, etc. Some of the women are not mentioned in direct terms and are rather stated as wives of men engaged in particular vocations, for example, wives of *caranas*, *talavacaras*, *matsya*, *lubdhakas*, *gopalakas*, *prasrsta*, *natas*, *nartakas*, *gayana-vadaka*, *vakjivana*, *kustlavas*, *plavaka*, *saubhikta*, etc.

A survey of the aspects like what categories of women were engaged in different kind of economic activities can be helpful in understanding their economic status. Interestingly, we find that it is the women with little or no hopes of a regular married or domestic life that are engaged in various kinds of state employments and activities, though this is not to suggest that there were no working householders. Herein, we can take a look at three important state employments, namely courtesans, spies and women employed in weaving industry.

Courtesans/*Ganikas* by very nature of their profession cannot be expected to be in an idealised marital or family relationship as has been canonized by the brahmanical codes. The provisions concerned with their sons, daughters and mothers show that their family system was not the one that was prevalent in the society at large (KA II.27.2, 29). Further, they were deployed as spies as well. The idealized chaste wife participating in ritual activities and looking after the household is so far away from this category that the two roles cannot even be expected to converge.

Women spies were of varied kinds and it is tough to infer anything with respect to their personal life. Some of them might have had to live in households of internal or external enemies for years on end, keeping their real identities under cover. Some of them were expected to enter into carnal relationships with strangers, enemies or suspects for the purposes of digging out information. The morality prescribed by the brahmanical codes did not work for them. Some of the spies were expected to work as murderers as well. How the professional life of these women affected their personal life is tough to judge, but we sure can expect something different from the ordinary.

Looking at the women employed in the weaving industry we find that there were different kinds of employment which this industry offered. Interestingly, different categories of destitute women seem to have benefited from employment in this sector. The examples mentioned in the text include 'crippled women and maidens, women who have left their home, women who are paying their fine through personal labor, through mothers of courtesans, through old female slaves of the king and through female slaves of temples whose service of the gods has ceased' (KA II.23.2, 11).

These destitute women were given extraordinary protection from the possible prying eyes of men. Perhaps these were the women whose honourable existence was a separate imperative for the state irrespective of their economic conditions. These could have been women of the higher *varna*, and also women whose existence was required for the smooth functioning of the state like the women who were employed as palace servants, spies, female attendants and the guards. The political and social hierarchies were interlinked and they re-enforced each other. It is perhaps for this reason that we find special employment provisions for these women. The list does not seem to contain any category that could be into family life as these are mostly socially or economically marginalized groups, and even here the very fact they had to earn a living for themselves in old age hints at their economic plight. Old female servants and young maidens would not have to earn a living in the patriarchal set up unless they were left with no other option. The very fact that these women were left to fend for themselves in a patriarchal society, wherein women are generally economically dependent on men in family, shows that their family life was either long over or was not possible at all.

Other important sectors of state employment for women were the roles of female attendants, palace servants and 'female guards bearing bows' (KA I.21.1). Amongst these the first two can be expected to lead a family life, but no certain statements can be made as regards female guards. This mention of female guards is perhaps the only one that we find with regard to early Indian history. Jaiswal suggests that these women perhaps came from *Bhila* or *Kirata* tribe.[1] What were the possible reasons for these women to join in the service of the king and what impact it had on their domestic and social life need to be explored in greater detail.

Courtesans (*Ganikas*) figure as an important category of state employees. The provisions relating to their training in skills (KA II.27.28–30), management of their establishment, safeguards provided to them (KA II.27.11–18) and the duties entrusted to them show that they were not merely prostitutes to satisfy carnal desires of men (KA II.27). We find that they were highly paid, particularly if we notice that the perks their work got them were also considerably high (KA II.27.1, 28). Their beauty and youth was a valued asset which was both an object of display and valuable commodity. This is evident from the fact that most beautiful and ornamented courtesans were to get maximum turns for attendance with various status symbols such as parasol, water jug and fan (KA II.27.4). Their ransom price was also very high (KA II.27.6). Furthermore, the state earned revenue through them as it is stipulated that 'actors and prostitutes shall pay half their wage' (KA 5.2.23).

However, it may be noted that despite all the protective provisions, courtesans had little say in choosing their clients. It is expressly laid down that 'a courtesan, not approaching a man at the command of the king, shall receive one thousand strokes with the whip, or a fine of five thousand *panas*' (KA II.27.19). They were, therefore, 'employees' bound by the orders rather than free enterprisers.

A perusal of the employment provided by the state can help us understand two very important aspects of women and work. Firstly, this exercise helps us to locate the ways in which state made use of the productive potential of women. Secondly, it helps in understanding the negotiation between the state and the society vis-à-vis regulating the roles of women in a patriarchal society.

According to Kautilīya,

> [T]hose women who do not stir out, those living separately, widows, crippled women or maidens, who wish to earn their living, should be given work by sending his own female slaves to them with (a view to) support (them). Or, if they come themselves to the yarn-house he should cause an interchange of goods and wages to be made early at dawn. The lamp (should be there) only for the inspection of the yarn. For looking at the face of the woman or conversing with her on another matter, the lowest fine for violence (shall be imposed), for delay in the payment of wages, the middle fine, also for payment of wages for work not done. (KA II.23.11–14)

We need to identify all these women.

'Those who did not stir out' of their home must have been those who were bound to their homes and hearth. The cue to their identity lies in the social system which can be gathered from the *dharmaśāstras* and relevant provisions of the *Arthaśāstra*. Jaiswal's suggestion

[1] Suvira Jaiswal, 'Female Images in the Arthaśāstra of Kautilīya', *Social Scientist* 29, no. 3/4 (March–April 2001): 55–56.

that these women (*aniskasini*) belonged to upper castes[2] is fairly tenable in the light of the various textual sources as well commonly held view that once a women steps into her marital home, she does not step out but for cremation. However, the term caste needs to be used with qualification. Also, possibly women married in *pratiloma* marriages can be enlisted here.

'Those living separately' (*prositas*) is an interesting category to look at especially because it has direct nexus with the possibilities that women had for moving out of marital homes and matrimonial alliances. Marriage in the *Arthaśāstra* echoes the *dharamsastric* views and mentions the same eight form of marriages as described in the *dharmaśāstras* (KA III.2.2–11). It is interesting to note that the *Arthaśāstra* states that 'maintenance and ornaments constitute woman's property' (KA.III.2.14). The inclusion of maintenance in the women's property is an important aspect. In a way it accords economic value to their role and gives them economic security. This is further evidenced by the fact that Kauṭilya fixes the upper limit to this value when he stipulates that 'maintenance is an endowment of a maximum of two thousand (*panas*); as to ornaments, there is no limit' (KA.III.2.15). The inclusion of maintenance provisions for women in monetary terms is an express acknowledgement of their contribution to the household as well as the state economy. However, justifiability of the quantum of the amount can be explored further as and when historical enquiries can be made. The crucial question is whether this maintenance was paid (or was meant to be paid) to the wife living within the marital home or to wife who had separated and shifted out? According to the *Arthaśāstra*, women's property could be used for maintenance of sons and daughters-in-law (KA.III.2.16). Why would a women living in a marital home need to maintain such dependents? Or were there women who were the breadwinners? If yes, did these women belong to particular social categories?

It is difficult to find the complete answers to these questions, but we do find a cue in the provisions mentioned in the text itself. It is stated,

> [I]f it (woman's property) has been used for three years, the (wife) shall not question, in the case of a pious marriages. If used in the *Gandharava* and *Asura* marriages, the (husband) shall be made to return both with interest, if used in the *Raksasa* and *Paisaca* marriages, he shall pay (the penalty for) theft (KA.III.2.17–18)].

Thus, we see that use of a woman's property is linked with the kind of matrimonial relationship she entered into, which in turn is related to her *varna* status.

The relative importance assigned to the father and mother in case of approval for different forms of marriages needs to be mentioned here. Mothers have a voice in the unapproved form of marriages (KA III.2.11–12). Since these marriages could be practiced only by the lower *varnas*, it can be said that women of lower *varnas* could have been living separately and bringing up their families. This can be substantiated by the fact that barring 'pious marriages' (KA III.2.18), Kauṭilya permits divorce by mutual consent to disaffected husband and wife (KA III.3.16).

Jaiswal's suggestion that '*prositas* were apparently not divorced but deserted or disaffected wives of upper caste men living on their own' seems to overlook the above-mentioned independent women who might have worked and raised not only their little children but

[2] Ibid., 51.

also married sons and their spouses. Jaiswal's suggestion as regards the deserted or disaffected wives is also corroded by the fact that such wives were not only to get maintenance but also compensation. According to the *Arthaśāstra* the husband was required to wait for eight years if the wife did not bear children or did not bear a son or was barren, for 10 if she gave birth to dead progeny, for 12 years if only daughters were born to her (KA III.2.38). Thereafter, he could marry a second wife with the object of getting a son (KA III.2.39). In case of transgression of these rules, the husband was to hand over the dowry, the woman's property and half that as compensation for supersession, and pay a fine of 24 *panas* maximum (KA III.2.40). With these many protective provisions for disaffected and deserted wives, it is difficult to agree that they were left destitute and had to live on their own. The sanction against renunciation and leaving family without making necessary economic provisions for wife (KA II.1.29–31) also suggests that maintenance of wife was a responsibility to be duly carried out even in case of desertion.

Further, it should be noticed that besides the provision for divorce, Kauṭilya provided that 'a husband, who has become degraded or gone to a foreign land or has committed an offence against the king or is dangerous to her life or has become an outcast or even an impotent one may be abandoned' (KA III.2.48). The women married to such men can also be categorized as *prositas*.

Besides *aniskasini* and *prositas*, widows formed the next important category employed or supported by the weaving industry. A study of rich widows in this context can shed more light on the issues of working women. The rules regarding the remarriage of widows and the devolution of their women's property in such circumstances shed light on the nexus between control of productive and reproductive capabilities of the women.

According to the *Arthaśāstra*, 'when the husband is dead, the (widow), if desirous of leading a life of piety, shall forthwith receive the endowment and ornaments and the remainder of the dowry' (KA III.2.19). But 'if, after receiving (these), she marries again, she shall be made to return both with interest' (KA III.2.20). Thus, we see that largely, if a widow was to remarry, she could do so only if she was ready to part with her property/assets and also to pay interest as penalty. Given the bias against women in general and widows in particular, the matrimonial alliance at the risk of economic security was hardly an option. However, under such conditions reproductive resources of a woman would have been wasted. The provisions that Kauṭilya provides to resolve this predicament is yet another clear example of the negotiated position between the state and the society. Accordingly, if the widow wished to have a family, she was to receive at the time of her remarriage 'what was given to her by her father-in-law and her (late) husband' (KA III.2.21). However, if she remarried against the wishes of her father in law, she was required to forfeit what was given to her by her father-in-law and her (late) husband (KA III.2.23).

In this way, the productive and reproductive resources of the widows were subordinated to a patriarchal state and society and she was disabled from keeping both the choices with her. 'The *Arthaśāstra* state is of course concerned to control family and sexual relations but it does so in the interest of the state for maximizing population and production.'[3] The

[3] Gail Omvedt, 'God as Political Philosopher: Buddhism's Challenge to Brahmanism', *Economic and Political Weekly* 36, no. 21 (May 26–June 1, 2001): 88.

importance that these provisions carried can be gathered from the fact that these are repeated and reasserted. For example, it is stated that 'a (widow remarrying) shall forfeit what was given by her (late) husband' (KA III.2.26). Similarly, 'if a widow who had sons were to marry again, she was required to forfeit her woman's property' (KA III.2.29). The comforts of a material life could only be kept if she forfeited her right to find companionship.

Other women employed in the weaving industry were crippled women, maidens, women who are paying their fine through personal labour, mothers of courtesans, old female slaves of the king and female slaves of temples whose service of the gods has ceased (KA II.23.2). Even these women had little scope of being accepted in the larger social milieu that was biased against the women in general. A huge bias is evident against the crippled people in the ancient texts, for example, the characters like Manthara in the Rāmayana and Shakuni in the Mahābhārata are presented in bad light. In the *dharamśāstra* literature, we come across graphic descriptions of women who were eligible brides, and with all the demands regarding the physical beauty and health, crippled women had little scope of getting married in such a social order.

Mothers of courtesans were generally entrusted with the duty of looking after their establishments and their household cannot be expected to have supported usual patriarchal family set up. The mention of the 'female slaves of the temple/*devadasis*' has rightly been described as 'euphemism for temple prostitution'[4] by Jaiswal. The way this institution developed and spread in later times makes it obvious that *devadasis* were denied a marital life.

'Women who are paying their fine through personal labor' present an interesting category. Firstly, it shows that these women were not convicted for grave offences, for in that case they would have been awarded more than monetary punishment. Women committing grave offences might have been kept in jail for the *Arthaśāstra* mentions separate apartments for women in prison houses (KA II.5.5). Secondly, it shows that these women perhaps had little other economic resources and were obliged to work for state in case they committed some offence.

Interestingly, the offences for which women were required to pay fine under the provisions of the *Arthaśāstra* were largely those activities wherein they chose to move out of the restrictions imposed on their movements outside home. For example, it was provided that 'on occasion of her enjoying herself outside the home out of jealously, the penalty shall be laid down' (KA III.3.11). Similarly, for a woman who left the house of her husband, the fine was six *panas*, except in case of ill treatment (KA III.4.1). In case a wife left the house of her husband and went to another village she was to pay a fine of 12 *panas* (KA III.4.16). In case she went in the company of a man with whom sexual-intercourse was permissible, the fine was 24 *panas* and the loss of all rights, except the giving of maintenance and approaching during the period (KA III.4.17). Thus, we see that state not only controlled the women as the chief patriarch but also regulated the productive energies of the women who tried to move out of the authority of the patriarchal set up.

[4] Jaiswal, 'Female Images in the Arthaśāstra', 55.

It is important to note that the *Arthaśāstra* explicitly states that these women were to be given work with a view to support them (KA II.23.11). Thus, only needy women could find employment in such work. In order to make sure that these women did not fell prey to any men, strict rules were provided as regards the dealings with them. The state officials were not only to mind their behaviour with these ladies, but also were warned by various penal provisions of various kinds that were supposed to guard the economic and social interest of these women. However, it is important to note that while state was required to take care of these women, it was equally strict with these women and severe punishment were spelled out for misappropriation, stealing or breach of contract by these women workers (KA II.23.15). This limited sate protection was available to 'needy' women but only when all norms of patriarchal set up stringently followed.

Women spies were an important tool available for guarding and furthering the interests of the state. They could be deployed for keeping a watch over both internal and external enemies, as well as for the purposes of checking the integrity of the ministers, etc. The *Arthaśāstra* mentions a number of conspiracies that could be hatched with female spies being instrumental in achieving the goal. They were instrumental in collection of information and were integral part of communication networks of spies. It is stipulated that amongst others 'women should by own end ascertain the indoor activity' and 'nuns should communicate that information to the spy establishments' (KA I.12.9). Only 'in case of prohibition of entry into the house for nuns, secret agents appearing at the door one after another or appearing as the mother or father of servants in the house, or posing as female artists, singers or female slaves' were entrusted with the task of gathering information that was spied out and conveyed outside by means of songs, recitations, writings concealed in musical instruments or signs (KA I.12.13).

Women worked both as stationed agents as well as roving spies (KA I.10.4, 5, 7). A woman could be a wandering nun who has won the confidence of the ministers (KA I.10.7), the begging nun (KA I.11.1), a wandering nun seeking a secure livelihood (KA I.12.4–5), etc. Prostitutes could also be employed as spies and the *Arthaśāstra* envisages their deployment for the purposes of foreign policy. For example, it is provided that 'keepers of prostitutes should make the enemy's army chiefs infatuated with women possessed of great beauty and youth. When many or two of the chiefs feel passion for one woman, assassins should create quarrels among them' (KA XII.2.11–12).

At times the stratagems required male and female spies to work in sync, for example, an agent appearing as an astrologer was required to declare to a high officer, whose confidence had been gradually won, that he is possessed of the marks of a king. In turn, a female mendicant was to declare to his wife that she would be the wife of a king or the mother of a king (KA XII.2.18–19). Female spies were employed for the purposes like ascertainment of the integrity or the absence of integrity of ministers by means of secret test as mentioned in Book I Chapter 10 Section 6, or for drawing out the enemy by means of stratagems as mentioned in Book XI, XII and XIII.

Female spies were not only to gather information and relay it to proper channel, but also to carry out assassinations. This must have required proper training for them. However, a closer look at the text shows that there were different classes of female spies engaged for different purposes. Amongst others 'women skilled in arts were to be employed as spies living inside their houses' (KA I.12.21). Others were required to work as assassins (KA V.1.19, XII.5.48). Some were to the play the roles of young and beautiful widows to tempt the lust of greedy enemy (KA XIII.2.42).

Some were to win confidence of the target and then to test their integrity and character. For example, the *Arthaśāstra* provides that a wandering nun, who had won the confidence of the ministers and was treated with honour in the palace, was to secretly suggest to each minister individually that the chief queen being in love with him has made arrangements for a meeting and there were possibilities of gaining wealth through such a liaison. This was the test of lust (KA I.10.7). Apart from professional spies, prostitutes and other women could be employed for the purposes of ploy. For example, a woman of bad character, appearing as the queen, was to be caught in the quarters of the enemy at night and so on (KA V.1.28). Similarly, courtesans and other women appearing as wives find mention as an important part of the espionage system (KA.VII.17.38).

Prostitutes and women of acrobats, actors, dancers or showmen employed as agents could be used for various conspiracies. These women were used to infatuate chiefs of the ruling council. Since it is opined that these could be 'infatuated with women possessed of great beauty and youth' (KA XI.1.34). 'When passion was roused in them, they were to start quarrels by creating belief about their love in one and by going to another, or by staging a forcible abduction by the other' (KA XI.1.35). During these quarrels, the assassins were to do their work (KA XI.1.35). Similar other conspiracies are mentioned in the text of the *Arthaśāstra* in chapters dealing with measures of foreign policy.

Besides, the female spies in the service of state (whether professionally employed or hired for particular projects), other women were also expected to work as informers. For example, traders of spirituous liquors were to employ female slaves of beautiful appearance to find out the intentions of strangers and natives (KA II.25.15). Similarly, prostitutes were directed to give lodging only to one thoroughly known to them and they were required to report about the men who spent lavishly and those who did rash deeds (KA II.36.8–9).

While courtesans, prostitutes, 'women of bad character', 'women of actors, acrobats, etc.', *Aditikausika* women, dancers, and songstresses (KA XI.1.42) are expressly mentioned as a part of the espionage system, it is difficult to judge whether all spies came from these categories. Suvira Jaiswal's suggests that women from the lower sections of society could be easily pressed into these services for state[5] and possibly these women along with female slaves formed the largest part of the espionage system, but we cannot discount the possibility of women from higher *varnas* being actively engaged in the intelligence services. Also, it remains to be established that any of these was 'pressed' to take up the role, since it is pretty much possible for any of them to be interested in extra income. Also, the state would have been anxious to have reliable spies.

While enlisting the roving spies the *Arthaśāstra* mentions 'a wandering nun, seeking a secure livelihood, poor, widowed, bold, Brahmin (by caste) and treated with honor in the palace' (KA I.12.4), and further states that 'by her office are explained similar offices for the shaven nuns of heretical sects' (KA I.12.4–5). These provisions might refer to the spies

[5] Ibid., 52.

playing these roles, but there is nothing that debars the possibility of Brahmin women or the Buddhist or Jaina nuns being employed in the intelligence department.

Female slaves formed an important part of the workforce both in the royal establishment and in the common households. In the royal establishment, 'female slaves of proved integrity' were to do the work of bath-attendants, shampooers, bed-preparers, laundresses and garland-makers; otherwise, they were required to supervise the artists doing these jobs (KA I.21.13). Further they were to offer garments, flowers and other cosmetics after first putting them on their own eyes, bosoms and arms (KA XXI.14–15). Thus, they were not only personal attendants but also a security check.

The *Arthaśāstra* has many important provisions on law-concerning slaves and labourers in Book III Chapter 13 Section 65. Interestingly, while many protective and emancipating provisions were spelled out for the female slaves in the common households, there was nothing that guarded the interests of the slaves in royal service. It is provided that,

> [M]aking a women (pledged) give bath to a naked person, giving corporal punishment to them and dishonoring them shall result in the loss of the capital, and shall result in freedom for a nurse, a female attendant, a woman tenant tilling for half the produce and a maid.

But it is difficult to imagine a king being subjected to any of these provisions.

Safeguards provided to female slaves are important for understanding the general conditions of women. These women represent the lowest rung in terms of economic and social status. The *Arthaśāstra* contains various provisions which make it clear that female slaves might have been sexually exploited. This practice was however sought to be contained and various protective and emancipating provisions were spelled out. For one approaching a pledged unwilling nurse, the punishment was the lowest fine for violence if she was under his control, and the middle if she was under the control of another (KA III.13.11). If one, himself or through another, defiled a maiden who was pledged, he was liable to lose the capital, and was required to pay her dowry in addition to a fine double the amount of dowry (KA III.13.12). In case the master was to beget a child on his own female slave, both the mother and the child were to gain independent status (KA III.13.23). If the mother was attached to the house and looked after the affairs of the family, her siblings were also given freedom (KA III.13.24). The *Arthaśāstra* required the master to provide nourishment for the foetus of an expecting female slave (KA III.13.20). This is perhaps the earliest reference to maternity care provisions for a female employee.

Amongst the employments mentioned for women in the non-state sector, we find little mention of professionals. Mention can be made of midwives, prostitutes, women of people who lived on secret means of earning, 'women who tilled for half the produce' and 'female slaves of temple' and other female slaves. Unfortunately, apart from prostitutes and women of certain specified occupational groups, these women are mentioned only once in the text. This leaves us with a sketchy picture, which can be supplemented with information about the economy and society in general.

An important indicator of economic status of women is the juristic personality accorded to them. Juristic personality refers to the capacity of suing and being sued. In other words, it can be defined as the liability a person incurs that can be enforced through judicial mechanisms, or simply the acts and omissions for which a person can be held liable. A liability is always coupled with a capacity. Thus, if a woman is held responsible for economic transactions, it is evident that she has a right or capacity to indulge in these transactions.

The *Arthaśāstra* provides that transactions concluded by a woman dependent on her husband or son were not to succeed, excepting the women to whom authority for transaction is given (KA III.1.12). This provision makes it clear that dependent women by themselves had no capacity to enter into a contract of any kind. We find similar references in the brahmanical codes as well. However, they could be vested with this capacity by getting authorization of the men in family. The women got this capacity not only by express permission but also by omissions of their husbands for Kauṭilya provides stipulates that the husband was liable for the debt incurred by the wife if he went abroad without providing for her (KA III.11.24). Thus, possibly women, unless dependent economically on male relatives, could indulge in economic transactions and seem to have enjoyed capacity to contract on their own as well as on behalf of men when authorized to do so. It is interesting to note that dependent women at least have been recognized as bearing the capacity even if it is to be exercised only on authorization.

It seems that, women in the family had a subordinate economic status and their dependence on men was related to the lack of social independence. As we have noticed earlier, most of the working women seem to be those who were either destitute or were not into regular matrimonial or family system. Thus, we can hardly be surprised that transactions concluded by the women who did not stir out of their homes were held enforceable (KA III.1.7). Since these women are fending for themselves it can be inferred that they are not dependent on men. Similarly, we find an exception stating that 'the wife shall not be held liable for the debt incurred by her husband, if she has not assented to it, except in the case of cowherds and farmers tilling for half the produce' (KA III.11.23). Perhaps equal participation in work towards earning livelihood in these categories accorded these women the capacity as well as the liability of economic nature. Women of these occupational/social groups were engaged in economically productive activities and hence cannot be regarded as dependent on their husbands. Similarly, we find that courtesans as well women indulging in prostitution of different kinds had greater authority over the disposal of their property, which is related to their capacity to contract.

While most of the mentioned occupations lacked longevity and would leave the women jobless in the later years of their life, the other involved are regular work that could be carried on till the age/health permits. For example, courtesans were to be young and beautiful, while an opportunity in weaving sector was available to the old palace servants. The elaborate instructions for employing destitute women in the weaving industry show that indeed there were a large number of women who fell on hard days. On the other hand, men in the *Arthaśāstra* are engaged into professional work and we find mentions of washermen (KA IV.1.14–23), tailors (KA IV.1.25), goldsmiths (KA IV.1.26–43), physicians (KA IV.1.56) and others (KA IV.1.65, IV.4.3).

The differences in opportunities available to men and women are evident from these options. The statements concerning the women of certain occupational/social groups bring out the basic texture of society. Almost everywhere we find a presumption that the women of dancers, wandering minstrels, fishermen, fowlers, cowherds, vintners and others who give freedom to their women, etc., are engaged in prostitution. This might have been true, but this provision also points to an important aspect of women and work, which is the fact that the predominant asset these women were thought to have had was their sexuality. The prolific mention of different kinds of prostitutes and women of men engaged in various low status works, who were thought to earn by accompanying strangers, shows that women in economic sphere were generally sex workers, exceptions being those specifically mentioned. As we have already noted, those specifically mentioned are either those who are being deployed by state for its own purposes or those rural women who were engaged in the agricultural sector. Both these categories were economically and politically essential for state.

The detailed survey of the women and work as found in the *Arthaśāstra* will remain incomplete without the very important category that has not found mention as yet, namely the queens. Their importance in economic and political set up is hinted at by the mention that 'the king's mother and the crowned queen should receive forty-eight thousand (*panas*)' (KA 5.3.3). Considering the anxious effort at maximum utilization of resources, we can be sure that such a huge amount would not have been allocated without reason. The concern for their security re-emphasizes their importance. It is provided that 'under no circumstances must the king make himself or the queen the target for the sake of ascertaining the probity of ministers' (KA 1.10.17). Their functions are not elaborated upon but the mentions of the ways in which a number of conspiracies could be hatched successfully with someone impersonating the queen shows that they must have been very active and involved in important matters. It will take a separate analysis to determine whether the emolument for the queen was just an honorarium to match their status or a compensation for the responsibilities they shouldered.

CONCLUSION

Any study of the *Arthaśāstra* brings out the prime concern for the security and maintenance of the state. The elaborate layout of socio-political structures and economic organization is directed towards furthering the vested interests of social and political elites wherein everything and everyone within the territory of the state is a resource to gain the politico-economic power and to maintain the same. Women accordingly figure in the *Arthaśāstra* primarily as objects and instruments for furthering the ends of the state.

Though the political and legal structure (both social norms and administrative apparatus) reinforce each other, yet the economic necessities and social dynamics made the state overlook or ignore the social norms. The state can be seen to propagate and protect the women in roles condemned by the *dharma* texts. *Arthaśāstra* gives us a better idea of the visibility of the women in the public spheres and economic roles as compared to the *dharmasastric* literature, and reveals a hierarchy therein. For example, the difference in the position of the royal ladies and the women belonging to certain working/professional classes is made conspicuous by provisions relating to them.

The most important point to be noted is the presence of women in productive activities in almost all the classes. On the one hand, we have mention of queens with a salary of 48,000 *panas* and on the other we have poor women employed in the weaving industry. Women did not only earn for themselves and family but also contributed a good share in the state revenue and constituted significant part of the workforce. The social status of the women was linked with their economic status and opportunities in a twisted way. The higher social status made women economically dependent on men while the comparatively poor agrarian women were seen as equal participants in the household. The former category could enter into contracts independently while the latter could be made liable even for the debts incurred without their prior approval! The exception in favour of women of higher *varna* from legal responsibility is a poor substitute for the restriction imposed on their economic freedom. This smacks of the reinforcement of *varna* and gender hierarchy envisaged in the brahmanical law codes. As has been pointed out by Gail Omvedt, 'Marriage and the family are very much concerns of the state, but the state is more interested in seeing that young women marry and produce children than that they be testaments to their family's purity.'[6] Such provisions highlight the concern of the state for managing the reproductive potential of the women for the stability of the socio-political order.

A few important remarks can be made as regards the composition of working women. Firstly, they came from all rungs of the society and their occupations differed in the early phase of life. The spectrum ranges from certain poorer classes whose sexuality was looked upon as the economic asset, while in cases of upper *varna*, concerns of chastity made it imperative to stick to the heavily regularized weaving industry. However, old age and lack of options got women across social categories into the same fold of working for the weaving industry in the hard days. Secondly, a vast number of women worked only when they fell on hard times or had no economic support, for example, the weaving industry largely seems to be supporting destitute women. There is hardly any mention of women professionals outside the folds of prostitution and espionage. But it still does not preclude independently working women who supported not just the grown up sons but also their wives. Thirdly, courtesans and spies had access to both men with power and rich property but the varied disguises that were taken by the women spies hint at the mobility of women. Possibly, a study can be taken up to find economic functions of the seemingly non-economic categories of women, and also deeper research into how the maintenance was fixed for disaffected women and what the quantum of 2000 *panas* meant in economic terms.

Fourthly, it is interesting to note that women protects the women who choose to maintain themselves through hard work and lets the men to have responsible indulgence with various categories of sexual service providers. Last but not the least, provisions regarding the protection of women's property on a careful analysis suggest that certain women enjoyed economic independence and supported their families. The mobility of the women also seems to suggest their vibrant social life. The provisions regarding wives, whether in conjugal happiness or disaffected on some account, seem to put matrimony on a very high pedestal with due acknowledgement of their economic worth. Nonetheless, lack of professional roles and education points towards the murky world where women's worth was associated with her body rather than the mind. All the accomplishments that women were to make were basically to enhance their appeal to men rather than to carve an identity of their own. A specific study into agrarian economy of this period can, however, enhance our understanding of the socio-economic dynamics of the majority population.

---

[6] Omvedt, 'God as Political Philosopher', 188.

BIBLIOGRAPHY

K. P. Kangle, *The Kautilīya's Arthaśāstra*, 3 Vols (Bombay: University of Bombay, 1965–1972).

Patrick Olivelle, *Manu's Code of Law* (New Delhi: Oxford University Press, 2005).

Sukumari Bhattacharji, 'Prostitution in Ancient India', *Social Scientist* 15, no. 2 (1987, February), 32–61.

Uma Chakravarti, 'Beyond the Altekarian Paradigm: Towards a New Understanding of Gender Relations in Early Indian History', *Social Scientist* 16, no. 8. (1988, August), 44–52.

Uma Chakravarti, 'Conceptualising Brahmanical Patriarchy in Early India: Gender, Caste, Class and the State', *Economic and Political Weekly* 27, no. 14 (1993, 3 April): 579.

D. D. Kosambi, 'The Text of the Arthaśāstra', *Journal of the American Oriental Society* 78, no. 3 (1958, July–September), 169–73.

I. W. Mabbett, 'The Date of the Arthaśāstra', *Journal of the American Oriental Society* 84, no. 2 (1964, April–June), 162–69.

Narasingha Prosad Sil, 'Kautilya's Arthaśāstra: A Comparative Study', *Journal of the American Oriental Society* 107, no. 4 (1987, October–December), 838–39.

Ludwik Sternbach, *Juridical Studies in Ancient Indian Law,* Parts I and II (Delhi: Motilal Banarsidass, 1965).

Thomas R. Trautmann, 'A Metrical Origin for the Kauṭilya Arthaśāstra', *Journal of the American Oriental Society* 88, no. 2 (1968, April–June), 347–49.

Women and Economic Resources: Women's Property Rights

Section III

Chapter 11 Proprietary Rights during Coverture*

ANANT SADASHIV ALTEKAR

The study of the evolution of the proprietary rights of women is a very fascinating subject. It has a vital importance to the historian of the woman, for economic independence and prosperity have usually an important bearing on the well-being of a class. The reader is already aware how the general position of women went on deteriorating after the beginning of the Christian era. He will now be surprised to learn that, in spite of this general setback, their proprietary rights were gradually becoming more and more extensive in course of time.

In early times, proprietary rights of women were recognised very tardily in almost all civilisations. This was the case specially in patriarchal societies. For a long time there was no question of the woman holding any property; she herself was an item in the movable property of the husband or the patriarch. This was the case among the Teutons. The Frisians used to give their women and children in payment of their taxes to Rome, when they had no other means to discharge their liabilities. At Rome the husband could sell his wife in early times, the right being taken away only at the beginning of the Christian era. For a long time the wife was under the tutelage of her husband and could possess no separate property at all, if she was married according to the orthodox religious rites. Even after the husband's death she did not become a *sui jure*, but passed under the tutelage of other male relatives. During the feudal age in Europe, women could no doubt inherit and hold even landed property.

This was, however, a nominal right. Women were really pawns in the hands of kings. Land was for military service, which women were incapable of rendering. So the emperor would take immediate steps to marry the daughters or widows of his barons or knights to whomsoever he liked.

When in his Spanish campaigns a number of his noblemen died, Charlmaigne immediately married their widows to the barons of his own choice. He was anxious that land should not be under the ownership of those who could not fight in his wars. Whether the widows

* Previously published in Anant Sadashiv Altekar's *Position of Women in Hindu Civilization: From Pre-Historical Times to the Present Day*, Motilal Banarsidass Publishers, Varanasi and Delhi (1959), pp. 212–33.

concerned wanted to marry, and if so, whether they had approved of the proposed new husbands, was a matter which he did not stop to enquire. Women were a sort of vitalised deed of conveyance. They were hardly as important as horses, which were so useful in war, save as living titles to landed property.[1]

In India too in very eariy times women were regarded as chattel. They were given away as gifts in the Vedic age, as would appear from several hymns, which glorify the gifts of generous donors.[2] In the *Mahābhārata* we find Dhṛitarāshṭra proposing to give hundred female slaves of Kṛishṛa as atoken of his regard for him.[3] The husband was deemed to have a natural proprietary right in the wife. It is on this undisputed assumption that Hariśchandra proceeds to sell his wife to the Domb at the Banaras Ghat and Dharma proceeds to stake Draupadi in the gambling hall. It may be further pointed out that even this proud and haughty queen does not think of disputing this right of her husband, when she is dragged to the court of Dhṛitarāshtra. She does not at all maintain that she has not lost her freedom because the husband has no right to sell or stake away his wife. She only wants to know whether her husband was a free man, when he had staked her.[4]

In the *Ṛigveda* also in the famous gambling hymn, we find the wife being staked away by the husband (X, 34).

The *Mahābhārata*, however, states that the assembly began to hiss loudly when Dharma proceeded to stake his wife.[5] It would therefore appear that though the husband's proprietary right in the wife was theoretically recognised, its actual exercise met with a stern social disapprobation. It was felt that only intoxicated or inhuman persons could think of exercising it.[6] In the Vedic age also, it was only a confirmed gambler who would sometimes stake his wife. In cultured circles the wife was regarded as the co-owner of the family property along with her husband, as the term *dampatī* would show.

Apart from the rather exceptional cases, referred to above, which really reflect the state of society in prehistoric times, there is no evidence of women being regarded as chattel in ancient India. The Dharmaśāstra writers of the first and the second centuries AD, leave no scope for an enterprising husband to utilise the results of his research in prehistoric social customs and institutions to the disadvantage of his consort; they have definitely declared that women and children cannot be objects of gift or sale under any circumstances.[7]

Let us now consider the proprietary rights of the wife, vis-à-vis her husband. The theory approved by the Hindu culture as early as the Vedic age was that the husband and the wife should be the joint owners of the household and its property. The husband was required to

---

[1] The reader will get more information on the points discussed in this para from George, *Story of woman* and Müller Lyer, *Family*.

[2] उप माष्टयावा स्वनयेन दत्ता वधूमन्तो दष्ठा राथसोऽस्युः। I, 126, 3.

[3] दासीनामप्रजातानां शुभानां रुक्मवर्चसाम्।
शतमस्मै प्रदास्यामि दासानामपि तावताम्।। V. 86, 8.

[4] किंतु पूर्व पराजैषीरात्मानमथवा नु माम्। II, 89, 19.

[5] एवमुक्ते क्ते तु वचने धर्मराजेन धीमता।
धिण्धिगित्येव वृद्वानां सभ्यानां निसृता गिरः।। II, 86, 40.

[6] को हि दीव्याद्भार्यया राजपुत्रो मूढो राजा दूतमदेन मत्तः। II, 89, 17.

[7] स्वं कुटुंबावरोषेन देयं दारसुतादुते। raj., II, 175.

take a solemn vow at the marriage that he would never transgress the rights and interests of his wife in economic matters.

The theory of the joint ownership of the couple should have led to a number of important corollaries, and fortified the position of the wife against an unreasonable or vicious husband.

This, however, does not seem to have taken place. One Dharmasūtra writer concludes from the joint ownership theory that the wife is entitled to incur normal expenditure on the household during her husband's absence.[8] Another concedes to her a third share of the husband's property, in case she was superseded unjustly.[9] But no further deductions were drawn.

The theory of joint ownership helped the wife only in securing a number of minor rights and privileges. It invested her with an absolute right of maintenance against the husband. A verse attributed to Manu, but not to be found in the present *Manusmṛiti*, goes to the extent of declaring that the husband ought to maintain the wife, even if there were no family property. He may have recourse even to questionable means, if there was no other alternative.[10] The husband could not proceed on a journey without making proper provision fop her maintenance and the household expenditure. If he married a second time, the first wife had to be properly provided for. If the wife had the misfortune of being assaulted, the liability of the husband to maintain her did not come to an end.[11] Early jurists no doubt held it improper for a wife to vindicate her claims against the husband in a court of law; later jurists like Vijñāneśvara, however, differed from this view and maintained that if a husband abandons a virtuous wife, or wilfully misappropriates her property and refuses to restore it, she can move a court of law to get her grievances redressed.[12]

The theory of the joint ownership of the couple secured only the above minor advantages to the wife.lt was not pressed to its logical conclusion in order to secure her an absolute equality with the husband in the ownership of the family property. Hindu jurists were not prepared to entertain such a claim on behalf of the wife. Only one amongst them, Yājñavalkya, permits her to claim a one third share, if she is unjustly superseded.[13] But this claim does not appear to have been either actually conceded in practice by society, or sanctioned by other jurists. The wife had no right to incur any substantial expenditure during her coverture without her husband's permission. Even the *Mitāksharā* expressly declares that she can spend out of

---

[8] पाणिग्रहणत्वाद्धि सहत्वं कर्मस...द्रव्यपरिग्रहेषु च । न हि भर्तुर्विप्रसवासे नैमितिके दाने स्तयमुपदिशंति
A. D. S., II, 6,14,16–20.

[9] आज्ञासंपादिनीं दक्षां वीरसू प्रियवादिनीम्।
त्यजन्दाप्यस्तृतीयांशमद्रव्यो भरणं स्त्रियाः।।
Yāj. II, 76.

[10] वृद्धौ च मातापितरौसाध्वी भार्या सुतः शिशुः।
अप्यकार्यशतं कृत्वा भर्तव्या मनुरसवीत् ।।

[11] स्वयं विप्रतिपत्रा वा यदि वा विप्रवासिता ।
बलात्कारोपभुक्ता वा चोरहस्तगतापि वा ।।
न त्याज्या दूषित नारी नास्याास्त्यागो विधीयते ।।
V. D. S., 28. 2, ff.

[12] त्तु गुरोः शिष्ये पितुः पुत्रे दंपत्योः स्वामिभृत्ययोः। विरोधे तुमियस्तेषां व्यवहारो न सिध्यति तदपि अत्यंतव्यवहारनिषेधपरं नं भवति । यदि दुभिक्षादिव्यतिरेकेण स्त्रीधनं व्ययीकृत्य विधिमानधनोइपि याच्यमानो न ददाति तदा दपत्योरिष्यत एव व्यवहारः ।
Mit. on *Yaj*., II, 32.

[13] See *ante*, p. 215 n. 2.

the family property only with the concurrence of the husband.[14] Hindu jurists have further failed to protect the wife's right to a maintenance or a share; they do not invalidate a sale or a mortagage of the family property by the husband, if it was prejudicial even to her right of maintenance. They would have regarded such a procedure as immoral and reprehensible; they have however failed to make it invalid *ab initio.*

General circumstances in society were very unfavourable to the theory of the joint ownership being utilised to invest the wife with the above powers and rights. Landed property was for a long time being owned either by village communities or by large joint families. Individual ownership was but slow in coming into general recognition even in the case of males. By the time individual coparceners could assert their individual rights in the estate of the family, the husband had come to be deified; so it became very difficult for jurists to invest the wife with any susbstantial rights as against the husband. The joint ownership of the husband and the wife thus practically remained a legal fiction. In effect the husband was the sole owner of the family property and the wife had no legal remedy, if he proceeded to squander it and defeat her right to a maintenance or a share. The modern law courts also have not come forward to afford any protection to the wife in such cases. It is only in Portugese India, where the Code Napoleon prevails, that the consent of the wife is a condition precedent to any valid disposal of the family property by the husband. It is now high time that the Indian Legislature should proceed to amend the Hindu Law, and invest the wife with full powers over her own share of the family estate, rendering its sale without her express consent illegal. The old Vedic theory of the joint ownership of the husband and the wife will fully justify such a legislation.

It was only with reference to immovable property that Hindu society was for a long time unwilling to invest the wife with full or exclusive ownership. The reasons for this have been already indicated. As far as movable property like ornaments, jewelry, costly apparel, etc. was concerned, women's right to own it was recognised at a very early date. All this property went under the category of Strīdhana or Women's Special Property. The story of its development is a very interesting chapter in the history of Hindu law.

It is very difficult to define Strīdhana precisely; Hindu jurists only proceed to describe its different varieties. Sufficient to state that the term is used to denote property over which women are allowed to have their own more or less absolute sway in normal times.

In its origin, Strīdhana was vitally connected with the custom of the bride price (*śulka*). We have already shown (*ante*, pp. 39–41) that this custom is of hoary antiquity, and that it continued to persist for a long time in spite of its vehement denunciation: The custom was up doubt a bad one, but it had one relieving feature.

It helped the development of Strīdhana. Owing to the affection, which parents naturally felt for their daughters, they used to return usually a part, and sometimes even the whole of the bride price to the bride, to be enjoyed by her as her separate estate during her own life. If she died leaving some children behind, her father would not object to the property devolving upon them, as they were also his own grand-children. If, however, the daughter left no issue

[14] तस्मादभर्तृरिच्छया भार्याया अपि द्रव्यविभागो भवत्येव न स्वेछया ॥
Ibid., *on Yaj.*, II, 52.

behind, her father would claim the property back from the son-in-law, who was expected to contract a fresh marriage in due course. Smṛiti writers expressly declare that the Strīdhana of a woman, married according to the Āsura form of marriage, where bride price has to be paid by the husband, would revert to her parents or brothers, if she left behind no issues.[15] This rule makes it quite clear that one of the ingredients of Strīdhana was a portion of the bride price, returned to the bride by her father. The husband therefore had to recognise his bride's ownership in it. The bride used to spend this gift usually in the purchase of ornaments for herself and utensils and furniture for her new household.[16]

Even when no bride price was paid, the bride used to receive some wedding gifts in the Vedic age. *Pāriṇṇhya* was the term used to denote them, and Vedic texts declare that the wife was to be their owner.[17] Gifts given on such occasions usually consisted of ornaments and clothes that could be worn by women alone. Men could have utilised them only by sale. In Hindu society there is, however, a deep prejudice against this procedure in connection with ornaments and clothes worn on auspicious occasions. Women therefore were naturally allowed to own these gifts. Whether the Vedic age allowed them to dispose of these articles without their husbands' consent, we do not know. Probably such a procedure was not permitted.

In course of time the scope of Strīdhana was enlarged. Gifts given by the husband even subsequent to the marriage were included in it. These were often extensive and would sometimes include even the whole of the husband's property. Women came to be gradually invested with full powers over the property thus conveyed to them. At, the time of his impending retirement Yājñavalkya proceeds to divide his whole property equally between his two wives. Under similar circumstances Dharmadinnā was informed by her husband that she could take away as much of his property as she liked, and retire to her parent's house (*Thg*., 12). In both these cases the clear intention was to convey full rights of ownership to the wife over the whole of the family property.

That women could exercise absolute control over such gifts which constituted their Strīdhana, was a principle that came to be recognised fairly early in Hindu society There were no doubt archaic texts which declared that wives, like sons and slaves, could own no property; whatever they acquired would be the property of their husbands.[18] Commentators, however, boldly declared that these texts had no application to the present. age. It is interesting to note that even writers like Baudhāyana, who refuse to recognise the wife's right

---

[15] अप्रजस्त्राधन भतुर्ब्राह मादिषु चतुर्ष्वपि
।दुहितृणां प्रसूता चेच्छेषेशु पितृगामि तत् ।।

Yāj., II, 145.

[16] The Gerade of the Saxons, which corresponded to Strīdhana, also usually consisted of women's dress, ornaments and household furniture.

[17] पत्नी, वै पारीणाहचस्य ईशे ।

T. S., VI, 2, I, I.

[18] भार्या पुत्रश्च दासश्च त्रयएवाधनाः स्मृताः।
त्ते समधिगच्छन्तियस्य तै तस्य तद्धनम् ।।

Manu, VIII, 416.

of inheritance, freely concede her title to Strīdhana[19]. Manu also does the same, though he does not recognise the widow as an heir to her husband. It is needless to add that writers like Vishṇu and Yājñavalkya, who recognise the widow as an heir, naturally concede proprietary rights to women over Strīdhana. All later writers do. the same.

The Vedic literature is silent about the precise scope of Strīdhana. We get an idea of its scope only from the Dharmaśāstra works. Manu is the earliest writer to give a comprehensive description of Strīdhana. According to him it consists of six varieties; (1–3) gifts given by the father, the mother and the brother at any time; (4) gifts of affection given by the husband subsequent to the marriage and (5 and 6) presents given by anybody either at the time of the marriage, or at the time when the bride is taken to her new home.[20] Gifts under most of these categories would consist usually of ornaments and costly apparel, and Manu is very vehement in denouncing those who would deprive women of these presents after their husbands' death.[21] Vishṇu (XVII, 18) adds three more categories to Strīdhana, (a) gifts given by the son, (b) or any other relation (c) and the compensation given to the wife at the time of her supersession on the occasion of her husband's second marriage. The above distinction in the different varieties of Strīdhana are not of great importance; suffice it to say that it mainly consisted of gifts given by relations, either at the time of the marriage or subsequent to it.

It is interesting to note that gifts given by non-relatives subsequent to the marriage, and the wages earned by the wife for her work are not included in Strīdhana. The exclusion of these two items is not difficult to understand. It was not advisable to encourage women to elicit presents from outsiders, for it would have led to serious complications in families presided over by jealous husbands. Inclusion of wages in Strīdhana would also have been unfair. They were usually earned only by the women of the working classes, whose budgets can never be balanced even today without including the earnings of women and children. Under these circumstances it would have been manifestly unfair to credit the wife's wages to her Strīdhana and call upon the husband to shoulder the entire burden of the family. Hindu jurists felt that the earnings of both the husband and the wife should be dedicated to the needs of the family. They have, however, failed to provide relief to the wife in case her husband were to squander his own earnings and compel the wife to support the family by her own wages. The law is still defective on this point and requires to be amended.

---

19 मातुरलकार दुहितरः सांप्रदायिकं भजेरन्नन्यद्वा ॥
B. D. S., II, 2, 44.

20 अध्यग्न्यध्यावहनिकं दन्तं च प्रीतिकर्मणि।
भ्रातृमातृपितृप्राप्तं षड्विधं स्त्रीधनं स्मृंतम्॥
IX, 194.

21 स्त्रीधनानि तु ये मोहादुपजीवन्ति मानवाः।
नारीयानानि वस्त्रं वा ते पापा यान्त्यधोगतिम् ॥
III, 52.
पत्यौ जीवति यः स्त्रीभिरलंकारो धृतो भवेत् ।
न तं भजेरन्दायादा भजमानाः पतंति ते॥
IX, 200.

From about the seventh century AD, we find a general tendency to enlarge the scope of Strīdhana. Devala is seen including maintenance and accidental gains under it.[22] But it was left to Vijñāneśvara to propose most extensive additions to the scope of Strīdhana. Taking advantage of the word *ādyam* 'etcetera' which Yājñavalkya has used at the end of the enumeration of the usual six varieties of Stridhana, this commentator declares that the expression in question is used in order to include the property acquired by inheritance, purchase, partition, chance, and adverse possession.[23] This amplified definition of Strīdhan is so comprehensive that it will include every type of property in the possession of a woman, howsoever it may have been acquired by her.

There can be no doubt that the original verses in *yājnavalkya smṛiti*, which are quoted in the foot note below,[24] did not contemplate the inclusion of any of the categories mentioned by Vijñāneśvara within the scope of Strīdhana. It is even doubtful whether the crucial term *ādyam*, which is Vijñāneśvara's sole justification for the amplification of the definition of Strīdhana, really occurred in the original verse of Yājñavalkya. Jīmūtavāhana contends that the correct reading is '*Ādhivedanikaṁ chaiva*' and not *Ādhivedanikādyam cha*' The word '*ādyam*' is generally used in Sanskrit at the end of an enumeration, so it should have come not after '*ādhivedanika*' in v. 143, but after, '*anvādheyakam*' in v. 144, which is the last specific category of Strīdhana mentioned by Yājñavalkya. Aparārka, who is one of the earliest commentators of Yājñavalkya, also reads *chaiva*, which seems to be the genuine reading of the verse.

But even supposing that the reading of Vijñaśvara is the genuine one, we have to concede that Yājñavalkya could hardly have intended to include items like inheritance and share at partition under the term 'etcetera'. These were very important items, which not only increased extensively the woman's rights, but circumscribed those of the coparceners. Yājñavalkya would surely have specifically and prominently mentioned them in his description of Strīdhana, instead of smuggling them surreptitiously under the term 'etcetera'. The word etcetera, if at all used by him, must have been obviously intended to include items like bride price, gifts from grandfather and other relation, and presents received after the marriage, which are mentioned in the immediately following line.

The above discussion will show that Vijñāneśvara has used one of the usual devices of Sanskrit commentators in order to enlarge the scope of Strīdhana. The credit of liberalising the law of Strīdhana therefore belongs to him and not to Yājñavalkya.

Hindu jurists of medieval times are divided as to the acceptability of the extended definition of Stridhana, as propounded by Vijñāneśvara. Majority of them, however, concur with him; Aparārka, Nanda Pandita Mitramiśra and Kāmalākara are prominent among them. Some, however, have refused to recognise his interpretation; Viśvarūpa, Devaṇabhaṭṭa and Jimūtavāhana are the chief among them.

---

22 वृत्तिराभरणं शुल्कं लाभश्च स्त्रीधनं भवेत् 11

23 आद्यशब्देन रिक्थकयसंविभागपरिग्रहाधिगमप्राप्तेमेतत्स्त्रीधनं मन्वादि-भिरुक्तम्।।
On *Yaj.*, II, 143.

24 पितृमातृपतिभ्रातृदत्तमध्यग्न्युपागतम्।
आधिवेदनिकाघदयं च स्त्रीधनं परिकीर्तितम्।।
बन्धुदत्तं तथा शुल्कमन्वाधेयकमेव च।।

This cleavage in the opinions of the jurists shows that society was following no uniform practice in the matter of recognizing the scope of Strīdhana. There are, however, no actual recorded cases to show how far the items mentioned by Vijñāneśvara were actually included within the scope of Strīdhana in medieval, times. The fact, however, that a large number of his successors uphold his opinion, would show that society was to a great extent following his lead.

Let us now consider the extent of the power which women possessed over their Strīdhana. We have no discussion about this point in early works. Vedic literature, for instance, is silent as to whether the wife could dispose of her property (Pāriṇāhaya) without her husband's permission. As secular law and its literature developed in course of time, the question began to be discussed by jurists. Early Smṛiti writers were not prepared to invest the woman with full powers over her Strīdhana. Manu for instance, declares that a wife ought not to alienate even her own property without her husband's sanction.[25] In course of time it was felt that this prohibition was not equitable. With a view to be fair to all the parties, later jurists divided Strīdhana into two categories, *saudāyika* and *asaudāyika.* Free gifts of affection given by relations like the father, the mother, or the husband were included in the first category[26] and were declared to be under the complete control of women.[27] The rest of the Strīdhana was *asaudāyika* Stridhana; women could not alienate it, but only enjoy its usufruct during their life time.

Originally Strīdhana consisted usually of ornaments and costly clothes. In course of time landed property also began to be conveyed to women as Strīdhana property. Jurists of the 7th and the 8th centuries discuss the question as to whether women possess full powers of ownership over the immovable property so acquired. As may be expected, opinion was divided on the point. Kātyāyana holds that women possess the power of sale and mortgage even over the immovable property included in their Strīdhana.[28] Nārada differs from him and declares that women can dispose of only the movables in their Strīdhana.[29] Medieval writers generally concur with this view.[30]

The reason why women were not granted full rights over the landed property included in their Strīdhana are not difficult to understand. In the vast majority of cases, it used to be a gift from the husband, and so it originally belonged to the property of the joint family. It was not in the interest of the latter to allow a coparcener to fritter away its resources by allow-

---

[25] न निर्हारं स्त्रियः कुयुः कुटुम्बाद्बहुमध्यगात्।
स्वकादपि हि विताद्वि स्वस्य भर्त्तरमाशया।।
IX, 299.

[26] ऊढया कन्यया वापि पत्युः पितृगृहेऽथवा।
भ्रातुः सकाशात्पित्रोर्वा लब्धं सौदायिकं स्मृतम्।। Kātyāyana in *Dāyabhāga*.

[27] सौदायिकं धनं प्राप्य स्त्रीणां स्वातंत्र्यमिष्यते।
यस्मातदानृशंस्यार्थं तैर्दत्तं तत्प्रयोजनम।। Kātyāyana in *Dāyabhāga*.

[28] सौदायिके सदा स्त्रीणां स्वातंत्र्यं परिकीर्तितम्।
विकये चैव दाने च यथेच्छं स्थावरेष्वपि।। Kātyāyana in *Dāyabhāga*.

[29] भर्त्ता प्रीतेन यद्दत्तं स्त्रियै तस्मिन्मृतेऽपि तत्।
सा यथाकाम्मश्नीयाद्यद्याद्वा स्थावरादृते।। Queted in Vyavahāramayūkha, p. 97.

[30] एवं च सौदायिके स्थावरेतरप्रीतिदते च स्त्रीणां स्वातंत्र्यमन्यत्र तु स्त्रीधनेऽपि अस्वातंत्र्यमिति मन्तव्यम्।। *S. C. V.*, p. 650.

ing him to make an unconditional gift to his wife from the family property. The gifts were regarded as valid only during the life of the donees. The latter were not allowed to alienate them to any of their cognatic relations. Similar considerations operated when the property in question was received by the woman from her father. The latter's agnatic relations were not prepared to tolerate his conduct, if he proceeded to permanently alienate a portion of the immovable property of the family. Patriarchal joint families in ancient times were too much attached to their ancestral possessions to allow their transfer to a cognatic relation.

The question of the power of alienation of the Strīdhana property was approached by the Bengal school of the medieval times on different lines. Its famous exponent Jīmūtavāhana felt that it was illogical to increase the scope of Strīdhana, and then to curtail women's powers of disposal over it. He argued that it would be proper to describe only that much property as Strīdhana, which women are allowed to dispose of according to their own free will. He therefore limited the scope of Strīdhana by refusing to recognise its amplified definition, as given in the Mitāksharā school, but conceded to women full proprietary rights over its time-honoured six varieties.

Did Vijñāneśvara intend to invest women with full proprietary rights over the whole of his amplified Strīdhana? It is a great pity that he should not have specifically discussed this important question. We are therefore driven to mere inferences. It is possible to argue that there is nothing improbable in Vijñāneśvara having intended to give full rights to women even over the landed property acquired by inheritance or partition, and included in their Strīdhana. Women will get property by inheritance, usually when their husbands had separated from the joint family and died without leaving any male issues. The husband's action in effecting a separation from the joint family had put an end to its interest in his separated the family was in great distress, the husband could utilise his wife's Strīdhana to tide over the difficulty. No other member of the family, however, could do so. Jurists differ as to whether the Strīdhana utilised by the husband to meet abnormal times was to be returned back to the wife. Yājñavalkya thinks that it need not repaid.[31] Kātyāyana holds that if the husband had promised to return it, he ought to keep his word. [32] An agreement by husband to give some property as Strīdhana was binding on his estate; if he died without completing it, his next heirs were required to carry it out.[33] Adverse possession could not deprive a woman of her title to Strīdhana.[34]

---

[31] दुर्भिक्षे धर्मकार्ये च व्याधौ सम्प्रतिरोधके ।
गृहीतं स्त्रीधनं भर्त्ता न स्त्रियै दातुमर्हति ।।
Yāj., II, 147.

The *Mitāksharā* explains:
भर्तु व्यतिरेकेण जीवन्त्या धनं न केनापि दायादेन ग्रहीतव्यम्।

[32] व्याधितं व्यसनस्थं च धनिकैर्वोपपीडितम्।
ज्ञात्वा निसृष्टं यत्प्रीत्या दद्यावात्मेच्छया तु सः ।।
Quoted in *S. C. V.*, p. 659.

[33] भर्त्रा प्रतिश्रुतं देयमृणवत्स्त्रीधनं सुतैः ।
Kātyāyana in *scv*., pp. 658 9.

[34] स्त्रीधनं च नरेन्द्राणां न कथंचन जीर्यते। *Nārada*, III. 83.
अनागमं भुज्यमानं वत्सराणां श्तैरपि ।

It is only rarely that we come across a discussion of the effects of unchas l tity on the right to Strīdhana. Devala has discussed this topic and declared that an unchaste woman forfeits her title to Strīdhana.[35] This seems to have been the general view. British courts, however, refused to follow it and recognised women's title to Strīdhana in spite of her unchastity.

The scheme of the inheritance of Strīdhana is a very complicated one and it has many provincial variations. We need not discuss the details of the problem here, as they would interest only the professional lawyer; it is sufficient for our purpose to refer to general principles. If a woman dies without leaving any issues, and if her marriage had taken place by any of the unapproved forms of marriage like the Āsura, Rākshasa, etc., her Strīdhana reverts to her parents or brothers.[36] The reason for this rule is the general presumption that the Strīdhana in such cases must have mainly consisted of the bride price, which was voluntarily returned by the father to his daughter for her use during coverture. If she dies leaving some issues behind, her Strīdhana would devolve upon them. Her father or brother would not naturally mind allowing the property to be inherited by them; but if she died issueless, the Strīdhana or the bride price was demanded back. The law at present presumes that all marriages take place by the approved forms, and so this rule of inheritance of Strīdhana is only of historical interest. Strīdhana now reverts to the husband, if the wife dies without issues.

A vast majority of jurists from, early times lay down that Strīdhana should devolve upon daughters. It usually consisted of ornaments and clothes, which could be used by women alone; so it was deemed to be in the fitness of things that they should be inherited by daughters. It is true that if they had devolved upon sons, their wives could very well have utilised the articles concerned. But women feel a greater affection for their daughters than for their daughters-in-law, and this circumstance determined the line of the succession. Among daughters, unmarried ones were to be preferred to married ones, and among the latter, the first claim was of those who were not well-to-do.[37] This devolution is governed just by those principles, which would appeal to an impartial and affectionate mother. In some schools, if there were no daughters living, the Strīdhana devolved upon daughter's daughters. Such cases, however, were few in practice.

ln patriarchal societies there is a general prejudice against property passing to female heirs; so this principle of allowing Strīdhana to devolve on daughters did not appeal to a large section of Hindu community. As long as Strīdhana consisted of a few gifts given at the time of the marriage, its devolution upon daughters did not meet with much opposition. In course of time, however, gifts given by the husband during the married life came to be included in Strīdhana. The motive of the husband was no doubt to provide. the wife against

---

35 अपकारकियायुक्ता निर्मर्यादार्थनाशिका ।
व्यभिचाररताया च स्त्रीधनं न च सार्हति ।
Quoted in *VMV.*, p. 98.

36 अप्रजस्त्रीधनं भर्तुर्ब्राह्मादिषु चतुर्ष्वपि।
दुहितृणां प्रसूता चेच्छेशेषु पितृगामि तत्।।
Yāj., II, 145.

37 तत्र चोढानूढासमवाये अनूढैव गृहह्णाति । तदभावे परिणीता । तत्रापि प्रतिष्ठिताप्रतिष्ठितासमवायेप्रतिष्ठिता गृह् णाति । तदभावे प्रतिष्ठिता ।
Mitāksharā on *Yāj.*, II, 145.

a rainy day, but he rarely intended to do so at the cost of his sons. His usual expectation was that the property should pass on to his sons after the death of his wife. Some jurists therefore felt that the most equitable course was to allow both the sons and the daughters to inherit the Strīdhana of their mother. This course is recommended by Manu;[38] we may well presume that he is very probably referring to the Strīdhana property given by the husband, though he does not say so in so many words. The Bengal, Mithilā, Madras and Gujarat schools of the Hindu Law rely upon the above view of Manu, when they lay down that Strīdhana consisting of gifts received from the husband subsequent to the marriage should devolve equally upon daughters and sons.[39]

There are many other minor details about the inheritance of Strīdhana. As they do not throw any light on the position of women, they are of interest only to the practising lawyer. We therefore need not discuss them here.

The above survey of the history of Strīdhana shows that it was recognised very early in the history of Hindu civilisation. Maxims of prehistoric times declaring that women can hold no property independently of their husbands were no doubt included in law books down to the fifth century AD; but they were not allowed to affect the development of Strīdhana. Its scope went on gradually increasing, till eventually, in some schools at least, it came to include all the varieties of property that a woman may happen to own. It is probable that the jurists, who included in Strīdhana even the property acquired by inheritance and partition, did not intend to invest women with the right of its alienation. Nevertheless it is indisputable that the allowed them at least a life estate in it; this concession was indeed a remarkable one for the age. Over Strīdhana in its narrower sense women possessed absolute ownership; they could dispose of it at their own will, and their husbands had no right over it. It is true that in times of exceptional difficulties Strīdhana could be used for the general needs of the family, but that was a liability that could not be equitably avoided It is worth noting that some jurists have laid down that Strīdhana spent even on such occasions ought to be refunded to women on the return of prosperity to the family.

The survey of the scope and the development of Strīdhana discloses that a considerable regard was shown to the economic needs of the weaker sex. The law, as it was developed by Vijñāneśvara, was no doubt remarkably liberal for his age, for it included all property, howsoever acquired, under the category of Strīdhana. It is true that Vijñāneśvara probably did not intend to give women the full right of disposal over the immovable property, acquired through inheritance or partition. Women, however, had no right to complain in the matter, for male coparceners also had no such unrestricted right even over their own self acquired property.

This history of Strīdhana is undoubtedly a proud and glorious chapter in the story of Hindu civilisation. It discloses a constant and continuous tendency in Hindu society to increase the scope of Strīdhana, usually at the expense of men's rights.

---

[38] जनन्यां संस्थितायां तु समं सर्वे सहोदराः ।
भजेरत्मातृकं रिक्थ जनन्यश्च सनाभयः ॥

[39] IX, 192.

2. *Dāyabhāga*, IV, 9–12, *Mayūkha*, IX; *SCV*., p. 656.

Women were also invested with the right of its independent disposal; even the husband could not touch it save under exceptional circumstances. This state of affairs compares very favourably with that in England, where down to 1870 AD, marriage suspended the very legal existence of the wife, whose entire property, whether inherited or self-acquired, automatically passed under the husband's control at the very moment of her marriage, unless secured by a previous settlement.

Only a few words are necessary in connection with the future development of the Strīdhana law. All the categories included in Strīdhana by Hindu jurists have been recognised by modern courts. They however hold that the property, which the widow inherits from her husband, is not Strīdhana in the technical sense, and that she cannot therefore dispose of it at her own free will. How far the law should be changed in this respect will be considered in the next chapter, where the widow's right of inheritance will be discussed in detail.

Smṛitis have laid down that any income, which a wife will acquire by her own exertions, will not be her Strīdhana, but will be merged in the general income of the family. We have already shown above (*ante*, pp. 220–21) how this apparently unreasonable rule came to be laid dawn. Circumstances have, however, changed now. It is but fair to admit that what an educated wife earns as a teacher, or a professor, or a doctor, or an uneducated wife as a field labourer or a factory worker, should be primarily regarded as her own property. The husband should have no right over it. It should be left entirely to the wife, as to what portion of her earnings she would devote to the general family expenditure. In. actual practice it would be found that a woman factory worker, for instance, will spend a lesser amount on herself than her husband would do, out of the wages they receive from their employer. The modern woman has developed her own individuality and would not like to surrender the ownership over her own earnings even to her husband. Married women, who earn a livelihood, are however few. Gifts received at the time of marriage are not many or valuable in the present age and they are not useful for daily expenditure. Strīdhana obtained as an heir to the husband after his death becomes available during widowhood when a woman has hardly any enthusiasm to utilise it. Instead of enlarging the scope of the old items in Strīdhana, the modern woman would desire the recognition of a new item, viz., a share in the monthly or annual income of her husband.

In spite of the spacious theory of the joint ownership the husband is usually the *de facto* controller of the family purse. The present age is an individualistic one and the modern wife, whether educated or uneducated, often feels that it should not be necessary for her to get the sanction of her husband for every little expenditure that she may have to incur on her behalf. In order to get over the embarrassing situations often arising on such occasions, she often feels that it would have been much better if she had a share in her father's property, the income of which she could have spent at her own free will. There are, however, several serious difficulties in the way of giving the daughter a share in the patrimony, as will be shown in the next chapter (Section I). It has, however, to be admitted that owing to inherited traditions, the husband is often inclined to assume a patronising air when sanctioning any expenditure for the wife which is not relished by him. It has further to be recognised that whether in the west or in the east, there is not yet a proper appreciation of the unpaid work for the household, which the wife ungrudgingly does for the common welfare of the family.

Gifts from the husband form an important item in the Strīdhan as envisaged by Hindu jurists, and its scope went on gradually increasing in course of time. The difficulties of the modern sensitive wife, above referred to, will disappear if the law enjoined that a small percentage of the monthly income of the husband shall be given to the wife as her Strīdhana, to be spent by her at her own sweet will, either for her own sake of for the sake of the family. An orientation in the development of Strīdhana on this line is necessary in the modern individualistic age. It will immensely help in increasing the happiness of many a family.

Chapter 12

Proprietary Rights: Inheritance and Partition*

ANANT SADASHIV ALTEKAR

We shall continue here our story of the development of the proprietary rights of women. We surveyed in the last chapter the position of the wife, *vis-à-vis* her husband, regarding the ownership of the family property, and discussed the evolution of Strīdhana. It was all along a story of gradual but continuous progress. In this chapter we shall discuss the rights of inheritance and partition, which are undoubtedly more important than the right to Strīdhana. As already shown in previous chapters, the angle of vision with which the daughter, the wife and the widow were looked upon varied in different ages. Naturally, therefore, the development of their rights of inheritance and partition proceeded on different lines. It would be therefore convenient to discuss it separately. The present chapter is therefore divided into four sections; the first three deal with the rights of inheritance of the daughter, the widow and other female relations respectively, and the last one with the rights at partition.

SECTION I: DAUGHTER'S RIGHT OF INHERITANCE

A reference has been already made to an old saying that a son, a wife and a slave can own no property independently of the father, the husband and the master (*ante*, p. 219, n. 1). The daughter is obviously intended to be included here under the son. In more than one place in the later Vedic literature we come across the view that women have no right of inheritance.[1]

There is no doubt that in very early times there was a general prejudice against property devolving upon female heirs by inheritance. The daughter formed no exception. She was often expected to increase the assets of her father's family by bringing a bride price. That she

* Previously published in Anant Sadashiv Altekar's *Position of Women in Hindu Civilization: From Pre-Historical Times to the Present Day*, Motilal Banarsidass Publishers, Varanasi and Delhi (1959), pp. 234–78.

[1] तस्मात्स्त्रियो निरिन्द्रिया अदायादी: ।

T. S. VI, 5, 8 2.

ता (स्त्रिय)नात्मनश्चैशत न दायस्य चैशत । *S. Br.*, IV, 4, 2, 13.

should get a share in and decrease the corpus of her father's property would have appeared as very preposterous to men at the down of civilisation. The very conception of Strīdhana shows that women could normally get property only by way of gifts from their relations at or subsequent to their marriage. There was no possibility of their acquiring any estate either by inheritance or by partition.

Among the female heirs the brotherless daughter was the first to succeed in establishing her right of inheritance. Circumstances were more favourable for the recognition of her right than that of the wife or the widow. As shown in the last chapter in the patriarchal atmosphere the wife could advance no claim in competition with her husband. The widow often used to marry or get a son by Niyoga; so the problem of her inheritance did not arise in society in anyacute form. We have already shown (*ante*, pp. 10–11) how the daughter in the Vedic age was well educated and possessed full religious privileges. Probably she could not herself offer funeral oblations to the manes, but she could get this done by her son. For all religious purposes the Vedic father could thus regard a daughter to be as good as a son.[2] He had a strong prejudice against adopting a son.[3] He therefore preferred property passing to his own daughter in preference to a stranger, who by a religious fiction, was to be regarded as an adoptive son. He could also usually arrange for the perpetuation of his own family by making an agreement with the son-in-law that he should send backhis first son to continue his maternal grandfather's family.

Amongst women, a brotherless daughter was thus the first to get her right of inheritance recognised. This happened as early as the time of the *Ṛigveda*, for there is no doubt that one of its early hymns refers to a brotherless daughter getting her share of patrimony.[4] This right of inheritance, however, was not an unmixed blessing. The Vedic age put a high premium on the son, and sons-in-law were unwilling to allow their first-born son to revert back to the families of their maternal grandfathers. In the present age there is a keen competition for the hand of a maiden, who is her father's heir; in the Vedic age she found it not always easy to marry and had often to remain a spinster.[5] Even when the father of a brotherless daughter gave an assurance that he did not regard her as a Putrikā and would not claim her

---

[2] It is true that in Dharmaśāstra literature, generally the son of a Putrikā is classed as a substitute for a real son; in early times, however, in some localities the daughter herself and not her son was regarded as the substitute. Thus *V.D.S.* XVII, 15 states तृतीया पुत्रिका and not पुत्रिकापुत्र. A similar conclusion can be drawn from *Manu* IX, 134. From the *Rājataraṅgiṇī* we find that Queen Kalyāṇadevi, wife of King Jayāpiḍa, was herself regarded as a Putrikā by her father. A nineteenth century Pandit of Kashmir had done the same at the same time of Dr. Būhler's visit to that state.

[3] न हि प्रभायारण: सशेवोऽन्योदर्यो मनसा मन्तवा उ ।

R.V., VII, 4, 8.

[4] अभ्रातेव पुंस एति प्रतीची गर्तारूगिव सनये धनानाम्

R.V., I, 124, 7.

[5] अमूर्या: सन्ति जामय: सर्वा लोहितवासस: ।
अभ्रातर इव योत्रास्तिष्ठन्तु हतवर्त्मन: ।।

A.V., I, 17, I.

यास्क comments: अभ्रातृकाया अनिर्वाह औपमिक:।

III, 5.

son, prospective bridegrooms feared that there might be a mental reservation behind the promise.[6] They would usually refuse to accept the daughter and her estate.

There is evidence to show that the right of a brotherless daughter to inherit her father's estate continued to be recognised down to c. 400 BC. In the *Therīgāthā* we come across an interesting incident. We find a mother trying to dissuade her daughter Sundarī from entering the nunnery by pointing out that she had become a full heir to her father's extensive estate as the latter had become a monk; she should therefore think of marriage and pleasure, and not of nunnery and penance.[7] It is clear from this story that a brotherless daughter was recognised as an heir in north-eastern India during the fifth century BC.

By about 200 BC girls ceased to be educated and began to be married at an early age. There was a general deterioration in the status of women, who were gradually losing their religious privileges. All this tended to adversely affect the proprietary rights of the daughter. A school came into existence which opposed her right of inheritance, even when she had no brothers. Āpastamba reluctantly allows daughter to inherit, but only if there is no *sapiṇḍa* or teacher or pupil to claim the property. This was a very remote possibility, for agnates include relations up to the seventh degree. He would rather prefer the property to be given to a public cause than to a daughter.[8] Vasishṭha (XV, 7) and Gautama (XXVIII, 21) do not mention the daughter in the list of their heirs. The same is the case with Manu.[9]

The majority of jurists, however, wanted to continue the old tradition, and allow the daughter to inherit her patrimony, if there were no son.

The *Mahābhārata* in one place maintains that it would be manifestly unfair and inequitable to allow a subsidiary son to get an inheritance, when there was a daughter to claim it.[10] She must at least get half the property, if not the whole.[11] Kauṭilya is also inclined to recognise the daughter as an heir, though perhaps to a smaller share (III, 5).

Yājñāvalkya, as may be expected, warmly champions the cause of the daughter and lays down that she should be the next heir after the son and the widow (II, 135). Bṛihaspati tries to disarm the opposition by sweet reasonableness. He points out that the daughter springs from one's own body just like the son; how then can anyone inherit the property, when she

---

[6] अभिसंधिमात्रात्पुत्रिकेत्येके
G.D.S. XXIX, 17; see also *V.D.S.*, XV, 5.

[7] पिता पब्बजितो तुम्हं भुंज भोगानि सुन्दरि त्वं दायादिका कुले।
Thg. no. 327.

[8] पुत्राभावे यः प्रत्यासत्रः सपिण्डः । तदभावे आचार्यः। आचार्या-भावे अन्तेवासी हत्वा धर्मकृत्येषु योजयेत् । दुहिता वा ।
II, 14, 234.

[9] न भ्रातरो न पितरः पुत्रा रिक्थहराः पितुः ।
पिता हरेदपुत्रस्य रिक्थं भ्रातर एव च ॥
Kullūka takes the expression पत्नीदुहितृरहितस्य as understood in the second line in order to support his view that Manu admits the daughter as an heir to her father. There is nothing in the text or context to support this assumption.

[10] यथैवात्मा तथा पुत्रः पुत्रेण दुहिता समा ।
तस्यामात्मनि तिष्ठन्त्यो कथमन्यां धनं हरेत ।
XIII, 80, II.
दुहितान्यत्र जातादि पुत्रादपि विशिष्यते ।

[11] अभ्रातृका समग्राह्रा चार्धार्हेत्यपरे बिदुः ।
XIII, 88, 22.

is still alive (XXV, 55)? Nārada advances a similar argument. Is not the daughter as much the child of her parents as the son[12]? How then can her right of inheritance be defeated in the absence of the latter?

There was a school of jurists which suggested that a brotherless daughter should be regarded as an heir only till she was married and well settled in life. Kātyāyana was its chief exponent.[13] Hindu society, however, refused to accept this opinion, and the school of Yājñavalkya, Nārada and Bṛihaspati eventually carried the day. From c. 500 AD nobody has called into question a daughter's right to inherit her father's property in the absence of a brother. The right has been recognised also by the modern courts.

The estate which a daughter inherits is usually a limited one. It is an absolute one only in the Bombay State. Everywhere else she acquires only a life estate. The Bombay custom of allowing the daughter to become an absolute owner of her patrimony is at least as old as the thirteenth century.

An inscription of this period, discovered in Kolhapur, refers to the sale of a piece of land by a woman, who had inherited it from her father.[14] The Bombay law on this point has been working smoothly and has caused no havoc in the joint family. It is now high time that it should be extended to other states as well.

DAUGHTERS WITH BROTHERS

Let us now consider the rights of inheritance of a daughter who has brothers. Patriarchal traditions were reigning supreme at the dawn of the Aryan history, and they were not favourable for the recognition of a daughter's right of inheritance in competition with a brother. From c. 300 BC marriage became obligatory for girls, and society felt that they should get proprietary rights in the families of their husbands and not in those of their fathers.

In the earlier period, however, girls were fairly well educated, and very often they would remain unmarried either by choice or by the force of circumstances. In such cases it was recognised that they ought to be allowed to have a share in their fathers' property. A Vedic stanza expressly refers to an old maiden claiming her share in her patrimony.[15] Usually, however, daughters married, and then they did not get any share in their patrimony. A Vedic

---

[12] पुत्राभावे तु दुहिता तुल्यसंतानकारणात्।
XIII, 50.

[13] पत्नी पत्युर्धनहरी या स्यादव्यभिचारिणी ।
तदभावे तुदुहिता यधनूढा भवेत्तदा ॥
Quoted in the *Mitāksharā* on *rāj.* II, 135–36. See also SCV., p. 687.

[14] सोमेश्वरभट्टस्य दुहितुः सकाशाद्गृहीत्वा पूर्वोक्तब्राहाणेभ्यो दत्तवान ।
E.I., Vol. III, p. 215.

[15] अमाजूरिव पित्रोः सचा सती समानदा सदसस्त्वामिये भगम्।
कृधि प्रकेतमुप मास्या भर दद्धि भागं तन्वा येन मामहः ॥
R.V., II, 17, 7.

poet expressly informs the brother that he should not give any share to his sister; she is after all to migrate to a different family.[16]

It has been argued that there was a school of jurists, no doubt representing a small minority, which favoured the recognition of the right of inheritance of the daughter along with the son as early as c. 500 BC. The only evidence for this view is a passage in the *Nirukta*. where arguments are undoubtedly advanced to support the daughter's claim. The passage in question is, however, a clear interpolation. We may nevertheless examine here the arguments advanced in it. We find that the champions of the daughter's claim were mainly relying on the authority of two old verses. The first of these occurs in the *Ṛigveda*.[17] Unfortunately it is a very obscure stanza difficult to interpret with certainty. It appears to refer to an agreement by the father of an only daughter with his son-in-law to the effect that his first son will revert to the maternal grandfather to continue his family. At any rate it does not refer to any right of inheritance of a daughter, who had brothers as well. The second authority relied upon by this school is a stanza, which it attributes to Manu.[18] This verse does not, however, occur in the present *Manusmṛiti* and it contradicts its views on this point enunciated elsewhere in the book. Further, it has to be pointed out that it does not at all support a daughter's right to inherit along with sons. To argue that the term *mithunānām* in this verse governs the word *putrāṇām*, the joint expression *mithanānām putrāṇām* meaning children of both the sexes, is a procedure that can hardly be justified. The expression *mithunānām* refers to parents, and the author of the verse opines that parents should divide their estate equally among their sons, without assigning a special share to the first-born, as recommended by some early jurists.

It therefore appears that if there was really a school of jurists in the sixth century BC, which wanted to champion the cause of daughters' inheritance, even when they had brothers, it could adduce no really authoritative texts in its support. The passage in the *Nirukta*, where this discussion occurs, is very probably a later interpolation. It is therefore extremely doubtful whether any such school at all existed in early times.

The general opinion of Hindu society was that sisters should get no share in the patrimony, if they had brothers. This is the opinion of the Dharmaśāstra literature, and Kauṭilya concurs with it.[19] There is only one writer, who assigns a small share to the daughter along with sons. It is Śukra. Śukrāchārya, the famous teacher of the Asuras, loved his daughter Devayānī

---

[16] नजामये तान्वो रिफ्माश्मारैक चकार गर्भ सनिंतुर्निधानम

R.V., III, 31, 2.

[17] शासद्वह् निर्दुहितुर्नप्त्यं ब्तस्य दीधिति. सपर्यन् ।
पिता यत्र दुहितुः सेकमृज्जन् संशग्म्येन मनसा संदधन् वै ॥

III, 31, I.

[18] अविशेषेण पुत्रणां दायो भवति धर्मतः
मिथुनानां निसर्गादौ मनुः स्वायं भवस्त्रतीत।। स्वायंभवस्त्रतीत ।

Nirukta, III, 4.

[19] अयादा दुहिता ।

III, 6.

dearer than his own life. It is therefore in the fitness of things that he should have been the only Smriti writer to assign a small share to the daughter, even when she had brothers.[20]

Śukra lays down that if a person divides his property in his own life time, he should assign one share each to his wife and sons, half a share to his daughters, and one fourth a share to his daughters's sons. If the division took place after his death, the sister was to get one eighth the share of the brother.[21] In actual practice the division of property usually takes place after the death of the father; so even under Śukra's dispensation, the daughter got only a very small share in the patrimony.

Śukra seems to be the only jurist, who has championed the cause of a daughter's share in her patrimony, even if she were not brotherless.

Vishṇu[22] and Nārada[23] also apparently seem to have recommended the same course; but their intention does not appear to have been to allow the daughter to take away her share after the marriage. Nārada expressly declares that the daughter's share in the patrimony was intended only for her maintenance till her marriage.[24]

Though Śukra was in a hopeless minority, his scheme of inheritance appealed to some sections of the community. There is evidence to show that some fathers used to follow the principle recommended by Śukra and divide their property both among their sons and daughters. This was probably the case when the property was self-acquired. We actually come across such a case in a Mysore epigraph. An inscription, dated 1188 AD, refers to a gentleman named Māchi, partitioning his landed property both among his sons and daughters. The sons of the latter encroached upon the lands of the sons of the former; the epigraph refers to the settlement of the dispute.[25]

Smṛitis and inscriptions, which attest to a daughter being assigned a share in the patrimony, are exceptions and not the rule. The general opinion of society was that women should get shares, directly or indirectly, in the property of their husbands and not in that of their fathers. Marriages had become obligatory for girls by c. 300 BC, and so the cases of spinsters remaining unprovided did not at all arise in society in the subsequent period.

---

[20] *Sukraniti* as a whole is as late as about 1300 AD, and it is not impossible that its scheme of inheritance, which assigns the daughter a share equal to half that of the son, may be due to the influence of the Muslim law.

[21] समानभागा वै कार्या: पुत्रा: स्वस्य च वै स्त्रिय: ।
स्वभागार्धहरा कन्या दौहित्रास्तु तदर्धनाक् ।।
मृताधिपे तु पुत्राद्या उक्तभागहरा: स्मृता: ।
मात्रऽदधाच्च्तुर्थाष्ठं भगिन्यै भगिन्य मातुरधिकम् ।।
IV, 5, 299–300.

[22] मातर: पुत्रभागनुसारेण भागहारिण्य: । अनूढा दुहितरश्च ।
XVIII, 34.

[23] ज्येष्ठायांशो्धिको देय: कनिष्ठायावर: स्मृत: ।
समांशभाज: शेषा: स्युरप्रत्ता भगिनी तथा ।
XIII, 13.

[24] या तस्य दुहिता तस्या: पिज्योत्यो भरणे मत:।
आसंस्कारं भजेरस्तां: परतो विभृयात्पति:।।
XIII, 27.

[25] *E.C.*,VI Mudgere No. 24.

Since marriages had become obligatory for girls, it was naturally laid down that reasonable expenses in connection with them should be a charge on the family property. If a father died before his daughters had been wedded, the sons were bound to spend reasonable amounts for their suitable marriages out of the family estate. What precise amount a brother ought to spend for his sister's marriage could not obviously be laid down in the law books; it used to vary with the status and circumstances of each family. A general rule, however, has been laid down that a brother should spend for his sister's marriage an amount equal to a one fourth share.[26] The language used in this connection is rather vague, and is capable of the following three divergent interpretations. (a) Each brother should forswear one fourth the share he has received, and the amounts so pooled together should be equally divided among the sisters and spent for their marriages. In practice this principle was likely to lead to anomalies, if the sons and daughters in a family were not equal in number. Thus if there was only one sister and she had four or more brothers, her marriage portion was bound to be greater than the individual share of her brothers. If the above ratio of the brothers and sisters were reversed, the marriage share of a sister would have been very inadequate; it would have been one sixteenth the share of the brother or even less. (b) A second interpretation of the rule suggested that the property should be divided into as many shares as there are children, and daughters should be given one fourth of the share thus ascertained, This arrangement also is likely to produce anomalies similar to those mentioned in connection with the first interpretation. (c) A third school therefore has pointed out that the real intention of the jurists in laying down this rule is that the patrimony should be so divided that ultimately the resulting marriage share of each sister should be equal to one fourth the share of each brother. This interpretation is probably the one intended by our jurists.[27]

Hindu jurists, however, declare that their intention is not so much to assign a one fourth share to the daughter, as to make adequate provision for her marriage.[28] To get his sister married was the sacred duty of the brother, and if her one fourth share was insufficient for the purpose, the brother was required to spend an amount even equal to his own share.[29] Some jurists go to the extent of laying down that even if there were no family estate the brother ought to meet the marriage expenses of his sister from his self-acquired property.[30] If, on the other hand, the family property was extensive and the reasonable expenses of a suitable marriage did not amount to the legal one fourth share, the sister was not to take away with

---

[26] असस्कृतास्तु संस्कार्या भ्रातृभिः पूर्वसंस्कृतेः ।
भगिन्यश्च निजादंशाछत्वाशं तु तुरीयकम्।।
rāj., II, 124.
See also *Manu*, IX, 118.

[27] See *SCV*, pp. 625 ff; *VMV*., pp. 58I ff.

[28] कन्याभ्यश्च पितृद्रव्ये देयं वैवाहिकं वसु ।
Devala in *SCV*., p. 625.

[29] यदि संस्कारपर्याप्तमपि पितृधनं नास्ति तदा पुत्रसमभागितैव दुहितृणाम् ।
VMV., p. 582.

[30] अविघमाने पित्रर्ये स्वांभाादुद्धृत्य वा पुनः।
अवश्यकार्याः संस्कारा भ्रातृभिः पूर्वसंस्कृतैः।।
Nārada, XIII, 34.

her the balance unspent.[31] It will be thus seen that while anxious to make adequate provision for the marriage of a sister, Hindu jurists have disapproved of the principle that she should inherit a share along with her brothers, and carry it away with her after the marriage.

The reasons for this attitude are not difficult to understand. Marriage had become absolutely necessary for daughters. So there was no possibility of spinsters remaining unprovided. There was a general prejudice against the introduction of an outsider among the landholders of a village since early times. This, however, was inevitable if the daughter, who was usually married to some outsider either in a near or a distant village, was allowed to claim a share. We must further remember that down to the middle of the nineteenth century, communications were difficult and expensive, and it was not easy for a daughter or her husband to manage her landed property situated in a distant village. To give a share to the daughter in immovable property was thus not a feasible proposition. As far as the movables were concerned, she used to get a fair share in them as presents at the time of her marriage, or as an heir to Strīdhana estate. Hindu society therefore felt that the best way to provide for women was to invest them with proprietary rights in their husbands' estates, and not in their fathers' property.

Circumstances have however now changed, and the law of inheritance requires some alterations with regard to the daughter.

Marriage is no longer a necessary event in the life of every woman. A class of educated women is coming into existence who, either owing to the desire for social service or through the force of circumstances, do not get married. These ladies cannot obviously get any proprietary rights through the husband. The law, as it stands today, does not allow them any share in their fathers' property as well. So they remain altogether unprovided for. As we have shown above (*ante*, p. 239), such women used to get a share in their patrimony in Vedic times. We should revive this right today. As these women lead a single life, their family responsibilities would be naturally less than those of their married brothers; their share in the patrimony should be smaller than that of a married brother, who will have a family to provide for. It is therefore reasonable to suggest that the share of the unmarried sister should be half that of her married brother.

Should a daughter, who gets married, also receive a share in her patrimony even when she has a brother? In 1936 a bill was introduced in the Imperial Legislative Assembly, which *inter alia* sought to give the daughter the same share in the patrimony as the son. This clause, however, had to be withdrawn, as the public opinion was not in its favour. Later on a draft by the B. N. Rao Committee proposed, as suggested in the 1st edition of this work, that an unmarried daughter should get half a share; but this measure also could not pass. The same was the fate of a third bill (1952) which sought to give to the daughter half a share unconditionally. The Hindu Code Bill, now before the Parliament (Feb. 1956) seeks to give even to the married daughter a share in the patrimony equal to that of the brother.

[31] तस्मात्संस्कारोपयुक्तद्रव्यस्यैव दानमात्रं विवक्षितम् 1

VMV., p. 582.

अनूढा इति विशेषोपादानाच्च विवाहार्थे पुत्राभागानुसारिभागहरणं न पुनर्भ्रातृणामिव दुहितणां दायविभागर्थमिति गम्यते।

SCV., p. 625.

Opinion in society and the Parliament is sharply divided on this point and it is difficult to state whether the Bill will pass, if free voting is allowed.

A careful analysis of the whole situation will show that on the whole it will not be in the interest of society to grant this right to the daughter. In the first place she will find it difficult to exercise it. Division of the family property usually takes place after the death of the father. A daughter, who has been married, say ten years before this event, will not be having a precise idea of the movable property of her paternal family, as she will be spending most of this time in her new home. It may be that during this period her father's family may have sold part of its ornaments to tide over some difficulties. If, as a consequence of these transactions, which are usually kept secret, the movable property brought forward at the time of the partition is less than what it was at the time of her marriage, the daughter would feel that her brothers have conspired to cheat her of her legitimate share. On the other hand, it is very easy to conceal cash, jewellery and ornaments, and crafty brothers can easily defeat their sisters' rights by producing only a part of them. There are very few families that keep their movable property in the form of cash balances in banks. Misunderstanding and heartburning will therefore be difficult to avoid between brothers and sisters at the time of partition.

The allotment of a share in the immovable property is also fraught with difficulties. Holdings of land in India are already very small and uneconomic; their size will be reduced to half, if the daughter receives a share in the patrimony equal to that of the son. This will be a national calamity. It may be argued that the rights of the weaker sex should not be sacrificed even for avoiding a national economic calamity. There is a force in this argument But we would point out that there are further difficulties in the way. The daughter after her marriage will usually go away to a different village or town to live with her husband. She will therefore be an absentee landlord. The absentee landlord is already being expropriated in Bombay, and other States will soon adopt the same course. The daughter will thus not materially benefit by a share in the lands of her father.

It has further to be admitted that soon after her marriage, the centre of interest and affection of the daughter naturally shifts to her new home. She becomes more and more immersed in her own family and children, and has no opportunities as before of noticing the financial transactions of her father's family. It would be unfair to saddle her with any liabilities which her parents' family may have incurred as a consequence of certain steps taken after her marriage and without her knowledge. To suggest that the consent of the daughter should be previously obtained on such occasions is impracticable. For usually the members of a family do not like its transactions like sale or mortgage of family property to be discussed by or communicated to even their near relations.

The present situation, however, is very unfair to the woman. She has no share in her patrimony and her condition becomes pitiable, if her husband abandons her and contracts a second marriage or takes to a vicious life. He can even escape his liability to give her a maintenance on the plea that she refuses to live with him. And what woman of self-respect will welcome her husband's home, if she is to be treated there merely as an unpaid and unwanted maid-servant? The best way, however, to meet the situation is not to assign a share to the woman in her patrimony, but to improve and enlarge her economic rights in her new family, of which she becomes an important member, and with the interests of which she becomes absolutely identified. It should no longer become possible for a husband to institute a suit for the restitution of conjugal rights, and escape his liability to maintain his wife on the plea that she refuses to obey the decree of the court to live with him. If it is proved that the wife has to stay away from the husband for no fault of her own, she should become entitled to get not merely a maintenance, but also a share equal to that of a son. It may be recalled that Yājñavalkya allows the wife a one third share in the husband's property under such circumstances.[32] As marriages usually take place between families of approximately equal financial status, the share which the wife will receive in her husband's property is not likely to be smaller than the one which she would have obtained as a daughter from her patrimony.

If the present law is amended on the above lines, it will not become necessary to complicate matters by giving the daughter a right to a share in her patrimony, which may be of doubtful benefit to her in actual practice, and which may also sometimes land her into financial liabilities. If her father dies after contracting debts subsequent to her marriage, she will be called upon to pay its share. Her liability will of course be limited by her share, but she will have to face a litigation. Serious difficulties may arise in the marriages of girls from poorer families. Would be bridegrooms accepting daughters from poor families now know that they will receive few or no presents at the marriage; they are sure that there is no liability. When the daughter gets a share, they must be prepared to face the music of a civil litigation after the death of their fathers-in-law. All would-be sons-in-law may not welcome this eventuality.

Normally speaking, more than 90 per cent couples can pull on well with each other, and there would be no necessity in such cases for the wife to demand a separate share from her husband. Unnecessary fragmentations of holdings, which would become necessary if all daughters are given a right of inheritance in their patrimony, will thus be avoided. In the few abnormal cases above referred to, where the condition of women at present becomes pitiable on account of their having no share in the patrimony, they would obtain the necessary relief by getting definite rights in their new families available even against the husband during the coverture.

For several centuries the Hindu wife has been occupying a position of subordination to her husband on account of her illiteracy and want of general knowledge and experience. There is an unconscious tendency in the average husband, both in the east and in the west, to assume a slightly condescending air when any money is to be sanctioned for the normal or special needs of the wife. Educated wives naturally resent this tendency and feel that they should have an income of their own, which they should be able to spend at their own free will. The best way to avoid this difficulty and consequent unpleasantness is not to grant a share in the patrimony, but to create a new variety of Strīdhana from the husband's income, which the wife should be at liberty to spend without his sanction. As a natural corollary of the principle that the husband and the wife are the joint owners of the family property, and as a recognition of the valuable unpaid work which the wife ungrudgingly does for the household, she should be entitled to receive a small percentage, say 5 per cent, of the income of the family as her own Strīdhana, to be spent by her at her own sweet will, either for her own sake or for the sake of the family. An orientation in the development of Strīdhana on this line will remove the difficulties of the modern sensitive wife. It will also render unnecessary

[32] आज्ञासम्पादिनी दक्षां वीरसू प्रियवादिनीम् ।
त्यजन्दाप्यस्तृतीयशिमद्रव्यो भरणं स्त्रियाः ।
I, 76.

the creation of the new right to a share in patrimony, which in practice will be difficult to exercise, and will lead to unnecessary and harmful fragmentations of landholdings.

To conclude, the following changes are desirable in the law of inheritance, as far as the daughter is concerned:

1. The daughter should have the right to demand that the same amount from patrimony should be spent on her education as is spent in her brother's case.
2. Education expenses apart, the daughter should have the right to a share equal to half that of her brother, if she remains unmarried. The usual presumption should be that the normal expenses of a daughter's proper marriage are equal to half the share of her brother in the patrimony. So a daughter who marries after the partition will not have to pay anything back after her marriage. This will avoid any devesting of the property subsequent to the marriage of the daughter.

SECTION II: WIDOW'S RIGHT OF INHERITANCE

The proprietary rights of the wife during the coverture have been already considered in the last chapter. We shall discuss now her rights during widowhood. Let us first take up the question of her right to inherit her husband's property.

We have already seen that there was a general prejudice in early times against allowing women to hold property. Even the wife, who was regarded as the husband's joint owner in the family property, had only very limited rights as against her consort. It is then no wonder that for a long time widow's right to inherit her husband's property should have remained unrecognised. Vedic texts, which declare women to be incapable of inheriting any property,[33] are particularly aimed against the widow. Joint family of the patriarchal type was the order of the day; males alone could be coparceners in it, women being allowed only a maintenance. In early times the custom of Niyoga was very common; so widows without sons were very few. A vast majority of widows therefore used to get their husband's shares, if not directly as their heirs, at least indirectly as the guardians of their minor sons. Very often they used to marry, and so the question of giving them a share in their dead husbands' property would not arise at all. The refusal to recognise the widow as an heir to her husband was thus causing not much actual hardship in society.

We therefore find that down to c. 300 BC, the right of the widow to inherit her husband's property was not recognised by any jurist. Vedic texts were definitely opposed to this right. Most of the Dharmasūtra writers adopt the same attitude. Baudhāyana expressly rejects the widow's claim on the authority of the Vedic texts referred to in the last para. Āpastamba

[33] तस्मात्स्त्रियो निरिन्द्रिया अदायादाः ।

T.S., VI, 5, 8, 2.

ताः (स्त्रियः) नात्मनश्चनैशत न दायस्य चनैशत ॥

S.Br., #IV, #4, #2, #13.

तस्मात्पुमान् दायादः स्त्री अदायादी ।

M.S., IV., 6, #4.

lays down that in the absence of the son the property should devolve, not upon the widow, but upon the nearest *male sapiṇḍa*. If none such within seven degrees is in existence to claim the property, it should devolve upon the preceptor. If he also is dead, then it should be taken over by a disciple of the deceased to be spent for charitable purposes.[34] This detailed scheme of Āpastamba about the devolution of property nowhere mentions or provides for the widow. The same is the case with Manu. He lays down that the property of a sonless person will first devolve upon his father, then upon his brother, and finally upon a *sapiṇḍa* and a *sakulya* in accordance to his propinquity. When none of these is forthcoming, first a preceptor, then a disciple, and finally the king should take it away.[35] Elsewhere he recognises the mother also as an heir;[36] the widow is, however, nowhere mentioned as possessing any rights of inheritance. It is true that Kullūka, a fifteenth century commentator no doubt contends that in *Manu smṛiti* IX, 185, though not expressly mentioned, the widow is intended to be understood as an heir after the son;[37] he is however obviously reading later ideas in the earlier text. There can be no doubt that Medhātithi, the ninth century commentator of Manu, is correct when he maintains that Manu has not recognised the widow as an heir at all.[38]

At about the beginning of the Christian era, both the Niyoga and the widow remarriage fell into disrepute as shown in Chapter V (*ante*, p. 146; p. 153). It was deemed to be more honourable for a widow to spend her remaining life in penances of religion than in pleasures of the family life. Leaders of society began to feel that if the widow was not to marry or get a son by Niyoga, she ought to be assigned a definite share in the family property. Early Dharmasūtra writers, however, were inclined to assign only a maintenance to the widow. This is the case with Kauṭilya also, who makes the widow's maintenance a charge upon the husband's estate, when it was resumed by the state.[39]

---

[34] पुत्राभावे यः प्रत्यासत्रः सपिण्डः। तदभावे आचार्यः। आचार्या-भावे्न्तेवासी हत्वा धर्मकृत्येषु योजयेत् । दुहिता वा ।
II, 14, 2–4.

[35] पिता हरेदपुत्रस्य रिक्यं भ्रातर एव च ।।
अनन्तरः सपिण्डाघस्तस्य तस्य हरेद्धनम् ।
अतः ऊर्ध्वं सकुल्यः स्यादाचार्यः शिष्य एव वा ।
X, 185, 187.

[36] अनपत्यस्य पुत्रस्य माता दायमवाप्नुयात्।
IX, 217.

[37] न भ्रातरो न पितरः पुत्रा रिक्थहराः पितुः।
पिता हरेदपुत्रस्य रिक्थं भ्रातर एव च ।।
While commenting upon this verse Kullūka says:
अविघमानमुख्यपुत्रस्य पत्नीदुहितृरहितस्य च पिता धनं गृह्णीयात्।
It will be noticed that there is nothing in the verse to justify the words
पत्नीदुहितृरहितस्य

[38] Medhātithi's commentary on this important verse is lost; we know of his views only from Kullūka's reference to them; cf:
अतो यन्मेवातिथिना पत्नीनामंशभागित्वं निषिद्धमुक्तं तदसंबद्धम् ।-भागित्वं बृहस्पत्यादिसंमतम् । मेवातिथिर्निराकुर्वत्र
प्रीणाति सतां मनः ।।
on *Manu*, IX, 187.

[39] अदायादकं राजा हरेत्स्त्रीवृत्तिप्रेतकदर्यवर्जम् ।
III, 5.

It was, however, being felt that this was not a satisfactory arrangement. Jurists gradually began to come forward to plead for a better recognition of the widow's claim. Gautama puts forth a modest proposal that the widow should be regarded at least as a coheir with other *sapiṇḍas*.[40] In course of time the opinion in favour of the recognition of the widow's right began to grow stronger. Why should she get only a portion of the husband's estate, and not the whole of it? It was felt that she ought to be the sole heir and not a co-heir. This view has been for the first time advocated by Vishnu at about the beginning of the Christian era. He definitely lays down that the widow shall inherit the whole estate on the failure of sons.[41] About a couple of centuries later Yājñavalkya joined Vishnu in championing the widows' right; it is his verses which were mainly relied upon by British courts, when they recognised the right of inheritance of the widow on the failure of sons.[42] It may be pointed out that the Upanishadic sage Yājñāvalkya had divided all his property between his two wives, when he had renounced the world. It would therefore appear that the Yājñavalkya school was since early days more favourably inclined to recognise women's rights than was the case with other jurists.

The proposal of Vishṇu and Yājñavalkya to recognise the widow as an heir was a sensational one. It affected the vested interests of male coparceners and therefore immediately provoked considerable and determined opposition. During the period 400–1000 AD jurists were divided into two schools, the orthodox one, which was not prepared to recognise the widow as an heir and the reformist one, which was bent upon agitating for the popularisation of its new reform.

Nārada, Kātyāyana and king Bhoja of Mālwā (c. 1015 to c. 1055 AD) were the chief advocates of the orthodox view. Nārada lays down that if a man dies without any issue or heir, his property should ultimately escheat to the king, who was to provide only a maintenance to the widow.[43] It is clear that Nārada did not mind property escheating to the crown; he would not, however, allow it to be inherited by the widow; Kātyāyana apparently held an identical view.[44] Bhoja would allow the widow to be an heir only if she submitted to

---

[40] पिण्डगोत्रर्षिसम्बन्धा रिक्तं भजेरन्स्त्री चानपत्यस्य । If we read here स्त्री वानपत्यस्य (instead of स्त्री चानपत्यस्य) as is done in the Ānandāsrama edition of the work, the widow will be an alternative heir, and not a coheir.

[41] अपुत्रस्य धंन पत्न्यभिगामि । तदभावे दुहि तृगामि ॥

XVII, 43.

In the *Pūrva-Mīmansā*, VII, 6, 14, Jaimini recognises the right of the wife to hold property. He is, however, probably referring to wives With husbands living, who alone were eligible to perform sacrifices according to him. It does not seem that Jaimini was inclined to recognise the widow as an heir to her husband. *Vishnusmṛiti* would therefore be the first work to recognise this right, as stated in the text above.

[42] पत्नी दुहितरश्चैव पितरौ भातरस्तथा।
तत्सुता गोत्रजा बंधुशिष्यसब्रह्मचारिणः ॥
एषामभावे पूर्वस्य धनभागुत्तरोतरः ॥
स्वर्यातस्य हचपुत्रस्य सवेवर्णेष्वयं विधिः ॥

II, I35–36.

[43] अन्यत्र ब्राहाणात्किन्तु राजा धर्मपरांयणः ।
तत्स्त्रीणां जीवनं दघादेष धर्मः सनातनः ।

XIII, 52.

[44] अंदायिकं राजगाम योषिद्भृत्यौर्ध्वदेहिकम् ।
अपास्य श्रोत्रियद्रव्यं श्रोत्रियेभ्यस्तदर्पयेत्॥

Niyoga. This virtually amounted to denying her the right of inheritance, for Niyoga had become very obnoxious since 500 AD, and no woman would have agreed to be a party to it. And even if she had consented, her ownership would have been a short-lived one; it would have terminated with the birth of the expected son.

There were several thinkers who recognised this state of affairs as unsatisfactory, but had not the necessary courage to recommend that the widow should be recognised as a full heir. They proposed half way measures. Some of them recommended that the wife should be allowed to inherit property worth about 2,000 or 3,000, in addition to any Strīdhana that may have been given to her by her husband.[45] Others thought that she should be permitted to inherit the movables only.[46] A third view was that the widow may be a deferred heir; she should be allowed to inherit on the failure of brothers-in-law, if her parents-in-law had no objection to the property devolving on her.[47]

The school of reformers, however, was not prepared to accept any such compromises. It insisted that the widows's right to inherit the full share should be recognised. It based its case on logic and reason. Bṛihaspat pointed out that the Vedas, the Smṛitis and sages of antiquity have unanimously declared that the husband and the wife are the joint owners of family property and together constitute one legal personality. A man therefore cannot be said to be completely dead as long as his wife is alive. How then can property pass on to another in the life time of the widow?[48] Vṛiddhamanu points out that the widow can offer

---

Quoted by Vijñāneśvara on *rāj.*, II, 136.

Kātyāyana and Brihaspati exist only in quotations and we often come across verses attributing contradictory views to them. Thus Vijñāneśvara at the above place also attributes the following verse to Kātyāyana, which clearly supports the widow's right: —

पत्नी पत्युर्धनहरी या स्यादव्यभिचारिणी ।
तदभावे तु दुहिता यघनूढा भवेत्तदा ।।

Similarly Devaṇabhaṭṭa ascribes a verse to Bṛihaspati, which concedes only a partial right of inheritance to the widow. See below p. 255 n. 2. It would appear that these books were not very carefully preserved and interpolations were often made in them by interested parties to support their own views.

45 द्रिसाहस्त्र: परो दाय: स्त्रिय दयो धनस्य वे।
भर्त्रा यच्च धनं दत्त सा यथाकालमाप्नुयात् ।।

Vyāsa in Aparārka, p. 752.

Silver Pana, roughly equal to a six Anna piece, is the coin referred to in the verse. Its purchasing power at that time was equal to that of Rs. 2 today. Property worth 2,000 would be thus equal to property worth about Rs. 10,000 today.

Mahābhārata, XIII, 82, 24 puts the limit at 3,000.

46 यद्विभक्ते धनं किंचिदाध्यादि विविधं स्मृतम् ।
तज्जाया स्थावरं मुक्त्वा लभेत मृतभर्तृका ।।
वृत्तस्थापि कृतेप्यंशे न स्त्री स्थावरमर्हति ।

Brishaspati in *SCV.*, p. 007.

This text of Bṛihaspati is opposed to a number of other verses attributed to him, and may be of doubtful authority.

47 स्वर्यातस्य हापुत्रस्य भ्रातृगामि द्रव्यम्। तदभावे पितरौ हरेयाताम् ज्येष्ठो वा पत्नी ।

Śaṅkha in *Mit.* on *raj.* II, 136.

48 आम्नाये स्मृतितन्त्रे च पूर्वाचार्येश्च सूरिभि: ।
शरीरार्घ स्मृता भार्या पुण्यापुष्यफले समा ।।
यस्य नोपरता भार्या देहार्ध तस्य जीवति ।
जीवत्यर्धशरीरे तु कथमन्य: स्वमाप्नुयात्।।

funeral oblations to her husband, and so she should be allowed to inherit his property.[49] To remove any doubt in the matter, Prajāpati lays down that the widow has a natural right to inherit all her husband's property, including movables, immovables, bullion, ornaments, stores, etc. Her right is not in the least affected even if her elderly relations, male or female, are alive. She will of course show them proper reverence, but hold the property in her own possession. If any male relation obstructs her peaceful enjoyment of the estate, it is the bounden duty of the king to punish him as a thief.[50]

It is perhaps Jīmūtavāhana, who argues the widow's case in the most masterly fashion. 'There is no authority to hold that the ownership in the husband's property, which the wife acquires at the marriage, terminates with the husband's death. How then can it be argued that the wife's right is destroyed the moment she is widowed? Nor can it be maintained that she is to utilise just as much of the income as may be necessary for her bare maintenance. Vishṇu says that the property of a person dying without sons will first devolve upon the widow, and then upon the daughter, parents, etc. Now it is admitted that in the above text the term property denotes the whole income of the estate, when construed with all other heirs like the daughter, the brother, parents, etc. How then can it have a restricted meaning when it is construed with the widow alone?[51]

We have seen already how there were early texts, which did not recognise the widow as an heir and allowed her only a maintenance. The new school cleverly explained them away as referring to concubines or unchaste wives. The chaste widow, it was argued, could never be deprived of her inherent right to inherit the entire property of the husband.[52] Now there can be no doubt that this interpretation, though ingenious, is altogether unjustifiable; earlier writers did undoubtedly intend to exclude from inheritance not only concubines and unchaste wives, but also chaste widows. Later champions of women's rights could not follow the straight forward course of refusing to accept the opinions of their predecessors; they had

---

Quoted in *Dāyabhāga*, Section XI,

49 अपुत्रा शयनं भर्तुः पालयन्ती पतिव्रता ।
पत्न्येवे दघात्तत्पिण्डं कृत्स्नमंशं हरेत च ।।

Quoted in *Mit*, on *Yaj*, II, I35–36.

50 स्थावरं जंगमं हेम कुप्यं धान्यरसांबरम् ।
आदाय दापयेच्छाद्ध मासंवत्सरादिकम् ।।
पितृव्यगुरुदौहित्रान्भर्तृ स्वस्त्रीयमातुलान् ।
पूजयेत्कव्यपूर्ताभ्यां वृद्धनाथातिथोंस्तथा ।।
तत्सपिण्डा ब्राहाणा वा ये तस्याः परिपंथिनः।
हिंस्युर्धनानि तान् राजा चीरदण्डेन शासयेत्।।

Quoted in *Parāśaramādhava*, Vol. III, p, 536.

These verses have been attributed to Bṛihaspati in the *Dāyabhaga*, Section XI.

51 परिणयनोत्पत्रं भर्तृधने पत्न्याः स्वामित्वं भर्तुमरणान्नश्यतीत्यत्र च प्रमाणाभावात् सति पुत्रे तदधिकारशास्त्रादेव पत्नीस्वत्वनाशोवगम्यते |......| न च वर्तनोपयुक्तधनमात्राधिकारार्थ पत्नीवचनमिति वाच्यम्। 'अपुत्रस्य धनं पत्न्यभिगामि तदभावे दुहितृगामि तदभावे पितृगामि''इत्यत्र सकृच्छ्रुतस्य धनपदस्य पत्न्यपेक्षमकृस्नपरत्वं कृत्स्नपरत्वंच भ्रात्राद्यपेक्षमिति तात्पर्यभेदस्या-न्याय्यत्वात्।

Dāyabhāga, Section XI.

52 यदुक्तं 'स्त्रीणा तु जीवनं दद्याद् इति संवर्धनमात्रवचनं तछशशी लाघार्मिकसविकरायौवनस्थपत्नीविषयम् ।

Kullūka on *Manu*, IX, 186.

यदपि नारदः तत्स्त्रीणां जीवनं दद्यात् इति तदवरुद्धास्त्री परं पत्नीपदाश्रवणत् ।

VMV.... sanraihandadanai

to devise some means, whereby they could explain away the earlier contrary texts without showing any disrespect to their writers. Reform in Hindu social customs and institutions has usually taken this peculiar course owing to the great conservatism of the race.

Let us resume our subject. The new school maintained that the widow's right of inheritance was an inherent one. The only circumstance that could defeat it was unchastity. When we note the ideas current on the subject at that time, this condition would not appear to be an unexpected one. The modern law on this point is very peculiar. It allow an inheritance to devolve upon a widow, only if she is chaste at the time of its opening. Her subsequent unchastity, however, does not devest the estate.

In spite of the able advocacy of the cause of the widow by the reform school, it took several centuries for her right to be recognised throughout India. The Deccan was more advanced in this respect than northern India. A writer of the sixth century BC observes that it is customer for the southerners to recognise the proprietary rights of women.[53] Among the champions of widows' rights the provenance of BṛihasPati, Vyāsa and Prajāpati is not known, but Yājñāvalkya was a southerner, and his commentator Vijñāneśvara hailed from the Deccan, as he was the Chief Justice of the Chālukya emperor Vikramādiya VII. That the widow's right of inheritance, so enthusiastically advocated in the *Mitākshar*ā, was actually recognised in contemporary Deccan can be proved from epigraphical evidence. A twelfth century inscription from Karnataka, while describing the scheme of devolution of property current in a certain village, mentions the widow as the heir immediately after the son (*E. I.*, V, p. 28). An inscription from Tanjore district, belonging to the same century, declares that a lawfully wedded wife inherits the whole property of the husband,including land, cattle, slaves, jewels and other valuables (*S. I. E. R.*, for 1919, pp. 79–88).

The causes for this earlier recognition of the widow's right of inheritance in the Deccan can only be inferred. As shown before in Chap. VI, Women were taking an active part in the administration in the Deccan even as governors of districts and towns. It is quite likely that many of the princesses, who were acting in these capacities, were themselves widows. If society had no objection to widows being governors and collectors, it could also reconcile itself to the recognition of the widow's right of inheritance as well. The existence of matriarchy in some communities may also have helped to liberalise the views of the Deccan society in this respect.

The widow's right of inheritance came into recognition in northern India somewhat later. In the days of Kālidāsa (c. 400 AD), if a person died without leaving a son, his property used to escheat to the king, who had to provide merely a maintenance to the widow. This is quite clear from the Śākuntala episode of the merchant dying in the shipwreck, whose property was proposed to be immediately resumed by the zealous ministers of king Dushyanta. In Gujarat the widow's right of inheritance was not recognised down to c. 1200 AD King Kumārapāla of that province (1144–73) admits frankly that his subjects were justified in their impression that their king always desired his rich subjects to die issueless, so that he may resume their

[53] गर्तारोहिणीव धनलाभाय दक्षिणाजी। *Nirukta* III, 5.

property.[54] A poet of his court tells us that it was this king who showed a magnanimity of mind, shown not even by kings born in the golden age like Raghu and Nahusha, and voluntarily forswore his right to the property of the 'weeping widow.[55] It would be thus seen that this reform met with considerable opposition from the governments of the day, because it adversely affected their revenues. As a partial compensation, some of them introduced a death duty on the property of persons dying without sons (Graham, *Kolhapoor*, p. 333).

Most of the digest writers, who wrote subsequent to c. 1200 AD, have recognised the widow's right of inheritance. We may therefore conclude that by c. 1300 AD, the right had come to be sanctioned throughout the whole country.

The Mitāksharā school recognised the widow's right of inheritance, only if her husband had separated from the joint family before his death.[56] An examination of the context of the verse in which Yājñavalkya mentions widow as the next heir, makes it clear that he intended to recognise her right, only if her husband was not a member of the joint family at the time of his death. This conclusion becomes further irresistible from v. 138, where Yājñavalkya lays down that when members of a family have reunited after separation, the surviving male coparceners will succeed the deceased, and not his wife.[57] Vijñānesvara. is therefore correct in holding that according to Yājñavalkya only the widow of a separated coparcener can become an heir to her husband. Of course he could have liberalised the law still further by drawing further deductions from the text of Bṛihaspati, which declares that none can touch the property of a person as long as his wife is alive. He could have argued that whether the deceased was a member of the joint family or not, was an immaterial question. As long as the wife was alive, the husband ought to be too regarded as living; the inheritance will not open at all till the death of the wife. She must be therefore allowed to enjoy the property of her husband irrespective of the consideration, whether he had separated from the family or not before his death.

Vijñāneśvara, however, was not prepared to take this step. He had included inherited property under Strīdhana, and he was probably reluctant to sanction a scheme of succession, where under extensive property would have automatically and very frequently passed out of the family to female Strīdhana heirs. He probably felt that if a coparcener effected a separation from the joint family, its members should have no grievance if his separated share passed as Strīdhana to his daughter. If, however, no separation had been effected, and the share of an undivided coparcener were still allowed to devolve on his wife, it would have passed out of the family with an alarming frequency, since unlike the Dāyabhāga school, the Mitāksharā school had declared this share as the Strīdhana of the wife. Most of the medieval jurists agree with the Mitāksharā and recognise the widow's right of inheritance only when her husband was not a member of the joint family at the time of his death.

---

[54] निष्पुत्रं म्रियमाणमाढ्यमदनीपालो हहा वाञ्छति।

Mohaparājya, Act III.

[55] न मुक्तं यत्पूर्वं रघुनहुषनाभागभरतप्रभृत्युर्वीनाथैः कृतयुगकृतोत्पत्तिभिरति। विमुन्त्र्यसन्तोषात्तदिह रूदतिवित्तमपुना कमारक्मापाल त्वमसि महतां मस्तक-मणिः।।

Kumārapālapratibodha, p. 43.

[56] तस्मादपुत्रस्य स्वर्यातस्य विभक्तस्य असंसृष्टिनो धनं परिणीता स्त्री संयता सकलमेव गृहणाति इति स्थितम्। On *Yaj*., II, 136. On *raj*., II, 136.

[57] संसुष्टिनस्तु ससृष्टो सोदरस्य तु सोदरः।।

To Jīmūtavāhana, the founder of the Dāyabhāga school, belongs the credit of liberalising the law still further in favour of the widow. We have seen above (*ante*, p. 225) that he would not include inherited property under Strīdhana. This was so, because he wanted to disarm society's opposition to his revolutionary proposal to make the widow an heir to her husband, even when the latter was a member of the joint family at the time of his death. While anxious that every widow should inherit her husband's share in the joint family property, he wanted to prevent it from going outside the family to Strīdhana heirs; He therefore did not include it under her Strīdhana.

The Dāyabhāga law undoubtedly marks a further step in the expansion of the widow's rights. It lays down that the widow can get her husband's share in the family property, even if he happened to be a member of the joint family at the time of his death. Jīmūtavāhana relies upon a text of Bṛihaspati, which is silent about separation and declares that the property of a person can devolve upon his brother, only when he dies without leaving a son or a widow behind.[58] He further points out that even when brothers are living as members of a joint family, according to his conception of this institution, each one has got his own share clearly determined, though not specifically separated by metes and bounds; it is then but fair that it should be earmarked for his wife.[59] There is further nothing to prove that the wife's co-ownership in the husband's property, that arises at the marriage, automatically terminates at his death, if it happens while the family is still joint.[60] It is therefore but fair that she should be allowed to inherit her husband's share irrespective of the consideration as to whether he had separated from the joint family or not.

If the texts, on which Jīmūtavāhana had relied, had been utilised to their fullest capacity, they would have easily enabled him to declare that the estate which the widow inherits is an absolute and not a limited one. The widow is the living half of the husband, savs Bṛihaspati; and therefore no one can get the right to inherit the deceased's property as long as she is alive. Now Jīmūtavāhana could have easily argued that the powers of the surviving half (the widow) cannot be less than those of the expired half (the husband), and so the widow's estate would be as absolute as that of her husband, she having the power of sale, mortgage or gift. He however did not take this step, but maintained that the widow had only a life estate in her inheritance. She could utilise its full income in any way she liked, but she could not touch its corpus.

To understand Jīmūtavāhana reluctance to grant to the widow a full estate in inheritance, we shall have to discuss the history of the question. The early jurists like Vishṇu and Yājñāvalkya, who have recognised the widow as an heir, have nowhere used any expressions to show that they regarded her as a limited heir. It is therefore possible to argue that they intended to invest her with the same full powers which they granted to other heirs like

---

58 यदा कश्चित्प्रमीयेत प्रवजेद्वा कथंचन ।
न लुप्यते तस्य भागः सोदरस्य विधीयते।
अनपत्यस्य धर्मीऽयमभार्यापितृकस्य च।
Quoted in Section XI.

59 न हि संसृष्टतवेऽपि यदेवैकस्य तदेवापरस्यापि किन्तु अविज्ञातैकदेशं तद्द्वयोः न तु समप्रमेव।
Dāyabhāga, XI

60 See *ante*, p. 237 n. 1

the son, the father or the brother whom they, have mentioned along with her. In the long discussion of the subject in the *Mitāksharā*, Vijñāneśvara also nowhere states or hints that the widow was a limited heir, having no right to dispose of the corpus of the property. In the concluding sentence of his discussion he states, 'Therefore the chaste and regularly married wife of a person, who has died without leaving behind any sons, and who had separated from the joint family and not reunited with it, inherits his entire property.[61] He has introduced here several qualifying adjectives, very carefully chosen; but among them there is none to suggest that he regarded the widow's estate as a limited one.

A number of other jurists, however, declare definitely that the widow is a limited heir. An authority quoted by the *Mahābhārata* states that the widow can only utilise the income of the property she has inherited; she can under no circumstances dispose of it.[62] Kātyāyana states that the inheritance will revert to reversioners after the death of the widow, she having no power to dispose of it.[63] Bṛihaspati, we have seen, was a fervent champion of the widow's rights, but even he expressly declare that her powers over her inheritance are limited; she cannot sell, mortgage or gift it away. He, however, permits a gift for religious purposes, which presumably was to be of a small portion only.[64] Nārada declines to concede full powers to the wife even over her Strīdhana, if it comprised of any immovable property. The wise have declared, says this sage, that transaction of landed property like sale, mortgage or gift, if made by women, are, automatically invalid.[65]

To conclude, we find that even some of the warmest champions of the widow's right of inheritance like Bṛihaspati definitely declare her to be a limited heir, while others like Yājñavalkya and Vishṇu are merely silent on the point. No one specifically invests her with the power to dispose of the immovable property in her inheritance, gifts for religious purposes being the only exception. It is therefore clear that down to the twelfth century, the widow was intended to be given only a limited power over her inheritance. Society was, as shown already, very reluctant to recognise the widow as even a limited heir; it would have summarily rejected the case of her champions, if they had suggested that she should be invested with absolute powers over her inheritance.

Late medieval period, c. 1200–1800 AD, was the most conservative one in the history of Hindu customs and institutions. It, however, can claim the credit of attempting to extend the widow's powers over her estate in one direction. We have seen above how down to

---

[61] तस्मादपुत्रस्य स्वर्यातस्य विभक्तस्यासंसृष्टिनो धनं परिणीता स्त्री सकलमेव गृह्णाति। *On Yāj*., II, 136.

[62] स्त्रीणां स्वपतिदायाद उपभोगफल: समृत:।
नापहारं स्त्रिय: कुर्यु: पतिवितात्कथंचन।। XIIII, 82, 25.

[63] अपुत्रा शयनं भर्तु: पालयन्ती पतिव्रता।
लभेतामरणात्क्षान्ता दायादा ऊर्धार्वमाप्नुयु:।। Quoted in *SCV*., p. 677.

[64] मृते भर्तरि भर्त्रंशं लभेत कुलपालिका।
यावज्जीवं हीनस्वाम्यं दानाधमनविक्रये।। व्रतोपवासनिरता ब्रह्मचर्ये व्यवस्थिता।
धार्मदानरता नित्यमपुत्रपि दियं व्रजेत।।
Quoted at Ibid.

[65] भर्त्रा प्रीतेन यद्दतं रित्रर्प तस्मिम्मूतेंडपि तत् ।
सा यमाकाममबनीयात्द्याद्वा स्थाख्यावृते ।।
स्वीकृतान्यप्रमाणानि कार्याव्याहुर्मनीषिर्ण: ।
विशेषतया नंदुहक्षेत्रदानाधभनबिक्रप्रा: ।।
I, 26–27.

c. 1200 AD, jurists were unwilling to concede to the widow the right to alienate her estate. Writers of legal digests after that date are seen to encourage the tendency to recognise this right under certain circumstances. There was a text of Bṛihaspati which, as pointed out already, permitted the widow to gift away a portion of her property for religious and spiritual purposes.[66] Medieval writers like Devaṇabhaṭṭa and Nīlakaṇṭha particularly emphasise on this right. The former states that when sale or mortgage of the immovable property was prohibited to the widow, what was meant was that she should not gift it away in one form or another to persons of questionable character like singers, dancers and actors[67]. The latter maintains that women have inherent powers to make gifts for spiritual purposes[68]. Neither Devaṇabhaṭṭanor Nīlakaṇṭha however states whether the consent of the next reversioners was necessary for validating such a transaction. The language which they have used would suggest that if the gift was a bonafide one for religious purposes, the widow could give it herself without the consent of the reversioners. The actual practice seems to have varied considerably. We haveno recorded cases for northern India, but south. Indian inscriptions of the medieval period show that the silence of the authorities was interpreted differently by different persons and localities.

There was one view that the express permission of the reversioners was an essential prerequisite for such a transaction. It would be therefore better if the gift was formally made jointly by the widow and the reversioners. Some inscriptions from South India show that this opinion was acted upon in practice on several occasions. Thus a tenth century epigraph from Mysore records a gift of land given by a widow and her brother-in-law (*E. C.*, IX, Holkere No. 33). The brother-in-law is obviously introduced here to show that the transaction had the full consent of the next reversioner. The widow alone could not have sold the property. A twelfth century inscription from the same state records the donation given by a widow to a temple along with her brother-in-law and Śrīvaishṇavas. Here it is clear that the consent of not only the next reversioner but of the whole caste was deemed necessary to validate the transaction (Ibid., X, No. 100 A). A thirteenth century inscription from Madura district narrates how two childless widows wanted to give a garden to a temple, how their relations would not sanction the transaction, and how eventually they could achieve their object only by securing the permission of some other reversioners (*S. I. E. R.*, 1916, No. 401). It is quite clear from the above cases that the widow's estate was regarded as a limited one. The permission of the next reversioner, if not of the whole caste, was necessary to enable her to gift it even for a religious purpose.

There are, however, other records equally numerous and hailing from the same part of the country, which record sales or gifts of landed property by widows made for religious purposes, but which are silent about any permission of the reversioners. A twelfth century inscription

---

[66] See *ante*, p. 263 n. 3.

[67] मृते भर्तरीत्थशदृष्टबानप्रतिरोय: । अदृष्टार्थदश्वानविथानात्तदितरदृ
इंटार्थनर्तकाबीनां दानादौ अस्वातन्यप्रतिपावनार्थभिति मन्तव्यमृ । एवं च धमदान
स्वातंत्यमसयेव । अपुत्रा शफ्तमादिकात्यायनोक्तमविभदतदशाविषए ।

S. C. V. pp. 667–7

[68] अदृष्टार्थदानाबलियाधमनादि भवत्येव ।

Vvavahāramayūkha p. 86.

from Trichiniopoly district records the gift of a piece of land by a Brahmana widow made in favour of a temple; a thirteenth century inscription from Kolar district refers to a sale by a widow of her own share in her landed property[69]; a fifteenth century record mentions a Brahmana widow building a temple and giving to it a gift of land for the spiritual benefit of herself and her husband; a seventeenth century inscription describes how a Brahamana lady gifted away a whole village to a temple. In none of these records it is anywhere mentioned or suggested that any of the widows had obtained the consent or permission of any reversioner for disposing her landed property. Had any such permission been received, it would have been surely mentioned, as was done by the persons who drew up the documents referred to in the last para. It is to be noted that these epigraphs were lithic deeds of title, intended to last for centuries; it is natural to presume that they would have carefully mentioned all relevant circumstances that would have been necessary to prove that the transactions recorded were valid ones, and the donees had acquired full and unquestioned titles.

The epigraphic evidence then shows that the custom differed with different castes and different localities in south India. Some sections of society felt that the permission of the reversioners was necessary to validate even a religious gift; others thought that it might be dispensed with. When we note that our jurists all belonged to the priestly class, it need not be wondered that their general tendency should have been to give the widow an unrestricted power in the matter.

While pleading for an unrestricted power to the widow to make gifts for religious purposes, Mitramiśra, a seventeenth century jurist of Uttara Pradesh, uses some expressions, suggesting that he was half inclined to sanction bonafide sales or gifts made even for non-religious purposes. 'To those who contend' says he, that women have no right to sell or gift away their husband's inheritance, we ask; do you mean to maintain that even if the gift or sale in question has already become an accomplished fact, it could become invalid merely because it was made by a woman? This is unfair…[70] Texts prohibiting sales etc. refer to the disposal of landed property made to vicious persons with the malicious purpose of defeating the rights of coparceners. They do not invalidate gifts etc. properly made. 'Ownership gives the right of disposal as much over the immovables as over the movables, and an accomplished transaction cannot be unsettled even by a hundred sacred texts'. This principle would have undoubtedly invested the widow with full rights of disposal even over immovable property. But Mitramiśra not only does not draw its natural corollary, but proceeds immediately to circumscribe its application. For he concludes his discussion with the observation, 'It therefore follows that a widow can dispose of her

---

[69] *I. M. P.* III, p. 1544; *E. C.*, X, Kolar No. 103; *I. M. P.*, I. p. 56; *E. C.*, XI, Holkere No. 80.

[70] संपृखमैय यननार्यमग्दग्य नास्तरेंव स्तिया भद्देरिड़्थं वानविक्रयब्ब-
अधिकार इत्याहुः । तवैदं वद्रज्यन् । किं तस्य तया कृतैडपि दस्नादौ ततचरूपकृ-
द्गनष्पत्तिरेंब्रा मन्याश्चिनैः सकत्भतृधिनग्रहर्ण तस्या उव्रर्त सति तस्या अस्व-
तंत्रस्वत्ये वांनादिस्वख्यानिष्यर्त्तर्वाश्वीपैतत्यात्......। बान1टिप्रतिर्षधवचनानि
दुर्मुतं पुरुवं प्रति कुटुम्बदुश्वबानार्थर्म९व दस्वक्रियादिप्रपृत्तिर्दनेर्षधकाद्गन न
बानादिस्वख्यानिष्पदित्तप्रलिपादफगंने । ......श्यर्यष्टविनिसोब्वद्रपहँत्वलक्षणस्वत्वस्य
द्रन्यान्तर इव टियेंरऊदृयद्गवरुरेंषादृब्रनशर्तनद्भद्गप. वस्तुनौन्यथाकरणब्वरुरुक्टयक्व तटांति-
पावनानुपयरिति निरुपितन् :

VMS., p.628–9

immovable property either for making a religious gift or for maintaining herself or for other proved necessities:[71] he does not add "or for any other purpose she may like"'. In spite of his liberal principles Mitramiśra was thus prepared to invest the widow just with those powers, which have been recognised in modern courts. It is clear that society was not yet prepared to grant the widow an unrestricted power over her immovable inheritance.

Should we now change the law and invest the widow with full powers over the immovable property inherited by her? This is a question on which opinion is divided at present. Dr. Deshmukh's bill, introduced in 1936 in the Imperial Assembly sought to invest the widow with this power, but the effort failed. The educated woman naturally feels it an insult that she should not have a power over her inheritance, which is conceded to the most illiterate and inexperienced villager. We must, however, note that even at present the widow can sell or mortgage her property for genuine necessities. The disability is that her powers in this connection are not unrestricted. This is of course a disability from one point of view, but also a protection from another. In the Punjab and Palestine, for instance, male peasants had unrestricted powers of alienation; the result was that many of them sold away their valuable lands and eventually became paupers, as they could not properly utilise or invest the sale proceeds. Eventually the governments of these provinces had to restrict these powers in the interests of the peasants. themselves. We should not forget that 95 per cent widows are still uneducated, inexperienced and altogether innocent of the provisions of law. If they are given the right to dispose of the landed property, many of them will be induced by interested parties to enter into unwise transactions. The money realised from sale will not last long, and the majority of widows disposing of their property will eventually find that they have lost both the lands and their sale proceeds. Their condition will then become very pitiable. In the present circumstances, therefore, it is not in the interests of the widows as a class that they should have unrestricted power of alienation. A beginning, however, should be made by giving it to those widows, who possess certain minimum educational qualifications. This of course will often adversely affect the prospective rights of reversioners, but they have been already annihilated by the ruling of the Privy Council, which has given the widow in many parts of the country an unrestricted power of adoption. If coparceners cultivate friendly and cordial relations with the widow, there is no reason why she should wantonly defeat their expectations. She would then take as much interest in her husband's family as her coparceners, and would not normally stand in the way of its continued prosperity after her death by selling or willing away her share.

Till 1937 it was only in Bengal where the Dāyabhaga law prevailed, that the widow could inherit her husband's property, even if he had died as a member of the joint family. Outside Bengal, she was recognised as an heir, only if her husband had effected a separation from the joint family before his death. This was the law as it was laid down in the *Mitāksharā* and enforced in modern courts. The latter, however, were anxious to help the widow as much as they could, and sought to facilitate matters in her favour by decreeing that a person should be regarded as being separated from the joint family, not only when

[71] तस्माढ़दृष्टायें दाने दृष्टदष्टावायकार्यार्वमाती विक्रपै चारुत्येव पब:
सकलभतृ धनविषयेंश्र्वयधिशारः । नियमस्तु नमीर्तकाविबानानावायकाधिविक्रिय-
निवृत्त्वर्थमिति सिध्दमृ ।

VMS., p. 630

he had actually severed his connection, but also when he had merely communicated his intention of doing so to his other coparceners. This used to enable many persons, who did not share the traditional regard for the sanctity of the joint family, to secure the devolution of their shares upon their wives. Those wives, however, who did not advise their husbands to take this rather unpleasant step, got as a reward for their regard for the joint family, the misfortune of losing their right of inheritance to their husbands. This was un doubtedly an undesirable and anomalous state of affairs. The Hindu Women's Right to Property Act of 1937 extends the Dāyabhāga principle to the whole of British India, and invests the widow with the right to inherit her husband's share in the family property, irrespective of the consideration as to whether he had effected a separation from the joint family or not. This is a step in the right direction and widows all over the country now possess this right.

SECTION III: OTHER FEMALE HEIRS

We have considered so far the right of inheritance of the daughter, the wife and the widow. The cases of remaining female heirs need not be considered in detail in the present work. Only some words will be necessary about a few of them.

The right of the mother to inherit the property of her son was recognised fairly early. Manu, who does not recognise the widow as an heir, concedes to the mother the right to inherit the property of a son dying without any issues (IX, 217). All the jurists concur with Manu in this matter. Some of them do not even allow sons to partition family property as long as the mother is alive. In practice the widowed mother was regarded as the sole controller of the estate, though the sons were its legal heirs and owners. Hindu culture held the mother in very high reverence; so her right of inheritance came to be recognised much earlier than that of the wife or the widow. In every day life, however, occasions were very few when property passed to a mother as the next heir of an issueless son. The recognition of this right did not therefore give rise to many exceptions to the general view of early times that women should not be recognised as heirs. The grandmother's claim to inherit her grandsons' property was also recognised very early for reasons similar to those which operated in favour of the mother. In actual practice, however, not even one grandmother in a million could have got an opportunity of being benefited by this concession. For she was a fairly distant heir and came only after the parents and brothers of the deceased. The recognition of the widow, on the other hand, as the next heir to an issueless husband was a revolutionary step, as it was sure to give rise to a large number of female heirs in actual practice. A long time therefore had to elapse before it could be taken.

We have seen above that the Deccan was the pioneer in recognising women's rights of inheritance. She continues her lead even today, for the Bombay school recognises a larger number of female heirs than any other school of Hindu Law. It is the only school which gives the right of inheritance to the widows of the agnates (Gotraja Sapiṇḍas). It is interesting to note that even the *Mitāksharā* does not support their claim to inheritance.[72] In Bombay Presidency, however, the right of the widows of agnates was recognised, mainly because local enquiry showed that it was actually conceded in practice. The courts were

[72] The *Mitākshara* does not at all mention the paternal uncle's wife or her daughter-in-law as an heir. Neither Devaṇabhaṭṭa nor Mitramiśra recognises Gotraja Sapinda widows as heirs. *SCV.*, p. 694; *VMV.*, p. 671.

also influenced to some extent by a wrong translation of a passage in *Manusmṛiti* by Sir William Jones. He had translated the line in question as 'To the nearest Sapinda, *male or female*, the inheritance next belongs'. The italicised words are not in the original text at all;[73] Sir William Jones had added them on the authority of Kullūka, who has explained the term Sapiṇḍa as *pumān strīvā*',[74] 'either male or female'. It will be seen from this incidence how adventitious circumstances connected with early translations have in some cases considerably affected the development of Hindu Law in modern times.

The sister has been placed much higher in the line of succession in the Bombay school than anywhere else. She comes immediately after the grandmother, mainly on account of an ingenious argument advanced in the *Mayūkha.*[75] It is clear that Nīlakaṇṭha is here trying to justify a known usage with the help of some spacious arguments.

Among the heirs of the descending order, Hindu jurists have been the hardest on the widowed daughter-in-law. Only one among them, Nanda Pṇḍdita (c. 1575 AD), recognises her as an heir.[76] The rest found it difficult to grant her any relief. The reasons are easy to understand. The Mitāksharā recognised the widow as an heir only when her husband had already separated from the joint family. It was regarded as highly indecorous for a son to separate from his father or grandfather; so there were hardly any widowed daughters-in-law in society who could claim a share under the Mitākshara scheme of succession. Under the Dayābhāga law, the separation of her husband from the family was no doubt not necessary for a widow to get a share; there was, however, another fatal difficulty in the way of the widow of the predeceased son. Under the Dayābhāga scheme, the son could get no right in the family property till after the death of the father; the widowed daughter-in-law could claim no share in the family property, because her husband himself was entitled to none at the time of his death. Thus both the Mitākshara and the Dayābhāga schools could extend no relief to the widow of a predeceased son. The British courts followed faithfully the medieval authorities on this point, and were therefore unable to liberalise the law in her favour. The situation has changed in 1937 with the passing of Hindu Women's Right to Property Act; now the widow of a predeceased son can get a life estate in the share to which her husband would have been entitled.

It is not necessary to consider the rights of inheritance of any more female heirs for the purpose of our present work. We therefore now pass on to consider women's rights at partition.

SECTION IV: PARTITION

The theory of joint ownership should have invested the wife with the right to demand a partition against her husband in case it became impossible for her to live with him. No such right was however recognised. Yājñavalkya lays down that a wife should get a third share

---

[73] Cf: अनन्तरं सपिण्डाद्यस्तस्य तस्य हरद्धनम्। IX, 187.

[74] 7 *Indian Appeals*. pp. 212–39.

[75] तस्या अपि भातगान्नेउत्पन्नत्वेन गोत्रजत्वाविशषाच्च।

[76] श्वश्रूमरणे श्वश्रूस्नुषयोः स्वत्वसाम्येन श्वश्रूमरणे स्नुषाया एव रुसाधारणसाम्यात।

Nanda Paṇḍita bases his case for the widowed daughter-in-law on Bṛihaspati's dictum,

जीवत्यर्धशरीरे तु कथमन्यः स्वमाप्नुयात्।

Kane. *History of Dharmaśāstra Literature,* I, p. 212.

in her husband's property, if she is unjustly superseded.[77] He is, however, the only jurist to recognise such a right, and it is quite possible that in actual practice, husbands may have managed to escape this liability under the plea that the wives superseded were disobedient ones. It may be, however, pointed out that to demand a partition was regarded as a very unbecoming procedure; even a grown up son could not ask for it, if his father were living jointly with his grandfather or other elderly collaterals. The wife thus suffered from the same disabilities as against her husband, as the son suffered as against the father. It is however high time to invest the wife with an incontestible right to demand her full share in the property, if she is compelled to live separately owing to her husband's misdemeanour. In such cases, she ought to get a share equal to that of a son.

Let us now consider normal cases of partition and women's rights on such occasions. The Vedic literature occasionally refers to a partition made by the father during his life time;[78] there is, however, nothing to indicate whether the wife used to receive a share on such occasions. Very probably, in spite of the general prejudice against allowing a share to women in inheritance, the father must have assigned an adequate share to his wife, if she were living at the time. In actual practice, the assigning of a share to the wife must have merely amounted to the patriarch reserving two shares for himself as against one assigned to each son. The wife probably got no independent control over it.

While describing partition, many of the Dharmaśāstra writers expressly include the mother, the wife and the daughter among the parties entitled to a moity. Among these the case of the daughter has been already considered (*ante*, pp. 239 ff.). As far as the wife is concerned, both Yājñavalkya and Kātyāyana allow her a share. If the partition had taken place during the husband's life time, very probably the wife must be allowing her husband to be in possession of her share; it must have therefore merely increased her husband's moity. It is interesting to note that Nārada allows two shares to the husband at partition[79]; the second one was probably intended for his wife.

Yājñavalkya allows the widowed mother a share equal to that of her son.[80] Śukra allows her only a one fourth share (IV, 5, 297), but his view is not shared by the vast majority of jurists, who insist that the mother should receive one full share. Some writers attempted to curtail the full share allowed to the mother by suggesting that the expression 'equal share' is not to be interpreted literally; it is really intended to mean just as much money as may be necessary for her maintenance. The *Mitākshara*, however, rightly points out the utter unreasonableness of this interpretation and maintains that the widowed mother must get a full share[81]. Most of the jurists have accepted this view, as also the modern law courts. The

---

[77] आज्ञासंपादिनीं दक्षां वीरसू प्रियवादिनीम्।
त्यजन्दाप्यस्त्रितीयांशमद्रव्यौ भरणं स्त्रिय:।। I, 76.

[78] पितुर्न जिव्रेवि वेदो भरन्त।
R. V., I, 70, 5; see also *T. S.*, III, 1,9,4–5.

[79] द्वाबंशौ प्रतिपद्येत विभजन्नात्मन: पिता। XIII, 12.

[80] यदि कुर्यात्समानंशान्पल्य: कार्या: समांशिका:।
न दत्तं स्त्रीधनं यासां भर्त्रा वा श्वशुरेण वा।। I, 115.
पितुरूर्ध्वं विभजतां माताप्यंशं समं हरेत्। II, 123

[81] अथ 'पत्न्य: कार्या: समांशिका'इत्यत्र 'माताप्यंशं समं हरेत्' इत्यत्र च जीवनोपयुक्तमेव धनं स्त्री हरतीति मतं तदसत्। अंशशब्दस्य समशब्दस्यच आनर्थक्यप्रसंगात्। On *Yāj.*, II, 136.

latter, however, had given the ruling that the widow could get this share only if her sons sued for a partition; she could not herself bring the suit. This was clearly against the Spirit of the Hindu law. Manu and Kauṭilya do not even permit brothers to effect a partition during the mother's lifetime;[82] they would have been shocked to be told that the mother could get her share only if her sons chose to effect a partition. The law therefore needed a change in the direction of allowing the mother to sue for her share, in case she could not pull on well with her sons. This desideratum was achieved by the Hindu Women's Right to Property Act passed in 1937 by the Indian Legislature.

We have now finished the history of the proprietary rights of women. It has no doubt detained us rather long, but it has made many interesting disclosures. We found that it did not take long for Hindu society to set aside primitive theories about women being mere chattel. It recognised their right to Strīdhana fairly early and went on expanding its scope; till eventually by the twelfth century AD, all varieties of property were included in it all over India, except in Bengal. In normal times the husband was not allowed to touch this property of his wife. The only development necessary in modern times in this connection is the recognition of the right of the wife to a small percentage in the husband's income as her *bhaṛtridatta strīdhana*, in recognition of the joint ownership of the family property and her valuable service in the household management. This would remove the difficulties of the modern sensitive wife, who does not like that for every little expenditure which she may have to incur, she should have to secure expressly or impliedly the permission of her husband.

The position of the wife vis-à-vis the husband was not satisfactory. She could not enforce a partition against him, if he persistently misbehaves or embarked upon a second marriage. Yājñavalkya, no doubt, allowed the wife a one third share in the family property, if she was unjustly superseded. He was, however, in a hopeless minority. We must, however, now follow his lead and allow the wife to claim a share at least equal to that of a son, if she is forced to live separately for no fault of her own. This would remove the proprietary disabilities from which such wives suffer at present on account of their having no share in the patrimony. We must further render it impossible for the husband to mortgage or sell his wife's share in the family property without her express consent.

Hindu jurists held marriage to be indispensable for the daughter, and therefore felt that they should merely provide for it. They went to the extent of laying down that a brother should provide for his sister's marriage even if there were no ancestral assets for the purpose. They were, however, opposed to give her a right of inheritance in the patrimony along with her brothers. The religious theory was that the marriage completely transfers the bride to the new family, and the jurists therefore felt that she should be provided for from its assets. We have shown above (*ante,* pp. 245–48) how on the whole this is a reasonable and satisfactory arrangement. There are many difficulties to encounter and few benefits to accrue from giving a daughter the right of inheritance along with her brothers. The present law gives rise to certain anomalies in some abnormal cases, but the correct remedy is to enlarge the wife's rights as against the husband on the lines indicated above. Of course, as far as daughters

See also *V. D. S.*, XVIII, 34, *Kātyāyana-matasaṁgraha*, v, 693.

[82] *Manu*, IX, 104; *Arthāsāstra*, III, 5.

who remain unmarried are concerned, they should be given a share in patrimony equal to half that of their brothers. The Hindu Code Bill is however seeking now (Feb. 1956) to give them a full share, and a section of the Hindu community is in favour of this innovation.

The brotherless daughter has been regarded as an heir since very early times. In Bombay presidency she takes the property as an absolute heir. This law should now be extended to the whole of the country.

For a long time the widow was not recognised as an heir, dian for whom she could hold her husband's share in the family property. When the custom of Niyoga disappeared and the childless widow came on the scene, Hindu society soon became alive to the necessity of recognising her as an heir. The fervour and zeal with which the battle of her right of inheritance was fought, are creditable for Hindu culture. The widow was no doubt regarded as a limited heir. She could, however, utilise the full income of the property, howsoever large it may be; only she could not alienate it without sufficient cause. When we consider how the vast majority of Hindu widows were illiterate at this time, the limitation must be pronounced to have been more a protection than a disability. The time has not yet come when we can effect a wholesale change in the law on the point. A beginning should, however, be made by allowing women the right of alienation, if they possess certain minimum educational qualifications.

The Bengal school was most liberal to the widow; it allowed her to become an heir, even if her husband had not separated from the joint family. This principle has been extended to the whole country since 1937; so a legitimate grievance, from which the widows under the *Mitāksharā* law were suffering, has been now removed.

It will be thus seen from the above survey that the proprietary rights of women have been developing fairly satisfactorily. As circumstances changed, they were being enlarged by Hindu jurists without any agitation whatever on the part of women. Society was actuated by a genuine desire to improve their economic lot, and did not hesitate to adopt measures that considerably curtailed the time-honoured rights of male coparceners. The courage that was shown in investing the widow with the right of inheritance, even when her elderly relations like brothers-in-law were alive, was really of a high order, when we consider the prevailing patriarchal atmosphere in society. The progress made cannot be of course regarded as adequate by the modern woman, but we must recognise that each age has its own limitations and cannot easily rise above them. Modern Hindu society has been showing a keen desire to enlarge the proprietary rights of women; the legislatures in India both Provincial and Central, began to champion measures to liberalise the law since 1936. The States of Baroda and Mysore led the way in the matter under the inspiration of their enlightened rulers. And now (February 1956) we have a measure before the Indian Parliament, sponsored by the Government, which seeks to give the married daughter a share in patrimony equal to that of the brother. What will be the fate of this measure cannot be anticipated; but it seems to be reasonably certain that at least the unmarried daughter will get a share in the patrimony equal to half that of her brother.

Chapter 13 The Legal Status of Women: Their Right of Inheritance*

M. A. INDRA

In the following two chapters we propose, very briefly indeed, to discuss the legal position occupied by women in ancient India. It appears that at an early stage of social evolution women were treated as chattels. They had no rights of their own. They were generally thought to be inherently incapable of holding any property. The Hindu women lived as slaves in their husband's household. In later times they could be bought and sold[1] and conceivably let out for enjoyment.[2] The position of women is summed up in the two texts, one from Baudhayana and another from Katyayana, which are cited by all later commentators as the last word on woman's capacity and her legal rights. The first authority lays down that 'the Veda declares therefore, that women are devoid of the senses and incompetent to inherit'.[3] Katyayana observes, 'Let the childless widow preserving unsullied the bed of her lord and abiding with her venerable protector, enjoy with moderation the property until her death. After her death, let the heirs take it. But she has no property therein to the extent of gift or sale'.[4] Narada, another lawgiver pronounces almost the same verdict.

Says he, 'women's business transactions are *null and void*, except in case of distress. Women are not entitled to make gift or sale. A woman can take only a life-interest whilst she is living together with the rest of the family'.[5]

* Previously published in M.A. Indra's *The Status of Women in Ancient India: A Vivid and Graphic Survey of Women's Position, Social, Religious, Political, and Legal, in India*. Motilal Banarasidass Publishers (1955).

[1] Narada, XII—19.

[2] Vishnu, VI—5.

[3] Baudhyana, II—2—3—46. Also Taittariya Samhita VI—5—82. *Tasmat Sriya Nirindriya adayadah.*

[4] Katyayana cited in Dayabhaga, X—1—56.

[5] Yaska, III—I. In this connection Yaska the most ancient and authoritative exegetist on the Vedas, recorded views of different schools of thought who agree on the point that woman is incompetent to inherit and it is for the same reason that she is gifted away by her father, whereas a son is not. But brotherless women appear to be fully entitled to the right of succession.

The recognition of woman's right of inheritance is comparatively of recent origin. In the old ages it is manifest, women had no such right. The Rig Veda in a clear passage denies that the widow has any right to succeed to her husband. It gives, however, a widow the right to inherit as the daughter of her parents.[6] But in this case, the daughter was generally made to beget a son by *Niyoga*.[7] The later lawgivers such as Gautama,[8] Vasishtha,[9] Baudhayana[10] and Manu,[11] all give her the option of *Niyoga* and recognise the daughter's right of inheritance.

Vishvarupa, the commentator of Yajnavalkya, who preceded the author of Mitakshara denies that the widow, unless pregnant had any right to succeed to her husband and that the daughter other than the appointed daughter, could succeed to her father. About Yajnavalkya and Mitakshara we shall presently show that they have not been so illiberal in granting women their due legal rights.

The practice of *Niyoga* limited the widow, to obtain a son by her husband's younger brother and failing him by the nearest agnate. For, the rule was that on the husband's dying issueless the wife had merely the usufruct of her husband's property till she could beget a son. If she did, the son became the heir. If she could not, the estate passed to the husband's younger brother and failing him his nearest *sapinda*, who was her guardian. The female *sapindas* were excluded from inheritance, as they were not to remain in the family in which they were born. They were not *gotrajas* in as much as their *gotra* changed after marriage.[12]

Manu also subscribes to the same view that women have no proprietary rights of their own. According to one of his clear injunctions, a *wife*, a son and a slave—these three are declared to have no property; the wealth which they earn is acquired for him to whom they belong.[13] This idea of Manu has been copied by the later authority, that is, Shukra, even to the letter.[14]

Thus according to the ancient Hindu law, woman was hardly considered to be a legal person and was thus almost incapable of possessing any right. She was treated as a perpetual minor, one over whom man was always entitled to exercise control. The result is that up to the present day the Hindu law recognises limited proprietary rights of a woman.

Now we proceed to elucidate, at some length, the law of inheritance as it affected woman in the capacity of a daughter, a wife, a mother and a widow. From the code of Manu it appears that unmarried daughters in ancient India were entitled to one-fourth of the shares of patrimony received by brothers.[15] That is, if there were many brothers and sisters, then

---

[6] Rigveda, II—2—7.
[7] Rigveda, III—31—1.
[8] Gautama, XXVIII—18.
[9] Vasishtha, XVIII—15.
[10] Baudhyana, II—2—3—45
[11] Manu, IX—127.
[12] In general *Gotrajas* only are considered as entitled to inheritance. The Smriti Chandrika included both male and female in the word '*Gotraja*'.
[13] Manu VIII—416.
[14] Shukra, IV—5—295.
[15] Manu, IX–118. See also Kautilya (BK III—5), 'Unmarried daughters shall be paid adequate dowry, payable to them on the occasion of their marriage'.

the brothers were severally to give portions to their sisters, each out of his share one-fourth part. Medhatihi censures those commentators who think that one-fourth share need not be given actually but only as much as will suffice to defray the marriage expenses.[16]

In the Vedic ages also, it appears that the unmarried daughter, who lived all her life in her parents' house called *Amuja*, generally demanded and got a share of the ancestral property for inheritance.[17] But ordinarily she could not claim any share with her brothers for it is clearly laid down in the Rigveda that 'a son born As regards the maternal estate, it is said by Manu, that when the mother dies, all the uterine sisters (who according to Kulluka are unmarried) equally of the body, does not transfer wealth to sister'.[18]

As regards the maternal estate, it is said by Manu, that when the mother dies all the uterine sister (who according to Kulluka are unmarried) equally divide the mother's estate with uterine brothers.[19] According to Brihaspati, married daughters receive only a 'token of respect'. But Narada says that issueless daughters do receive some portion of the deceased mothers' share. Manu allows even daughters of daughters to get something out of the estate of their maternal grandmother on the score of affection. According to the interpretation of Kulluka these granddaughters should be unmarried.[20] To the separate property of a mother, known technically as *Stridhana*, the detailed consideration of which we postpone to the next chapter, only unmarried daughters (*Kumaris*) are heirs.[21] But Narada observes that *Kumari* in reality means a daughter who has no sons. Hence such daughters also receive *Stridhana.* The rule of Gautama,[22] so often quoted in the Mitakshara also lays down almost the same injunction. According to it, if the competition be between the unprovided and the enriched daughter, then the unprovided one inherits, but on the failure of such the enriched one succeeds. Thus it is clear that the unmarried daughter excludes the married daughter, whether she is rich or poor. In default of unmarried daughters, the married daughters succeed and among them the poor excludes the rich.

The position of Yajnavalkya who is still the most respected legal authority, may also be stated in a few words, as regards the daughter's right of inheritance. According to him unmarried sisters must be provided by their married brothers with expenses of marriage by giving one fourth part of their shares of patrimony.[23] The Mitakshara commenting on the above says, 'It is thus clear that daughters too after the death of their fathers have the right of succession'.[24] It also emphatically declares that this is not a provision for marriage, but a right to share in the heritage. About the mother's estate Yajnavalkya observes that all the property of a mother except her debts belong to her daughter.[25] The Mitakshara's reason for

[16] Medhatithi, on the above verse.
[17] Rigveda, II—17—7.
[18] Rigveda, III—31—2.
[19] Manu, IX—192.
[20] Kulluka on Manu, IX—193.
[21] Manu, IX—131.
[22] Gautama, *Stridhanam Duhitrinam Aprattanam Apratish thitanam.*
[23] Yajnavalkya, II—124.
[24] Mitakshara on the above.
[25] Yajnavalkya, II—117.

the mother's property going to daughters is that whereas daughters are born with greater portions of the blood of their mothers than with those of their fathers, therefore daughters must be the recipients of their mothers' *Stridhana*.[26]

Discussing the order of succession in case of a man dying without a son, the Mitakshara declares That the patrimony passes to the wife but in her absence to daughters, preferably the unmarried ones.[27] This rule has been supported by Brihaspati as well as Manu who says that the wife is the pronounced successor to the wealth of her husband and in her default the daughters. As a son so does the daughter of a man proceed from his several limbs. How then when one's self is alive in the form of one's daughter should any other person take her father's estate? Katyayana another lawgiver also holds the same view that the widow should succeed to her husband's wealth, provided she is chaste and in default of her, let the daughters inherit, if unmarried. The married daughters also got the right to inherit the paternal share. According to the Smritichan drika's interpretation of a Yajnavalkya text, the share was to be handed over to the husband.[28] But the author of the Viramitrodaya[29] refutes this view and declares that shares of the married daughters should be regarded as their *Stridhana.* Both the Madhviya and the Vivadatandava later legal digests also are opposed to the view of the Smritichandrika.

The doctrine of the Dayabhaga school in this matter also is worth being recorded. It says that a daughter who is mother of a male issue or who is likely to become so is only competent to inherit and not one who is a widow or is barren or fails in bringing none but daughters. The school argues that in reality daughters confer no benefit but they succeed because their sons do. It is the daughter's son who is the giver of a funeral oblation, not his son, nor the daughter's daughters, for the funeral oblation ceases with him. But it must be remembered that every daughter is presumed to be likely to get male children. If therefore she was married and was not past the child-bearing age, she would succeed to her father. It is then immaterial that she becomes a widow or is barren since an estate once vested cannot be devested by subsequent, disability.

There was in ancient India a peculiar class, known as appointed daughters. He who had no son might make his daughter in the following manner an appointed daughter. Addressing his son-in-law he might say, 'The male child born of her shall perform my funeral rites'[30] Between a son's son and son of an appointed daughter, there was regarded no difference, neither with respect to worldly matters, nor to sacred duties, for their father and mother both sprang from the body of the same man. The fundamental concept of inheritance was. 'Let one offer *Pindas* and take the wealth' (Manu).[31]

---

[26] Mitakshara on the above.

[27] Yajnavalkya, II—135–36. Also Manu (IX—130) 'Just as a person is born through a son, so is he through a daughter; the daughter and son are therefore equal. If the daughter is alive, how can anyone else take away the estate of the father?'

[28] Smritichandrika, II—115.

[29] Viramitrodaya—59, 60.

[30] Manu, IX—127. Baudhāyana also disqualifies a daughter from inheritance, even where she is the only child of the family. It is her son who can inherit the property who was called *putrika-putra* (II—2—3—15). He was entitled to offer funeral cakes to his grandfather. Also see Apastamba. II—6—14—2, 3, 4. Vasishtha XVIII—21 and XVII—12, 15.

[31] Manu, IX—133.

The interpretation by Vasishtha of an appointed daughter (*Putrika-putra*) is quite different. He declares on the authority of the Vedas that the only daughter belongs to her father's family and becomes the son of her parents. Such a *Putrika-Putra* (daughter, considered as a *putra*) is charged by her father to perform the customary obsequies to him after his death and consequently to become his heir herself. She comes to be counted as a son, her place among the twelve sons being second only to the son of the body (*aurasa*). Professor Jolly in his book *The Hindu Law of Adoption, Partition and Inheritance* (p. 149) refers to the prevalence of this custom in Kashmir, even in very recent times. He gives a passage of the Rajatarangini which mentions cases where the only daughter was installed as a son, where even her name was changed into that of a boy in order to obtain through her the same religious advantages as if she had been a son. Thus the name of Kalyandevi—a princess was converted by her royal father into the masculine form Kalyanmalla and all rites to be performed by a *Putra* were performed by her.

The son of an appointed daughter received the full estate of his grandfather who left no other son. On him was enjoined the duty of offering two funeral cakes to his own father and his maternal grandfather. But if after a daughter has been appointed a son be born to her father, the division was to be equal, for there was no right of primogeniture for a woman.[32] If an appointed daughter by accident died without leaving a son, the husband of the appointed daughter could without hesitation take that estate.[33]

Thus from the foregoing paragraph it is clear that daughters whether married, unmarried or appointed had some rights of succession in ancient India. They were not altogether excluded from inheritance, as their sisters certainly were in the later ages. The repeated argument in favour of the daughter's claim was that she too like the son was born of the limbs of her father. How hould any other, person inherit her father's property while she lived.[34]

Now, our next consideration is the legal status of woman as a wife and a widow. From the perusal of *Dharma Shastras* it appears that wives were generally thought to be without property. Manu[35] and later Shukra[36] agree on this matter. Their distinct verdict is that women as wives have no right on any estate except *Stridhana*, which generally goes to daughters. The logic of the above proposition is as follows. Upon her marriage the wife not only leaves her parental home, but severs her connection with it as completely as if she had never been born therein. She abandons the *gotra* of her parents and passes into and assumes that of her husband into whose family she is received as a daughter. But in it she has no individuality apart from that of her husband. She therefore, is entitled to no separate ownership. Over the property of her husband also she has no right during his lifetime beyond the right of maintenance and residence. This right to maintenance arises out of the jural relationship between the husband and wife created by marriage which is indissoluble. Besides it is based on humanitarian grounds as well. With regard to forsaken wives Yajnavalkya observes that 'he who forsakes a wife though obedient to his commands, diligent in household management,

[32] Manu, IX—134.
[33] Ibid., XI—135.
[34] Ibid., IX—30.
[35] Manu, VIII—416.
[36] Shukra, IV—5—295.

mother of an excellent son and speaking kindly shall be compelled to pay the third part of his wealth, or if poor to provide a maintenance for that wife'.[37] In the matter of partition however, the Mitakshara law allows a wife to get an equal share with her own son or sons when the division is made in the lifetime of her husband. In case she has *Stridhana* from her father-in-law, then she is entitled to half the share.

The aphorisms of Jaimini have been, however, not so half-hearted in granting to women their dues. They clearly pronounce that the one effect of marriage is to give each of the parties thereto, control over the other's wealth. On the seventeenth aphorism, Shabara the commentator observes as follows; 'The wife is entitled to wealth earned by the husband and *vice versa.* Hence sacrifice must be performed by both jointly, because if one of them is unwilling to perform it, the gift cannot be valid. Therefore, gift or money, even earned by the husband, is invalid if the wife's consent is not obtained'.

This quotation shows that both Jaimini and Shabara entertained more liberal views with regard to the right of the wife than the Smritikaras of the later ages.[38]

Now women as widows had ample rights to inherit their husbands' property. After the husband's death the first successor was the widow. Yajnavalkya,[39] Vishun,[40] Brihaspati,[41] Briddha Manu[42]—all are of the opinion that it is the wife who preeminently deserves to succeed to the estate of her deceased husband. One of the above-mentioned lawgivers argues that when the wife is half of the husband, then after husband that half is perfectly entitled to the property of the deceased half. Kautilya also supports widow's right of inheritance by saying, 'A barren widow who is faithful to the bed of her husband, may under the protection of her teacher enjoy his property as long as she lives, for it is to ward off calamities that women are endowed with property. On her death her property shall pass into the hands of her kinsmen' (BK III—2).

Medhatithi is against the widow's right of inheritance but his views are disputed by all and held as unreasonable. Katyayana believes that the widow's right of succession is incontestable.[43] So does Harita emphatically declare in an unmistakable passage.[44] The truth is that the widow's rights are very deep-rooted in the Aryan society. They go back even to the Vedic ages when even a childless widow was entitled to succession to her husband's estate.[45] In case she had sons, she was to divide the property of her husband with sons equally.[46] Brihaspati's assertion in this respect, however, is very explicit. Says he, 'In Vedas, Smritis

---

[37] Yajnavalkya, I—76.

[38] Gautama, XXVIII—21

In the absence of any issue or even an appointed daughter, the wife could inherit the property of her deceased husband. Gautama gives to the wife the right of inheritance and names her as one of the successors to the property of the deceased.

[39] Yajnavalkya, II—135, 36.

[40] Vishnu, in Mitakshara.

[41] Brihaspati, Ibid.

[42] Bridha Manu, Ibid.

[43] Katyayana in Mitakshara.

[44] Harita, Ibid.

[45] Rigveda, IX—102—11.

[46] Yajnavalkya, II—123.

and practice of people, a wife is considered by wise men as half the body of her husband, sharing equally the fruits of his good deeds and misdeeds. Half body of his, which is not dead, lives. How then can anyone else obtain his wealth, when half of his body survives?'

Manu[47] and Narada, however, appear to hold the opinion that brothers should have the property of a deceased brother and not his wife, who is to get only maintenance. But the widow who was given to a sinful life was not to be given any maintenance at all. In fact, unchastity in any female heir be she a daughter, a wife a widow or a mother, disqualified her for inheritance. Whosoever was in keeping of a man when the succession opened was excluded from inheritance, even though she might have married him afterwards. The Mitakshara,[48] the Dayabhaga,[49] and in fact all the legal authorities agree on this point. Otherwise, the maintenance of a widow who, not suspected of any misconduct, was commonly a charge on her husband's estate. The widow as of a right was entitled to reside in the family-dwelling house. This is clear from Katyayana's passage in which he says that the family-house cannot be sold. The widow's right of a residence could not be defeated even by offering her a separate house to live in, on the ground of her quarrelsomeness.

The Mitakshara commentary has with regard to the right of a widow's inheritance, raised a very interesting legal controversy. The contention of Shankha, Narada and Katyayana appears to be that brothers of a deceased person, have as compared to his widowed wife, a preferential right of succession to his property. But Briddha Manu and Vishnu hold a contrary opinion. A reconciliation between the conflicting views is brought about by the Mitakshara, by interpreting the former law as applicable to co-parcenary brothers, whereas the latter holds good, in the case of separation.

Again the widow's rights are assailed by Gautama and Vasishtha, who opine that only those widows are entitled to the right of inheritance, who make it definitely known that in order to have progeny they will resort to the practice of *Niyoga.* But the Mitakshara treats such line of thinking as inconsistent and ridiculous. In the explicit case of sonlessness only Yajnavalkya has conferred the right of succession on widows. The law, as expounded by him, is obviously dealing with widows who could not have any *Kshetriya* male offspring during the lifetime of their husband.

Still another objection as regards widow's competence to inherit is made by saying that whereas they are disqualified by all to *Shastras* to attend sacrifices or *Yajnas* and whereas all wealth has performance of religious rites as its objective, therefore, they are to be interdicted from inheritance of all property. This queer argument is disposed of by the Mitakshara with a word that gaining of virtue is the end of all human activities and not of mere performance of sacrifice.[50]

In the end, a word may be said about woman's rights as a mother. Obviously they were very limited, for a mother invariably was a wife. In the presence of her husband, she had

[47] Manu, IX—185.

[48] Mitakshara, II—3.

[49] Dayabhaga, XI—1—47, 48.

[50] Mitakshara, II—135, 36.

no separate property except her *stridhana.* However, a widowed mother had ample rights which can easily be understood.

In both the cases a mother obtained the inheritance of a son, if he died without leaving an issue.[51] She also inherited a daughter's property, if the daughter was married in the *Asura* form and died without an issue.[52] The mother's claim has been much strongly supported by the Dayabhaga school. According to it, if the father be not living the succession devolves on the mother. Vishnu's text also declares that if the father be dead, succession appertains to the mother.[53] It is argued that a mother's claim precedes that of brothers and the rest, since it is necessary to make a grateful return to her for benefits which she has personally conferred by rearing the child in her womb and nurturing him during his infancy and also because she confers benefits on him by the birth of other sons, who may offer funeral oblations in which he will participate.

Thus we may conclude that the legal position of women as daughters, wives, widows and mothers was by no means, one of complete disability, but one dictated by justice and fairness, as far as the circumstances of the ancient ages allowed. This much at least is certain that taking into view the contemporaneous conditions of other countries in this respect, ancient India had no reason to be less satisfied with the legal status, which she allotted to her women.

[51] Manu, IX—217.
[52] Ibid., IX—197.
[53] Vishnu cited in Dayabhaga, XI—IV—1, 2. Smritichandrika (II—38, 39) a later commentary on Yajnavalkya, however, asserts the view on the strength of a Vedic text, that a mother has the right to maintenance only and not to any succession.

Chapter 14

Property Rights of Women in Ancient India*

N. N. BHATTACHARYYA

There has been no dearth of work on *Strīdhana* or 'woman's property' in India, written from a purely legalistic point of view, since the establishment of the East India Company's rule in India. William Hicky who came to Calcutta as a legal practitioner during the time of Warren Hastings observed that the Indians were impressed by the British system of the administration of justice and that the ever-increasing lawsuits offered a wide scope of earning to the European legal practitioners who came to seek their fortune in this country. It was for their convenience that need was felt to compose treatises on Hindu and Muslim laws. The first work of this kind was *A Code of the Gentoo Law,* which was an English rendering of *Vivādārṇavasetu*, compiled under the direction of Warren Hastings, by a team of Brāhmaṇa legal experts, done by N. B. Halhed and published in the year 1776. The first authoritative work on Hindu law was H. T. Colebrooke's *A Digest of Hindu Law on Contracts and Succession*, with a commentary by Jagannath Tarkapa Panchanan, which was published in four volumes from Calcutta in 1797–98. This work contains, with other aspects of Hindu law, sections on Strīdhana. Colebrooke also edited and translated two Smṛtis and wrote few papers on legal topics. It should also be noted that in the list of the earlier publications in the Bibliotheca Indica series, ancient legal texts occupied a leading position. It was probably due to the fact that the European legal practitioners, as well as their Indian counterparts, were required to know the basic contents of the Dharmaśāstras and their commentaries, frankly for their professional interest.

Among the nineteenth century major publications of legal treatises, dealing with *Strīdhana* as well, mention may be made of Thomas Strenge's *Hindu Law* which was published as early as in 1830. *The Digest of Hindu Law,* written by West and Buehler and published in 1867–69, was also a landmark in modern legal literature of India. But the most authoritative work, which suits the purpose of the present paper, was Sir Gooroo Das Bannerjee's

* The reference list of this chapter has been prepared by Dr Ranjeeta Datta, Associate Professor, Centre for Historical Studies, JNU, in the absence of detailed references and bibliography in the original text.

Hindu Law of Marriage and Strīdhana, which was originally published in 1878 and had undergone numerous editions as had been in the case of J. D. Mayne's *A Treatise on Hindu Law and Usage*, another important legal publication of the nineteenth century. Rao Saheb V. N. Mandlik's *Hindu Law* which was published in 1880 had also been a standard work for many years. The Tagore Law Lectures, instituted by the University of Calcutta, were instrumental in bringing out a good number of legal publications. Among these the lectures on the *Outlines of the History of Hindu Law of Partition, Inheritance and Adoption as Gontained in Original Sanskrit Treatise*s, which were delivered in 1885 by J. Jolly, came out in a book form in 1888. Next to the work of Sir Gooroo Das Bannerjee it has been the most useful work on Strīdhana. Another work of Jolly is also important for our purpose. It was written in German and published in 1896 from Strassburg under the title *Recht und Sitte* which was subsequently rendered into English by B. K. Ghosh and published from Calcutta in 1928 under the title *Hindu Law and Custom.* Another important work, having bearing on our subject, was G. C. Sarkar's *Hindu Law of Adoption,* which was published in 1891.

In the present century there has been a multifarious increase in the publication of legal literature in most of which the question of Strīdhana has been seriously dealt with. Among such publications mention should be made of Priyanath Sen's *General Principles of Hindu Jurisprudence* (1918), K. P. Jayaswal's *Manu and Yājñavalkya: A Comparison and a Contrast* (1930), Radha Binod Pal's *History of Hindu Law* (1938), P. V. Kane's *History of Dharmaśāstra,* Vol. II (1941) and Vol. III (1946), N. C. Sengupta's *Evolution of Ancient Indian Law* (1953), L. Sternbach's *Judicial Studies in Ancient Indian Law* (1965–67), D. M. Derret's *Religion, Law and State in India* (1968) etc. This abundance of modern studies on the ancient legal tradition of India amply testifies that Strīdhana or Women's property was never a neglected subject. It should also be remembered in this connection that a considerable bulk of the civil suits has always been concerned with women's property and as such the concept of Strīdhana has been the subject of wide discussion and controversy. So goes a proverb in India that the lawyers fill their coffers with women's money, and this is not without any significance. In fact, all the studies on Strīdhana have been from a legalistic and professional point of view. The only exception is the work of P. V. Kane, in which there has been an attempt to view the whole thing in an historical perspective. Without much exaggeration it may be said that most of the well-known modern treatises on Hindu law purport in a subtle way to devise endless ways and means to deprive the women, especially the widows, of their property right, and these cunning devices have been given the status of law in the name of the interpretation of the ancient texts rather than what the texts suggest by themselves. As Kane has rightly said: 'It is also to be regarded that owing to the ignorance of Sanskrit on the part of the most judges that had to decide cases of Hindu Law, the opinions of individual learned authors…were followed without personal examination by judges on the authorities on which the opinions of authors were based' (Kane, III, 757 n.). The best way to deprive a woman of her property right is to make the scope of Strīdhana as narrow as possible so that it might comprise no more than a few clothes and ornaments. Thus, while according to the Mitākṣarā, the property inherited by a woman or obtained at a partition should fall definitely within the category of Strīdhana and pass automatically to her own relations after her death, the modern jurists have taken just a different stand saying that the property inherited by a woman from her parents or parents-in-law or husband or anyone should not fall within the category of Strīdhana and that it should pass after her death not to her own relations or natural heirs but to the next heir of the person from whom she inherited it.

While dealing with the property rights of ancient India, one should not forget that it took a long time for the primitive customs and conventions, by which the ancient societies were governed, to get streamlined into a widely acceptable legal system, that quite for a long time the whole matter of inheritance was not regulated by any general state power and that different regions of the country had and still have different legal traditions. Even in a single region laws and customs vary from caste to caste, community to community. Everywhere in India, there is a wide gulf of difference between the codified and customary laws. The former consists of the laws and customs as codified in the Dharmaśāstras or Smṛtis and is followed mostly by the dominant section comprising about 20 per cent of the total population of India. Others follow various customary laws and traditions for the study of which we are to depend on the vast mass of anthropological literature including correspondences, notes and queries, gazetteers, memoirs, journals, census reports, surveys and individual monographs on tribes and castes. Specially important in this connection are the regional studies on tribes and castes made by L. K. Ananthakrishna Iyer, William Crooke, R. E. Enthoven, D. C. J. Ibbetson, H. H. Risley, H. A. Rose, H. V. Nanjundayya, R. V. Russell, Rai Bahadur Hira Lal, E. Thurston, K. Rangachari, etc., which contain details about the laws and customs of the simpler peoples not belonging to the culture of dominant section. Apart from these, in the works of E. Steele, G. K. Raychaudhuri, G. Oppert, J. E. Padfield, S. C. Bose and a few others, the laws and customs of the popular traditions make frequent appearance.

Matrilineal inheritance which is prevalent among various tribes and castes of India is a typical example of customary laws. P. R. T. Gurdon and A. Playfair have given details of this form of inheritance in their works entitled *The Khasis* and *The Garos of Meghalaya* which were published respectively in 1907 and 1909. Among these tribes the entire property belongs to the mothers and it is transmitted in the female line from mother to daughters, the youngest one having the largest share. Such form of inheritance has been noticed among various tribes and castes of Madhya Pradesh, Karnataka and Kerala, details of which are found in such works as *The Tribes and Castes of the Central Provinces of India* (1916) by R. V. Russell and Rai Bahadur Hira Lal, *The Mysore Tribes and Castes* (1928–35) by H. V. Nanjundayya and L. K. Ananthakrishna Iyer, *The Castes and Tribes of Southern India* (1909) by E. Thurston and K. Rangachari and *The Cochin Tribes and Castes* (1909) by L. K. Ananthakrishna Iyer. In Kerala, the Nayar joint family or *tarwad* consists of a woman, her daughters and grandchildren in the female line, and when it grows unusually big it often splits into smaller family units called *tavazis*. A thorough study of the rules of matrilineal inheritance was made by Baron Omar Rolf Ehrenfels in his *Mother-right in India*, which was published in 1941. The custom of matrilineal inheritance has also been extensively dealt with in Debiprasad Chattopadhyaya's *Lokāyata* (1959), K. M. Kapadia's *Marriage and Family in India* (1966) and the present writer's *Indian Mother Goddess* (1970, 1977). In certain cases again, we come across a transitory phase between matrilineal and patrilineal forms of inheritance in which the sister's son gets the property of his mother's brother. Reference to such a typical system is found in the Mahābhārata (VIII. 45.13) in which it is stated that this form of inheritance was in vogue among the Āraṭṭas and Bāhīkas. In southern India this system was known as *alia-santāna* which was followed even by the kings of Travancore. What we want to suggest is that, so far as the question of inheritance and ownership of property was concerned, the doctrine of *patria potestus* so intensely crystallised in the Smṛtis was never a universal phenomenon in India.

From the internal evidence of the Ṛgveda it appears that the concept of individual ownership was not prevalent in the early Vedic age. References to 'common wealth' or 'collective ownership' are found abundantly in the Ṛgveda (cf. I. 141.1; III. 2.12; VI. 26.1; VII. 76.5; VIII. 99.8, etc.). Tribal bond of kinship was an essential feature of the early Vedic society and as such tribal wealth was divided among the constituent clans and subclans. This is attested by the passages referring to *vārya* and *bhāga* which were the Ṛgvedic terms of division. Land was not any form of property in the early Vedic age, because agriculture was then hardly known. Even when agriculture was introduced in the later Vedic age land was subject to joint or corporate holding, so the question of individual ownership and inheritance of land could not arise at all. The Vedic tribes were mostly pastoral warriors and they counted wealth in terms of cattle. The pastoral societies have, however, greater scope to develop the sense of property and individual ownership since cattle could be preserved and multiplied, used as the best medium of exchange, increased by wars and raids, and divided among clans, families, even individuals. Evidence of some kind of individual possession is found in the later books of the Ṛgveda. That in the later period of the Ṛgveda even women were entitled to have some share of cattle wealth as marriage gift is suggested in the 'wedding hymn' (X.85.13–38). The term mentioned there is *vahatu* which has been explained by Sāyaṇa as 'cow and other gifts given for pleasing the girl'.

Needless to say that the Vedic society, owing to its pastoral background, was essentially patriarchal which is attested by the abundance of misogynistic passages in the Vedic texts. For example, in the Śatapatha Brāhmaṇa (IV.4.2.3) it is stated that 'women own neither themselves nor an inheritance'. Yāska in his Nirukta (III.4) says that women are not entitled to partition and inheritance. But whatever was the attitude towards women, it was not possible in practice to suppress all their property rights, especially owing to the fact that there were parallel traditions everywhere in which women were treated differently and the influence of which could not be ignored by the Vedic lawgivers. The term *pāriṇāhya* has been used in the Taittirīya Saṁhitā (VI.2.1.1) indicating the authority of the wife on family resources. This recurs in the Pūrvamīmāṁsāsūtras (VI.10.10) of Jaimini which has been explained by Śabara in terms of possessing certain forms of property by the wife, and almost in the same sense the term has been used by Manu (IX.11). It should, however, be stressed that although the concepts of property and division are found in the Vedic texts, especially the later ones, in that formative period of economic life there was a natural contradiction between the social and individual ownership. The Dharmasūtras are openly in favour of an extremely patrilineal form of inheritance in which in the absence of sons the property will rather go to the near and remote agnates (*sapiṇḍa* and *sakulya* relations) of the property holder than to the daughters of his own seed. The Dharmasūtras of Āpastamba (II.6.14.19), Baudhāyana (II.2.49) and Vasiṣṭha (XVII.48–49), however, say that the ornaments and such wealth as bestowed upon her by her relations, both agnate and cognate, should be absolutely owned by her.

It is in the Dharmaśāstras or Smṛtis that we come across a distinct codification of the rules relating to ownership, inheritance and partition. The codes of Manu are the first systematic expositions of all these, and his basic approaches to these questions were followed in principle, with certain conservative or liberal reservations, by the later lawgivers. The Manusmṛti must have been composed before the beginning of the Christian era, while the Smṛtis of Yājñavalkya, Nārada and Bṛhaspati were composed within the limit of the Gupta age, and those of Kātyāyana, Vyāsa and Pārāśara in the post-Gupta period. Manu made the Dharmasūtra traditions up to date. But while dealing with the Dharmasūtra injunctions regarding the property rights of women he faced two apparently contradictory principles. The first is that Dharmasūtras allow women to become exclusive owners of such wealth as is obtained by them as gifts from their relations. This formed the basis of his famous formulation of the six-fold concept of Strīdhana (IX.194). The second principle of the Dharmasūtras was rather difficult for him to accept. The Dharmasūtras categorically say that property should be transmitted only through the male line and that women have no right to inherit their paternal property by themselves. Manu was no less patriarchal than the authors of the Dharmasūtras, but as the first universal lawgiver he had to take into consideration the existing laws belonging to other popular traditions, apart from the Vedic sources, which speak of women's right to inherit their ancestral property. So he had to make a compromise. Thus, on the one hand, nowhere in his codes he says that sisters are equally entitled to the patrimony as their brothers but, on the other, he says that for the purpose of the marriage of their sisters the brothers should forego one-fourth of their own shares in favour of the sisters (IX.118). Obviously, this does not mean that the daughters are the natural heirs of their father. The father is, however, at liberty to give any amount of wealth as gift to his daughter and such gifts are regarded as belonging to the *pitṛdatta* and *anvādheya* categories of Strīdhana. Apart from this, if a man is sonless, he can regard his daughter as *putrikā* or 'daughter functioning as son' who will be his legitimate heir (IX.127). The wealth owned by the mother will pass to the daughter (IX.131). It is surprising to note that Manu is completely silent about the rights of the widow.

The codes of Manu had a tremendous impact not only on the subsequent lawgivers but also on others belonging to different disciplines. Even a philosopher like Śaṅkara unconditionally says that in regard to social matters Manu is final. Of course, among the subsequent lawgivers some differences from Manu in approach are found. For example, Yājñavalkya supports Manu's insistence on the doctrine of primogeniture, but he holds that the father and sons have equal ownership of ancestral property which subsequently led to the emergence of *janma-svattva-vāda*, peculiar to the Mitāksarā school. He says in conformity with Manu's view that after the father's death the sons shall divide property among themselves, the mother taking an equal share and the sisters a fourth part of the son's share. Like Manu, Yājnñavalkya does not make any clear statement whether this one-fourth share, enjoyed by the sisters, is owing to a natural succession or to a moral obligation for which the brothers should forego their one-fourth. So far as Strīdhana is concerned Yājñavalkya clarifies the stand of Manu and insists categorically on the exclusive right of women of their Strīdhana. The husband can make use of it only in case of a famine, or for the performance of some specially efficacious religious rite, or during illness or under such severe conditions when he has no other way to save himself without the help of his wife's money.

Later lawgivers like Nārada, Bṛhaspati and Kātyāyana, and their successors follow either Manu or Yājñavalkya with diminishing importance on the doctrine of primogeniture upheld by the earlier authorities. In regard to inheritance and partition, so far as the shares of women are concerned, they also speak of the one-fourth share conventionally without any further clarification. However, in regard to Strīdhana some of them are more particular. Among them Kātyāyana (594 ff., 895–920) makes the most elaborate treatment of Strīdhana making improvement of what was suggested by *Manu and Yājñavalkya* and his version has been accepted by all digests including the Dāyabhāga. He defines Strīdhana under the following categories: *adhyagni* or what is given to a woman at the time of marriage before the nuptial fire; *adhyāvahanika* or what she obtains when she is being taken from her father's house to the bridegroom's; *prītidatta* or what is given to her through affection (to this category Manu includes gifts from the husband during love-making); *śulka* or what is given to her as the bridal price (which includes household articles as well); *anvādheya* or what is given to her after marriage from the family of her husband or of her own parents (to a certain extent it corresponds to Manu's *pitṛdatta*, *mātṛdatta* and *bhrātṛdatta* categories, though he refers to a seventh category under the title *anvādheya* meaning 'gift-subsequent'); and *saudāyikā* or what is obtained by a married woman in her husband's house or by a maiden in the house of her father. In other words, 'all property (whether movable or immovable) obtained by a woman, either as a maiden, or at marriage, or after marriage, from her parents or from husband and his family (except immovable property given by husband) is included within the scope of *strīdhana*' (Priyanath Sen, 335–36).

From the tenth century onwards there was a qualitative change in the approach towards property and property relations. It was possible after the advent of Jīmūtavāhana (c. AD 1100–50) and Vijñāneśvara (c. AD 1080–1100). The Dāyabhāga of Jīmūtavāhana and the Mitākṣarā of Vijñāneśvara became so important that throughout the successive ages these two works and their legal interpretations came to be regarded as almost the sole source of the Hindu laws relating to ownership, partition and inheritance. According to the Dāyabhāga of Jīmūtavāhana, ownership implies absolute competence of the owner to dispose of his property at his will. The owner is the sole lord of his property having the right of its alienation without the consent of his sons or relations. Jīmūtavāhana has also brought a significant change in the concept of *sapinda* relation. He says that there is no reason to hold that this relation should evolve only among the strictly patrilineal agnates. Rather those who are more intimately associated with the family, notwithstanding cognates of different male descent, like the daughter's son, father's daughter's son, maternal uncle, etc., should be regarded as belonging to the *sapinda* relation. This is a revolutionary departure from the approach of the previous lawgivers. Jīmūtavāhana accepts Kātyāyana's definition of Strīdhana allowing every right to the woman to give, sell or enjoy it independently of her husband. Jīmūtavāhana also categorically says that if the owner of the Strīdhana does not bestow her property at her own will to her chosen person or persons, the property will devolve equally upon the sons and unmarried daughters.

The Mitākṣarā of Vijñāneśvara, which is actually a commentary on the Yājñavalkyasmṛti, is of more complex character than the Dāyabhāga of Jīmūtavāhana. Vijñāneśvara, unlike Jīmūtavāhana, does not admit absolute ownership of an individual over the property and holds that certain relations acquire ownership at the moment of their birth. As soon as a son is born he becomes co-owner of the property enjoyed by the father. In the field of succession agnates are preferred to the cognates. Vijñāneśvara has given the sonless widow the right to succeed to the whole property of her husband. As between the claims of the daughters he prefers unmarried to the married and unprovided to the endowed daughter. His rule of succession is mainly based upon the principle of propinquity or proximity of relationship and as such he allows to daughter's son to succeed immediately after the daughter and before the mother and the father, and the mother to succeed before the father. According to Vijñāneśvara's concept, the Strīdhana is that form of property which is acquired by a woman 'by inheritance, purchase, partition, seizure and finding'. Among the six categories of Strīdhana, in the case of those belonging to *anvádheya* and *prītidatta* categories, daughters are allowed to succeed equally and in their absence the sons. Strīdhana belonging to four other categories will be succeeded in the following order—unmarried daughter, unendowed married and endowed married daughter. The Strīdhana of a childless woman goes to the husband.

Although there was not so much anomaly in the case of Strīdhana which could be accrued in the hand of a woman through a variety of sources and after her lifetime possession and enjoyment of it, it could be succeeded by her heirs in the female line on the basis of the principle of propinquity, the question of a woman's natural right to succeed her father's property directly, as that happened in the case of her brother's, has not been clearly answered in the Smṛtis and their commentaries. From the bewildering variety of statements found in these texts what actually emerges, as has rightly or wrongly been understood by the present writer, may be reproduced as follows. Regarding direct inheritance of the father's property the Dharmaśāstras or the Smṛtis and their commentaries follow the Dharmasūtra tradition according to which property will devolve only among the sons and in their absence among the agnates in the male line. That the sisters were entitled to get one-fourth of their brothers' share on account of their marriage was more an expression of moral obligation than of a legal compulsion. When all the Smṛtis and their commentaries unanimously say that what a woman obtains through inheritance becomes a category of her Strīdhana it does not mean direct inheritance of her father's property; rather it means the direct inheritance of her mother's Strīdhana. What she obtained from her father, brothers and paternal relations was gift rather than inheritance, and the wealth thus accrued in the Strīdhana might be turned into a property to be inherited by her daughters. The question of a daughter's direct inheritance could arise only when the father was sonless. But the Smṛtis and their commentaries are not at all unanimous on the question whether in the case of a sonless person his daughter can be natural heir of her father's property or it will go to the agnates of the paternal line according to the principle of propinquity. Even Manu's concept of *putrikā*, that is, sonhood ascribed to the daughter by the sonless father, has been subject of keen controversy among the commentators. This remained a floating question, causing innumerable law suits, till the enactment of the Hindu Code. Again when all the Smrāti writers agree that what is obtained by a woman owing to the partition of a property will form a category of her Strīdhana, it undoubtedly implies an inheritance, but it pertains to the wife, widow, mother and even grandmother and not to the daughter. The wife, the widow, the mother or the grandmother could not demand a partition by themselves but were entitled to a share when the partition took place. The wife's share in most cases was equal to that of a son. The widow of a deceased coparcener was a member of the coparcenary, Kātyāyana (926) allows a sonless widow to become the sole owner of her husband's property, though this stand is not maintained in all the Smrātis. The Dāyabhāga holds that the widow of a sonless member of a joint family is entitled to have a share of the property while the Mitāksāarā allows absolute ownership of the widow over the movable property of her deceased husband.

SANSKRIT TEXTS AND TRANSLATIONS

J. R. Gharpure, trans., *Balambhatti*, 3 Vols, *Being a Commentary by Balambhatta Payagunde on The Mitaksara of Sri Vijnaneswara on the Yajnavalkya-Smrti* (1920).

F. W. Thomas, ed. and trans., *Brihaspati Sutra, or, the science of Politics According to the School of Brihaspati* (Lahore: Motilal Banarsidass, 1921). (The Devanagari text prepared from his edition (in Roman script), with introductory remarks and indexes by Bhagavad Datta.)

H. T. Colebrooke, trans., *Dayabhaga of Jimutavahana: The Hindu Laws of Inheritance in Bengal* (1818).

P. V. Kane, trans., *Katyayana Smriti on Vyavahara (Law and Procedure)*, Sanskrit with English Translation (Bombay, 1933).

Julius Jolly, trans., *Naradiya Dharmasastras or The Institutes of Narada*, translated for the first time from the Unpublished Sanskrit Original (London: Trubner & Co, 1878).

Max Muller, ed., *Rig-Veda-Sanhita, the Sacred Hymns of the Brahmans, Together with the Commentary of Sayanacharya*, published under the Patronage of the Hounorable East India Company (London: W. H. Allen and Co, 1849).

Ganganath Jha, trans., *Shabara Bhasya*, 3 Vols (Baroda: Baroda Oriental Institute, 1939).

H. T. Colebrooke, ed. and trans., *The Law of Inheritance According to the Mitakshara* (Calcutta: Thacker Spink and Co, 1869).

Max Muller, ed., *The Laws of Manu.*, translated with extracts from Seven Commentaries, *Sacred Books of the East,* Vol. 25 (Oxford University Press, 1886).

Kisari Mohan Ganguli, trans., *The Mahabharata of Krishna-Dwaipayana Vyas* (Calcutta: Bharat Press, 1883–96).

B. D. Basu, ed., *The Mimamsa Sutras of Jaimini*, *Sacred Books of the Hindus*, trans. Pandit Mohan Lai Sandal (Allahabad: The Panini Office).

Max Muller, ed., *The Minor Law Book.* Vol. 33 of *Sacred Books of the East*, trans. Julius Jolly (Oxford: The Clarendon Press, 1889).

Lakshman Sarup, ed. and trans., *The Nighantu and The Nirukta of Sri Yaskacarya: The Oldest Indian Treatise on Etymology, Philology and Semantics* (London: H. Milford, 1920–29).

The Purva-Mimansa Sastra of Gemini (Allahabad: The Panini Office, 1916).

Max Muller, ed., *The Sacred Laws of the Āryas as Taught in the School of Apastamba, Gautama, Vâsishtha, and Baudhâyana*, Vol. 1 of 2. Part 1: *Āpastamba and Gautama. The Dharmasutras*, Vol. 2 of *Sacred Books of the East*, trans. Georg Buhler (Oxford University Press, 1879).

Max Muller, ed., *The Sacred Laws of the Āryas as taught in the school of Apastamba, Gautama, Vâsishtha, and Baudhâyana*, Vol. 2 of 2. Part 2: *Vāsiṣṭha and Baudhāya*. Vol. 14 of *Sacred Books of the East*, trans. Georg Buhler (Oxford University Press, 1882).

Max Muller, ed., *The Satapatha Brahmana. According to the Text of the Mâdhyandina School*. Vol. 2 of 5, Books III and IV, Vol. 26 of *Sacred Books of the East*, trans. Julius Eggeling (Oxford University Press, 1885).

A. B. Keith, *The Vedas of the Black Yajus School entitled Taittiriya Sanhita*, translated From the original Sanskrit prose and verse (Cambridge, MA, 1914).

J. R. Gharpure, *Yajnavalkyasmriti or the Institutes of Yajnavalkya, Together with the Commentary of the Mitaksara by Sri Vijnaneswara. Book the Second. An English Translations with Notes, explanations etc: Collection of Hindu Law Texts*, no. 2 (Bombay).

SECONDARY WORKS

Sir Gooroodas Banerjee, *The Hindu Law of Marriage and Stridhan. Tagore Law Lectures* (Calcutta: Thacker, Spink &Co., 1879).

N. N. Bhattacharya, *Indian Mother Goddess* (Calcutta: Indian Studies Past and Present, 1971). (Formerly printed in ISPP 11, 4 July–September 1970).

N. N. Bhattacharya, *Indian Mother Goddess* (Columbia: South Asian Books, 1971).

Royal Asiatic Society of Bengal, *Bibliotheca Indica* (Calcutta: Royal Asiatic Society of Bengal, 1907).

S. C. Bose, *The Hindoos as They Are*, 2nd ed. (Calcutta, 1883).

Debiprasad Chattopadhyaya, *Lokayata: A Study in Ancient Indian Materialism* (New Delhi: People's Publishing House, 1959).

H. T. Colebrooke, *A Digest of Hindu Law: On Contracts and Successions, with a Commentary by Jagannát'ha Tercapanchánana*, 2 Vols (Madras: J. Higginbotham, 1864). (Vol. 1, London, 1801).

H. T. Colebrooke, *Miscellaneous Essays, by H. T. Colebrooke, with Life of the Author. By his Son, Sir T. E. Colebrooke* (London: Trübner & Co., 1873).

William Crooke, *The tribes and castes of the North-western Provinces and Oudh*, Volume I–IV (Calcutta: Office of the Superintendent of Government Printing, 1896).

J. Duncan M. Derret, *Religion, Law and State in India* (London: Faber and Faber, 1968).

Reginald Edward Enthoven, *The Tribes and Castes of Bombay*, 3 Vols (Bombay: Government Central Press, 1920–22).

N. B. Halhed, *A Code of Gentoo laws, or, Ordinations of the Pundits: From a Persian Translation, Made from the Original, Written in the Sanskrit language* (London, 1776).

D. C. J. Ibbetson, *Panjab Castes* (Lahore: Printed by the Superintendent, Government Printing, Punjab, 1916).

L. K. Ananthakrishna Iyer, *Tribes and Castes of Cochin* (1912).

L. K. Ananthakrishna Iyer, *The Cochin Tribes and Castes* (Madras, 1909).

L. K. Ananthakrishna Iyer, *The Mysore Tribes and Castes* (Mysore: Mysore University Press, 1930).

K. P. Jayaswal, *Manu and Yājñavalkya—A Comparison and a Contrast: A Treatise on the Basic Hindu Law*, 1st ed. (London: Butterworth & Co., 1930).

Julius Jolly, *Outlines of an History of the Hindu Law of Partition, Inheritance and Adoption* (Calcutta: Thacker, Spink &Co; Madras: Higginbotham & Co and London: W Thacker and Co., 1885).

Julius Jolly, *Recht and Sitte* (Strassburg: Karl J Tubner, 1896).

P. V. Kane *History of the Dharamsastras* (Poona: Bhadarkar Oriental Research Institute, 1968–75).

K. M. Kapadia, 'The Matrilineal Family', in *Marriage and Family in India*, ed. K. M. Kapadia (Bombay: Oxford University Press, 1966), 336–54.

Rao Sahib V. N. Mandalik, *Hindu Law, or Makyukha and Yajnavalka* (Bombay: Education Society Press, 1880).

John D. Mayne, *A Treatise on Hindu Law and Usage*, 7th ed., revised and enlarged (Madras: Higginbotham & Co., 1906).

H. V. Nanjundayya and Rao Bahadur L. K. Ananthakrishna Iyer, *The Mysore Tribes and Castes*, 3 Vols (Mysore: Government Oriental Library; Bangalore. Government Book Depot, 1928–35). (Published Under the Auspices Of The Mysore University).

Omar Rolf Leopold Werner Freiherr von Ehrenfels, *Mother-Right in India* (H. Milford, Oxford University Press, 1941).

J. E. Padfield *The Hindus at Home. Being Sketches of Hindu Daily Life* (London, 1923).

Radha Binod Pal, *History of Hindu Law in the Vedic Age and in Post Vedic Times down to the Institutes of Manu: Tagore Law Lectures* (1930).

Peter Quennell, ed., *The Memoirs of William Hickey* (London: Hutchinson, 1960).

Recht and Sitte, *Einschliesslich der einheimischen Litteratur in Grundriss der Indo-arischen Philologie und Altertumskunde. Translated as Hindu Law and Customs by Bata Krishna Ghosh* (Calcutta: Greater India Society, 1928).

H. H. Risley, *The Tribes and Castes of Bengal* (Bengal Secretariat Press, 1891).

Horace Arthur Rose and Edward Douglas MacLagan, *A Glossary of the Tribes and Castes of the Punjab and North-West Frontier Province* (Lahore: Samuel T. Weston at the Civil and Military Gazette Press, 1911–19).
R. V. Russell and Rai Bahadur Hira Lal, *The Tribes and Castes of the Central Provinces of India*, 4 Vols (London: Macmillan and Co., limited, 1916).
G. C. Sarkar, *Hindu Law of Adoption* (1891).
Priya Nath Sen, *The General Principles of Hindu Jurisprudence: Tagore's Law Lectures* (1918).
N. C. Sengupta, *Evolution of Ancient Indian Law* (London: Probsthain, 1953).
L. Sternbach, *Judicial Studies in Ancient Indian Law*, Parts 1 and 2 (Delhi: Motilal Banarsidass, 1965).
Thomas Strange, *Hindu Law*, 2 Vols (London: Parbury & Co, Payne & Co., Butterworth, 1830).
E Thurston and K. Rangachari, *Castes and Tribes of Southern India* (Madras: Government Press, 1909).
Sir Raymond West and Georg Buhler, *A Digest of the Hindu Law of Inheritance, Partition, and Adoption, Embodying the Replies of the Sastris: With Notes and Introduction* (London: Sweet and Maxell, 1919).

Chapter 15

Turmeric Land: Women's Property Rights in Tamil Society since Early Medieval Times*

KANAKALATHA MUKUND

As with many questions relating to the status of women in Indian (and specifically Hindu) society, the simple question, 'what rights did women have to property?' becomes an extremely complex one with no uniform answers which are valid for all regions, castes or classes. To begin with, there is no unanimity on this question even among the various Smṛtis and texts of jurisprudence. That there should be a considerable variance between theory and customary practice is understandable. What is difficult to reconcile is the general perception that women have no property rights in Hindu society, even though there have been several legal cases about women's property rights and the *strīdhana* which even went up to the Privy Council[1] This paper is an attempt to examine the issue of women's property rights in the specific regional culture of Tamil society. Inscriptional evidence and other sources allow us to trace some aspects of how women have controlled and used property since early medieval times. In spite of large gaps in data, this evidence can be related to usage in recent times. Accordingly, we can try to capture, even though imperfectly, the arrangements which were in vogue prior to the Hindu Act of Succession, 1956. To understand the nature of rights in land or other property, we need to examine both customary and legal rights, the extent of direct control, and the power of alienation. No surprisingly, what comes across is that, in spite of some general, common features there is endless variation in customs and practices.

* Reproduced with permission from the author. Previously published in *Economic and Political Weekly*, vol. 27, Sameeksha Trust, 1997. Reproduced in Kumkum Roy, *Women in Early Indian Societies*, Manohar Books, Delhi, (1999); pp. 123–40.

Thus, what this preliminary investigation reveals is that the diversity of women's property rights across regions/sub-regions/castes/classes/families can be dealt with only through a series of microstudies. What I have tried to do is to point to the diversities and hazard some tentative hypotheses which may instigate other scholars to explore these challenging untrodden paths.

WHAT IS WOMEN'S PROPERTY?

In the ancient Smṛtis and Dharmaśāstras (for the most part dating back to 200 BC–AD 400), which were the first systematic treatment of Hindu law, the question of property rights and inheritance formed one of the important aspects of civil law, with the more controversial question of women's rights also being discussed.[2] Even the *Manusmṛti* recognised women's property or *strīdhana*, and the right of unmarried daughters to a share of the father's property. Yājñavalkya, Kātyāyana and Nārada were the important jurists who, though by no means unanimous in their views, further developed and defined women's property rights. To condense their views in the simplest form, women could acquire property in four principal ways: (a) what was given to them at the time of marriage (*adhyāgni*); (b) gifts given after marriage, either by the parents, husband or husband's family, 'through affection'—often referred to as *saudāyika*, *prītidāna* or *prītidatta;* (c) through inheritance and (d) by working.

The earliest recognised form of women's property was *strīdhana* or what was given to the bride at the time of marriage. There seems to be a sound basis to believe that this *strīdhana* was originally part of the bride price or *kanyāśulka* paid by the bridegroom, a part of which was passed on to the bride by her parents. The ready acceptance of this without reservation as the property of the woman also derived from the general disfavour in which the practice of *kanyāśulka* came to be held (so that, by excluding the husband from the right to this property, the habit could be discouraged). Other gifts which were given on the occasion of a wedding were also denoted as *strīdhana*, mainly because they tended to be small in value.

Saudāyika was also included in *strīdhana.* This specific allusion to a *gift* is in itself an indication that a woman had no automatic right to this wealth, as an inheritance right. There was also a further rider that if any immovable property had been gifted by the husband, the wife had only limited, at best usufruct, rights in that property. *Strīdhana*, on the other hand, was the absolute property of the woman and it is a matter of interest that husbands were forbidden to use or sell the *strīdhana*, except in times of dire need.

The earnings of a woman were universally stated to belong to the family and could not be considered *strīdhana.* In this context it is interesting to note that in present-day Tamil Nadu, in common perception, *the only class of women* who were thought to have property rights were the *devadāsīs*[3] These women and their immediate kin usually constituted self-supporting, female-headed households whose property (in legal language) was acquired by 'self-exertion and mechanical arts'. Courtesans (*gañikās*), of course, were certainly prominent on the social scene even in ancient times, but the debates on women's property rights seem to have been located only within the patriarchal system.

The really thorny issue in women's property rights was the question of inheritance rights to family property—of daughters to the father's property and of married women/widows to the husband's property. Again there was no consensus on these rights, but slowly the view gained ground that while daughters were normally entitled only to their marriage portions, they could inherit property when there were no sons in the family or if they were unmarried at the time of the death of the father. Somewhat reluctantly, widows were also accepted as having the right to a share of the husband's property, but, on the death of a widow her share reverted to the heirs of her late husband.

Two major schools of thought on property rights emerged in the early twelfth century—the Dāyabhāga school of Jīmūtavāhana and the Mitākṣarā school of Vijñāneśvara. The Dāyabhāga school gave more comprehensive inheritance rights to widows, while the Mitākṣarā school specified that *strīdhana* went by succession from mother to daughter (the preferred line of succession was unmarried daughters first, married, but not well-off daughters next, married daughters, sons and other heirs). The main significance of these works was that they became the basis of Hindu law on these issues under the British courts, which referred to these authorities for establishing what constituted women's property. They ultimately developed the idea of two kinds of women's property. The first was that of *strīdhana* (as defined in the older texts), which on the death of the woman would pass on to *her* children/heirs—that is, she constituted an independent stock of descent. Most often, the recognised succession was down the female line, but according to some schools, all children shared equally in the property. The other form of property, termed 'woman's estate', referred to the share of the widow, over which she had no power of alienation (except under extenuating circumstances)[4]

These rights also varied from region to region, depending on whether local usage subscribed to *Mitākṣarā* or *Dāyabhāga.*

Thus, traditionally there was no definitive or uniform code relating to women's property rights. Even among the Smṛti writers there was an ongoing debate as to whether customary practice or śāstras should take precedence. We gather that what was being laid down as law tended to be prescriptive and not always a record of what existed in practice; equally, that the modifications which were made in *strīdhana* and widows' rights derived at least in part from *de facto* recognition of customary rights. That the usage varied from region to region was also acknowledged, and even from very early times commentators pointed out that in the *dakṣiṇa* (southern) region women's rights were more broad-based.[5] By the twelfth century, when the *Dāyabhāga* and *Mitākṣarā* texts were being authoritatively codified, there also existed a large corpus of inscriptions in south India. This coincidence in time makes it possible for us to juxtapose the actual with the prescriptive, and to understand the historical experience relating to women's property rights in south India.

INSCRIPTIONAL EVIDENCE

There are many references to women and their use of property in inscriptions in Tamil Nadu.[6] Their range and sheer volume indicate that inscriptions can indeed be used as a sound basis for reconstructing social history. The 348 inscriptions used here are very suggestive of local customs in this context. In order to understand the social background of the women, a combined caste/class ordering has been drawn up.[7] By and large, class, rather than caste, is used as the reference point, so that even though most local chiefs and local elite families were *vēḷālas*, and occasionally Brāhmaṇas, they are designated by the class and not by caste (Tables 15.1 and 15.2). In 21 cases it has not been possible to identify either caste or

Table 15.1 Distribution of Women Property Owners

District	Century	Status	Number
Chingelpet	0	Brāhmaṇa	2
Chingelpet	8	Major Royalty	2
Chingelpet	9		1
Chingelpet	9	Brāhmaṇa	1
Chingelpet	9	Local chief	5
Chingelpet	9	Major royalty	1
Chingelpet	10	Tēvaraṭiyāl	2
Chingelpet	10	Local chief	1
Chingelpet	10	Major royalty	6
Chingelpet	11	Brāhmaṇa	9
Chingelpet	11	Tēvaraṭiyāl	3
Chingelpet	11	Local chief	2
Chingelpet	11	Local elite	1
Chingelpet	11	Maidservant	1
Chingelpet	11	Major royalty	2
Chingelpet	11	Palace maidservant	1
Chingelpet	12		3
Chingelpet	12	Brāhmaṇa	2
Chingelpet	12	Tēvaraṭiyāl	4
Chingelpet	12	Local chief	1
Chingelpet	12	Major royalty	1
Chingelpet	12	Temple servant	1
Chingelpet	13		1
Chingelpet	13	Tēvaraṭiyāl	6
Chingelpet	13	Local chief	1
Chingelpet	13	Local elite	1
Chingelpet	13	Religious/Hindu	1
Chingelpet	14	Tēvaraṭiyāl	2
Chingelpet	14	Local chief	2
Chingelpet	16	Tēvaraṭiyāl	1
Chittoor	9	Major royalty	1
Chittoor	12	Local chief	2
Chittoor	13	Local chief	4
Chittoor	15		1
Chittoor	18	Local chief	1
Chittoor	19	Local chief	1
Coimbatore	11		2
Coimbatore	12	Major royalty	1
Coimbatore	12	Vēḷāḷ	2
Coimbatore	13	Tēvaraṭiyāl	1
Coimbatore	13	Local elite	1
Coimbatore	13	Palace maidservant	1
Cuddapah	12	Local chief	1
Cuddapah	12	Military leader	1

District	Century	Status	Number
Madurai	8	Local chief	1
Madurai	8	Shepherd	1
Madurai	11	Major royalty	2
Madurai	13	Local chief	2
Madurai	18	Local chief	2
Madurai	18	Major royalty	2
Madurai	19	Tēvaraṭiyāl	1
Nellore	17	Local chief	1
North Arcot	9	Local chief	1
North Arcot	9	Major Royalty	4
North Arcot	10	Major royalty	4
North Arcot	10	Religious/Jain	1
North Arcot	11	Tēvaraṭiyāl	1
North Arcot	11	Local chief	1
North Arcot	11	Major royalty	1
North Arcot	11	Merchant	1
North Arcot	13		1
North Arcot	13	Local chief	6
North Arcot	13	Local elite	1
North Arcot	14	Tēvaraṭiyāl	1
North Arcot	14	Local chief	1
North Arcot	16		1
North Arcot	16	Local chief	1
North Arcot	16	Local elite	1
Pudukottai	10	Local chief	2
Pudukottai	11	Local chief	1
Pudukottai	12	Tēvaraṭiyāl	2
Pudukottai	13	Tēvaraṭiyāl	1
Pudukottai	13	Local chief	1
Pudukottai	14	Tēvaraṭiyāl	1
Pudukottai	15	Temple servant	2
Ramnad	8	Brāhmaṇa	1
Ramnad	11	Brāhmaṇa	2
Ramnad	11	Tēvaraṭiyāl	1
Ramnad	11	Local chief	1
Ramnad	12	Major royalty	1
Ramnad	14	Local chief	1
Salem	12	Local chief	1
South Arcot	9	Local chief	2
South Arcot	10		2
South Arcot	10	Brāhmaṇa	1
South Arcot	10	Tēvaraṭiyāl	1
South Arcot	10	Local chief	9
South Arcot	10	Local elite	1
South Arcot	10	Major royalty	2
South Arcot	10	Palace maidservant	1

District	Century	Status	Number
South Arcot	11		1
South Arcot	11	Tēvaraṭiyāl	3
South Arcot	11	Local chief	4
South Arcot	11	Major royalty	4
South Arcot	11	Palace maidservant	1
South Arcot	11	Temple servant	1
South Arcot	12	Tēvaraṭiyāl	2
South Arcot	12	Local chief	3
South Arcot	12	Merchant	1
South Arcot	13	Tēvaraṭiyāl	4
South Arcot	13	Major royalty	1
South Arcot	18	Merchant	1
Tanjavur	9	Local chief	2
Tanjavur	9	Major royalty	2
Tanjavur	10	Brāhmaṇa	1
Tanjavur	10	Local chief	2
Tanjavur	10	Local elite	1
Tanjavur	10	Major royalty	36
Tanjavur	10	Military leader	1
Tanjavur	10	Palace maidservant	4
Tanjavur	11	Tēvaraṭiyāl	5
Tanjavur	11	Local chief	2
Tanjavur	11	Major royalty	37
Tanjavur	11	Palace maidservant	3
Tanjavur	12		4
Tanjavur	12	Tēvaraṭiyāl	2
Tanjavur	12	Major royalty	1
Tanjavur	12	Palace maidservant	1
Tanjavur	13		2
Tanjavur	13	Brāhmaṇa	2
Tanjavur	13	Tēvaraṭiyāl	2
Tanjavur	13	Local chief	1
Tanjavur	13	Religious/Hindu	1
Tanjavur	17	Tēvaraṭiyāl	1
Tanjore	11	Brāhmaṇa	1
Tanjore	12	Local chief	1
Tiruchi	0		1
Tiruchi	10	Brāhmaṇa	1
Tiruchi	10	Local chief	2
Tiruchi	10	Major royalty	13
Tiruchi	11	Brāhmaṇa	2
Tiruchi	11	Local chief	1
Tiruchi	11	Local elite	1
Tiruchi	11	Maidservant	1
Tiruchi	11	Major royalty	3
Tiruchi	12	Brāhmaṇa	1

District	Century	Status	Number
Tiruchi	12	Tēvaraṭiyāl	2
Tiruchi	12	Major royalty	1
Tiruchi	13	Local chief	3
Tiruchi	13	Major royalty	1
Tiruchi	13	Temple maidservant	1
Tiruchi	14		1
Tiruchi	14	Local chief	1
Tiruchi	17	Major royalty	2
Tiruchi	18	Tēvaraṭiyāl	1
Tiruchi	18	Local chief	1
Tirunelveli	8	Local chief	1
Tirunelveli	12	Brāhmaṇa	1
Tirunelveli	13	Brāhmaṇa	1
Tirunelveli	18	Major royalty	1
Total			348

Source: *SITI* and VRR.

Table 15.2 Class/Caste Background of Women Property Owners

Status	Number
Brāhmaṇa	28
Tēvaraṭiyāl	50
Local chief	79
Local elite	8
Maidservant	2
Major royalty	132
Merchant	3
Military leader	2
Palace maidservants	12
Religious/Hindu	2
Religious/Jain	1
Shepherd	1
Temple maidservants	1
Temple servant	4
Vēḷāḷa	2
Total	327

Source: SITI and VRR.

class background. 'Major royalty' refers to dowager queens, or queens and princesses of the imperial dynasties (predominantly Coḷas, Pāṇḍyas and Pallavas). The temple dancers are referred to by their old Tamil name *tēvaraṭiyāl* rather than the more familiar *devadāsī*. This has been done intentionally because the word *tēvaraṭiyāl* specifically means a servant of god and clearly, the dancer was only one of the many kinds of *tēvaraṭiyār* (the masculine and plural form) who served in the temple in various capacities—in the kitchen, arranging the flowers, keeping the temple clean, etc. The local chief and local elite were the dominant landowning classes; in modern terminology they might be termed dominant peasant classes. Their power base derived from their landownership and their relationship with the royal families, since most of the queens came from these families.

The inscriptions refer to several kinds of property transactions—gifts to the temple, sales, and assignment of property and/or land revenues to the *tēvaraṭiyāl* for their services. These transactions also indicate that the ownership rights of women with regard to their property extended to the power of alienation through gifts and sales. Women also bought property in addition to acquiring property through inheritance or being employed, so that virtually all the forms of women's property rights were found to operate among the Tamil people, though the Smṛtis did not acknowledge some of these rights.

The temple was the focus of social and economic life of the locality, and was the beneficiary of major patronage and endowments from the royal houses and the state as well as a variety of more modest offerings, usually for the 'merit' of the donor or a specified beneficiary (such as husband, son, brother, king, etc.). The latter were necessary to finance a variety of routine temple services: lamps which burned day and night (*nantā viḷakku*) or at dawn/dusk (*sandhyā dīpam*), food offering to the various *mūrtis* in the temple, or flowers, etc., to the devotees and Brāḥmanas.[8] Gifts were sometimes made directly in kind—gold and silver jewellery or vessels, lamps, etc., but were more often given indirectly in a two-stage process, in which the service was maintained through the income earned or interest on an asset which was assigned to the temple, or farmed out to specific individuals/groups or local assemblies. For instance, the normal assignment for a specified measure of oil or ghee to be given per day to the temple for burning an eternal lamp was 90 sheep or 32 cattle. The recipient of the livestock would have to ensure that the oil or ghee, as specified, was regularly given to the temple. Similarly money (gold coins or gold) would be donated which would be given out to individuals or groups or even the local assemblies who would undertake to pay 15 per cent interest (or an equivalent value in ghee or oil) to the temple. Strict fines (up to 25 per cent of the value of the endowment) were specified for even one day's failure to keep up the payment and groups which had received the money but had been unable or unwilling to fulfil these terms and conditions would have to sell some land of equivalent value to the temple. Since the scope for malfeasance was very large under these arrangements, audit committees were often appointed to check the temple accounts.

Against this general background, we can also get a more detailed picture by referring to some specific information in the inscriptions. Coming to the class background of the donors, two groups (Table 15.2) are predominant—the ruling classes (royalty, local chiefs, local elite and military) account for 63.5 per cent (221) of the donors. Women of the royal families were involved actively in the construction and maintenance of temples. The extent of their endowments precludes the facile assumption that they were only utilising some kind of a personal 'allowance' made to them. The earliest reference to a queen who constructed a temple was to the Pallava queen Raṅgapatākā in the eighth century.[9] The local feudal chiefs, whose daughters married into the royal families, maintained a steady and continuous tradition of patronage to temples, but the most vigorous and emphatic patronage came from the Coḷa queens and princesses. A look at Table 15.1, for instance, shows that in Tanjavur district alone there are 73 inscriptions (in the tenth and eleventh centuries) and 13 in Tiruchi district (tenth century) which record their gifts to temples. Since dowager queens and princesses were also actively promoting these activities, it seems reasonable to argue that they must have been making these endowments out of their personal property (most likely inherited on the maternal side from the local landowning elite families).

Three significant personalities in this respect were Cempiyanmādevī, mother of King Uttama Coḷa, Lokamahādevī (or Olokamahādevī), Dantiśakti, queen of Rājarāja Coḷa, and Kuntavai, his sister. The dowager queen Cempiyanmādevi, in addition to her numerous gifts and endowments, exercised such authority even in the reign of her grandnephew Rājarāja that she could command one of the temple managers to donate money to meet the expenditures incurred in the daily rituals of the temple, besides fixing the emoluments of the temple servants, and arranging for various items of temple expenditures to be met from land assignments.[10] Queen Lokamahādevī not only built a temple in her own name (Lokamahādevīśvaram), but she also took a keen interest in the day-to-day management of the temple. Even as a dowager queen she ordered the reclamation and cultivation of waste lands in a village, the income to be used for special festivals in the temple.[11]

The other important class of women referred to in the inscriptions were the employed women (19.8 per cent). While the most numerous group was the *tēvaraṭiyāl*, it is clear that women were employed in various capacities in the palaces, households of the elite, in the temples and in their capacity as wives of temple servants. In all cases they obviously could exercise ownership rights over their income/property, although this was not accepted by the Smṛtis, once again highlighting the dichotomy between the law in theory, and the practice.

The *tēvaraṭiyāl*, of course, represents a case worth studying in itself. In the early period, the temple dancer had both a secular and religious significance in the social milieu which revolved around the temple. She was clearly regarded as an employee of the state who served in the temple at par with other temple servants. The dancers could be transferred from one temple to another and were paid either by being assigned shares in land; the revenue from specified taxes, or '*kāṇi*' (landholding) rights in temple lands.[12] Paying for a *tēvaraṭiyāl* to dance in the temple was considered to be an act of religious merit even in normal times, and especially when temples had suffered after the Muslim invasions in the fourteenth century and the consequent disruptions in social and political life.[13] There are several references to the property owned, sold and bought by the *tēvaraṭiyāl* which indicate that they had property independent of the temple.[14]

Contemporary consciousness tends to locate the temple dancer within the social structure, primarily with reference to her sex life. The earlier evidence indicates a far more complex reality. There is even a reference to a married *tēvaraṭiyāl*, while the sister of another was evidently a favourite wife/concubine of a local chief.[15] The most common arrangement, as in later times, may well have been that they became the mistresses of the local landed elite. But this seems to have been not only an accepted, but even a respectable social practice, and there are several references to the concubines (*pōkiyār*) of local chiefs who made gifts to temples in their own right. At least one reference shows that property was transferred to the 'unofficial' family as gifts given out of affection or *prītidāna*.[16]

Though we thus have convincing evidence of women's property rights, it is also equally clear that such rights were not universal or uniform for all women. The extent to which women could control their property depended on the usage current in their immediate social circle. Among the well-to-do, land was given as *strīdhanam* to the daughter on her marriage—there is even a reference to it and gifted as *strīdhanam* to the goddess in the temple—but, as this gave the husband the status and the right of doing service in the temple and the privileges due to that in local affairs,[17] it was clearly he who was regarded as the landholder.

Two contemporary inscriptions of c. 1270 capture the anomalies in women's status very well. One refers to a woman who was a member of the local committee of justice (*niyāyattār*): the other to two Brāhmaṇa widows without sons who were forced to sell their land.[18] The latter gives the bare outlines of what was perhaps a fruitless struggle on the part of the widows to retain their land. They were, however, not given any help by their relatives (*jñātis*) and finally had to sell the land. The fact that they were represented by close male relatives—one by her father, the other by her son-in-law who was also her brother—in the sale negotiations indicates that there was strong social and intra-family opposition to their owning land when they had no sons. While the rights of the women of the royal families at one end of the social spectrum, or of the *tēvaraṭiyāl*, a special group, were not questioned, in the middle classes these rights were not equally well protected or accepted.

The inscriptions (Table 15.1) also throw up some tentative inferences. One noteworthy fact is that, with the beginning of Hoysala/Vijayanagar rule, there is a sharp decline in the number of references to women (after the fourteenth century). The inescapable inference seems to be that Vijayanagar society was far more restrictive when it came to women's property rights. Even though women probably continued to enjoy the more open traditional arrangements in Tamil Nadu, the culture of the rulers discouraged the public display of these rights through recorded endowments, sales, etc. Another point to note is that the inscriptions are most numerous in the heartland of imperial power—Tanjavur, Tiruchi, South and North Arcot and Chingelpet districts. It would be interesting to investigate whether significant sub-regional variations existed within Tamil country.

URBAN PROPERTY, 'MAÑCAL KĀṆI' AND OTHER RIGHTS

The temple economy was primarily structured on the power relations of the agrarian society; from the inscriptional evidence it is not possible to reconstruct the nature of the property rights of urban women. For the more recent period, some scattered evidence exist which indicate that women did inherit non-agricultural property, both movable and immovable. The records of the mayor's court in Madras[19] contain the details of several cases when women were involved in litigation concerning money given on loan, urban property which was mortgaged, division of property, etc. Just to cite one instance, the widow of Beri Timmanna, the chief merchant of the English at Madras, had sued borrowers for repayment of loans which amounted to more than 15,000 *pagodas*. In another case initiated by her son, the property in contention was a house which she had made over to her daughter.[20] There was also an intriguing case in which a woman claimed the estate of her 'first husband's first wife's son' (which he had inherited from *his* mother) as the natural heir, because the son was mentally deranged.[21] Almost all the more complex cases involving inheritance claims to property were arbitrated by the caste councils, which shows that while customs may have differed from caste to caste, women's rights to inherit, own and manage property were accepted. On the other hand, the almost contemporary diaries of the famous *dubash*, Ananda Ranga Pillai, also record several cases where widows were disinherited, mistreated and denied even maintenance rights.[22] Family customs, local social mores and, in these times, the attitudes of the colonial rulers all seem to have been important in the effective realisation of women's rights. The English at Madras, as the eighteenth century progressed, seem to have abandoned their earlier deference to local customs and caste decisions. This probably explains why, at the end of the century, the litigation over the estate of the extremely wealthy merchant and *dubash*, Pachaiyappa Mudaliar, dragged on, though he was survived by two widows and a daughter, until all the claimants to the estate died.[23]

In contemporary Tamil society, one of the most important rights of women is the right to inherit land. This again was *strīdhanam*, which devolved on the female heirs, and passed from mother to daughter. Usually handed over to the girl when she got married, this land was called *mañcal kāṅi* (*mañcal* means turmeric). The origin of this name in itself would be interesting to investigate. I have been told that the reference to turmeric indicates that this was land, probably not a part of the patrilineal property, on which minor cash crops like turmeric could be grown. The more plausible explanation seems to be that this was meant to provide an independent income to the daughter which would be enough at least for personal expenses (*mañcal* and *kumkumam*). In almost all cases, the income from this land certainly seems to go to the woman; the extent of control or decision-making right that she has over this land would, however, seem to vary from individual to individual, and family to family. It would also be interesting to explore whether the practice of cross-cousin marriage as well as marriage with the maternal uncle was an attempt to keep the property which went to the daughter within the control of the natal family.

How did this line of female property originate? One possibility is that in almost every family at some time there must have been a generation with only daughters, who would accordingly succeed to the property. This is a hypothesis which instinctively I tend to reject. The rights of women without brothers tend more often to be appropriated by other male relatives than to be protected, and there have even been cases which went up to the Privy Council when the male members of a family disputed the right of an only daughter to her father's property. Was this custom then the legacy of a distant, matrilineal social system which existed in this region (as it still does in neighbouring Malayalam country)? These questions need to be investigated in much greater depth. Sadly, many of these practices seem to have degenerated in the past few decades, even before the enactment of the 1956 law. Dowry seems to have replaced traditional *strīdhanam* almost completely, weakening the rights and status of women.

Another form of property over which a woman had absolute control was her jewellery and personal belongings. Jewellery inherited from the mother, almost always, was handed over to the daughters, while jewellery presented by the in-laws or husband could be given to daughters-in-law or their children. The extent to which these norms of preserving the line of descent were adhered to seems to vary, again, from family to family. I have been told of instances when a signed release was obtained from all the granddaughters on the female line by a lady who wanted to gift her *strīdhanam* jewellery to her son's daughters. More often, this seems to have been less rigidly observed; women usually gave their jewellery to their daughters and their daughters' daughters, but not invariably so.

In addition to these inheritance rights, women also have some customary rights in Tamil society. Among all castes and classes in Tamil Nadu the bride receives a gift from her mother's family, usually from the maternal uncle, known as the *amman cīr*, which includes the bride's *sārī*, a gold ring and silver toe rings. Married daughters similarly continue to receive *poṅkal cīr* from their brothers each year, besides having several other claims to ritual gifts from the natal home. These may be small in value, but are important in that they establish a continued claim on the family property.[24]

One community which stand out from the rest are the Nattukottai Chettiars, a traditional mercantile caste, whose activities mainly centred on moneylending and trade. The men would travel extensively in the course of their trading operations, often being away from home for several months or years. The moneylending activity, which was essentially home-based, would be managed by the women. This was particularly common once the Chettiars established themselves in trade in Burma (Myanmar) and Malaysia (in the last decades of the nineteenth century). In the mayor's court records series, there are also extant some account books in Tamil dating back to the 1790s, where the accounts of some Chettiar women are recorded, indicating that this practice is not of recent origin. Yet, the traditional property rights of Chettiar women seem to be particularly weak. Since the community, by and large, was not an agriculture-based community, at the time of her marriage, the girl would receive a large cash settlement which was theoretically her property. In most cases this was absorbed into the business capital of the in-laws' family enterprise, and there does not seem to have been the concept of her individual property rights. In fact, as long as the daughter-in-law stayed in a joint family, her natal family would provide for the personal expenses of the girl and her children. There was a curious case of women managing and controlling large amounts of money and substantial business transactions but without individual property rights.

Another example of a unique locality-specific system is found in Kilakkarai, in southern Tamilnadu.[25] This is a small coastal town where the local population, mostly Muslims, have traditionally been chank divers. Here, there is a strong tradition of property which is passed on from mother to daughter. On marriage, each girl receives a house, household necessities and jewellery from her mother. When there are several daughters, the house property has to be sub-divided. Whatever money is left over after all the daughters are provided for is divided according to the *shariat.* Yet, the entire arrangement of women controlling property and forming the line of descent is entirely at variance with Islamic law.

CONCLUDING REMARKS

It is obviously difficult to conclude with definitive comments or analysis of the nature or basis of women's property rights in Tamil society. A common factor which these women share with women all over India is that the property rights seem to be acquired only on marriage. In traditional society, there are so few instances of women remaining single that the rights of an unmarried woman are, at best, notional. The condition of widows and their inheritance rights is again difficult to capture. The common experience seems to be that few widows actually received their just dues from the husbands' families, though here again the experiences varied from family to family.

One significant feature of the usage in Tamilnadu which needs to be stressed is that, even though the daughter was given her property when she got married, this took the characteristics of an inheritance right and not a marriage settlement or dowry, arrived at on the basis of mutual bargaining between the two families.[26]The notion that a woman has a continued right to small gifts and *cīr* from her father or brother is again not ubiquitous in north Indian society. One can also tentatively link the traditional rights of women to own land in Tamil society with recent research findings which point out that only in Tamilnadu and Kerala do women directly supervise cultivation, for control and management go with ownership. Thus, even as we answer some questions, many unanswered and until now unanswerable ones emerge, which need much more intensive exploration.

NOTES

[I wish to thank all the women who have generously shared their family experiences with me. Special thanks are due in this regard to Sakuntala Jagannathan and Sarojini Varadappan, and to Lalitha Iyer for sharing her research experience and notes.]

1. For the legal background on women's property rights, see Paras Diwan, *Dowry and Protection to Married Women*, New Delhi: Deep and Deep, 1987, Chapter 4: '*Strīdhana*'. An oft-cited legal work on the same issue is Gooroodas Banerjee, *Hindu Law of Marriage and Strīdhana*, Calcutta, 1923.
2. A. S. Altekar, *The Position of Women in Hindu Civilisation*, Delhi: Motilal Banarsidass, 1991 (rpt.), Chapters VIII and IX offer a clear discussion of the various aspects of women's property rights. See also Diwan, op. cit.
3. This general perception seems to have really crystallised during the debate on the proposed Devadasi Abolition Bill in the 1940s, and has now become part of popular wisdom.
4. 'Women's estate' has also been converted into '*strīdhana*'—that is, with full property rights for the woman—under the Hindu Succession Act, 1956, Diwan, op. cit., p. 121.
5. Both Yājñavalkya and Vijñāneśvara of the Mitākṣarā school, who were more liberal in their views, were from the south, Altekar, op. cit., p. 258.
6. The two sources for inscriptions are: T. N. Subramaniam (ed.), *South Indian Temple Inscriptions*, Madras: GOML, 1953–57, 3 vols. (hereafter *SITI*) and V. R. Rangacharya, *A Topographical List of the Inscriptions of Madras Presidency*, New Delhi: Asian Education Service, 1985 (rpt.) 3 vols. (hereafter VRR). I have taken care to see that the inscription which are cited in both—and these are, surprisingly, very few—are used only once. The 'border' districts of Cuddapah, Nellore and Chittoor have been included, partly because during the linguistic reorganisation of states some *tāluks* in these districts became a part of Tamilnadu. The original classification of districts, including Pudukottai (in VRR, III) have been retained for simplicity.
7. The basic limitation is that only women of property-owning classes are considered here. There are references to women/families who are 'donated' to the temples for various kinds of service (like husking paddy), etc., but these are not included because of the limited terms of reference of this paper.
8. The terms and conditions of the endowments, as outlined here, were common for male and female donors. However, only the references to the gifts made by women are studied.

9. In the Kailasanatha temple in Kanchipuram. Making a pun on her name, the inscription describes her as an exemplary 'flag (*patākā*) among women'.
10. Inscriptions from Tirumananjeri, in Tanjavur district, VRR, vol. II, Tanjore, 672, 673 and 687.
11. *SITI*, vol. II, 610 and VRR, vol. 1, Chingelpet, 727.
12. VRR, vol. II, Tanjore 1363 and *SITI*, vol. III-2, 1299.
13. VRR, vol. I, Chingelpet, 567.
14. Ibid., Chingelpet, 214, refers to a *tēvaraṭiyāl* who was forced to sell her land by public auction to pay a fine. Such matters were obviously a collective local responsibility for, when neither the local people nor the local assembly would buy the land, the temple management (*tānattār*) had to buy it.
15. VRR, vol. I, Chingelpet, 1016 and *SITI*, vol. I, 537.
16. *SITI* vol. III-1, 1102, dated AD 1374.
17. *SITI*, vol. II, 1008.
18. VRR, vol. I, Chingelpet, 771 and *SITI*, vol. II, 819.
19. Records of Fort St George, Tamilnadu Archives, Series under mayor's court records, proceedings and pleadings, dating, but not continuously, from 1689.
20. Fort St George, Diary and Consultation Book, 22 March 1694, (Tamilnadu Archives); mayor's court proceedings, 1717–19.
21. Pleadings in the mayor's court, 1744–45.
22. Lalitha Iyer, 'Glimpses of Women's Lives in Eighteenth Century Tamilnadu', paper presented at a symposium on Ananda Ranga Pillai's diaries at Pondicherry in February 1991.
23. K. Srinivasa Pillai, *Kāñcipuram Paciyappa Mutaliyār Carittiram* (Ripon Press Madras, 1911) (Tamil) (from Lalitha Iyer).
24. Louis Dumont (*Affinity as Value*, Oxford, Delhi, 1988, p. 87) comments that the function of gift-giving and gift-receiving come down by one generation. A woman gets gifts from her parents, who are later replaced by her brother. The brother/maternal uncle also becomes the gift-giver to his sister's daughter and other children.
25. Personal communication from Lalitha Iyer, who passed on her research notes to me.
26. It is interesting to compare this with the practices in several parts of Andhra Pradesh. In Nellore district, the women inherit the equivalent of *mañcal kāṇi* which is referred to as *pasupu kumkumamu*, with a striking similarity even in the name. Further north, in coastal Andhra, *pasupu kumkumamu* is the *strīdhanam* which is given as dowry to the bride, but the woman retains complete right to this property.

Chapter 16

Property Rights of Women in Medieval Andhra*

A. PADMA

EDITOR'S NOTE

A. Padma, the author of this essay, had originally combined the themes of both 'profession' and 'property' in relation to women in medieval Andhra. Her perspective was primarily to highlight economic empowerment and financial independence. We have, however, split this essay into two parts in order to make it more comprehensive to students. The editor felt that this would better serve the purpose of young scholars. The present section on women's property rights in medieval Andhra comprises the second part of Padma's essay.

***

The evolution of women's property rights has witnessed several stages. Initially, a woman is regarded as an item in the movable property of the husband and is along with sons, slaves considered as money less.[1] They were given away as gifts to the priests in lieu of their services or sold as slaves to clear the debts made by their husbands.[2] By the first century of Christian era, the Dharmasastra writers made it very clear that wife and children are not to be tendered as objects of gifts or sale under any circumstances.[3] Āpasthambha's theory of wife and husband as the joint owners of the family property secured minor rights for a wife but they were conditional as she had no right to spend money or incur normal expenditure even on household without the consent of her husband.[4] Among the other Smṛti writers, Yājñavalkya came forward with more liberalised principles regarding property rights of women. *Mitākshara*, a medieval digest on the same further enlarged the scope of women's right over property.

* Reproduced with permission from the author. Previously published in 'The Socio-Cultural World of Women in Medieval Andhra (from eleventh to thirteenth centuries AD)', Bharatiya Kala Prakashan, Delhi (2001); pp. 71–84.

There are two sources of property for women, inheritance and acquired (*strīdhana*). Available evidences from ancient test and legal treatises point to the prevalence of both these rights. However, references to the term *strīdhana* are more commonly found.

INHERITANCE

Inheritance can be the property that is inherited by a woman as an heir to the parental property. Different views are expressed by the legal text writers on this issue. From Manu, it is known that a daughter cannot become an heir to the paternal property under normal circumstances.[5] She can become so only when she is duly appointed by her father in the absence of male issue with a view to beget a son through her, who shall take on to the estate of his grandfather besides offering funeral cake to him. Such an appointed daughter is called *Puṭrika.*[6]

Mitākshara, on the contrary, gives a different picture on this issue. It says that the property shall pass on to the successors depending on their relationship with the owner of the property. They are of two categories—those who get share through *Apṛatibaṅdha dāya* (sons, grandsons, great grandsons… who are presumed as coparceners to one's property by birth) and those who get their share through *Sapṛatibaṅdha dāya* (wife, daughter and such others who become owners of the property only after the death of the owner.[7] Thus, in the absence of male heirs, the wife (widow) becomes the first heir. Next to her in order of succession are, daughter, mother, father, brothers, their sons or persons of the same *gōtṛa*, disciples, co-students in the respective order.[8] It is here that a great change is brought by Vijñāneśvara by making widow as the first heir of her sonless deceased husband's property, provided she be pious, chaste and religious minded.[9] It appears that the laws of *Mitākshara* were closely followed in Āndhradeśa, as the same is translated into Telugu by Ketaṇa as *Vijñānēśvaramu* which formed the basic source of law during Kakatiya period.

Both Manu and Vijñāneśvara converge on few issues of daughter's nomination as natural heir, providing maintenance allowance to the widow of the deceased to the extent that her share in the property shall be equal to that of the sons' and setting 1/4th of each son's share towards marriage expenses of unmarried daughters.[10]

One of the Mukhalingam temple inscriptions refers to the distribution of property of a deceased *desi* trader among his heirs. The widow was provided maintenance allowance and some amount was set apart for the marriage expenses of unmarried daughters.[11]

Mitākshara further states that the ownership of a woman on such property is complete in all respects whether the heir belonged to *Apṛatibatidha* or *Sapṛatibatidha* category. In other words, the holder of the property had the rights of *Dāna* (giving in charity), *Damana* (overpowering-destruction), *Bhōga* (enjoying), *Vinimaya* (consuming) and *Vikṛaya* (selling).[12] Questioning Manu's theory of dependence of a woman on man at every stage of her life, Vijñāneśvara states that she may be dependent on her male counterpart due to her weak physical nature, but that should not fall in the way of her economic independence or her claims to parental property of whatsoever kind.[13] In the case of the community of temple dancing girls and those women whose profession is prostitution, daughters become the *Ap ṛatibaṅdha dāya* holders (natural heirs) and succession is in the female line. Sons become *Sapṛatibaṅdha dāya* holders.[14]

ACQUIRED PROPERTY

Besides property obtained through inheritance, women also acquire property through various means. The origin to the acquisition of property by women can be traced to Vedic times. The wedding hymns of *Ṙgvēda* indicate that gifts are to be sent to the bridegroom's house with the bride and over such articles the wife is the mistress.[15] Ornaments, costly dresses and household articles constitute those and they are generally kept under the control of women. Gradually, such kinds of property went on increasing in extent and value necessitating the early jurors to be specific on the claims on such property, which is otherwise called *Sṭridhana.*

Manu defines *Sṭridhana* as the six folded property of a woman—that which is obtained through gifts before the *nuptial* fire, on the bridal procession, what was given in token of love, and what was received from her brother, mother or father.[16] This concept is elaborated greatly by the jurors Yajñavalkya and Kātyāyana.[17] Accepting these definitions, Mitakshara also included inherited property under *strīdhana*. Furthermore, gifts given by husband out of love, the amount due to her at the time of his second marriage superseding her and the property acquired through general methods of earning such as *Ṙikhta* (inheritance), *Kṛaya* (purchase), *Saṁvibhāga* (partition), *paṛigraha* (chance) and *Adhigama* (adverse possessions), bride price (*ōli* or *sulka*), *uṅkuva* and *Aṛaṇamu* are included under woman's property.[18] The provisions of Dharmasastras are supported by plenty of contemporary, literary and epigraphical sources.

An epigraph dated 1255 AD recorded a gift of a land containing *Pōka* trees as *sṭrīdhana* by Achanta Sūraparaju to his daughter. This *strīdhana* is referred to in the grant as *Aṛaṇamu.*[19] The Bayyāram, Niḍigoṅḍa and Kuṅdavaram inscriptions refer to the villages Bayyāram, Niḍigoṅḍa and Kuṅdavaram as *aṛaṇamu* lands given to the donors Mailama and Kuṅdama at the time of their marriage with Natavaḍi chief Rudra.[20] *Palnāṭi Viracharitra*, refers to *aṛaṇamu* on many occasions. At the time of the marriage of Mahadevarāju, a Haihaya chief of Palnad, the bride's father gave several cows and many bōya servants as *aṛaṇamu* to the bride.[21] On the occasion of Mailama's marriage with Anugurāju, her father, the Velanāḍgu chief Goṅka gave *Palanāṭisīma* as *aṛaṅamu.*[22] Similarly, Anugurāju's son Mallarāju was married to Kālāchūri princess Sirādevi who brought 1000 cows, 1000 sheep and the necessary bōya attendants as *aṛaṇamu* along with her. [23] Nannechoḍa, in his *Kumārasaṁbhavamu*, mentions that Parvati's father gave several valuable presents to her in lieu of her marriage with Lord śiva.[24] *Raṅganātha Rāmāyaṇamu* also has a reference to *aṛaṇamu* paid to Sitā by her father in lieu of her marriage with Lord Rama.[25]

Ōli, Uṅkuva are the other terms found in the contemporary literary sources as well as in the epigraphs. These correspond to the *Sulka* or the bride-price which is included under *strīdhana* by the legal writers. However, it appears that the demand seemed to be very high from the parents of the girls. Because of this, the caste associations decided the amount of *Ōli* to be paid to the bride's father. An epigraph from Malleśvara temple, Vijayawada records one such arrangement made by the *Telikivēvuru* (Teliki/Telaga community association) of the regions of Koṇḍavīḍu, Koṅḍapalli and Rājamahēndravaramu. It is decided that for the first marriage, the *Ōli* should be 21 *chinnamāḍalu* (gold coins) and certain amount of silver.[26] *Palnāṭi Vīracharitra* also has a reference to this practice. At the time of Balachandra's marriage with Manchala, the bride's mother demanded huge sums of money towards *Ōli.*[27]

Uṅkuva too finds frequent mention in the contemporary literary works.[28] Generally, it is the amount paid by the groom to the bride or her parents at the time of marriage.[29] However, the use of the term is often associated with the business of prostitution in terms of the money paid to the mother of the girl.[30]

WOMEN'S DOMINION ON *STRĪDHANA*

The treatises on Dharmasastras and moral literature not only dealt with the property rights and possessions of women but laid some restraints and limitations on their appropriation. For the sake of deciding the dominion of a woman on her *stṛīdhana*, the property received by her is divided into two categories based on its source (a) *Saudāyika* that which is received by a woman whether as a maiden or as a married woman, from her parents or husband and over which she had complete control and (b) *Non-saudāyika*, the property received by all other means. On this she has only the right to enjoy.[31] A maiden is free to dispose of *Saudāyika* as well as *non-saudāyika* property at her pleasure.[32] A widow too can dispose of every kind of *strādhana* including movable property but not immovable.[33] However, she can alienate a portion of immovable property towards religious purposes or for *śraddha* rituals for her husband.[34] A married woman, if her husband is alive can dispose of at her pleasure only *Saudāyika* property.[35] The husband's rights on *strīdhana* also are determined by this division. The *non-saudāyika* property is subject to husband's dominion during his life and may be taken by him even when there is no distress.[36] If, however, the property is of *saudāyika* category, he has no domain except under certain circumstances of distress, disease, famine or religious purposes.[37] For all other purposes he is liable to return the same. No other person has any right to use it under distress or otherwise.[38] If he takes away the ornaments by force, he is liable to be punished in the courts.[39]

The succession to *strīdhana* again varies according to the marital status of a woman and the form of marriage. Generally, *strīdhana* devolves in the line of females only.[40] The order of succession to *strīdhana* except for *Sulka* and maiden's property is:

1. unmarried daughter,
2. married daughter who is indigent,
3. married daughter who is well provided for,
4. granddaughters through daughter,
5. daughter's son,
6. sons,
7. son's sons,
8. husband (in approved form of marriage), and
9. *sapiṅḍas* of husband[41]

The paternal gifts given to the deceased women can be claimed by the husband in the event of absence of daughters provided the marriage is one of the approved forms.[42] Nādiṅḍla inscription records an interesting issue of parent's claims on a married woman's property after her death and reasserts the husband's right on the same.[43] Guilds like *Teliki Samayamu* as in the above instance decide such issues. However, if the marriage is not approved by the legal traditions, the property claims can be made by the parents.[44] The property specified under *Oli* or *Sulka* has a separate course. It generally devolves on brothers and parents, and the husband has no dominion on the same.[45]

Though Vijñāneśvara did not intend to give women, the full rights of disposal over the immovable property, both inherited and acquired, they are to a limited extent exercising their property rights as revealed from the extensive inscriptional evidences registering grants.by women of all classes of the society. We even have few instances of the purchase of lands by women paying suitable price and donating the same to the deities. A record from Nilakaṁṭeśvara temple, Nārāyaṇapuram registers grant of a piece of wet land to the temple by Nagava, a *Sānikāpu* woman.[46] It is mentioned in the record that she bought the same by paying a suitable price. Another record refers to the purchase of land by one Komaṛasāni, though details are not given.[47] An epigraph mentions that a couple obtained sale deed of a piece of land on which both their names are written as partners of the property.[48]

As the purpose is religious for which both husband and wife enjoy equal status, it is very difficult to arrive at the economic independence of women. The case of temple girls too cannot be viewed in isolation to the temple and their economic independence is always related to their status in the temple and their conditions of service. In this connection, the observation of Dhrama Kumar is worth mentioning, 'In the medieval period, there existed no legitimate private property rights worth the name as the king reserved the right of eviction of land for certain reason'.[49] Thus, even the male coparceners had no unrestricted right over their self-acquired property.

REFERENCES

1. A.S. Altekar, *The Position of Women in Hindu Civilisation* (Delhi, 1962), p. 213.
2. *Ibid.*
3. *Ibid.*, p. 214.
4. S. Bhattacharji, 'Economic Rights of Ancient Indian Women', in *EPW,* March, 2–9, 1991, pp. 507–512.
5. Bühler, *Laws of Manu,* IX, verse 134.
6. *Ibid.,* IX, 127. Also, for a detailed description on the issue, Arudra, 'Puṭrika Elāṇti Kūtuṛu' *Vyāsapitham,* (Vijayawada, 1985), pp. 54–59.
7. *Saṁgrahāṅdhra Vijnakośamu*, pp. 174–179.
8. *Ibid.*
9. The chastity of a widow's life is given great emphasis. It is stated that she should observe fast, make gifts in the name of her husband and perform such other good deeds and lead a virtuous life. Then only she would become the heir of her sonless deceased husband's property. P.V. Kane, *Op. cit.*, Vol. III, 1974, pp. 735–738.
10. Buhler, *Laws of Manu,* IX, 118.
11. *Temple Inscriptions of Andhra Pradesh (TIAP),* Vol. I, (Srikakulam Dist), No. 35.
12. *Saṁgrahāndhra Vijñāna Kosamu*, pp. 174–179.
13. *Ibid.*
14. *Ibid.,* Also G.R. Kuppuswamy, *Economic Conditions in Karnataka* (A.D. 973–A.D. 1336), (Dharwar, 1975), FN 126, 'A note on Mitākshara' p. 40.
15. A.S. Altekar, *Op. cit.*, 1962, p. 218.

16. Buhler, *Laws of Manu*, IX, 194.
17. Yajñavalkya is the foremost among the promoters to the cause of women's property rights. Kātyāyana defines *Strīdhana.*as the property acquired through *-Adhyagni* (nuptial fire), *Adhyāvāhanika* (bridal procession), *Pādavaṁdanika* (doing obeisance at the feet of elders), *Prītidatta* (out of love), *Sulka* (bride price) and *Anyādhēyaka* (received after marriage). *Mitākshara* includes a wider range of definition, making *strīdhana* as applicable to all kinds of money that belonged to a woman.
18. *Saṁgrahāṅdhra Vijñana Kosamu*, pp. 174–179.
19. *South Indian Inscriptions (SII),* Vol. X, No. 349.
20. *LAP: WD.* No. 57, 58 and *Epigraphia Andhrica*, Vol. I, 'Bayyaram Tank Inscription of Kakati Mailama', pp. 71–94.
21. *Palnāṭi Vīracharitra*, p. 139.
22. *Ibid.*, p. 24.
23. *Ibid.*, p. 56.
24. *Kumārasaṁbhavamu*, 7th canto, verses 139, 140.
25. *Raṅganātha Rāmāyaṇamu*, Bālakāṅḍamu, p. 67.
26. *SII,* Vol. VI, No. 797.
27. *Palnāṭi Vīracharitra*, pp. 341–343.
28. *Kumārasaṁbhavamu*, 7th canto, verse 136.
29. *Raṅganātha Rāmāyaṇamu, Bāla Kmṅḍamu*, p. 55.
30. *Daśakumāracharitramu*, 6th canto, verse 51. Also, *Palnāṭi Viracharitra,* pp. 341–344.
31. N. Aruna Kumari, 'Concept of Stridhana in Mitakshara' in *PAPHC*, 8th Session, (Kakinada, 1984), pp. 42–44.
32. P.V. Kane, *History of Dharamasastra,* Vol. III, 197, p. 784.
33. *Ibid.*
34. Generally permission from the king or the members of village assembly or elders is necessary for such an act. *Andhra Pradesh Government Report on Epigraphy*, 1965, No. 4 records the confirmation of the grant of land by one Srimahādevi by the king, while her husband Vijayaditya predeceased her.
35. P.V. Kane, *Op. cit.*, Vol. III, 1974, p. 784.
36. *Ibid.*, p. 785.
37. *Ibid.*
38. *Ibid.*, p. 787.
39. *Vijñāneśvaramu,* Vyavaharakāṅḍamu, verses 53, 54.
40. *Ibid.*, verse 138.
41. *Mitākshara* on Yaj. II, 145, quoted from P.V. Kane, *Op. cit.*, Vol. III, 1974, p. 794.
42. Buhler, *Laws of Manu*, IX, 196. *Mitākshara* also agrees with Manu on this issue.
43. *SII*, Vol. X, No. 221.
44. *Bühler, Laws of Manu*, IX, 197, *Mitākshara* too opines the same.
45. P.V. Kane, *Op. cit.*, Vol. III, 1974, p. 793.
46. *SII*, Vol. X, No. 654. Also, *Ibid.*, Vol. VI, Nos. 967 & 979 are of the same nature.
47. *Hyderabad Archaeological Survey (HAS),* Vol. XIX, Km. 17, Ramakrishnapuram.
48. *SII*, Vol. V, No. 1014.
49. Dharma Kumar, 'Private Property in Asia? The case of Medieval South India', in *CSSH* Vol. XXVII, No. 2, (April, 1985), pp. 340–366.

Contextualising Women's Work in the Public Domain

Section IV

Chapter 17

State of the Field: Perspectives on Women and Work in Early South India*

VIJAYA RAMASWAMY

This essay is intended to be a long duree 'thick' description of women and work in South India. It is a broad mapping of what has been perceived as women's work from the early Christian era correspondingly roughly to the period of the Sangam literature[1]. Medieval literature such as Vallabharaya's *Kreedabhiramamu* and Srinatha's *Palnattuvira Charitra* from the Vijayanagar period, apart from inscriptions, have been the primary sources for salvaging information on women's work and women and work from the tenth to the seventeenth century. The accounts of women's involvement in specific economic sectors sometimes get carried forward into the early colonial era. The primary economic domains within which this study is located constitutes the primary sectors of economy in the pre-colonial era such as 'women and farm work', women in dairy farming and women in crafts especially the textile sector. The study also looks at the role of the Devaradiyar in Tamil economy and culture and secondary areas of women's work such as catering, inn-keeping, fisheries and liquor distilling and tertiary levels of women's work such as acting as wet-nurses or as official mourners. All these activities, while they could be seen as women's work fell under the two seminal categories of domestic work and non-domestic 'paid' work. Work within the household included such activities such as spinning apart from cooking, child-rearing and home economics while women's work in the public domain included women's participation

* Previously published in 'State of the Field: Perspectives on Women and Work in Pre-Colonial South India', *International Journal of Asian Studies*. Vol 7, No. 1, Cambridge University Press (2010), pp. 51–79.

Dhiraj Knite, Eugenia Vanina, Chitra Joshi and Rohan de Souza made sharp critical comments on the draft which helped me to re-form my arguments. Divya Narayanan provided me with valuable references on Mughal society. To all of them much thanks.

All translations from Tamil texts and folk songs are mine unless otherwise stated.

[1] See my article on economic transition in this collection for a critical definition of the Sangam Age and Sangam literature.

in agricultural and craft activities outside the household as well as the range of economic activities carried out by temple women.

WOMEN AND FARM WORK

The Sangam texts[2] provide us with several instances of women's participation in the rural economy, especially agriculture. Weeding and planting (this includes the task of transplanting), guarding of the crops (which is exclusively the work for young, unmarried girls), husking and winnowing and pounding (of the paddy) were women's tasks. Women also participated equally with men in the work of irrigation and harvesting. The Perunkadai[3] which is one of the five great Tamil epics (based on the Sanskrit *Brihatkatha*) belonging to the Post-Sangam period and authored by Konguvelir, states that women were particularly skilled in planting seeds. The *Perumpanattruppadai*[4] anthology gives a detailed description of the Eyirriyar women smoothening and weeding the fields with furrows which had an iron tip called *kozhu*.[5] The Eyirriyar women in the post-Sangam era constituted low-caste agricultural labour but for the period of this text (which may be roughly dated between the second and fourth centuries CE), it is not clear whether they were working as agricultural labour or tilling their own land. The *Narrinai*[6] describes the Uzhavan and Uzhatti, the farming couple, leaving for their fields at dawn, after a simple meal of rice gruel with fish. However the term 'uzhatti' was not applied exclusively to the farming wife but also to a woman working as an agricultural labourer.

Farm work related women's folk songs provide a major source of alternative history in reconstructing the lives of women in Tamil society and economy. Interestingly, women's farming songs are also found in the Sangam literature itself. The *Malaipadukadam*[7] and the *Kurunthogai*[8] refer to the women pounding the grain rhythmically to the accompaniment of a song. This genre is called *vallai pattu*.

The technological transition from hoe agriculture to plough agriculture has been recorded as an important marker in changing gender balance within the agricultural domain in the context of traditional Asian (and African) economies. This is a major plank of the arguments raised by Ester Boserup in her discursive analysis of *Women's Role in Economic* Development.[9] She talks about the marginalisation of women with the coming of the plough essentially in the traditional Asian economy. To quote from Boserup[10]:

---

[2] See my article in Nathan ed. 1997, pp. 223–228 on classifying Sangam texts on the basis of historical blocks and locating women within these blocks.

[3] *Perunkadai,* stanza I; 413, p.234, stanza I.163–4 vide Hanumanthan 1979, p. 100.

[4] *Perumppanatruppadai* in *Pattupattu* lines 90–7.

[5] *Perumpanatruppadai,* 90–97 vide Ramaswamy 1989, pp. 81–99.

[6] Natrinai stanza 60: 1–8.

[7] *Malaippadukadam* from the *Pattupattu*, 342.

[8] *Kuronthogai* verse 89:1.

[9] Boserup 2007 pp. 12–14 of the section 'The Plough, The Veil and the Labourer'.

[10] Ibid. pp. 13–15.

> The main farming instrument in those regions, the plough, is used by men helped by draught animals, and only the hand operations—or some of them—are left for women to perform....The land is prepared for sowing by men using draught animals, and this thorough land preparation leaves little need for weeding the crop, which is usually the women's task. Therefore women contribute mainly to harvest work and to the care of domestic animals... Sometimes such women perform only purely domestic duties, living in seclusion within their own homes and appearing in the village street only under the protection of the veil, a phenomenon associated with plough culture, and seemingly unknown in regions of shifting cultivation where women do most of the agricultural toil.

I have argued in an earlier essay that the evidence of the Sangam texts could itself be divided into three historical blocks[11] which indicate a gradual transition from a society in which women were co-sharers with men in most farming activities to a patriarchal society in which women (along with the lower castes) were beginning to be marginalised. In literary terms this change can be perceived in the movement from the *Ettutogai* anthology to the *Pattupattu* anthology. The eventual emergence of a patriarchal structure can be roughly assigned to the period between the fifth and seventh centuries CE, marked by the last block of the Sangam texts called *kizhkannu.* The predominance of plough agriculture or settled cultivation and the gradual displacement of shifting cultivation based on the hoe in which women were active participants, resulted also in the gradual emergence of a patriarchal and caste based society. The increasingly significant concepts of purity and pollution meant that women (because of their menstrual cycles) should not be allowed to handle the 'sacred' plough. Women therefore came to be called '*Kalam toda magalir*'[12] literally 'women who do not touch the plough'.

A major shift occurred in production organisation between the Sangam and late-Sangam period (late-Sangam or post-Sangam period can be situated between the third century CE to the fifth century CE) and the beginnings of medieval state formation under the Pallava and Chola dynasties in around the eighth century. The movement of Tamil society from a loosely stratified clan and kinship-labour based production system to a much more economically stratified and socially and ritually hierarchical society, dominated by Brahmanical ideology and brahmadeya land systems, resulted in a new production system. This was based increasingly on the exploitation of the labour of landless lower castes like the Pallar, Kadaiyar, Tudiyar and Paraiyar. Epigraphical records throw up new terms for servile labour such as 'kudiyar', 'vettiyal' and 'muttal'[13]. This shift had a major impact on the position of women and social perceptions of their labour. From being co-sharers in farm work, women came to be perceived as domestic subordinates. The new (read non-Brahmanical/Brahminical upper caste) cultural markers in society celebrated the 'subordinated labour' of the woman as evidence of her virtuous commitment to her hearth, husband and children while rendering invisible her work-participation in the home. Increasingly, the upper caste women came to be confined to their domestic chores and extolled in their re-productive functions as producers of males. The iconisation of the upper-caste/upper-class housewife in medieval canonical

[11] Ramaswamy 1997, pp. 223–246.

[12] Puramnanuru: 299 vide Hanumanthan 1979, p. 32.

[13] It is interesting that the term 'muttal' (pronounced as in the English word 'tall') today means 'a stupid person' in Tamil, in the same manner in which the medieval English term 'villein' or serf, becomes transformed in modern parlance into 'villain', the obvious inference being that poverty breeds both ignorance and crime.

and literary texts, as chaste wife and self-sacrificing mother, goes hand in hand with her marginalisation in the economic domain.

The differential impact of these changes on lower caste women, the 'kadaisiyar', like the Pallar and Paraiyar, is striking. While undervaluing their labour, it brought them into the public domain as waged workers. It seems likely that some of women's farm related activities such as irrigating the fields, harvesting crops and the pounding of grain to the rhythmic music of the *vallai pattu* may have changed from unwaged to waged labour in the case of lower caste women from the medieval period onwards. While pounding of grain may have constituted a part of the 'domestic' duties of women whether upper caste or lower caste, it is likely that this became a paid profession for low caste/untouchable women sometime in the medieval period. The *Periyapuranam,* a twelfth century hagiographical text, refers to the Pulatti singing while husking paddy while her husband the Pulayan was employed in the field[14]. The Pulaya and the Pulatti were clearly categorised as 'polluting castes' associated with death, scavenging etc. They were also invariably landless agricultural labourers and the term used for them is 'kadaisiyar' or the 'lowest'. It can therefore be logically inferred that both the Pulayan and the Pulatti were being employed in agricultural labour by the landlord. A similar inference can be made for the Parayan and his wife the Parchchi. This is the sense in which Chekkizhar uses the word in the *Periyapuranam* where in the story of the Paraiya saint Nandanar, the Uzhatti is described by the poet as resting under a Marutu tree while her baby slept on a leather sheet.[15]

WOMEN AND FARM WORK IN THE TAMIL FOLK SONGS

The folk song genre in women's work situations constitutes an important source for mapping women's farm related work. These folk songs specifically reflect the predicament of low caste and/or destitute women (primarily widows with children) who had to labour for their survival. The *natru padal* (seed planting songs) and *etra padal* (water lifting songs) are still to be heard in the Tamil Nadu countryside. In reconstructing the history of women and work, these songs can become a major source of alternate history because most agricultural songs relate to women from the lower strata of society.[16] In terms of the class structure identifiable in the majority of these work songs as clearly 'lower class', this genre becomes crucial to the study of women's labour history.

There is a complete absence of the woman's voice in most of what is classified as high literature (broadly canonical/Sanskritic), within which one would locate the majority of upper-caste women, working within domestic spaces and secluded from the public gaze. These women lacked access to the means of creating, disseminating or preserving their own history. As Maria Mies points out, the process of 'housewifization' rendered women's

[14] *Periyapuranam*, vide Sastri 1975, pp. 568–69. The passage contains a brief description of Adananur village's low-caste settlement where Nandanar lived.

[15] *Periyapuranam* 5:22–4 and 6:206–7 vide Sastri 1975 pp. 568–69.

[16] One does occasionally come across songs by upper class rural women engaged in domestic chores in what is now described as 'unpaid' or 'unwaged' labour.

(in the Indian context I would qualify this with 'upper caste' women) 'unpaid' household work, 'invisible'. To quote her, 'The construction of woman as mother, wife and housewife was the trick by which 50 per cent of human labour was defined as a free resource. It was female labour.[17] 'In contrast, the work songs (literally '*tozhil paadal*'), which would include voice of both lower caste and destitute upper-caste women, which are a part of Tamil folk tradition, provide us with a grassroots perception of women's place in historical societies as perceived by women themselves.[18]

I would like to give an example here. In the case of women with infants, the task of working in the hot mid-day sun was rendered doubly painful. The following is a cradle song reflecting this mood:

While harvesting if
I strap you to my shoulders
in the noon-day heat
Will you not feel faint?
while I work in the fields
and leave you by the side
Will you not begin to cry?
I am a low-paid labourer (term used is chital)
The overseer (kangani) will be enraged
And if the overseer were to scold
will not my child feel sad.[19]

The work of lifting water for the agricultural fields was performed either *by bullocks or by women* (the equating of animal power with woman power is interesting) by moving up down a plank in order to rotate the wheel with the chain of buckets. The tedious work of lifting water required enormous staying power which was to be found only in the draught animals and in women. This set of *etra padalgal* are sung by women punctuated by the rhythm of the buckets being drawn up. A woman sings:[20]

If I become an old hag
Where is the fragrance in me?
For him there will be one without the home
And one within.
Forty six, forty seven, forty eight.

The song indicates several aspects of a working woman's life—the tedium of her work situation, a typical domestic situation of a patriarchal home where the man moves freely between his wife and his mistress, seen in the phrase 'one without the home and one within', and the

[17] Mies 1998 (originally 1886). intro. p. ix.
[18] Ramaswamy 1993, pp. 113–129.
[19] Tamizhannal 1956, p. 99. The translation of the song is mine.
[20] Vanamamalai 1964, p. 417. For more such examples from Tamil work songs see Ramaswamy 1994, pp. 23–24.

compulsions under which a woman has to work in order to survive. The longish folk song eventually takes the bucket count beyond hundred.

WOMEN AND WORK IN THE NON-FARM AGRICULTURAL SECTOR

Mullai: The Pastoral Tract and Dairy Farming:

A familiar sight in the Tamil countryside even in my childhood (1950's and early 1960's) was the *'morkari'* and *'neykari'*, literally 'the buttermilk woman' and 'the woman who vends clarified butter' (ghee). These women are itinerant peddlers and generally carry their wares on an earthen vessel on their heads. Women's predominance in the production and sale of dairy products goes back a long way in Tamil culture. In the Sangam period poetry of the Mullai (pastoral) *tinai,* consists of extensive metaphors and imageries pertaining to women churning buttermilk, milking cows and selling curds and butter. The *Perumpanattrupadai*,[21] which can roughly be ascribed to the fourth century CE, gives a detailed account of the work-day of a shepherdess. In a somewhat clumsy simile it compares the rhythmic churning of the curds by her to a tiger's roar! The shepherdess in the Tamil country is known by names such as 'Aaichchi', 'Kovichchi', 'Idachchi' etc. Starting her day at dawn, she churns the curds to take out butter. She then sells the buttermilk from door to door in the kurinji and Marudam regions and with the money she gets, she buys food grains and other necessities. Elsewhere in the *Purananuru* it is said that curds were directly exchanged for foodgrains with the farmer's wife.[22] Women were therefore key participants in the rural barter economy.

The process of setting curds by curdling the milk, is used as a simile in the *Purananuru* where it says 'Like the curd being squirted into a pot of milk from the fingers of a tired shepherdess'[23]. The same anthology contains another poem, which says that in the Pandyan country the prosperous housewife exchanged her paddy for the goat meat brought by the shepherdess from Mullai.[24] In the *Perumpanattrupadai*[25] it is said that the Aaichchi is not satisfied with the gold she saves up from her dairy sales but uses the 'capital', to buy a good milch buffalo, a good cow and a black buffalo in order to expand her business. The term used is '*mudal*' which literally translates as 'capital'. This indicates that some women went beyond simple barter and actually set up dairy business.

In the religious literature of the early medieval Bhagavata movement (commencing around the seventh century CE), the image of the shepherdess figures very strongly. In the *Tiruppavai* (a lyrical religious composition) of the woman saint Andal (seventh century), the picture of the dusky shepherdess, with her heavy chains and clinking bracelets, churn-

---

[21] *Perumpanatruppadai* ed. Swaminathayyar 1931, lines 156–60.

[22] *Purananuru* ed. Swaminathayyar 1935, stanza 33, lines 1–6.

[23] *Purananur* in ibid., 276, lines 5.

[24] Ibid., lines 166–68.

[25] *Perumpanatruppadai* edited by Svaminathayyar 1931, 164–65.

ing the curds at dawn, occurs repeatedly[26]. Andal's home was Tirumullaivayil which was a pastoral zone specializing in dairy products. The very name mullai connects it with the pastoral economy as evident from the Sangam eco-zones analysed earlier. In course of time it may have gained the status of a small town. Today Tirumullaivayil constitutes a suburb of Chennai and is a sacred site. It is noteworthy that Krishna or Mayon, the deity of the pastoral tract called Mullai, became a central cult figure of the Bhagavata movement. The centrality of the 'milk maids' who milked the cows, churned buttermilk and sold their products such as milk, curds (yogurt) and butter, is bound up with the medieval bhakti movements and the devotion of the gopis or milkmaids towards Krishna. If one were to look for parallels from other regions, the milk maids of Brindavan (Mathura) come in for a close comparison.[27]

The evidence regarding the persistence of the pastoral zone with its predominantly dairy economy in the medieval period can therefore be logically deduced, both as a result of historical evidence of these towns and the flourishing of Krishna bhakti signifying the popularity of Mayon, the pastoral deity. However the nature of pastoral women's share in the overall medieval economy is more difficult to determine. European sources for the medieval period suggest that due to the proximity of the pastoral and agricultural tracts, the women from poor peasant families often hired themselves out as servants in the dairy sector in the emerging European towns. As the housewife became free from labour in the larger dairy farms, milking, cheese making and butter making became the work of hired women workers. An experienced cook would carry her spoon or ladle in her apron and a dairymaid a stool. Daniel Defoe commented on the attention attracting techniques of these 'working women' as 'eminently impudent'.[28]

Neydal: Women in the Coastal Economy

Women living in the coastal terrain have traditionally played an active role in salt panning and sale of salt. Women engaged in salt production and sale were known as *umanapendir*.[29] The *Perumpanatruppadai*[30] describes how the umanar couple extracted the salt, loaded it on carts and sold it in the neighbouring eco-regions. The *umanapendir* also hawked the headleads of salt from door to door getting in exchange paddy and other essentials[31].

Fisheries is another economic sphere in which women played a major role in traditional society. In early Tamilaham (which includes the regions of Kerala and Andhra Pradesh) women played a key role in fishing and in hawking the fish. The Paradaiyar women caught and sold fish. Young girls of this community kept watch over the fish drying in the sun.[32] The

[26] Andal's *Tiruppavai*, songs 7, 8, 12 etc. I have translated from the Tamil text in *Nachchiyar Tirumozhi and Tiruppavai,* 1985.

[27] Mukherji 1982, pp. 325–331.

[28] Hufton 1993 on p. 18 cites Daniel Defoe's '*The Behavior of Servants in England',* London 1724, pp. 1–9.

[29] *Perumpanatruppadai* ed. by Svaminatha Iyer 1931, lines 61–65.

[30] ibid. lines 50–60.

[31] *Ahananuru:* 390: 8–10; 140; *Kurunthogai:*269: 5.

[32] *Ahananuru*, 9, 20.

Ahananuru[33] refers to these women as *panimagal*, literally 'working women' and says that they sat in street corners selling fish. This does suggest that the more affluent fisherfolk may have hired women to carry out the actual task of hawking the fish. There are also references to fisherwomen exchanging fish for paddy from the Marudam tinai. The *Aingurunuru*[34] says that the Valaiyar (another fishing community) women sold *viral* fish (regarded as a delicacy) and got year-old white rice (that is, high quality rice) in return.

The Handloom Sector

While weaving has been a male preserve in most traditional Indian societies, (the exception being hill regions and tribal belts), spinning has been exclusively women work. Vedic texts however, refer to women weavers as 'vayatri'[35]. While the overall number of women weavers vis-à-vis men, remains ambiguous, canonical literature like the *Shatapatha Brahmana*[36] makes it clear that spinning was the exclusive domain of women.

Sangam literature refer to spinner as *parutti pendugal* literally 'the spinning women'. Spinning was particularly the occupation of destitute widows, and single women, interestingly those categories of women who had to sustain themselves through their own earnings.[37] The *Purananuru*, a Sangam text datable to anywhere between the third century BCE and the third century CE, uses the expression: *Parutti pendir paruvalenna* for the thread spun by spinsters[38] and says that spinsters spun late into the night with the aid of a lamp[39]. Another text *Natrinai* referring to windows/spinsters, as '*alil pendir*' which means 'women without men' says that they spun fine yarn.[40] A celebrated more or less contemporaneous text from Northern India, *Arthashastra* of Kautilya, states that the Devadasi, who was too old to perform any service in the temple, was employed to card cotton for her livelihood. Devadasis and old maid servants were also employed to cut wood, pick cotton, hemp and flax.[41]

The Virasaivite movement in Karnataka which began in the twelfth century provides a refreshing perspective on professional women spinners. The movement has two prominent *vachanakaras* from this profession—Kadire Remmavve and Kadire Kayakada Kalavve. Both women have prefixed their names with their profession '*kadire*' meaning spinner and this is quite in keeping with the social philosophy of Virasaivism. A celebrated dictum of the religion is '*Kayakave Kailasa*' which in idiomatic English would be 'work is workship'. Virasaivism holds as its cardinal principle the necessity to work and be self-reliant. In so saying it challenged the Brahmanical notion of mendicancy and alms-taking as a path to

---

[33] *Ahananuru*, 126.

[34] *Aingurunuru* ed. Swaminathaiyyar and Sundaranar, 1957, 47: 1–3 and stanza 48. See also *Purananuru*, 343:1.

[35] *'gnas tva krantann apaso tanvata vayitriyo vayan'* says the *Panchavimsha Brahmana*—vide Rau 1970, p. 16, n.13.

[36] *tat vai etat strinam karma yad urnasutram'* 12.7.2.11, vide Rau 1970, p. 16.

[37] In this connection, the English word 'spinster' for a single woman provides an interesting parallel since the word originates precisely in the same context, as a woman who had to spin for her survival.

[38] *Puramnanuru* ed. Swaminathaiyyar, Madras, 1935, song 61:line 1.

[39] ibid. 327.

[40] *Nattrinai* ed. Narayanaswami 1952, 353: 1–2.

[41] *Arthashastra* of Kautilya II: 23 vide Tyagi 1994, p. 105.

salvation. For the first time the working woman gained her own identity and social space despite the fact that the movement functioned within a patriarchal framework.

Kadire Remmavve used the imagery connected with her occupation to describe not only her faith but her social situation as well. She says:[42]

Fast turning spinning wheel
Listen to the caste and lineage (kula jati)
of the spinning wheel I turn
The plank below is Vishnu
The wooden idol (bobbin winder) Maha Rudra
The two threads that pass through constitute intellect
awareness is the spindle
You turn the wheel by the handle called devotion
The threads turn and the bobbin is filled.
I cannot turn the spinning wheel
because my husband has beaten me
What can be done, My Lord Gummisvara!

Kadire Kalavve says that the spindle of spirituality will break if one mixes with *vrataheena* or persons with the faith and devotion. The 'Charkha Namah' (Spinning Loom Songs), popular among Muslim women in the North Deccan during the medieval period, also belongs to the same genre. The medieval historian Isami in his *Futuhat-us-Salatin* has a very interesting passage on women and the profession of spinning. Talking about the failure of Razia Sultana, the ruler of Delhi Sultanate, Isami writes 'a woman cannot acquit herself well as a ruler, for she is essentially deficient in intellect. It is better for a woman to occupy herself with the *charkha* since the attainment of high position on her part would make her intoxicated.'[43]

Spinning continued to be the exclusive professional preserve of women during the medieval Vijayanagar period. Srinatha in the *Palnattu Viracharitra* (circa fifteenth century), says that in Palnad while the farmers ploughed the field, their wives spun thread. Women spinning thread must have been such a common sight in the region, for Srinatha[44] comments, that even if the celestial dancer Ramba were to come to Palnad, she would perforce have to rotate the spinning wheel!

A. I. Chicherov in his path-breaking monograph on medieval craft and trade[45] between the sixteenth and eighteenth centuries brings together evidence from diverse regions, especially Bengal, to show that spinning was the profession of upper caste women, more particularly impoverished Brahmin widows. In the pre-colonial period spinning was by and large a part of the informal sector of the economy. Women did the spinning within their domestic space and then either sold them directly at the local fairs or delivered them to the middlemen (agents of Master-Weavers or merchants) who collected the spun yarn from them.

---

42 Ramaswamy 1996, p. 54. Remmavve's term 'wooden idol' clearly indicates a bobbin winder.
43 *Futuhat-us-Salatin* 1976, vol. II, pp. 253–54. For an overview see Siddiqui in Pawar ed. 1996, pp. 87–101.
44 *Palnattu Viracharitra* of fifteenth century poet Srinatha in Sastri and Venkataramanayya 1946, vol. III, p. 52.
45 Chicherov 1971, pp. 52–56.

In the handloom sector the bleaching and washing of cloth has also been a predominantly women's activity. The washerwomen came from the lowest caste and were called 'Pulatti'. The *Purananuru*[46] say that the Pulatti washed the clothes in the particular area called *'kalar'* whose mud was a good purifying and whitening agent. Their use of the *kalar* mud for washing, earned them the name 'kalayar'. The texts describe how she prepared starch from rice[47] and dipped the clothes in the starchy solution[48]. Finally with her long tapering fingers she removed the lumpy or excess starch from the clothes.[49] The *Ahananuru* also refers to washing and starching of cloth by the Pulatti.[50] *Natrinai* says that the Pulatti worked far into the night, drying clothes and/or starching them.[51]

Washing of clothes was done by both men and women of the Pulaya caste. Washerwomen were called Vannati or Pulatti in the Tamil country and as 'Chakali' in Andhra. It is repeatedly stated both in Sangam texts and early medieval texts that apart from bleaching woven cloth, the washermen washed the clothes of people and presumably were paid for it. The Pulatti are clearly mentioned as women who washed impure clothes[52] (rendered impure by neo natal ceremonies following birth or by death). Her male counterpart, the Pulayan, was usually the one who handled the dead body and the Pulatti cleaned the house of death with cow dung etc. It was logical in the traditional social structure dominated by fear of death pollution, for the Pulayar to be regarded as an 'untouchable' (located below and beyond the four varnas) caste.

There are a few medieval inscriptional references to them.[53] It is clear that the washing of clothes was a paid service but there is no indication of what was the nature and mode of payment. There are hardly any historical references to this. One can only logically assume that like other menials and professional of the village community they were being paid from the grain heap. An isolated piece of evidence is a document from the Mackenzie Collection which says that the Pulatti was paid three sheep and three rupees collectively by the village community as her wages.[54]

A sociological facet to the professional and social status of the Pulatti is provided by the comments in the medieval twelfth century hagiographic text *Periya Puranam*. It refers not only to their drinking habits but says that they frequently went into a state of possession' and danced in frenzy 'jumping about the cattle'[55]! An analysis of 'possession' behaviour has shown that it was quite often the means adopted by the disempowered and unprivileged

---

46 *Purananuru,* 311: 1–2. Also *Ahananuru* 89 which says that the washermen were called kalaiyar because of the mud they used for washing.

47 *Natrinai* 90: 2–4 vide Ramaswamy 1989, p. 87.

48 *Kurunthogai,* 330: 1, ibid., p. 87.

49 *Ahamnanuru,* 34: 11–12 ibid., p. 87.

50 Ibid. *Ahananuru:* 34 and 387.

51 *Natrinai:*353 vide Balambal 1998, p. 39.

52 *Ahamnanuru:* 387: 6–7 and Purananuru: 368: 15–16 vide Hanumanthan, 1979, p. 131–132.

53 *South Indian Inscriptions* (henceforth *S.I.I.*)., vol. IV, No. 1384.

54 Appadorai 1936, vol. I, p. 280 cites Colin Mackenzie, 'The Village Feast', *Indian Antiquary,* III, pp. 6–9.

55 *Periyapuranam* vide Sastri 1975, pp. 568–69.

to seek empowerment and social recognition. The logic would certainly hold true in the case of the Pulatti.

WOMEN IN CRAFTS: POTTERY, BASKETRY, MAT-WEAVING, PITH WORK AND GARLANDS

A major poet of the Sangam period called Venni Kuyattiyar (literally 'the potter of the Venni region') became well known for her poem celebrating the victory of Karikala Chola (circa second century CE) at the battle of Venni (in Tanjavur district). An inscriptional reference to Kumbari or the potter's wife who assisted her husband in smoothening the clay and baking the pots, is found from the Andhra region.[56]

Basket-making and mat-weaving have been traditionally associated with women. Both are part of cottage industries and are very poorly paid professions. In the *Kalittogai* roughly datable to the sixth century CE, it is said that besides washing it was the work of the Pulatti to make baskets out of 'korai' weeds[57] In inscriptions there is reference to *Medari*, meaning female basket weaver.[58] In the Karnataka and Andhra regions the basket weavers belonged to the Medara caste. There is a reference to women basket weavers whose work is known as 'kantakara vritti' in the Vallabharaya's *Kreedabhiramamu*[59] (fifteenth century). The same text also states that many of these Medara women were so poor that they took to prostitution out of economic compulsions. Basketry is the auxiliary craft of the Parava (fisherwomen) of Kerala.

Pith work called *netti* in the south was also done by women. The plant known as shol-apith has soft flexible stems with spongy cellular tissues in them and also in the branches. The Sangam texts refer to the many crafted items made out of *netti* including hair decorations and garlands. The *Silappadikaram* refers to the *netti* work done in Pumpuhar and the sale of *netti* products in the markets of Pumpuhar.[60] With *netti* were made flowers, toys, hair decorations especially marriage coronets etc. Although the text does not specifically state that *netti* workers were women, one can logically presume so, since women are still engaged in *netti* work in South India. In Karnataka among the Gudagara caste, the men carve wooden figures while the women engaged in pith/*netti* work.[61] Whether it is basketry, mat-weaving or netti-working, evidence indicates that while the production was dominated by women, their labour was informal and extremely underpaid, compounded by economic and sometimes sexual exploitation.

[56] *S.I.I.,* vol. IV, No. 677.

[57] *Kalittogai*, Nachchinarkiniyar commentary, ed. Anantharaman 1925, Marutam: 13–14 and also verse 117.

[58] *Journal of the Andhra Historical Research Society*, vol. VI, Pt.3 and 4, p. 205 vide Hemlatha 1991, p. 41.

[59] *Kreedabhiramamu* of Vallabharaya,ed. Sastry 1952, verse 67. The first English translation of *Kreedabhiramamu* was by Rao and Shulman in 2002.

[60] *Silappadikaram*, 4: 45–51 and 5: 28–34.

[61] Chattopadhyay 1985, p. 111.

Garland making and flower selling was and continues to be predominantly women's occupations. The *Ahananuru* says that Vettuva (feminine of Vedar, hill tribe) girls gathered the flowers in bamboo pipes and went to the villages to sell them.[62] Devaradiyar usually undertook the task of garland making in the temples. A eleventh century record from the Abhiramesvara temple in Tiruvamattur[63] in South Arcot district refers to women being employed for picking flowers and making garlands. The same record says that while male workers employed by the temple for drawing water and irrigating the fields were paid at 8 nalis of rice per day, the women workers were given exactly half the rate, that is 4 nalis of rice. The *Kreedabhiramamu*[64] also refers to women engaged in the profession of garland making and flower selling.

'Dancing Girls' as Working Women: From Devaradiyar to Tevadiya

The changing phases of the Devaradiyar and the nature of the work associated with the community of temple women is crucial to the theme of women and work.

In Sangam literature, dancing girls are called Parataiyar and, Madhavi, the rival protagonist of the 'chaste' wife Kannagi, in the epics *Silappadikaram* and *Manimekalai*, (dated roughly between the second century CE and fourth century CE) was a well-known dancing girl of Kaveripumpattinam.

It is important to point out that nowhere in early medieval inscriptional records does the term 'Devadasi' actually figure. This term which dominates our understanding of women temple workers, begins to be encountered only in the nineteenth century. In the inscriptions and early texts, they are known by various terms such as 'Devaradiyar', Soole, Sani, Paatra and sometimes Ganika or Dasika. Historically, temple women seem to have been divided into three categories—Devaradiyar, Padiyilar and Ishtabhattaliyar. There is clear inscriptional and literary evidence that some Devaradiyar did get married.[65] The *Dashakumara Charita* of Dandin refers to this practice.[66] There is even reference to a Devaradiyar having married a king of the Velanadu family whose territoriality comes under the Eastern Chalukyas of Vengi.[67] The category of women called 'Padiyilar' remained single and their name literally means 'those who are without husbands'.

Inscriptions suggest that there was a hierarchy of the devaradiyar as well as the nature of the temple work assigned to them, ranging from slaves and prostitutes to temple attendants/servants at one end of the trope to affluent, land-owning devaradiyar.

There are several instances recorded in inscriptions of the sale of dancing girls to the temple indicating that their status must have been that of virtual slaves. A record dated 1119 CE states

[62] *Ahananuru* ed. with commentary by Nattar and Pillai 1943, song: 231.
[63] *Annual Report of Epigraphy (henceforth A.R.E.),* 1922, No. 18 dated CE 1030.
[64] *Kreedabhiramu*: 174.
[65] *S.I.I.,* vol. V, No. 1102.
[66] *Dashakumara Charita* pp. 74–75, 86, 125, 150, 163, 167 etc. vide Gupta 1972, p. 222.
[67] Venkataramanayya, 1950, p. 287.

that an army captain called Alagiya Pallavarayar gave the girls of his family to the Tiruvallan temple after branding them on their foreheads with a trident[68]. A similar sale of four women as Devaradiyar to the Tiruvalangadu temple for a sum of 700 Kasu is reported in an inscription date 1175.[69] Another record from Tiruvorriyur[70] refers to the gift of five women and their descendants as 'Devaradiyar' to the Tiruvorriyur temple, who were employed in husking paddy by the temple authorities. These records indicate that the devaradiyar were drawn from divergent castes ranging from Kaikkolar to Isai-Vellalar.

Inscriptional evidence is, however, equally clear on the point that while slaves may have constituted one rung of female temple servants, the other rung consisted of independent women professionals. Even among the professional female temple servants, the work structure was not monolithic but hierarchical. The inscriptional record dated 1265 from Tiruvorriyur[71] (Chingleput district) of the period of Rajanarayana Sambuvaraya refers to a strike by the Devaradiyar, Padiyilar and Ishtabhattaliyar as a result of the confusion over the allocation of duties and their ritual hierarchy. A committee constituting of Nattar, Maheshvaras, Sthanathar, Virachola Anukkar and Kaikkolar headed by a Mudaliyar of Bhiksha Matam of Chidambaram enquired into the charge and allocated the functions of the Devaradiyar and regulated their status. The arbitration was necessitated by the fact that the Padiyilar were dying of poverty and had become greatly reduced in number. The committee appointed the Ishtabhattaliyar to assist the Padiyilar. It however appears that the Devaradiyar may have been at the top of this hierarchy because they were specifically exempted from such menial chores such '*taligai vilakku'* or 'rice cleaning and 'tiruvillakku tirumelugu' meaning 'cleaning the lamps with cow dung'. The Devaradiyar were to carry the flower plate '*pushpataligai'* and '*tirunirkappu'* (?) while the Ishtabhattaliyar, the lowest in the hierarchy made the *varikkolam* that is decorating the temple floor with rice flour and cleaning vessels. Holding the mirror before the deity, fanning the deity with the fly whisk[72] and holding the 'Sripadam'[73] (literally the auspicious feet of the Lord represented in gold) were performed by the 'superior' dancing girls. The dispute continued, necessitating another arbitration committee under the aegis of Vittappar of Anegondi, an official of Kampana Udaiyar and yet another committee three years later under Tunaiyirunda Nambi Kongarayar. The task of dancing and singing in the temples was assigned to the dancing girls with the Ishtabhattaliyar dancing before the god and the Devaradiyar before the goddess. The same Tiruvorriyur inscription refers to Devaradiyar being assigned the task of singing Tiruppadiyam in 'aagamamargam'[74] (literally the path of the Agamas) style to wake up the deity.

68 *A.R.E.,* 230 of 1921–22, part two, para 19.

69 *A.R.E.,* 80 of 1913.

70 *A.R.E.,* 122 of 1912.

71 *A.R.E.*, 196 of *A.R.E.* 1912–1913, p. 128 ff para 51 of part two.

72 *S.I.I.,* vol. XI, no. 1035 from Simhachalam (in modern Waltair in Andhra Pradesh).

73 *A.R.E.,* Nos. 373 and 380 of 1919 published in Subramanian 1957 as Nos. 358 and 369.

74 The Agamas are theoretical treatises as well as practical manuals on modes of ritual temple worship.

Considering the wide trope of economic and social activities engaged in by these 'temple-women' it becomes important to locate these women as active agents in the temple economy whether in a subordinate or controlling capacity.[75]

Therefore historical evidence makes it amply clear that not all temple women were slaves or of a lowly status. Many of them enjoyed a high status, property and a respectable position in society. Inscriptions from the Chola-Pandya period, refer to the land holdings of Devaradiyar. The eleventh-century Rajaraja inscription[76] states that the Devaradiyar were invited to serve the Thanjavur periya koyil and given house site and land near the temple. In 1337, the task of conducting the celebration of an important festival at the temple of Alumelumagamma in Tiruchchanur (Tirupati) was jointly given to the Devaradiyar and the Kaikkolar.[77] The Devaradiyar also enjoyed the rare privilege of an exclusive audience with the king.[78] These women were then, powerful, financially independent and apparently socially respected.[79] There are records which testify to them as land owners as well as generous donors of land to the temples.[80]

The position of dancing girls in the context of the economic domain has to be determined in terms of the data, however sparse, of the structure of work and wages. An inscription from the Tiruvorriyur temple[81] clarifies that the women employed as garland makers were paid 10 nalis of rice each per day together with 1½ kalanju of pon per annum for buying clothes. One of the earliest inscriptions which refers to the grant of house sites and paddy shares to the Devaradiyar is the tenth-century record of Rajaraja I from Brahadisvara temple.[82] An undated inscription from Malkapuram states that Kasisvara Siva Ayyamgaru (village community) made a gift of one *khandika* and ten *tumus* of land to each of the eleven Sanis.[83] The Srikurmam inscription dated 1250 CE provides us with valuable information regarding the wages paid to the Sanis stating 'to each of the thirty Sanis, 42 puttis of paddy per year, two tambulams every day and three appanas per month'.[84] The Chebrolu inscription of Jayappa, the general of Kakatiya Ganapati dated 1235 CE, records the construction of double storied houses for the sixteen best ganikas of the temple of Chodisvara at Tamrapura.[85]

---

[75] Interesting perspectives on temple Devaradiyar in the Chola period is provided in Orr 2000. Apart from discussing 'Temple Women as Servants of the Lord' she also engages with 'Temple Women as Temple Patrons' and 'property and piety'. Orr has looked at the material assets especially landed properties of the Devadasi. Her work can therefore be seen as a break-away from traditional historiographies which tend to conflate the categories of temple women, ritual dancers, temple servants and 'sacred' prostitution.

[76] *S.I.I.,* vol.II, part two, no. 66.

[77] Tirumalai Tirupati Devasthanam Inscriptions (henceforth *T.T.D.I.*), vol. I, No. 108.

[78] *A.R.E.*, 229 of 1919. The inscription dating to the period of king Deva Raya II of the Vijayanagar empire states that the Devaradiyar alone, among women, enjoyed the privilege of a direct audience with the king.

[79] This is the thrust of the article by Sen 1993, pp. 240–277.

[80] For example *S.I.I.,* vol.V, Nos. 1026, 1027, 1102 etc.

[81] *A.R.E.*, 146 of 1912. The 1912–13 volume of the *A.R.E.* series is particularly rich in its information on the Devaradiyar of the Tiruvorriyur temple.

[82] *S.I.I.,* vol. II, pt. 2, No. 66.

[83] *S.I.I.,* vol. X, No. 396 vide Reddy 1991, p. 74.

[84] *S.I.I.,* vol. V., No. 1188 vide Reddy 1991, pp. 74–75.

[85] *Epigraphica Indica,* vol. VI, pp. 38–39, text lines 152 to 155 in Reddy 1991, p. 75.

A very interesting inscription from Mangalore dated 1204 CE states that if the dancing girls did not turn up to perform their specified duties in the temple they were to be fined 5 ½ coins as penalty.[86] It is said of the dancing girls coming under the purview of the Sanula Samayamu, literally, the collective organisation of Sanis, that any ethical violation of the professional/social code could result in the expulsion of the dancing girl.[87] Medieval inscriptions which refer to the 'Soolevala'[88] suggest that this must have been an official specifically appointed to supervise the duties of the dancing girls.[89]

Prostitution was and continues to be a female preserve. Since this is the only profession, which has been recognised as a woman's profession, there is a plethora of literature on prostitution. The fee collected by the prostitutes for their services was called *roya* and the non-payment of fees to the prostitute was punishable by law as was the charging of excess money from the customers by the prostitute. Reference to special courts called Jara Dharmasasanamu which dealt with issues of justice[90] concerning prostitutes comes from both inscriptions[91] and literature.[92] The Shiva Sharanes within the Virasaiva movement, which originated in Karnataka in the twelfth century but spread over much of Andhra as well, includes a few who were professional prostitutes such as Gangamma, Soola Sankavve and Virasangavve.[93] One of them called Soola Sankavve in her vachana speaks of professional ethics:

In my harlot's trade,
having taken one man's money
I daren't accept a second man's, Sir.
and if I do,
they will stand me naked and
kill me, Sir.
And if I cohabit
with the polluted,
my hands, nose, ears
they'll cut off
with a red hot knife, Sir.
Ah, never, no
knowing you, I will not.
My word on it
Libertine siva!

---

[86] *S.I.I.*, vol. VII, No. 185 Gururajachar 1974, p. 246.
[87] *S.I.I.*, vol. VI, No. 1202
[88] *S.I.I.*, vol. IX, i. 80 (introduction) and *Hyderabad Archaeological Series* (*HAS*) 18, p. 35. See P.B. Desai's introduction in Gururajachar 1974, p. 246–247.
[89] The office is similar to the 'Ganikadyaksha' meaning 'Head of the Courtesans', referred to in Kautilya's *Arthashasthra* (Sanskrit text dated between third century BCE and second century CE) ed. Kangle 1965, lines: 2.27.1.
[90] A brief but interesting article on this theme is by Padma in Satyanarayana and Reddy 2005, pp. 12–15.
[91] Hyderabad Archaeological Series, vol. XIX, Warangal 3, Koravi inscription, pp. 135–138 vide Padma, Ibid., p. 14.
[92] *Kreedhabiramamu* of Vinukonda Vallabharaya 1960, verses: 265, 272 vide Padma, Ibid., p.14.
[93] I have briefly discussed this aspect under the section on 'Social Philosophy' in my book 1996, pp 52–55.

(translated by Susan Daniel in Susie Tharu and K.Lalita ed. Women Writing in India 600 BC to the Present, OUP, 1991, pp. 81–82).

Perhaps the only professional women's guild consisted of the temple women and the inscriptions characterise them as Sani Munnuru.[94] The guild seems to have enjoyed some power because a thirteenth-century record (dated 1292) from Peddakallepalle in Krishna district[95] even indicates that the Sani Munnuru along with the Sthanapatis (also called Sthanathar, i.e., temple trustees) were part of the temple management. In another record the collective organisation of the Sani is referred to as 'Nibandhakaralu' in the context of temple managers/trustees.[96] Two records from the Narasimha temple at Simhachalam dated 1427 and 1447 respectively refer to them as 'Sanula Sampradayam' literally 'hereditary/traditional temple dancers'.

The ubiquitous presence of devaradiyar as 'professionals' functioning in the public domain, makes the trope of these so called 'dancing girls', vital to an understanding of the nature of women and work within and beyond domestic spaces.

Maids and Menials

The references to low caste women employed as domestic workers are fewer in the Sangam period essentially because while the texts mention the poorer classes and low castes as 'kadaiyar' and 'kadaisiyar', there is no clear evidence that they worked as domestic labour. This can only be logically inferred from Sangam texts like *Mullaipattu* which refer to the employment of girls for lighting of huge lamps and for serving as handmaidens in war-camps.[97] Maids in the capacity of female attendants or companions do figure in a number of Sangam texts. In the *Ahananuru,* the maid chastises a philanderer for trifling with the affection of her mistress and then abandoning her 'like an evil man who falls out with a friend who has lost his wealth[98]. For northern India however, there is a plethora of evidence of servant-maids, especially from Buddhist sources[99]. The women employed as servants or menials were both free and unfree (slaves). According to the canonical text *Narada Smriti,* 'impure work' like scavenging, cleaning the house of death or the giving of 'message' was to be performed by slaves while 'free' servants were exempt from such socially 'de-meaning' tasks[100]. Finley describes domestic servitude as 'Between Slavery and Freedom'[101] and this would also be an accurate description of the karmakaris in the Indian situation.

---

[94] *S.I.I.,* vol. V, No. 161.

[95] *S.I.I.,* vol. VI, No. 84.

[96] *S.I.I.,*vol. X, No. 10.

[97] *Mullaipattu:* 45–49 Vidyanandan 1954, op.cit, p. 265.

[98] In the *Ahananuru,* both 'Aintinai Elupatu' and 'Aintinai Aimpathu' have a number of references to female attendants/companions. See Krishnan 2000, pp. 239–245.

[99] Important investigation on the nature of the work undertaken by the dasis, karmakaris and other categories of women workers have been made by Uma Chakravarti in her many writings on women. See especially her essay 'of Dasas and Karmakaras' in her book 2006, pp. 70–100.

[100] *Narada Smriti,* Chapter V: 23–42 vide Hanumanthan 1979, p. 55.

[101] Finley 1964, pp. 233–249.

The twelfth-century Sanskrit text *Manasollasa*[102] written in north Peninsular India by the Chalukyan king Somesvara, recommends the employment of women for such menial tasks as drawing water, serving food (women cooks would be of a superior strata), sweeping and swabbing of the premises, washing feet, messaging, hair dressing etc. In Tamil inscriptions these maids are referred to as *atiyar, totti* (untouchable caste?) or *panimakkal*. In Sanskrit the commonly used terms are *paricharika* or *dasi*. According to the medieval text *Basava Puranamu,* carrying water and taking the cattle to graze also seems to have constituted the maid's duties.[103] Women also worked as construction labour. One Chola inscription from Tiruvamattur (in South Arcot district) says that at a site where there were both male and female labourers, the women were to be paid half of what the men got.[104] The record specifies the work as lifting water from ponds and canals etc and irrigating the gardens and fields as also gathering flowers and making garlands. For all such labour the male workers were to be paid eight *nazhis* of rice perday while the women workers were to be paid only four nazhis. Similarly another inscription states that among daily wage workers, women were to be paid half of the wages given to men.[105] Servants including those employed to sing in the temples, were granted lands as service tenures[106]. Female musicians would of course be in a slightly higher category of servants than the unskilled maids. However, a record dated 1235 CE states that even female attendants were given house sites.[107] A thirteenth-century Pandyan inscription refers to a curious case involving a murder where the Pandyan State also confiscated the lands of the male and female servants of the murderer.[108] A remarkable record belonging to the fourteenth regnal year of Rajadhiraja II from Achchalpuram[109] defines the lowly status occupied by workers and servants in medieval society. The record says that workers should not use titles such as 'Vel' or 'Arasu', should not beat the drums on sad or happy occasions and that even wealthier servants cannot own slaves. The medieval text *Yasatilaka* refers to the employment of elderly and experienced women as supervisors over the maid servants of the royal household.[110]

Within the Bhakti tradition there is an interesting reversal of this lowly status accorded to servants, both men and women, in secular life. Basavanna, the twelfth-century saint who spearheaded the Virasaivite movement, says in one of his vachanas or poems that 'it is far better to be a *totti* (maid) in a devotee's house than a queen in the palace.[111]

---

102 *Manasollasa* of Somesvara III, ed. Shrigondekar, Baroda 1939, verses: 1817–18.

103 Early medieval references to this are found in *Tattvasaram and the Basava Puranamu* cited in.Kamat 1980, p. 63.

104 *A.R.E.,* 18 of 1922.

105 *A.R.E.,* 223 of 1917.

106 *S.I.I.,* vol. II. No. 66.

107 Epigraphica Indica, vol. VI, pp. 38–39 vide Appadorai 1990, vol. I, p. 279.

108 *A.R.E.,* 301,302 and 303 of 1923 and part. II, para 77.

109 *A.R.E.,* 538 of 1918, 1919 part II, pp. 97–98. For an interesting analysis of this inscription see Pandarattar 1974, pp. 572–73.

110 Handiqui, K.K., *Yasatilaka and Indian Culture*, Sholapur, 1949, p. 28 vide Kamat 1980, p. 119.

111 *Bhakti Bhandara Basavannavara Vachanagalu* vide Kamat 1980, p. 118.

Wet-nurses, Foster Mothers and Midwives

Wet nurses are important protagonists in the entire corpus of Sangam literature. The term used is 'chevili thai'. Though it is logical to presume that only indigent women took to this profession, the nurse seems to have enjoyed the respect as well as affection of the family she served. The *Ahananuru*[112] refers to women adopting the profession of wet-nurse. The *Perumpanatruppadai*[113] lists the duties of the nurse which included amusing the child, feeding it and soothing it to sleep etc. A beautiful poem from the *Natrinai*[114] has a mother's reminiscence about her daughter who had just got married:

> *'Is this my child behind whom the wet-nurse used to run, with a golden cup of rice mixed with honey and milk in her hands, alternately coaxing and threatening the child.'*

In the *Kurijipattu*[115] the daughter of the house, first confides her love affair to her wet nurse or foster mother who then convinces the mother and the marriage takes place. Wet nurses also wielded some power in Peninsular politics. Devakabbe, the wet nurse of chief Irebedenga, donated seventy *dramma* and land at Choppadandu which went towards the excavation of a tank.[116] The children of wet nurses also came to occupy administrative positions. An inscription dated 1235 CE records grants made by a royal servant, who was the son of the wet-nurse of king Kota Manmaketa.[117] To provide a significant later day parallel from Northern India, wet nurses played a crucial role in Mughal history. Much has been written about the political involvement of Maham Anaga, the wet nurse of emperor Akbar and her natural son Adam Khan, in sixteenth-century Mughal politics.

It appears that the 'dhatri' referred to in medieval inscriptions and texts indicate the traditional midwife called 'dai'. An inscription refers to women being employed as midwives in the prasutishala which can roughly be translated as 'maternity home'.[118] The dhatri or dai is referred to in Vijayanagar period for instance in the text *Vaddaradhana* of Sivakotyacharya[119] as well as in the *Adipurana* of Pampa.[120] The role of the dai must have been ubiquitous at all birthings in traditional societies but, because this is a process that involves extreme privacy and secrecy, historical evidence is extremely sparse.

Oil Extraction, Toddy Making and Culinary Profession

The history of early Peninsular India suggests strongly that certain types of work were considered an extension of the 'domestic' and therefore women's profession. This included cooking

[112] *Ahananuru*, op.cit., 105.
[113] *Perumpanatruppadai,* op.cit., 247–253.
[114] *Natrinai*, op.cit., 110.
[115] Kuriniipattu in *Pathupattu,* op.cit., 1–26.
[116] Inscriptions of Andhra Pradesh, Kurnool district, No. 8 vide Padma 2001, p.60.
[117] *A.R.E.,* 484 of 1913.
[118] *S.I.I.,* vol. V, No. 395.
[119] *Vaddaradhana* of Sivakotyachary, vol. II, p. 34 vide Kamat 1980, p. 119.
[120] *Adipurana* of Pampa, verse: 21 vide Kamath 1980, p. 119.

and hawking of sweetmeats, extraction and sale of oil, the preparation and sale of liquor made at home from old rice or fruits and the making of pickles and pappad which were also hawked by women. Extraction and sale of oil as well as extraction and sale of toddy involved women's labour. This equation changed in the later-medieval period when the profitability increased in tandem with greater capital imput and improved technology. As a result of these developments, these traditional domains of female enterprise were gradually taken over by men.

A. Oil Extraction

In the Sangam period the extraction and sale of fish oil seems to have been done by fisher-women called Valachchi. The *Porunaratrupada*[121] says that fish oil and toddy were exchanged for honey and edible roots. The *Kreedabhiramamu* says that Teliki women extracted and sold 'champangi nune', that is, oil from the Champangi flower.[122] Reference to Telika or women oil mongers also occur in medieval inscriptions.[123] The *Keyurabahucharitamu* of Manchanna describes a Vaishya girl bartering oil for rice in a small shop.[124] In the course of the colonial period traditional techniques of oil extraction by women gradually died out and the building of oil distilleries meant the movement of this work altogether away from women's work spaces into the larger domain of mechanised oil extraction, dominated by male labour.

B. Liquor Distillation

Sangam texts are replete with references to the preparation of liquor from fermented rice and fruits by women. They also state that women hawked toddy from door to door, carrying it on their heads. The coastal Valaiyar women, from the Neydal region, are said to have processed and sold toddy made from Palmyra juice or from rice. In the Marudam region women were specifically associated with the production of rice toddy which was called *toppi*. The *Perumpanatrupadai*[125] clearly states that women enjoyed drinking the *kallu* or *toppi*, which they prepared at home. The process is also detailed in this text. First, a kind of rice starch was prepared which was allowed to ferment for a day or two. When impurities were drained from this liquor it was called *nerumpili.*[126] A mild toddy prepared from the palm fruit was called *pennai* while liquor prepared from honey was called *tekkal-tenal*. Women also hawked the liquor that they had prepared. The *Ahananuru*[127] says that the Ariyal girls sold toddy which they carried on their heads in pots. Like oil, the toddy was also exchanged for paddy or rice.[128] Since women prepared all varieties of liquor their consumption of alcohol

---

[121] Ramaswamy 1999, pp. 150–171.

[122] Kreedabiramamu of Vallabharaya verse 103. vide Rao and Shulman 2002, p. 48. I must add however, that the description is of a purely sensuous nature and adds nothing materially to the theme of women and work.

[123] *S.I.I.,* vol. V, Nos. 1051 and 1076.

[124] *Keyurabahucharita* of Manchanna, second canto, verses 11–15 vide Padma 2001, p. 61.

[125] *Perumpanatruppadai*, line 142.

[126] Ibid. Lines 274–281.

[127] *Ahananuru*: 157.

[128] Porunaratruppadai vide Pattupattu, Swaminathayyar 1937, lines: 214–15.

was logical.[129] The *Pattinappalai* says that the Paratavar women (fisherfolk) of the *Neydal*, first offered the liquor to the gods and then consumed it.[130]

The tenth-century medieval text *Takkayakkapparani*[131] says that women consumed strong rice liquor called *neruvu*. As cited earlier, the thirteenth-century hagiographical work *Periyapuranam*[132] refers to Pulatti women dancing and jumping around in an inebriated state. Even in the medieval period, liquor distilling was apparently still considered an extension of a woman's domestic chores although liquor was also made for the local market and sold by women.

As liquor distilleries separated from the rural sector and became professionally more profitable, they were almost entirely taken over by men. This process was a gradual one commencing from the late-medieval and moving into the early colonial times. This argument finds an interesting echo in Judith Bennett's book on 'Ale-Wives' and breweries in Medieval England and the passing of the trade, in the course of the seventeenth century, into male hands as it came to be dominated by better technology, more capital and greater profitability.[133]

WOMEN COOKS AS PROFESSIONALS

In the patriarchal register the kitchen has always constituted woman's space and cooking is seen as a woman's primary occupation and pre-occupation. That besides constituting 'wifely' duties as enumerated in the *Tolkappiyam*, this was also perceived as woman's profession can be seen by the reference to the 'appakkari' (the *aappam* resembling pancakes) in the *Maduraikanchi*[134] as well as *Silappadikaram.*[135] There are references to the appointment of female cooks in the medieval period. An inscription from Talagunda in Karnataka dated 1158 CE states that three female cooks were appointed as cooks in an agraharam and were paid money as well as given clothes.[136] These could only have been destitute Brahmin widows since no one in an agraharam (a Brahmin settlement) would eat food cooked by a non-Brahmin. A late-Chola inscription from Tiruvorriyur (Chingleput district) refers to the employment of four cooks to cook in the temple kitchen.[137] Medieval inscriptions from Tirupati Devasthanam provide evidence of female cooks.[138] The *Kreedabhiramamu* refers to women who maintained Pootakulla illu or small inns where the usual charge was one ruka per meal.[139] This reference clearly states that these cooks/inn owners were destitute

---

129 *Pattinappalai* in *Pattupattu*, line 108.

130 Ibid. Lines 80–85.

131 *Takkayakkapparani* vide Rajamanikkanar 1970, p. 507.

132 *Periyapuranam* Sastri 1975, p. 568–69.

133 Bennett 1996.

134 *Maduraikanchi:* 405–406.

135 *Silappadikaram:* 13: 122–23.

136 *Epigraphica Carnatica:* Vol. VII, Sk. 185.

137 128 of 1912–1913, p. 103 vide Raman 1959, p. 170.

138 *T.T.D.I.,* ed. Sastri and Viraraghavacharya 1931–38, vol. II, No. 135 dated CE 1496.

139 *Kreedabhiramamu* 2002, lines 158–60; 161–166. A Telugu *ruka* is more or less the same as the Tamil *panam,* roughly 0.15 or 0.16 of the seventeenth century rupee. Another reference to 'women cooks' is in line 189 of the same text.

Brahmin women. Elsewhere the same text also refers to the *Tammadi Sani Mandiramu*[140] which may have been rest houses run by the Devaradiyar. A Kannada text refers to an old woman Pitavve who sold 'dosa' (similar to pancakes) while her neighbour Ammavve sold cowdung cakes.[141] Medieval Persian sources also refer to inns run by women. *Tazkiratul Muluk* of Rafiuddin Shirazi (written between 1608–12) describes the women of the bhatiyara caste as maintaining themselves by keeping inns.[142]

PROFESSIONAL WOMEN MOURNERS: UNIQUE TO THE INDIAN SOCIO-ECONOMIC LANDSCAPE

There is one very important dimension of women's work in the Indian context which not only feminist historians but also feminist film makers are looking at now. This is the occupation of the professional mourner, a profession which seems to have been a women's preserve. In India, even in early historical times, professional mourners have almost always been women. In fact, a thirteenth-century inscription from Pudukottai state records that when death occurred in any household, the Valaichchi women (low caste/untouchables) put a cloth over their heads and mourned the dead with loud wails.[143] The singing of these lamentation songs constituted a special repertoire since songs meant for young wives dying in child birth would be very different from the songs on the death of the master of the household or the almost celebratory tone of the dirges sung at the death of elderly persons. Cleaning of the death-polluted house with cow dung the next day was also their job. They were paid for both. Professional mourning as women's work has no parallel in Western societies to the best of my knowledge and has therefore escaped the critical gaze of Western feminist scholars.

CONCLUDING REFLECTIONS

In recent years critiques of everyday life, where women's work and the process of houswifization occupies centre stage, has become a key concept within post-colonial discourse. This encompasses not only feminist writings on the theme of women's work space but also sociological writings endeavouring to theorise 'Everyday Life'. Written in 2000, Michael E. Gardiner's book *Critiques of everyday life*,[144] brought together some of the perspectives on everyday life from Mikhail M Bakhtin to the feminist sociologist Dorothy E. Smith. In her writings[145] Smith contends that mainstream institutionalised forms of sociology (this would be true of most disciplines) present us with versions of the social world that are systematically exclusionary and distorting. She uses the term 'malestreaming' for this

[140] Ibid., verse 273.

[141] *Vachanadharmasara:* 223 vide Kamat 1980, p. 118.

[142] Divya Narayanan cites many such instances in her unpublished M.Phil dissertation 2006.

[143] Inscriptions of the Pudukottai State, No. 601.

[144] Gardiner, 2000.

[145] Smith 1987 and Smith 1990, to cite just two out of her many writings on this theme.

insidious process of epistemological conditioning. These 'malestream' accounts of everyday life effectively rob women of any real agency of understanding and thereby transforming their world. Smith stresses the immediacy of developing a woman-centred ontology that respects the integrity of every life, and hence the 'lived' character of female existence and experience. The challenge lies in steering clear of all abstracted textual forms which feed directly into the requirements of either capitalism or bureaucratic power and control. Such efforts in the context of Indian history must perforce remain very tentative. A panoramic survey of women and work in Peninsular Indian history up to the beginnings of colonialism should be seen as initial steps towards a much more ambitious feminist enterprise. The primary endeavour has been to salvage available data on women's work both paid and unpaid, both visible and less-visible in order to highlight South Indian women's contribution to the work domain and indicate directions of movement and change in women's work/labour history.

REFERENCES

Original Texts (in Sanskrit, Tamil, Kannada or Telugu)

Tamil Works:

Sangam Texts

(The Sangam texts referred to in this article can be dated roughly between third century B.C and third century A.D.)

Ahananuru ed. with commentary by Venkataswami Nattar N. M. and Venkatachalam Pillai, R. Madras: Saiva Siddhanta Kazhagam, 1943.

Aingurunuru ed. Swaminathaiyyar U. V. and Kalyana Sundaranar, S., Madras: Kapir Achchukootam, 1957.

Kuronthogai ed. U. V. Swaminathaiyyar, Madras: Kapir Achukootam, 1962.

Kalittogai, Fourteenth century commentator Nachchinarkiniyar's commentary, ed. Anantharaman, E. V., Madras: Saiva Siddhanta Kazhagam, 1967.

Malaippadukadam from the *Pattupattu*, Anthology, ed. U. V. Swaminathaiyyar, Madras: Kapir Achukootam, 1965.

Natrinai *Nanuru* ed. by A. Narayanaswami, Madras: Saiva Siddhanta Kazhagam, 1962.

Perumppanatruppadai in *Pattupattu,* Anthology, ed. by U. V. Swaminathaiyyar, Madras: Kapir Achukootam, 1965.

Perunkadai, ed. by U. V. Swaminathaiyyar, Madras: Publishers not known, 1924

Porunaratruppadai in the Pattupattu Anthology, ed. Swaminathayyar, U. V., Madras: publishers not known, 1937.

Purananuru ed. U. V. Swaminathayyar, Madras: Kapir Achukootam, 1963.

Silappadikaram of Ilango Adigal (a Post-Sangam text) ed. Dikshitar, V. R. Ramachandra. New York: New York University Press, 1954 (originally published in 1939).

Sanskrit Texts

Arthashastra of Kautilya (third century to second century A.D.) ed. and transl. in three parts by Kangle, R.P., Bombay: University of Bombay, 1965.

Manasollasa (12th century Sanskrit text) of Somesvara III, ed. Shrigondekar, Baroda: 1939, verses: 1817–18.

Manusmriti as *Manu's Code of Law: A Critical Edition And Translation of the Manava-Dharmasastra* ed. By Patrick Olivelle with the Editorial Assistance of Suman Olivelle, Oxford University Press, New Delhi, 2006, chapter IX, verses 10–12.
Manusmriti, (commentary by Kulluka), ed. Narayan Ram Acharya Kavitirtha, tenth edition, Nirmaya Press, Bombay, 1946, IX: 10–12.
Vimalakirtinirdesa Sutra, 1974.

Medieval Texts

Andal's *Tiruppavai*, (Tamil Poetry, written in the seventh century CE by the Vaishnava woman saint Andal) songs 7, 8, 12 etc. Tamil text in *Nachchiyar Tirumozhi and Tiruppavai in Sri Andal: Her Contribution to Literature, Philosophy, Religion and Art*—All India Seminar on Andal, published by the Sri Ramanuja Vedanta Centre, Chennai, 1985.
Kreedabhiramamu of Vinukonda Vallabharaya ed. and transl. Rao, Velcheru Narayana and Shulman, David under the title, *Kreedabhiramamu: a lover's guide to Warangal,* New Delhi, Permanent Black, 2002.
Kreedabhiramamu of Vinukonda Vallabharaya, ed. Veturi Prabhakara Sastry, Muktiyala: (Hyderabad), Manimanjari, 1960.
Futuhat-us-Salatin ed. A.S. Usha and trans. Agha Mehdi Hasan, Three volumes, Aligarh, Aligarh Muslim University, 1976–77.

Epigraphical Records (inscriptions on rocks and copper plates)

Annual Report of Epigraphy, Southern Circle (abbreviated as *A.R.E.* in the footnotes), 1887 onwards, Madras: Govt. of Tamil Nadu.
Inscriptions of the Pudukkottai State translated and ed. K.R. Srinivasa Aiyar, Pudukkottai: Pudukkottai State Press, 1941–1946 (originally published in 1929 by the Sri Brihadamba State Press of Pudukkottai).
South Indian Inscriptions (abbreviated as *S.I.I.* in the footnotes) published from the 1890 onwards, Madras: Govt. of Tamil Nadu.
Tirumalai-Tirupati Devasthanam Inscriptions, (abbreviated as *T.T.D.I.* in the footnotes) ed. Sastri, S. Subramanya and.Viraraghavacharya, V 6 vols., Madras: 1931–38.
Subramanian, T.N. ed. *South Indian Temple Inscriptions*, Madras: Madras University, 1957.

Secondary Works (in Tamil) *Note that Chennai and Madras refer to the same place but most Tamil publishers prefer to use the term 'Chennai' rather than the anglicised 'Madras'.

Rajamanikkanar 1970.
Rajamanikkanar, M. *Pattupattu Araichi*, Chennai: Tamil Nadu Text Book Society, 1970.
Tamizhannal 1956
Tamizhannal, S. *Taalattu,* Karaikkudi in Tamil Nadu, Mathili Pathippagam, 1956.
Vanamamalai 1964
Vanamamalai, N. *Tamizhar Nattu Padalgal,* Madras: Madras University, 1964.
Vidyanandan 1954
Vidyanandan, S. *Tamizhar Salbu,* Chennai: Pari Publications, 1954.

Secondary Works (in English)

Appadorai 1990
Appadorai, A. *Economic Conditions in Southern India,* 1000–1500 AD, Madras: University of Madras, reprint 1990 (originally published in 1936).
Bachelard 1964
Bachelard, Gaston. *The Poetics of Space: The Classic Look at How We Experience Intimate Places,* tr. By Maria Jolas from French, Beacon Press, Massachusetts: 1964 (French original in 1958).
Bader 1964
Bader, Clarisse. *Women in Ancient India: Moral and Literary Studies,* tr. by Mary E.R. Martin. reprinted under the Chowkhamba Sanskrit Series, vol. 44, Varanasi: Chowkhamba Publishers, 1964. (originally published in French in 1867 and the English translation in 1925).
Balambal 1998
Balambal, V. *Studies in the History of the Sangam Age,* Delhi: Kalinga publications,1998.
Bennett 1996
Bennett, Judith. *Ale, Beer and Brewsters in England: Women's Work in a Changing World,* New York and Oxford: OUP, 1996.
Billington 1973
Billington, Mary Francis. *Women in India,* New Delhi: Amarko Book Agency *(Reprint)*, 1973 (originally published in 1895).
Boserup 2007
Boserup, Ester. *Women's Role in Economic Development,* Earthscan, London: Sterling, 2007 (first published in 1970).
Chakaravarti 1989
Chakaravarti, Uma. 'Whatever Happened to the Vedic Dasi?' in Sangari, Kumkum and Vaid, Sudesh. *Recasting Women: Essays in Colonial History*, New Delhi: Kali for Women, 1989.
Chakravarti 2006
Chakravarti, Uma. *Everyday Lives, Everyday Histories: Beyond the Kings and Brahmanas of 'Ancient' India,* New Delhi: Tulika Books, 2006.
Chattopadhyay 1985
Chattopadhyay, Kamaladevi. *Handicrafts of India* (rpt) New Delhi: Indian Council of Cultural Relations, 1985.
Chicherov 1971
Chicherov, A.I. *India: Economic Development in the 16–18th centuries–Outline History of Crafts and Trade,* Nauka Publishing House, Moscow: 1971, pp. 52–56.
Ekejiuba 1995
Ekejiuba, Felicia. 'Down to Fundamentals: Women-Centred Hearthholds in Rural West Africa' in Deborah Fahy Bryceson, ed. *Women Wielding the Hoe,* Oxford: Oxford University Press, 1995.
Finley 1964
Finley, M.I. 'Between Slavery and Freedom', *Comparative Studies in Society and History,* Vol.6, No.3, 1964, pp. 233–249.
Gardinaer 2000
Gardinaer, Michael E. *Critiques of everyday life,* London and New York: Routledge, 2000.
Gupta 1972
Gupta, D.K. *Society and Culture in the Time of Dandin,* New Delhi, Meharchand Lachamandas, 1972.
Gururajachar 1974
Gururajachar, S. *Some Aspects of Economic and Social Life in Karnataka – 1000–1300,* Mysore: Prasaranga Publications, 1974.
Habib 2000
Habib, Irfan. 'Exploring Medieval Gender History', Calicut: Symposium on Gender History, Indian History Congress, 2000.
Hambley 1998

Hambley, Gavin. R.G. *Women in Medieval Islamic World: Power, Patronage and Piety,* New York: St. Martin's Press, 1998.
Hanumanthan 1979
Hanumanthan, K.R. *Untouchablity: A Historical Study up to 1500 AD*, Madurai: Koodal Publishers, 1979.
Hemlatha 1991
Hemlatha, B. *Life in Medieval Northern Andhra,* New Delhi: Navrang Publishers, 1991.
Hufton 1993
Hufton, Olwen. '*A History of Women* in the West', in General Editors Georges Duby and Michelle Perrot, volume III, *Renaissance and Enlightenment Paradoxes* edited by Natalie Zemon Davis and Arlette Farge, Cambridge Masschusetts and London: The Belknap Press of Harvard University Press, 1993, pp. 15–45.
Kamat 1980
Kamat, J.K. *Social Life in Medieval Karnataka,* New Delhi: Abhinav Publications, 1980.
Krishnan 2000
Krishnan, A. *Tamil Culture: Religion, Culture & Literature,* Delhi: Bharatiya Kala Prakashan, 2000.
Law 1981
Law, Bimla Churn. *Women in Buddhist Literature,* Varanasi: Indological Book House, 1981.
Mies 1998
Mies, Maria. *Patriarchy and Accumulation on a World Scale: Women in the International Division of Labour,* London & New York: Zed Books Ltd, 1998 (originally published 1886).
Moosvi 1994
Moosvi, Shireen. 'Work and Gender in Pre-Colonial India' in Fauve-Chamoux and Sogner Solvi ed. *Socio-Economic Consequences of Sex-Ratios in Historical Perspective, 1500–1900*, Proceedings of the Eleventh International Economic History Congress, Milan: Universita Bocconi, 1994.
Mukherji 1952
Mukherji, Lily. 'Social Life in Mathura and Vrindavan in the Medieval Ages', *Proceedings of the Indian History Congress*, Kurukshethra: 1982, pp. 325–331.
Narayanan 2006
Narayanan, Divya. M.Phil dissertation (unpublished) titled *A Culture of Food: Aspects of Dietary Habits and Consumption in the Urban Centres of North-West India Between the Sixteenth and Early Seventeenth Centuries,* New Delhi: Centre for Historical Studies, Jawaharlal Nehru University, 2006.
Orr 2000
Orr, Leslie. *Donors, Devotees and Daughters of God: Temple Women in Medieval Tamil Nadu,* New York: Oxford University Press, 2000.
Padma 2001
Padma, A. *The Socio-Cultral world of Women in Medieval Andhra: from 11th to 13th centuries*, New Delhi: Bharatiya Kala Prakashan, 2001.
Padma 2005
Padma, A. 'Women and Social Justice – A Study of the Kakatiya Period' in A. Satyanarayana and P. Chenna Reddy ed. *Recent Trends in Historical Studies: Festschrift to Professor Ravula Soma Reddy*, Delhi: S.K. Pathak for Research India Press, 2005.
Pandarattar 1974
Pandarattar, Sadasiva. *Pirkala Cholargal* (Tamil), Chidambaram: Annamalai University, 1974.
Raman 1959
Raman, K.V. *The Early History of the Madras Region*, Chennai: University of Madras, 1959.
Ramaswamy 1999
Ramaswamy Vijaya. 'Women and the 'Domestic' in Tamil Folk Songs', *Man in India*, 74(1) 1994, pp. 21–37 and reprinted in Kumkum Sangari and Uma Chakravarti ed. *From Myths to Markets: Essays on Gender*, pp. 41–42, Shimla: Manohar and the Indian Institute of Advanced Study, 1999, pp. 39–55.
Ramaswamy 1997
Ramaswamy, Vijaya. 'The Kudi in Early Tamilaham and Tamil Women from Tribe to Caste' in Dev Nathan ed. *From Tribe to Caste*, Shimla: Indian Institute of Advanced Study, 1997, pp. 223–246.

Ramaswamy 1996

Ramaswamy, Vijaya. *Divinity and Deviance,* Delhi: Oxford University Press, 1996.

Ramaswamy 1993

Ramaswamy, Vijaya. 'Women and Farm Work in Tamil Folk Songs', *Social Scientist,* Vol.21, Nos. 9–11, September–November, 1993, pp. 113–129.

Ramaswamy 1989

Ramaswamy Vijaya. 'Aspects of Women and Work in Early South India', *Indian Economic and Social History Review,* No. 23, 1989, pp. 81–99 and reprinted in Kumkum Roy ed. *Women in Early Indian Societies,* New Delhi: Manohar: 1999, pp. 150–174.

Rau 1970

Rau, Wilhelm. *Weben und Flechten in Vedischen Indien,* Weisbaden: University of Wiesbaden, 1970.

Reddy 1991

Reddy, Nagolu Krishna. *Social History of Andhra Pradesh: 7–13th centuries,* New Delhi: Agam Kala Prakashan, 1991.

Sangari 1989

Sangari, Kumkum and Vaid, Sudesh ed. *Recasting Women: Essays in Colonial History,* New Delhi: Kali for Women, 1989.

Sastri 1946

Sastri Nilakanta K.A. and Venkataramanayya, N., ed. *Further Sources of Vijayanagar History,* 3 vols, Madras: University of Madras, 1946.

Sastri 1975

Sastri, Nilakanta K.A. *The Colas,* Madras: University of Madras, 1975 (originally published in 1935).

Sen 1993

Sen, Aloka Parashar. 'Temple girls and the Land Grant Economy', in Sen, Aloka Parashar edited *Social and Economic History of Early Deccan: Some Interpretations,* New Delhi: Manohar, 1993, pp. 240–277.

Siddiqui 1996

Siddiqui, I.H. 'Socio-Political Role of Women in the Sultanate of Delhi' in Pawar, Kiran ed. *Women in Indian History,* Patiala-New Delhi: Vision & Venture, 1996, pp. 87–101.

Smith 1987

Smith, Dorothy E. *The Everyday World as Problematic: A Feminist Sociology,* New England: North Eastern University Press, 1987.

Smith 1990

Smith, Dorothy E. *The Conceptual Practices of Power: A Feminist Sociology of Knowledge,* Toronto: University of Toronto Press, 1990.

Tyagi 1994

Tyagi, Anil K. *Women Workers in Ancient India,* New Delhi: South Asia Books, 1994.

Venkataramanayya 1950

Venkataramanayya, N. *The Eastern Chalukyas of Vengi,* Madras: Vedam Venkataraya Sastri and Bros., 1950.

Woolf 1974

Woolf, Virginia. *A Room of One's Own,* London: Hogarth Press, 1974 (first published in 1929).

Chapter 18

Women's Profession in Medieval Andhra*

A. PADMA

EDITOR'S NOTE

The second part of A. Padma's essay, dealing with women's property rights in medieval Andhra, has been placed under Section III. The first part which deals with various professions open to women in medieval Andhra is being dealt with here. It must be pointed out that although this Reader has a separate section on prostitution, I have felt that in the case of this particular essay the logical and historical flow is better maintained by retaining the section on prostitution here rather than moving to Section V.

***

Indian tradition determines the space of men and women in public and private domains respectively. However, interchangeability of gender roles is observed at times. Even in the classical tradition though a man is deemed to succeed to the throne, in the absence of a male heir/co-regent, his wife becomes the ruler to ensure continuity of rule. Women belonging to the weak sections of the society take up economic activities along with men to supplement the family income. Thus, it appears that there is no clear-cut demarcation between the gender roles and they are very much influenced by the demands of the situation.

The law givers too provided ample space for women making them political heirs under certain circumstances. They enabled women to enter into valid contracts or pledge their husband's property for the purpose. Not only these, they have also allotted certain rights on property to women whether inherited or acquired by them. This largely explains the economic participation of women in the medieval times.

* Reproduced with permission from the author. Previously published in 'The Socio-Cultural World of Women in Medieval Andhra (from 11th to 13th centuries A.D.)', Bharatiya Kala Prakashan, Delhi (2001); pp. 71–84.

PROFESSIONS

In the primitive societies, no division of labour is found between the two sexes. Anthropological studies project women of ancient societies as food gatherers and food processors.[1] In due course, agriculture and crafts which necessitated a *heavy* muscular power and labour were taken by men and the works which involved patience, skill and forbearance were practiced by women.

Certain leisure time activities of women, like spinning, weaving, stitching clothes, etc. contributed for the family economy. The dharmic literature also provided space for different occupations to be held by different categories of women. For example, entertainment maids in the royal courts.[2] The duty of attending to the personal works of a king and his family members was also assigned to women. Similarly, the profession of dance in the courts became exclusive of women, with the result that a new class of courtesans came into existence. Some of the wealthy and learned courtesans were patronised by kings as their concubines. Concubinage became an established and respectable profession in the medieval times. By about the same time, the temple too emerged as an important feudal institution creating provisions for temple dancing girls and women attendants for carrying out various ritual services to the temple deities, thereby widening the scope for their participation in almost all spheres of socio-economic, politico-cultural lives.

The occupations held by different categories of women can broadly be discussed under 3 heads; Occupations of *Kulastreelu* (family women), Women as *Bhōogastṛreelu* (entertainment maids) and the temple girls. Under each category folk-elite variation and integration are discussed.

OCCUPATIONS OF *KULASTREELU* (FAMILY WOMEN)

Occupations taken up by women belonging to both elite and common sections of the society whose marital status (maiden, married or widow) is specific are included in this category.

Generally women of elite group did not take up any profession. The exception being women of ruling elite who entered into administrative jobs. This can be viewed more as hereditary right to that of profession. However, women of the common sections of the society had to take up various economic activities to supplement the income of their husbands and to help them in the smooth running of the family. These include:

(a) Service in Royal Palace

A king's household is a big affair. Royal palace served as the biggest employer with several attendants for each type of work. Women are employed in the inner circles of the palace. *Manu* holds that well trained women and whose toilet (attire/garments) and ornaments examined should be appointed as entertainment maids by a king.[3] They should attend to him with such works as serving with fans, water, and perfumes. *Mānasōllāasa,* recommends employing women in the royal households for cleaning rice and serving food, washing feet, massaging, dressing hair, applying unguents and for providing entertainment with programmes of music, dance, instrument playing.[4] The medieval dance treatise *Nrittaratnākaramu* of Jāyapasēnani suggests that the king should be attended upon by maids alone while he watched programmes of music and dance and there should be a woman who is perfectly talented in these arts in order to explain the significance of the programme to the king.[5] Contemporary epigraphical and literary evidences throw much light on the different duties of women in the royal households.

The wet-nurse is entrusted with the duty of bringing up the infant prince/princess to the early years of its childhood. Preferably old and experienced women are appointed for the purpose. *Dādi* is the term associated with these women. Epigraphical and literary references provide more details of the post and the importance attached to it.[6] Women attendants of the palace performed tasks like giving oil or scented bath to the king, massaging hair or other parts of the body, cleaning grains or such other works in the royal kitchen.[7] A record mentions the donor as the son of *Aḍupulotteḍi Aṅgāṅḍi* (one who massages the feet) of king, Kulottungachoḍa Deva.[8] Women are appointed sometimes to look into the catering services of the royal kitchen. An undated epigraph from Amarāvati refers to the wife of Prolaya as *Vaṅṭala* Kāmasāni, probably in charge of royal kitchen.[9] Serving meals for the members of the royal family, especially the king, is also one of the duties of women attendants of the palace. Such women who arrange the meal plates for the king are referred to as *Taḷiya*[10] It appears that the court of Prataparudra II, the Kakatiya emperor had 3,200 women attendants.[11]

Women alone are appointed as guards for the inner apartments of the palace and as personal body guards for royal women.[12] Mānasōllāsa, prescribes elderly and experienced women to supervise the work of the maids of the palace.[13]

Āndhra Mahābhāratamu mentions a post, Sairaṅdhri, (a woman engaged to decorate the queen). According to Tikkana, often women who are deserted take up this job. They stay for a specific period in the harem. Their duty is to decorate the queen and the job requires perfect talent in arts like hair dressing, beautification processes and making different kinds of garlands.[14] This post probably had its origin in Vedic period. No specific payment is prescribed but she was maintained within the palace and was given a respectable treatment.

Women belonging to *Bōya, Eṛuka, Cheṅchu* communities too are appointed for various services in the royal palaces. *Bōya* women wrap clothes to the palanquins, while their husbands were the palanquin bearers.[15] The services of *Eṛuka* women were utilised to learn the plans of rival political powers in the war fields.[16]

Details regarding the mode of payment, amount of salary paid to each of these women employees are however not available. It appears that they are maintained out of royal income and residential accommodation is also provided to them within the palace compound. Moreover, the children or husbands of these women were assigned administrative posts such as *Talāṛi* and *Daṅḍanāyaka.* An inscription dated AD 1235 records grants made by a royal servant and son of the wetnurse of king Kōṭa Maṅmaketa.[17] Another similar reference indicates that the husband of one Itasāni, a servant of Ganapatideva was the horse-man of the king.[18]

(b) Other General Occupations

During medieval times, professions are mostly caste oriented. The contemporary sources provide us with evidences of women's direct involvement in most of them. The village fairs and *tiṛunāḷḷu* held near the temples and pilgrim centres provided sufficient market ground for carrying out their economic activities. In addition, some of them are involved in selling their goods in the streets of the cities and towns. The contemporary literature provides abundant examples of women vendors.

Krīdābhirāmanu refers to women of *Teliki* community whose traditional occupation is extraction of oil, selling hair oil made of Saṁpeṅga flowers (Michelia Champaka).[19] From the same work it can be gathered that few women sold herbal medicines and cosmetics for beautification in the *Maila-saṅta* (market for the out castes).[20] Women selling flowers are termed as Pushpalāvikalu.[21] Generally they sold flowers in the streets of the city during evening or twilight hours. At times they also ran shops to sell flowers.

In *Keyūrabāhucharitramu*, a *vaisya* girl is described as selling oil in exchange to rice in the shop.[22] Srinatha's *Cātu* verses refer to women running shops in the village fair to sell fruits like mangoes,[23] betel leaves,[24] bangles,[25] etc. Poor widows of brahman community stitched meal-plates with broad leaves and earned money by giving them in the houses of brahmans.[26] In addition inns and rest houses are run by poor and destitute women mostly of brahman community. Krīdābhirāmamu refers to *Pōotakūḷḷa illu* (inn) maintained by brahman widows where delicious food was offered at cheaper rate.[27] The work further refers to a rest house called *Tammaḍi sāni Maṅdiramu.*[28]

Women belonging to *Mēdara, Eṛuka,* Cheṅchu, *Sabara* communities too probably made monetary use of their craft skills. *Mēdara* women were experts in basket weaving.[29] *Eṛuka* women were proficient in future telling.[30] Sabara and *Cheṅchu* women probably earned their livelihood through selling tanned animal skins, combs, false hairs and other forest products.[31] Women of *Dommari* and *Goṛaga* classes were expert jugglers. *Krīdābhirāmamu* depicts them as performing gymnastic feats in the streets of Ōṛugallu.[32] They were very clever tumblers and tight rope dancers exhibiting their skills as they travel about. Some of them sold date mats, cane baskets and combs of horn and wood.[33] Basavapurāṇamu refers to a *golletha (Bōya womaṅ)* selling milk, curd and butter in the streets.[34]

Literary and epigraphical sources refer to maids employed for domestic works like bringing water,[35] cooking,[36] etc. The elite class, concubines and wealthy courtesans are the employers for those maids. The maids of concubines and courtesans are supposed to acquire sufficient knowledge in fine arts and instrument playing.[37] *Basavapurāṇamu* mentions women in bonded labour.[38] Their occupation seems to be permanent for the family of the maid based on the term *Ilupuṭṭubānisa* found in *Paṅḍitārādhyacharitra.*[39] Large monastic establishments running residential schools, choultries attached to the temples too employed women for petty works like cleaning grains and vessels. An epigraph from Drākshārāmam registers a grant of 3 *kuṅchamulu* of rice, 1 *jīvita māḍa* and 3 *chinnālu* as salary for the two women employed for pounding rice grains, cleaning vessels and to bring water in the *Kuloṭṭuṅga Choḷa satramu* attached to the temple.[40] Another epigraph, also from the same place records grants of lands in lieu of salary to two women for pounding rice in the temple choultry.[41]

While these occupations are characterised by the direct involvement of women in earning money for the family, certain others like domestic service, rearing cattle, bringing up children, assisting their husbands in craft occupations and agricultural processes remained as supplementary roles as they are not recognised as works or paid jobs. Palkuriki Somanatha, in his Basavapuṛāṇamu gives a detailed description of how medieval women brought up their children, their care for the infants and concern about the general ailment of small children.[42] A mother's voice is considered important in deciding issues like marriages of children.[43]

Within the artisan tradition too women played a passive role in assisting their husbands in the preparatory processes. Their work is not a full time wage employment as production was not commercial. The woman worked in a joint endeavour with her husband. For example, if a potter turns the wheel and moulds the clay into shapes, his wife paints them and dries them.[44] Similarly in other fields like weaving,[45] dairy farming,[46] oil industry,[47] fishing, nut processing,[48] and such other domestic craft occupations, women's subsidiary role went un-noticed and remained hidden. Thus, her contribution to the income of the family did not come to light.

Similar is the case of agricultural processes wherein a woman's contribution is inevitable at every stage of crop production. Planting of seeds, weeding of plants, husking and winnowing of paddy and such other sundry jobs were done entirely by women.[49] *Kumārasaṁbhavamu* contains a description of young and unmarried girls keeping a watch over the paddy fields to drive off the birds and other stray animals.[50] Literary works refer to women singing songs while engaged in agricultural activities such as pounding the grain.[51]

The occupations of family women are thus direct as well as indirect economic activities. In addition, midwifery and nursing, are the other professions taken up by women who are elderly and experienced. The Gōḷakimaṭha established by Viśveśvara Śiva Dēsika at Malkāpuram had one *Prasūtiśāla* (maternity home) attached to it. Though no other details are available in the grant, it can be assumed that women were probably working in the said maternity home as mid-wives and carrying out the duty of attending to child-birth.[52]

WOMEN AS BHŌGASTṚEELU (ENTERTAINMENT MAIDS)

All ancient works including Dharmasastras, mention a separate class of women working as entertainment maids. It was a part of the traditional culture of having women with a separate social status for the purpose of providing enjoyment to men. To this category are included the courtesans, concubines and the prostitutes. Their professions are recognised by law and are brought under its protection by framing rules of succession, maintenance and such other property rights, distinct from those of family women. Laws are also made for protecting them from the dangers of their profession.

In the medieval period, the increasing feudal character of the state necessitated the king to be more authoritative on local chiefs. The existence and stability of the kingdom depended on the king's exercise (exhibition) of right and might. He had to undertake wars for the purpose, assume titles, extend patronage to religious institutions, scholars and poets. Along with these, it became a regular practice to maintain a number of beautiful and talented women as courtesans in the courts or as concubines in the harems. The prowess of the king is reflected in the number of women in his harem, thus creating a great political significance to the institutions of courtesans and concubinage. Gradually the men of elite as well as common sections of the society too maintained women besides lawfully wedded wives. While courtesans and concubines of the king enjoyed higher social status and privileges, prostitutes could not claim so. Even the classical tradition depicts them as money minded. Thus it appears that there are three categories of entertainment maids, courtesans, concubines and prostitutes.

Courtesans

The appointment of a group of dancers in the king's court was a customary practice of the ancient and medieval times. Āndhradeśa too is no exception to this. They are referred to as *Vārāṅganalu*,[53] Vāravilāsinulu,[54] Gaṇikalu.[55] Vatsayana defines *Gaṇika* as a woman expertised in all 64 arts.[56] Mānasollāsa ordains that the *Gaṇikas* along with women of royal family, dancers, priests and feudatories are to attend the king's assembly on special occasions.[57] The very presence of the courtesans brought gracefulness to the court. Ekamranatha mentions that there are as many as 8000 *Biṛudu Pātralu* (courtesans whose profession is to sing/dance in courts to the tunes in praise of the king) and 500 entertainment maids in the court of Prataparudra.[58] Though exaggerating, but the figure indicates the popularity of the dancers in the courts of medieval period.

The contemporary literary sources indicate that every royal court had a contingent of courtesans whose *Nṛityāgana Vinōdamulu* is a daily routine in the court.[59] Girls proficient in fine arts were appointed for the purpose. Courtesans were one among the tributes paid by the feudatories to their overlord. Instances from *Siṁhāsanadvātṛiṁsika* refer to the vassals sending girls as part of their tributary payments offered to their lords.[60]

The courtesans lived in separate streets in the capital cities. Their houses were well furnished and beautifully decorated giving great appearance to the city itself. Literary and epigraphical references show that capital cities like *Vikramasiṁhapura*,[61] *Tsandavole*,[62] *Amarapuramu*,[63] were appearing graceful because of the beautiful houses of the courtesans. This is suggestive of the higher socio-economic status of these women. They were a class by themselves due to the nature of their profession. They received specialised training through teachers appointed for the purpose. (For further information, readers can refer to Chapter 5 in Ref. 64.) Their higher social status and greater economic independence is reflected in their patronising scholars, poets and involvement in religious services through gift making.

Concubinage

On the origin of this institution, N.Venkataramanayya says, 'The existence of courtesans in large numbers in the courts of kings and nobles and those attached to temples must have fostered its growth and encouraged people to form irregular unions with members of this community without any social opprobrium'.[65]

The kings maintained rich, learned women and those skilled in fine arts as their concubines in the harem. They are variously referred to as Bhōgastrēelu,[66] *Bhōgamahishi,*[67] *Lañjapeṇḍlamu,*[68] *Lanjiya,*[69] *Vārakanta,*[70] etc. No social stigma is attached to this practice. Even the kings and nobles patronising concubines took pride in assuming such titles as *Vāranāri* manōrañjana,[71] *Rāya* vesyābhujaṁga,[72] *Vāranāriyauvana Vasaṁthudu,*[73] *Kāminījana Manōvallabha,*[74] etc. as indicated in the contemporary epigraphs. A Telugu Choda chief from Cuddapah region claimed that he was *Vilāsavibhavabhōgapuraṅdara,* and *Chātuṛvidha Kāminī—janaratīśvara.*[75] Another record from Drākshārāmam gives the epithet of the king as *Vāravanitājana Chitta Bhavudu.*[76] This gives support to the argument that patronising concubines is considered as a status symbol of royalty during the period. This practice of the kings is followed even by petty ruling chiefs and nobles.

The harlots lived in separate localities called Āryavāṭikas. Their houses were beautifully decorated with paintings, ornate furniture, soft beds, decorated foams, comfortable chairs, large mirrors and painting halls. They dressed themselves in the most elegant manner.[77] Patronising scholars, poets, painters, musicians, holding literary assemblies, contributing to the state's development through their munificent grants to religious and charitable institutions were part of their regular activities.[78] Prataparudra's concubine Māchaldevi was a famous woman. She commanded a great respect in the society and was described as *Pratāparudra dharaṇīsopatta Gōshtipratishta Pāriṇa.*[79] Kota Keta's concubines gave grants to Buddhadeva at Amarāvati.[80] The concubines of the kings took no hesitation to call themselves the *Bhōgastṛeelu* of the ruling chiefs. Even their children who were generally appointed in the royal service claimed identity through them. In the of Gañjam plates of Gōkaṛṇa and Mātuṛa grant of Nārāyaṇa, the donees claimed themselves as *Veśya Vamsodhbhava.*[81]

The concubines demanded money in the form of *Uṇkuva,* while their men participated in the wars. It is quoted in *Palnāṭi Vīracharitra* that Syāmāṅgi, the concubine of Blachandra (son of Brahmanayudu) demanded a silk saree and Rs. 12,000 as *unkuva* at the time of his leaving for the war field.[82] She claimed that the amount was charged as she had to accompany him to the heaven as *velayalu.*[83] *Unkuva* forms a part of *strīdhana,* a woman's property.[84]

Despite their economic stability and social security in royal courts as courtesans and concubines, there was a need for their legal security and protection. Dharmasastras provide maintenance allowance for the concubines of the deceased besides recognising their sons as illegitimate heirs to the parental property.[85] They also made strict regulations to check the irregularities of the practice. Yājñavalkya prescribes a fine of 50 *panas* against a person cohabiting with the concubine of another.[86] Generally patronised by the men of elite section as part of their privileges, these concubines enjoyed a higher socio-economic status whereas prostitution differs from this in its operational manner.

Prostitution

Commonly referred to as *Veśya, Vārāṅgana, Velayālu, Lañjiya,* these women constitute a professional group by themselves. At times there is no clear distinction between a concubine and a girl who practices prostitution as a profession. They trace their origin from the heavenly nymphs called *Apsaras.*[87] Not a single procession whether of political, social, religious or of festive significance advanced without the programmes by the girls of this group.[88] Raṅganātha Rāmāyaṇamu refers to a *Gaṅikānikāyamu* (an association of *Gaṇikas*) on the occasion of the marriage of Lord Rāma with Sitā.[89]

Women following the profession lived in separate localities of the cities called *vesyavśṭikas.* The Thousand pillar temple inscription of Hanumakonda describes one such *vesyavatika* of Ōṛugallu.[90] A similar account is given in the literary work, *Krīdābhirāmamu.*[91] *Pratāparudracharitra,* quotes that there were about 1,27,000 houses of *veśyas* in Ōṛugallu.[92] The figure seemed to be too high, but, at the same time is suggestive of the wide spread nature of the profession. Contemporary poets described prostitutes of the temple city of Drākshārāmam in their works.[93]

The material prosperity achieved through stabilised feudal political relations during Kakatiya rule in Āndhradeśā could have given rise to the amorous nature of the class of elite. The rulers and their officers needed company of women even during times of war to provide them with relief through their programmes of music/dance and to give them strength and relaxation of the mind. Common men too followed suit. The Saivite movement recognizing the Pañchamakāras as forms of devotion to God, accorded a sort of religious legitimation to this practice.[94] Saivite scriptures identified one's sexual pleasure as that belonging to the Lord, it being one form of devotion of God.[95] *Basavapurāñamu* reflects that Basaveśvara, used to send presents, delicious food preparations to the Saivite priests who spend their whole day in the company of prostitutes.[96] From the various sources we gather that there were about 12,000 such priests who were referred to as Miṅḍa *Jaṅgamas.*[97] The large number only indicates the wide religious sanction by the sect to prostitution.

From the very young age a harlot is trained properly, the syllabi of which is designed in such a way as to make her occupation profitable. In addition, they are supposed to eat little, observe vows for prosperity, learn tricks to deceive men and earn more money.[98] The most important guide and mentor for a harlot is her mother. The *veśyamātha* teaches her daughter that money, costly garments and precious ornaments are compulsory for women following this profession.[99] She trains her daughter to be specific regarding matters of money and makes efforts to prevent her from being carried away by the promises of *Magalajiyalu* (men who try to save money through deceiving the innocent prostitutes), or by religious sentiments.[100] She keeps guard over her daughter and protects her from unpecunious customers.

However, the practices of the mothers of the girls are not held in esteem by many of the contemporary poets. They highlighted the greediness of the Vaśyamātha with great contempt. This shows their male bias as they have not reflected the fear and foresight of the mother for the security of her daughter based on the age bound and temporary nature of their profession. They do not have any other occupation except utilising their youthfullness for earning their livelihood. Once they cross their youth, their plight becomes miserable. Moreover, in the continuous expansion of the institution they have to face competition in their profession from the youngsters. A girl has to accumulate profits to the maximum extent possible during this period of her life. Having realised this need, the *veśyamātha* guides her daughter to be particular in demanding money from the customers. This is evident from the story, of *Chaturika,* in *Kēyūrabāhucharitramu,* who very cleverly organised her profession and earned money.[101] *Daśakumāra charitra* mentions Kuṅṭineelu probably women brokers.[102] The fee collected from the customer is referred to as Rōyi. It can either be in cash or kind. As long as the contract for which *Rōyi* was paid holds good, the girl cannot entertain any other person.[103] Generally the amount of *Rōyi* depends on the demands of the girl. *Krīdābhirāmamu* quotes one Kaṛnāṭi *veśya* demanding *satīhātakanishkamu* (one sari and some amount of gold) and another *veśya* asking for two *sonnāṭaṅkamulu* (two gold coins).[104] Sometimes their demands were so high that a person had to mortgage landed property.[105] *Paṅḍitārādhyacharitra* contains another practice called *Vāḍapottu* wherein men of a particular street enter into a specific contract with a harlot as regards the person who should visit her. The girl was thus maintained by the men of that street.[106]

The dangers of the profession and its temporariness lead the prostitutes going for unfair means of earning money. *Krīḍābhirdmāmu* refers to a *veśyamātha* sending her daughter to another person after collecting fee from a person. For controlling such practices the state appointed officers and a separate court was established for the purpose, which is referred to as *Jāradharmāsanamu.*[107] The Koṛavi inscription and *Vijhañeśvaramu* of Ketana mention laws made by the state to punish greedy mothers of the harlots and to control their unfair practices of earning money.[108] Generally a specific amount of fine is levied on the accused together with such punishments as cutting the nose, ears or shaving the head.[109] At the same time laws are also made to protect women from the evil attempts of men. It is declared that for women of this class having sex with men is not a sin.[110] A customer who promises to pay the amount to a *veśya* but fails to comply with is penalised with double the amount to be paid to her and an equal amount as penalty to the king.[111] Similarly, for impersonification, one gold *masaka* is to be paid.[112] Fines are also imposed for causing physical injury to the girls.[113] Thus, the protection offered is dual, protection of prostitutes against exploitation by customers and society and protection of the public from the treacherous or dubious nature or the prostitutes.

The contemporary literature provides instances of certain veśyas religiously inclined towards Saivism. They took *Dīksha* from *Jaṅgama* priests and dedicated the whole of their life in their service, not entertaining any other customer. Such girls were respected and accorded motherly treatment from the disciples of the priests, who gave them initiation.[114] Through references in the literary works of the period it appears that courtesans and concubines of elite men enjoyed recognition in the society whereas prostitutes had to struggle hard to earn money. Moreover, the state collected a tax on the mirrors used by the girls of this community.[115]

WOMEN IN TEMPLE SERVICE

By medieval times, the temple achieved great institutional status linking itself closely with the rise of devotional sects. It became a principal site for sect activity. The temples are provided with support and protection by the ruling warrior groups.[116] This involved a diverse body of functionaries with substantial pilgrim participation. In turn the temple culture firmly established the agrarian feudal order. The rise of devotional bhakti literature of the times too is suggestive of the new feudal class relationships and the corresponding ideology. The deity in the temple is equated with the king and a parallel world of authority is reconstructed on the spiritual plane. Ritual worship in the temple is conceived on the same lines of ritual services offered to the king. Thus, attempts are made to authenticate and legitimise the new feudal polity of the period through a parallelism between the deity and the king.[117]

Since, the temple and God are homologised with royal court and king respectively, the *dēvasthāna* maintained the same bureaucracy as that of the *Rājasthāna.* This aspect gains further support from the inscriptional references indicating interchangeability of women in temple service with those of the king's court. An inscription from Srikalahasthi temple registers orders of a king transferring a dancing girl and her descendants from his service to the temple.[118] Another record from Mukhalingam temple mentions that Vāsama, the Guḍisāni of Madhukisvara temple was also the *Lańjiya* of Doḍḍapanāyaka, an officer of the Velanāḍuchoḍa king Rajendra Choḍa.'[119] This interchangeability can be understood in terms of the ritual exchange of honours between the king, his officers and the temple in the feudal political background.

The God and the king had to follow elaborate rituals before they start their routine. The temple rituals are of two types—*Aṅgabhōga* (the general worship services) and *Raṅgabhṅga* (the ritual services specially in the *Raṅgamaṅṭapa* built for the purpose daily or on festive occasions). Women are employed in both categories, however, in large numbers in the latter.

Big temples of the period in Āndhradeśa like Pālakolanu, Chēbṛolu, Drākshārāmam, Siṁhāchalam maintained as many as 300 to 500 temple girls. They are generally donated by the kings, vassals or their generals. 30 daughters from the *Nāyaka* families of Kaliṅga maṅḍala were donated to the temple at Mukhaliṅgam by an officer of Eastern Gaṅgas to execute various deeds specified in the record.[120] General Jāyapa donated 300 girls of the age of 8 years to the temple at Chēbṛolu.[121] Another record indicates the donation of a girl called Bhaṅdaramu Akkama as Sāni, to the temple at Velpūṛu by Ganapatidevaraja, son of Kōṭa Bayyaladevi. Lands and gardens were also donated by him as *vṛitti* (maintenance expenses) to her.[122]

Sometimes girls are brought from different places of the country and are given employment in the temple as in the case of the Viśveśvara temple at Malkāpuram where the singers were brought from Kashmir.[123] Apart from these, it is also observed that many women enter into temple service for employment probably for the sake of the shares in temple property and a portion of *prasādamu* of the deity offered to them in lieu of their services in the temple. A merchant at Elēśvaram donated his two granddaughters to the temple.[124]

The temple girls are commonly termed as *Sānulu, Sāni Saṁpradāyamuvāru, Guḍisānulu* or sometimes indicating the numerical status as *Munnūṭi Sānulu, Pedamunnūṭti Sānulu, Sāni Munnūru,* etc.[125] The term does not indicate any caste status, though an inscription from Simhachalam relates them to the sudra caste.[126] *Pātra* is another term used generally to denote the dancing girls of the temple.[127] *Dvādasa Sēva Vilāsini* refers to women performing 12 prescribed duties.[128]

It appears that women temple employees performed a variety of functions in the temple both of *Aṅgabhōga* and *Raṅgabhōga* services. They are paid generally in kind, with a share in the temple property, a part of the *prasāda* offered to the deity. Occasionally they are paid in cash. Sometimes the donors specify the manner of enjoying share in the temple lands by the temple girls and deposit certain money in the temple treasury for their maintenance.

Further it is seen that most of the lady temple professionals of the temple appear to be married. But certain services of *Raṅgabhōga* needed elaborate and intensive training from childhood, through dance master, for which purpose, they are generally dedicated to the temple service unmarried and young.[129]

After passing through a prescribed test conducted on completion of training, they are inducted into actual service which involved singing and dancing on particular occasions of worship both in the morning and night and performing special programmes on festival days.[130] The professional and marital status of the temple girls is generally reflected in the grants given by their relatives, father, husband or sons claiming matronymic identity.[131]

Due to their continuous service requirements at the temple for most part of the day, these temple women are provided with quarters in the vicinity of the temple. The locality is termed *Sānivāḍa.*[132] Epigraphical references indicate that temples like Srīkūrmam, Kollūṛu, Nādiṅḍla, Juttiga, Ghaṅṭasāla, Chēbṛōlu had separate quarters built for the temple dancing girls.[133] Chebrolu inscription of general Jayapa records construction of two rows of double storeyed buildings for 16 lady temple attendants.[134] Pillalamaṛṛi inscription of Rēcheṛla chief Nāmireḍḍi records construction of houses to temple girls in the fort of Pillalamaṛṛi where the temple of Eṛakeśvara was constructed by him.[135]

It is further observed that the services of these temple girls are hereditary.[136] They enjoyed a higher socio-economic status as revealed through their grants, which included not only cash or kind but immovable property too. Their sons are generally appointed in the royal service. The two sons of Sokkama, the *naṛtaki* of Paṅḍīśvara temple were in the service of the king Goṅka II and her daughter Kāmidevi was one of the queens of the king.[137] Similarly, the son of sāni Bayyāṁmbika, of the same temple was in the service of the king Goṅka II.[138]

The expansion of temple building activity, the presence of temple girls in large numbers in most of the temples together with their higher socio-ritual status necessitated an organisational operation for them. They formed into a professional guild called *Sānula Samayamu* or *Sāni Munnūṛu* which was found in every big temple of Āndhradeśa.

These include, maintaining temple properties, supervising the grants or other endowments of the temple, mobilising temple resources (through leasing out the lands, animals, etc.) in addition to determining the rules and procedural aspects of the services of the temple girls who were members of the guild.[139] Gradually, their association became a part of the temple administrative functionaries of the higher-rank referred to as *Mānulu* and figured in most of the matters relating to the appropriation of temple property.[140]

Thus we can say that the involvement of women in economic activities was more prominent in medieval Āndhra. Ketana's *Vijñaneśvaramu,* the legal digest of the period giving permission for women to enter into contracts with the prior consent of their husbands is worth mentioning in this connection.[141] Moreover, contemporary epigraphs contain ample references to the involvement of women in gift making as part of their attempt to gain religious merit.

Can this be taken to mean the economic independence of women? It is doubtful, as Dharmasastras, quote that the wages earned by a woman on her own exertion are not included in her property but they become part of the joint property of the family. However, they have provided for certain rights to women on property both inherited and acquired in the form of gifts given to them on specific occasions such as marriage. Therefore, to understand the extent of economic independence enjoyed by women more clearly, it becomes necessary first to study the rights on property allowed to them by tradition and to understand a woman's domain on the same.

REFERENCES

1. Monika vonder Meden and Kathee Myers, 'The Hidden Talent, Women Creators and Inventors' in *Women's World,* No. 10 (US June, 1986), pp. 5–8.
2. Buhler, *laws of Manu,* VII, verse 219.
3. *Ibid.*
4. Sōmeśvaradeva, *Mānasōllāsa,* (Trans.) S. Visvanathasarma, (Hyderabad, 1961), 3rd canto, Chapters, 1,4, 13, verses 956, 958, 993, 1529, 1530 and 1531.
5. Jāyapa Sēnani, *Nrittaratnākaramu,* translation by Rallapalli Ananta Krishna Sarma, (Hyderabad, 1969), Chapter VIII.
6. We find references to wet nurses in the literary works of the period like *Kēyūrabāhucharitramu, Siṁhāsanadvātrmsika, Kumāra saṁbhavamu,* etc. They are supposed to maintain the secrecy of the personal matters of king. Generally they were treated with much respect and their children were appointed in important posts of administration. In the epigraph they figured as donors of lands. Devakabbe, the wet nurse of Iṛivebeḍeṅga granted 70 Ḍṛammas and land at Choppadaṅḍu, wherein a tank was constructed. (*IAP : KD,* No. 8).
7. *Mānasōllāsa,* Chapters, 1, 4, 13.
8. *South Indian Inscriptions (SII),* Vol. IV, No. 1249.
9. *Ibid.,* Vol. VI, No. 240.
10. *Ibid.,* No. 178.
11. *Pratāparudracharitra,* p. 46.
12. A.S. Altekar, *The Position of Women in Hindu Civilisation,* (Delhi, 1962), p. 180.
13. Jyotsna K. Kamath, *Social Life in Medieval Karnataka,* (Delhi, 1980), p. 119.
14. Tikkana, *Andhra Mahābhāratamu,* (Virata, Udyoga Parvamulu), (ed.), K. Laxmi Ranjanam and Divakarla Venkatavadhani, (Hyderabad, 1970), 1st canto verses 289–335 give a detailed description of the responsibilities of the post of *Sairaṅdhri.*
15. K. Chengalraya Chetti, *Āndhradeśa Sāṅghika Āaṛdhika Charitra* (A.D. 1300–1600), (Tirupati, 1991), p. 198.
16. Ambati Subbaraya Chetti, 'Kakatīyulanāti Saṁghika Charitra' in *Kakatiya Samchika,* (Hyderabad, Reprint, 1992), pp. 141–149.
17. A.R. 484 of 1913.
18. A.R. 558 of 1925.
19. *Krīdābhirāmamu,* verse 102.
20. *Ibid.,* verse 77.
21. *Ibid.,* verse 173, also Nannechoda, *Kumārasaṁbhavamu,* (ed.), Korada Mahadeva Sastri, (Hyderabad, 1987), 8th canto, verse 122.
22. *Kēyūrabāhucharitramu,* 2nd canto, verses 11–15.
23. Veturi Prabhakara Sastri; (ed.), *Cātu Padya Maṇimaṅjari,* (Hyderabad, 1988), verse 314, p. 134.
24. *Ibid.,* verse 313, p. 134.
25. *Ibid.,* verse 353, p. 144.
26. *Ibid.,* verse 325, p. 136.
27. *Kriḍabhirāmamu,* verses 161–166. The details of the food preparations are given in verse 166.
28. *Ibid.,* verse 273.
29. *Ibid.,* verses 68–69.
30. K. Chengalraya Chetti, *Op. cit.,* 1991, p. 65.
31. Palkuriki Somanatha, *Sri Paṅḍitārādhyacharitra,* (ed.), Chilukuri Narayana Rao, (Madras, 1939), Paṛvata Prakaranamu, Jōgula Naḍakalu, pp. 235–236.

32. *Krīdābhirāmamu,* verses 143–144. The woman belonging to Goṛaga caste was able to take out the nose-ring put in a tub of water with her nose and with her back facing the tub. Simialrly, she was able to string the black beads into a chain within no time.
33. Edgar Thurston and K. Rangachari, (ed.), *Castes and Tribes of Southern India,* Vol. II, (Madras, 1987), pp. 185–190.
34. Palkuriki Somanatha, Basavapurāṇamu, (ed.), Nidadavolu Venkat Rao, (Madras, 1952), 2nd canto, pp. 41–42.
35. *Ibid.,* 4th canto, Nimmavva Katha, pp. 103–105.
36. *Ibid.,* Siriyāḷuni Katha, pp. 100–102.
37. *Ibid.,* 3rd canto, Mugdhya Sangayya Katha, pp. 50–53. The harlot asks her maids to bring various musical instruments and to play different tunes together with singing and dancing to entertain the devotee of Siva, who came to her house.
38. *Ibid.,* 4th canto, Piṭṭavva Katha, p. 115. Also 3rd canto, Nāṭyanamittaṅḍi Katha, p. 66.
39. *Paṅḍitārādhyacharitra,* Purātana Prakaraṇamu, Gurubhaktāṅḍāri Katha, pp. 78–83.
40. *SII,* Vol. IV, No. 1015.
41. *Ibid.,* No. 1288.
42. *Basavapurānamu,* 3rd canto, Bejjamahādevi Katha, pp. 58–61. There is a detailed description of the way in which small children were given bath, the procedure for feeding them and steps to be taken to prevent the general ailments like indigestion, cold, etc.
43. *Ibid.,* Also see Nannaya, *Āndhra Mahābhārtamu,* Adiparvamu, 8th canto, verse 254. At the time of the marriage of Draupadi, importance was given to be mother's voice which was equated by the poet to that of *Vidhāta* (creator)., A similar opinion was conveyed through *Kumara Saṁbhavamu* also at the time of the marriage of Parvati.
44. Papul Jayakar, 'Handi Crafts' in Tara Ali Baig, *Women of India,* (Delhi, 1958), pp. 212–220.
45. *Catu Padya Maṇimaṅjari,* verse 31 pp. 139–140.
46. K. Radhakrishna Murthy, *The Economic Conditions of Medieval Āndhradeśa* (Tirupati, 1987), pp. 131–132. The idea is also based on few sculptures depicting women feeding animals, milching cows and churning curds, available from the temples of Srisailam & Tirupati.
47. *Krīdābhirāmamu,* verses 102–103 contain the description of a Teliki woman moving along the mortar probably while pressing the oil.
48. Though there are no exact references for the involvement of women either directly or indirectly in this industry, we can presume that women played their part in cleaning the nuts and processing them. Because, we find plenty of references in the inscriptions of the period to the gardens of *Poka* trees (areca nut) and thus it could be one of the popular occupations of the period.
49. Generally, these works are associated with the beliefs in the fertility cult prevalent among the village people and was reflected in the songs sung by them. And therefore, they are performed only by women (An interview with Dr. Nayani Krishnakumari).
50. *Kumārasaṁbhavamu,* 7th canto, verse 92.
51. These songs are commonly called as *Taṛuvōja,* Arugra, *St nagra Āndhra Sāhityam,* Vol. I, (Madras, 1977), p. 77.
52. *SII,* Vol. X, No. 395. It is quite possible that Śaivism, during its process of propagation into the common sections of the society, opened up maternity homes for their help and could have recruited women as midwives for providing assistance during the course of delivery. However, this assumption can not be proved as there are no evidences for the same in the contemporary inscriptions or literary sources.
53. *Pratāparudracharitra,* p. 47.
54. Maineni Krishnakumari, 'Rājarāja Deveṅdravarmuni Yudhapura Tāmrasāsanamu', *Bharati* (Jan, 1986), pp. 30–33.
55. *Kēyūrabāhucharitramu,* 1st canto, verse 57.
56. Vatsyana, *Kāmasutra,* I. 3.20, quoted in P.V. Kane, *History of Dharamasastra,* Vol. III, 1974, p. 639.
57. Someśvaradeva, *Mānasōllāsa,* I p. 155, verses 3–5, quoted from Jyostna K. Kamat, *Op. cit.,* 1980, pp. 115–116.
58. *Pratāparudracharitra,* p. 45.
59. *Ibid.,* p. 47.
60. Koravi Goparaju, *Siṁhāsanadvatṛmsika,* (ed.), Gadiyaram Ramakrishna Sarma, (Hyderabad, 1982), 2nd canto, verse 131, and 11th canto, verse 172.
61. Ketana, *Daśakumāracharitra,* (ed.), Kandukuri Viresalingam, (Madras, 1975) 1st canto, verse 11.

62. *Keyūrabāhucharitramu,* 1st canto, verse 18.
63. Maineni Krishna Kumari, *Op. cit.,* pp. 30–33.
64. A. Padma, *The Socio-Cultural World of Women in Medieval Andhra,* Delhi, 2001.
65. Nelaturi Venkataramanayya, *The Eastern Chalukyas of Vengi,* (Madras, 1950), p. 287.
66. *SII,* Vol. V, No. 290–252.
67. *Ibid.,* Vol. VI, No. 55.
68. *Ibid.,* Vol. V, No. 249.
69. *Ibid.,* Vol. VI, Nos. 1083, 1090.
70. *Ibid.,* No. 210.
71. *Ibid.,* Vol. X, No. 258.
72. *Ibid.*
73. *HAS,* Vol. XIII, Vardhamānapura Inscription of Malyala Guṇḍadaṇḍādhisa.
74. *SII,* Vol. X, No. 258.
75. *IAP : CD,* (Hyderabad, 1977), No. 159, pp. 241–248.
76. *SII,* Vol. IV, No. 1039.
77. *Kridābhirāmamu* depicts the description of the house of Machaldevi, the concubine of Prataparudra II in verses 183, 187, 191, 192, 193 (pp. 50–55).
78. *SII,* Vol. VI, No. 669 refers to Viraṁba, *Prēyasi* of king Nṛisiṁha donating a kitchen to the temple at Paṅchadhārala.
79. *Krīḍābhirāmamu,* verse 180.
80. *Epigraphia lndica,* Vol. VI, No. 15A.
81. *AR,* 1952–53 (1958), No. 7.
82. *Palnāti Vīracharitra,* pp. 341–344.
83. *Ibid.,* p. 341.
84. *Uṅkuva* is another term for *Sulkamu* or the bride-price. Also referred to as *Oli* in certain circumstances. It is the money given by the bride-groom to the parents of the bride. It is a part of *Strīdhana* in the sense of *Sulkamu.* (*Saṁgrahāṅdhra Vijñāna Kosamu,* pp. 174–179). We find references to this term in the other literary texts of the period like *Kumārasaṁbhavamu,* 7th canto, verse 136, *Daśakumāracharitramu,* 6th canto, verse 51, *Raṅganātha Rāmāyaṇamu,* Bālakaṅḍamu, p. 55, etc.
85. Nārada, Kātyāyana, Yāgñavalkya are the earlier Smṛiti writers who argued on this point. *Mitakshara* provides further details of the maintenance to be provided to the concubines of the deceased. For more details, P.V. Kane, *Op. cit.,* Vol. III, 1974, pp. 808–812
86. *Ibid.,* p. 812.
87. *Ibid.,* p. 638.
88. B.S.L. Hanumatha Rao, *Āndhrula Charitra,* (Guntur, 1983), p. 282.
89. *Raṅganātha Rāmāyaṇamu,* Bālakaṅḍamu, line 75.
90. P.V. Parabrahma Sastry, *Kakatiya Sasana* Sahityamu (Hyderabad, 1981), Thousand pillar temple inscription, pp. 7–16.
91. Such streets where prostitutes live are also referred to as *Bhōgamu Vīdhi. Krīḍābhirāmamu,* verses 114–117.
92. *Pratiāparudracharitra,* p. 43.
93. *Paṅditārādhyacharitra,* Purātana Prakaraṇamu, Gurubhaktaṅḍāri Katha, p. 80. Also, *Catu Padya Manimanjari,* pp. 121–126.
94. According to R.S. Sharma, *Paṅchamakāras,* the five orgiastic rites. of Tantric religion are introduced into Saivism due to socio-political changes of the medieval period. For details R.S. Sharma, 'Material Milieu of Tantricism'in R.S. Sharma, (ed.), *Indian Society, Historical Probings, Essays in memory of D.D. Kosambi,* (New Delhi, 1984), pp. 175–189.
95. K. *Satyanarayana, A Study of History and culture of Andhras,* Vol. II, (Delhi, 1983), p. 76.
96. *Basavapurāṇamu,* 3rd canto, Mugdhasaṅgayya Katha, pp. 50–53. Also, 3rd canto, pp. 48–49. Basaveśvara, without any hesitation, concedes to the demand of one such *Jaṅgama* priest, and gives with pleasure, the silk sari of his wife.

97. R.N. Naṅdi, 'Origin of Virasaiva Movement' in *IHR,* Vol. II, No. 2 (Delhi, 1976), pp. 32–46.
98. *Daśakumāracharitramu,* 5th canto, verse 1028. Hemadri, in his *vṛata khāṅḍ* of *Chātuṛvaṛga Chiṇtāmaṇi,* mentioned one *Vāravṛata* to be observed by the girls for prosperity in their profession. H.V. II, 541–548, quoted from P.V. Kane, *Op. cit.,* Vol. VI, Part I, 1975, p. 417.
99. *Daśakumāracharitramu,* 6th canto, verse 114.
100. *Kumārasaṁbhavamu,* 8th canto, verses 136–144.
101. *Kēyūrabāhucharitramu,* 2nd canto, Chaturika Katha, verses 42–74.
102. *Daśakumāracharitramu,* 5th canto, verse 49.
103. *Paṅḍitrārādhyacharitra,* Purātana Prakaraṇamu, Malhaṇa Katha, pp. 84–86. Also a. Gurubhaktāṅḍari Katha, pp. 78–83.
104. *Krīdābhirāmamu,* verses 91, 286, 290.
105. *Ibid.,* verse 245.
106. *Paṅditārādhyacharitra,* Purātana Prakaraṇamu, Gurubhaktaṅḍāri Katha, pp. 78–83.
107. Krīdābhirāmamu, verses 265, 272.
108. *Vijñāeśvaramu,* Prāyaschitta Kāṅḍamu, verse 110, Also, HAS, Vol. XIX, Wg 3, Koṛavi, pp. 135–138
109. *Ibid.,* Also, *Krīdābhirāmamu,* verse 270.
110. P.V. Kane, *History of Dharamasastra,* Vol. III, 1974, p. 638.
111. *Matsyapurāṇa,* 227-144-146 quoted from P.V. Kane, *Op. cit.,* Vol. III, 1974, p. 481.
112. *Ibid.*
113. *Vijñāeśvaramu,* Prāyaschitta Kāṅḍamu, verse 113.
114. *Basavapurāṇamu,* 3rd canto, Mugdha Sangayya Katha, pp. 50–53.
115. Gade Narsing Rao, Chāḷukyula Kalamnati Rajyanga Paristhithulu' in *Rajaraja Pattabhisheka Samchika,* (Rajahmundry, 1922), p. 132. *Andhra Mahabharatamu Santiparva,* 6–88 also refers to tax on prostitutes.
116. Burton Stein, 'Social Mobility and Medieval South Indian Hindu Sects' in Burton Stein, (ed.), *All the King's Mana*: *Papers on Medieval South Indian History* (Madras, 1984), pp. 282–301.
117. M.G.S. Narayanan and Veluthat Keshavan, 'The Bhakti Movement in Medieval South India' in D. N. Jha, (ed.), *Feudal Social Formation in Early India,* (Delhi, 1987), pp. 348–373.
118. *Inscriptions of Āndhradeśa,* Vol. II, Part I, (Tirupati, 1968), No. 669.
119. *SII*, Vol. V, No. 1083.
120. *Temple Inscriptions of Andhra Pradesh (TIAP),* Vol. I (Srikakulam Dist), No. 264.
121. V. Yasodadevi, 'A History of Andhra Country', *JAHRS,* Vol. XXV, p. 147.
122. *SII,* Vol. X, No. 344.
123. *Ibid.,* No. 395.
124. Abdul Waheed Khan, *A Monograph on Yēlēśvaram Excavation,* (Hyderabad, 1963), No. 25, p. 62.
125. The term 'Sāni' is very frequently mentioned and with various meanings in the contemporary inscriptions. It was used as a suffix to the married women in the sense of *Svāmini* (wife) or to denote the courtesans or the temple girls. The term *Munnūṛu* refers to 300 probably indicating the numerical status of the group. As their post in the temple appeared to be hereditary, we find another usage – *Saṁpradāyam Sānulu.*
126. *SII,* Vol. VI, No. 1202.
127. Girls whose function is exclusively dancing and those who expertised themselves in the art of dancing are called *Pāṭra.* We find several references to this term in the contemporary epigraphs in connection with providing *vṛittis* to them. For instance *SII,* Vol. VI, No. 1052.
128. *Ibid.,*Vol. X, No. 74. For more details regarding the 12 services which are supposed to be performed by the girls, see Alladi Vaidehi, *Āndhrula Saṁghika Āardhika Charitra,* (Madhya Yugam) *(A.D. 1000–A.D. 1250),* (Hyderabad, 1978), pp. 61–62.
129. *Saṁgrāhaṅdhra Vijñāna Kōsamu,* Devālaya Nṛityamulu, pp. 708–717.
130. *Ibid.,* The Syllabi of education for a temple girl is discussed in the next chapter.
131. The donor of a record from Tsandavole was the son of the *Guḍi Sāni* Bānāṁbika and he was also employed with the king Kulōttuṅga Chola Goṅka. *SII.,* Vol. IV, No. 1130, Similarly other references like *SII.,* Vol. V,

No. 1027, Vol. X, No. 5, 189, Vol. VI, No. 169 and many more are of the same nature, given by the children of the temple girls. A record from Mukhalingam temple registers a grant by the father of *Guḍi Sāni,* (*TIAP,* Vol. I, (Srikakulam Dist.), No. 165), and another from the same region records a grant by the husband of Sāni Mādali Rekama (SII., Vol. V, No. 117).

132. *AR,* No. 164 & 1893 (SII, Vol. IV, No. 989).
133. *SII,* Vol. IV, 989. Also, Vol. X, Nos. 5, 107, No., 115, 116, etc.
134. V. Yasoda Devi, 'A History of Andhra Country', *JAHRS,* Vol. XXV, p. 147.
135. R.N. Sastri, *Rēcheṛla Reḍḍy Vaṁsa Charitra, Sāsanamulu,* (Hyderabad, 1989), Pillalamarri inscription, No. 5.
136. M. Ramarao, *Inscriptions of Āndhradeśa,* Vol. II (Tirupati, 1968), No. 135.
137. V. Yasoda Devi, 'A History of Andhra Country', *JAHRS,* Vol. XXV, p. 146.
138. *Ibid.*
139. A record from Siṁhāchalam, mentions the various regulations of the guild It is stated that if these instructions are not obeyed properly the girls would be expelled from the guild. (*SII,* Vol. VI, No. 1202).
140. The term *Māni* refers to a person having a vow of celibacy.The temple administrative functionary containing male members, together with the female functionaries form the unit *Sānulu Mānulu,* which takes care of the temple properties. Please see Chart V for more details of their functions.
141. *Vijñāeśvaramu,* Vyavahāra Kāṅḍamu, verse 61.

Chapter 19

Temple Women and Work in Medieval Kēraḷam

ANNA VARGHESE

INTRODUCTION

The region of Kēraḷam in the time period from eighth to seventeenth centuries CE is marked by the growth, proliferation and transitions in the history of the temples and various occupational groups associated with it. The study of temple women in particular is interesting as it gives a powerful addition to the study of gender among the temple servants and donors to the temples. This paper is an attempt to classify, contextualize and situate the temple women of Kēraḷam of medieval time period.

I would like to attempt to answer a few set of questions in this paper, like, what did it mean by the phrase temple woman in Kēraḷam region? What did the title 'temple woman' mean to the woman and to the larger society? Were the positions held by these women honorific or ritual? What were its characteristics? What is the nature of the narrations in acci caritams? How rooted were Kēraḷam's temple women in the notions of patriarchy? Even though Kēraḷam was the land of matriarchy for certain sections of the society, what was the nature of property rights of the temple women? How effective was their power over their resources, their body and sexuality? The tēvaṭicci was the representative of women engaged and reflected in the accounts related to the temple society. How far can we take the term tēvaṭicci as a generic term to point to temple women in Kerala?

I

There has been a popular debate among Kerala historians and literary critics about the presence and absence of dancing girls in Kerala temples. In Elamkulam Kunjan Pillai's opinion, *tēvaṭiccistānam* was a respectable position obtained by knowledgeable, artistic and noble ladies in association with the temples.[1] Kunjan Pillai through an analysis of Uṇṇunīlisandēśam argues that there were female temple dancers who existed on a large scale in Kēraḷam region. He says that Cerukara Uṇṇiyāḍi, who is mentioned in 101 verse of Uṇṇunīlisandēśam, lived just west side of Kaṇḍiyūr temple. Muttūṭṭu Iḷayacci who is another *dēvadāsi* who is mentioned in 102 verse of Uṇṇunīlisandēśam lived north to Cerukara Uṇṇiyāḍi.[2] The four women of Kuṛuṅgāṭṭu house would be *dēvadāsis* of Maṭṭom temple.[3] These women had high sounding titles like '*mahitacirutēvi*' denoting high position.[4]

M. G. S. Narayanan acknowledges the presence of dancing girls and opines, 'the association of dancing girls known as Naṅgacci or Tēvaṭicci as found in several temple inscriptions, with the temple deserves notice as it shows that the temple, which was primarily a religious institution, also catered to the needs of scholarship and culture.'[5] Narayanan observes that in a number of medieval Maṇipravāḷam poems, *cāttirār* or brahman students appear as heroes and lovers of dancing girls and courtesans.[6] At any rate 'the rise of the Dēvadāsi system in the South India may be dated to a period not later than the 8th century AD'.[7]

Kalamandalam Kalyanikuttiyamma sees the term *tēvaṭicci* as acci of *tēvan's aṭi* or *dēvapadadāsi* (maid servant at the feet of God).[8] Rajan Gurukkal, even after observing that the temple courtesans were of high birth and material status, has ruled away the idea of comparing them with the *dēvadāsis* of other South Indian temples.[9] Rajan Gurukkal and Raghava Varier says that the *dēvadāsi* of the Tiruvalla temple borrowed gold from the temple of which the interest was 290 *para*[10] of paddy and he argues that the *dēvadāsi* would have had land worth the interest to borrow such gold from the temple.[11] Varier and Gurukkal talk about *dēvadāsi* and *naṅga* as *dēvadāsi*, those associated with temples. Both these categories received rice as *jīvitam*,[12] as seen from the Neḍumpuram Taḷi inscription and Tiruvalla Copper Plates.[13]

K. N. Ganesh traces the natural expansion of temples and the provision of dancing girls to them as a process. He says that when the temples spread their ideological and economic

---

[1] Elamkulam Kunjan Pillai, *Kerala Charithrathinte Iruladanja Edukal* (Kottayam: Sahitya Pravarthaka Sahakarana Sangam Ltd., 1957), 75.

[2] Elamkulam P. N. Kunjan Pillai, *Unnuneeli Sandesam—From the Historical Perspective* (Trivandrum: Sahityaniketan, 1969), 113.

[3] Ibid.

[4] Ibid.

[5] M. G. S. Narayanan, *Perumals of Kerala, Political and Social Conditions of Kerala under the Cera Perumals of Makotai (c800–1124 AD)* (Calicut: Xavier Press, 1996), 190.

[6] Ibid., 192.

[7] Ibid., 193.

[8] Kalamandalam Kalyanikuttiyamma, *Mohinoyattom Charithravum Attaprakaravum* (Kottayam: D.C. Books, 2008), 49.

[9] Rajan Gurukkal, *The Kerala Temple and Early Medieval Agrarian System* (Sukapuram: Vallathol Vidyapeetham, 1992), 55.

[10] A measure.

[11] Rajan Gurukkal and Raghava Varier, *Keralacharithram: A History of Kerala* (Sukapuram: Vallathol Vidyapeetham, 2011), 167.

[12] Daily allowance.

[13] Gurukkal and Varier, *Keralacharithram*, 132.

influence, the number of persons attached to the temples also increased, who were to be provided by the lands. As an example, he says that the temples of Nāñjināḍu provided a number of dancing girls who were settled as *kuḍis* and they were provided with the income from temple lands.[14] K. N. Ganesh opines that in the medieval Kerala context, apart from *aḍiccutaḷi*[15] and women artists, the entire temple service personnel were men.[16] In the medieval *maṇipravāḷam* works, in many of the heroines' houses, it was right in the female line that existed. In temple arts, the position of the *naṅgyār* was matrilineal.[17] From an analysis of the maṇipravāḷam kāvyam heroines, K. N. Ganesh opines that they do not have similarity with *tēvaraṭiyāḷ* or *gaṇikas* found outside Kerala. These women belonged to households with female line rights. Women who were called *accikaḷ* and their homes are indications of female line rights. Some of them were singers and dancers. Just like the war skills, the skill in music and dance was considered indications of gender positions in South Indian *gōtra* society. Importance given to songs and *kūttu* was a symbol of this. These female line rights can be seen as part of *tara* rights.[18] Ganesh argues that if we put aside *naṅgyār*, there is no evidence of *tēaraṭiyāḷ kuḍikaḷ* in Kerala, as similar to those in Tamil Nadu. Naṅgyār kūttu was seen as an independent dance form. Apart from that there were no evidences of hereditary *dēvadāsi* lineages in Kerala.[19]

The basic argument of P. Soman was that there did not exist a *dēvadāsi* system in Kēraḷam just like the fact that there did not exist large kingships or huge temples or temple urbanism in Kēraḷam like the other places in South India.[20] Soman argues that the creation of a *dēvadāsi* system which was never existent in Kerala by Elamkulam Kunjan Pillai and other historians of his school to exaggerate the sensual desires of the *nampūtiris* (brahmans) were not right. He argues that stating that all nampūtiris of Kerala delighted in women and were lascivious was a very biased way of writing history.[21] Soman argues that the female dancers of Kēraḷam do not figure in folk songs or glorious stories of temples or northern ballads.[22] The *kūttambalams* in Kēraḷam were built for cākyār kūttu and not for dēvadāsiyāṭṭom. The naṅgyār women who took part in Kūḍiyāṭṭom and naṅgyār kūttu were not *dēvadāsis*.[23] In Kerala temples, there was no performance rite of *dēvadāsi* dance during *dīpārādhana* (the waving of lamps to an idol).[24]

P. Soman argues that it was Nair *dāsis* who pounded paddy in temples and on those *marumakkattāyam accimar* (matrilineal accimar) *tēvaḍiccittam* was inflicted upon and were

---

[14] K. N. Ganesh, 'Agrarian Relations and Political Authority in Medieval Travancore AD 1300–1750' (Ph.D. thesis, Centre for Historical Studies, School of Social Sciences, Jawaharlal Nehru University, New Delhi, 1987), 221.

[15] This term referred to women who did menial services in the temple like sweeping and mopping the premises.

[16] K. N. Ganesh, *Keralathinte Innalekal* (Thiruvananthapuram: Dept. of Cultural Publications, Government of Kerala, 1997), 220.

[17] Ibid., 222.

[18] Ibid., 222.

[19] Ibid., 228.

[20] P. Soman, *Devadasikalum Sahitya Charithravum* (Thiruvananthapuram: The State Institute of Languages, 2009), 35.

[21] Ibid., 25.

[22] Ibid., 55.

[23] Soman, *Devadasikalum Sahitya Charithravum*, 59.

[24] Ibid., 63.

mentioned as *tēvaraṭiyāḷ* and *tēvaḍiśśikaḷ* in inscriptions.[25] By charging *gaṇika* traits on *marumakkattāyam accimar*, *marumakkattāyam* sexuality (sexuality as part of inheritance through female line) became accepted. The brahman children born out of *marumakkattāyam accimar* were never accepted as legitimate children. If Nairs or ambalavāsis called a brahman as father, it was a sin equivalent to killing a brahman.[26]

Soman says that the *devādāsi* system in temples and the dance and dance-related rituals for Śiva who is Naṭarāja began in Tamil country in the medieval times with the establishment of Śiva temples which were centres of the Śaiva bhakti movement.[27] This postulation is, however, not to be taken without a pinch of salt because we come across sources which speak of instances where the girls associated to dance and Śiva worship are mentioned, in the case of Orissa, Andhra, Karnataka and Kerala.

II

In the second section, I would like to look at the class of women addressed as *peṇkaḷ* in the inscriptions. *Peṇṇu* is the singular term for woman where as *peṇkaḷ* is the plural term indicating women, or is used as a term of respect. The term *peṇkaḷ* was used to denote a female attendant in the context of a temple inscription of Southern Kēraḷam. The inscription is from the temple of Udaiyār Śivīndaramuḍaiya-Nayinār in Śucīndram (the Śucīndram inscription of Venrumankoṇḍa Bhūtalavīra Ravivarman 1537 CE).[28] The inscription calls the female attendant, Śrī-Parpanāda-Perumāḷ, by the term *peṇkal*. She is described as the daughter of Nāchchiyār[29] and her lineal descendants were to receive 12 *nāḷi*[30] of rice food hereditarily. Here, the post and *virutti*[31] were hereditary. This was a royal order by the Travancore ruler, Ravivarman. Śucīndram, under the reign of Travancore rulers is also famous for the presence of dancing girls.[32] Here, the inscription mentions the individual name of the female attendant as Śrī- Parpanāda-Perumāḷ. This is significant because often the epigraphical evidences about women servants of the temples are seen as a collective mention of the group of women, not on an individual basis.

III

The third section is on the term *peṇṇumpiḷḷaikaḷ* from the inscriptions which also mean female attendants. The Arrur copper plate of Ravivarman Siraivaymuttavar, Kollam year

25 Ibid., 79.

26 Ibid., 79.

27 Ibid., 27.

28 Suchindram Inscription of Venrumankonda Bhutalavira Ravivarman, dated Kollam 721 from Suchindram, Travancore Archaeological Series, hereafter TAS, Vol. 4, No. 21, p. 104.

29 The term refers to goddess. Temple women were considered wives of gods and daughters of goddesses.

30 A measure.

31 Allotment of land as service tenure, usually with hereditary rights.

32 Kalyanikuttiyamma, *Mohinoyattom Charithravum Attaprakaravum*, 34.

821 (1646 CE),[33] records that *peṇṇumpiḷḷaikaḷ* (female attendants) were taken in processions during the *pārivēṭṭai* (hunting day) of the holy deity of the temple of Muttalakkuṟichchi alias Śrī-Vīrakēraḷapuram.[34] They were taken along under the charge of Vikkiraman Śēgaran, the *cīpaṇḍāram* (temple accountant). The copper plates of the Travancore Kings were related to the accountant family of Kāriyatturai Kaṇṇan Vikkiraman of Pūvanga viḷāgattu Kōvikkal. Vikkiraman Śēgaran was given the hereditary right with privileges to conduct the *Aśvati* festival in the temple, taking with him the *peṇṇumpiḷḷaikal*, and discharge the arrow on the hunting day. Neither the number of female attendants nor indications of any *virutti* to them is mentioned.

The translation of a Tamil record from Viravanallur[35], Kollam year 811 (1636 CE), records that few women servants were set apart for menial work in the temple of God Karpaka Vināyakar, Nayinār Tirunellaināttar and goddess Alagiyanāchchiyār-ammai in Vīrakēralanallūr.[36] The conduct of worship in this temple was done from the land grants by Śettu Tirunelvēlipperumal Venrumālaiyitta-perumāl of Vīrakēralanallūr. I was able to identify the proper names of four women, Nallakuṭṭi, Ayyanayinān Uḷḷittār, Kāḷi and Maruti. Nallakuṭṭi is the daughter of Āndicci and Ayyanayinān Uḷḷittār is her sister. Kāḷi is the daughter of Aṇṇaiñji and Maruti is her sister. They were taken into service with the presence of Ūr and Kaṇiyālar (accountant).[37] The record is significant in terms that it gives the names and details of the women servants appointed. However a close reading of the inscription proves that the word signifying 'women servants' is absent. Another inscription from the same Śiva temple at Vīrakēralanallūr of a later date, Kollam 854 (1679 CE),[38] records that Rama-Nāchchiyār, the daughter of Āndichchi, made gifts of land for maintaining *maṭha* and conducting worship to Mahēśvara in the *ambalam*. We doubt whether the Āndichchi is the same person mentioned in the inscription of Kollam 811 whose daughters are referred to as women servants. If one daughter can be in a wealthy position as to donate lands, we doubt whether the other daughters were given as servants or were they somebody higher in status.

The Arrur plate of Vīra Ravi Udaiyamārttāṇḍavarman (1251 CE)[39] mentions that all temple servants had to accompany the procession for *paḷḷiveṭṭai* and *ārāṭṭu* taken by God Mahādevar at Nayinār Muttalakkurichchi/Śrī Vīrakēraḷapuram. The same inscription mentions about female attendants to the temple. In the record which gives RaviKēralavarma Udayar the *kōyinma, ūranmai* and *sthāna* by King Vīra Ravi Udayamarttāndavarman Śiraivāy Mūttavar, king of Vēṇadu, it is mentioned that the female attendants had to be taken along with the paraphernalia for the God for two occasions. One was the *paḷḷiveṭṭai* on the 9th day of festival. In this the God was taken in procession accompanied by all temple servants, those in

[33] Arrur copper plate of Ravivarman Siraivaymuttavar, Kollam year 821 (1646 CE) from Arrur in Padmanabhapuram Division, TAS, Vol. 4, No. 44, p. 160.

[34] Vīrakēralapuram was in Śengaḷunīr-valanādu, a sub division of Malai-mandalam. It was near Kannanur, a panchayat town in Tiruchirappalli, now in Tamil Nadu. See Ibid., 153.

[35] Viravanallur, a short form of Vīrakēralapuram, is a village in south Travancore.

[36] Viravanallur record from Viravanallur near Kannannur, TAS, Vol. 7, No. 26, p. 40.

[37] I have tried to translate the inscription which is in Tamil and Grantha script, published in Viravanallur record from Viravanallur near Kannannur, TAS, Vol. 7, No. 26, p. 40.

[38] Viravanallur inscription dated Kollam 854 from Viravanallur, TAS, Vol. 7, No. 28, p. 41.

[39] Arrur plate of Vira Ravi Udaiyamattandavarman dated Kollam 426 from Arrur in Padmanabhapuram Division, TAS, Vol. 4, No. 15, p. 86.

charge of the sacred treasury with female attendants, and the other was *ārāṭṭu*, the sacred bathing ceremony of the deity, where there was a similar procession to the river.

Leslie C. Orr says that there is no evidence that temple woman were dedicated or married to the God, and only a small percentage of these women identified themselves as spouses of men.[40] This observation is interesting because it is contrary to the popular belief about *dēvadāsis* that they are married off to Gods. The whole practice of 'marrying off' to the deity would have begun quite late than the Cōḷa period to which Orr has assigned the book, that is, 850–1300 CE. The *dēvadāsis* were rarely associated with dance.[41] They performed menial works or 'attendance functions' like fly-whisk bearing. The fly-whisk bearing women were called *kavarippiṇākkaḷ* and were assigned residences in the temple precincts.[42] Orr points to two sorts of temple service in which women were predominant and were involved—menial service associated with food preparation and cleaning, and attendance functions. 'In the former, the tasks were of extremely low status, and in the latter, they were nonessential, occasional, optional, incidental—and perhaps ornamental'.[43] *Peṇkaḷ* or *peṇṇumpiḷḷaimar* from Kēraḷam are significant in the context that there were women attendants in the region of Kēraḷam also who were employed in the temples. My attempt is not to compare Leslie C. Orr's description about women who performed menial services with *peṇkaḷ* because the epigraphical evidences are from different time periods. However, the practice of having women servants in temples continued in the later centuries in the region of Kēraḷam as we find them in the earlier centuries in the Cōḷa country.

IV

The fourth section of the paper is on the term *peṇvaḻikku avakāśam*. This denotes that the properties were handed over to the next generation in the female line. James Heitzman finds one feature about *dēvadāsis* as fascinating from Orr's book that is 'many identified themselves within female-focused family groups and matrilineages, with some inscriptions mentioning several generations connected to the same temples'.[44] This is similar to the instance where rights were passed on to future generations of women servants through *peṇvaḻikku avakāśam* or rights through female line.

We find inscriptional evidence of the cleansing works of a temple entrusted to female members of a family, that also in *peṇvaḻikku* (in the female line). The services of cleaning the *mahāmaṇḍapa* and the sacred kitchen of the temple and of supplying turmeric for the *ārāṭṭu* festival (holy bath) of the temple of Bhagavati at Tiruchchāranam was a right of the

[40] Leslie C. Orr, *Donors, Devotees and Daughters of God: Temple Women in Medieval Tamilnadu* (New York: Oxford University Press, 2000), 74.

[41] Ibid., 105–26.

[42] Ibid., 89.

[43] Orr, *Donors, Devotees and Daughters of God*, 125.

[44] James Heitzman, review of *Donors, Devotees and Daughters of God: Temple Women in Medieval Tamilnadu* by Leslie C. Orr, *Journal of the American Academy of Religion* 70, no. 3 (September, 2001): 660. Retrieved 1 January 2014, from http://www.jstor.org/stable/1466540

family of Dhanmaseṭṭi Narāyanan Kāḷi of Tirukkuḍakkarai.[45] The inscription of Kollam year 540 (1365 CE) from Chitaral[46] records that certain lands were given for the enjoyment of female members of the family of Dhanmaseṭṭi Nārāyanan Kāḷi of Tirukkuḍakkarai for their services of sweeping and sprinkling with water the premises of the temple. This inscription transferred these lands to the *pādamūlam*[47] of the same temple in Kollam year 540. If any default in service was made, the lands were to be reverted to the family of Nārāyanan Kāli, in the female line. It may have been an attempt to concentrate the temple services within the ritual group and gain the *kārāṇmai* rights. However, a default of duties accounted for a fine of 5 *kaḻañju* of gold to be paid to the king and a reversal of the order. Here we see that the names of the *peṇkal*, the women who were temple servants, were not mentioned again, but that of the head of the family was recorded, even though the *kārāṇmai* land was given for their services. We can read this fourteenth century CE inscription in association with the matrilineal system in Kēraḷam that existed among certain sections of the society. This system in the region gave the sole authority of properties in the hands of the *Kāraṇavar*, the senior male member of the family. However, this particular inscription cannot be read in that light because most probably the women mentioned were from the family of a merchant as the name of the family head suggests (Dhanmaseṭṭi Nārāyanan Kāḷi, seṭṭi indicating a surname of a merchant). And this region in the modern context being in Tamil Nadu is suggestive that this particular family may have Tamil origins. So to link them with matriarchy and the women's right over property is problematical in this case. Even though the name of the king is not mentioned, the gifting of *kārāṇmai* land is a case of royal patronage.

V

From the copper plate records of Travancore kings related to the temple of Tiruppāṟkkaḍal-Bhaṭṭāraka of Kilimanur of the twelfth century CE we come across the term *tēvaṭicci* referring to a woman servant of the temple. This is interesting as the copper plates of the temple of Tiruvallavālappan of the twelfth century CE had references to *tēvaṭicci* as dancing girls.[48] The *tēvaṭicci* in Kilimanur plates (1168 CE) was a woman servant who pounded the paddy and carried the hand lamps.[49] This *tēvaṭicci* received a daily *virutti* of 2 *nāḻi* of rice from the daily offerings every day. She is listed as a temple servant among the others as vāriyan, tirupallittāyam, tirumanikāval and uvachchar. A noteworthy point here is that the *tēvaṭicci* was mentioned in the list of the functionaries, not with the ritual personnel of the temple, like the *mēlśānti* (head priest), *kīlśānti* (assistant priest) or *tirukkuḍa* (umbrella bearer). Mostly,

[45] Chitaral Inscription of Kollam 540 from Chitaral, TAS, Vol. 4, No. 42, p. 149.

[46] The village of Chitaral is 4 miles to the north-east of Kuḻitturai, the headquarters of Viḷavangōd taluk of the Padmanabhapuram division of South Travancore, now in Tamil Nadu.

[47] Servants of the god, men who wore silk cloth for purity sake, devoted to service in central shrine and the regular conduct of worship.

[48] Huzur plates of Tiruvalla from Tiruvalla dated c. eleventh or twelfth century CE, TAS, Vol. 2, P. 3, p. 151.

[49] Kilimanur copper plates of 1168 CE from Trivandrum, TAS, Vol. 5, No. 24, p. 72.

there was only one *tēvaṭicci* as the record uses the singular form *tēvaṭicci* (woman servant) unlike the other plural forms of words, *tirumanikāval* (watchmen) and *uvachchar* (drummers).

VI

The sixth section of the paper is on temple dancing girls. There is a belief that the famous Odissi dance which has captured the world's attention is an improved form of Māhārī (*dēvadāsi*) dance.[50] Kalamandalam Kalyanikuttiyamma who has written on the dance form Mōhiniyāṭṭom, and traced the origin of this classical dance form, from *tēvaticciyāttom*, the dance performances done by the temple dancing women of early Kēraḷam, records that the Śucīndram temple had 32 dancing women attached to it. They sang *aṣṭapadi*[51] from South to North *nadās* (temple entrances) in *śrībali*[52] procession after *attaḷapūja*[53] put the deity to sleep and danced for all special occasions. They were taught dance by appointment of *naṭṭuvanmār* from the *dēvaswom*. But this is the case of the temple in the twentieth century CE; in the sixteenth century the *peṇkal*, as we saw in the first section of this paper, may have been ancestors to the dancing girls, as she is called the daughter of Nāchchiyār (goddess) which indicates that she was consecrated to the temple.[54]

The two main references to dancing girls from Kēralam region come from Cōlapuram or Kōttaru[55] or Mummudiśōlanallūr, a village in Nāñjināḍu within Travancore. A Cōlapuram inscription of Kollam year 428 (1253 CE) records that Kōmaḷavalli, dancing girl of the temple of Rajēndraśōlisvaramudaiya-Nayinār at Tirukkōttaru alias Mummudiśōlanallūr, received four *naḻi* of rice as cooked food daily and this was installed on a hereditary basis.[56]

---

[50] Benudhar Patra, 'Devadāsī System in Orissa: A Case Study of the Jagannātha Temple of Puri', *Annals of the Bhandarkar Oriental Research Institute* 85(2004): 166. Retrieved 1 January 2014, from http://www.jstor.org/stable/41691949

[51] A song from Geetagovindam. See Sreekantesvaram. G Padmanabha Pillai, *Sabdataravali Malayalam Dictionary* (Kottayam: Sahitya Pravarthaka Co-operative Society Ltd., 1993), 232.

[52] The term *śrībali* in the inscriptions which later became *śīvēli* in the colloquial usage refers to the procession of the miniature of the main temple deity, usually three times during the course of the daily *pūjas*.

[53] In Malayalam, *Attaḷam* is supper, *Pūja* is worship. *Attaḷapūja* is the last worship of the night, after which the sanctum sanctorum and the temple is closed. See Pillai, *Sabdataravali Malayalam Dictionary*, 99.

[54] For a detailed account of the dedication of temple dancing girls to South Indian temples; see Kay Jordan K., *From Sacred Servant to Profane Prostitute: A History of the Changing Legal status of the Devadasis in India, 1857–1947* (New Delhi: Manohar Publishers, 2003), 1–2.

[55] Kōttaru, situated near the Aruvaymoli mountain pass which was a highway of commerce and travel between Travancore on the western side and plains of the Coimbatore, Madura and Tinnevelly districts, was a flourishing town of commerce. This pass was frequently used by the Pāndyas, Cholas, Vijayanagara generals and Nāyaka kings for entering Travancore. It was also a Chola military outpost with a permanent garrison (*nilaippadai*) to guard the Chola interest there. Since the place had a close affinity with the culture and people of other areas of the South, the presence of the dancing girls can also be attributed to it. See Ramanatha A. S. Ayyar, *Travancore Archaeological Series*, vol. 6, part 1 and 2 (Thiruvananthapuram: Department of Cultural Publications, Government of Kerala, November 2003), 1, 3.

[56] Cholapuram Inscriptions from Cholapuram dated Kollam 428, TAS, Vol. 6, No. 16, p. 26.

The rice was given to the temple by Vaḍugan-Guṇavan alias Rajēndraśōla-Vaiśravaṇan of Tirukkōṭṭāru alias Śōlakēralapuram, the brother of Kōmaḷavalli. As the term Vaiśravaṇan indicates, Vaḍugan Guṇavan might have been a merchant in all possibility. He gave 61 *achchu* for providing 5 *nāḻi* of rice for offerings and vegetables for curry to the images of God Periyadēva-Nayinār and goddess Nāchchiyar, consecrated by him in the temple. For this 61 *achchu*, Vaḍugan Guṇavan obtained land on lease from Vīrapāṇḍiya Pallavaraiyan for cultivation. From its produce he measured daily, without fail, 5 *nāḻi* of rice and supplied vegetables also. With this stipulated quantity of rice, the offerings were provided and also 4 *nāḻi* of rice as cooked food to Kōmaḷavalli.[57] Even after the lease expired, the temple servants, supervisors and Vaḍugan Guṇavan invested the lease amount and additional loan aggregating to 61 *achchu* on some property, and Vaḍugan took it to cultivation on a hereditary basis and provided the 5 *nāḻi* of rice and vegetables for offerings without fail. Here, the brother of the dancing girl is more prominent as it is he who consecrates the Nāchchiyār as well as gives the donation of 5 *nāḻi* of rice daily and vegetables for the land he obtains on lease for the 61 *achchu* he paid.

This instance makes another point also clear, that even if Kōmaḷavalli has received patronage from the kings or landlords (which in itself is not clear from the inscription), the wealth was handled by the brother. Even if she did not receive patronage and was a member of a wealthy family and was thus offered to the temple,[58] the wealth was managed and transacted by her brother Vaḍugan Guṇavan. It is he who earns the right of hereditary cultivation of the land even after the loan expires. Here we can problematise the matrilineal societal set up of the region and the power of women. There are chances that she would have not been a Nair woman and might have been one from the Tamil region also. However, the evidence again reveals the fact that the power ultimately rested in the hands of the *Kāraṇavar* or the senior male member of the family. Even though the dancing girls may have been wealthy, they would not have been the actual power holders of the family. This inscription points to the fact that the *tēvaṭicci* of the Kēralam was different from the *dēvadāsis* of the other regions of South who were wealthy donors who wielded the power of decision and execution. From the thirteenth century CE, 'Amman Gods' were revoked as Nāchchiyār-partners of *Dēvan* and were consecrated. Amman Gods were goddesses of agriculture who were worshipped throughout South India.[59]

Absence of inscriptional and literary evidences makes it clear that the *tēvaticcikal* of Kēralam, even though were wealthy and donors, were not similar to the rich *dēvadāsi* donors of Tamil and Andhra regions.[60] To read them in association with the socio-economic situation of the Kēraḷam region, we should infer that the dancing *Tēvaṭiccikaḷ* of the region were not

---

[57] Cholapuram Inscriptions from Cholapuram dated Kollam 428, TAS, Vol. 6, No. 16, p. 26.

[58] Kay K. Jordan opines that the dedication of *dēvadāsis*, the female ritual specialists to the deity, came as expressions of gratitude for the conception and safe delivery of the child or the recovery of family member from illness. See Jordan, *From Sacred Servant to Profane Prostitute*, 1.

[59] Soman, *Devadasikalum Sahitya Charithravum*, 29.

[60] For an account of dēvadāsi donors of Tamil Nadu see Orr, *Donors, Devotees and Daughters of God*, 171. For the Andra region see Cynthia Talbot, 'Temples, Donors, and Gifts: Patterns of Patronage in the 13th c South India', *The Journal of Asian Studies* 50, no. 2 (May 1991): 308–340.

as powerful as their counterparts in other areas of the South. Since they lacked the power, they could not have had much say in the decision making of the society or temple affairs.

These dancing girls were entitled to *virutti* from the temples. Sometimes more than one *tēvaṭicci* shared the fixed *virutti*. During festive occasions specially, dancing girls were appointed by the temple authorities and paid *virutti* collectively. The Tiruvalla copper plates mention four *Tēvaṭiccikaḷ* in association with the festival of Ōṇam,[61] who were given 12 *nāḷi* of rice during the occasion. They may have shared this rice and taken 3 *nāḷi* each. Here we should note that while the ritual functionaries in the higher rungs of the hierarchical ladder were paid individually and these were carefully recorded, these women were given a collective *virutti* and we often do not know the details of number of them appointed or the scale of distribution of their *virutti*. No mention is made about their families or how they shared this rice.

The appointment of dancing girls in temples during festive occasions can be corroborated from literary evidences also. Kalamandalam Kalyanikuttiyamma,[62] with the help of oral traditions, says that the women dancers from the Śucīndram temple (Southern Travancore, now in Tamil Nadu) used to dance in Saraswatiamman Kōvil in Pūjapura for *navarātri pūja* and in Padmanābhaswami temple (both in Thiruvananthapuram taluk) in the month of Tulām and received special rights for that. They were said to have received the *paḍaccōru* (share of cooked rice) of 2 *idaṅgaḷi* of rice as wages. The aspect of migration is very prominent in the case of dancing girls. During the Travancore kings' rule, the *dāsis* and artists who performed mōhiniyāṭṭom and kēḷikka came from Tamil Nadu, particularly Tanjāvūr.[63] Most of the old writs or documents are records of giving encouragement and expenditure to South Indian *dāsis* and artists. They do not contain mentioning about temple *dāsīs* or women artists of Kēraḷam.[64]

Regarding the Śucīndram temple and the dancing girls there, P. Soman argues that the *tēvaraṭiyāḷ* mentioned in the Śucīndram temple inscriptions were pounders of paddy in the temple and it was from this group that *dēvadāsis* were recruited.[65] There were different hierarchical divisions among the *dēvadāsis* as seen from the studies about Śucīndram temple.[66] While mentioning about the customs related to *dēvadāsis* in the temple, Soman says that *tōḍa* denoted youth and was the symbol of *dēvadāsi*. *Tōḍavaykkal* was when the *dēvadāsi* removed the *tōḍa* before the *yōgam* due to old age or terminal illness. *Taikiḷavikaḷ* were those who had resigned with a particular pension, mostly in kind.[67] *Dēvadāsis* got land without taxes and paddy as wages for jobs in temples. The *dēvadāsis* had a right over the *paḍaccōru* or rice offered to the Dēvan (God) in Śucīndram temple as a mark of right over the leavings or leftover of her husband's meal.[68]

---

[61] See note 48.
[62] Kalyanikuttiyamma, *Mohinoyattom Charithravum Attaprakaravum*, 34.
[63] Soman, *Devadasikalum Sahitya Charithravum*, 57.
[64] Ibid.
[65] Ibid., 31.
[66] K. K. Pillai, *Suchindram Temple*, A Monograph (Chennai: Kalakshetra Publications, 2002).
[67] Ibid., 32.
[68] Ibid., 32.

The dancing girls sometimes accompanied the *isthakabal* party (welcoming group) of the Maharaja at major temples like Sivaganga at Melkote.[69] This is equivalent to the evidences from Uṇṇunīlisandēśam that dancing girls used to receive the Travancore *rājas* when they were out with their paraphernalia. When the Vēṇāḍu king Ādityavarma came through the south side of the Umayanallūr temple and entered the Kollam town, he was greeted by a *dēvadāsi* named Veḷḷūr Nāṇi.[70] Before Ādityavarman leaft Thiruvananthapuram, a beautiful woman named Uṇṇiyāḍi is said to have come and waited for him. Elamkulam Kunjan Pillai is of the opinion that this woman would have been part of the matilakam dancers.[71] He further argues that there are references in Uṇṇunīlisandēśam that throughout Ādityavarman's journey from Thiruvananthapuram to Kaḍandhēri, whenever he was near temples, there were women who came and received him.[72] Since there was a custom that prevailed in Śucīndram and Kēraḷapuram temples that when the Vēṇāḍu kings visited, *dēvadāsis* of these temples received them, Elamkulam argues that these women who received Ādityavarman throughout his journey near the temples were also temple dancers.[73]

Tēvaṭiccikaḷ were also a significant part of the temple economy. The donative inscriptions[74] which showcase their names are also indications of their not-so-ignored roles in the temple life. *Tēvaṭiccikaḷ* here were dancing girls who sometimes made handsome money and land donations to temples. The girls' families often earned fame and respectable status due to her good deed. They claimed and often partook the share of sacred offerings from the temple.

Cynthia Talbot[75] reads from the thirteenth century Andhra inscriptions that patronage of religion may have been the only public activity women could have engaged in. Leslie C. Orr, through a study on the Cōla inscriptions (850–1300 CE) states that temple women's relationships with the temple were secured through their donations.[76] There is an argument that the unmarried status of the temple women gave them the economic autonomy that helped them to act as temple patrons, while the donative activities of other women were curtailed.[77] At the same time we come across women donors in Andhra region who were royal women—the wives of powerful kings and princes, and the non-royal women of

---

[69] Janaki Nair, 'The Devadasi, Dharma and the State', *Economic and Political Weekly* 29, no. 50 (10 December 1994), 3161. Retrieved 1 January 2014, form http://www.jstor.org/stable/4402128

[70] Pillai, *Unnuneeli Sandesam*, 95.

[71] Ibid., 104.

[72] Ibid.

[73] Ibid.

[74] Donative Inscriptions had a public significance, for they were highly visible documents situated on temple walls and columns or on separate slabs and pillars within the temple compound. See Talbot, 'Temples, Donors, and Gifts', 333.

[75] It is noteworthy that the thirteenth century Andhra inscriptions praise men mostly in terms of their military accomplishments, where women are eulogized almost solely for their religious beneficences. See Talbot, 'Temples, Donors, and Gifts', 329.

[76] Temple women's patronage was diffuse and individualistic. They used donations as a way to forge and strengthen connections with the temple in their locality, connections that were critical to their status and identities as temple women. See Orr, *Donors, Devotees and Daughters of God*, 162.

[77] Orr, *Donors, Devotees and Daughters of God*.

the humbler descent—the wives and daughters of peasant leaders (reḍḍis), warrior chiefs (nāyakas), herders (bōyas) and merchants (seṭṭis).[78]

In the erstwhile Kēralam regions, which had a close affinity with the Tamil culture, we find dancing girls installing the image of goddess and making cash donations for daily offerings in the temples. The Cholapuram inscription of Kollam 428 (1253 CE) mentions Śeṅgōḍan-Pūvāṇḍi, a dancing girl of the temple of Rājēndraśōḷīśvaramuḍaiya-Mahādēva in Tirukkōttaru alias Mummudiśōlanallur (part of Nāñjināḍu, one of the 13 malaināttunāḍukal, now in Tamil Nadu). She installed the image of the consort (nāchchiyar) to the God Kuṉṟameṟinda Piḷḷaiyār in the temple and gave 3 *śalāgai* (or) 10 *achchu* and 10 new *achchu* of gold, 20 *achchu* in total, for the expenses of providing the sacred offerings to this goddess. The temple servants and supervisors of the temple accounts who received the amount agreed to give her daily 5 *nāḻi* of paddy as interest for the 2 *nāḻi* of rice she gave for sacred offerings to goddess Nāchchiyār. If she measured out this 2 *nāḻi* of rice on the *palakaittalai*,[79] she was given cooked food of one *nāḻi* of rice after making the offerings to the goddess. She was also presented with a cloth on the bathing day (*tīrttam*) of the annual festival. This supply of cooked food, cloth and paddy was to be continued on a hereditary basis to the descendants of Śengōdan-Pūvandi.[80] The temple servants and temple account supervisor received 20 *achchu* and gave in writing an agreement on stone and copper to this dancing girl that 2 *nāḻi* of rice will be provided forever. This inscription proves that Śeṅgōḍan-Pūvāṇḍi had active interaction with the temple authorities and the fact that she got the agreement written on stone and copper was a part of the attempt to ensure the hereditary interactions and to proclaim her name. The present of cloth on the *tīrttam* day was a public acknowledgement of her position as the dancing girl of the temple. The economic significance of her act cannot be lessened as she received an interest of 5 *nāḻi* of paddy for the 2 *nāḻi* of rice she gave daily for the sacred offerings daily.

'Muttakuḍi occurs in the Kēraḷapuram inscription where it refers to a family of dancing girls attached to the Siva temple at that place'.[81] The Kēraḷapuram inscription of Kollam year 782 (1607 CE) records that two women, Nīlammaikuṭṭi, daughter of Māḍammai, and Māḍammai, daughter of Ichchakuṭṭi, set up the pillar bearing the image of Kulaśēkhara Perumāḷ in the south-western corner (*kanni-mūlai*) of the Rishabha—maṇḍapa of Śiva temple at Śengalunir valanāḍu, near Padmanābhapuram.[82] These two women belonged to the *mūttakuḍi* (family) of dancing girls attached to the temple of Mahādēva at Kēraḷapuram. These dancing girls attached to the temples would have been wealthy and holding high position in the society then to have made donations to the temple.

---

[78] Talbot, 'Temples, Donors, and Gifts'.
[79] A plank on which paddy was measured.
[80] Cholapuram Inscription dated Kollam 428 from Cholapuram, TAS, Vol. 6, No. 15, p. 25.
[81] Cheramangalam records of Jatavarman Sundara Chola Pandya from Cheramangalam in Eraniel Taluk of Padmanabhapuram Division dated eleventh century CE, TAS, Vol. 5, No. 7, p. 29.
[82] Keralapuram Inscriptions from Keralapuram, a suburb of Muttalakurichchi near Padmanabhapuram dated Kollam 782, TAS, Vol. 5, No. 27, p. 94.

We come across few instances of female patronage to temples from an inscriptional study of the region of Kēralam. An inscription of Rajasekhara of eighth century CE[83] mentions one Kaṇṇan Śaṅkaran, who held the position of Kāvadi. It says that the *puraiyiḍam*[84] that belonged to Śankari, the daughter of the Kāvadi Kaṇṇan, which yielded a hundred and fifty *tūnis* of paddy and three *dināras*, was given to the God of Kailāsa. This instance can suggest that the accountant would have been wealthy enough to grant her daughter with plots of land. It can also be suggestive that the family of the accountant was in close association with the temple and gave generous grants to the temple.

It was recorded in the Tirunandikkarai inscription of Vijayaragadeva of tenth century CE[85] that Kīlanadigal, the daughter of Kulaśēkharadēva and queen of Vijayaragadevan, gave thirty *kalañju* of gold to maintain a perpetual lamp in the temple of Tirunandikkarai Bhatāra. The accountant was among others present while the donation was made. Tiruvalla copper plate records the gift of Rāmanmādevi of Muññinādu, the lands Iñjaitturutti and Kulikkādu together with their tenants to the God Tiruvalla vālappan.[86] With the income from these lands, a food offering of 4 *nāḻi* was to be made to the god.

Here, the relationship status of female donors was clearly mentioned that they were either daughters of wealthy members of the society or wife of a king. The panels of evidences where lay women or nuns were seen to contribute, as in the case of western Indian social set up of Buddhist influence[87] is missing in Kēraḷam.

VII

Accimār are a category of women who can be seen as having similar characteristics of *dēvadāsis*. Some historians have called the *accimār* as *dēvadāsis*. However, they are distinct and different from *dēvadāsis* in the sense that they were more subjugated to the interests of landlords and men of power in the society even though they were sometimes attached to temples. The *dēvadāsi* system formed as a sub institution related to the temples in the medieval times. There is an opinion that many *dēvadāsis* belonged to Nair *taravaḍus* (matrilineal ancestral homes) which were rich and privileged. It is said that the *dēvadāsis* to *Padmanabhaswami* temple in Thiruvananthapuram were selected from a particular Nair community with a status called *pādamaṅgalam*.[88] When a girl gets selected as a *dēvadāsi* to a temple, her mother or close relative forms a contract called *jātakam* with the temple

83 An Inscription of Rajasekhara from Changanasseri dated eighteenth century CE, TAS, Vol. 2, No. 2, p. 14.

84 Site of habitation.

85 Tirunandikkarai Inscription of Vijayaragadeva from Tirunandikkarai in Kalkulam Taluk dated tenth century CE, TAS, Vol. 4, No. 38, p. 145.

86 Huzur plates of Tiruvalla from Tiruvalla dated eleventh century or twelfth century CE, TAS, Vol. 2, P. 3, p. 153.

87 Vidya Dehejia, 'The collective and popular basis of Early Buddhist patronage: sacred monuments, 100 BC–AD 250', in *The Powers of Art. Patronage in Indian Culture*, ed. Barnara Stoler Miller (Delhi: Oxford University Press, 1992), 23.

88 P. V. Velayudhan Pillai, *Manipravalakavitha (History of Manipravala Literature)* (Thiruvananthapuram: The State Institute of Languages, 2003), 21.

administration. Later on at an auspicious time, she is wedded as wife of god and is accepted by the temple. All the music and dance training of the girl happens in the temple. Dance masters called *naṭṭuvanmār* were appointed in major temples for this purpose. On the attainment of proper knowledge of dance and music, the young woman is accepted as a *dēvadāsi*. 'According to the tradition recorded in the Mādalāpānji (the chronicle of the Jagannātha temple at Puri) recitation of Gītagōvindam was introduced in the Jagannātha Temple of Puri as a daily service of the Devadāsīs by Narasiṁhadeva I (AD 1238–1264)'.[89] Kalamandalam Kalyanikuttiyamma refers to the dancing women of Travancore who danced to the tune of lyrics from Gītagōvindam.

Dēvadāsis acquired higher education and were proficient in music, dance, instruments, *kāvyas* and *śāstras*. They were always married women without widowhood and hence were considered to be a good omen. There existed a practice that when Vēṇāḍu kings came, the *dēvadāsis* in different temples on his way should come out and receive him. This may be because the kings were considered at par with or just below the status of gods and the maid servants to gods were considered to be servants to kings as well. In southern Travancore, the *dēvadāsis* of Keralapuram and Śucīndram temples are said to have had relationships with Nair men.

Dēvadāsis were of different hierarchical statuses. Those of the higher status danced before god only on festival days and respectfully received the kings and chiefs who visited the temples. Those of the lower orders did services like holding the lamps for lights, worship in the evenings, sweeping the room for *śrībali*, sing during *attāḻa śrībali*, bring water to the temple and dance when the god comes out in procession. A woman, accepted as *dēvadāsi* in a temple, received *kuḍi* and *paḍi*, *kuḍi* denoting the house to stay and *paḍi* her salary. Very famous *dēvadāsis* received the status called *rāyar*. When they wanted to retire from work due to illness or old age, they could do so by submitting their ear ring along with 12 gold coins to the temple administrative assembly.

Vaiśikatantram, written in the twelfth or thirteenth century CE, discusses about the custom of *vaiśikavritti* or prostitution and narrates the outlook of a *vaiśya* or prostitute.[90] In the text, the grandmother educates the granddaughter that the *dēvadāsi* should be smartly talented enough to perform on stage evoking in every member of the audience the feeling that it is me whom she likes the most. This text, even though exaggerated, shows the presence of women well versed in dance and music, which pleased men and were an integral part of the social system.

Uṇṇiyacci caritam is an accicaritam text written in the first half of the thirteenth century CE. Uṇṇiyacci, who was the *dēvadāsi* of Tirumarutūr temple in northern Kerala, belonged to Atimayanallūr in Tamil Nadu and came with her mother Acciyār to Kerala. A *gandharva* (heavenly being) sees her on the *Aṣṭami* festival in the *Kumbha* month in Tirumarutūr temple and develops interest in her. The *dēvadāsi* should have had important role to play in this temple festival.

---

[89] Patra, *Devadāsī System in Orissa*, 163.

[90] In Vaiśikatantram, a grandmother narrates the principles and rites of prostitution to her granddaughter. She says that her family has a rich tradition of about eight generations of hereditary knowledge in the occupation and reminds her how difficult it is to learn and master the occupation of prostitution. See K. Ramachandran Nair, *Vaisikatantram* (Trivandrum, 1969).

It is recorded in *Uṇṇiyacci caritam* that the *dēvadāsis* lived in houses which were close to temples. It also refers to rōhiṇi who is a girl of nine years. 'In a time when the *dēvadāsi* system was prominent, a virgin of nine years had a very high status in the society'.[91]

A medical practitioner who was at the house of Uṇṇiyacci claims to have treated and cured a *dēvadāsi* who gave him 50 *accu* (gold coin). '*Dēvadāsis* lure men through their sweet talk'.[92] The men assembled in front of Uṇṇiyacci's house describes about a *dēvadāsi* of Kāḷambaḷḷiyil house. That young woman bit the man on his lower lips and took his gold ring and got rid of him. She said if he gives more gold, he will be allowed to sleep with her. The man gave a gold coin to the *dēvadāsi's* man in secret and that man said it is for her and the gold and money given is not enough. This shows that a male member of the *dēvadāsi's* family took undue money from her seekers and tried to extract more money and gold from men in her name. Here, the sexuality of the *dēvadāsi* is made just as a pawn in the hands of the male member in the family to obtain maximum wealth from men who came to spend time with her.

Uṇṇiyacci caritam also refers to the young daughter of Nīli who was much able. She was a *dēvadāsi*. She is described as being clean, decorated and very smart. The men discussed about going there. The men tried to appease the female attendants of Uṇṇiyacci hoping to find entrance to her house.

Uṇṇicirutēvi caritam was written in the second half of the thirteenth century CE. Uṇṇicirutēvi, the heroine of the text, was born as the daughter of Rāyirampillai and was the granddaughter of Nangayya and belonged to the Poyilam village and Tōṭṭuvāyppaḷḷi house. Uṇṇicirutēvi's grandmother is described to be proficient than Lord Śiva in dance. Poets in *Unnicirutevicaritam* are referred to as saying that they could receive the *naivēdyam* (food offering) made to temple as reward for writing poems about women proficient in dance. This may be taken as a clear reference to direct association between *dēvadāsis* and temples.

There were men who sold all their earnings and were ready to submit it before Uṇṇicirutēvi. Poets who claim to have written poems about Uṇṇicirutēvi and are ready to present it before her were many. Brahman men with vermilion marks, gold rings, nicely worn dhotis and sacred thread were also present.[93] Some cruel brahmans dressed up like clowns got embarrassed describing their sexual desire. It was almost like a practice where the women with divine nature and high status in the society gave a vision of themselves to the common man that was to happen in Uṇṇicirutēvi's house.

Uṇṇiyāḍi caritam was written in the second half of the fourteenth century CE by Damodaracakyar who was patronized by Kerala Varma, the king of Kayamkulam. Uṇṇiyāḍi belonged to Cerukara *illam* and her mother was Uṇṇikuṭṭatti. The wide acceptance of the *dēvadāsi* system is evident from the fact that a famous *dēvadāsi* called Kuṭṭatti was married by *Kēraḷa Varman*, king of Kayamkulam, and their daughter Uṇṇiyāḍi turned out to become another famous *dēvadāsi*.

---

91 Mughathala Gopalakrishnan Nair, *Unniyacci caritam* (Thiruvananthapuram: The State Institute of Languages, 2011), 47.

92 Ibid., 72.

93 Sundaram Dhanuvachapuram, *Unnichiruthevi charitham* (Thiruvananthapuram: The State Institute of Languages, 2005), 7.

Poet says that the beautiful women of the Ōḍanāḍu region have been obtaining the wealth of men which is the men's courage. These beautiful women daily steal the hearts of young men. Even the female attendants of Uṇṇiyāḍi are very beautiful. They bear the box of betel leaves, hold a fan in the shape of umbrella made of peacock feathers, wear head ornaments and are fully decorated in ornaments and they talk sweetly. Uṇṇiyāḍi is narrated to be beautiful as a deer who won over the clan of heavenly dancers in her beauty.[94]

The Brahmeśvar Temple Inscription from Orissa describes the beauty and grace of the *dēvadāsis* offered by queen Kalāvatī as those who appeared graceful by wearing various types of ornaments, and at the time of dance flashes of lightning were revealed in their movements.[95] This can be seen in corroboration with the beauty of the *tēvaṭicci* and *accimār* described in the acci caritams so elaborately.

A poet who waits at the doorstep of Uṇṇiyāḍi is referred to as boasting to have written a *taivampāṭṭu* (poem) about the beautiful young damsel. Among the people impatiently waiting to see Uṇṇiyāḍi are many poets who have written *Maṇipravāḷa ślōkas* about her, *bhaṭṭanmār* who are young brahman scholars who have come with their bundle of books, rich *nampūtiris* (brahmans), chiefs and poor literary men.

P. Soman says that the ambalavāsi[96] groups followed the practice of *tālikeṭṭu* as marriage practice.[97] When the ambalavāsi women maintained sexual relations with nampūtiri, embrāntiri or paṭṭar, the ambalavāsi men had sexual relations in their own group or with Nair women. For ambalavāsi women, *sambandham*[98] with nampūtiri men was merit from their previous lives.[99]

VIII

Leslie C. Orr refers to the term *naṭṭuvar* mentioned in the thirteen Cōḷa period inscriptions that she located. In every case, the *naṭṭuvan* was male and was described as receiving support from the temple for his services, and in two of the inscriptions, the *naṭṭuvan's* service rights were transferred to male relatives. She argues that the *naṭṭuvar* were not linked to temple women in the inscriptions, but in some cases they were associated with *uvacccar* (drummers) or other musicians.[100]

Pertaining to the Kēraḷam region, P. Soman argues that men who belonged to the *dēvadāsi* group performed as singers, and musicians as background supporters of *dāsiyāṭṭom*. They were called *naṭṭuvanmār*.[101] The *naṭṭuvan* taught dance and music, conducted the initiation ceremony into dancing and played background music. The people who sounded *kuḷal* were

---

[94] Sundaram Dhanuvachapuram, *Unniyadicharitham* (Thiruvananthapuram: The State Institute of Languages, 2007), 186.

[95] Patra, *Devadāsī System in Orissa*, 167.

[96] Many of the temple women later crystallized themselves into ambalavāsi caste.

[97] Soman, *Devadasikalum Sahitya Charithravum*, 75.

[98] Here sambandham means marriage.

[99] Soman, *Devadasikalum Sahitya Charithravum*, 76.

[100] Orr, *Donors, Devotees and Daughters of God*, 107.

[101] Soman, *Devadasikalum Sahitya Charithravum*, 30.

called *parvaśanmār* and the musicians were called *ōccanmār*.[102] He argues that the *naṭṭuvar* of Kēraḷam were cākyār and mārārs. They were never the male counterparts or the men of the *dēvadāsis*.[103]

Literary evidence of *naṭṭuvanmār* from the Kēraḷam region is very scarce. However, there is mention of male attendants of *accimār* in the caritam literature. But we are not sure if they were dance masters—*naṭṭuvanmār*. There is a reference where the male attendant of Uṇṇiyacci was approached by a man who had come to meet her. He gave a golden coin into the attendant's hands in order to meet her fast. The man seems to have promised that he would not tell this matter to anyone and the coin was for her. But later the man said that the *accu* (golden coin) and money was not sufficient for meeting her.[104] Here the reference indicates that this might only have been Uṇṇiyacci's attendant and most probably not her dance master.

However this does not deny the fact that there were dance masters who taught the *dēvadāsi* girls from the age of 9. The age of 9 was significant for the dancing girls as mostly they were dedicated to the god when the virgin girls were 9 years old.[105]

IX

CONCLUSION

We can see from the following study that the term *tēvaṭicci* cannot be used as a generic term to indicate temple women. On the one hand, we come across the *tēvaṭicci* who was the dancing girl and donor and on the other, we see *peṇkal* and *peṇṇumpiḷḷaikaḷ* who were the female attendants and cleaners of temples. We see a clear hierarchical division among them, the dancing girl being the donor and receiving the higher *virutti*, whereas the female labourers, often mentioned collectively without any mention of their names, were attributed a collective *virutti*. The dancing girl acquired a ritual status in the worship in temples. The *tēvaṭicci* was part of the *Śrībali* in few instances. However, the actual control of these dancing girls rested with senior male members of their families who possessed the real power over their *virutti* lands.

Interesting is the instance where the term *tēvaṭicci* is used to denote the woman temple servant. Here, the temple utilizes the labour of these women for low wages, often in kind. The power play of the women was subtle as we see the hand of the *Kāraṇavar* as a controlling agency over the feminine. The king is evident as the generous patron, giving *kārāṇmai* lands to the families of women servants. The hereditary rights on female donors was stressed and recorded.

The *accimār* enjoy the attention given to them by their seekers which includes a wide range of men like landlords, warriors, brahman scholars, brahman students, singers, poets,

---

[102] Ibid., 33.

[103] Ibid., 55.

[104] Nair, *Unniyacci caritam*, 77.

[105] Ibid., 47.

rich and poor lovers who were ready to submit all their earnings before the *accimār* whom they were eager to meet. However, male members of their family are seen to have extracted money and gold from their seekers and their life reduced to giving pleasure by their dance, songs and sexual favours to men wielding power. In society during the eighth to twentieth century CE, Kerala was conditioned and tuned by its political, social, economic, intellectual and literary dimensions which accepted and accredited the exploitation of these categories of women as a natural phenomenon. There might have been voices of dissent and conflicts, but they are carefully silenced in the sources of written history. An open analysis of the lives of these women brings out a vivid narrative of these scenes of exploitation, marginalization and subjugation through the thin layers of cleverly woven descriptions of glory, heavenly beauty, high status, divine duties and just wages.

We can see that the inscriptional references to individual names of women as part of service classes are very few, considering the fact that women may have been employed in tying the *paḷḷittāmam* (sacred garland) and would have been among the *śīkkol* or *aṭikkumavar* (sweepers). We see that they were mentioned, though in a collective term of *peṇṇumpiḷḷaikal* or *peṇkaḷ*, as a very important part of sacred processions for *paḷḷiveṭṭai* and *ārāṭṭu*, significant rituals involving the deity. Though the degree of their representation in the inscriptions is low when compared to the ritual personnel and other functionaries, still we cannot close our eyes towards the less visualized, yet rich images of the women among temple functionary groups.

I am also making an attempt to see the transition of the temple women through the centuries from the eighth to seventeenth CE. When in the initial centuries we see dancing women and women donors, later we do not have inscriptional evidences on them. The *caritams* and *sandēśa kāvyams* which are dated from the thirteenth, fourteenth and fifteenth centuries CE contain a colourful description of *accimār* and heroines who were epitomes of beauty. Some of them we have clear indications of being associated with temples. For others, it is difficult to postulate that way. Hence, it is difficult to assume a picturesque description of the temple women as dancing girls of medieval Kerala. However, the pounders of paddy and the women who did services like sweeping and mopping—the *aḍiccutaḷi*—continued to exist in the temples. The British attempt to showcase them as one category was not right because they assumed various roles and various shades of womanhood absorbed in various sizes and shapes in varied functional roles.

BIBLIOGRAPHY

Subrahmanya K. V. Aiyar, *Travancore Archaeological Series*, Vol. 4, Parts 1 & 2 (Thiruvananthapuram: Department of Cultural Publications, Government of Kerala, February 1999).

Ramanatha A. S. Ayyar, *Travancore Archaeological Series*, Vol. 5, Parts 1, 2 & 3 (Thiruvananthapuram: Department of Cultural Publications, Government of Kerala, February 1999).

Ramanatha A. S. Ayyar, *Travancore Archaeological Series*, Vol. 7, Parts 1 & 2 (Thiruvananthapuram: Department of Cultural Publications, Government of Kerala, December 2004).

M. G. S. Narayanan, *Index to Cera Inscriptions: A Companion Volume to Thesis on 'Political and Social Conditions of Kerala under the Kulasekhara Empire'*, (submitted for the Degree of Doctor of Philosophy of the University of Kerala, University of Kerala, Thiruvananthapuram, 1972).

Gopinatha T. A. Rao, *Travancore Archaeological Series*, Vol. 2 & 3 (Trivandrum: Department of Cultural Publications, Government of Kerala, 1992, March).

Chapter 20

Gender, Caste and Labour: Ideological and Material Structure of Widowhood*

UMA CHAKRAVARTI

In this essay, I attempt to explore the relationships among gender, caste and labour in the context of widowhood. I look mainly at widowhood among the upper castes, an issue that has dominated our consciousness for over a century, but try to understand the larger structure of relations—material and ideological—in which patriarchal practices enforced permanent widowhood on women. I argue that patriarchal practices among the different castes, though dissimilar, are part of the larger structure of caste, production and reproduction. Thus, traditional patriarchal practices could be distinctive for various castes, to make for a hierarchy of cultures and a system of production in which the low castes labour and reproduce labour, whereas the high castes do not labour and reproduce only specialists—ritual specialists—or a literati which performs specific types of non-manual work.

Further, I suggest that the distinctive cultural codes form a basis for the hierarchy of castes in which not only are castes ranked in an elaborate hierarchy, but there is an ideological and material rationale for the hierarchy. The stringent control of female sexuality among other 'non-labouring' high castes with permanent enforced widowhood at the apex of the cultural codes becomes the index for establishing the highest rank in the caste system. Conversely, the range of marriage patterns practised in the case of widows among the lower castes, which the higher castes often impose upon them, nevertheless becomes the ideological rationale for ranking these castes as low. This serves a double purpose: not only does it establish distinctions between castes and legitimize the hierarchy of caste, it also establishes a firm demographic basis for production relations. Thus a single-caste framework functioning both at the level of ideology and material arrangements requires distinctive patriarchal arrangement and cultural codes among the hierarchy of castes, to reproduce both the ideological and material arrangements of a certain structure of production.

* Reproduced with permission from the author and the publisher, from *Everyday Lives, Everyday Histories: Beyond the Kings and Brahmanas of 'Ancient' India*. Tulika Books, New Delhi, 2006, pp. 156–79.

This essay was first published in *Economic and Political Weekly,* Vol. XXX, No. 36 (September 1995), pp. 2248–56; it was republished in Martha Chen (ed.), *Widows in India* (Delhi: SAGE, 1998).

I argue in this essay that the experience of widowhood must be firmly situated in a certain kind of production relations apart from its patriarchal context, as the discussion below will amplify.

CONCEPTUALIZING WIDOWHOOD: WIDOWHOOD AS SOCIAL DEATH

Widowhood in India among the upper castes is a state of social death.[1] The widow's social death stems from her alienation from reproduction and sexuality, following the loss of her husband and her exclusion from the functioning social unit of the family. Once a woman ceases to be wife (especially a childless wife) she ceases to be a 'person'—she is neither daughter nor daughter-in-law. The problem posed by Brahmanical patriarchy therefore is: since the wife has no social existence outside of her husband's house, then, as a widow, who or what is she? The texts and rituals attempt to work the problem out. The problem itself is simply that although the widow is socially dead, she remains an element in society; the question then is how to incorporate her. One way could be to constitute a separate community of widows, a non-sexual community, such as that of female ascetics. Another could be to retain her in society but place her on its margins and then institutionalize her marginality. This is what Brahmanical patriarchy did with the widow. The widow's institutionalized marginality, a liminal state between being physically alive and being socially dead, was the ultimate cultural outcome of the deprivation of her sexuality as well as of her personhood.

The widow's marginal state meant that she was, in a manner of speaking, functionally incorporated into the household while being considered an out-sider. Thus, while the widow was functionally incorporated either into the natal or affinal family, she was, especially in the affinal household, the 'domestic enemy'. At the same time, she was the 'insider' who had fallen, one who had ceased to belong and been expelled from normal participation in the community (for failing to prevent her husband's death). She was the object of divine and social disfavour. Widowhood was perceived as a disrupter of the social order and a potential violation of the moral order. There were two modes of representing the social death of widows: one was intrusive, in which the widow was conceived of as someone who did not belong because she was an 'outsider' (as in the affinal home); and in the extrusive mode, the widow who had left her natal home following marriage became an outsider because she no longer belonged. The widow was both simultaneously—in the affinal and in the natal home she became the outsider who now no longer belonged, and she thus shared the sense of being an outcaste. It was not, however, the rules of purity and pollution but those of inauspiciousness that were the means of maintaining social distance in the case of the widow. The widow was socially differentiated by prescribed behaviour which she had, at all costs, to follow.

Symbolic ideas of a cultural system are usually given social expression in ritualized patterns. The death of the husband (without whom the widow ceased to be a social entity) among upper-caste Hindus was ritually expressed through special ceremonies involving the marginalization of the erstwhile wife who, as a widow, was defined as socially dead. The rituals of widowhood incorporated certain basic features signifying the symbolic rejection/deprivation of the widow's sexuality. The rituals included the imposition of some visible mark to define and highlight this new status. Following the assumption of the new status, the widow was relocated within the household of her dead husband. Unlike the marriage rituals marking the woman's entry into legitimate sexual activity, which are elaborate, the rituals marking the renunciation of the widow's sexuality are simple but always deeply humiliating and traumatic. The most dramatic and visible 'ritual' for Brahmana women is tonsure, or the shaving of the head. The unique practice of tonsure, prevalent among many South Indian and West Indian Brahmana communities, requires some analysis of the notion of widowhood in Brahmanical patriarchy so that we may unfold the cultural meaning of this highly symbolic act. It may be argued that to enforce permanent widowhood upon women the community needs to continuously reiterate its authority over the widow; enforced tonsure is a way of doing that. It is a reiteration by the community of their power to control the widow's sexuality. Meyer Fortes and R. Firth[2] have suggested that symbols, both private and public, constitute a major instrument of power when used directly or indirectly. This is true of tonsure, which was deeply resented by widows and perceived by them to be an indication of their utter powerlessness in the hands of a cruel system, insisted upon by Brahmana men.[3] Here tonsure represents the social aspect of symbolic behaviour, referring to ritual processes by means of which symbolic ideas are acted out in terms of real human interaction. That such actions are always highly formalized and ceremonial is evident in the removal of the hair of widows.

Widowhood is clearly a highly symbolized domain in the experience of upper-caste Hindu society. While there are many elements of the widow's existence that are symbolized, there is an overwhelming concentration on the profound danger represented by the sexuality of the widow. The continued existence of the widow after the death of her husband was to convert what was most valuable to the husband in his lifetime into an awesome threat to his community. The theme that dominates the ceremonies and rituals of widowhood is the sexual death of the widow. And since the upper-caste woman in Brahmanical patriarchy is primarily a vehicle for reproduction, the sexual death of a woman is simultaneously a social death. The customs and rituals mark a social and ideological resolution of the tensions inherent in a conceptualization of widowhood in which the widow continues to exist but is sexually a non-being.

WIFEHOOD, WIDOWHOOD AND *STRISVABHAVA* IN BRAHMANICAL PATRIARCHY

From the evidence of the classical texts it is clear that the upper-caste Hindu widow was an anomaly in traditional Hindu society, since she had no place and no function in the Hindu social order. The death of a woman's husband marked the woman's transition from wife to widow, taking her from a central place in the family to its margins. In order to understand the upper-caste widow's marginal/liminal place, it is thus necessary to look at the wife, who is the obverse of the widow in the Brahmanical texts.

The Wife in Brahmanical Patriarchy

The wife is the most important focus of attention among the different categories of women in the prescriptive texts: symbols, rituals and norms are all concentrated in the person of the wife. A woman is recognized as a person when she is incorporated into her husband—only then does she become a social entity and in that state she is auspicious, a *sumangali*, a *saubhagyavati.* It is therefore not surprising that marriage is the only ritual prescribed for the woman. Together with her husband she performs rituals and procreates a son or many sons.[4] These two acts define her as a social being and for both, the presence of the husband (who makes her complete) is imperative. Outside of the husband, the wife has no recognized existence in Brahmanical patriarchy.

The performance of rituals, and procreation, are acts in which women are perceived as agents or inferior partners through whom men discharge two of their three debts. The three debts are: to the sages, to the gods and to the '*pitr*'. The debt to the sages is discharged through *brahmacharya*, a compulsory stage that precedes marriage; the debt to the gods is discharged by performing *yajnas;* and that to the pitr by reproducing sons.[5] The wife thus helps her husband in discharging two of his three debts, by associating with him in sacrifice and by procreating sons. The role that the wife is assigned in participating in the ritual itself stems from her primary function of procreating sons. Manu states the relationship quite explicitly: 'To be mothers are women created and to be fathers men; religious rites therefore are ordained in the Veda to be performed [by the husband] together with the wife.'[6]

While men discharged their debts and ensured their salvation, women helped men to achieve immortality and heaven through the son, and thus discharged their obligation. The goal of the life of women was thus to get married and procreate sons—in fact, according to the texts, women are created for the sole purpose of procreating sons (*Stripumsa*, V.19).[7] It is not surprising that the *Dharmasutras* permit or, rather, recommend that the husband marry again even when the first wife is living, if she has no son. The sonless wife should not be an obstacle in the fulfilment of the husband's goal.[8] That she was merely the medium through which the husband's goals were achieved, and that she herself had neither personhood nor religious or social goals, is evident from the denial of children (and through sons to immortality) to her in the event of her husband's death.

The rituals at the time of marriage explicitly recognize the crucial place of procreation. This is evident in the Brahmanical texts,[9] and anthropological analyses of the Hindu marriage ceremony repeat the centrality of reproduction in the rituals so evident in the Brahmanical texts. For example, in the crucial *haldi* ceremony that precedes the actual marriage rites, the spouse is smeared with turmeric. According to informants, the effect of the turmeric application is that the body is heated up for sexual intercourse. The source of sexual energy that haldi is believed to create is located unambiguously in women, in which sense they are perceived as active agents in the process of reproduction.[10] Further, the colour most often associated with brides is red: red is the colour of vitality because of its connotation of blood. It is appropriate where something important and life-giving is about to take place. The red *kumkuma* or *sindoora* applied only by married women symbolizes the sexually active or sexually potent female. The bride's red sari and kumkuma together represent the fluids of creation, life, female creative power and, specifically, the capacity to bear children.[11]

It is significant that the symbolism of marriage rites represents women not only as a source of sexual energy, but also as having fertility closely identified with the fertility of nature and possessing qualities that are juxtaposed with other qualities supposedly held by men. However, these are held in such a way as to render them relatively 'wild' and 'disorderly'.[12] A concomitant of the ceremonies is that only in their relations to men as wives and mothers do they become fully cultural or, indeed, fully human.

In handling the concept of wifehood, the prescriptive texts too constantly attempt to resolve the basic contradiction that women represent, between their nature and their function. A demoniac and innately promiscuous nature is ascribed as their lot due to the previous bad *karma* that produces female birth; it must be suppressed in favour of their function as wives.[13] Women are perceived as being caught in a trap caused entirely by their karma; they are the sites of conflict between *strisvabhava*, their innate demoniac nature which is lustful, and *stridharma*, their function as wives.[14]

The innate promiscuity of women requires the legitimate channelization of their sexual energy in a stringently organized system of reproduction, without which the social order would collapse. Thus, to ensure the absorption of the wife's sexual energy, frequent satiation is required, and the husband who does not approach his wife after the purificatory bath following the end of menstrual pollution is to be punished. This is a race case of punishment advocated by the Dharmasutras to an 'erring' husband'.[15] Even so, the innate sinfulness and lustfulness of women can easily lead them to adultery, which is severely punishable by every form of humiliation to be publicly heaped upon the adulterous wife. Surveillance of the wife within marriage is regarded as necessary and its repeatedly recommended in the prescriptive texts.[16]

It was to channelize the overflowing sexual energy of women that early marriages became so crucial in the structure of Brahmancial patriarchy. If a girl did not marry by the time she reached puberty, she would easily and inevitably be led 'astray'. As Selwyn states, an unmarried, menstruating girl eventually becomes an object of 'moral panic'. Such a women, 'untamed by wifehood and motherhood, is...a liability to her kin, her caste, and to society in general'.[17] The Brahmanical textual position is unambiguous in the responsibility it places on the girl's family if she remains unmarried after puberty.[18] The parents and, eldest brother go to hell in a such a situation. If a girl is married after this point, her husband is to be socially excommunicated. According to some texts, the father or guardian incurs the sin of destroying an embryo at each appearance of the menses as long as the girl remains unmarried.[19]

Marriage is thus imperative for women: within it alone can women's innate sinfulness and lustfulness be channelized, and thereafter, through legitimate reproduction, women enable men to discharge their debts to the gods and ancestors and achieve heaven. Through wifehood and motherhood, women discharge their functions in society, acquire personhood and, in this capacity, perform rituals with their husbands as *sahadharminis.* Within marriage, as true followers of stridharma and *pativratadharma*, women can achieve great powers. Through marriage and wifely devotion, the 'biological' woman—a wild, untamed and disorderly entity—can be converted into the 'cultured' woman—a social entity who has vanquished all the demoniac forces within her.[20] Only thus can women overcome the inauspicious marks of female birth and acquire the necessary karma to be reborn as men, preferably *dvija* (twice-born men), entitled to seek the goal of immortal heaven.[21]

The overflowing sexual energy of women, containable and legitimately expressible only in marriage, is regarded as assuming dangerous dimensions when the husband is away. Like the unmarried, menstruating girl, the wife whose husband is absent is an object of moral panic. The didactic Sanskrit and Pali literature abounds in stories of women's licentiousness in the absence of husbands, thus bringing about moral and social disorder.[22] The way the prescriptive texts deal with this situation prefigures the manner in which the sexuality of women in widowhood is handled. All the advice given to the wife to make herself attractive and to invite the sexual attention of her husband is explicitly prohibited in his absence. Her movements are severely curtailed and so too her behaviour.

The contrast between the prescription to the wife while the husband is home and when he is away is telling. The texts, for instance, prescribe a purificatory bath after her menstrual pollution is ended and she is exhorted to make sexual advances to her husband that night.[23] But when the husband is away, the 'chaste' woman—'*sati*'—is expected to forgo perfumes, garlands, collyrium, the chewing of betel and even the use of the teeth-cleaning stick. According to one authority, the face of the wife whose husband is away should look pale and distressed, she should not embellish her body, she should be devoted to the thought of her husband, she should not eat a full meal, and she should emaciate her body.[24] These traditional injunctions were repeated in the eighteenth-century text for women which lays down that the woman whose husband is away 'should abandon playing, adorning her body, attending gatherings and festivals, laughing and going to other people's houses, and even laughing with the mouth open'.[25] These are also the general prohibitions observed by menstruating women and by widows. Such actions are regarded as making a woman attractive[26] and providing occasion for interaction with others, making the wife vulnerable to her own passions, and so must be avoided when the husband is unavailable either because he is prohibited from touching his wife, or is away, or is dead.

The Widow in Brahmanical Patriarchy

As we have noted earlier, the wife who becomes a widow creates an anomalous situation in the Brahmanical prescriptive texts. Since the wife represents the core of womanhood, she is the real focus of attention both in the prescriptive texts and in mythology. The texts concern themselves with converting biological entities into social or cultural entities. Once the ideal of wifehood is achieved, the woman becomes a prototype and model for other women, epitomizing '*sativa*', the wifely power of the chaste woman. It is significant that there is no widow in traditional mythology except Kunti. But even she, although important, is not central to the narrative in the *Mahabharata.*[27] The only woman who comes close to such a position is Savitri, who is doomed to widowhood in the narrative. But the focus of the story is how Savitri fights off her husband's death. By implication, the narrative lays the groundwork for the widely held belief that women who are widowed fall into that state because they bring it upon themselves. To that extent, they are responsible for the death of the husband.

The mythology of chaste wives who predecease their husbands is consistent with the general position in the Brahmanical prescriptive texts that widowhood is solely attributed to *purva karma* and is the punishment for a sinful existence in the past. A true pativrata can never be widowed because she will never leave her husband, not even in death. She will either die before him as a sumangali or will accompany him in death.[28] Indeed, the wifely power of the pativrata lies in the woman's ability to snatch her husband from the jaws of death, as Savitri did with Satyavan; the texts tell us that just as a snake-charmer forcibly draws out the snake from its hole, so too the spiritual power of the pativrata snatches her husband from the messengers of death and reaches heaven with him. On seeing such a pativrata, the messengers of death beat a hasty retreat, knowing that they have been thwarted by her devotion.[29] The ideal type of woman in the Brahmanical texts is one who is imbued with the qualities of a sati. She is a woman whose chastity makes her a living sati and gives her the power to ensure that she dies before her husband. Alternatively, if her husband dies before her, she has the power and will to accompany him in death as a sati and thereby reject widowhood.

This is the background to the religious sanction for sati, the immolation of the wife to overcome widowhood. All the major texts exhort the wife to accompany her husband in death by performing *sahagamana* or *sahamarana.* The husband is to be followed always: like the body by its shadow, like the moon by moonlight, like a thundercloud by lightning. In order to achieve this state, the wife is prepared for such an action right from the time of the marriage vows.[30] There is no doubt that the woman who gladly follows her husband from his house to the cremation ground attains, with every step, the rewards of the horse sacrifice.[31] The woman who rejects widowhood can purify and rescue the most sinful and evil husband. Even the woman who has been a bad wife, who has until then, because of her wicked mind, despised her husband – even she, through the act of dying with her husband, confers merit on herself. The act destroys her earlier sin even if she does it out of anger or fear. This then becomes the scriptural justification for forcing women to burn themselves. It is the ultimate and only effective *prayaschitta* for the bad wife; through it she redeems herself and escapes the future misery that her bad karma would normally have brought her.[32]

Following these arguments, it is clear that according to the ideology of brahmanical patriarchy, if a wife is widowed, she has certainly not been a pativrata, nor vanquished her innate weakness and sinfulness (which her birth as a female entails), nor availed of her last chance for redemption through satihood: in short, she is an outcaste. She is therefore a doubly condemnable creature: to be feared and despised. The widow must thenceforth atone for her sins, for bringing widowhood upon herself. Through bodily mortification and steadfast devotion to her departed lord, she must stringently monitor her sexuality and master the promiscuity that inheres in all women. To enable others to have proof of her virtue, she must occupy the darkest recesses of the house and submit herself to the constant surveillance of the patriarchal gaze, even as it might work through the women of the household, with everyone committed to upholding the notions of family honour inscribed in the gender and caste codes.[33]

The Widow in Prescriptive Texts

Since a woman becomes a social entity only when, as a wife, she is united with her husband, the death of the husband represents the cessation of her social existence and the end of her personhood. Once the husband dies, the wife's sexuality, which within marriage served familial and social goals, is of no use to the community. The death of the husband thus marks a dramatic shift in the perception of the community towards the woman. Even more than the unmarried, menstruating girl or the nubile wife whose husband is away, the widow is an object of real moral panic. While the sexuality of these other categories can be held in abeyance, the sexuality of the widow cannot: she must therefore be completely de-sexed. And because this is not easy to achieve, the widow must be represented as the most repugnant and despicable of characters. Feared and hated, she must henceforth be confined to 'dark spaces' where she is inaccessible.

The prescriptive texts lay down stringent codes of behaviour in order to ensure that the widow's sexuality is repressed, mastered or forcibly contained. These prescriptions are outlined in all the major texts beginning with Manu, until which time the texts had recognized the possibility of redeploying the sexuality of the widow after a specified period of celibacy and mourning. The institution of '*niyoga*', or levirate unions, is mentioned in the *Rgveda* and survived into the first millennium AD. However, the *Dharmasutra* literature indicates that the practice was conditional upon the absence of a son from the woman's first husband, and had to have the sanction of the elders in the family.[34] Many condemned the practice, and upheld the norms of a celibate and perpetual widowhood. Following Manu, the emergence of the norm of celibacy became the basis for all the individual prescriptions: the widow must give up all ornaments, observe fasts, emaciate her body and remain steadfastly loyal to her dead husband.[35]

The *vriddha Harita* is more explicit about the marked nature of the widow's appearance and behaviour. 'She should give up chewing betel-nut, wearing perfumes, flower, ornaments, and dyed clothes, taking food from a vessel of bronze, taking two meals a day, applying colloyrium to the eyes; she should wear only a white garments, curb her senses and anger, and sleep on the ground.'[36]

The prescriptive texts provide only one models for the widow who continues to live after her husband. and that is the model of the ascetic widow. This model closely corresponds to two categories of males in the Brahminical texts who, like the widow, must transcend or renounce their sexuality: the '*brahmacharya*' and the *'sannyasi'*.[37] The first is a male who has not yet entered an active sexual phase, and the second is a male who has renounced sexual life after completing his duties as a householder and begotten sons, and is therefore free to pursue his salvation goals.[38] For both these categories, celibacy is compulsory and underpins all the codes to be followed. Indeed, the widow's way of life is specially called the renouncer's life or, in the widest sense, a celibate life. But there is a crucial difference because the widow cannot leave home as a true renunciate.[39] Unlike the true '*pravratiya*', she has no individual salvation goals apart from those of her dead husband. The widow's asceticism and, bearing no personal results equivalent to that of the male ascetic, that is, cessation of rebirth or '*moksha*', is nevertheless necessary in order to ensure the peace of mind and happiness of her dead lord. Devotion and loyalty to one's husband remains the key point of a widow's life; the widow's asceticism celibacy are thus negative, not positive. Her 'stridharma' continues in widowhood and requires her to master her sexuality. it will ensure her salvation by ensuring her husband's salvation, otherwise he will descend to hell.[40] For this reason, the widow's celibacy is not transient but must last as long as she lives. Thus, although there is a certain similarity between the asceticism of the widow and that of the renouncer, the goals are so distinct that the widow is not an ascetic; the transformative space available to women within the ascetic tradition[41] is denied to the widow.[42]

In brief, the prescriptive texts clearly outline only two models of widowhood: that of the of the dying sati who mounts the pyre, rejects widowhood and proves herself to the best follower of 'stridharma'; and that of the living sati who becomes an ascetic within the home, remaining a celibate, steadfastly devoted to her husband till she dies. There is no third model, certainly not of the true renunciate, at least in the brahmanical prescriptive texts.

The two models—the dying sati who mounts the pyre and the living sati who mortifies the body—are repeated through the centuries in all the later texts of the brahmanical tradition. Of the two, the first remained the more valued ideal for a variety of reasons. The devotion of the dying sati who mounted the pyre and the merits such an action brought to her relatives were no doubt greater than those of the ascetic widow. At the same time, it must be remembered that the dying sati also solved the problem of the sexually active women whose sexuality must not be expressed. The hazard of the sexually active widow forced in to celibacy were ever-present in the texts.[43]

In the eighteenth century, Tryambaka took an unambiguous position on the issue of the sati versus the ascetic widow. The practice of dying with the husband was commended for all women. But if, for some reason, the wife did not follow her husband, then Tryambaka exhorts that her virtue must be protected, for, as he puts it, if her virtue is lost the woman falls down into hell. More important, the loss of her virtue causes her husband to fall down from heaven to hell.[44] The rewards for good behaviour are both material and spiritual. The ascetic widow gains heaven for herself and her husband. Further, she ensures rebirth as a high-status man for herself. Only the chaste widow is entitled to maintenance or the enjoyment of property during her lifetime. According to Katyayana, 'A sonless widow, preserving the bed of her husband unsullied and being self-controlled, should enjoy her husband's property till her death.'[45] (This position was upheld in judgements in the eighteenth and nineteenth centuries.[46])

The limited and conditional rewards, one necessary for her survival and the other to secure an unseeable future, go along with an otherwise humiliating existence. While the rules minutely regulate the widow's conduct, it is clear from references that the lawgivers could not effectively restrain men from violating the injunctions regarding strict celibacy for widows. The *Adi Parva* (of the *Mahabharata*) recognizes that, 'just as birds flock to a piece of flesh left on the ground, so all men try to seduce a woman whose husband is dead'.[47] Taken together, the inherent sinfulness of women, their lustfulness and the predatory character of men required the segregation, isolation and marking of the widow.

It is in the context of the above discussion that the rites and customs associated with widowhood acquire meaning. These rites and customs were prevalent in different degrees in the case of most widows, but were highly concentrated in the person of the high-caste Hindu widow and included the rite of tonsure. Control over female sexuality was almost obsessively applied among high-caste women because the danger to the structure of brahmanical patriarchy was great in their case. The reproduction of the hierarchical caste order with its horror of miscegeny subverting the entire edifice necessitated such stringent control. Unlike the lower-caste woman, the high-caste woman did not labour outside the home or participate in primary production. She was regarded solely as a receptacle through whom reproduction could take place. The death of the husband of the high-caste woman and the consequent cessation of her reproductive potential created a dangerous situation. The anxiety about monitoring her sexuality doubled; while, as we have seen, the wife's sexuality had to be channelized, the widow's sexuality had to be abruptly terminated. The rites reflect the dramatic transition from one stage to another: from a controlled and channelized sexual life and personhood, to sexual death and social obliteration.

THE SYMBOLIC STRUCTURE OF WIDOWHOOD

The passage of a woman from the position of a wife and sahadharmini to that of a widow is marked by various rites. These rites are not the subject of sustained attention in the early sacred texts, as the focus of attention was concentrated on the male corpse. However, the texts do indicate that soon after the death of the husband, the appearance of the widow was distinctly marked off from other women, as well as from those customs or symbols that were associated with the marriage of a woman. These included the 'kumkuma', the red mark on the forehead, the 'sindoora' applied in the parting of the hair in certain parts of India, and the use of 'haldi', among other banned items. These items, as we have noted before, are associated with sexuality and reproduction. Haldi, for example, has a strong relationship with fertility and prosperity, and is considered so auspicious and powerful that 'naturally', widows could not be allowed to use it.[48]

Other customs not specifically mentioned in the texts are also widely prevalent, such as the breaking of glass bangles and the breaking of the *'mangalsutra'*, the sign of a married woman in many parts of India.[49] These acts are performed with a degree of violence that adds to the humiliation the widow must undergo for the rest of her life, and which she begins to experience immediately after the death of her husband. Two other markers of widowhood are the white, ochre or occasionally maroon, coarse garment prescribed for widows, and, among the high castes in southern and western India, the tonsured head. The colour codes of red and white are systematically sustained in the wife/widow opposition. Whereas red symbolizes fertility and sexuality, white symbolizes asexuality. In place of the red kumkuma which is banned for widows, it is customary for them to use '*vibhuti*', or ash, to mark their foreheads. The white or ochre sari symbolizes purity, coolness and the asexuality of the non-bride, more pertinently, the renouncer. White is also the colour of death; the 'vibhuti' or white ash is associated with the funeral pyre,[50] and the exclusive use of this colour by widows among women indicates their continued association with asexuality and death.[51]

The ritual of the tonsure marks a more extreme resolution of the asexuality of the widow. It is significant that there are no references to the tonsure of widows in the early prescriptive texts. On the other hand, these texts rule that the widow should not adorn her hair with flowers and must keep it bound; so it is obvious that tonsure was not prescribed initially and certainly not for all castes. There is every possibility that widows of royal families kept their hair unbound during the period of pollution and mourning. Unbound hair appears frequently as the sign of widowhood in the *Mahabharata.* When Draupadi kept her hair unbound for twelve years she was symbolically proclaiming a state of widowhood and mourning.[52]

As a custom, the tonsured head appears to have been taken over from a very early practice among the Tamils. The *Purananuru*, a second-century AD text, portrays widows as subject to many restraints: they did not wear ornaments, slept on beds of stone and caked their shaved heads with mud.[53] The custom is mentioned in Sanskrit texts for the first time in the *Madanaparijata*, a commentary on the *Skandapurana* written in the fourteenth century.[54] The text states that the widow, like the son of the deceased, had to shave her head. Up to this point in the account, the widow is depicted as sharing pollution or mourning along with her sons.[55] However, the text further states that widows are required to tonsure themselves continually at periodic intervals till their death.[56] The eighteenth-century Tanjore text, the *Stridharmapaddhati* of Tryambakayajvan, argues that the rules prescribing shaving of the head applied only to Brahmana widows and that women of other castes kept their hair.[57] In eighteenth-century Maharashtra, the state enforced it in the case of Brahmana widows,[58] and the custom was widespread among Brahmana widows in Maharashtra, Tamil Nadu and Karnataka.

The notion that both sin and pollution lodge in the hair appears to be widespread; it is, for example, a ubiquitously held belief among Hindus and has been documented in the case of the Hindus of Banaras.[59] It is for this reason that funeral rituals require that on the last day the hair is shaved off, thus ensuring the removal of the pollution. Normally, on more everyday occasions of pollution, the ritual washing of the hair is considered enough. However, death pollution for the upper castes requires more effective forms of ending the pollution (as in the shaving of the head).[60] In the case of widows, however, the requirement of periodic shaving must necessarily have connotations other than mere death pollution.

Anthropological evidence provides us with some clues to the relationship between hair, pollution and sex. Paul Hershman's field observations of hair-grooming practices in Punjab show that such practices are particularly important in the case of women.[61] A similar notion of pollution is prevalent even where tonsure is practised. It was enforced by the popular belief that if the widow did not shave her head, every drop of water that fell on her hair polluted the husband's soul as many times as the number of hairs on her head.[62] Hair is thus a major marker of the state of pollution, or purity and auspiciousness, and of the possible shift from one to the other, especially in the case of women.

In this context of the symbolism regarding hair, it is notable that of all the parts of the body, hair has the most mystical association. There is hardly a culture in which hair is not, for males, a symbol of power, manliness, freedom. It is the seat of strength in many myths and cultures, the most well-known being the case of Samson. It is also held to have fertilizing powers, as evident from Greek myths. At puberty the hair, already the seat of strength, is considered to be enhanced and containing a double portion of vital energy, since at that point it is an outward manifestation of the newly acquired power of reproducing the species. Abundant hair is a sign of vigorous sexual energy, idealized as the essence of feminine beauty, but indicative also of the wantonness of women.[63] Since abundant hair is a symbol of life-power, the way one handles it is a marker of what one does with this life-power. The grooming or exhibition of hair, for example, has a pronounced erotic element in Melanesia.[64] A shorn head is, conversely, symbolic of the loss of power and freedom, even of castration.

While Berg has analysed the unconscious meaning of an individual community's attitude towards hair, Leach[65] and Obeyesekere[66] have explored the symbolic structure of hair and its relationship to sexuality in the context of renunciation, asceticism and sexual restraint. Both argue that symbols have meanings at different levels and that, apart from their personal meaning for individuals and groups, they have a socio-cultural message which is public. Leach argues that while the private has indeterminate meaning, the essence of public symbolic behaviour is that it is a means of communication in which the actor and the audience share a common language—a symbolic language; every member of a certain culture will attribute the same meaning to any particular item of culturally defined symbols.[67] Leach and Obeyesekere thus contest Berg on the unconscious symbolism of hair. On the basis of anthropological evidence from South Asia, they argue that hair behaviour embraces a widely understood set of conscious sexual symbolizations. It is because of this that hair plays such an important part in rites of passage involving the formal transfer of a person from one social–sexual status to another.[68]

The tonsured head, both in the case of men and widows, is clearly a public symbol—one that is recreated each time upon an individual. It is also part of a larger symbolic set in which the tonsured head, the half-shaven head of the Brahmanas and the matted hair of the ascetic have different but related meanings; they are all linked within a unit of specific cultural meanings attributed to hair and sexual behaviour.

In the case of the shaven head, Obeysekere and Leach accept Berg's analysis of the unconscious meaning of hair as symbolic castration. Leach argues further that allowing the dishevelled state is an ascetic repudiation of the very existence of sex. Referring to the practice of keeping a young girl's hair short in Assam and Burma, whereas married women wear their hair long, he suggests that short-haired women are those whose sexuality is under restraint.[69] Similarly, the elaborate half-shaved, half-haired head-grooming of the Brahmana indicates the simultaneous control of sexuality and the legitimate raising of off-spring. In the symbolic system of Brahmanism, the tuft means sexual restraint, matted hair means total detachment from sexual passions, and the shaven head means celibacy. At least in South Asia, then, sex behaviour and hair behaviour are consciously associated from the start.[70]

Obeyesekere argues strongly for a sharp distinction between the shaven head and matted hair which, according to him, are not interchangeable, as their meaning is not confined to chastity alone. It is only the shaven head that implies castration, although it implies chastity and renunciation at the same time. The difference between the shaven head of the Buddhist monk and the matted-haired ascetic is indicative of the gradations within restraint in sexual behaviour. In the case of the celibacy of the monk, sexual passion must be eliminated, not just held in abeyance, as in the Shiva mythology—the archetype of the symbolism of matted hair. The biologically obvious way for the complete elimination of sexual passion is castration. Coming close to that is expressing it indirectly and symbolically, through a non-literal interpretation, as tonsure. Obeyesekere concludes that the primarily psychogenetic meaning of the shaven head is castration, its further cultural meaning is chastity and its extended interpersonal meaning is renunciation. While all three meanings are contained within the act of tonsure for widows, the most important level of meaning is that of castration.[71]

The tonsure of the widow, with its attendant meanings of castration, chastity and sexual death, was, at the same time, a visible marker of the widow's entry into a state of social death. For the upper-caste widow, sexual death was social death, as there was no other role assigned to her apart from that of reproduction. Such an ideology entailed the enforcement of grim conditions upon the widow's existence. Symbols and rituals of marriage and widowhood, along with material arrangements affecting widows, were linked together to form a structure that governed the lives of upper-caste widows, which survived into the nineteenth and twentieth centuries.[72] This structure had a counter, but complementary, set of relations that applied to lower-caste widows, as the field-based studies analysed below demonstrate.

MATERIAL RELATIONS AND THE IDEOLOGY OF WIDOWHOOD: TWO CASE STUDIES

Widowhood in a South Indian Brahmanical Community

Anthropological analysis of the belief structure of a Brahmana community with regard to gender relations provides a case study about latent ideas on widowhood among havik Brahmanas in the Malnad area of south India.[73] The study uncovers complex emotions of fear and guilt located within a structure of power in which men wield total authority over women who are economically completely dependent upon, and subordinated to them, in every way; the most vulnerable section among women are widows. The study suggests that those who wield power over others in real life invert the actual relations in their belief system, and portray as malicious and dangerous the very people over whom they wield power, as in the case of havik Brahmana men and havik Brahmana widows. At the same time, the study shows that such beliefs are unique to havik Brahmana society, and are absent among those communities in which gender relations are relatively less authoritarian and women have relatively higher status within their caste than do havik women.

It is believed by havik Brahmanas that widows, who occupy the lowest status position, poison others at random with a substance obtained secretly by them from a strange reptile. Widows without male issue are particularly suspects. The victim is said to develop an incurable stomach ailment leading to a distended stomach. In young women, the symptoms approximate to a pregnancy; treatment is not usually secured till it is too late. A number of havik Brahmana informants hold that widows poison others to ensure that in their next incarnation they will have many sons and will predecease their husbands.[74] The implication seems to be that Brahmana widows are unhappy in this life and that many of them perform a harmful act in order to be happier in their next life. What is significant is that the alleged victims are not selected for purposes of revenge or hatred; the widows act not against someone but for themselves, to secure a different and better life in the future than the one in which they have been widowed and subjected to infinite misery.

Havik Brahmanas occupy the highest position in society in the villages where they reside, and derive their livelihood from the possession of small areca-nut plantations and from land that they lease to the agricultural castes. Since havik Brahmanas never accept food from any other caste, their poisoners have to be members of their own caste. Only widows are believed by the havik to have indulged in this practice at some time or the other. The deep-seated belief may be interpreted as representing the destructive potentialities of havik

Brahmana widows. According to Harper, the fear itself can only be explained in the context of the havik social structure, especially its gender relations.[75]

All women, particularly widows, are feared by havik men. Women are a potent source of pollution for havik men, for whom ritual defilement is a major concern. Menstruating women and women who have recently given birth to a child—in other words, women in states that emphasize their 'femaleness'—must be segregated. Even inadvertent contact with them causes much greater ritual pollution than does contact with a member of the untouchable castes. In a state of ritual impurity women can cause untold harm to their families; should an impure woman accidentally contaminate a god or a deity, it may cause illness or even death to members of her family.[76]

At a more general level, all women are inherently dangerous because they are sexually passionate and demanding: as temptresses of the flesh, they sap male vitality and stand between brahmana men and their goals of salvation. In the context of everyday relations, women are believed to disrupt fraternal solidarity, a cherished ideal among havik Brahmana men but hardly ever actualized in real life, and not because of women: this is a stereotype which, in Harper's view, has no bearing on the breakup of the fraternal household.[77] But it is brahmana widows who are most feared amongst women. The very sight of the widow is inauspicious, so inauspicious that if sighted at the start of an auspicious venture, the venture must be postponed; even dreaming of a widow augurs ill. Further, in the system of religious beliefs all female deities are, in general, more dangerous and malicious than their male counterparts. Mariamma, the goddess of smallpox and the deity who has the highest malevolence potential, is in local mythology represented as a Brahmana widow. It is of utmost significance that according to the narrative she slew her husband in a fit of rage when she discovered that she had been deceived by him. Mariamma thus became a widow by murdering her own husband. This is clearly linked to a deeply held belief in brahmanical society that should a husband predecease his wife it is somehow, in some mystical way, the wife's fault.[78]

The belief in poisoning by widows is thus part of a more complex constellation of ideas around the theme of fear of women, but particularly widows. In the havik Brahmana household, the authority of males over females is absolute. At marriage, performed ideally before puberty, authority over the bride is completely transferred from her natal family to her husband's family. Post-marital residence is virilocal for women and patrilocal for men; women are excluded from inheritance and, except for certain types of jewellery, they do not own property.[79]

Divorce is prohibited, polygamy is permitted but rare, widows must never remarry, widowers are expected to remarry and often do. Since, at marriage, a woman is transferred from one patrilineage to another, her natal kinsmen have no jural control over how she is treated. A mistreated daughter-in-law (who, as a bride, occupies a position of low status and power within her new house, where the male kinsmen have the right to discipline her severely) should not complain to her natal kinsmen because this would only cause them grief about a situation over which they have no control. The only recourse she has is to bring dishonour upon her husband's family through suicide. It is not surprising, then, that all havik families prefer to marry their daughters to less wealthy families in order to maximize their influence over their girls' new social environment.[80]

Havik women labour only within the household, unlike women of nearly all other castes in the region, who perform agricultural labour. Also, they do not handle financial matters. Havik males characterize women as weak-willed, superstitious and constantly in need of male protection. Prohibited from possessing sacred religious knowledge, they are characterized as having 'shudra minds'.[81] The perception of havik men about the subordination of women and girls expresses itself in a dual manner: positively with regard to comprehension and behaviour towards daughters, and negatively when it constructs widows as malevolent.

Havik men hold deeply ambivalent and contradictory attitudes towards women. Mothers are revered, sisters and particularly daughters are regarded as dependents towards whom there is much affection. Harper argues that the havik male's fear of women is linked to guilt about the subordinate status of females compared to males. This recognition of status difference accounts for the compensatory behaviour exhibited towards daughters—the expressed sentiment is that because daughters may suffer after marriage, they must be made as happy as possible before the event.[82] In the value system of the male havik, there is thus a great disparity between the attitudes expressed towards wives and women in general, and towards close agnatic kinswomen.

The fear about wives in particular is evident also in the way in which every structural mechanism, ideological and organizational, is used to prevent women from uniting in opposition to the male dominance within the marital household. Women from the same patriarchal family are barred from marriage into one household; indeed, brothers should not marry girls even from the same village. These conventions prevent sisters, female patrilateral parallel cousins and childhood friends from residing together in the same house after marriage. The bride's isolation in the new house must be complete for the subordination to be effective. The life-cycle of women, however, has a certain progression even within the husband's family. After a period of trial and tribulation occupying the lowest position in her husband's family, a woman may, and often does, gain in respect, especially if and when she produces a son. She may ultimately become a mistress in her own house and a mother-in-law with power over her daughters-in-law. Time thus appears to be in her favour.[83]

But, as Harper points out, if she is widowed, especially without having borne a son, even time cannot lift her out of her oppressive situation. She will be permanently deprived of even the little she had as a wife—a husband and children. Forced to wear a distinctive garment and tonsure her head to symbolize her degraded status, she is publicly defeminized. More offensive than anything else, the widow is never again referred to as 'she' but, instead, by the neuter 'it'. The widow is ridiculed and is commonly the butt of jokes. She is called a '*prani*', an animal.[84] A symbol of inauspiciousness, she can no longer participate in the domestic ceremonies that form a part of women's culture. Everyone concedes that the life of the widow is one of unalleviated misery. But this does not merit real sympathy. The fate that befalls a widow is believed to be deserved. Expected to pray daily that she should predecease her husband, a woman is considered to be at fault if widowed. 'It ate up its husband', is what people would say.[85] Any move up or relatively high status she might have gained through time is instantly diminished. That havik society would regard widows to be sufficiently bitter and resentful to harm others in order to escape the sufferings (future) entailed by widowhood, is thus entirely 'rational'.

In the larger structure of relations governing caste, gender, widowhood and belief systems, there is a crucial but inverse connection between the widow's real powerlessness and her imagined power to strike back. The subordinated status of the woman as widow is expected to breed the desire for revenge. The overt submission of the widowed woman is perceived as a mask which hides her suppressed anger and makes her infinitely dangerous, in some cases even bloodthirsty.

It is notable that the structure of ideas with regard to widowhood among Brahmanas grows out of the material and social position of widows in high-caste society. In marked contrast, widowhood is not pitiable, nor are widows regarded as particularly dangerous, among the different categories of women in the lower castes. Widowhood in non-brahmanical society is not marked by the kind of dramatic break in the life of a woman as in high-caste society: it is a different state, but the structural opposition between wife and widow does not exist. Widowhood is organisable in the case of the non-Brahmana castes along the axes of production and reproduction, rather than reproduction alone. Widows from these castes are thus incorporated in the social and economic order. This is strikingly evident if we look at the labouring castes who work for the havik Brahmanas in the Malnad region. Post-marital residence in the case of the labouring castes is determined by individual economic factors, and, sometimes, may even be in villages where neither the man nor the wife has close ties but where work is available. Extended families are not glorified among the shudras as among the haviks. Among untouchables, the extended family is almost never found. Post-puberty marriages are the norm and divorce may be initiated by either party. Family authority is more equally divided between the husband and the wife: women earn and handle family finances. Menstrual taboos are less rigorous, and payment of bride price is frequent.

Shudra and untouchable widows do not shave their heads, nor are they set apart by distinctive dress, referred to as animals or excluded from auspicious ceremonies. In these castes, widows and divorcees may, and do, contract second marriages. The status of a woman who enters into a secondary marriage is only slightly less than that of a virgin bride. It is significant that non-Brahmana widows in the Malnad region are absorbed into productive and reproductive activities (if they belong to such an age-group); they are not considered dangerous or inauspicious; women's status is relatively higher than is the case with havik women and, unlike the latter, they are not considered dangerous or inauspicious.[86]

Widowhood among Low-Caste Labouring Groups in North India

The manner in which material and social factors differentially organize conceptions of widowhood is examined and analysed at length by Pauline Kolenda in the context of a north Indian village. Kolenda's essay is comparative with regard to region, and explores the connection between present practice and historical texts which make references to widowhood, the levirate and remarriage of women.

Kolenda examines widowhood among high-caste Rajputs and low-caste chuhras in a north Indian village.[87] Drawing from other anthropological works, especially on south India, she notices that widowhood as well as the status of women in the high castes are related, among other things, to control over property inherited by men, which may foster the degradation of women in order to exclude them from a share in the inheritance. Ideologically, this is portrayed as women being 'assimilated' to their husbands and becoming one flesh with them. In contrast, the lower-caste women are not 'assimilated' to their husbands in marriage but remain equal and opposite to them. An important factor responsible for the differences between high and low castes is the contrast between high castes as landowners and low castes as wage earners. There is here an equality between adult son and father, and between husband and wife, which comes from their separate and more or less equal status as wage earners. The lower-caste woman's economic role accounts for her more equal rights both in her marital and natal homes. Thus, the difference between high-caste and low-caste women is caused by differences in relation to production.[88]

Kolenda carries forward the analysis of gender, caste and the economy with a close look at widowhood, but particularly relating it to enforced widowmating among the low castes. To begin with, the chuhras do not necessarily follow patrilocal residence. There is much flux in the population as families change residence: chuhra families may settle in the wife's village, in other villages where one might find kin, or just anywhere that work is available. Lack of land has resulted in the chuhras being more mobile and less anchored to locality than the high-caste Rajputs in the area. Because of their poverty, chuhra women work outside the home: it is they who do the '*jajmani*' work. A chuhra widow can support herself and her children as long as she can continue the jajmani work. There is no dramatic change in the chuhra widow's lifestyle or standard of living.[89]

The Rajput widow, on the other hand, is stripped of her jewels, is allowed to remain on her dead husband's property contingent only on 'good' behaviour, and is forbidden to marry again. Only one sexual partner is envisaged for a Rajput woman during her lifetime, and that is her husband. To him she is given in sacred ceremony, with community sanction and a dowry. A woman, along with her family, is made impure by any subsequent sexual relationships she might have. An adulterous Rajput wife or widow can be cast out and even executed. Sati is an ideal, and worshipping at a sati shrine is the first ceremony in the marriage of every Rajput woman.[90]

The main contrast between Rajput and chuhra women is with regard to work, marriage and widow-mating. All chuhra women, along with other shudra or untouchable castes, can remarry, and the practice of levirate is common among these castes. In the structure of ideas, widow remarriage is one of the key defining practices that constitute the impurity of low castes. But, significantly, as has been documented elsewhere, low castes were expected to conform to the custom.[91] The insistence on such a practice was in part a reinforcement of closely guarded upper-caste privileges, including enforced widowhood, which ensured higher ritual status for them. But it was also a means by which the upper castes manipulated and controlled the demographic structure of all castes—high and low. Patriarchal formulations were closely tied to caste and class formation.

That caste, class and patriarchy worked together to organize the sexuality of all women is evident from widow-mating practices among the chuhras. Chuhra widows of child-bearing age are expected to re-mate. Only the widow with grown children, that is, well past the child-bearing age, is permitted to remain unmated, if she makes a declaration to the community to be a celibate.[92] This is not a recognition of the sexual needs of widows, but an arrangement to utilize the productive and reproductive labour of widows. While maintaining land structures intact, as among agricultural castes such as the Jats (who were restricted to levirate widow marriage), such an arrangement would ensure the full productive potential of a woman to ensure maximal replenishing of the labouring and servicing castes.

Key elements in chuhra widow-mating are a hierarchy of mating patterns according to the distance of the second mate to the dead husband, and a set of rules for the disposal of the widow's sexuality. The power to dispose of a widow's sexuality lies with the patrifraternal contingent of her husband's paternal family. The preferred mate to whom the widow will be assigned is the dead husband's unmarried younger brother. If there is no unmarried younger brother, she may be assigned to a married brother with his, his wife's, the widow's and the widow's father's consent. She may be also given to a patrilateral parallel cousin or a matrilateral cross-cousin of the dead husband, but here too, her consent as well as that of her father are required. In the case of the latter, the new mate must pay for her. Both the patrilateral parallel cousin and matrilateral cross-cousin have the right to sell her once she has mated with them. A married woman or a widow who commits adultery can also be sold. Once a woman is sold, she may be re-sold repeatedly.[93]

The hierarchy of marriage types are: (1) marriage by '*pheras*' (the first marriage); (2) secondary marriage to husband's brother; (3) secondary marriage to husband's patrilateral parallel cousin; (4) being sold to a man who is a matri-lateral cross-cousin of the husband; and (5) being sold to a stranger.[94]

It is evident from the above summary that, despite the relative economic independence and security of the chuhra woman, it does not make her 'close to equal to men',[95] as Kolenda establishes so decisively: the men can pressure her to take another mate, and they can even sell her so that she is separated from her kin. Her inferiority is established through the mating rules, but more so through rules regarding the buying and selling of widows. Control over the sexuality and labour of the widow lies not with the widow but in the hands of the husband's family. Kolenda's analysis of chuhra widow-mating customs also considers the relationship of such practices to textual evidence; she suggests that the customs among the low castes are not an aberration accountable to unsanskritic patterns, but, rather, are an archaic survival of prevalent mating patterns before the brahmanical codes proceeded to lay down definite and distinctive sexual codes for different categories of women.[96] While they prescribed ascetic widowhood, defeminization and the sexual death of the upper-caste widow, and thereby raised the status of the entire caste in relation to others, they characterized widow-mating, conceptualized in the practice of *niyoga* (the traditional term of levirate) as fit only for 'cattle' and shudras.[97] It then became a crucial index of caste status in a deeply hierarchical order. The reproductive practices of the labouring classes were simultaneously castigated and utilized; multiplying cattle and those who must labour was consistent with the brahmanical caste order. Patriarchal formulations for women of the high castes and women of the low castes were structurally integrated into the ideology and material relations of the caste system. The high castes were required to restrict reproduction so that there was no pressure on the resources in their control. Equally, since they did not labour, the increased reproduction of the labouring classes would expand the potential to exploit resources under the control of the upper castes. Chuhra widows, like all low-caste widows, were socially subordinated but did not face sexual death (or social death) at the death of their first husbands; the chuhra widow was the structural opposite of the Brahmana or Rajput widow who faced sexual and social death when her husband died. While enforced widowhood was the rule among the high castes, enforced cohabitation may be said to have been the rule for widows of the lowest castes.

The apparent difference in widow marriage and widow-mating patterns between high castes and low castes may lead to the conclusion that there were different patriarchies according to the respective caste status. This is only partly true; it needs to be stressed that these differences were arranged within a larger. single, conceptual and material organizational structure. Within the larger rubric of a Brahrnanical patriarchy, caste, gender, land control and demography were tied together inexorably both conceptually and in terms of material and social arrangements.

This paper was first presented at a conference on 'Widows in India' held in March 1994 at the Institute of Management, Bangalore. I am grateful to Patricia Uberoi for comments on an earlier draft, as well as for drawing my attention to certain anthropological writings on the symbolism associated with hair. I am also indebted to Gerda Lerner for extended discussions on gender which have helped to shape some of the arguments in this paper.

NOTES

1. I have made a free and associational use of this term, borrowing from Orlando Patterson's classic work on slavery. Although the upper-class widow was far removed from the slave—someone who was uprooted from family and alienated from her/his culture—I find the concept of social death useful in capturing the peculiar status of the widow: that of a non-being. The social death of the widow makes her permanently into a non-being, an indelibly defective state that weighs endlessly upon her destiny, someone who can never be brought to life again. See Patterson, *Slavery and Social Death*, p. 38.
2. Cited in ibid., p. 37.
3. *Inamdar et al., Position of Widows.*
4. Kane, *History of the Dharmashastras*, Vol. II, Part I, pp. 428–29.
5. Ibid., p. 560.
6. *Manu Dharmashastra,* IX.96.
7. Narada, *Stripumsa,* V.19, cited in Kane, *History of the Dharmashastras*, p. 561. As early as the *Shatapatha Brahmana*, it is said that a sonless wife is possessed with nirrti, ill-luck or destruction.
8. *Apastamba Dharmasutra*, 11.5; 11.12–13.
9. According to the marriage rules of the *Asvalayana Gryhasutra*, the husband leads the wife thrice round the fire and the water jar (a symbol of fertility), keeping their right sides turned towards it, and murmurs, 'I am heaven thou art the earth. I am '*saman*' thou art the *'rk'* Let us both marry here. Let us beget offspring.' (Kane, *History of the Dharmashastra*, pp. 528–30).

   Later, when the bride enters her husband's home, the husband chants, 'Here may happiness increase to you through offspring.' Then he kindles the nuptial fire and, as his wife is seated on a bull's hide, he makes oblations, chanting, 'May Prajapati create offspring to us.' As the bride enters her husband's house she breaks her silence and says, 'May my husband live and may I secure offspring.' (Ibid., p. 530.)

   The rites that relate to the *'garbhdanam'* or the '*chaturthikarma'* ceremony performed before the marriage are consummated following the first menstruation of the girl. After the wife has bathed, her husband makes her pound rice, which is then boiled and eaten. Then the husband fills a water jar and sprinkles the wife thrice with the water, and repeats certain *mantras*: 'May Vishnu ready your parts, may Tvasta frame your beauty, may Prajapati sprinkle and may Dhata implant an embryo unto you. May the Asvins plant in thee an embryo. As the earth has fire inside it, as heaven has India inside it, so I plant a garbha in thee.' *Brihadaranyaka Upanishaa* (translated by Max Mueller), V.1413. 19–22.

In the rite of the *chaturthikarma*, three nights after marriage the husband performs certain acts and murmurs, 'into thy breath I put the sperm, may the male embryo enter the womb as an arrow into the quiver, may a man be born here, a son after ten months'. (Kane, *History of the Dharmashastras*, pp. 202–03.)

10. Selwyn, 'Images of Reproduction', p. 684.
11. Fuller and Logan, 'Navaratri Festival in Madurai'.
12. Selwyn, 'Images of Reproduction', p. 687.
13. Leslie *Perfect Wife*, pp. 248, 266.
14. See 'Conceptualizing Brahmanical Patriarchy' in this volume, pp. 147–48.
15. *Apastamba Dharmashastra,* I. 10, 28, 19.
16. Chakravarti, 'Conceptualizing Brahmanical Patriarchy'.
17. Selwyn, 'Image of Reproduction', p. 688.
18. According to Parasara, an unmarried girl beyond the age of ten is described as a *rajasvala* (a menstruating women). If the father has not given a girl in marriage by the time she is twelve, his 'pitr' (ancestors) have to drink her monthly discharge. (Kane, *History of the Dharmashastras*, p. 444.)
19. Ibid., p. 442.
20. In one of the rituals at the time of marriage the husband says to the wife, 'Be firm like a stone, overcome the enemies, trample down the foes.' (Ibid., p. 528)
21. Leslie *Perfect wife*, pp. 266–72.
22. Chakravarti, 'Conceptualizing Brahmanical Patriarchy', pp. 145–53.
23. The *Agni Purana* says, 'anointed with unguents of ground turmeric and saffron, wearing bright garments, thinking only of her husband, beautifully ornamented, she goes to bed' (Kane, *Histiry of the Dharmashastras*, p. 565).
24. Ibid., p. 566.
25. Leslie, *Perfect Wife,* p. 291.
26. Ibid., p. 97.
27. Kunti was the senior wife of King Pandu and mother of the Pandavas. Kunti's wife dowed status is not important in the *mahabharata*. The significant aspects of kunti's life are: first, her power to conceive through invoking the gods; second, the conception of Karna before her marriage to pandu and the consequent abandonment of karna which causes her much anguish, particular when great war takes place, since Karna fights on the side of the kauravas and against her other sons; and third, her important role as mother of the pandavas. For an insightful interpretation of Kunti, see Karve, *Yuganta*, pp. 37–55.
28. A *Pativrata*, for instance, is defined by Brihaspati as one who is emaciated when her husband is away on a journey and who dies on the death of her husband. Leslie, *Perfect Wife*, pp. 293–94.
29. Ibid.
30. According to Tryambaka's *Stridharmapaddhati*, the Brahmana priests should recite the words, 'may you be the one who accompanies your husband always, when he is alive and even when he is dead'. According to the same text, there are great rewards in store for the pious sati: 'if when her husband has died a women ascends with him into the fire she is glorified in heaven, as one whose conduct is equal to that of Arundhati'. Leslie, *Perfect Wife*, pp. 293–94.
31. Ibid., p. 292.
32. Ibid., p. 295.
33. *Chtkravari* 'Social Pariahs and Domestic Drudges'.
34. Kane, *History of the Dharmashastras,* p. 599.
35. *Manu Dharmashastra,* V 157–60.
36. *Vriddha Harita*, XI.205–10, cited in Kane, *History of the Dharmashastras*, p. 584.
37. Fuller and Logan, Navaratri Festival in Madurai', p. 89ff.
38. Leslie, *Perfect Wife*, p. 299.
39. A widow who for forsakes sons, brothers and other male relative after her husband's death and lives independently incurs great condemnation, according to Tryambaka. Ibid., p. 300.
40. Ibid., p. 299.
41. Chakravarti, 'Rise of Buddhism as Experienced by Women'.

42. That the widow is not an ascetic is evident from the observations of parvatibai Athavale, a widow writing about widowhood in 1928. Describing the forced tonsure of widows, Parvatibai distinguished between the voluntary acceptance of the renunciate status and the coerced celibate status of the widow as embodied in her tonsure. The voluntary shaving of the head as an initiatory rite for those who 'give up' the worldly lite was regarded by Parvatibai to be a 'rightful religious act', but not the compulsory shaving of the head of the widow against her volition. Volition, therefore, was the crucial difference between a true renunciate existence and a simulated renunciate existence of the widow based on coercion exerted by others. In her view, the renunciate within the home was a contradiction in terms.
    Athavale, *Hindu Widow*, p. 242.
43. As early as the second century ad, Tamil poems portray the austerities required to keep the dangerous power possessed by women under control. One poem describes the hazards of a young, chaste, high-born woman attempting such control: unable to do so, she wanders towards the burning ground – only there is she freed from the passions of her youth and able to protect her chastity. Hart, 'Woman and the Secred', p. 242.
44. Leslie, *Perfect Wife*, p. 298.
45. Kane, *History of the Dharmashastras*, p. 586.
46. Honama vs Timannabhat, *Indian Law Reports (ILR),* I, Bombay 559; Bhikhubai vs Haribhai, ILR, 49, Bombay 459.
47. Kane, *History of the Dharmashastras,* pp. 584–85.
48. Beck, 'Color and Heat in South Indian Ritual', p. 559.
49. The breaking of glass bangles and the '*mangalsutra*' is now the most common form of representing the transition from the wife as suhagan or sumangali to that of the widow in the visual medium. In Indian cinema it is the transformative symbol for widowhood followed by the donning of a stark white sari.
50. Fuller and Logan, 'The Navaratri Festival in Madurai', pp. 89–92.
51. Beck, 'Color and Heat in South Indian Ritual', p. 571, n. 13.
52. Hiltebeitel, 'Draupadi's Hair', pp. 179–214, 208.
53. Hart, 'Woman and the Sacred in Ancient Tamilnadu', p. 241.
54. Kane, *History of the Dharmashastras,* p. 587.
55. Berg, *Unconscious Symbolism of Hair,* p. 26.
56. Kane, *History of the Dharmashastras,* p. 587.
57. Leslie, *The Perfect Wife*, p. 303
58. Chakravarti, *Rewriting History*, p. 24.
59. Fuller and Logan, 'Navaratri Festival in Madurai', p. 94.
60. Ibid., p. 95.
61. According to Hershman, there are certain times when pollution occurs for women: at the death of the husband, during menstruation and following intercourse. The end of the pollution period is marked by a ritual bath when it is crucial that the hair is washed, groomed and bound in the proper fashion, 'Hair, Sex and Dirt', pp. 274–98, 285–89.)
62. Personal communication from my maternal grandmother, C. Alamelu.
63. Berg, *Unconscious Symbolism of Hair*, pp. 29–30.
64. Ibid., p. 22.
65. Leach, 'Magical Hair', pp. 147–64.
66. Obeyesekere, Medusa's Hair.
67. Leach, 'Magical Hair', p. 148.
68. Ibid., and Obeyesekere, pp. 45–50.
69. Leach, '*Magical Hair*', p. 154.
70. Ibid., p. 156.
71. Obeyesekere, *Medusa's Hair*, pp. 33–34, 45–50. In an influential nineteenth-century novel in Marathi, the young widow's resistance to the range of practices associated with widowhood is finally broken by her forcible tonsure, executed brutally by her cruel and orthodox uncle. At the end of the tonsure the uncle says, 'You want to remarry! Go and remarry now. This is how one has to cut off the noses of the likes of you.' Apte, *Pan Lakshyant Kon Gheto*, p. 484.

72. Chakravarti, 'Social Pariahs and Domestic Drudges'.
73. Harper, 'Fear and the Status of Women', pp. 81–95.
74. Ibid., pp. 81–83.
75. Ibid., pp. 87–88.
76. Ibid., p. 85.
77. Ibid., pp. 89–90.
78. Ibid., p. 86.
79. Ibid., pp. 87–88. The material condition of women as permanent dependents of men is a crucial component of women's vulnerability. This is compounded when a woman is widowed because she is then regarded as losing even her limited entitlement to food and clothing to which she had access as a wife. She also loses the power she may have wielded as manager of the domestic domain. Cultural values legitimize a low allotment of food as widows are expected to fast often and eat minimally. In return for the 'maintenance' they receive from their male official kinsmen (or even natal kinsmen), they must render labour which is invisibilized. Widows are often taunted with the allegation that they are 'drudges', eating up the resources of a household. For an extended discussion of the material dimensions of widowhood, see Chakravarti, 'Social Pariahs and Domestic Drudges'.
80. Harper, 'Fear and the Status of Women', p. 88.
81. Ibid., p. 89.
82. Ibid., p. 92. See also Pandita Rainabai's perceptive observations, especially on the relations between mothers and daughters, in *The High Caste Hindu Woman,* p. 17.
83. Harper, 'Fear and the Status of Women', p. 90.
84. Ibid.
85. Ibid., p. 91.
86. Ibid., pp. 91–92.
87. Kolenda, 'Widowhood among 'Untouchable' Chuhras', pp. 289–354.
88. Ibid., pp. 299–300.
89. Ibid., pp. 306–07.
90. Ibid., pp. 316–19.
91. Chakravarti, *Rewriting History*, pp. 52–53.
92. Kolenda, 'Widowhood among 'Untouchable' Chuhras', p. 329.
93. Ibid., pp. 329–36.
94. Ibid., p. 336.
95. Ibid., p. 315.
96. Ibid., 326.
97. *Manu Dharmashastra,* IX, pp. 65–67.

WORKS CITED

Agrawala, V.S. (1953), *India as Known to Panini,* Lucknow: University of Lucknow.

Aitareya Brahmana (1879), edited by T. Aufrecht, Bonn: Marcus.

Alavi, Hamza (1981), 'Peasants and Revolution', in A.R. Desai (ed .), *Peasant Struggles in India,* Bombay: Oxford University Press.

Aloysius, G. (1998), *Religion as Emancipatory Identity: A Buddhist Movement among the Tamils under Colonialism,* Delhi: New Age.

Alsdorf, L. (1974), 'The Impious Brahman and the Pious Candala', in L. Cousins *et al.* (eds), *Buddhist Studies in Honour of J.B. Horner,* Holland: Reidel.

Altekar, A.S. (1987), *The Position of Women in Hindu Civilization,* Delhi: Mocilal Banarsidass, reprint.

Ambedkar, B.R. (1957), *The Buddha and His Dhamma,* Bombay: Siddhartha Publications.

Amore, R.C. and Larry D. Shinn (1981), *Lustful Maidens and Ascetic Kings,* New York: Oxford University Press.

Anderson, Perry (1974), *Passages from Antiquity to Feudalism,* London: Verso.

Anguttara Nikaya (1885–90), in five volumes, edited by R. Morris and E. Hardy, London: Pali Text Society.
———. (1932), translated by F.L. Woodward and E.M. Hare as *The Book of Gradual Sayings,* Vol. V, London: Pali Text Society.
———. (1959), in four volumes, edited by Bhikkhu J. Kashyap, Nalanda Devanagari Pali Series, Bihar Government.
Anitha, S. *et al.* (1995), 'Interviews with Women', in Tanika Sarkar and Urvashi Butalia (eds), *Women and the Hindu Right: A Collection of Essays,* Delhi: Kali for Women.
Apastamba Dharmasutra (1975), translated by George Buhler, in *Sacred Laws of the Aryas,* Delhi: Motilal Banarsidass, reprint.
Apte, Hari Narayan (1961), *Pan Lakshyant Kon Gheto* (in Marathi), translated by Srinivas Kochar into Hindi as *Karm Dhyan Deta Hai,* New Delhi: Sahitya Akademi.
The Arthashastra. See *The Kautilya Arthashastra.*
Arudra (1992), *Sita Ram ki Kya Lagti Thi* (in Hindi), Delhi: People's Publishing House.
Ashtadhyayi of Panini (1962), in two volumes, edited and translated by S.C. Vasu, Delhi: Motilal Banarsidass.
Atharvaveda (1936), edited by Dr Raghuvira, Lahore.
Arhavale, Parvatibai (1986), *Hindu Widow,* Delhi: Reliance, reprint. Bacchetta, Paola (1996), 'Hindu Nationalist Women as Ideologues: The Sangh, the Samiri and Differential Concepts of the Hindu Nation', in Kumari Jayawardena and Malathi de Alwis (eds), *Embodied Violence: Communalizing Women's Sexuality in South Asia*, Delhi: Kali for Women.
Bader, Clarisse (1925), Women in Ancient India, London: Longmans Green. Bagchi, Jashodhara (1985), 'Positivism and Nationalism: Womanhood and Crisis in Nationalist Fiction, Bankim Chandra's *Anandmath', Economic and Political Weekly*, Review of Women's Studies, Vol. 20, No. 43.
Bahmana Vagga, Dhamma pada (1881), translated by F. Max Mueller, *Sacred Books of the East*, Vol. X, Oxford: Clarendon Press.
Bailey, H.W. (1959), 'Iranian Arya and Daha', *Transactions of the Philological Society*, London, pp. 71–115.
Balagopal, K. (1993), 'Why Did December 6, 1992 Happen?', *Economic and Political Weekly*, Vol. 28, No. 17.
Ballhatchet, K.A. (1956), 'Some Aspects of Historical Writing on India by Christian Missionaries', paper presented at South Asia Seminar, School of Oriental and African Studies, London.
Barna, B.M. (1970), *Pre-Buddhist Indian Philosophy*, Delhi: Motilal Banarsidass, reprint.
Basham, A.L. (1971), *The Wonder that Was India*, Delhi: Rupa and Co.
———. (1981), *The History and Doctrine of the Ajivikas*, Delhi: Morilal Banarsidass, reprint.
Baudhayana Dharmasutra (1986), translated by George Buhler, in *Sacred Laws of the Aryas*, Vol. II, Delhi: Motilal Banarsidass, reprint.
Beck, Brenda (1969), 'Color and Heat in South Indian Ritual', *Man*, New Series.
———. (1986), 'Social Dyads in Indic Folktales', in Blackburn and Ramanujan (eds), *Another Harmony*, Delhi: Oxford University Press.
Benveniste, Emile (1973), *Indo-European Language and Society*, translated by E. Palmer, London: Faber and Faber.
Berg, C. (1951), *The Unconscious Symbolism of Hair*, London: Allen Unwin.
Berlin, H. Ludders (1973), *A List of Brahmi Inscriptions*, Varanasi: Indological Book House.
Bhagavad Gita (1968), edited by S.K. Belvalkar, Poona: Bhandarkar Oriental Research Institute.
Bhagavata Purana (1905), Bombay.
Bhagvati Sutra (1918–21), Bombay.
Bharucha, Rustom (1994), 'On the Border of Fascism: Manufacture of Consent in Roja', Economic and Political Weekly, Vol. 29, No. 23, pp. 1389–95.
Bhattacharji, Sukumari (1994), *Women and Society in Ancient India*, Calcutta: Basumati Corporation.
———. (1999), 'Prostitution in Ancient India', in Kumkum Roy (ed.), *Women in Early Indian Societies*, Delhi: Manohar.
Bhattacharya, Santwana (1995), 'Retelling Epic Tales' (an interview with Nabaneeta Dev Sen), *Indian Express*, 16 July.
Biardeau, Madeleine (1969), 'Etudes de Mythologie Hindou: II', *Bulletin de!' Ecole Frmifaised' Extreme-Orient*, Vol. 55, pp. 59–105.
———. (1981), 'The Salvation of the King in the Maha bharata', *Contributions to Indian Sociology*, Vol. 15, pp. 75–97.

Blackburn, Stuart H. and A.K. Ramanujan (eds) (1986), *Another Hannony: New Essays on the Folklore of India*, Delhi: Oxford University Press.

Blackstone, Kathryn R. (2000), *Womenin the Footsteps of the Buddha: Struggle for Liberation in the Therigatha*, Delhi: Motilal Banarsidass.

The Book of Discipline (1941), in five volumes, translated by LB. Horner, London: Luzac and Co.

Borthwick, Meredith (1984), *The Changing Role of Women in Bengal 1849–1905*, Princeton: Princeton University Press.

Bose, A.N. (1942), *Social and Rural Economy of North-East India*, in two volumes, Calcutta: University of Calcutta.

Bottomore, Tom *et al.* (1983), *A Dictionary of Marxist Thought*, Oxford: Basil Blackwell.

Bougie, Celestin (1971), *Essays on the Caste System*, Cambridge: Cambridge University Press.

Brihadaranyaka Upanishad (1881), translated by F. Max Mueller, in *The Upanishads*, Vol. XV, Oxford: Clarendon Press.

———. (1950), translated by Swami Madhavanand, Almora: Advaita Ashram.

Brihaspati Sutra (1941), edited by I.V. Rangaswami Aiyangar, Baroda: Oriental Institute.

Buike, Father Kami! (1996), *Ramkatha*, Allahabad: Indian Press.

Burke, Peter (1978), *Popular Culture in Early Modem Europe*, London: Temple Smith.

Burlingame, E.W. (1921), *Buddhist Legends*, Harvard Oriental Series, Vol. 29, Cambridge, MA: Harvard University Press.

Byres, T.J. (1986), 'The Agrarian Question and the Differentiation of the Peasantry', Foreword in Atiur Rahman, *Peasants and Classes: A Study in Differentiation in Bangladesh*, London: Zed Books.

The Cambridge Economic History of India (1982), Vol. I: *c. 1200–c. 1750*, edited by Tapan Raychaudhari and Irfan Habib; Vol. II: c. 1757–1970, edited by Dharma Kumar, Cambridge: Cambridge University Press.

Chakraborty, Haripada (1973), *Asceticism in Ancient India*, Calcutta: Punti Pustak.

Chakravarthy, Venkatesh and M.S.S. Pandian (1994), 'More on *Roja*', *Economic and Political Weekly*, Vol. 29, No. 11, pp. 642–44.

Chakravarti, Uma (1981), 'The Rise of Buddhism as Experienced by Women', *Manushi*, No. 8.

———. (1983a), 'The Development of the Sita Myth: A Case Study of Women in Myth and Literature', *Samya Shakti*, Vol. 1, No. 1; also in this volume.

———. (1983b), 'Renouncer and Householder in Early Buddhism', *Social Analysis*, No. 13, pp. 70–83; also in this volume.

———. (1985a), 'The *Agrihinis* of Ancient India', *Teaching Politics*, Vol. 11, No. 2.

———. (1985b), 'Of *Dasas* and *Karmakaras*: Servile Labour in Ancient India', in Ursa Patnaik and Manjari Dingwaney (eds), *Chains of Servitude: Band age! and Slavery in India*, Delhi: Orient Longman, pp. 35–75; also in this volume.

———. (1985c) 'Towards a Historical Sociology of Stratification in Ancient India', *Economic and Political Weekly*, Vol. 20, No. 9, 2 March, pp. 356–60; also in this volume.

———. (1986), 'The Social Philosophy of Buddhism', *Social Compass*, Vol. 23, Nos 2–3, pp. 199–221; also in this volume.

———. (1987), *The Social Dimensions of Early Buddhism*, Delhi: Oxford University Press.

———. (1989), 'Whatever Happened to the Vedic *Dasi*?: Orientalism, Nationalism and a Script for the Past', in Kumkum Sangari and Sudesh Vaid (eds), *Recasting Women: Essays in Colonial History*, Delhi: Kali for Women, pp. 27–87; also in this volume.

———. (1993a), 'Conceptualizing Brahmanical Patriarchy in Early India: Gender, Caste, Class and Stace', *Economic and Political Weekly*, Vol. 28, No. 14, 3 April, pp. 579–85; also in this volume.

———. (1993b), 'Social Pariahs and Domestic Drudges: Widowhood among Nineteenth-Century Poona Brahmanas', *Social Scientist*, Nos 244–46, September–November.

———. (1993c), 'Women, Men and Beasts', *Studies in History*, Vol. 9, No. 1, pp. 43–70; also in this volume.

———. (1995), 'Gender, Caste and Labour: The Material and Ideological Structure of Widowhood', *Economic and Political Weekly*, Vol. 30, No. 36; also in this volume.

Chakravarti, Uma (1996), 'In Search of the Peasant in Early India: Was the *Gahapati* a Peasant Producer?', in V.K. Thakur and Ashok Anshouman (eds), *Peasants in Indian History: Theoretical Issues and Structural Enquiries* (Essays in Memory of Professor R.K. Chaudhary), Patna: Janaki Prakashan, pp. 150–78; also in this volume.

———. (1998), *Rewriting History: The Life and Times of Pandita Ramabai,* New Delhi: Kali for Women.

———. (1999), 'Of Hegemonic Agendas and Contesting Voices: Towards Recovering a Sitayana', unpublished MS.

———. (2003), *Gendering Caste: Through a Feminist Lens,* Kolkata: Scree.

———. (2005), 'Re-inscribing the Past: Inserting Women into Indian History', in Kamala Ganesh and Usha Thakkar (eds), *Culture and the Making of Identity in Contemporary India*, Delhi: Sage.

———. (2005), 'Women's Histories in South Asia', in Prem Poddar and David Johnson (eds), A *Historical Companion to Postcolonial Thought in English*, New York: Columbia University Press.

Champakalakshmi, R. (1996), *Trade, Ideology and Urbanization: South India 300 BC to AD 300*, Delhi: Oxford University Press.

Chanana, D.R. (1963), *The Spread of Agriculture in Northern India*, Delhi: Suman Prakashana.

———. (1990), *Slavery in Ancient India*, Delhi: People's Publishing House, reprint.

Chandogya Upanishad (1930), edited by E. Senart, Paris: Les Belles Lettres.

Chandra, Pratap (1978), *Metaphysics of Perpetual Change: The Concept of Self in Early Buddhism*, Bombay: Somaiya Publications.

Chandra, Sudhir (1987), 'Lake of Palms: An Essay in Understanding Early Indian Nationalism without the Imperialist Discourse', paper presented at the seminar on Communication and Society, Nehru Memorial Museum and Library, Delhi.

Chartier, Roger (1982), 'Intellectual History or Socio-cultural History? The French Trajectories', in D. La Capra and S.L. Kaplan (eds), *Modern European Intellectual History*, New York.

Chattopadhyaya, B.D. (1990), *Aspects of Rural Settlements and Rural Society in Early Medieval India*, Calcutta: Centre for Studies in Social Sciences.

———. (1994), *The Making of Early Medieval India*, Delhi: Oxford University Press.

Chattopadhyaya, D.P. (1968), *Lokayata*, Delhi: People's Publishing House. Chattopadhyaya, Gautam (1965), *Awakening in Bengal: Early Nineteenth Century Selected Documents*, Calcutta: Progressive Publishers.

Chaudhuri, Nirad C. (1974), *Scholar Extraordinary: The Life of Rt. Hon. Friedrich Max Mueller P.C.*, Delhi: Oxford University Press.

Chayanov, A.V. (1987), *The Theory of Peasant Economy*, Delhi: Oxford University Press.

Chowdhry, Prem (1994), *The Veiled Women: Shifting Gender Equations, Haryana 1880–1980*, Delhi: Oxford University Press.

Clark, T.W. (1961), 'The Role of Bankimchandra in the Development of Nationalism', in C.H. Philips (ed.), *Historians of India, Pakistan and Ceylon*, London: Oxford University Press.

Coburn, Thomas (1995), 'Sita Fights while Rama Swoons: A Shakta Version of the Ramayana', *Manushi*, No. 90.

Cohn, Bernard (1985), 'The Command of Language and the Language of Command', in Ranajit Guha (ed.), *Subaltern Studies IV*, Delhi: Oxford University Press.

Colebrooke, H.T. (1795), 'On the Duties of the Faithful Hindu Widow', *Asiatic Researches*, 4.

———. (1805), 'On the Vedas, or Sacred Writings of the Hindus', Asiatic Researches, 8.

Cone, Margaret and Richard F. Gombrich (1977), *The Perfect Generosity of Prince Vessantara*, Oxford: Oxford University Press.

Coomaraswamy, Ananda (1916), *Buddha and the Gospel of Buddhism*, New York: Harper Torchbooks.

Cullavagga (1956), edited by Bhikkhu J. Kashyap, Nalanda Devanagari Pali Series, Bihar Government.

———. (1958), in *Vinaya Pitaka*, Nalanda: Pali Publication Board. Cunningham, J.D. (1849), *History of the Silihs*, London: John Murray.

Dandekar, R.N.(ed.) (1990), *The Mahabharata Revisited*, Delhi: Sahitya Akademi. Das, Arvind (1988), 'Electronic Religiosity: Meaning of Goswami Ramanand Sagar', *Times of India*, 5 August.

Das, R.M. (1962), *Women in Manu and His Seven Commentators*, Varanasi: Indological Book House.

Das, Veena (1976), 'Indian Women: Work, Power and Status', in B.R. Nanda (ed.), *Indian Women from Purdah to Modernity*, Delhi: Vikas, pp. 129–45.

———. (1977), *Structure and Cognition: Aspects of Hindu Caste and Ritual*, Delhi: Oxford University Press.

Das, Veena (1981), 'Kama in the Scheme of Purusarthas', *Contributions to Indian Sociology*, New Series, Nos 1–2.

Dasgupta, Madhusra ba (2000), 'Usable Women: The Tales of Amba and Madhvi', in Mandakranta Bose (ed.), *Faces of the Feminine in Ancient, Medieval and Modern India*, Delhi: Oxford University Press.

Davids, T.W. Rhys (1970), *Buddhist India*, Delhi: Indological Book House, reprint.

———. (1972), *History of Indian Buddhism*, Allahabad: Rachana Prakashan, reprint.

Davis, Natalie Z. (1975), *Society and Culture in Early Modern France*, Stanford: Stanford University Press.

Dehejia, Vidya (1988), *Slaves of the Lord*, Delhi: Munshiram Manoharlal.

Deshpande, C.R. (1978), *Transmission of the Mahabharata Tradition*, Shimla: Indian Institute of Advanced Study.

Dev Sen, Nabaneeta (1997), 'Rewriting the Ramayana: Chandrabati and Molla', in Geeti Sen (ed.), *Crossing Boundaries*, Delhi: Orient Longman, pp. 163–77.

Dhammapada Atthakatha (1906), Vol. I, edited by H.C. Normann, London: Pali Text Society.

Dhaniya Sutta, Sutta Nipata, Khuddaka Nikaya (1959), Vol. I, edited by Bhikkhu J. Kashyap, Nalanda Devanagari Pali Series, Bihar Government.

Dhannakosa, Vol. I, edited by Laxman Shastri Joshi, Wai.

The Dialogues of the Buddha (1973), *Digha Nikaya*, in three volumes, translated by T.W. Rhys Davids, Delhi: Motilal Banarsidass.

Digha Nikaya (1958), in three volumes, edited by Bhikkhu J. Kashyap, Nalanda Pali Devanagari Series, Bihar Government.

———. (1976), edited by E. Carpentier, London: Pali Text Society.

Doniger, Wendy and Brian Smith (1991), *The Laws of Manu*, Delhi: Penguin Books.

Drekmeier, Charles (1962), *Kingship and Community in Early India*, Stanford: California University Press.

Duff, Grant (1826), *History of the Marathas*, London: Longmans Green. Dumont, Louis (1972), *Homo Hierarcbicus*, London: Paladin.

———. (1976), 'World Renunciation in Indian Religions', *Contributions to Indian Sociology*, Vol. 4.

Dutt, R.C. (1888), *A History of Civilization in Ancient India*, Delhi: Vishal.

———. (1943), *Pratap Singh: The Last of the Rajputs*, Allahabad: Kitabistan. Dutt, 5. (1924), *Early Buddhist Monachism*, London: Kegan Paul.

Epigra phica Indica (1970), edited by Jas Burgess, IX, No. 5, 45, 1.29, Delhi: Motilal Banarasidass, reprint.

Erndl, Kathryn M. (1991), 'The Mutilation of Surpanakha', in Paula Richman (ed.), *Many Ramayanas: The Diversity of a Narrative Tradition in South Asia*, Delhi: Oxford University Press.

Feer, M.L. (1963), *A Study of the Jatakas*, Calcutta: Susil Gupta.

Femia, Joseph V. (1987), *Gramsci's Political Thought: Hegemony, Consciousness, and the Revolutionary Process*, Oxford: Clarendon Press.

Fick, R. (1920), *The Social Organization of North-east India in Buddha's Time*, Calcutta: University of Calcutta.

Finley, M.I. (1964), 'Between Slavery and Freedom', *Comparative Studies in Society and History*, Vol. 6; republished in *Economy and Society in Ancient Greece*, Harmondsworth: Penguin Books, 1983.

Fiske, Adele M. (1976), 'Buddhism in India today', in Heinrich Dumoulin and John C. Maraldo (eds), *Buddhism in the Modern World*, London: Collier Macmillan.

Fuller, C.J. and Penny Logan (1985), 'The Navaratri Festival in Madurai', *Bulletin of the School of Oriental and African Studies*, Vol. 47, Part I.

Ganesh, Kamala (1985), 'Women's Seclusion and the Structure of Caste', paper presented at the Asian Regional Conference on 'Women and the House hold', Delhi.

Gautama Dharmasutra (1975), translated by George Buhler, in *Sacred Laws of the Aryas*, Vol. I, Delhi: Motilal Banarsidass.

Ghose, J.C. (1885), *The English Works of Raja Rammoham Roy*, Calcutta: Oriental.

Ginzburg, Carlo (1980), *The Cheese and the Worms*, London: Routledge and Kegan Paul.

Gokhale, B.G. (1968), 'Dhamma as a Political Concept', *Journal of Indian History*, Vol. 46, Part II.

Guha, R. (1963), *A Rule of Property for Bengal: An Essay on the Idea of Permanent Settlement*, Paris and The Hague: Mouton.

———. (ed.) (1981), *Subaltern Studies: Writings on South Asian History and Society*, Vol. I, Delhi: Oxford University Press.

Guha, R. (1987), 'Chandra's Death', in R. Guha (ed.), *Subaltern Studies* V, Delhi: Oxford University Press.

Gupta, Dipankar (1981), '"Caste", Infrastructure and Superstructure', *Economic and Political Weekly*, Vol. 16, No. 51.

Habib, Irfan (1982), 'The Peasant in Indian History', Presidential Address to the 43rd session of the Indian History Congress held at Kurukshetra; republished in Essays in *Indian History: Towards a Marxist Perspective*, Delhi: Tulika, 1995.

———. (1995), *Essays in Indian History: Towards a Marxist Perspective*, Delhi: Tulika Books.

Hansen, Kathryn (1988), 'The *Virangana* in North Indian History: Myth and Popular Culture', *Economic and Political Weekly*, Vol. 23, No. 18, pp. ws 25–33.

Hardy, Friedhelm (1983), *Viraha Bhakti: The Early History of Krsna Devotion in South India*, Delhi: Oxford University Press.

Harper, Edward B. (1969), 'Fear and the Status of Women', *Southwestern Journal of Anthropology*, Vol. 25.

Hart, George (1973), 'Woman and the Sacred in Ancient Tamil Nadu', *Journal of Asian Studies*, Vol. 32, No. 2, February, pp. 233–50.

Hatalkar, V.G. (1973), 'M.G. Ranade', in S.P. Sen (ed.), *Historians and Historiography in Modern India*, Calcutta: Institute of Historical Studies.

Heesterman, J.C. (1964), 'Brahmin, Ritual and Renouncer', *Wiener Zeitschrift fur die Kunde Si,dund Ostasiens*, Vol. 8, pp. 1–31.

———. (1981), 'Householder and Wanderer', *Contributions to Indian Sociology*, Vol. 15, pp. 251–71.

Heimsath, Charles (1964), *Indian Nationalism and Hindu Social Reform*, Princeton: Princeton University Press.

Herrenschmidt, Olivier (2004), 'Ambedkar and the Hindu Social Order', in Surendra Jondhale and Johannes Beltz (eds), *Reconstructing the World: B.R. Ambedkar and Buddhism in India*, Delhi: Oxford University Press, pp. 42–43.

Hershman, Paul (1974), 'Hair, Sex and Dirt', *Man*, New Series, Vol. 9, No. 2. Hiltebeitel, Alf (1981), 'Draupadi's Hair', *Pumshartha*, Vol. 5, pp. 179–214.

Hilton, Rodney (1973), *Bond Men Made Free: Medieval Peasant Movements and the English Rising of 1381*, London: Methuen.

Hobsbawm, Eric (1983), 'Introduction: Inventing Traditions', in Eric Hobsbawm and Terence Ranger (eds), *The Invention of Tradition*, Cambridge: Cambridge University Press.

Hocart, A.M. (1950), *Caste: A Comparative Study*, London: Methuen.

Horner, LB. (1975), *Women under Primitive Buddhism*, Delhi: Motilal Banarsidass, reprint.

Huilgol, Glynn (1979), 'The Sanctification of Sita', Women's Sociological Bulletin, Vol. 1, No. 3.

Hultzsch, E. (1969), Vol. I, *Corpus Inscriptionum Indicarum*, Delhi: Indological Book House.

lnamdar, Radhabai *et al.* (1911), *Position of Widows*, typescript, Eur. MS D 356, India Office Library.

Jain,J.C. (1947), *Life in Ancient India as Depicted in the Jain Canon*, New Book Company.

Jain, P.C. (1971), *Labour in Ancient India*, Delhi: Sterling.

Jaini, P.S. (1970), '*Shramanas*: Their Conflict with Brahmanical Society', in J.W. Elder (ed.), *Chapters in Indian Civilization*, Dubuque, Iowa: Kendall Hunt.

———. (1991), *Gender and Salvation: Jaina Debates on the Spiritual Liberation of Women,* Berkeley: University of California Press.

Jamison, Stephanie (1999), *Sacrificed Wife, Sacrificer's Wife*, New York: Oxford University Press.

Jan Yun Hua (1962), 'Hui Chao's Record on Kashmir', *Kashmir Research Bi Annual*, 2.

The Jataka (1957), edited by E.B. Cowell, translated by R. Chalmers *et al.*, London: Pali Text Society.

Jataka (1964), in six volumes, edited by V. Fausboll, London: Pali Text Society. Jha, V.V. (1974), 'From Tribe to Untouchable: The Case of the Nishadas', in R.S. Sharma and V.V. Jha (eds), *Indian Society: Historical Probings*, Delhi: People's Publishing House.

Jones, Kenneth (1976), *A1ya Dharma: Hindu Consciousness in 19th Century Punjab*, Delhi: Manohar.

Jones, William (1807), 'On the Chronology of the Hindus', in Lord Teignmouth (ed.), *The Works of William Jones*, London: John Stockdale, Piccadilly and John Walkes.

Jordens, J.T.F. (1978), *Dayananda Saraswati: His Life and Ideas*, Delhi: Oxford University Press.

Kakar, Sudhir (1978), *The Inner World*, Delhi: Oxford University Press.

Kamasutra (1929), edited by Damodar Shastri, Banaras: Chowkhamba Sanskrit Series Office.

Kane, P.V. (1941), *History of the Dharmashastras*, Vol. II, Part I, Poona: Bhandarkar Oriental Research Institute.
Karve, Irawati (1974), *Yuganta: The End of an Epoch*, Delhi: Sangam Books.
Kaul, Shonaleeka (2005), *The City in Early India: A Study of Literary Perceptions*, Ph.D. thesis, Jawaharlal Nehru University, Delhi.
The Kautilya Arthashastra (1986), in three volumes: Part I, text critically edited by R.P. Kangle; Part. II, translation by R.P. Kangle; and Part III: A Study, by R.P. Kangle, Delhi: Motilal Banarsidass.
Kaviraj, Sudipta (1987), 'The Myth of Infinity: The Construction of the Figure of Krishna in *Krishnacarita*', Occasional Papers, Nehru Memorial Museum and Library, Delhi.
Kolenda, Pauline (1987), 'Widowhood among "Untouchable" Chuhras', in *Regional Differences in Family Structures in India*, Jaipur: Rawat Press.
Kopf, David (1969), *British Orientalism and the Bengal Renaissance*, Calcutta: Firma K.L. Mukhopadhyaya.
Kosambi, D.D. (1957), *Exasperating Essays: Exercises in the Dialectical Method*, Pune: Mudra Press.
———. (1962), *Myth and Reality: Studies in the Formation of Indian Culture*, Bombay: Popular Prakashan.
———. (1975a), *The Culture and Civilization of Ancient India*, Delhi: Vikas, reprint.
———. (1975b), *An Introduction to the Study of Indian History*, Bombay: Popular Prakashan, reprint.
Latyayana Srautasutra (1872), edited by Anandachandra Vedantaragesa, Calcutta.
Leach, E.R. (1958), '*Magical Hair*', *Journal of the Royal Anthropological Institute of Great Britain and Ireland*, Vol. 88, pp. 147–64.
Lerner, Gerda (1986), *The Creation of Patriarchy*, New York: Oxford University Press.
Leslie, Julia (1989), *The Perfect Wife: The Orthodox Hindu Woman according to the Stridharmapaddhati of Tryambakayajvan*, Delhi: Oxford University Press.
Ling, Trevor (1976), *The Buddha*, Middlesex: Penguin Books.
Ludden, David (1989), *Peasant History in South India*, Delhi: Oxford University Press.
Macdonell, A.A. and A.B. Keith (1912), *Vedic Index of Names and Subjects*, London, published for the Government of India.
Mackay, E. (1948), *Early Indus Civilization*, London: Luzac and Co.
Mahabharata (1933–39), critical edition by V.S. Sukhtankar *et al.*, Poona: Bhandarkar Oriental Research Institute.
Mahabhashya of Patanjali. See *Vyakarana Mahabhashya of Patanjali.*
Mahavagga (1956), edited by Bhikkhu J. Kashyap, Nalanda Devanagari Pali Series, Bihar Government.
———. (1958), in *Vinaya Pitaka*, Nalanda: Pali Publication Board.
———. (1974), translated by T.W. Rhys Davids and H. Oldenberg as *Vinaya Texts*, Part I, *Sacred Books of the East*, Vol. XIII, Delhi: Motilal Banarsidass, reprint.
Maitra, Prita (1991), 'Master of the Game', *Sunday*, 22 October–2 November, pp. 44–53.
Majjhima Nilwya (1958), in three volumes, edited by Mahapandita Rahula Sankritayan and P.V. Bapat, Nalanda Devanaga ri Pali Series, Bihar Government.
———. (1958), in three volumes, Nalanda: Pali Publication Board.
———. (1976), translated by LB. Horner as *The Middle Length Sayings*, London: Pali Text Society
Majumdar, R.C. (1961), 'Nationalist Historians', in C.H. Philips (ed.), *Historians of India, Pakistan and Ceylon*, London: Oxford University Press.
Malalasekhara, G.P. (1960), *Dictionary of Pali Prnper Names*, in two volumes, London: Pali Text Society.
Mallik, A.R. (1961), 'Modern Historical Writing in Bengali', in C.H. Philips (ed.), *Historians of India, Pakistan and Ceylon*, London: Oxford University Press.
Mani, Lara (1986), 'Production of an Official Discourse on Sati in Early Nineteenth Century Bengal', *Economic and Political Weekly*, Review of Women's Studies, Vol. 26, No. 17.
Manu Dharmashastra (1984), translated by George Buhler as *The Laws of Manu, Sacred Book s of the East*, Vol. XXV, Delhi: Motilal Banarsidass, reprint.
Marshall, J. (1931), *Mohenjodaro and the Indus Civilization*, Vol. I, London: A. Probsthain.
Masud, Iqbal (1992), 'Images of Dominance', *Indian Express*, 16 August. Matilal, B.I. (ed.) (1993), *Moral Dilemmas in the Mahabharata*, Shimla: Indian Institute of Advanced Study.

Max Mueller, F. (1859), *A History of Sanskrit Literature*, London: Longmans Green.
———. (1892), *India: What It Can Teach Us*, London: Longmans Green.
Max Mueller, Georgina (1902), *Life and Letters of F. Max Mueller*, London: Longmans Green.
Medick, Hans and David Warren Sabean (1984), *Interest and Emotion: Essays on the Study of Family and Kinship*, Cambridge: Cambridge University Press.
Mehta, Ratilal (1939), *Pre-Buddhist India*, Bombay: Examiner Press. Meenakshi, K. (1986), 'Old Inda-Aryan to Middle Indo-Aryan', in Sabyasachi Bhattacharya and Romila Thapar (eds), *Situating Indian History*, Delhi: Oxford University Press.
Menon, Dilip, (1993), 'The Moral Community of the Teyyattam: Popular Culture in Late Colonial Malabar', *Studies in History*, Vol. 9, No. 2, pp. 187–219.
Milindapanha (1962), edited by V. Trenckner, London: Pali Text Society.
———. (1964), translated by I.B. Horner as *Questions of King Menander*, Vol. I, London: Luzac and Co.
Mill, James (1840), *The History of British India*, with notes by H.H. Wilson, fifth edition, London: James Madden.
Morgan, L.H. (1958), *Ancient Society*, Calcutta, reprint.
Mukherjte, Prabhati (1988), *Beyond the Four Varnas: The Untouchables in India*, Delhi: Motilal Banarsidass.
Murcott, Susan (1991), *The First Buddhist Women: Translations and Commentary on the Therigatha*, Berkeley: Parallel Press.
Murshid, Ghulam (1983), *Reluctant Debutante*, Rajshahi: Rajshahi University.
Murri G.S. and A.S.K. Aiyangar (1950), *Edicts of Asoka*, Madras.
Nandy, Ashis (1983), *The Intimate Enemy: Loss and Recovery of the Self under Colonialism*, Delhi: Oxford University Press.
Naradasmriti (1889), translated by J. Jolly in *The Minor Law-Books, Sacred Books of the East*, Vol. XXXI, Oxford: Clarendon Press.
Nehru, Jawaharlal (1982), *The Discovery of India, Delhi*: Oxford University Press.
Neufeldt, Ronald W.(1980), *Max Mueller and the Rig Veda: A Study of its Role in His Work and Thought*, Calcutta: Minerva.
Neumayer, E. (1983), *Prehistoric Indian Rock Paintings*, Delhi: Oxford University Press.
Nidana Katha (1973), translated by T.W. Rhys Davids as *Buddhist Birth Stories*, Delhi: Indological Book House.
Niranjana, Tejaswini (1994), 'Integrating Whose Nation? Tourists and Terrorists in *Roja*', *Economic and Political Weekly*, Vol. 29, No. 3, pp. 79–82.
Obeyesekere, Gananath (1981), *Medusa's Hair: An Essay in Personal Symbols and Religious Experience,* Chicago: University of Chicago Press.
O'Flaherty, Wendy D. (1976), *The Origins of Evil in Hindu Mythology*, Berkeley: University of California Press.
———. (1985), *Tales of Sex and Violence*, Delhi: Motilal Banarsidass.
———. (1999), *Splitting the Difference: Gender and Myth in Ancient Greece and India*, Chicago: University of Chicago Press.
Oldenberg, H. (1882), *The Buddha: His Life, His Doctrine, His Order*, London: Williams and Norgate
———. (1920), 'On the History of the Indian Caste System', *Indian Antiquary*, Vol. XLIX.
Olivelle, P. (1976), 'A Definition of World Renunciation', *Wiener Zeitschrift fiir die Kunde Sudund Ostasiens*, Vol. 20, pp. 75–83.
Pacittiya (1940), translated by LB. Horner as *The Book of Discipline*, Oxford University Press.
———. (1958), Vol. I, *Vinaya Pitaka*, edited by Bhikkhu J. Kashyap, Nalanda Devanagari Pali Series, Bihar Government.
Padma Purana (1950), edited by Ravisenacharya, translated by Daulat Ramji, Delhi: Veer Sena Mandali.
Pande, G.C. (1974), *Studies in the Origins of Buddhism*, Delhi: Motilal Banarsidass.
Pandita Ramabai (1887), *The High Caste Hindu Woman*, published by Pandita Ramabai, Philadelphia.
Parajika (1958), in *Vinaya Pitaka*, edited by Bhikkhu J.Kashyap, Nalanda: Pali Publication Board.
Parasher, Aloka (1991), *The Mlecchas in Early India*, Delhi: Munshiram Manoharlal.

Patil, S. (1982), Dasa-Sudra Slavery: Studies in the Origins of Indian Slavery, Delhi: Allied Publishers.
Patterson, Orlando (1982), Slavery and Social Death: A Comparative Study, Cambridge, MA: Harvard University Press.
People's Union for Democratic Rights (PUDR) (1983), Inside the Family, Delhi. Philips, C.H. (1961), 'James Mill, Mountstuart Elphinstone and the History of India', in C.H. Philips (ed.), Historians Piggott, S. (1948), Pre-historic India, Harmondsworth: Penguin Books.
Pillai, J.M. Somasundaram (1959), Two Thousand Years of Tamil Literature, Madras: The South India Saiva Siddhanta Works Publishing Society.
———. (1968), A History of Tamil Literature with Texts and Translations, Annamalainagar, published by the author.
Poddar, Arvind (1976), Renaissance in Bengal: Search for Identity, Shimla: Indian Institute of Advanced Study.
Pollock, Sheldon (1993), 'Ramayana and the Political Imagination in India', Journal of Asian Studies, Vol. 52, No. 2, May.
Prasad, Jaishankar (1974), Dhruvaswamini, Allahabad: Leader Press.
Pushp, P.N. (1980), 'Ramayana in Kashmiri Literature and Folklore', in V. Raghavan (ed.), Ramayana Tradition in Asia, Delhi: Sahitya Akademi, pp. 534–45.
Raghavan, V. (ed.) (1980), The Ramayana Tradition in Asia, Delhi: Sahitya Akademi.
The Raghuvamsa of Kalidasa (1985), translated by C.R. Devadhar, Delhi: Motilal Banarsidass.
Rai, G.K. (1976), 'Forced Labour in Ancient and Early Medieval India', The Indian Historical Review, Vol. 3, No. 1, pp. 16–42.
Ramanujan, A.IC (1985), Poems of Love and War, Delhi: Oxford University Press.
———. (1985), Speaking of Siva, Harmondsworth: Penguin Books.
———. (1991), 'Three Hundred Ramayanas: Five Examples and Three Thoughts on Translation', in Paula Richman (ed.), Many Ramayanas: The Diversity of a Narrative Tradition in South Asia, Delhi: Oxford University Press, pp. 22–49.
Ramaswamy, Vijaya (1989), 'Aspects of Women and Work in Early South India', Indian Economic and Social History Review, Vol. 26, No.1, pp. 81–99.
———. (1996), Divinity and Deviance: Women in Virasaivism, Delhi: Oxford University Press.
———. (1997), Walking Naked: Society, Spirituality in South India, Shimla: Indian Institute of Advanced Study.
The Ramayana of Valmiki (1957), Vol. II, translated by H.P. Shashi, London: Shanti Sadan.
———. (1958), edited by S. Kuppuswami Sastrigal et al., Madras.
———. (1976), translated by Makhan Lal Sen, Delhi: Munshiram Manoharlal.
The Ramayana of Vabniki: An Epic of Ancient India (1986), Vol. II, Ayodhyakanda, edited by Sheldon Pollock, Princeton: Princeton University Press.
Rao, Velucheri Narayana (1991), 'A Ramayana of Their Own: Women's Oral Tradition in Telugu', in Paula Richman (ed.), Many Ramayanas: The Diversity of a Narrative Tradition in South Asia, Delhi: Oxford University Press, pp. 114–36.
Ramagar, Shercen (1991), Enquiries into the Political Organization of the Harappan State, Pune: Ravish Publishers.
Raychaudhari, H.C. (1972), Political History of Ancient India, Calcutta: University of Calcutta.
Reddy, Snehalata (1973), Sita; republished in The Other Side, September 1985.
Rgveda (1971), edited by R.T.H. Griffith, Varanasi: Chowkhamba Sanskrit Series Office.
Richman, Paula (ed.) (1991), Many Ramayanas: The Diversity of a Narrative Tradition in South Asia, Delhi: Oxford University Press.
Riseew, Carla and Rajni Palriwala (1997), Shifting Circles of Support, Delhi: Sage.
Robinson, E.J. (1957), Tamil Wisdom: Traditions Concerning Hindu Sages and Selections from Their Writing, Madras; reprint, Delhi: Asian Educational Services, 2001.
Rosselli, John (1980), 'The Self-Image of Effeteness: Physical Education and Nationalism in 19th century Bengal', Past and Present, Vol. 86.
Rowbotham, Sheila (1976), Hidden History: Rediscovering Women in History from the 17th Century to the Present, New York: Vintage Books.
Roy, Kumkum (1987), 'Women in Early India', unpublished typescript.

Roy, Kumkum (1992), 'The King's Household: Structure/Space in the Sastric Tradition', Economic and Political Weekly, Vol. 27, Nos. 43–44, pp. WS55–60; reprinted in Kumkum Sangari and Uma Chakravarti (eds), From Myths to Markets: Essays on Gender, Shimla: Indian Institute of Advanced Study and Delhi: Manohar, 1999.

———. (1994), The Emergence of Monarchy in Early India 800–400 BC, Delhi: Oxford University Press.

———. (1998), 'Unravelling the Kamasutra,' in Mary E. John and Janaki Nair (eds), A Question of Silence?: Sexual Economies of Modern India, Delhi: Kali For Women.

———. (2002), 'Goddesses in the Rgveda: An Investigation', in Nilima Chitgopekar (ed.), Invoking Goddesses: Gender Politics in Indian Religion, Delhi: Shakti.

———. (2003), 'Of Theras and Theris: Visions of Liberation in the Early Bud dhist Tradition', in Vijaya Ramaswamy (ed.), Re-searching Indian Women, Delhi: Manohar.

———. (2005), 'Recent Writings on Gender Relations in Early India', in Kirit Shah (ed.), History and Gender: Some Explorations, Jaipur: Rawat Press.

Ryan, Bryce (1953), Castes in Modern Ceylon, New Jersey: Rutgers University Press.

Sadharma Pundarika (1953), edited by Nalinaksha Dutta, Calcutta: Asiatic Society.

Samyutta Nikaya (1952), translated by F.L. Woodward and C.A.F. Rhys Davids as The Book of Kindred Sayings, in five volumes, London: Pali Text Society.

———. (1959), in four volumes, edited by Bhikkhu J. Kashyap, Nalanda Devanagari Pali Series, Bihar Government.

Sangari, Kumkum (1999), 'Consent, Agency and Rhetorics of Incitement', in Politics of the Possible: Essays on *Gender;* History, Narratives, Colonial English, Delhi: Tulika Books, pp. 364–409.

Sarkar, S.C. (1958), 'Derozio and Young Bengal', in A.C. Gupta (ed.), Studies in Bengal Renaissance, Jadavpur: National Council of Education Bengal.

Selwyn, Tom (1979), 'Images of Reproduction: An Analysis of a Hindu Marriage Ceremony', Man, Vol. 14, No. 4, December

Sangari, Kumkum and Uma Chakravarti (eds) (1999), From Myths to Markets: Essays in Gender, Shimla: Indian Institute of Advanced Study and Delhi: Manohar.

Sankalia, H.D. (1967–68), 'Archaeology and the Ramayana', Puratattva, Vol. 1.

Saraswati, Dayananda (1915), Satyarth Prakash, translated by Chiranjiva Bharadvaja, Agra: Arya Pratinidhi Sabha.

Sarkar, Jadunath (1928), India through the Ages; reprint, Calcutta: Orient Longman, 1979.

Sarkar, S.C. (1958), 'Derozio and Young Bengal', in A.C. Gupta (ed.), Studies in Bengal Renaissance, Jadavpur: National Council of Education Bengal.

Selwyn, Tom (1979), 'Images of Reproduction: An Analysis of a Hindu Marriage Ceremony', Man, Vol. 14, No. 4, December.

Sen, Sukumar (1977), The Origin and Development of the Rama Legend, Calcutta: Rupa and Co.

Sen, Sunil (1961), 'Romesh Chandra Dutt', in C.H. Philips (ed.), Historians of India, Pakistan and Ceylon, London: Oxford University Press.

Senivaratne, Sudarshan (1978), 'The Mauryan State' in H.J.M. Claessen and P. Skalnik (eds), The Early State, The Hague.

Shanin, Teodor (1972), 'Chayanov's Message: Illuminations, Miscomprehensions, and the Contemporary "Development Theory"', in A.V.Chayanov, The Theory of Peasant Economy and the Awkward Class: Political Sociology of Peasantry in a Developing Society, Russia 1910–25, London: Oxford University Press.

Shanin, Teodor (ed.) (1971), Peasants and Peasant Societies, Harmondsworth: Penguin Books.

Sharma, R. (1971), A Socio-Political Study of the Valmiki Ramayana, Delhi: Motilal Banarsidass.

Sharma, R.S. (1958), Sudras in Ancient India: A Social History of the Lower Order Down to circa AD 600, Delhi: Motilal Banarsidass; second revised edition, 1980.

———. (1965), 'Usury in Early Medieval India (AD 400–1200)', Comparative Studies in Society and History, Vol. 3, No. 1.

———. (1965), Indian Feudalism, Delhi: Macmillan.

———. (1977), 'Conflict, Distribution and Differentiation in RgVedic Society', The Indian Historical Review, Vol. 4, No. 1.

———. (1983a), Material Cultureand Social Formations in Ancient India, Delhi: Macmillan.

Sharma, R.S. (1983b), Perspectives in Social and Economic History of Early India, Delhi: Munshiram Manoharlal.
Shastri, Shakuntala Rao (1959), Women in the Sacred Laws, Bombay: Bharatiya Vidya Bhawan.
Shatapatha Brahmana (1964), edited by A. Weber, Varanasi: Chowkhamba Publishers.
Singh, Pankaj K. and Jaidev (1999), 'Decentering a Patriarchal Myth', in Kumkum Sangari and Uma Chakravarti (eds), *From Myths to Markets: Essays in Gender*, Shimla: Indian Institute of Advanced Study and Delhi: Manohar.
Sinha, Mrinalini (1986), 'Colonial Politics and the Ideal of Masculinity', paper presented at the Third National Conference of Women's Studies, Indian Association of Women's Studies, Chandigarh.
———. (1995), Colonial Masculinity: The 'Manly' Englishman and the Effeminate Bengali in the Late Nineteenth Century, Manchester: Manchester University Press.
'The Sita Who Refused the Fire Ordeal,' (1981), Manushi, Vol. 8.
Mrs Speier (1856), *Life in Ancient India; reprinted as Phases of Indian Civilization*, Delhi: Cosmo.
Spivak, Gayatri Chakravorty (1987), 'A Literary Representation of the Subaltern: Mahasweta Devi's "Stanadayani"', in R. Guha (ed.), *Subaltern Studies V*, Delhi: Oxford University Press.
Stein, Burton (1980), *Peasant State and Society in Medieval South India*, Delhi: Oxford University Press.
Stephens, Julie (1992), 'Feminist Fictions: A Critique of the Category "Non-Western Woman" in Feminist Writings on India', in R. Guha (ed.), *Subaltern Studies VI, Delhi*: Oxford University Press.
Stokes, E.G. (1961), 'The Administrators and Historical Writing on India', in C.H. Philips (ed.), *Historians of India, Pakistan and Ceylon*, London: Oxford University Press.
Sukhtankar, V.S. (1957), *On the Meaning of the Mahabharata*, Bombay: The Asiatic Society of Bombay.
Sutherland, Sally (1992), 'Seduction, Counter Seduction and Sexual Role Models: Bedroom Politics and the Indian Epics', Journal of Indian Philosophy, Vol. 19, pp. 53–61.
———. (1996) 'The Political and Social Ramifications of the Construction of Gender in the Valmiki Ramayana', paper presented at the Ramayana Conference, University of Hyderabad.
Sutra Kritanga (1895), translated by Hermann Jacobi, in jaina Sutras, Vol. II, Sacred Books of the East, IX.V, Oxford: Clarendon Press.
Sutta Nipata (1958), Khuddaka Nikaya, Nalanda: Pali Publication Board.
———. (1977), translated by V. Fausboll, Sacred Books of the East, Vol. XI, Part II, Delhi: Motilal Banarsidass.
Sutta Pitaka (1958), comprising the Digha Nikaya (three volumes), the Majjhima Nikaya (three volumes), the Samyutta Nikaya (four volumes) and the Anguttara Nikaya (four volumes), Nalanda: Pali Publication Board.
Syed, A.J. (ed.) (1985), D.D. Kosambi on History and Society: Problems of Interpretation, Bombay: University of Bombay.
Talbot, Cynthia (1995), 'Rudraina-devi, the Female King: Gender and Political Authority in Medieval India', in David Shulman (ed.), Syllables of Sky: Studies in South Indian Civilization, Delhi: Oxford University Press.
Tambiah, S.J. (1970), Buddhism and the Spirit Cults of North-East Thailand, Cambridge: Cambridge University Press.
Thapar, Romila (1978a), 'Dana and Dakshina', in Ancient Indian Social History: Some Interpretations, Delhi: Orient Longman.
———. (1978b), Exile and Kingdom: Some Thoughts on the Ramayana, Bangalore: Mythic Society.
———. (1978c), 'Renunciation: The Making of a Counter Culture?', in Ancient Indian Social History: Some Interpretations, Delhi: Orient Longman.
———. (1981), 'The Householder and the Renouncer in the Brahmanical and Buddhist Traditions', Contributions to Indian Sociology, Vol. 15.
———. (1983), From Lineage to State, Delhi: Oxford University Press.
———. (1990), A History of India, Vol. I, London: Penguin Books.
———. (1999), Sakuntala Texts, Readings, Histories, Delhi: Kali for Women.
Theragatha, Khuddaka Nikaya (1958), edited by Bhikkhu J. Kashyap, Nalanda: Pali Publication Board.
Therigatha (1948), translated by C.A.F. Rhys Davids as Psalms of the Sisters, London: Pali Text Society.
Thorner, Daniel (1971), 'Peasant Economy as a Category in Economic History', in T. Shanin (ed.), Peasants and Peasant Societies, Harmondsworth: Penguin Books.
Thorner, Daniel (1972), 'Chayanov's Concept of Peasant Economy', in A.V. Chayanov, The Theory of Peasant Economy and the Awkward Class: Political Sociology of Peasantry in a Developing Society, Russia 1910–25, London: Oxford University Press.

Threatened Existence: A Feminist Analysis of the Genocide in Gujarat (2003), International Initiative for Justice in Gujarat, December.
Tod, James (1920), Annals and Antiquities of Rajasthan, 1829–1830, edited by William Crooke, London: Oxford University Press.
Tripathi, R.S. (1937), History of Ancient India, Delhi: Motilal Banarsidass. Tyagi, Jaya (2001), Women in the Grihyasutras, unpublished Ph.D. thesis, University of Delhi.
Uberoi, J.P.S. (1969), 'The Five Symbols of Sikhism', in Darshan Singh Maini (ed.), Sikhism, Patiala: Punjabi University.
Uberoi, Patricia (ed.) (1994), Family, Kinship and Marriage in India, Delhi: Oxford University Press.
The Uttararamacharita of Bhavabhuti (1993), edited by M.R. Kale, Delhi: Motilal Banarsidass.
Vasan, S.S. (1953), Avvaiyar (film).
Vasishtha Dharmasutra (1975), translated by George Buhler, in Sacred Laws of the Aryas, Vol. II, Delhi: Motilal Banarsidass.
Vasudevan, Geeta (1981), Women in the Ramayana, unpublished M. Phil.paper, Jawaharlal Nehru University, Delhi.
Vinaya. Pitaka (1879-93), edited by H. Oldenberg, London: Pali Text Society.
———. (1958), Volumes I–IV:Vol. I, Parajika; Vol. II, Pacittiya; Vol. III, Mahavagga; Vol. IV, Cullavagga, Nalanda: Pali Publication Board.
Vinaya Texts (1881), edited by T.W. Rhys Davids and H. Oldenberg, Oxford: Clarendon Press.
Vishnttsmriti (1880), translated by J. Jolly as *The Institutes of Vishnu, Sacred Books of the East,* Vol. VII, Oxford: Clarendon Press.
Vivekananda, Swami (1958), *Complete Works,* Vol. II, Calcutta: Advaita Ashrama.
Voigt, Johannes H. (1967), *F.M. Max Mueller: The Man and His Ideas,* Calcutta: Firma K.L. Mukhopadhyaya.
Vriji, K.J. (1952), *Ancient History of Saurashtra,* Bombay.
Vyakarana Mahabhashya of Patanjali (1892), edited by Franz L. Kielhorn, Vol. I, Bombay: Central Book Depot.
Wagle, N.N. (1966), *Society at the Time of the Buddha,* Bombay: Popular Prakashan.
Warder, A.K. (1956), 'On the Relationship between Buddhism and Other Contemporary Systems', *Bulletin of the School of Oriental and African Studies,* Vol. 18.
———. (1970), *Indian Buddhism,* Delhi: Motilal Banarsidass.
Weber, Max (1960), *The Religion of India,* New York: The Free Press.
Wheeler, R.M. (1953), *The Indus Civilization,* Cambridge: Cambridge University Press.
Yajnava lkyasmritisamvat) (1986), Banaras: Chowkhamba Sanskrit Series Office.
Yalman, Nur (1963), 'On the Purity of Women in the Castes of Ceylon and Malabar', *Journal of the Royal Anthropological Institute of Great Britain and Ireland,* Vol. 93, pp. 25–28.
Zinn, Howard (1999), *A People's History of the United States,* New York: Harper Collins.

Chapter 21 Work and Gender in Mughal India

SHIREEN MOOSVI

The study of women as a component of the labour force in pre-colonial India is in infancy as yet. Monographs on women in Mughal India and other pre-modern regimes have tended to concentrate more on their social status, customs, clothing and fashion, or on individual women.[1] The inadequacy of secondary work is partly explained, perhaps, by difficulties of source material. The kind of profuse documentation which exists for political and fiscal history of the sixteenth–eighteenth centuries is not available for either labour or demographic history. There is no way one can reconstruct sex ratios in the general population or in the non-domestic labour force.

One has, therefore, to cut one's coat according to one's cloth. Where some information is available, though this had not so far been brought together, is in respect of the kinds of work that women did. Incidental references in Indo-Persian and other literature from the fifteenth to eighteenth century provide us with general statements or individual facts from which general conditions may be inferred. Such material has been explored for this paper, notably, Abū'l Faẓl's *Ā'īn-i Akbarī* (c. 1595) and other historical works. Deserving of special mention is Muḥammad Shādiābadī's dictionary, *Miftāh-ul Fuẓala,* written in Malwa in 1468–69, with the explicit purpose of explaining words relating to things of everyday life. Its unique manuscript in the British Museum was illustrated probably early in Akbar's reign (1560s and 1570s), and these illustrations often help us when the text itself is silent.[2] In 1825, James Skinner wrote at Hansi (Haryana) his Persian work on castes, the *Tashrīh ul-Aqwām*. The splendid illustrations he provided from hands of Mughal-school artists in

[1] Rekha Misra, *Women in Mughal India (1526–1748)* (Delhi, 1965); G. Rumer, *Gulbadan, Portrait of a Rose Princess at the Mughal Court* (New York, 1980); C. Pant, *Nur Jahan and Her Family* (Allahabad, 1978); J. Brijbhushan, *Razia Sultan of Hindostan* (New Delhi, 1990); A. Bulenschon, *The Life of a Mughal Princes, Jahan Ara Begum* (London, 1931); J. Brijbhusan, *Muslim Women* (New Delhi, 1980); S. Thomas, *Women of Destiny* (New Delhi, 1979).
[2] British Museum MS Or. 3299.

the British Museum copy add to the detailed textual information which relates mainly to Haryana and the Delhi region.[3]

These two illustrated works exemplify the importance of pictorial evidence, notably offered by miniatures of the imperial Mughal school of the sixteenth and seventeenth centuries. Its well-known tradition of accuracy and realism invests this school's portrayals of scenes of the court and of everyday life with particular significance for our purpose. The miniatures of the later Mughal-influenced Rajput and hill schools (eighteenth century) supplement the Mughal school.

The third principal body of evidence comes from British surveys and reports of the early nineteenth century, where conditions and traditions of the pre-colonial society were observed and noted. Most noteworthy among these is Francis Buchanan's set of celebrated *Journey from Madras* (1800–01)[4] and his detailed surveys of districts of the lower and Gangetic basin, prepared between 1806 and 1812.[5] These can be said to form the initial point of all modern economic and anthropological enquiries in India.

What follows is a classified presentation of information of the gender division of labour as one can reconstruct for pre-colonial northern India from this material. At the end, I hope to examine the broad inferences one can derive from the description.

AGRICULTURE

Our evidence shows ploughing to be a man's operation: all illustrations from the Mughal and hill (*pahari*) schools, for example, show only men drawing the plough. In line with the current practice, a Mughal miniature of c. 1610 depicts a woman sowing seed broadcast, walking directly behind the man who is driving the plough.[6] In 1811–12, Buchanan reported that in Bihar women earned some wages through sowing seeds, though this was for them a part-time job in addition to spinning.[7]

The work in the field that the women did in the eighteenth century included transplanting, weeding and helping in harvesting.[8] Though the actual operations carried out by women are not always clear enough in Mughal miniatures, women working in the fields form part of the typical rural scene depicted by the artists. Such illustrations may be seen in the *Anwār-i*

[3] British Museum Add. 27,255.

[4] Francis Buchanan, *A Journey from Madras through the Countries of Mysore, Canara, and Malabar, & C.*, 3 vols (London, 1807). I have not used the very rich material contained in this work, because my present paper is confined to northern India only.

[5] Francis Buchanan, *An Account of the District of Purnea in 1809–10* (Patna, 1986 [reprint]); *An Account of the Districts of Bihar and Patna in 1811–12* (Patna–Gaya Report) (Patna, 1986 [reprint]); *An Account of the District of Shadabad* (Shahabad Report) (1832); *An Account of the District of Bhagal*pore (Bhagalpur Report) (1832); see also Motgomery Martin, ed., *The History, Antiquities, and Statistics of Eastern India*, 3 vols. (London, 1838), where these and other district surveys are reproduced in an abridged form.

[6] T. Falk and S. Digby, *Paintings from Mughal India* (London, n.d.), Plate 18.

[7] Buchanan, *Patna–Gaya Report*, Vol. II, 618.

[8] Buchanan, *Purnea Report*, 444 and 446.

Suhailī illustrated in 1575[9] and *Razmnāma*, c. 1600.[10] A line drawing of early nineteenth century from Kashmir very clearly depicts a woman transplanting paddy along with a man.[11]

Both men and women were hired for weeding and transplanting work, and, at least in District Purnea (Bihar), c. 1810, their wages were equal, though both were paid generally in kind. Buchanan estimates that a man able to work 270 days in a year could earn about 12 rupees a year. His wife doing the same job could 'make fully as much'.[12]

Besides these direct field operations, there was another task performed by women that too merits classification as field work. They not only cooked food for their men working in the fields, but also carried it to the field. In an illustration in the *Anwār-i-Suhailī*, a woman is shown bringing food to her husband standing on the well irrigating the fields.[13]

After the produce was collected from the field, it apparently called for more work from women than men. The beating of rice was exclusively a woman's job, and in the illustration of pestle and mortar (*okhlī*), the *Miftāh-ul Fuẓala,* shows a woman working with it.[14]

Buchanan writing about Bihar and eastern Uttar Pradesh, c. 1810, says that the cleaning of rice was 'performed entirely by the women'. The separation of husk from rice was done by three methods, namely, by a wooden foot-worked hammer, called *dhengli*; by beating by hand in mortar and pestle (*okhlī*), and by boiling. The first of these methods according to Buchanan was 'very laborious and was generally carried out by two women'. The beating of rice in mortar with a wooden pestle was a comparatively lighter work, but the method was less efficient. Only the winter or coarse varieties of rice were cleaned by boiling that was the easiest method but considered most inferior.[15] The payment for the work was made in kind; A woman called upon to furnish 9 or 10 measures of husked rice for every 23 or 24 measures of paddy simply had as her wages the husked rice that she had left with her after she had delivered to her employer the fixed measures. Buchanan estimates that the woman was usually left with less than one-fifth of the rice she cleaned (Dinajpur, c. 1810).[16] In Purnea, a woman by cleaning rice, around 1810, earned not more than a quarter of a rupee a month and allowing for sickness, etc., she worked about 10 months a year, and thus earned not more than ₹ 2.50 in a year.[17]

Rice husking was not a full-time job as women did it along with their other domestic duties and spinning. In any case, beating rice by working the *dhengli* was so laborious that the women were only able to exert themselves for a limited number of hours.[18]

Not only the cleaning of rice but the milling of all food-grains as well was considered a woman's job. The *Miftāh-ul Fuẓala* (1468–69) shows a woman turning a rotary hand-mill,

[9] Bharat Kala Bhavan, Varanasi, No. 9069, f. 18.
[10] Prince of Wales Museum, Bombay, Acc. No.43. 35 (dispersed copy).
[11] D. D. Kosambi, *An Introduction to the Study of Indian History* (Bombay, 1956), 319, Figure 41.
[12] Buchanan, *Purnea Report*, 446.
[13] *Anwār-i Suhailī*, Kala Bhavan, Varanasi, MS 9069, f. 61.
[14] Or. 3299, f. 89a.
[15] Martin, *Eastern India*, Vol. II, 822.
[16] Ibid., 823.
[17] Buchanan, *Purnea Report*, 444.
[18] Martin, *Eastern India*, Vol. II, 822.

with a single handle.[19] In 1676, Fryer noted about India generally: The Indian Wives dress their Husbands, Victuals, fetch Water, and Grind their Corn with an Hand-Mill, when they sing, chat, and are merry.[20]

When Buchanan says that two women used to sit on the hand-mill, the labour being very hard and the work restricted to three hours a day, he must be referring to a larger hand-mill used for grinding of grain for non-domestic use or for the market. He adds that both men and women were employed at such hand-mills.[21]

Fetching water for domestic needs, as Fryer observed, was another customary chore of Indian women. The way the village women in India carried pitchers, filled with water, balancing them one over the other on their heads, became a popular theme for artists and was a feat remarkable enough to draw the attention of Emperor Akbar who commended Indian women for it.[22] The pictorial representations show women drawing water from wells either by throwing down a rope tied to a pot and pulling it up (c. 1570)[23] or by drawing it over a pulley set-up on the well (c. 1700).[24] Some of these and other paintings from the eighteenth century show women carrying filled pitchers.[25]

In the 1810s, Buchanan found in Bhagalpur 'a great many poor women' who made their living by 'carrying water for wealthy families' and were called *panibharin*' (water-fillers). The usual payment for supplying one pitcher daily was 2 paisa (1 rupee = 64 paisas) a month and the women were thereby able to earn about half a rupee a month. This income they generally supplemented by some spinning. In Patna, the wages for water-carrying were higher.[26]

Looking after cattle and making milk products formed another major sector of women's work. Explaining the term for butter (*maska*), the illustration in the *Miftāh-ul Fuẓala* shows a women sitting and churning butter-milk.[27] In a Kangra painting showing Krishna steeling butter, women are shown making butter.[28] A man is never shown in any illustration similarly preparing butter or butter-milk.

Feeding cattle was also a part of women's domestic chores. A miniature of Kangra school, c. 1750, shows women feeding cows.[29] However, milking cows was a job which men and

[19] Or. 3299 f. 119a.

[20] J. Fryer, *A New Account of East India & Persia being Nineteen Year's Travels, 1672–81*, ed. W. Crook, Vol. II (London, 1912), 118.

[21] Buchanan, *Patna–Gaya Report*, Vol. II, 637.

[22] Blochmann, ed., *Āʾīn-i Akbarī*, Vol. II (Calcutta, 1867), 228.

[23] Basil Gray, ed., *Rajput Paintings* (Faber Gallery of Oriental Art, n.d.), Plate 2.

[24] Laurence Binyon, *The Court Painters of the Grand Moguls* (London, 1921), Plate XVII; Falk and Digby, *Paintings from Mughal India*, Plate 26; T. Falk and M. Archer, *Indian Miniatures in the India Office Library* (Delhi, 1981), Plate 42d, 514.

[25] L. Hajek and W. Forman, *Miniatures from the East* (London, n.d.), Plates 46 and 47. E. Kuhnel, *Miniatumalerei Im Ishamischen Orient* (Berlin, 1923), 147.

[26] Buchanan, *Patna–Gaya Report*, Vol. I, 287.

[27] Or. 3299, f. 89b.

[28] M. S. Randhava, *Kangra Paintings of the Bhagvata Purana* (New Delhi, 1960), Plate III (colour).

[29] Ibid., Figure 4 (black and white).

women both performed; and there seems no strict division of work here, for the paintings show men and women both milking cows and goats.[30]

The women did a number of other sundry jobs related to agriculture for which we have traditions but little literary or visual evidence. The jobs included feeding oil seeds or pieces of sugarcanes in the press worked by men, cooking sugarcane juice for making jaggery, etc. Their role could be so important that Akbar's official historian, Abū'l Faẕl writing about Bengal, says that the entire agricultural work depended upon women.[31] Bengal being mainly a paddy-producing area, this statement might not be an exaggeration, since weeding, transplanting, harvesting and beating rice all essentially fell to the women's share. Women helped in irrigation as well: a nineteenth-century drawing from Kashmir shows a man drawing water from a well while the woman cuts and makes water channels to irrigate the field.[32]

It appears that the women of common peasants invariably worked along with their men. Only the castes who claimed a higher status tended to keep their women indoors, as in the case of higher ranks among the Jats, according to the *Tashrīh ul-Aqwām*.[33]

An interesting evidence of women carrying out actual cultivation comes from the Middle Himalayas, where only hoeing, not ploughing, could be practised to loosen the soil. Here, in 1624, it was reported that 'the women cultivate the soil, while men are weavers'.[34] The conditions in the Kashmir Valley were not identical, but a number of nineteenth-century drawings from Kashmir show women performing almost all agricultural operations along with men, except ploughing.[35]

TEXTILES

The process of textile manufacture, after cotton was removed from the field, followed fairly well-marked stages. First of all, there was the process of separating the fibre from the seed, a function which seems to have been performed mainly by women. The Ajanta frescoes of the sixth century show a woman using the Indian cotton-gin, now called *charkhī* (two rollers horizontally mounted on a stand, but without worm-gearing).[36] In an eighteenth-century painting a woman is shown carrying the same instrument, now provided with worm-gears as well.[37]

After the seeds were expelled, the fibres had to be separated from each other (scutched). The Ajanta frescoes mentioned above show a woman working with a roller and a board,

---

[30] D. Barret and B. Gray, *Paintings of India* (British Museum, 1963), 74, 88 (c. 1595), 156 (c. 1690).

[31] Blochmann, *Ā'īn*, Vol. I, 389.

[32] Kosambi, *An Introduction to the Study of Indian History*, Figure 43, 321.

[33] Add. 27,255, f. 157a.

[34] C. Wessels, *Early Jesuit Travellers in Central Asia, 1603–1721* (The Hague, 1924), 52.

[35] Kosambi, *An Introduction to the Study of Indian History*, 318–19, 321.

[36] Reproduced in G. Yazdani, *Ajanta, the Colour and Minochrome Reproductions of the Ajanta Frescoes, Based on Photography*, Part I, Plate XII.

[37] L. Hajek, *Miniatures from the East* (London, 1960), Plates 48 and 49.

to obtain the separation;[38] but this was a laborious process, which could also damage the fibres. By medieval times, the bow-string device was in wide use for this purpose. This was invariably operated by men so that a semi-itinerant class of men, *dhunyās* or *naddāfs*, went around scutching cotton. In the fourteenth century we are told how, after obtaining cotton, a mother gave it to a *naddāf* (male scutcher) to scutch it.[39] Pictorial representations show that the cotton-bow was used exclusively by men.[40] But it appears that the bow did not altogether replace hand-beating, and in the 1660s according to an English factor, women scutched fibres by this process.[41] Buchanan, c. 1810, too reports women beating cotton to separate fibres. He adds, however, that 'for greater part' scutching was done by men using the bow.[42]

Not all *dhunyās* (carders) went door-to-door selling their services; a considerable proportion of them (around one-third, according to Buchanan) purchased cotton and scutched it at home.[43] In the case of these 'self-employed' carders the women were entrusted with the job of hawking the cotton scutched at home by their men.[44]

The next process, namely, spinning, was done almost exclusively by women, by hand-spindle or by wheel. Writing at the close of the fourteenth century, Amīr Khusrau likens the needle and spindle to a young woman's spear and arrow.[45] In the dictionary Miftāh-ul Fuẓala, written in 1468–69 and illustrated about a hundred years later, where the text explains the terms for spindle (*duk* and *praiti*), the illustration depicts it as being worked by women.[46] The same work defines the *charkha*, or spinning wheel, as the device 'by which women spin yarn'.[47] The earliest reference to spinning wheel in India dates back to 1350, when while censuring Queen Raziyya for claiming to act as sovereign, the historian Isāmī says that a women is suited only to work on the spinning wheel.[48]

From the succeeding centuries, continuous pictorial evidence of women working on the spinning wheel grows in profusion, through the miniatures of Mughal painters as well as other Indian schools. A selection is listed below:

(a) A woman spinning on wheel with no crank handle: illustration in *Miftāh-ul Fuẓala*.[49]
(b) Village women carrying spinning wheels, c. 1590.[50]

---

[38] M. K. Dhavalikar, *Ajanta: A Cultural Study* (Pune, 1973), 2.
[39] K. A. Nizami, ed., *Khair-ul Majālis* (Aligarh, 1956), 190–91.
[40] Or. 3299, f. 66.
[41] Foster, ed., *English Factories in India 1665–7* (Oxford, 1927), 174.
[42] Buchanan, *Patna–Gaya Report*, 647.
[43] Ibid.
[44] Buchanan, *Purnea Report*, 536. A day's sale proceeds are estimated as ₹1 to ₹ 2.
[45] M. Sulaiman Ashraf, ed., *Hasht Bihisht* (Aligarh, 1918), 28.
[46] Or. 3299 f. 151a.
[47] Ibid., f. 94b.
[48] A. S. Usha, ed., *Futūḥ us Salāṭīn* (Madras, 1948), 134. Spinning wheel, originally a Chinese device, came to India, probably through the Islamic civilization. Interestingly enough, in the Persian poetry of twelfth–thirteenth centuries the wheel (*charkhī*) is invariably seen as an instrument worked by women. Cf. Irfan Habib, 'Medieval Technology Exchange between India and the Islamic World', *Aligarh Journal of Oriental Studies* II, nos. 1–2 (1985): 203–04.
[49] Or. 3299 f. 151a.
[50] *Razamnāma*, Or. 12076f.

(c) A woman with a spinning wheel with no handles, dated 1606.[51]
(d) Three women working on spinning wheels, in the foreground, 1617.[52]
(e) A woman and a wheel with a half handle, Shāhjahān's reign (1627–58).[53]
(f) A sturdy village woman sitting in front of a spinning wheel with handle, c. 1670.[54]
(g) Spinning wheel, with handle, being carried by a woman, Kangra painting depicting a scene from the Mahabharata, 1785–90.[55]

As in the case of scutching, the two devices for spinning also remained in use simultaneously. The hand spindle was used by women to spin fine yarn and silk thread even in the nineteenth century.[56]

Buchanan says that spinning was not a taboo for any caste and thus a large number of women from all castes used to spin.[57] We are told in the fourteenth century that Shaikh Nizāmuddīn mother, when making a turban for him, spun half of the yarn herself, while the other half was spun by her slave girl.[58] The *Tashrīh ul-Aqwām*, c. 1825, says that the women of the Kayasth caste also spun yarn.[59] Even if women did not spin for wages, they still spun for the use of the family.[60]

Spinning could be adjusted to the working time available to individual women. Thus, Buchanan noted that they spun 'when their other occupations permit', spinning often coming after the work of cooking, bringing up children and beating rice. On the other hand, 'the women of rank' who sat before the wheel for a whole day could do so because they were not obliged to attend to other work.[61] Wages in both cases naturally varied. Women, working part-time, on an average earned ₹ 3.25 a year in Bihar,[62] ₹ 2.37 in Gorakhpur[63] and a quarter rupee a month, that is, ₹ 3 a year, in Purnea.[64] As against this, those who worked full-time and spun fine thread earned 15 annas a month or ₹ 11.25 a year in Purnea.[65]

Women spinners did not usually work for wages, but as self-employed persons, obtaining the raw material themselves. At times they bought even unscutched cotton, had it scutched

---

[51] E. Kuhnel and H. Goets, *Indian Book Painting from Jahangir's Album in the State Library, Berlin* (London, 1926), Plate 1.
[52] A. K. Das, *Mughal Paintings during Jahangir's Time* (Calcutta, 1978), 235, Plate 2.
[53] Ivan Stchoukine, *La Painteors Indienne a l'Epoque des Grand Moghols* (Paris, 1929), Plate XLIV.
[54] F. R. Martin, *The Miniature Paintings and Painters of Persia, India, Turkey, from the Eighth to the Eighteenth Century* (London, 1912), Plate 207a.
[55] Randhava, *Kangra Paintings*, Plate V.
[56] Buchanan, *Purnea Report*, 536–37.
[57] Ibid., 536.
[58] Nizami, *Khair-ul Majālis*, 190–91.
[59] Add. 27,255 f. 105b.
[60] Buchanan, *Patna–Gaya Report*, Vol. II, 639.
[61] Buchanan, *Purnea Report*, 536–37.
[62] Buchanan, *Patna–Gaya Report*, 647–48.
[63] Martin, *Eastern India*, 558–59.
[64] Buchanan, *Purnea Report*, 536–37.
[65] Ibid.

on payment[66] and then spun the yarn and sold it.[67] It was perhaps more convenient and practical for women since this arrangement did not subject them to any strict time schedule or make them work outdoors. The spinning in case of part-time spinners was done usually in the afternoon, while beating rice occupied them during the mornings.

Cotton was not the only material for women to work in. They also worked at reeling and selling tasar-silk thread. The earnings estimated were 7.5 *annas* a month.[68]

In Kashmir shawl-wool was spun by girls who started work at the age of 10 and according to an estimate, a hundred thousand women (out of a supposed total population of 800,000) were engaged in spinning wool in the valley in 1822.[69]

Whereas spinning was strictly women's work, the actual weaving was done mainly by men, though women presumably assisted them in preparing the warp and weft-threads. Mughal and later miniatures show only men with the loom.[70] But Buchanan says that 'each loom requires one man and woman', the latter to wind and to assist in wrapping.[71]

In carpet-making, while spinning was again done by women, the weaving was reserved to men. The collective earnings of two men and two women were estimated by Buchanan at ₹ 17.89 in a month. Here, too, the raw material was their own.[72]

In blanket-making, the same division of work prevailed; women spun and men wove. A pair of shepherds (man and woman) in Bihar is reported by Buchanan to have produced a blanket worth one rupee in four days.[73]

It seems that in other processes after weaving, the division of work between men and women was not so sharply defined. In dyeing and perhaps bleaching both worked together. Writing in 1675–76, Fryer says that in Calicut, washermen were 'women as well as men': they were not only very competent but also cheap.[74] In Bihar, too, both men and women washed and bleached cloth for the English Company in c. 1810 and the earnings of husband and wife collectively were '1 anna short of 28 Rs' a year.[75] The women besides working with their husbands also washed the worn clothes of people, acting as domestic washerwomen.[76] Calico printing too was apparently carried out by both. Moti Chandra finds words for both male and female calico-printers, in the fourteenth–fifteenth century, namely, *chhimpaka* for female and *chhipa* for male printers.[77]

---

66 Martin, *Eastern India*, 558–59.

67 Buchanan, *Patna–Gaya Report*, 647–48; Buchanan, *Purnea Report*, 536–37; Martin, *Eastern India* (Gorakhpoor), 558–59.

68 Buchanan, *Patna–Gaya Report*, Vol. II, 651.

69 W. Moorcroft and G. Trebeck, *Travels in the Himalayan Provinces of Hindustan and the Punjab, in Laddakh and Kashmir from 1819 to 1825*, ed. H. H. Wilson, Vol. II (London, 1937), 174.

70 Or 3299, ff. 262a, 268; *Tutinama*, c. 1565–70, Chester Beatty Library, MS No. 21 f. 29.

71 Buchanan, *Patna–Gaya Report*, 651.

72 Ibid., 657.

73 Ibid., 651.

74 Fryer, *A New Account of East India*, 121–22.

75 Buchanan, *Patna–Gaya Report*, 616–17.

76 Ibid.

77 Moti Chandra, *Journal of Indian Textile History*, Vol. V, 51–52.

From the seventh century we have evidence of women putting patterns on cloth by the tie-and-dye process.[78] Women's role in this process has remained traditional, though often professional men and women worked together.

Another craft that the women pursued was embroidery. They stitched 'flowers' upon muslin, a profession said to be pursued by them at various places.[79]

BUILDING INDUSTRY

In its detailed description of the staff of the building establishment of the Mughal government, Abū'l Faẓl's *Ā'īn-i Akbarī* does not indicate, directly or indirectly, any participation of women labourers in construction work. But Mughal paintings provide firm evidence of their participation. In a depiction (c. 1590) of the building of Akbar's capital city of Fatehpur Sikri, women are shown performing heavy tasks like breaking stones and old bricks by pounding to prepare rubble, preparing bitumen mortar-cement and staining and mixing lime used to surface walls.[80] In another painting of the same time depicting Akbar's construction of the Agra fort, women are seen preparing lime-mortar, and carrying it in pans, held in hand or over their heads, to the masons at work. At least one of them walks up a slanted platform with the pan on her head.[81] It is worth noting that these jobs continue to be traditionally women's jobs in the Indian building industry even today.

Unfortunately, there is no information about women's wages. If the brick pounders (*surkhī kob*) in Abū'l Faẓl's account are women, we may take it that each woman worker earned 1.5 *dāms* (40 *dāms* = ₹ 1) for pounding 8 *mans* (200.70 kg) of bricks. If she then pounded 1.66 *mans* (267.62 kg), she would have earned the lowest daily wage specified for the same work for unskilled labourers.[82]

PETTY COMMERCE

Women's participation in petty commerce seems to have been considerable. Milk and its products were usually hawked by them. Buchanan writing, c. 1810, about Bihar, describes the division of work among pastoral castes as follows: The young men were 'farmers', the old and the children tended cattle, and women sold milk and the cakes of dung that were used for fuel.[83] In fact, the collection of dung and the making of dung cakes for fuel was a task traditionally assigned to women and children. The author of the *Tashrīh ul-Aqwām*, 1825, a work on castes, describing the Gujjar and Ghosi castes, differentiates between the

---

[78] Banabhatta, *Harshacarita*, ed. P. V. Kane, 2nd edn. (Delhi, 1965), Ucchvasa IV, 14. I owe this reference to my colleague Mr Ishrat Alam, who has also given me other help.

[79] Buchanan, *Purnea Report*, 544 and *Patna–Gaya Report*, Vol. II, 655.

[80] Binyon, *Court Painters*, Plate IX.

[81] Geeti Sen, *Paintings from Akbarnama* (Calcutta, 1984), Plates 31 and 61.

[82] Blochmann, *Å'ðn*, Vol. I, 170.

[83] Buchanan, *Patna–Gaya Report*, Vol. II, 635.

two castes according to the way their women sold milk, curd, butter, etc. According to him, the women of the Gujjars hawked the products from door to door, while those of the Ghosis sold these at their own houses.[84]

Men and women of the Kunjra caste sold green vegetables[85] while only the women of gardeners hawked fruits and green vegetable in the markets and went from door to door.[86] The women of gardeners' caste also sold flowers; the *Tashrīh ul-Aqwām* mentions this, and a miniature of the eighteenth century from Awadh depicts a female flowerseller.[87]

Bangle-makers sold bangles visiting the houses and hawking along streets and lanes: their women carried the basket of bangles while they emitted cries to attract customers' attention. The *Tashrīh ul-Aqwām* generally describes this as being the practice in Haryana around 1825.[88] Buchanan c. 1810 gives a similar account of the glass and lac bangle-makers in Bihar.[89]

At least in Bihar, about that time, all grain parchers and sellers of parched grains were women. They used to sit on the road sides with small fire places while the customers brought their own grain to get it parched, the parchers keeping back small amounts of grain. In this way, according to Buchanan, women earned no more than 2 paisas a day (that is less than a rupee a month). But some had their own grain that they parched and sold sitting at their shops, their earnings then being a good deal more.[90]

Selling fish either door-to-door or in the market was also traditionally a women's profession among the fisher folk.[91]

SUNDRY PROFESSIONS

There were various other professions where gender division of work was not well-marked, and men and women both carried the same professions either separately or together. The potter's wife, for example, kneaded clay for the potter working at the kiln, as shown in an illustration, c. 1850–60.[92]

Men and women both worked as sweepers.[93] In making ornaments out of lac, men and women worked together. Possibly, here women did not work full-time since, unlike men, they had other chores also to look after, for example, beating rice to supplement family earnings.[94]

[84] British Museum Add. 27,255, f. 150a.

[85] Ibid., f. 235a.

[86] Ibid., f. 232b.

[87] Falk and Archer, *Indian Miniatures in the India Office*, Plate 26.

[88] Add. 27,255, ff. 326a–27a.

[89] Buchanan, *Patna–Gaya Report*, Vol. II, 620–21.

[90] Ibid., Vol. II, 636.

[91] Ibid., 291.

[92] Reproduced in William Crooke, *A Glossary of North Indian Peasant Life*, ed. Shahid Amin (New Delhi, 1989), Plate X.

[93] Add. 27,255, f. 178b.

[94] Buchanan, *Purnea Report*, 522.

The leaves widely used for serving meals in were gathered, dried and stitched by men and women working together. A husband and wife making such platters earned approximately ₹ 3 a month.[95] In the manufacture of nitre salt, one man, one woman and two girls or boys were required to look after each furnace, though perhaps they performed different tasks.[96] In preparation of tobacco and charcoal balls, both the sexes were equally occupied.[97]

A profession where women had primacy, though it was not their sole preserve, was that of inn-keeping. The inn-keepers (*bhatyārdīs*) were traditionally women. Rafīuddīn Shīrāzī, a Persian merchant visiting India in the 1560s, tells us:

> On roads used by people at every *farsakh* (2.5 miles) or half *farsakh*, notables of this country have founded or left behind in trust *sarāis* (inns), where persons of the caste of *bhatiyārās* (male) reside so that whenever the travellers arrive, they can on payment stay there and give provisions for food to the *bhatiyårð* (female) who then cooks the food according to their taste and takes her wage.

He calls such inns '*bhatiyārī's* houses'.[98]

Manucci records a tradition that Sher Shāh (1540–45) assigned the duty of looking after the travellers to married slaves and their wives.[99] Withington, visiting India in 1612–16, mentions only women inn-keepers.[100] Peter Mundy in India, c. 1630, not only emphasizes that inn-keeping was the job of women but also informs us that their men were most commonly *Kahārs* (palanquin bearers), fowlers or fishermen.[101] G. Forster says more cautiously that 'many' of the inn-keepers were women.[102] In the 1810s, Buchanan still found inn-keeping as the job of old women.[103] The inn-keeping, of course, included the work of preparing and serving meals.

Women also served as wine-servers in taverns. There is an interesting pictorial representation in the *Miftāh-ul Fuẓala* of a tavern where women are serving wine and eatables and also entertaining the guests by singing with musical instruments. The fact that Emperor Akbar in 1582 appointed a woman belonging to the caste of wine-distillers to the official wine shop at the court[104] suggests that the *Miftāh-ul Fuẓala's* illustration was no fantasy, but depicted actual conditions.

Among the nomadic roadside entertainers called *nats* (male) and *natnðs* (female) forming a well-known caste of rope dancers and gymnasts, women performed various gymnastic feasts. Thevenot in the 1660s describes a performance by a pair in Nander (Maharashtra) where the major role was played by the woman-performer. He provides an illustration as

---

95 Buchanan, *Patna–Gaya Report*, Vol. II, 617–18.
96 Ibid., 667.
97 Ibid., 629.
98 *Tazkiratu'l Muluk*, Add. 23883, ff. 172a–74b.
99 N. Manucci, *Storia do Mogor, 1656–1712*, trans. W. Irvine (London, 1907–08), 115.
100 W. Foster, ed., *Early Travels in India (1583–1619)* (London, 1927), 225.
101 R. C. Temple, ed., *The Travels of Peter Mundy in Europe and Asia* (London, 1914), 121.
102 G. Forster, *A Journey from Bengal to England* (London), 86–87, 92.
103 Buchanan, *Patna–Gaya Report*, 635.
104 Badauni, *Muntakhab-ut-Tawarikh*, ed. Ahmad Ali, Vol. II (1865), 301–02.

well.[105] The *Tashrīh ul-Aqwām* shows a woman performing along with a man.[106] There was another class of female professional magicians (*bhānmati*) who showed their tricks and magical articles. A description of them, with illustration, is provided in the *Tashrīh ul-Aqwām*.[107]

Women of a number of lower castes went to upper class houses on occasion of celebrations of births and marriages to sing and dance 'in order to earn their livelihood.'[108] Women of lime-makers did this, according to the *Tashrīh ul-Aqwām*,[109] and those of *doms* (*domīnīs*), according to a contemporary narrative from Lucknow.[110]

Singing and dancing at a higher professional level was also carried out by women who worked as free entertainers for higher classes. In most cases, their men acted as musicians playing instruments or, in the case of less-accomplished persons, took other sundry professions. These women singers and dancers usually acted as prostitutes,[111] a profession whose prevalence was acknowledged. Emperor Akbar allotted a special locality in his capital, Fatehpur Sikri, for the courtesans and tried to restrict their visits as dancers to the houses of nobles and gentry.[112]

A crucial role was played by women as primitive doctors and physicians. They served as midwives and as nurses to babies. The midwife and nurses invariably appear in Mughal paintings depicting scenes of births of princes, as for example that of Emperor Akbar himself[113] and those of his sons,[114] as well as of the birth of Lord Krishna, painted during the eighteenth century.[115]

A popular notion was that a number of diseases originated owing to excess or bad blood and it had, therefore, to be sucked out by leeches. Mrs Meer Hasan Ali (c. 1820) observed 'leech-women' at Lucknow visiting homes with the insects and performing this operation, which required a certain amount of skill.[116]

It was common for women to work on wages as domestic servants. The practice of employing female domestic servants was certainly not confined to aristocratic establishments. A painting, c. 1740, depicts a rather modest home where a maidservant is seen killing a snake, the operation being observed by three other women, one of whom is apparently the mistress of house.[117] Describing the practice in Bihar and eastern Uttar Pradesh, Buchanan states that the wages given to women domestic servants were 'as high nearly as those given to men'.[118]

---

[105] *Travels of Thevenot and Careri*, 107 and 109.

[106] Add. 27,255, f. 304b (illustration) and f. 306a.

[107] Ibid., f. 123b (illustration), f. 124a.

[108] Ibid., f. 141a.

[109] Ibid.

[110] Meer Hasan Ali, *Observations on the Mussulmans of India*, Vol. II (London, 1832), 43.

[111] Add. 27,255, ff. 138a–141b.

[112] Badauni, *Muntakhab-ut-Tawarikh*, 186.

[113] Or. 12988, ff. 20b and 22a, Plate 44;

[114] Chester Beaty Library Ms No. 3 ff. 142b and 143b; Geeti Sen, *Paintings from the Akbarnama* (Calcutta, 1984), Plates 56 and 57.

[115] W. G. Archer, *Visions of Courtly India—the Archer Collection of Pahari Miniatures* (London, 1976), Plate 27.

[116] Meer Hasan Ali, *Observations on the Mussulmans of India*, 143–44.

[117] Falk and Archer, *Indian Miniatures*, 436, Plate 239.

[118] Buchanan, *Patna–Gaya Report*, Vol. I, 287.

ELITE PROFESSIONS

Women's occupations do not seem to have been confined to manual labour and arts alone. There are at least a few references to women pursuing trade and controlling agricultural land and urban property. In the seventeenth century, a Surat merchant left to his wife his merchandise and the conduct of his trade at Surat when he went to Mecca as the agent of another merchant. When he died there, the widow went to the court of a *qāẓī* to claim her right to manage her deceased husband's affairs.[119]

In the territory of the present state of Uttar Pradesh, a Khatri woman, Sabhanu, was found selling her village land, c. 1680. There is evidence of other brahman as well as Muslim women in the same region, who were proprietresses of village lands.[120] They also formed an important class of recipients of land grants from the imperial Mughal government.[121] Jahangir appointed a woman to process and recommend such grants.[122] Shāhjahān followed the practice and the head of department came to be designated as the *Œadru-n Nisa*.[123]

Sale deeds from Gujarat towns such as Surat, Cambay and Broach show that during the seventeenth and eighteenth centuries women owned urban property which they themselves purchased, sold or mortgaged.[124]

It was, perhaps, possible for women to fulfil responsibilities of such positions, whether by inherited ownership or grant or appointment, because among higher classes it was not uncommon for women to be lettered. The illustration depicting a school scene in the *Miftāh-ul Fuẓala* shows a young girl sitting with a boy learning to write the alphabet.[125]

Mughal court artists depict women reading letters and books.[126] From the Deccan School too comes similar pictorial evidence. Mughal royal ladies were learned enough to maintain their personal libraries and to compose poetry.[127] There are notices of accomplished Persian poetesses in the sixteenth and seventeenth centuries.[128] We know that some women worked as artists as well. Among Jahāngīr's (1605–27) court painters, there is mention of at least three women artists. The signed painting of one of them, Nādira Banū, survives in the

[119] Blochet, Supp. Pers. 482 ff. 185a–6b. For full translation of the document see my 'Travails of a Merchantile Community—Aspects of Social Life at the Port of Surat', *Proceedings of the Indian History Congress*, 52nd Session (Delhi, 1991–92), 408–09.

[120] For full references see *ASMI*, 191–92, f.n. 95.

[121] Ibid., 352–53 and *n*.

[122] S. Ahmad, ed., *Tuzuk-i Jahāngīrī* (Ghazipur, 1863), 21.

[123] Shāhnawās Khān, Ma'āsir-ul-Umarā, ed. Abdur Rahim and Ashraf Ali (Calcutta, 1881), 241.

[124] National Archives of India, Acquired Documents.

[125] British Library Or. 3299, f. 278b.

[126] Falk and Archer, *Indian Miniatures*, 386; M. C. Beach, *Mughal and Rajput Paintings* (Cambridge, 1992), Plate 68, 95.

[127] Gulbadan Bāno Begum (Emperor Bābur's daughter) wrote her memoirs, *A History of Humayun*, ed. A. S. Beveridge (London, 1902). A reference to her library is made in Bāyazīd Biyāt, *Tazkira-i Humāyūn-o-Bābur*, ed. M. Hidayat Hosaim (Calcutta, 1941).

[128] Badauni (*Muntakhab-ut-Tawārīkh*, Vol. III, ed. Ahmad Ali [Calcutta, 1869], 360–61) mentions a poetess, Nihānī, of the sixteenth century. From the seventeenth century, we have names of a number of poetesses, most of them royal princesses. See S. M. Jafar, *Education in Muslim India* (Delhi, 1972), 194–98.

Gulshan Album (Imperial Library, Tehran). The ascription on the painting describes her as daughter of Mīr Taqī, a well-known calligrapher at Jahāngīr's court; she was herself a pupil of Aqā Raẓā, a master painter of Jahāngīr's atelier.[129] There are also pictorial depictions of women doing painting.[130]

WOMEN IN ARISTOCRATIC DOMESTIC ESTABLISHMENTS

Service in aristocratic households was not an inconsiderable source of employment for women during the sixteenth–eighteenth centuries. Women were appointed to perform a variety of tasks, high and low, skilled and unskilled. Writing about Emperor Akbar's household Abū'l Faẓl gives the number of harem inmates as 5,000.[131] The number of royal ladies, out of 5,000 total harem inmates, could then not have been more than 500; and there was, therefore, a female labour force of 4,500 in the imperial household establishment alone. The establishments of the nobles were replicas of the imperial establishment in nearly all respects except in size; the latter naturally varied in proportion to the rank and status of the noble. Pelsaert goes on to say that Mughal nobles usually had three to four wives, and each wife was allowed 10 or 20 or 100 female attendants.[132] The contemporary paintings bear witness to this, by invariably showing large retinues of women attendants, waiting upon royal or noble ladies.[133] Eighteenth-century miniatures from different regional schools suggest that the same conditions prevailed among the regional aristocracies.[134]

In these pictorial depictions, we can often clearly identify the kinds of work they performed. On ceremonial occasions such as celebrations of births[135] or weddings[136] they are shown looking after the entire domestic arrangements except for the cooking of food, which seems to have remained largely men's work in the great establishments.[137] Abū'l Faẓl says that the meals in Akbar's entire harem establishment were distributed from one main kitchen, though some very high ranking royal ladies had kitchens of their own.[138] Pelsaert describes a similar distribution of cooked meals among the ladies of a noble's household from a single kitchen.[139]

Women attendants are shown fanning their mistress, massaging her feet and legs at bedtime, doing her bed, helping her walk, and serving meals, eatables and wines. The

[129] I am grateful to Professor S. P. Verma for this information. See also Das, *Mughal Paintings*, 235.

[130] Falk and Archer, *Indian Miniatures*, 531 and Ivan Stchoukine, *La Peinture Indienne, A L'Epoque Des Grands Moghuls* (Paris, 1929), Plate LXXV (Rajput School).

[131] Blochmann,*Ā'īn*, Vol. I, 40.

[132] Pelsaert, 'Remonstrantie', c. 1626, trans. W. H. Moreland and P. Geyl, *Jahangir's India* (Cambridge, 1925), 64.

[133] Falk and Digby, *Paintings from Mughal India*, Plates 31–40.

[134] Archer, *Visions of Courtly India*, Plates 12, 19, 29; Beach, *Mughal and Rajput Paintings*, Plate J.

[135] Sen, *Paintings from Akbarnama*, Plates 17, 18.

[136] Amina Okada, *Imperial Mughal Painters* (Paris, 1992), Plate 102, 98.

[137] M. S. Randhwa, *Paintings of the Babur Nama* (New Delhi, 1983), Plate XI.

[138] Blochmann, *Ā'īn*, 40.

[139] Pelsaert, 'Remonstrantie', 64.

attendants also entertained their mistress by singing and dancing or by narrating fables and stories.[140] Another very popular theme with the artists was that of a lady at her toilet, where she is shown attended by a large number of servants, doing her hair, holding the mirror to her, pouring out water, etc.[141]

The attire of the women servants, particularly those employed in the imperial establishment, seems to indicate a distinct hierarchy. In illustrations showing the celebrations at the birth of Emperor Akbar's son, a woman in a highly dignified dress is shown standing before a group of religious men (a pandit and mullahs) and appears to be a matron or housekeeper.[142] Even among singers and dancers, there seems to be a very clear distinction of rank. These appear to belong to two classes. One may be classified as that of artistes. These are usually shown dancing alone in classical styles or singing with the accompaniment of musical instruments or playing musical instruments themselves.[143] Others of the more ordinary class sang and danced in the popular fashion with drums and in rather ordinary dresses.[144]

In Akbar's household establishment, women employees were divided into two grades. Those in grade I received a monthly stipend ranging from ₹ 20 to 51 and those in grade II, from ₹ 2 to ₹ 40.[145] The lowest wage of unskilled women servant was ₹ 1.5 a month (2 *dams* a day); the women employed in the imperial harem appear to have been much better paid.

Pre-colonial India was not a uniform mass, though the caste system did further a uniformity amidst much social diversity. But we can recognize throughout a tendency to assign certain jobs or stages in the labour process to women. The general exclusive attribution of spinning to women can be attributed to the expectation that their smaller and nimbler fingers suited the operation better. Spinning seems to have been allotted to women in the same manner in practically all civilizations. Certain jobs fell to the women's lot because with childbearing and rearing, pure domestic duties, like cooking food, were undertaken by them, and not by men (a feature perhaps as universal as spinning). Women's restricted participation in certain other jobs seems to have been determined by the fact that they could only work part-time, or that the work required a momentary application of such heavy muscular power as they did not generally possess. Thus, they do not appear to have worked on the plough, or as weavers or blacksmiths, but assumed only supplementary roles in these spheres. Finally, male dominance, sanctified by faith and culture, determined that women should work as harem attendants, and as singers and dancers, and often combine the latter profession with prostitution.

---

140 Stchoukine, *La Peinture Indienne*, Plates LXXXV, LXXXI, LXXXIV; Archer, *Visions of Courtly India*, Plates 20, 25, 29, 46, 52, 73, 74.

141 Okada, *Imperial Mughal Painters*, Plate V; Welch, *Imperial Mughal Painting*, Plate 16; Archer, *Visions of Courtly India,* Plates 46, 56, 61.

142 Welch, *Imperial Mughal Painting*, Plate 16.

143 Stchoukine, *La Peinture Indienne* Plates IX, XXI, LVII; Sen, *Paintings from Akbarnama*, Plate 19; Beach, *Mughal and Rajput Paintings*, 132; Falk and Archer, *Indian Miniatures*, Plate 7.

144 Sen, *Paintings from Akbarnama*, Plate 3; Beach, *Mughal and Rajput Paintings*, Plate 86, 116, Plate 98, 132; Falk and Archer, *Indian Miniatures*, Plate 7.

145 Blochmann, *Å'ðn*, Vol. I, 40.

Women were an important component of the labour force, and among the labouring poor, an asset rather than liability. The insistence on remarrying a widow to the husband's brother, or alternatively the parents-in-law's right to marry a widow off to someone else, found in many castes,[146] implied this perception, which also meant the currency of bride-price, as against the pervasive dowry system of today's India. Women, as labourers, were not, however, mere extensions of their husband's persons. We have seen that they received wages themselves for their work, and often sold or hawked wares and goods produced by themselves or in conjunction with their menfolk. This suggested a certain amount of independence for the women of the lower orders in traditional India. This independence often was sharply curtailed and seclusion and the veil enforced among both Hindus and Muslims in the case of higher class women.

Even among higher classes, women were legal persons in both Hindu and Muslim law. As such, they could hold and, therefore, manage property. In the Mughal royalty and nobility, they received education, and some of them even took to literary and artistic professions, while others were assigned semi-bureaucratic or supervisory functions.

The colonial subjugation of the Indian economy, especially 'de-industrialisation' during the nineteenth century, brought about considerable change in the conditions we have summed up above. Certain professions of women, notably spinning, were practically eliminated; others like work in plantations, mines and factories (few and small as these still were) were created. The same women could not, of course, shift from the old sectors to the other new ones, and the process had therefore a most wrenching effect on women. A recognition of this made the Indian National Movement adopt the women's spinning wheel for its symbol, both as token of protest and declaration of intent. The fulfilment of the intention is, however, still a distant goal.

[146] See, for example, *Tashrīh ul-Aqwām*, British Museum Add. 37,255, f. 138a–41b.

Devaradiya: Hand-maidens of God or Sex-workers?

Section V

Chapter 22 Courtesans†

VATSYAYANA MALLANAGA

ONE: DECIDING ON A FRIEND, AN ELIGIBLE LOVER, AND AN INELIGIBLE LOVER

[1]Courtesans find sexual pleasure and a natural way of making a living in their sexual relations with men. [2]Doing it for sexual pleasure is natural, and for gain is artificial, [3]but she makes the artificial, too, appear natural, [4]because men trust women who are driven by desire. [5]In order to demonstrate that it is natural, she betrays no greed. [6]And in order to make the future secure, she do†t get money from him by objectionable methods.

[7]She is always well dressed as she looks out on the main street, easily seen but not too much exposed, because she is just like something for sale. [8]She makes friends with people through whom she can attract the man, cut him off from other women, ward off losses and rebound from them, get money, and avoid being treated with contempt by her lovers. [9]These friends are policemen, officers of the courts, fortune-tellers, bold men, heroes, men who know the same things as she knows, men who have a grasp of the arts,* libertines, panders, clowns, garland-makers, perfumers, wine-merchants, washermen, barbers, beggars, and

† Reproduced with Permission from Sudhir Kakar. Previously published as 'Book 6: Courtesans' in Vatsyayana Mallanaga's *Kamasutra*, Sudhir Kakar (ed.), pp. 131–59. The note cues and note explanations have been kept intact as per the original publication.

[4] Men become attached to a woman who lets them think, 'She is in love with me', but not to women who are driven by money.

[9] Policemen and officers of the courts ward off her losses and get money for her. Fortune-tellers bring men to her and urge them on by saying, 'If you make love with this woman, your fortunes will flourish.' Bold men and heroes ward off her losses and get money for her. Men who know the same things love her and get money for her. Men who have a grasp of the arts learn the arts from the woman and publicise them, which brings lovers to her. The panders and the others bring in money through their own work and bring lovers to her through their free access to the houses of other men.

whichever other men can be used to accomplish her goals. [10]Lovers who are eligible just for the sake of money are these: an independent man, a man who has just come of age, a rich man, a man whose source of income is transparent, an official, a man who obtains wealth without difficulty, a jealous rival, a man with a steady income, a man who believes he is lucky in love, a braggart, an impotent man, a man who wants to be known as a real man, a man who competes with his equals, a man generous by nature, a man who has influence with a king or a minister of state, a fatalist,* a man who despises wealth, a man who transgresses the instructions of his elders, a man who sets an example for his siblings, a rich only son, a man who wears the sign of a religious order, a man who conceals his sexual desire, a hero, and a doctor.

[11]But men who are rich only in love and fame are eligible lovers because of their good qualities. [12]The man's good qualities are these: he is born of a great family, learned, know ledgeable about all customs, a poet, a skilled storyteller, eloquent, resolute, skilled in the various crafts, concerned for his elders. He has ambition, great endurance, and loyalty, is generous but not envious, and loving to his friends. He is fond of crowds, salons, theatrical performances, parties, and all kinds of games. He is free of disease, sound of limb, full of

---

[10] These livers are for money and not for love, but their money can be used for sexual pleasure and fame. An independent man is not dependent on his elders. A man who has just come of age is not too old. When she wants something from a man whose source of income is not in public view, because it comes from some other region, even when he gives her money, it is a useless gift. An official can five her money derived from whatever money he officiates over A man whose wealth comes easily, either through an inheritance or by finding some treasure or through a favour from the king, fives it away easily, too. A jealous rival gives her a lot of money in competition with another lover. A tax-collector or usurer has steady income. A man who believes he is lucky in love, although he is unlucky in love, does not want people to think that he is unlucky in love, and so he gives the woman a lot of money in the course of getting her away from another man. An impotent man, a non-man, gives her a lot of money in order to proclaim his virility. A man who wants people to think he is a real man gives her a lot of money when she asks for it. When two men equal in family, knowledge, wealth or age are rivals, each thinks, 'That man who is my equal gave a lot to that courtesan; I will give her more her more Such a lover keeps spending more like a mare who always wants to be in front. If a man has the ear of a king or minister of state, even if he himself does not give her anything, he can get the king or minister to give her something, by saying, 'This is the woman I love.' A fatalist thinks, 'My fortune is drying up because my good luck is drying up, not because it is spent on pleasures and so he gives her a lot of money A man who transgresses his gurus' words gives her a lot even though he is doing wrong A rich only son is never restrained by his parents even if he gives her a lot, because they do not want him to go anywhere else. A man whose sexual desire is concealed thinks, People must not find out' but since he is tormented by desire, he gives her a lot. A hero makes friends and makes money. A doctor, even if he does not give the courtesan money, gives in fact by healing her when she is ill.

[12] The man's good qualities are described here in keeping with the statement above [at 1.5.28]: 'We will explain the good qualities and lack of good qualities in both [kinds of lovers] in the discussion of courtesans.' V calls him 'the man' here, and not 'the lover', to apply more generally; he also gives him other names, such as 'suitor' in his relationship to a virgin, 'successful suitor' in his relationship to a second-hand woman, 'paramour' in his relationship to the wife of another man, and 'lover' in his relationship to a courtesan. The man is learned, in logic and so forth. He knows all customs, even the customs of heretics. He composes poems in Sanskrit and other languages. He is skilled in crafts such as sketching. He does services for those who are mature in knowledge or in years. It is said: 'The qualities of a man of endurance are heroism, indignation, speed, and cleverness.' A Brahmin who does not drink makes a lot of profits. A 'bull' is sexually potent. The man flirts by glossing over the flaws in the condition of the women's bodies.

the breath of life, like a bull, friendly. He does not drink wine. He attracts women and flirts with them but is not in their power. He has an independent income, is not coarse, prone to anger, or nervous.

[13]The woman's qualities, on the other hand, are these: the woman is beautiful, young, with auspicious marks, sweet, in love with good qualities but not with money, by nature inclined to love and sex, with a steady mind, true to one type,* a seeker of special things, never living in a greedy way, and fond of salons and the arts. [14]The following are the common qualities that the woman has, in addition: intelligence, good character, good behaviour, honesty, gratitude, the ability to see far and long, no habit of interrupting or contradicting, a knowledge of the right time and place, and urbanity.* And she is free from depression, excessive laughter, malignant gossip, verbal abuse, anger, greed, dullness, and fickleness. She speaks only when spoken to and is skilled in the *Kamasutra* and its ancillary sciences.

[15]The inverses of these qualities are the faults. [16]These are not eligible lovers: A man wasting away, sick, with worms in his faeces* or 'crow's-mouth', in love with his wife, coarse in speech, miserly, or pitiless; a man whom the elders have thrown out, a thief, or a hypocrite; a man who is addicted to love-sorcery done with roots, who does not care about honour or dishonour, who can be bought for money even by people he hates, or is shameless.

[17]Scholars say: 'The reasons for taking a lover are passion, fear, gain, rivalry, revenge against an act of hostility, curiosity, partially, exhaustion, religion, fame, compassion, the words of a friend, diffidence, resemblance to someone loved, wealth allaying passion, a shared caste, living in a house together, continuity, and the future'. [18]Vatsyayana says: Gain, warding off

---

[13] Here, too, V says 'the woman', not 'the courtesan'. Auspicious marks indicate that she will have the good fortune to be loved. A woman inclined to love and sex is fond of both external foreplay and the sexual act. When a woman with a steady mind decides, 'This has to be done', she does it. A woman true to one type has one consistent form, not a deceptive one.

[15] The inverse of the common qualities are such faults as birth from a bad family and so forth, ugliness and so forth, stupidity and so forth.* And if he has these, a lover is not a lover.

[16] A man wasting away is suffering from tuberculosis ('the royal sickness'). Worms in the faeces is a condition generally called 'faeces-flies', in which worms appear in the opening from which faeces are excreted; when semen infected with the disease through contact with the faeces enters a woman, she gets a fever. Crow's-mouth is a foul-smelling mouth; or else it means that, just as a crow puts things both pure and impure into his mouth, so this man desires women without reflecting about it, and becomes ineligible for sex. A man who loves his wife does not give the courtesan money because he never becomes attached to anyone else. A man who can be bought even by people he hates is so greedy that he surely will not give her money.

[17] These are the reasons: passion, which sometimes arises naturally, by itself, fear of death, like the fear that afflicted Rambha because of Ravana, who said to her, 'If you do not satisfy my desire, I will kill you'; gain, getting land and so forth; rivalry, like that between the two women, Devadatta and Anangasena, who fought over Muladeva; curiosity, which arises when one hears that a man is debauched and wonders, 'Is he, really?'; exhaustion, for sex revivifies; religion, which is served by sex with a learned Brahmin who has nothing; compassion, taking pity on someone who says, 'I will die if you will not make love with me'; the words of a friend, who says, 'Someone to whom I owe a favour has arrived; do, please, sleep with him tonight': diffidence toward someone who has the status of an elder; allaying passion, for an excessive volume of semen* is dispelled by sex with any man.

[18] The author here is saying: This is a matter either of practical calculation or of abstract theory. Healing, friendship, dispelling sorrow, and cultivating the arts are matters of practical calculation; while gain warding off losses, and love are theoretical, for everything can be subsumed under them. The category of gain includes rivalry, curiosity,

losses, and love are the reasons. [19]Gain, however, should not be thwarted by love, since gain is the chief concern. [20]But the relative weight of fear and so forth* should be tested. That is how to decide on a friend, an eligible lover, an ineligible lover, and the reasons for taking a lover.

Getting a Lover

[21]Even when a lover propositions her, she does not accept him immediately, for men scorn what is easy to get. [22]In order to find out the lover's true feelings she sends him servants with masseurs, singers, and clowns, or people devoted to him. [23]If they are not available, she sends the libertine and so forth. From them she finds out if the man is pure or impure, passionate or not passionate, attached to her or not attached, generous or not generous. [24]And when she has found out about him, she offers him her love through the mediation of the pander.

[25]Under the pretext of a quail-fight, cock-fight, or ram-fight, or of hearing a parrot or a mynah talk, or of a theatrical spectacle or some art, the libertine brings the man to her home, [26]or her to his. [27]When the man arrives, she gives him a love-gift, something that will arouse his love or erotic curiosity, saying, 'This is for you alone, and no one else, to enjoy.' [28]She charms him through whatever sort of conversation pleases him and through courtesies. [29]When he has gone, she immediately sends after him a servant girl to joke with him and to give him a small gift. [30]Or she herself goes, with the libertine, under some pretext. That is how to get a lover.

[31]And there are verses about this:

When a man comes to her
she gives him, with love,
betel and garlands and carefully prepared fragrant oils,
and she engages him in conversation about the arts.
[32]She gives him things out of affection
and exchanges things with him;
and of her own accord
she lets him know that she wants to make love.
[33]Through love-gifts, hints,
and courtesies with just one meaning,
she becomes intimate with her lover, and after that
She gets him to love her.

---

partiality, exhaustion, religion, fame, the words of a friend, and allaying passion. The category of warding off losses includes fear, hostility, and compassion. All the rest [passion, diffidence, resemblance to someone loved, a shared caste, living in a house together, continuity, and the future] are subsumed under love.

21 And so there is a common saying:

He scorns the woman easy to get,
and desires the woman hard to get.
But when he has propositioned her over and over, she may accept him.

25 The art might be singing.

28 The conversation could be about poetry or about art. Giving him liquor, betel, and so forth are courtesies.

33 The pander and the others drop hints by saying, 'Why don't you sleep here?' These courtesies make direct suggestions about nothing but sex.

TWO: GIVING THE BELOVED WHAT HE WANTS

[1]Once united with the man, she behaves like an only wife in order to make him love her. [2]A brief saying sums it up:

She makes him love her but does not become attached to him, though she acts as if she were attached.

[3]And she represents herself as dependent upon a mother who is cruel by nature and cares about nothing but money, [4]or if she does not have a mother, upon a woman who is like a mother. [5]This other woman, however, is not too fond of the lover, [6]and tries to take her daughter away by force. [7]At this prospect, however, the woman continually exhibits displeasure, loathing, shame, and fear, [8]though she does not disobey the other woman's command. [9]She announces that she has a unique disease that has no apparent cause, is not disgusting, cannot be perceived with the eye, and is intermittent. [10]She makes this excuse when she has a reason not to go to the lover. [11]But she sends a servant girl for his leftover garlands* and betel.

[12]When making love, she expresses wonder at what he does for her. [13]She learns the sixty-four arts of love,* [14]and when he has taught her these methods, she practises them on him in return, with constant repetition. [15]When they are alone together she does what suits his individual personality. [16]She tells him her desires. [17]She conceals any imperfections of her hidden places. [18]In bed, she does not ignore him when he turns toward her. [19]She responds when he touches her hidden places. [20]She kisses and embraces him when he is asleep. [21]She watches him when his mind is elsewhere, and when she is standing on the rooftop porch of her house and he recognises her there from the main street, she becomes shy and no longer cunning.

---

[1] As it was said earlier [at 4.1.48], 'An only wife... even a courtesan'. But if she is not the only one, then V tells her how to give the man she loves what he wants, for when he is making love with her, she loves him.

[3] She implies that she must do what her mother says.

[6] She tries to take her daughter away to another lover.

[7] She exhibits these feelings towards the man she goes to.

[9] It is unique because it is artificial, a disease such as headache or stomach ache.

[10] When she wants to make love with another lover, she uses her disease as her excuse.

[11] The woman, who is not her mother, collects these things as if the courtesan wanted to say, 'Even with this I will find a kind of happiness'.

[13] When she becomes aware of the sixty-four erotic techniques of Babhravya of Panchala, she says, 'Teach me how to do it'.

[14] She uses them afterwards again and again on this very lover, so that he understands. 'She has made such an effort just for my pleasure!'

[16] When they are alone, she says, 'My desires were to make love and laugh with you all night long.'

[17] She does not let him see or touch anything flawed in her armpits, thighs, or sexual organ, for fear that it might dampen his ardour.

[18] To proclaim her affection, she sleeps facing him.

[21] She also watches him when he is on the main street, even when she is on the rooftop porch of her house. When he sees her, she thinks, 'My lover is looking', and she becomes shy, and that is what destroys her cunning. If she did not show her shyness, he would imagine that she was cunning, for he would think, 'Her affection is artificial, since she looks right at me all the time.

[22]She hates anyone he hates, and likes anyone he likes. She takes her pleasure in what gives him pleasure, and rejoices and sorrows as he does. She wants to know about his women. And her anger does not last long. [23]She worries that some other woman has left the marks of nails and teeth or him, even when she herself has made them. [24]She does not speak of her passion for him, [25]but shows it by her signals. [26]And when she is drunk, asleep, or ill, she talks about it* [27]and about the man's good deeds. [28]When he is talking, she grasps the point of what he is saying, and when she has considered it, and there is an opportunity to praise him, she speaks; she makes a reply to what he has said, if he is devoted to her. [29]She is attentive to all his stories, except when they are about another wife. [30]When he sighs, yawns, stumbles, or falls, she wishes him health; [31]when he sneezes, cries out, or is startled, she exclaims, 'Live!'* [32]If she becomes depressed, she pretends to be ill or to have the morbid longings that pregnant women have. [33]She does not praise another man for his good qualities, [34]nor blame another man for the flaws that he has in common with her man.

[35]She keeps anything he has given her. [36]When there has been a false* accusation of infidelity or some misfortune has occurred, she wears no jewellery and refuses to eat. [37]And she grieves in unity with him. [38]She chooses to leave the region with him and to be ransomed from the king. [39]She can live a long life only because she has him. [40]When he gets money, or achieves something he wants, or improves his physical strength, she makes an offering to her personal deity as she had promised in advance. [41]She always takes care to dress well and wear jewellery, and takes little food. [42]She mentions his name and his lineage in her

---

22 She sends spies to find out if he loves other women.

24 She does not say, 'I feel very passionate; make love with me!'

25 She does this so that he knows she is tormented by desire.

26 She feigns intoxication, feigns sleep and pretends she has become ill as a result of his failure to make love with her; she says, 'I have become ill from lack of sex.'

27 If he has done something to get religious merit, such as building a temple for the gods or a pool, she says, 'well done!'

28 She says, 'How well that was said! who else knows how to speak like that?' Responding to the speech of a man in whom affection has not yet arisen would be, on the other hand, an embarrassment.

29 In order to express her jealousy and anger, she does not respond to a story about another wife.

32 When she is depressed because she has heard something unpleasant about the man and he ask s her the cause of her depression, she says, 'I have had this illness for a long time; it is an old enemy that afflicts me.'

33 Or else he will think, 'She is attached to another man'

36 As long as he thinks, 'She has veen unfaithful' for that entire period in order to prove him wrong, she demonstrates the torment of her body by acting exhausted, anointing her limbs with oil fasting, and so forth. A misfortune might be the death of the man's son or brother and so forth, or his falling ill or getting a fever.

37 She laments, saying, 'How can this have happened to you when you have done nothing wrong' In this way she shows him, 'I too am miserable because of this misery.'

38 She says, 'My mother is truly perverse. Take me away from her and bring me to another country, where I Can live independently.' And if she is bound to the king, she gets him to like this idea: 'Ransom me from the hands of the king, or else he will have me brought back when I have run away.'

39 'Otherwise I will die at any moment', she says.

40 He gets back his physical strength after an illness. She says, 'Formerly, I asked the Goddess to fulfill my hopes for getting money and so forth, and that is why these wishes have been fulfilled; now I must make the offering to her.'

songs; when she is weary, she lays his hand on her breast and forehead, and she falls asleep in the pleasure that she experiences in that. [43]She sits on his lap and goes to sleep there, and when he gets up and moves away from her, she goes after him. [44]She wants to have a child by him, and does not want to live longer than he.

[45]When they are alone together, she does not speak of things that he does not know. [46]She restrains him from making a vow or fasting, by saying, 'It is my fault.' But if this is not possible, then she too takes on that role. [47]If there is a quarrel, she says, 'Even he cannot decide the matter.'* [48]She herself looks upon what is his and what is hers as indistinguishable. [49]She does not go to parties and so forth without him.

[50]She is proud of wearing leftover garlands and eating leftover food. [51]She admires his lineage, character, artistic skill, caste, knowledge, class, wealth, homeland, friends, good qualities, age, and sweetness. [52]She urges him to sing, and so forth, if he knows how. [53]She goes to him with no regard for danger, cold, heat, or rain. [54]On the occasion of making funeral offerings for reincarnation in other bodies she says, 'And let him alone be mine!'* [55]She does what he wants with regard to his wishes, tastes, feelings, and character. [56]She is suspicious of love-sorcery worked with roots. [57]She always argues with her mother about going to him, [58]and if her mother forces her to go elsewhere, then she longs for poison, fasting to death, a sword, or a rope. [59]And she convinces the man of this, through her secret agents, or she herself makes him grasp her situation. [60]But she does not argue about money, [61]and she does nothing without her mother.

[62]When he goes on a journey, she makes him swear to return quickly. [63]And when he is away, she makes a yow to abstain from washing and she refuses to wear jeweller, except for jewellery with religious meaning and power. Or she wears one conch-shell bangle. [64]She remembers things that happened in the past, goes to fortunetellers and oracles who channel supernatural voices, and envies the constellations, the moon, the sun, and the

[43] When he goes to a friend's house, or to see a deity, then she thinks, 'I cannot be separated from him for even a moment', and she herself follows him.

[44] She says, 'I am in my fertile period and so you should not sleep anywhere else!' and 'If my death comes before his, it would be a blessing.

[46] She takes the same vow.

[47] If there is a quarrel with someone about a fine point of meaning in some matter, she says, 'If anyone can do it, he is the one.'

[50] She says, 'Give me your leftover garlands and so forth. And when you are invited somewhere and do not take me with you always send me what you do not eat.

[56] When he says, 'You are always using love-sorcery to put me in your power, so that I will be totally submissive to you', she replies, 'No! I would never do anything like that!'

[58] Her mother forces her to go to another lover.

[59] She convinces him that it is all her mother's fault alone, not hers. Her position is that the lives of courtesans are despicable, because their mothers, thirsting for money, make them abandon a man they are fond of and join them with some other man.

[61] In the end, when her mother tells her even what to eat, she does not disobey.

[64] She envies them, thinking, 'They are being rewarded for their merit, for my lover sees them; I must have no merit, for he does not see me.'

stars. [65]When she has a dream-vision of what she longs for, she says, 'May I be united with him!' [66]If she is disturbed by a dream of what she does not long for, she performs the ritual to set it at peace.

[67]When he is coming home, she performs a ritual to honour the god Kama, [68]makes offerings to the deities, [69]brings out a full pot* with her girlfriends, [70]and performs a ritual to honour the crows.* [71]And right after he comes to her for the first time, she does this very same thing, without the ritual to honour the crows.

[72]To a man who is attached to her she says that she will follow him even beyond death.* [73]The signs of his being attached to her are that he trusts her with his true feelings, lives in the same way as she does, carries out her plans, is without suspicion, and has no concern for money matters.

[74]All of this has been said to give an example taken from the teachings of Dattaka. What remains unsaid is what a person learns from the experience of the world and from the nature of men. [75]And there are two verses about this:

Because of the subtlety and excessive greed of women.
and the impossibility of knowing their nature,
the signs of their desire are hard to know,
even for those who are its object.
[76]Women desire and they become indifferent,
they arouse love and they abandon;
even when they are extracting all the money,
they are not really known.

---

[65] If she sees an auspicious dream that is true, she tells her people about it in the morning. If she has a false dream, she tells them she did not have a dream. If her lover is in another region and has some wish that is not fulfilled, she knows of this by these various dreams.

[66] If she thinks, 'Something unwished-for has happened to him', she summons the Brahmins.

[71] She says, 'I am fulfilling the promise I made when I said, 'If my beloved comes back to me, I will give you a ball of rice.

[72] She says, 'When you have gone to heaven, it will not be possible for me to live.'

THREE: WAYS TO GET MONEY FROM HIM

[1]She has both natural and contrived ways of getting money from a man who is attached to her. [2]Scholars have said about this: 'She should not use contrived means for this, if she can obtain it naturally or get even more through inventiveness.' [3]Vatsyayana says: He will give double the agreed amount when it is embellished through a contrived means.

[4]She contrives the following pretexts to get money from him: She gets money in order to take from merchants, on credit against future payment, such things as jewellery, cooked food, raw ingredients, drinks, garlands, garments, and perfumes.* [5]She praises his wealth to his face. [6]She pretends to need money for such things as vows, trees, parks, temples, pools, gardens, festivals, and love-gifts. [7]She says that her jewellery was stolen by guards or thieves, as a result of her going to him, [8]that her property in the house was lost through fire, someone breaking through a wall, or carelessness, [9]and so was some jewellery that the owner has asked to have back, and the man's jewellery. And she lets him know, through spies, about the expenses she has incurred in order to go to him. [10]She incurs debts for his sake, and she quarrels with her mother about the expenses that he has caused her.

[11]She no longer goes to parties given by friends, because she has no presents for them. [12]And the valuable present that these friends previously brought her, which she had mentioned previously, now must be reciprocated. [13]She abruptly ceases her usual activities. [14]She engages artisans on the man's behalf. [15]She does favours for a physician and a minister of state for the sake of a particular project. [16]When disasters befall friends who have done her favours, she helps them out. [17]She carries out home improvements. She outfits

---

[3] She will get double what would come to her through natural means and discussion, and without deductions.

[4] He gives her the money but she does not actually get the things.

[7] She says this so that he thinks, 'She was robbed coming to my side', and gives her other jewellery.

[8] She reports to him, 'Through carelessness, a fire broke out and burnt up my property.' She herself must not set a fire, however, because then through her fault many lives might be lost. Or thieves, or people who pretend to be thieves, dig an opening in a wall to rob the house. She says, 'Through my carelessness, or my mother's, things were lost in the house.'

[9] Someone else had hidden jewellery there, for some reason, and now has asked to have it back; and the man had left his own jewellery there. But now that he learns that it has been destroyed by fire, of course he gives her money, and does not ask for his own jewellery. In front of the man, spies brought in by servants sent by the man say, 'To come to you, she spent these funds on rum, betel, and so forth.'

[12] She says, 'These friends brought valuable presents to me at my festival.' She had mentioned them to him before the friends' party had taken place. For when she asks for them in advance he gives them at the time of the affair, and if he does not give them, she certainly does not go to him then.

[13] She abruptly ceases her daily care of her body, so that he thinks, 'Now she is not even able to care for her body', and gives her money.

[14] She says, 'This excellent artisan demands a lot to do the work, and I do not have it, but if you give it, the work will be done; if not, I will have it done when I have the money.'

[16] These favours were do ne for the man, and those for whom the favours have been done will do favours for the man if disasters—of human origin or acts of gods—befall him.

[17] The pregnant woman is her girlfriend. The courtesan says to the man, 'Because of the death of a son (or whatever) of a friend of yours, I am so unhappy. Seeing this, you should cheer me up.' With this sort of pretext she manages the home improvements and so forth.

the son of a girlfriend on a ceremonial occasion. There are the longings that a pregnant woman has for special food. She is ill. She cheers up an unhappy friend. [18]She sells a part of her jewellery for the man's sake. [19]She shows a merchant the jewellery that she always uses, or the household goods and cooking utensils, in order to sell them. [20]When there is a pooling of similar household goods with those of rival courtesans de luxe, she takes the special ones. [21]She does not forget former kindnesses, and she speaks warmly of them in public. [22]Through spies, she makes sure that he hears about the abundant gains made by rival courtesans de luxe. [23]Then, in the man's presence, she describes to those women her own even greater gains, whether or not this is so, with an air of embarrassment. [24]She openly refuses men with whom she has had former connections, when they try to get her to come back to them again by offering her abundant gains. [25]She remarks on the generosity of the man's rivals. [26]And if she thinks, 'He will not come back', she begs like a child. Those are the ways to get money.

Signs That His Passion Is Cooling

[27]She always knows when his passion is cooling, from the changes in his natural feelings and the look of his face. [28]He gives her too little of too much. [29]He is close with those who are against her. [30]He pretends to do one thing and does something else. [31]He abruptly stops doing what he usually does. [32]He forgets his promises, or keeps them in the wrong way. [33]He speaks with his own people through signs. [34]He sleeps somewhere else, making the excuse that he has to do something for a friend. [35]He talks secretly with the servant of a woman who was previously his mistress.

---

[19] In the presence of the lover, the woman shows the jewellery and so forth to a merchant with whom she has a prior understanding, so that the man thinks, 'She must have nothing left at all, if she is trying to sell the things she uses all the time', and so he gives her money.

[20] Here V cites the teaching of Dattaka—'When there is a pooling of similar household goods, she takes the special ones'—and adds a phrase to clarify it: 'with rival courtesans de luxe.' Because the goods are similar, they accidentally get exchanged, and so that this should not happen again, in the presence of her lover she takes from the hand of the merchant, from time to time, some goods that are superior in both size and quality, so that the lover will give her money to pay for it. Generally, courtesans of the same class borrow one another's household goods as the need arises.

[21] She praises them in his presence, so that he says, 'The kindness that I did has not come to naught here', and he gives her money again.

[23] She does this so that he too becomes ashamed, and gives her money.

[24] She does this so that he hears about this, says, 'She loves me', and gives her money.

[26] Thinking, 'He will not come back to this house', she gets a child to request, 'Give this to me'. Or else it means that she abandons her shame, like a child, and begs him.

[29] He makes friends with those in the faction opposed to the woman.

[31] He does not give her what he has been giving her even day.

[33] He does not communicate with them with words, for he thinks, 'She must not hear this.'

[36]Before he realises it, she finds some pretext and gets her hands on his valuables.* [37]A creditor takes them from her hands by force. [38]If he argues about this, he can be sued in court. Those are the signs that his passion is cooling.

Ways to Get Rid of Him

[39]If a man is attached to her and has done favours for her in the past, even if he now yields but little fruit, she keeps him around by lying. [40]But if he has nothing left at all and no resources to do anything about it, she gets rid of him by some contrivance, without any consideration, and gets support from another man. [41]She does for him what he does not want, and she does repeatedly what he has criticised. She curls her lip and stamps on the ground with her foot. She talks about things he does not know about. She shows no amazement, but only contempt, for the things he does know about. She punctures his pride. She has affairs with men who are superior to him. She ignores him. She criticises men who have the same faults. And she stalls when they are alone together. [42]She is upset by the things he does for her when they are making love. She does not offer him her mouth. She keeps him away from between her legs. She is disgusted by wounds made by nails or teeth. When he tries to hug her, she repels him by making a 'needle' with her arms. Her limbs remain motionless. She crosses her thighs. She wants only to sleep. When she sees that he is exhausted, she urges him on. She laughs at him when he cannot do it, and she shows no pleasure when he can. When she notices that he is aroused, even in the daytime, she goes out to be with a crowd.

[43]She intentionally distorts the meaning of what he says. She laughs when he has not made a joke, and when he has made a joke, she laughs about something else. When he is talking, she looks at her entourage with sidelong glances and slaps them. And when she has interrupted his story, she tells other stories. She talks in public about the bad habits and vices that he cannot give up. Through a servant girl, she insults him where he is vulnerable.

---

[36] She does this before he realises, 'My passion for her is cooling'.

[37] She had taken the man's money from this creditor, who had had it as a debt; and by a previous agreement, the creditor took it back by overpowering her by force.

[38] If the man argues, 'But this is mine; why are you taking it?' the creditor sues him in court. And if he does not argue, the goal is achieved.

[39] She deceives him, because he is still attached to her. But even if he has previously done her many favours, she gets rid of him if he wants another woman.

[40] If someone should remark, 'How can she just throw him out, when he has given her sexual pleasure and profit?' V replies, 'She gets support from another man', and this man gives her both pleasure and profit.

[42] She crosses her two arms, places her hands on her own shoulders, and puts her two arms together to make a needle. When he tries to make love, with some difficulty, and she sees that he is exhausted, she urges him to go on, but does not help him out by offering to play the part of the man [2.8.1]. There actually is a kind of sexual donkey who makes love in the daytime even though it is forbidden. When she realises, from his gestures and signals, that he wants to make love, she goes out.

[44]She does not see him when he comes to her. She asks for things that should not be asked for. And at the end, the release* happens of itself. That is Dattaka's view of the liaison.

[45]And there are two verses about this:

The work of a courtesan is to test lovers and then join with them,
to enchant the man she joins,
to get money from the man she has enchanted,
and at the end to release him.
[46]A Courtesan who manages a liaison
according to this method
is not cheated by her lovers
but makes piles of money.

[44] It was Dattaka who set forth the rules for the relationship between the lover and the courtesan, up to this point; I did not invent it. For it was he who decided, through the commission of the courtesans, to make this condensation. But it was Babhravya who set forth in a useful form what I am going to tell now, about getting back together with an ex-lover and so forth.

FOUR: GETTING BACK TOGETHER WITH AN EX-LOVER

[1]When she is getting rid of her present lover after she has squeezed all the money out of him, she may get together with a man who was previously her lover. [2]If he still has money or has made money, and still loves her, she can get together with him. [3]If he has gone elsewhere, she must find out about him; he may belong in any of the six possible categories, according to the circumstances:

[4][*a*] He left her of his own accord and he left the other woman, too, of his own accord.

[5][*b*] He left both her and the other woman because they got rid of him.

[6][*c*] He left her of his own accord and he left the other woman because she got rid of him.

[7][*d*] He left her of his own accord and stayed with the other woman.

[8][*e*] He left her because she got rid of him and he left the other woman of his own accord.

[9][*f*] He left her because she got rid of him and he stayed with the other woman.

[10][*a*] If a man who left both her and the other woman of his own accord tries to talk her into taking him back, she should not take him back, because he has a fickle mind and has scorned the qualities of both women.

[11][*b*] A man who left both her and the other woman because they got rid of him has a constant mind. If the other woman got rid of him, even though he has money, because she could get a lot of money from another man, the courtesan may take him back, thinking, 'Since that woman insulted him, he will give me a lot of money out of spite.' [12]But if she rejected him because he has no money or is stingy, he is not a good prospect.*

[13][*c*] If he left her of his own accord and left the other woman because she got rid of him, and if he gives her more than he did the first time, then he is fit for a liaison.

[14][*d*] If a man who left her of his own accord, and stayed with the other woman, tries to talk her into taking him back, she must find out about him. [15]She may think, 'He went away because he was looking for something special, and now he wants to come back from her to me because he did not see that special something; and if he comes back because he wants to know me better, he will give me a lot of money, because of his love for me. or, because he has seen her faults and now sees that I have most of the good qualities being a man who recognises good qualities, he will give me the most money.' [16]But if she realises, 'He is a child, whose gaze never rests in a single place, or a man who generally breaks agreements, or someone who Joes anything he can do, as fickle in his passion as turmeric is in its colour',* then she either will or will not get back together with him.

[17][*e*] If a man who left her because she got rid of him, and left the other woman of his own accord, tries to talk her into taking him back, she: must find out about him: [18]If he comes back because he loves me, he will give me a lot of money. Since that other woman did not please him, my good qualities will win him over. [19]Or since, in the past, I got rid of him for no cause, now he wants to cultivate me and vent his hatred on me. Or he wants to get my confidence and get back, in retaliation, the wealth that I look away from him when he was courting me. Or he wants to get revenge by breaking me away from my present lover and

---

[15] 'He was looking for some special kind of sex, which he did not see in that woman, because she lacked sophistication. He wants to come back from her to me, because he has seen that special something in me.'

then abandoning me.' A man that has such unpleasant ways of thinking is not one to get back together with. [20]Time will reveal if he changes his way of thinking.

[21][*f*] A man who left her because she got rid of him, and stayed with the other woman, and tries to talk her into taking him back, has been covered by this last case. [22]Among those who try to talk her into taking them back, the one who stayed with the other woman is the one that she herself tries to talk herself into taking back: [23]'I got rid of this man for a false reason, and he went elsewhere, and now I should make an effort to bring him back.' [24]Or, 'Once he hears from me, he will break away from her [25]and he will stop her income.' [26]Or, 'He has now come into some money; he is living in a bigger house; he has an administrative job. He has separated from his wives. He has freed himself from those on whom he was dependent. He has split with his father or brother.' [27]Or, 'If I get together with him, I will get the wealthy lover whom he is now keeping away from me.' [28]Or, 'His wife has treated me with contempt; I will get him to leave her.'* [29]Or, 'His friendis in love with my co-wife, who hates me: I will use him to get his friend to break away from her.' [30]Or, 'I will make trouble for him by making him appear light-minded, because of his fickleness.'

[31]The libertine and the others explain to him that the woman got rid of him before because her mother was so evil-minded, and she herself was powerless, even though she was in love with him; [32]and that, although she sleeps with her present lover, she has no desire, and she hates him. [33]They try to get him back by playing upon his memories of her and his former love for her, [34]and they say, 'She vividly remembers what you did for her.' That is how to get back together with an ex-lover.

[35]Scholars say: 'Between two lovers, one who had an affair with her in the past and one who did not, the one who had an affair with her in the past is better. For she knows his character and has seen his passion, and he serves her well. [36]Vatsyayana says: A man who had an affair with her in the past does not give her very much money, because all the money has aiready been squeezed out of him, and it is hard to get his trust again; but a man who did not have an affair-with her in the past easily falls in love with her. [37]Nevertheless, there are exceptions according to the nature of the man.

[38]And there are verses about this:

She may wish to get back together again
to break another woman away from the lover,

---

[27] 'He is keeping him away from me now, because of his friendship with him.'

[28] When I had broken with him, he went back to his own wife. And I will treat her with contempt because of this, and by getting back together with him I will get him to leave her, and so I will get revenge for this insult'

[29] 'The friend of my ex-lover has power and possessions, and he is in love with my present or former co-wife, who wishes to harm me. By means of the ex-lover, I will get that friend to break away, so that she will have no profit and will have to do favours for me.'

[30] 'He left me to go elsewhere, and he also left her to go elsewhere.'

[34] They mention what he did for her, by giving money or warding off losses, to show that she is grateful.

[38] Breaking another woman away from the lover' refers to the situations in which 'his wife has treated me with contempt' [28] or 'his friend is in love with my co-wife, who hates me' [29]. 'Hurting the lover who stays with another woman' refers to the situation in which 'he will stop her income' [25]. 'Breaking the ex-lover away from another woman' states a reason for staying with the ex-lover.

or the lover from another woman,
and to hurt, again, the lover who stays with another woman.
[39]When a man is too deeply attached to her,
he fears that she will make love with another man
and he disregards her lies.
And, because of his fear, he gives her a lot.
[40]She welcomes the man who is not attached* to her
and scorns the man who is attached to her.
And if a messenger should come from another man
who is very experienced,
[41]a woman stalls for time with her former lover,
when he is trying to talk her into taking him back:
she makes sure that the connection is unbroken,
and does not give up the man who is attached to her.
[42]But a woman may talk with a man who is attached to her
and in her power and then, nevertheless, go elsewhere.
And when she has taken the money from him, too,
she enchants just the man who is attached to her.
[43]A clever woman gets back together with an ex-lover
only after she has tested, at the start,
the future outlook, the gain,
the abundant love, and the friendship.

---

[40] The man who is not attached to her is an ex-lover who is still very much in love with her; she welcomes him because his feelings for her are known. The man who is attached to her is not in love with her, and so she treats him with contempt. Another man, who is very clever, gives her a great deal of money, saying, 'Do not make a connection with another man.'

[41] Although he uses the more general term, 'a woman', he is referring only to a courtesan in this section. She does not make love with the man right then, or else there might be a break from her present, attached, profitable lover. And the previously intimate ex-lover is willing to wait for another time, because he loves her so much and has hope.

[42] She enchants just the man who is attached to her because she loves him for having stayed; she does not make any connection with the other man.

FIVE: WEIGHING DIFFERENT KINDS OF PROFITS

[1]If she has a multitude of lovers and can make a lot of money every day, she need not confine herself to a single lover. [2]Taking into account the place, the time, and the conditions, and her own qualities and luck in love, and whether she is charging more or less than other women, she establishes the price of a night. [3]She also sends messengers to her lover, and she herself summons men with whom he has some connection. [4]She may go two, three, or even four times to a single lover in order to take extraordinary profits, and then she establishes a liaison.

[5]Scholars say: 'When she has several lovers at once, however, who offer equal opportunities for profit, the obvious choice is the one who gives her whatever she-wants.* [6]Vatsyayana says: The one who gives gold is best, because gold cannot be taken back again and can buy everything that is needed. [7]Of gold, silver, copper, bronze, iron, furniture, utensils, bedding, blankets, special clothing, perfumed articles, sharp spices, dishes, ghee, sesame oil, grain, and the species of cattle, each should be chosen rather than the one that follows. [8]When the things are the same, or of the same quality, the choice should be made on the basis of a friend's advice, temporary needs, future needs, the lover's qualities, and love.

[9]Scholars say: 'Between a lover who is in love and another who is generous, the obvious choice is the generous one.' [10]Vatsyayana says: But it is possible to cultivate generosity in a man who is in love. [11]For even a greedy man, if he is in love, spends generously, but a generous man cannot be made to fall in love through mere persistence.

[12]Scholars say: 'In this case [of a man in love versus a generous man], too, between a wealthy man and one who is not wealthy, the choice is the wealthy man; and between a generous man and a man who does what she needs to have done at the moment, the clear choice is the man who does what she needs to have.' [13]Vatsyayana says: But the man who does what she needs to have done, when he has done it once, thinks that he has given satisfaction. A generous man, however, has no regard for the past. [14]In this case [of a generous man versus a man who does what she needs], too, the choice is for the man who takes care of future needs.

[15]Scholars say: 'Between a grateful man and a generous man, the clear choice is the generous man.' [16]But even when she has pleased a generous man for a long time, when he sees one false move or believes unjust slander by a rival courtesan de luxe, he has no regard for the trouble she went to in the past. [17]For in general, generous men are dignified, straightforward, and thoughtless. [18]Vatsyayana says: A grateful man has regard for the trouble she has taken in the past and his passion does not' suddenly cool toward her. And

---

[8] The woman chooses on the basis of her own love and the man's love for her.

[13] Because he is generous, he does not consider the past and say, 'I already gave money to her, and I will not give it again.'

[16] A false move is an infidelity committed by the woman.

[17] Because they are dignified, they do not disregard a false move. Because they are straightforward, they accept unjust slander, such as, 'That woman is always making false moves.' Because they are thoughtless, they have no regard for the pains a woman takes on their behalf.

[18] He does not accept unjust slander.

since his character has been tested and proven, he is not susceptible to unjust slander.* [19]In this case [of a generous man versus a grateful man], too, the choice is for the man who takes care of future needs.

[20]Scholars say: 'Between a friend's advice and getting money, the clear choice is for getting money.' [21]Vatsyayana says: Money will be gained in the future, too; but a friend whose advice is once disregarded may become offended. [22]In this case [of a friend's advice versus getting money], too, the choice is for the man who takes care of temporary needs. [23]In this case, she brings the friend around by showing what she needs to have done, saying, 'I will take your advice for what is going to happen tomorrow', and then she still keeps the money for her temporary needs.

[24]Scholars say: 'Between getting money and warding off losses, the clear choice is getting money.' [25]Vatsyayana says: Money gained has a limit; loss, however, once it breaks out, continues to move in directions that no one can predict. [26]In this case [of getting money versus warding off losses], too, the choice must be made with regard to the relative weight of each factor. [27]This means that the choice is for a loss warded off rather than a doubtful gain.

[28]The top courtesans de luxe spend their excess profits by building temples, pools, and gardens; setting up raised mounds and fire altars; giving thousands of cows to Brahmins through the mediation of people worthy to receive them; bringing and offering articles of worship to the gods, or providing money sufficient to spend on that worship. [29]Those who live on their beauty spend their excess profits by getting jewellery for all their limbs, decorating their houses elegantly, and glorifying the furnishings of their houses with expensive household goods and servants. [30]Servant women who carry pots of water spend their excess profits by having spotless clothes to wear all the time, buying food and drink to stave off hunger, using perfumed things and betel all the time, and wearing jewellery that is partly to made of gold. [31]Scholars say: 'This example of the top courtesans de luxe also applies to the excess profit of all of them, even the middle and lowest ones.' [32]Vatsyayana says: This is not a real livelihood, because the profit is not constant, depending as it does on place, time, ability, power, love, and people's customs.

[33]If she desires to keep a lover from going elsewhere, or if she desires to get a man away from some woman to whom he is attached, or if she wants to separate another woman from her gains, or if she thinks that by taking up with a man who is not eligible she will improve her own position, prosperity, future, and her sex appeal; or if she desires to get the man to help her ward off a loss; or if she wishes to betray another man who is attached to her, because she regards his former favours as if they had never been done; or if she simply wants love; then she will even take just a very small profit from a man of good intentions. [34]She will not, however, take anything at all if she is thinking of the future and seeks refuge with him in the hope of warding off a loss.

[26] A heavy gain outweighs a light loss, and a heavy loss outweighs a light gain.

[28] Mediation is given through the hand of another person, since a Brahmin cannot receive a gift from a courtesan.

[29] Those who live on their beauty do not know the arts.

[31] The middle and lowest are the women who live on their beauty and the women who carry water pots.

[35]But if she thinks, 'I will abandon him and take up a liaison with someone else'; 'He will go'; 'He will get together with his wives'; or, 'He will lose his money'; 'His supervisor or his master or father will come and work on him like an elephant goad'; or, 'He will lose his position'; or, 'He is fickle', then she wants to make her profits from him in the present moment. [36]If she thinks, 'He will get the favour that the ruler promised him'; 'He will obtain an administrative post or position'; or, 'The time for him to get his livelihood is coming near; his ship will come in; his landholding or grain will ripen'; 'What is done for him is not lost; he always keeps his word', then she wants him for the future, or she engages him in a liaison. [37]And there are verses about this:

For both future and present purposes,
she should avoid, at a great distance,
men who have amassed their wealth with difficulty
and men who are the cruel favourites of the king.
[38]She should make every effort to captivate
men whom it is disastrous to avoid
and prosperous to seek,
and she should use every pretext to get close to them
[39]And she should seek out, even by spending her own money
those who think on a large scale and have great energy,
those who, in a good mood, will give her money
even for some small matter, and without counting it.

SIX: CALCULATING GAINS AND LOSSES, CONSEQUENCES AND DOUBTS

[1]Losses result even from gains that are being amassed, and so do other consequences and doubts. [2]All of these come from weakness of mind; from excesses of passion, of self-importance, of duplicity, of honesty, of confidence, and of anger; and from carelessness, recklessness, and the workings of fate. [3]Their results are the failure to reap the fruits from expenditures that have been made; lack of a future; blockage of money that is supposed to come in; disappearance of what has been gained; development of a harsh temperament; sexual vulnerability; injury to the body; hair-loss; collapse; and mutilation of the limbs. [4]Therefore, from the very start one should try to root out these causes and pay attention to the factors that increase gains.

[5]The three gains are money, religious merit, and pleasure,* [6]and the three losses are loss of money, loss of religious merit, and hatred. [7]The production of something from something else, when these three gains are being amassed, is a consequence. [8]'Is it to be or not to be?' is a pure doubt about the uncertainty of achieving an object. [9]'Will this happen or that?' is a mixed doubt. [10]Two goals achieved when a single goal was being pursued make a two-sided result, [11]and something produced by a group is a group result. We will be referring to these. [12]The form of the three gains has been discussed. The three losses are precisely the opposite of them.*

[13]A gain that has the consequence of further gain occurs when she has a lover of the highest class and openly gets money from him but also becomes acceptable, sexually accessible, and sought after by other men and gets a future. [14]A gain that has no consequence occurs when she goes from one lover to another merely for profit.

[15]A gain that has the consequence of a loss occurs when a man attached to her gives her money from someone else, which cuts off her future and puts an end to her money; or when she has a lover who is low or hated by everyone, which destroys her future. [16]A loss that has the consequence of a gain occurs when, by spending her own money, she takes as a lover a hero or minister of state or a powerful man who is greedy; even though this liaison is fruitless, it brings a future with it and is undertaken in order to prevent some disaster or to allay some factor that might be greatly destructive of her gains.

[17]A loss that has no consequences occurs when she gratifies, even by spending her own money, a miser who thinks he is lucky in love, or an ungrateful man who by his very nature cheats, and in the end this is fruitless. [18]A loss that has the consequence of further loss occurs when she gratifies in that very way just such a man who is a favourite of the king, rich in cruelty and power, and in the end this is fruitless, but when she gets rid of him that also does her harm.

[19]The consequences for religious merit and pleasure can be calculated in the same way, [20]and each can be combined with one of the others in the appropriate way. Those are the consequences.

---

12 The gains have been discussed in the passage about the three aims of human life [1.1.2].

15 Because of his own lack of funds, the man who is attached to a woman gives her money that he took from another man and should give back to him, so that people say, 'She is living with a robber.'

20 There are twenty-four combinations of consequences: each of the six—gain, loss, religious merit, violation of religion, pleasure, and hatred—coupled with four of the others.

[21]The doubt about money is, 'Will he give it or not lower, even if he is fully satisfied?' [22]The doubt about religious merit is, 'Will I serve religion or not, by throwing out a man from whom no more money can be taken, once all the money has been squeezed out of him and he is no longer fruitful?' [23]The doubt about pleasure is, 'Will there be pleasure or not, if I go to a servant or some other low man whom I find attractive?'

[24]The doubt about loss is, 'If I do not go to a powerful but low man, will that cause me a loss or not?' [25]The doubt about the violation of religion is, 'If I abandon a man who is attached to me but is absolutely fruitless, and he goes to the world of his ancestors, does that violate religion or not?' [26]The doubt about hatred is, 'Will my passion cool or not toward a man whom I do not find attractive and who hesitates even to speak of passion? Those are the pure doubts.

[27]Now for the mixed doubts. [28]The doubt is: 'Will gain or loss result from gratifying a newcomer whose character is unknown or a newly arrived man who is powerful because he has the protection of a favourite?' [29]The doubt is: 'Will I serve religion or violate it if I go, on the sympathetic advice of a friend, to a Brahmin who knows the Veda, or to a man who is under a vow of chastity or consecrated for a sacrifice, or a man who has taken a vow or who wears the sign of a religious order, if he has seen me and conceived a passion for me and wants to die?' [30]The doubt is: 'Will pleasure or hatred result if I go to a man without knowing if he has or does not have good qualities, because people have not yet tested him?' [31]Each can be combined with one of the others. This ends the discussion of the mixed doubts.

[32]These are the two-sided results, according to Auddalakr. 'A two-sided gain occurs when she goes to another man and gain comes, also, from the man who is attached to her, out of rivalry.[33] A two-sided loss occurs when she spends her own money on a fruitless liaison with another man, and the man who is attached to her, unable to put up with that, takes back the money he, had given her. [34] A two-sided doubt about gain occurs when she has gone to another man and worries, "Will there be gain in this or not?" and "Will the man who is attached to me also give something, out of rivalry, or not?" [35]A two-sided doubt about loss occurs when she has gone to a man at her own expense: "Will my former lover, in his frustration and anger, do me harm or not?" and, "Will the man who is attached to me, unable to put up with it, take back the money he had given me or not?"'

[36]But the followers of Babhravya say: [37]'A two-sided gain occurs when gain comes both from the man she goes to and from the man who is attached to her to whom she does not go. [38]A two-sided loss occurs when she spends her money fruitlessly on going to another man and cannot recoup her loss of money from the man she does not go to. [39]A two-sided doubt about gain occurs when she has gone to another man, and she wonders: "Will he give me money without my incurring expenses or not?" and "Will the man who is attached to me and to whom I have not gone give me money or not?" [40]A two-sided doubt about loss occurs when she has gone to another man at her own expense, and she wonders: "Will my former lover, frustrated, demonstrate his powers or not?' and, 'Will the one I do not go to become angry and cause me a loss or not?"'

---

[26] He hesitates to say, 'There will be no pleasure', because he is tormented by passion. But he is not even attractive to her.

[27] He wants to die because he has reached the final stage of desire.

[40] She does not go to the man who is attached to her.

[41]Six mixed results are produced by combining these: gain on one side and loss on the other; gain on one side and doubt about gain on the other; gain on one side and doubt about loss on the other. [42]Considering among these, together with her helpers, she acts in such a way as to maximise gain, even when there is doubt about gain, or to cut her losses significantly, [43]She treats religious merit and pleasure in this same way: they can be combined, one with another, and paired with their opposites. Those are the two-sided results.

[44]When a group of voluptuaries keep one woman for all of them, that is a group liaison. [45]When she gets together with first one of them and then another, she gets money from them one by one, through their rivalry. [46]At occasions such as the spring festival, she announces, through her mother: 'My daughter "will go tonight to the man who does this or that for me."' [47]And from going to them in a way that causes rivalry, she targets what she needs: [48]gain from one and gain from all of them, loss from one and loss from all, gain from half and gain from all, loss from half and loss from all. Those are the group results.

[49]Doubt about gain and doubt about loss can be calculated as above. And religious merit and pleasure can be combined with them in the same way. Those are the gains and losses, consequences, and doubts.

NOTES

6.1.9, 13, 31 The arts here could refer either to the fine arts or to the arts of love, or to both. Y does not specify.

6.1.10 These fatalists are called Daicapramana ('those for whom fate, or the gods are the authority'); the fatalists mentioned at 1.2.26 are *Kalakarinikas* ('those who invoke fate, or time, as the cause').

6.1.13 Y glosses what we have translated as 'true to one type' (*ekajatiya*) as meaning that the woman does not keep changing her appearance (losing and gaining weight, one might suppose, changing her hairdo, etc).

6.1.14 These qualities are apparently appreciated in all women, in contrast with the qualities enumerated in 6.1.13, which are appreciated only, or specially, in courtesans.

---

[43] Two-sided results for religious merit occur when [6.6.29] she goes to the Brahmin who is going to die, for religious merit comes both from the fact that she is serving a Brahmin and that he is otherwise going to die of his love for her. Two-sided results for the violation of religion occur when [29] she goes to the man under a vow of chastity, both because he breaks his vow and because he is unwilling. Two-sided doubts about religious merit arise when [38] she goes to another man who has no money, and she worries, 'Will religious merit be served or not?' and [22] the man who is attached to her can give her nothing, because she has squeezed all the money out of him, and she worries, 'Will religious merit come from this or not?' Two-sided doubts about the violation of religion arise when [29] she goes to another man from a religious order and makes him break his vow, and she wonders, 'Will religion be violated or not?' and [29] the man attached to her, who has taken a vow, intends to give her a lot of money, and she wonders, 'Will religion be violated or not?'

Two-sided results for pleasure occur when [23] she goes to another attractive man and also [32–4] satisfies her desire with the attractive man who is attached to her. Two-sided results for hatred occur when [26] her passion cools both form going to another unattractive man and from going to the unattractive man attached to her. Two-sided doubts about pleasure arise when [30] she goes to another man, without knowing if he has good qualities or not, and she wonders, 'Will pleasure result or not?' and [33] the man attached to her is unrequited and she wonders, 'Will pleasure result or not?' Two-sided doubts about hatred arise when [26] she goes to another man and wonders, 'Will my passion toward this man cool or not, since he hesitates to talk about dispelling passion?' and [26] 'Will my passion cool or not toward the man attached to me, to whom I feel the same way?'

[y] 6.1.15 Y takes his examples from each of the three groups of qualities: bad family (the inverse of a great family, the first quality in 6.1.12), ugliness (in contrast with beauty 6.1.13) and stupidity (in contrast with intelligence 6.1.14). This means that the faults apply to both men (6.1.12) and women (6.1.13–14).

6.1.16 'Worms in the faeces' may offer a speculative explanation for some venereal disease.

[y] 6.1.17 Y assumes that women have semen, a belief that he and Babhravya express in the discussion of female orgasm (at 2.1.18). Ravana raped Rambha by threatening to kill her, but she cursed him so that he could never rape another woman again. This story is told in the *Ramayana*; see Doniger, *Splitting the Difference.* Devadatta and Anangasena are two courtesans, and Muladeva is a muster-thief, in Somadeva's tenth century work *Ocean of Story* and Kshemendra's eleventh century work the *Kalavilasa.*

6.1.20. 'And so forth' may refer to the twenty reasons for a courtesan to take a lover, listed in 6.1.17; though why 'fear' should come first and stand for the group in this case is puzzling, one would expect 'passion', the first reason listed there.

6.2.11 The word for leftover garlands also means the flowers left over from an offering to the gods, whose leftover food (called *prasada*) is distributed to worshippers together with the leftover flowers, or to a king, as described in 4.2.57.

6.2.13 These techniques are discussed in 2.2.3.

6.2.26 This can mean either that she expresses her passion for him by faking drunkenness and so forth and then blames them on her sexual deprivation, or that she uses those feigned conditions that strip away pretences as an excuse to tell him how she feels. Y takes the first two (drunkenness and sleep) in the first sense and the third (disease) in the second sense.

6.2.31 She says 'Live!' in the spirit of our 'God bless you', or *Gesundheit* and for a similar reason: the widespread folk belief that the soul temporarily leaves the body during a sneeze (when the heart does in fact stop for a split second).

6.2.36 The word *vrittha*, that we have translated as 'false' can also mean 'casual' or 'in Vain', and the compound as a whole can apply either to him or to her. Y takes it in the sense of 'false', and applies it to the woman's infidelity; but it could also apply to him in this sense, or it can be taken in the sense of 'casual', and can be applied to, either him or her: 'When s/he has been accused of a casual infidelity...' Her fasting in the context of his infidelity is well attested in Sanskrit literature, which makes it more likely that it is the man's infidelity that V intended. The word *vyasana*, that we have rendered as 'misfortune' may also mean 'addiction, evil passion, vice', presumably his, but, again, possibly hers.

6.2.47 Or, if this quarrel is between them, and about the vow mentioned in the previous passage, she may be arguing that it is too demanding even for him to carry out.

6.2.54 She asks that when she is reborn, he be reborn as her husband.

6.2.69 A pot full of presents is distributed to anyone who brings good news.

6.2.70 Crows are said to be auspicious omens with the power to make wishes come true.

6.2.72 To follow him beyond death means to die a natural death after his death and wait to be joined with him in heaven or the next rebirth. Only later, and very rarely, did it come to mean mounting his funeral pyre alive to burn to death with his corpse.

6.3.4 She gets the money ostensibly to pay for the things but actually buys them on credit and keeps the money; he sees the things and thinks she has bought them with the money he gave her.

6.3.36 This may also mean that she does this before he realizes that she is going to take the money and run.

6.3.44. The word 'release' (*moksha*) more generally refers to a person's spiritual release from the world of transmigration (as in 1.2.4); there may be an intended irony in its use here to designate the release of a man from a courtesan's thrall.

6.4.12 The idea seems to be that there is no more reason to take him now than there was when the other woman got rid of him, since he still has no money.

6.4.16 'As tickle in his affections as turmeric is in its colour' puns on the word *ruga*, which can mean either 'colour' or 'passion', and on the fact that turmeric cannot hold its colour for long.

6.4.28 There is some confusion in the editions of this passage about the person who is the object of contempt. According to Shastri's reading, it is the courtesan; according to Goswami's, it is the man (treated with contempt by his wife). And according to Y, it is the man's wife (treated with contempt by the courtesan). We have followed Shastri here.

6.4.40 The attitude to the man who is 'attached', according to this verse and, even more sharply, in the commentary on it, is far more cynical than the one expressed in earlier discussions of the attached man, as at 6.2.73. There, he was a willing devotee; here, he seems to be either entirely besotted or simply the man with her at the moment, or both. There, he was cherished; here he is taken for granted and scorned, explicitly contrasted with the man she does love. This may be an example of a different origin for the prose and verse passages of the text.

6.5.5 A series of choices is made here between paired alternatives, and there is a running disagreement about them between V and earlier scholars. In passage 5 the scholars rank at the top, the man who gives her what she seeks or needs, a general category that will be broken down, in passage 8, into those who fulfil temporary and future needs and that V, in passage 6, epitomizes in the man who gives gold. Passage 8 offers another set of categories, which are debated in the passages that follow, together with yet other criteria. In passage 9, the scholars rank the generous man over the man in love, and V disagrees in 10–11. In passage 12 (and again in 14, 19 and 22), the scholars rank the man who does what she needs to have done over the generous man, and V disagrees in 13. In 15 the scholars rank the generous man over the grateful man, and V disagrees in 16–18. In 20 the scholars rank the general category of getting money over a friend's advice, and V disagrees in 21. In 24 the scholars rank getting money over counteracting losses, and V disagrees in 25–27.

6.5.18 The text allows the reading that the man himself cannot be slandered, which is a more logical conclusion from his own good character, but V links it to passage 16 and takes it to mean that he does not believe slander against her.

6.6.5 This triad may well be a satirical twist on the famous triad of the three aims of human life (1.1.1), which here are reduced to three aspects of one of them: money or power—which (in Sanskrit, *artha*) itself also means 'gain'.

6.6.12 This triad is, theoretically, that of losses connected with money, religious merit, and pleasure, though V spells these out neither for gains (which he has discussed at 2.1.1) nor for losses. Significantly, V here reverses the usual order, putting *artha* first. One might also see a triad in situations that result in positive gain, (6.6.13–14) mixed gain and loss (6.6.15–16) and loss (6.6.17–18).

Chapter 23 Temple Women as Temple Servants*

LESLIE ORR

In the whole of the corpus of Chola period inscriptions, I have found only nine inscriptions like this one, which name women with responsibility functions. Three of these inscriptions date from the second subperiod, and the other six are from the last subperiod. Another 15 mention groups of people with responsibility functions, using 'temple woman' terms (e.g., *tevaraṭiyār*) which may refer to women (as well as to men). Inscriptions of this type are found especially in the first subperiod. The total of 24 inscriptions that refer to temple women with responsibility functions constitute 8 percent of all inscriptions that mention temple women, but there is little evidence to suggest a definite chronological pattern of their increasing or decreasing involvement in temple affairs. Mostly, they simply were not involved.

It is certainly clear that temple women were not part of the development characteristic for men—the very sharp increase between the second and third subperiods in the number of named individuals with responsibility functions. This increase between the early and later Chola periods seems to be the result, at least in part, of the fact that more and more men had the function of 'taking in hand' (*kaikkoṇṭa*) an endowment, receiving a gift on behalf of the temple. Women, in contrast, do not seem to have performed this function; the only case I have found is that of a temple woman (*tevaraṭiyār*) who 'took in hand' the gift that a queen made to a temple in Kanyakumari district in the thirteenth century (KK 194= TAS 8, 34). Another important administrative function in the temple that is quite commonly mentioned as belonging to men, either as individuals or in groups, is that of 'supervisor' (*kaṇk āṇi*). Here again, I have come across just one inscription in which a named woman has this function—the preceding translation—in which four temple women (*patiyilār*) shared the role of supervisor with other temple functionaries.

If these roles were extremely rare for women, what types of responsibility functions did temple women have? Table 23.1 shows the numbers of inscriptions that mention temple

*Reproduced with permission from the author. Previously published in *Donors, Devotees and Daughters by* Leslie Orr. OUP, New York, pp. 99–134.

women in connection with each of five types of responsibility functions, considering separately the nine inscriptions in which temple women are named (and definitely female) and the 15 in-scriptions that refer to groups of temple women (*tevaraṭiyār*, *emperumāṉaṭiyār*, etc.). I have arranged these types of responsibility functions roughly in order, beginning with those roles that seem to have involved the most decision-making powers and control and ending with those that were more nominal and honorific in character and peripheral to the workings of the temple.

The two functions already discussed, marked by the terms *kaikkoṇṭa* and *kaṇkāṇi*, are classified as functions of the first sort, administrative functions, as are other kinds of active engagement in the conduct of temple affairs. People charged with the second category of responsibility functions, collection of taxes and fines, received property on behalf of the temple but would not have been involved in decision making or management of the temple's wealth. The third category, people who 'tended' temple resources, are those with whom livestock, land, or gold was invested by the temple in expectation of a certain regular return in the form of ghee for lamps, paddy, or other supplies used by the temple. In Chola period inscriptions, there are many examples of shepherds involved in such 'tending' relationships with the temple. For example, at the great temple of Tanjavur, specific shepherds, together with their relatives, would be assigned 96 sheep or 48 cows, in exchange for which they would be expected to provide daily enough ghee to fuel a perpetual lamp; the shepherds, their relatives, and their relatives' relatives were supposed to maintain this arrangement in perpetuity (SII 2.63, 2.64, 2.94, 2.95). Temple Brahmans also frequently entered into these tending relationships.[1]

Neither the fourth nor the fifth category of responsibility functions necessarily involved any active hand in or control over temple affairs, although people with these functions were acknowledged to have at least some connection with and authority in the business of the temple. The fourth category includes individuals who acted as signatories to grants and groups that represented interests in the temple in drawing up agreements. People who were engaged in the fifth type of responsibility function, invariably in groups, were said to ensure the protection (*rakṣai*) of the grant recorded in an inscription; typically, *paṉmāheśvarar* or *śrīvaiṣṇavas* were said to exercise this role.

Table 23.1 Types of Responsibility Functions Performed by Temple Women

	Named	Group	Total
Administration	3	4	7
Collection of taxes and fines	—	4	4
Tending	4	2	6
Party to agreement	2	2	4
Protection	—	3	3
Total	9	15	24

Table 23.1 shows us that temple women as individuals were not closely linked to the inner workings of the temple. Of the responsibility functions that involved some degree of control over temple resources, individual temple women are named as temple administrators in three inscriptions and in the category of those who tended temple property in four inscriptions.

We find a few more references to control over temple resources, as well as to other types of responsibility functions, in inscriptions that refer to groups of people (particularly people termed *tevaraṭiyār*), who may have been temple women. Four inscriptions include such groups among supervisory or managerial personnel, and in four others, groups of *tevaraṭiyār* are given the responsibility for the collection of fines or taxes. There are three inscriptions, all dating from the first subperiod and found in Tirupati in Chittoor district (in the northernmost part of the Tamil country, in what is today Andhra Pradesh), in which we encounter the expression *emperu-māṉaṭiyār rakṣai.* Because *emperumāṉaṭiyār* is one of the 'temple woman' terms and was applied in other inscriptional contexts to people who were definitely women, it is possible that it indicates the designation of temple women as 'protectors' of grants. But even in the case of groups, only a very small number of inscriptions represent temple women—or groups that might include or consist of temple women—as performing responsibility functions.

We may contrast these small numbers not only with the much larger numbers of male temple officials who, as individuals or in groups, engaged in responsibility functions central to the workings of the Chola period temple but also with the numbers of temple women—referred to as *sānis*—who were involved in such functions in medieval Andhra Pradesh. In Telugu inscriptions contemporary with the Chola period inscriptions in Tamil, *sānis*, very often together with male temple officials such as *māṇis* or *sthānapatis*, or as a group termed the 'three hundred *sānis*,' frequently took charge of or supervised the administration of gifts to the temple (Talbot 1988b, 105–7; Ramaswamy 1989, 96–97). In the Tamil country, in contrast, the responsibility for temple affairs seems to have rested solely with men, and it is extremely rare to find managerial tasks, even of the most nominal sort, shared with temple women.[2]

The almost complete lack of engagement of temple women in responsibility functions means that they were not authorized to exercise power within the institutional structure of the temple nor to have direct access to the economic resources of the temple. But they were also denied the opportunity, which so many men took advantage of in the later Chola period, to use involvement in temple affairs as a means of gaining status and public prominence. The men whose names increasingly multiply in the records engraved on temple walls were—through the inscription of the record itself, as well as through the encounters, transactions, and solemn ceremonies of donation and witnessing that the record represents—accorded recognition by the temple and the local society, in terms both of their reputations and social connections in the short term and of their fame for posterity.[3] Temple women may have realized these aims through their activity as do nors—an avenue that temple men did not follow—but they did not acquire or enhance their status and position by participating in temple affairs, as temple men did. Temple women did, however, participate in temple service, and we now examine this aspect of their identity and activity.

SERVING IN THE TEMPLE

Dancing and Singing

In the third year of the reign of Ko Māṟapaṉmar alius Tiripuvaṉacakkaravattikaḷ śrī Vikkirama Pāṇṭiyatevar, the sacred order [of the deity] concerning the *patiyilār* and the *tevaraṭiyār* of the temple of Lord Tiruviraṭṭanamuṭaiya Nāyaṉār [was given]: that when the [deities] Chief (*mutaliyār*) Nāṭaṟkariyakūttar and Nāyakar are brought into the hundred-pillar *maṇṭapam*, the *patiyilār* are responsible for dancing before the raising of the curtain and the *tevaraṭiyār* are responsible for dancing after the raising of the curtain.—SII 8.333: this inscription was engraved in the thirteenth century on the southern *gopura* at the Viraṭṭaneśvara temple in Tiruvadi, South Arcot district.

In the ninth year of the reign of Śri Kulottuṉkacoladevar, it is agreed (this) first day of the ninth year that gold and paddy are to be provided as they were formerly provided for the *pāṇar* in this temple, at the rate of 1 *kalam* of paddy, measured by the *ūrkkāl*, per person, for the basic living allowance (*mutal kāṉipeṟṟapaṭi*) for Irumuṭicoḻaṉ Pirāṉ alias Acañcalapperayaṉ—who is to sing for the Lord of Tiruviṭaimarutu in Tiraimūrnāṭu in Uyyakoṇṭārvaḷanāṭu, who is to cause the *taḷiyillār tevaraṭiyār* to sing in the temple, and who is to dwell here as the person of this place responsible for the *pāṇar*—and for his descendents (*vaṅśattār*).

We, together with those servants of the temple (*palapaṇi nivantakkārar*) who are partners in this agreement, assign, as formerly to the *pāṇar*, the land necessary to produce this paddy and additional expense money—land that is part of the *tevatānam* of this god—as land for the support of *pāṇar* (*pāṇakāṇi*), as their 'livelihood' (*jīvitam*).

And, as a place of residence, a house is given for dwelling here, and the terms of this allowance (*paṭi*) are inscribed in stone as what is approved this ninth year and first day, according to royal order (*tirumukam*).

This royal proclamation (*tirumantira olai*) is signed by Malaiyappiryār and Putukkaṭaiyār, the tax accountants Neṭumaṇamuṭaiyāṉ, Ponnuḷāṉ, Paṇṇainallūruṭaiyāṉ, Veḷārkiḻ avaṉ, Aracūruṭaiyāṉ, and Ceṟṟūruṭaiyāṉ, [and others].

[The boundaries of the land are given and the yield in paddy.] Signed: the temple accountant Kuṇṭaiyūrkiḻavaṉ, the temple servant (*tevarkaṉmi*) Tirucciṟṟampalapaṭṭaṉ,the temple manager (*śrīkāriyam*) Mulaṅku-ṭaiyāṉ, and the *śrīmāheśvara kaṇkāṇi* Tiruviti Anpaṟkaracu. [More details of the land boundaries are given, and the names of these signatories are again inscribed].—SII 5.705: this inscription, which begins with a very long *meykkīrtti*, was engraved in A.D. 1142 at the Mahāliṅgasvāmi temple in Tiruvidaimarudur, Tanjavur district.

The art of the *devadāsīs*, their expertise in dancing and singing, has been at the center of much of the attention paid to these women in the last century. One frequently encounters the idea that the entire *devadāsī* institution is tied to the introduction of song and dance into rituals of worship, that the very raison d'être of the temple woman was to serve as a performer in the temple (e.g., Sadasivan 1993, 31). Several of the scholars who have made substantial contributions to our understanding of temple women in recent times have themselves been dancers, and their work conveys a vivid appreciation of the artistic tradition and professional skill of the surviving members of *devadāsī* communities.[4] But the *devadāsīs*' artistic heritage is not particularly ancient. Their traditions—including the repertoire of particular music and dance forms and the performance of dance at specified moments in temple ritual—seem to have been developed and codified in the eighteenth and nineteenth centuries (Khokar 1979, 64; Kersenboom 1987, 43–48; Meduri 1996, 40–45). It is not really possible to trace back to early times a continuous lineage for the *devadāsī* as we think of her today, as a temple servant whose ritual expertise was dance. Songs and dances do not seem to have been formal liturgical elements or offerings made to the temple deity in the temple ritual of early South India, as it is reflected in the Tamil *bhakti* literature of the sixth to ninth centuries, nor was the singing and dancing that was a part of early devotional life of the same character or performed by the same types of people as the temple songs and dances of later times (Young and Orr 1985; Orr and Young 1986). As we have seen in the analysis of Chola period setup grants at the beginning of this chapter, hymn singing did become a more established feature of temple liturgy in succeeding centuries, but dance seems to have been a minor component in the ritual life of the medieval temple. The Agamic texts similarly give the impression that dance was an optional element in temple ritual.[5] And between medieval and modern times, many factors have been at work which have altered the ritual contexts in which temple women had a part to play, the artistic traditions that shaped the forms of temple dance, and the associations between temple dance and temple women.

Despite the fact that temple women are so frequently referred to as 'dancing-girls'—or, more respectfully, 'temple dancers'—in scholarly and popular literature, the inscriptions of medieval India only rarely refer to them in this way. Of the 304 Chola period inscriptions that mention temple women, only 4 use terms that mean 'dancer.' In two of these inscriptions, both of which refer to groups of singers, as well as dancers, it is not even certain that these performers are female. The first, an early Chola period inscription from Chittoor district in the far north, records that *kūttu-āṭiṉār* ('*kūttu* dancers') and *pāṭiār* ('singers') were to receive payment for their services, apparently on the occasion of a festival for the god Indra (SII 8.529). The second is an eleventh-century inscription from Kolar district, in the northwest, which mentions the provisions made for the *āṭiṉār* and *pāṭiṉār* who were to perform at a festival (EC 10.Kl 108). These inscriptions, although separated in time, come from the same general geographical area, and the use of the term *aṭiṉār* for 'dancers' seems restricted to this region. In two other inscriptions that record arrangements for temple dance, and refer to the performers as dancers, there is much more certainty that these are women. Both are mid-twelfth century inscriptions from Tiruvengavasal in Tiruchirappalli district, which name the women who were commissioned to dance at temple festivals. In one of these inscriptions (IPS 139), the woman is referred to as a *cāntikkūtti. Kūtti* is the feminine form for 'dancer,' derived from *kūttu* ('dance, dancing'). A *cāntikkūtti* is a woman who performs the *cānti* dance; *cānti* (from Skt. *śānti*, 'peace') is perhaps best translated in this context as 'festival' (MTL, 1370).[6] The other inscription (IPS 128) names a woman who is to act as an *āṭuvāḷ* ('female dancer'), and specifies that she is to perform the *cāntikkūttu*.

Very few temple women are referred to as dancers, and it is equally the case that all female dancers were not temple women. Four Chola period inscriptions refer to *kūttis* or *cāntikkūttis* who do not appear to have had any connection with the temple. Two are eleventh-century inscriptions with references to a 'dancer-tax' (*kūtti kāl*) (EI 22.34; SII 7.467).[7] And two thirteenth-century inscriptions (IPS 219 and SII 17.463) record the donations of women said to be *cāntikkūttis* 'of our town' or 'in this place'—not 'of the temple.' One of these (IPS 219) describes the donor as the daughter of a man named (or titled) Periyanāṭṭācāriyaṉ, 'great teacher (*ācāriyaṉ*) of the district (*nāṭu*),' a name that indicates high professional standing. This man is not identified as a *cāntikkūttaṉ,* but there are several inscriptions in which male dancers are referred to by this term. In one (SII 2.67H), the *cāntikkūttaṉ*—who was employed to perform a play or a dance called the 'Rājarājeśvara-nāṭakam' at the big temple of Tanjavur—also has *ācāriyaṉ* ('teacher') as part of his name. In another (IPS 275), a *cāntikkūttaṉ* 'of this district (*nāṭu*)' is said to have received land from the same temple of Tiruvengavasal that employed the two female dancers (the *cāntikkūtti* and the *āṭuvāḷ*) already mentioned.

Although all the inscriptions that refer to men as *cāntikkūttar* do so in connection with support from or performance in a temple, it seems to me that there are a number of indications that *cāntikkūttar* were professional dancers who were independent of the temple, in family-based occupational groups in which both men and women were involved in performances in various contexts. The constellation of features shown by the inscriptions that reter to *cāntikkūttar*—their identification as being of the town or district rather than of the temple; the word *ācāriyaṉ* as part of the names of several ot the men; the employment of *cāntikkūttar* in the temple specifically for dance performances; the mention of a father-daughter kinship relation—suggest that the *cāntikkūttar* were an occupational group not primarily identified with temple service but employed by the temple as performers, especially during festivals.[8]

Among those—*cāntikkūttar* and others—who danced in the temple, men were more prominent than women, particularly in the earlier Chola period. Table 23.2 shows the numbers of inscriptions that refer to temple dancers or performers of drama (*nāṭakam*) in each of the four subperiods, indicating whether we can identify them as women, men, or neither. The first thing we notice in this table is how small these numbers are. That my careful scrutiny of the entire corpus of Chola period inscriptions has uncovered only 38 inscriptions that refer to temple dancers underscores the minor and inessential character of dance as an element of medieval temple ritual. In 12 of the inscriptions, it is not possible to ascertain the sex of the performer; I have nonetheless taken these inscriptions to refer to temple women in my overall tabulation because it seems quite possible that some of these anonymous dancers were women. When we turn to a comparison of the two groups of inscriptions in which the dancers are clearly male or female, we see that in the earlier Chola period men were much more frequently given the task of dancing in the temple than were women: nine inscriptions

Table 23.2 Temple Dancers in Chola Period Inscriptions

	Chola 1	Chola 2	Chola 3	Chola 4	Total
Women	1	1	6	4	12
?	2	2	5	3	12
Men	3	6	3	2	14
Total	6	9	14	9	38

refer to male dancers and only two to female dancers. In the later Chola period, however, the situation is reversed: twice as many temple dancers are identified as women than as men.

We see a similar and even more dramatic reversal in comparing male and female dancers with respect to the contexts of their performances. In the first two subperiods, six inscriptions assign men to the function of dancing at festivals, and only one assigns women to this function; in the last two subperiods, just 1 inscription designates men as festival dancers, whereas seven designate women. In the later Chola period, then, women became increasingly visible as temple dancers, and although they did not entirely monopolize temple dance, women seem to have effectively displaced men from a role that had formerly been largely a male preserve—dancing at festivals.

The seven inscriptions that describe temple women as festival dancers represent a small fraction of the total number of inscriptions that refer to temple women and their activities and an even tinier fraction of all the Chola period inscriptions that refer to temple ritual in general and to arrangements for festivals in particular. In other words, dancing at festivals was a relatively unimportant aspect of temple women's lives, and having temple women dance was not at all necessary for the conduct of temple festivals. Nonetheless, the pattern of displacement that these inscriptions reveal, in however minor a way, may be significant for our understanding of changes in both the circumstances of temple women and the organization of temple life. As temple women in the later Chola period were taking over from men the responsibility for performing festival dances, they were moving into a specialization that was to become in later centuries central to their identity and their place in the structure of temple service.[9]

But the way—or one of the ways—in which Chola period temple women accomplished this move sets them apart from their counterparts of a later age and from their male counterparts in their own times. In at least two of the seven inscriptions from the later Chola period that describe women performing festival dances, these women purchased from the temple the right to perform this service, as well as the right to sing the Tamil devotional song *Tiruvempāvai* (ARE 160 and 161 of 1940–41). These temple women were not inheriting the right to perform dance but were, instead, acquiring it by making a deal with the temple.[10] Thus, along with the shift in the identity of festival dancers from male to female, there was also a shift from the employment of members of a professional community, who were not necessarily associated with a particular temple, to the employment of temple women who regarded dancing at festivals more as a privilege and mark of status than a duty for which they would be remunerated. The first of the two inscriptions translated at the beginning of this section, fixing the order in which the *patiyilār* and *tevaraṭiyar* were to perform dance in the course of daily worship, provides another indication of the concern for rank and ritual rights that seems to characterize temple women's involvement with dance in the later Chola period.

Temple women were not, of course, the only people who regarded temple service in this light, and the structuring of temple life around concepts of privilege and honor was to become more and more important for all types of tasks and positions in the post-Chola period. But during the Chola period itself, we find a kind of patchwork in which some of the roles associated with the functioning of the temple seem to have had an honorary character, some were more in the nature of 'jobs' of either a menial or professional nature, and others were a mixture of these two types or were transitional from one type to another—tending in most cases toward becoming increasingly honorary. The complexity of this pattern becomes even greater when we take into account not only the different kinds of tasks there were to perform in the context of the temple but also the variety of people who might perform them and the possibility of competition among them. In the case we are considering here, I have suggested that the role of dancer, and particularly festival dancer, was in the early Chola period filled largely by members—mostly but not exclusively male—of a professional, family-based occupational group, the *cāntikkūttar*. In the later Chola period, the *cāntikkūttar* lost ground to women who were temple-rather than family-based and who regarded this role as a privilege rather than a profession. This is not to say that these women lacked skill in dance, but they differed dramatically from the *cāntikkūttar* in that their primary identity was not that of dancer.

Yet another group is associated with temple dance: the *naṭṭuvar*, or 'dance masters.'[11] They are different from the *cāntikkūttar* because they were not displaced from their role in the temple by temple women, and they are different from the temple women because their role continued throughout the Chola period to be a professional and family-based right rather than a matter of personal privilege. *Naṭṭuvar* are mentioned in 13 Chola period inscriptions that I have located. In every case, the *naṭṭuvaṉ* is male and is described as receiving support from the temple for his services, and in two of the inscriptions, the *naṭṭuvaṉ*'s service rights are transferred to male relatives. The *naṭṭuvar are* not linked explicitly to temple women in the inscriptions,[12] but in several cases *naṭṭuvar* are associated with drummers (*uvaccar*) or other musicians. An eleventh-century inscription (SII 8.644) records that a *naṭṭuvar* was assigned an *uvacca-kāṇi*, 'drummer's service right,' and a thirteenth-century inscription (EC 10.Bp38a) describes a *naṭṭuvaṉ* as the head of a group of *uvaccar*. We have seen, earlier in this chapter, how important drummers were in the ritual life of the temple. References to *uvaccar*, as key ritual specialists, are particularly abundant in the early Chola period, but by the early twentieth century, members of this community—who became known as Ōcchar—had suffered a marked decline in social status and had a much more marginal ritual status as drummers and priests who served village goddesses (Thurston and Rangachari 1909, 5: 419–20; Pillay 1953, 248).[13]

The inscriptions of the later Chola period that show *naṭṭuvar* as supervisors of groups of *uvaccar* or as possessors of *uvaccar*'s service rights may provide a clue to how the *uvaccar* lost their ritual status. As the *naṭṭuvar* maintained and strengthened their position within the temple structure, they may, in the later Chola period, have begun to compete with the *uvaccar* and take over some of their functions. Eventually, the *uvaccar* were entirely displaced as ritual specialists within the great temples. Another function with which the *naṭṭuvar* might have increasingly been involved, and which is related to drumming, was that of dance teacher: the Chola period temple women who were not members of *cāntikkūttar* families perhaps received instruction from *naṭṭuvar*—just as, in recent South Indian history, *devadāsīs* have been taught by *naṭṭuvaṉār*.[14]

When we consider the roles of temple women and other temple servants as singers in Chola period temples, we see a pattern of competition and displacement similar to that for dance but with the opposite result: whereas temple women appear to have been increasingly implicated in dance, particularly festival dance, they were progressively excluded from the role of hymn singer.

Just as temple women were rarely referred to as dancers, so, too, were terms that mean "singer" scarcely ever applied to them. Temple women were very different from male temple servants in this regard. In the Chola period inscrip-tions, two types of terms are used for 'singers': general terms, including those based on the Tamil verb *pāṭu* 'to sing,' and those derived from the Sanskrit *gandharva* (the term forthe celestial musicians who are, in myth, the companions of the *apsarās*); and technical terms, like *viṇṇappaṉ ceyvār*, those who "sing sacred hymns in the presence of the deity" (MTL, 3664). The general terms may be found in combination with expressions that provide somewhat more ritual specificity, with respect to the kind of song to be performed; for example, *tiruppatiyam pāṭuvar* are "those who sing (Tamil) hymns." In many cases, the plural form of these terms and the anonymity of the singers obscure their sex, but when we can ascertain whether those identified as singers are female or male, they are almost invariably the latter.

The technical terms are never applied to women,[15] and there are only two inscriptions in which women are referred to as singers, using the general terms. One of these, a tenth-century inscription from Travancore, in southern Kerala, records an agreement between the Chera king and the authorities of a Śiva temple about the payments to be made for various temple services and temple servants, including the *naṅkaimār kāntarpikaḷ*, the "lady singers" (TAS 8,43). The term used here for "singer," *kāntarpikaḷ*, has its male equivalent in the terms *gāndharvar* or *kāntarppar*, which are found elsewhere in Tamil inscriptions of the Chola period (e.g., SII 23.264 and SII 4.867). The second inscription comes from Kanchipuram in Chingleput district and records the gift of villages by a Telugu Choda chief to support the "women who sing (*pāṭum peṇṭukaḷ*) before the Lord"—who is in this case a form of Viṣṇu, Śrī Varadarājasvāmi (SITI 393). In contrast to this single inscription that applies terms derived from *pāṭu* to women,[16] I have found eight inscriptions in which they are applied to men. The term *pāṭuvar*, "singer," is used to refer to men in five inscriptions, but there are no cases in which it definitely refers to women.

Not only is there a preponderance of men among those who are identified as singers in Chola period inscriptions, but also the task of singing in the temple is assigned much more frequently to men than to women. The predominance of men as hymn singers has made me decide to handle the inscriptions in which the sex of the singers is unclear in a different way than I have for dancers: I have included in the category of temple women only those singers who are definitely female. Table 23.3 indicates the numbers of inscriptions that refer to singers in the temple, as women, as men, or as people whose sex cannot be ascertained. Men are more numerous as temple singers in all subperiods except the third, when an equal number of inscriptions describe women as filling this function. All six of the inscriptions in this subperiod that describe women as temple singers are from a single temple in Nallur,

Table 23.3 Temple Singers in Chola Period Inscriptions

	Chola 1	Chola 2	Chola 3	Chola 4	Total
Women	2	2	6	2	12
?	14	15	5	8	42
Men	4	13	6	5	28
Total	20	30	17	15	82

in South Arcot district, and they are all records of deals made by individual *tevaraṭiyār:* each of these women, having made a gift of gold to the temple, received the right to sing a particular portion of the hymn *Tiruvempāvai* and, in several cases—as we have already seen in the discussion of temple women's involvement in festival dance—to perform certain dances or to be otherwise involved in the conduct of festivals (ARE 143, 144, 149, 160, 161, and 176 of 1940–41).

Tiruvempāvai, a composition of the Śaiva poet-saint Māṇikkavācakar, is referred to not only in this set of inscriptions but also in an eleventh-century record from Tiruvorriyur in Chingleput district, in which 16*tevaraṭiyār* are given the responsibility for its performance (ARE 128 of 1912). It is striking that this is the only specific hymn mentioned by name as part of the temple liturgy to be performed by female singers. It may be that this particular devotional work, which is cast in the feminine voice, was regarded as being particularly appropriate for women to sing—as it continues to be in contemporary Tamilnadu (Orr and Young 1986; Young 1993). But other compositions—for example, *Tiruvāymoḻi*, part of the Vaiṣṇava canon of devotional hymns in Tamil—seem to have been considered as suitable only for male performers.[17]

Chola period inscriptions indicate that until the thirteenth century, many different types of people filled the role of hymn singer: in the early period, this task was assigned, on the one hand, to a woman who was a slave (ARE 149 of 1936–37), and, on the other hand, to high-status men, such as Brahmans (including those bearing the title *paṭṭar,* from Skt. *bhaṭṭar)* and *aṭikaḷmār* (ascetics or "honored devotees"). In the third subperiod, there continue to be hymn singers of various types and status: apart from the temple women who negotiated for the privilege of singing *Tiruvempāvai*, there are references to men who were *uvaccar* or *pāṇar* and who served as singers in this period. One of the inscriptions translated at the beginning of this section (SII 5.705) shows how members of this latter community were associated with hymn singing at a temple in Tiruvidaimarudur, in Tanjavur district, in the twelfth century.

The *pāṇar* are known to us from early Cankam literature as itinerant bards who sang and played the stringed *yāḻ,* but there are very few references to this group in Chola period inscriptions—not enough to shed light on the way in which, in Chola and post-Chola times, their social situation changed dramatically as they shifted in occupation from being musicians to being tailors and came to be considered of low caste (Kailasapathy 1968; Young and Orr 1985 and 1988). In the previous translation; a *pāṇaṉ* (or a man who is taking up the temple service rights of the *pāṇar*) is an active participant in temple life: he is to receive support from the temple, to sing for the temple deity, to oversee the singing of the *tevaraṭiyar* in the temple, and to be responsible for the group of *pāṇar* associated with the temple. But a century later, there are indications that the status of the *pāṇar* had declined[18] and that their eligibility to serve as singers in the temple was being more strictly defined.

In the thirteenth century, hymn singing was increasingly dominated by people of high status—Brahmans and others—and by members of new professional or temple service categories. Already in the eleventh century, in the middle of the Chola period, we begin to encounter the term *viṇṇappañ ceyvār*, which was to become one of the technical terms for hymn singer in the Śrīvaiṣṇ tradition (Jagadeesan 1967), and in the thirteenth century we find the earliest inscriptional references to *otuvār*, the hymn singers in the later South

Indian Śaiva tradition (ARE 203 of 1908; SII 23.92; TAS 6.14; Peterson 1989, 56–75). It appears that a relatively open and fluid notion of who might sing hymns in the temple had given way by the end of the Chola period to more restrictive ideas about the ritual qualifications and rights associated with this role. This development may have been tied to the canonization of the two bodies of devotional poems—composed by the Vaiṣṇava and Śaiva poet-saints—and their adaptation and entrenchment in temple liturgy, which took place during the Chola period.[19] Ritual chanting and singing were part of the traditional expertise of Brahmans, and as the Tamil hymns came to be acknowledged as equal in importance to the sacred Vedic texts, the definition of who was eligible to be a hymn singer may have been subject to increasing regulation and definition. In this atmosphere of competition and professionalization, temple women—as well, perhaps, as members of traditional performing communities, like the *pāṇar*—seem to have had little opportunity to further their activities and identities as singers in the temple.

It is clear that the temple women of medieval Tamilnadu were not primarily or originally dancers and singers. They did, nonetheless, occasionally perform songs and dances in the temple—in several cases actually paying for the privilege of doing so—and participated in the processes that were ongoing throughout the Chola period in which different kinds of individuals and groups laid claim to the task or the honor of performing for the deity. The rights to these temple service roles were not, even by the end of the Chola period, exclusively or permanently assigned to particular types of temple personnel, but certain patterns that would persist into later times were beginning to be established. Several groups that had been prominent as singers, musicians, or dancers in the pre-Chola or early Chola period—the *pāṇar*, the *uvaccar*, and the *cāntikkūttar*—had decreasing access to the ritual roles they once played in the life of the temple. The eclipse of these figures is not, however, attributable to a single cause; if, for the *pāṇar*, it was a case of displacement by Brahmans and new categories of professional temple servants, the *cāntikkūttar* may have had temple women to blame for their marginalization.

The increasing involvement of temple women with festival dance may have been possible because this was a service that was not ritually neces-sary but occasional and optional. We may contrast the role of festival dancing with hymn singing, which was becoming increasingly part of the formal liturgical structure of daily worship; dancing at festivals was an activity in which individual initiative, rather than membership in a particular community or professional group, might have provided the opportunity for participation. If temple women began to take advantage of this opportunity in the late Chola period, they did so only in small numbers. Their dancing at temple festivals was not central either to the definition of what they were or to what constituted a proper temple festival. It is only in retrospect that we can see that temple women's engagement with festival dance in this period was of great significance for their future roles as temple servants.

Temple Women as God's Attendants

In the fifteenth year of the reign of Śrī Uttamacoḻadevar Ko Parakesarivarmaṉ, [an image of] Śrībalidevar, eight trumpets, and fly whisk handles for the 24 fly whisk women (*kavarippiṇākaḷ*) were made out of gold and given to Mahādevar (the Great God) of Tiruvoṟṟiyūr, as graciously commanded by Uttamacoḻa and arranged by Ceṉṉiy Eṟipaṭaiccoḻaṉ Uttamacoḻaṉ. . . . [The rest of the inscription is broken off.]—SII 3.143: this inscription was engraved in A.D. 985 on a slab that is now built into the floor of the verandah around the central shrine of the Ādhipurīśvara temple in Tiruvorriyur, Chingleput district.

On the 116th day in the thirteeth year of the reign of Tribhuvuṉaviradevar, the emperor of the three worlds who seized Maturai, Īḻam, Caruvūr, and the crowned head of the Pandya king, and who performed the consecration (*abhiṣekam*) of victory and the consecration of the hero, the *tāṉattār* (temple trustees) and the *ūrār* (village assembly) met to determine the order of hymn singing (*tirup pāṭṭaṭaivu*), carrying the sacred lamps (*tiruvālatti*), and the order of personal attendance (*meykkāṭṭaṭaivu*) [on the deity] of the temple women (*teva aṭiyār*) of the temple of Lord Cuntaracoḻīśvaramuṭaiyār in Kūḻaikuḷattūr; this determination of rank (*muṟai*) before [Śiva's] sacred trident was conveyed to Vllavatāy.

[In] the first family (*kuṭi*).... rank are Māṇikkam and Tiruvampalam pirīyāti alias Catturukāla-māṇikkam.

[In] the second rank (*muṟai*) are Ammaiyāḻvi alias Aṟputakkūtta-māṇik kam and Nācciyāḻvi alias Villavatāy-māṇikkam.

[In] the third rank are Cuntara.... ṉuktavaḷate.... māṇikkam and her daughter Kaṇavati alias Kulottunkacoḻa-māṇikkam and Pollātapiḷḷai alias Tiruñāṉacampanta-māṇikkam and Ciṟuval. . . . yāṟkoyil-māṇikkam.

[In] the fourth rank are Valli alias Irājakempira-māṇikkam and Pollātapiḷḷai alias Coḻakoṉ-māṇikkam.

[In| the fifth rank are Āṭko. . . . ra-māṇikkam and Ciṟupa. . . . alias. . . . Tiruciṟṟampala-māṇikkam.

[In] the sixth rank are Ammaiyāḻvi alias Tiruveṇṇāval-māṇikkam and.... Tirukaḷiṟṟupaṭi-māṇikkam.

[In] the seventh rank are Poṟṟu . . . . liviṭṭa . . . . ṟṟucoḻa-māṇzikkam and Kūttāṭinācci alias Tirunaṭampuṟinta-māṇikkam.

For the sacred lamps on festival days (*tirunāḷ*)..... and for carrying.... on festival days, today. . . . [The rest of the inscription is defaced.]—IPS 162: this inscription was engraved in A.D. 1207 on the south side of the wall of the ruined Śiva temple in Kulattur, Tiruchirappalli district (Pudukkottai State).

Seventeen Chola period inscriptions refer to temple women as attendants in temple rituals. There are four types of attendance functions that temple women performed: bearing flywhisks (mentioned in eight inscriptions), being present at festivals (in four inscriptions), bearing lamps (in three inscriptions), and acting as a personal attendant on the deity (in two inscriptions). These tasks are similar to singing and dancing in their connotations of special privilege, entailing as they do participation in ritual and proximity to the temple deity, but they are rather different from singing and dancing in that they are entirely unskilled functions.

The most frequently mentioned type of attendance is bearing a flywhisk—the yaktail fan or "chowrie" (Ta. *kavari* or *cāmarai*, from Skt. *cāmarā*). To be fanned with the flywhisk is a mark of distinction particularly associated with kings and deities, who have frequently been depicted in the literature and art of North India, since the early centuries B.C., as flanked by beautiful, female flywhisk bearers (Tewari 1987, 52–70). The association of the flywhisk with both religious and royal contexts is attested to in South India at least since the ninth century A.D.[20] The inscriptional evidence of the Chola period indicates that temple flywhisk bearers were most often women but not exclusively so; at the Srirangam temple, for example, a man was appointed, in the late eleventh century, to do flywhisk service (SII 24.66).[21]

Of the eight inscriptions that refer to temple women as performing this service, three are from the early Chola period, and all three—including the first, the previous translation—use the term *kavarippina*, "flywhisk woman," for the temple women involved.[22] Even though a specific term is applied to these women, it does not appear to) entail any particular ritual qualifications or status. In one case, slave women, who have been donated to the temple by a local notable, perform this attendance function: "I have given, with pouring of water, my slave (*aṭiyāḷ*) Uraṉ Colai, her daughter Veḷāṉ Pirāṭṭi, and her daughter Aṟamaiyiṇtaṉ Kaṇṭi to sing hymns (*tiruppatiyam*) and [act as] *kavarippiṇāvarkaḷ* for the Supreme Lord of the temple . . ." (ARE 149 of 1936–37). This tenth-century record clearly spells out their status as chattel but also indicates the privileged character of the role these women are to fulfill by using an honorific double plural for the term "fly whisk women." The honor of attending the deity as a fly whisk bearer is also evident in the five inscriptions of the later Chola period that refer to temple women in this role. They are all thirteenth-century inscriptions from temples in Chingleput district that describe individual temple women as making deals—offering substantial donations to the temple in exchange for the privilege of being a flywhisk bearer (ARE 172, 180, 183, 210, and 211 of 1923).

The fact that these deals were made by temple women suggests that the task itself was not so much a critical ritual function as an incidental adjunct to temple ceremony, whose significance lay primarily in the fact that considerable honor was attached to this role. At the same time, inasmuch as it was a service of attendance borrowed from or shared with the royal context, flywhisk hearing did not need to be performed by a specially qualified or ritually pure person. This activity was an ornamental one, just as in a royal court, where it would be performed by female servants or palace women; the function in the temple was thus perhaps ideally carried out by women, and their identity or status—whether they were slaves or wealthy patrons—was not an issue.[23]

Four Chola period inscriptions refer to temple women's involvement in temple festivals, without specifying any particular function such as singing and dancing. In three of these inscriptions, this involvement means taking part in festival processions, and all three describe the temple woman's right to participate as the consequence of her donation to the temple—once again, a deal. It is clear that what was involved in these deals was the acquisition of a position of honor, of precedence and proximity to the deity in the procession. The fourth inscription mentions in rather vague terms the responsibility of temple women to be present at temple festivals. Chola period temple women seem not to have been extensively involved in festival rituals.[24] When they were involved, their participation had the same character as that of the temple women who bore flywhisks—that is, it was less a matter of performing a ritual function than of (literally) parading the status that had been accorded to them by the temple.

Three of the Chola period inscriptions that refer to temple women as attendants describe them as bearing lamps. In two cases, both from the far south, the task of carrying lamps (*vilakku*) was assigned to temple women (*tevaraṭiyār* or *tevaṭiccis*) along with menial tasks—weaving garlands or pounding paddy (SII 14.132; TAS 5.24—translations of both follow). In these cases, it is not at all obvious that bearing lamps was actually a ritual duty that involved proximity to the deity; it is possible, for example, that the lamps in question were simply for illumination. But a more formal ritual function for temple women is evident in the third inscription, which is translated at the beginning of this section. In this record, seven *tevaraṭiyār* are each assigned a turn (*muṟai*) to sing, wave the lamp (*ālatti*) before the god, and attend on him (IPS 162). The term *ālatti* that is used for "lamp" in this inscription is derived from the Sanskrit word *ārati*, and we find in this inscription the technical usage *tiruvālattiyeṭu*, "to wave light, etc., before an idol or important personage" (MTL, 246). The careful specification of the order of precedence for the temple women to perform this service indicates the honor associated with this role. But waving and bearing lamps was not a task assigned exclusively to female temple servants, and we find—at least in inscriptions of the early Chola period—men who performed this function, including Brahman men charged with waving the *ālatti* lamp (e.g., SII 3.149). Bearing or waving lamps does not seem to have been a very important role for temple women in the Chola period—in contrast to its apparent significance for South Indian temple women in more recent times[25]—nor does it seem to have been a function that was of particular importance in Chola period temple rituals.

Two thirteenth-century inscriptions refer to temple women who were personal attendants for the image of the deity. One of them has just been discussed, in which the duties assigned in rotation to the temple women of Kulattur included attendance on the god (*meykkāṭṭu*), in addition to waving the *ālatti* lamp before him and singing hymns (IPS 162). The other inscription is another thirteenth-century record, from Tirunelveli district in the far south of Tamilnadu, which assigns a series of roles to various temple women, including cleaning and decorating temple floors, as well as a task that I classify as personal attendance—applying *kāppu* (substances such as sandal paste for ritual protection or adornment) to the images of the deities in the temple (ARE 374 of 1972–73). In both of these inscriptions, in which the names of the temple women are given and their duties and ranks carefully specified, it is clear that personal attendance on the deities was a coveted honor.

This service, like the other attendance functions with which temple women were involved, could be, from the point of view of the person who performed it, a special privilege and, at the same time, from the point of view of the deity or the coordinator or sponsor of temple worship, an optional service, which could be done by a variety of people—or not done at all. Attendance functions do not loom large in the central patterns of ritual life of the medieval South Indian temple or in the range of roles with which temple women were engaged None of these attendance functions—bearing flywhisks, participating in festivals, bearing or waving lamps or personally attending the temple deity—was performed exclusively by women. Yet something may be said to be peculiarly feminine about these tasks: close to half of the 17 inscriptions that refer to temple women's involvement with these duties describe the acquisition of the right to perform these services as the result of a deal. Men may, on occasion, have been involved in the same tasks, but men never arrived at this involvement through these means. The fact that temple women made deals in order to serve in these roles—and that, in other cases, the exact nature of their right to perform these functions was carefully spelled out in the inscription—indicates that what was at stake was not the temple's effort to find someone to fill a job but rather the temple woman's effort to acquire recognition and status in the temple. The indications of the honorary character of these functions are particularly in evidence in the later Chola period; this was also the period of increasing involvement by temple women in these roles—13 of the 17 inscriptions date from the later Chola period.

It is also possible that the temple considered such roles suitable for women. It may be, for example, that the character of these attendance ser-vices as marginal or incidental to the basic temple ritual was significant in this regard; women could be allowed to participate in temple ceremony in a capacity that would not aggravate competition for more ritually central roles. Or it may be that women's engagement in these attendance functions was seen as bringing a special quality to the atmosphere of the temple that resonated either with the ornamental character of women's roles in the palace or the auspicious character of women's roles in the home.

Bearing fly whisks—the attendance function of temple women mentioned most frequently—was a "traditionally" feminine occupation that was connected particularly with the royal context. Having women adorn one's court, as part of one's entourage, as personal attendants, or in processions, was a feature of the display and ceremonial associated with the king.[26] Although parallels and mutual borrowings between the temple and the royal palace appear to be more characteristic of the post-Chola period than of the period under study here, it may be that the increasing involvement of temple women with ornamental attendance functions in the later Chola period reflected an early stage in the transfer of aspects of the royal idiom to the temple.[27] It is also possible that some of the attendance functions performed by women in the temple—such as bearing lamps or decorating shrines and images—reflected tasks characteristically performed by women as part of domestic or votive religious observances.[28] Because of these domestic associations, such tasks may have been regarded as auspicious, and because they were performed by women in the home, they may have been considered particularly appropriate activities for temple women.

Preparing Garlands for the Lord

In the fourth year of the reign of Ko Caṭayapaṉmar alias śrī Cuntaraco- ḻapāṇṭiyadevar, we the *mahāsabhaiyār* (Brahman assembly) of the *brah-madeyam* Srī Rājarājaccaturvvetimarikalam in Muḷḷināṭu, Muṭikoṇta- coḻavaḷanāṭu, Irācarācappāṇṭināṭu, met together in the hall (*ampalam*) to make a binding agreement.

We grant land for gardens and houses for the *uvaccakaḷ* (drummers) who are garden laborers (*nanāṉvdnak kuṭikaḷ*), for the potters (*kucavakaḷ*), for the temple women (*tevaraṭiyār pṇṭtukaḷ*) who carry sacred lamps (*tiruviḷakku*) and weave garlands (*tirupaḷḷittāmam*), for laborer-herdsmen (*veṭṭikkuṭikaḷ iṭaiyar*) who supply ghee for the lamps, and for other expenses of whatever kind for Lord (*āḻvar*) Śrī Rājendracoḷa-vinnakar. [The inscription goes on to describe the boundaries of the land granted; the end of the inscription is missing.]—SII 14.132: this inscription was engraved in A.D. 1025 on the north wall of the Gopālasvāmi temple in Mannarkoyil, Tirunelveli district.

The tasks associated with providing flowers for the temple—gardening and weaving garlands—present a kind of mirror image to attendance functions. Attendance functions were inessential and optional but brought high honor to their performers, whereas providing flowers was absolutely necessary for the conduct of temple ritual but was considered to be menial labor. Although this task, essential to worship from the earliest *bhakti* times, was viewed as a lowly one, in the "lowlier than thou" ethos of devotion that developed in the *bhakti* period, it was a task that the highest-born devotees felt honored to perform.[29] Something of this same spirit may have been carried forward or revived in the Chola period.

In Chola period inscriptions, most of the work of gardening, picking flowers, and making garlands seems to have been done by men. In only five inscriptions do women perform these functions, and in all of them women are responsible only for picking flowers and making garlands rather than tending the temple gardens. The previous translation illustrates this division of labor: men (in this case, interestingly, *uvaccar*, "drummer") are charged with taking care of the gardens and women (*tevaraṭiyār*) with making the garlands. This inscription is also typical of the handful of records that refer to women in this capacity in that it dates from the second subperiod, when three of the five inscriptions were engraved. In this early Chola period, the other people, apart from temple women, who were assigned to the task of gardening or garland making are, when they are identifiable, invariably men of relatively low status. They are not mentioned by name and are anonymous members of groups; often they are referred to, as in the case of the previous inscription, as *kuṭikaḷ*, "laborers."

In the later Chola period, however, the positions of gardener and garland maker were increasingly assigned to high-status people, including *tavaciyar* ("ascetics") and various categories of "honored devotees," such as *āṇṭār*, *nampis*, and *śrīvaiṣṇavas*.[30] In a number of the later Chola period inscriptions, including a thirteenth-century record that assigns a temple woman the task of weaving garlands (ARE 374 of 1973), those who acquired the responsibility for gardening or garland making are named. The designation of a particular individual usually indicates that some value or prestige was attached to the right to fulfill that role. Although they were essentially unskilled and menial forms of work, gardening and picking and plaiting flowers were forms of service that in the course of the Chola period increasingly involved high-status people interested in securing—in their own names—the right to perform these tasks. It is likely, then, that there was increasing competition for and more and more restricted access to these service roles. This increasing competition and restriction may account for the decline in the engagement of temple women with these tasks, although women had, in any case, never been more than marginally involved with these functions.

Menial Servants and Slaves

According to an earlier royal order, in the nineteenth year of the reign of Tribhuvaṉacakkaravattikaḷ Śrī Rājarājatevar, in the fifth month, on the third *tithi* of the bright fortnight, in the 26th *nakṣatra*, I, Vayalūr-kiḻavaṉ Tiruve-kampamuṭaiyaṉ Centāmaraik Kaṇṇaṉ alias Vayirātarāyaṉ of Virukaṉpakkam alias Ceṉṉinallūr in Poṟūrnāṭu in Puliyūrkkoṭṭam alias Kulottuṅkacoḻavaḷanāṭu, in Jayaṅkoṇṭacoḻamaṇṭalam, gave to [the deity] Lord Tiruvoṟṟiyūr-uṭaiya nāyaṉār five persons—Periyanācci, her daughter Māri, her younger sister Kavuttāḻvi, her younger sister Tiruvāṇṭi, and her younger sister Vaṭukāḻvi—to husk paddy for the feeding hall (*cālai*).

They are to husk paddy for the feeding hall of the god and those who are their descendents (*vaḻi*) are to continue this paddy husking for as long as the sun and moon shall shine.

I, Vayalūr-kiḻavaṉ Tiruvekampamuṭaiyaṉ Centāmaraik Kaṇṇaṉ alias Vayi-rātarāyaṉ, have had this inscribed in stone.—SII 4.558: this inscription was engraved in A.D. 1235 on the north wall of the second prakara of the Ādhipurīśvara temple in Tiruvorriyur, Chingleput district.

Paḻuvūr Nakkaṉ, having given the village of Nctuvāyil and the hamlets surrounding Neṭuvāyil to this deity, and taking responsibility for paying all taxes due from this holy temple and the village, now does obeisance and makes a further undertaking that paddy be measured out in the temple courtyard (*tirumuṟṟam*).... to the amount of 1,000 *kalam*, and that 100 *kaḻañcu* of fine quality gold be weighed out. . . . providing for the expenses of cloth, oil, taxes. ... the expenses [for feeding] 30 *śivayogi* Brahmans and 20 Brahmans—altogether 50 people.

[The inscription goes on to give an account of the amount to be fed to each person per day—of rice, ghee, *kaṟi* (curry), *puḷiṅkaṟi* (tamarind or sour curry), salt, betel, and arecanut—and how much paddy is required for each of these expenses, resulting in a total of 1,605 *kalam*, 2 *tūṇi*, 3 *kuṟuṇi*, and 2 *nāḻi* of paddy annually.]

For one man to bring firewood (*viṟakiṭuvāṉ*), I *kuṟuṇi* of paddy daily, and for one cook (*aṭnvan*), I *kuṟuṇi* of paddy daily—amounting, for the two men, to 60 *kalam* annually—and for each man an allowance for cloth of 1 *kācu* (money) and 10 *kalam* paddy—totaling 2 *kācu* and 20 *kalam* paddy.

For oil at the time of the solstices and of Saturn for the 30 *śivayogi* Brahmans and the 20 Brahmans—altogether 50 people... [a total of 54 *kalam* of paddy is required annually].

[The inscription continues with a detailed account of the amount of paddy required to meet the expenses of providing dal (*payaṟu*), black pepper, and asafoetida on a daily basis—totaling 155 *kalam* and, in money, 15 *kācu,* excluding the money required for "garden duty.")

For one woman to gather and smear and apply powder in the feeding hall (*cālai*), 2 *nāḻi* of paddy daily is required—amounting to 7 *kalam*, 1 *tūṇi*, and 1 *patakku* annually.

For one woman to remove the leavings and [clean] the eating place with earth and put ashes in the pot, 4 *nāḻi* of paddy daily is required, plus an allowance for cloth—amounting to 10 *kalam* annually.

For two hymn singers (*tiruppatiyam viṇṇappañ ceyvār*), 1 *patakku* and 4 *nāḻi* of paddy daily is required—amounting to 75 *kalam* annually. and going, the placement and eviction, of those wishing to eat in the feeding hall, 1 *kuṟuṇi* and 2 *nāḻi* of paddy daily is required, plus an allowance for cloth—amounting to 37 *kalam*, 1 *tūṇi,* and 1 *patakku* annually.

For a potter (*kucavaṉ*) who makes pots for the feeding hall, 2 *nāḻi* of paddy daily is required—amounting to 7 *kalam*, 1 *tūṇi*, and 1 *patakku* annually.

For a proclaimer (*cotivi colluvaṉ*) for 27 days of proclamation from the gopuram, 1 *kuṟuṇi* of paddy daily is required—amounting to 30 *kalam* annually.

For one Brahman man who performs recitation (*adhyayyaṇam*) while the Brahmans are dining (*uttamāgrattil uṇṇum*), 1 *kuṟuṇi* of paddy daily is required—amounting to 30 *kalam* annually, plus 5 *kalam*, or 31/2 *kācu* cloth money.

For sandal [paste] for the *śivayogi* Brahmans and the Brahmans who are dining, 1/2 *kācu* or 5 *kalam* of paddy is required.

[The inscription next provides details of the daily and annual expenses for offerings at the nighttime *śrībali* ritual—including rice, sugar, fruit, and tamarind.]

I, Irājarājapallavaraiyaṉ [= Paḻuvūr Nakkaṉ] made this gift as a tax-free "inner sanctum endowment" (*tiruvuṇṇāḻikaippuṟam*), in the 7th year of the reign of SrāIrājarajatevar, to this [god] Śrī Vijayamaṅkalatevar, the Great Lord of this *brahmadeyam*, whose temple I constructed in stone, and a record of these arrangements has been here engraved in stone.

[There follows a detailed account of the requirements for thrice daily offerings (to the deity), including rice, ghee, *poṟikkaṟi* (fried curry), areca nut, betel, and curds. Provisions are also made for five perpetual lamps and . . .]

For a cook, 2 *nāḻi* and 1 *aḻakku* of paddy daily, and for the writer of accounts, 4 *nāḻi* of paddy daily; for 2 lamps for the nighttime *śrībali*, [a certain amount of oil required daily—the total annual expense is 365 *kalam*, 7 *kuṟuṇi*, and 4 *nāḻi*]

Between religious acts and evil deeds there is no comparison. May this grant be protected by the *paṉmāheśvarur.*—SII 19.357 (lines 41–83): this inscription was engraved in A.D. 992 on the north and west walls of the central shrine of Guṅgājaṭādhura temple in Govindaputtur, Tiruchirappalli district. It is written in continuation of an inscription, dated eight years earlier, that records the gift by the same donor of the village mentioned at the beginning of this record. 18 Chola period inscriptions record the assignment of temple women to menial functions associated with cleaning and food preparation. In half, the women can he identified as slaves, having been sold or—as in the first of the two preceding inscriptions—given to the temple. Such cases are an exception to the rule that the specification of a temple servant's name is a mark of the honor attached to the service: slave women's names are recorded in inscriptions for the same reason that the boundaries of land sold or granted to the temple are indicated in detan—to pioviuw, a—property possessed by the temple.

In only one of the 18 inscriptions referring to temple women's involvement in menial tasks is there the slightest hint that the task is regarded as a privilege. In the thirteenth-century inscription already discussed (ARE 374 of 1972–73), 10 temple women were assigned to various duties, including applying *kāppu* (protective substances or adornments) to the deities—a task that I classified as an attendance function—as well as making decorations (*kolams*) in the great hall (*mahāmandapa*) of the temple and cleaning and applying *kāppu* in the first and second *prākāras* (surrounding courtyards). This is the only Chola period inscription that specifies that women performed the service of cleaning temple floors, although other people—men or anonymous groups—were often assigned to this task, and as we shall see, women were frequently charged with cleaning the floors of eating halls. Both Tamil and Sanskrit *bhakti* literature exhorts devotees to serve the Lord by cleaning the floors of his shrine,[31] but this is the only inscription that suggests through its careful assignment of duties to specific women—that cleaning the floors of the temple was considered an honored task in the Chola period. It is also the only inscription that indicates that making auspicious designs (*kōlams*) had a place in the Chola period temple or that this was a distinctively feminine task, as it is in contemporary South India.

For most of the temple women whose duties found them squatting or kneeling on floors, their work was more in the nature of drudgery than auspicious ritual activity. The preceding translation above outlines the specific duties that were required of two women employed by the temple to serve in a feeding hall: one was to smear the floor (probably with cow dung, as a means of purification) to prepare it before a group of Brahmans and *śivayogis* ate, and the other woman was to clear away the leavings and clean up afterward. Altogether 11 Chola period inscriptions refer to temple women acting as servants in feeding houses—*Cālais* or *maṭhas*—and although the women's precise tasks are rarely described, it is likely that they were similar to those in the preceding inscription, and that these tasks were normally assigned to women; men who worked in *Cālais* or *maṭ has* were typically artisans (especially potters), cooks, or watchmen. In seven of the 11 inscriptions, the women are said to he slaves, which was rarely the case for their male counterparts. It is clear that the type of service performed by temple women in feeding houses was of extremely low status.

In six inscriptions, temple women are involved in the preparation of food that was offered to human or divine recipients. One, an eleventh-century inscription from Chidambaram, specifies that a married woman (*vāḻvacci*) was to bring the water vessel as part of the arrangements made to feed Brahmans (SII 4.223; this inscription is translated at the beginning of the fol-lowing section). In five inscriptions, all from the later Chola period, temple women had the duty of pounding or husking paddy or dal; two of these. including me first record translated at the beginning of this section, identify the women involved with this work as slaves.

Food preparation tasks of this type were not carried out exclusively by women. But two related types of preparatory functions in the temple were monopolized by men. Both tasks seem to have had more honor attached to them than the work performed by women. The first is the preparation of offerings other than food. For example, while there is one inscription in which a woman fetches water to be used in cooking for Brahmans, numerous inscriptions describe Brahmans with the task of bringing water to bathe the image of the deity. And if temple women pounded paddy to prepare rice for cooking, when the substance pounded was sandalwood or turmeric, used to adorn the image of the deity, the people employed were invariably men—and, again, frequently Brahmans.[32]

The second kind of preparatory function from which women were excluded was the role of cook. The terms used to designate the person who cooked food for the deities or for human recipients in Chola period inscriptions—*aṭuvāṉ*, as in the preceding translation, which describes the arrangements for feeding *śivayogis* and Brahmans, or *maṭaiyaṉ,* as in the following inscription—are clearly masculine forms. It is surprising that the inscriptions contain so little information about the identities of temple cooks; most inscriptions that mention cooks do so in the same breath as potters or the men who were to fetch firewood, without indicating that their ritual status qualified them to prepare food of the requisite purity for gods and Brahmans (Orr 1994b). But the inscriptions do indicate clearly enough that temple cooks were men. Temple cooks and the men involved in the preparation of nonfood offerings may have been engaged in menial tasks, but the ritual location of these tasks was a good deal closer to the divine presence at the center of the temple than were the activities of the temple women. The rice husked by a slave woman in the temple courtyard had a long way to travel before it was transformed into food for the gods.

There are not very many references in Chola period inscriptions to the buying and selling of human beings or to the transfer of people as chattel, and such references are virtually nonexistent in the early Chola period. But almost all references to slavery involve women.

I have located 21 inscriptions that refer to slavery, and in only one (ARE 280 of 1927–28) are the slaves—"drummer slaves" (*uvacca aṭimai*)—exclusively male. All of the other 21 inscriptions refer to slave women attached to the temple. Slave men are almost invariably identified as the children of slave women....

It is not surprising that virtually all the slaves mentioned in Chola period inscriptions were owned by the temple, given that the inscriptional sources are predominantly focused on temple affairs. Some slaves had a brand or mark (*ilaiccinai*—from Skt. *lakṣanā*) on their bodies, which indicated their status.[33] As we have seen, the work of slaves that is mentioned most frequently is service in a feeding house attached fo a temple; there are also two inscriptions in which female slaves husked paddy for the temple, and one inscription, which we have encountered several times earlier in this chapter, in which the tasks of slave women were to sing hymns and bear fly whisks. It is likely that in the later Chola period, female slaves were owned not only by the temple but also by certain wealthy members of society, and these women performed domestic functions similar to those they carried out in the temple. This may have occured particularly in the core Chola region, where we have the most evidence for temple slaves and where the Chola court may have set a certain royal style for domestic arrangements, and perhaps for temple arrangements as well.[34]

Temple women's involvement with the menial work of cleaning and food preparation is mentioned with increasing frequency in the course of the Chola period: in the first subperiod, just a single inscription refers to these tasks, but by the last subperiod there are 10 such inscriptions. Most of these identify the women as slaves. The rise in this type of female temple service represents the dark underside of the increasing visibility of temple women and their increasingly well-defined status and specialized roles. If, on the one hand, some temple women in the later Chola period were mobilizing their energies and resources to secure special relationships with the temple and to acquire positions of honor, on the other hand, there were those whose connections with the temple were not of their own making and whose work underscored their debased status. Yet in some ways the woman who had the privilege of standing or dancing beside the processional image of the deity and the woman who swept and smeared the floor of the feeding hall may have been regarded in the same light: both might have been referred to as *tevaraṭiyār* and both might have been seen as considered to be carrying out typically feminine functions.

The Overlapping and Obscure Outlines of Female Temple Service

In the twenty-fourth year [of the reign of] Ko Virāca Kecaripaṉmār alias Lord Śrī Rāḻentiracoḻatevar, through the agreement here drawn up, [to last] as long as the moon and sun shall endure, Nakkaṉ Paravai, the "intimate" (*aṇukki*) of Lord Rājentiracojatevar, [gave] that part [specified herein] of Parākramacoḷanallūr, in Kiṭāraṅkoṇṭacoḻap-periḷamaināṭu, an eastern suburb of the *taṇiyūr* Perumpaṟṟappuliyūr of Rājentiraciṅkavaḷanāṭu, for the expenses on the festival day in [the month of] Āṇi when the Lord—who is the master of Tiruccirrampalam—graciously goes forth [in procession], for rice offerings for the Lord, for the distribution of a 1000 pots of rice for the *śrīmāheśvaras* at the time when the rice offering is graciously [accepted by the Lord], for the oil necessary lor the festival, for the gold which is graciously distributed [by] the Lord, and for the expenses including [provision of] the sacred cloth (*paricaṭṭam*)—totaling 20 *kācu.* A true copy of the deed of sale [of this land] was taken from the people of the town (*nagaram*) who reside in the place called Kuṇa meṅ kaipuram [and this deed of sale is recorded here].

[The following lines describe the boundaries of the land bought and donated by Nakkaṉ Paravai and her defrayal of the taxes due (in paddy) through a payment of gold. The inscription goes on to describe a further donation of gold by Paravai...] to provide for what is necessary for the Tiruvātirai festival in Mārkaḻi, including the cloths (*paricaṭṭam*) to be distributed—amounting to an expense of 120 *kacu;* for the rice offerings at the Tiruvāṉi festival, and for the cloths to be distributed, and for expenses including (provision of) 4 *nāḻi* (of paddy) for lamp oil—180 *kācu*; for reciters of *Tiruttoṇṭuttokai* at the Tirumāci festival—5 *kācu*—altogether 305 *kācu* were received and this agreement was drawn up.

The communities (*kuṭikaḷ*) who reside in Kuṇamehkaipuram, including merchants, *veḷḷāḷar*, oil sellers (*caṅkarappāṭiyār*), weavers (*cāliyar*), and *paṭṭiṉavar* (fish sellers?), and the artisan groups (? *kiḻkalaṉaikaḷ*) including carpenters, blacksmiths, goldsmiths, and weavers (*koliyar*) accept the terms of this agreement, and undertake to maintain it for as long as the moon and sun endure.

The inhabitants of this ūr (village) gave a part of the land of their ūr, called Caṅkoṭiyaṉ Paravainaṅkainallūr [named after the donor Paravai], to cover the expenses of feeding 20 Brahmans in the Ciṅkalāntakaṉ *cālai.*

[The following lines specify the amount of paddy this land will produce, how taxes are to be paid from part of this produce, and how the rest is to be spent to feed the 20 Brahmans: to provide rice, curry, and spices—black pepper, tamarind, salt, turmeric—ghee, curds, betel, arecanut, firewood, plantain, and oil, and to support several servants.]

For one cook for the *cālai* (*cālai-maṭaiyaṇ*) 6 *nāḻi* of paddy, and as clothing allowance for the aforementioned... [break in the inscription]... 8 *kalam* of paddy, for one potter (*kucavaṉ*) 4 *nāḻi* of paddy, for one married woman (*vāḻvacci*) who brings the water vessel 4 *nāḻi* of paddy, for five women doing service (*paṇiceyya peṇṭukaḷ*) 1 *kuṟuṇi*, and as clothing allowance for the aforementioned 10 *kalams* of paddy, and as clothing allowance for one honored (overseer of the *cālai?*) 10 *kalams* of paddy—altogether 3 *kalam* and 3 *kuṟuṇi* of paddy per day or 1,226 *kalam*, 7 *kuṟuṇi*, and 4 *nāḻi* of paddy per year, including all the expenses here specified.

[This] agreement shall remain in force, having been engraved in stone, from this twenty-seventh year [of the king's reign] henceforth, as long as the moon and the sun endure.—SII 4.223: this inscription, which begins with a very long *meykkīrtti*, was inscribed outside the first *prākāra* of the Nāṭarāja temple at Chidambaram, South Arcot district. in A.D. 1039. [This section of the inscription begins with an account of the quantities of paddy available for the temple, the produce of various lands, amounting to a total of 1,080 *paṟa* of paddy annually.]

Of this total of 1,080 *paṟa* of paddy, 3 *paṟa* are to be taken daily, to produce 48 *nāḻi* of rice, as measured by the god's *iraṭṭamaṭai*, and portions distributed in the following manner: for the *meṟccānti* (priest) 4 *nāḻi* and 1 *uri*, for one *kiḻccānti* (assistant priest) 3 *nāḻi* and 1 *uri*, for another *kiḻccānti* 3 *nāḻi*, for the sacred parasol [bearer] 2 *nāḻi*, for the feeding of the *vaiśvadeva* ("all gods") at the daily *śrībali* ritual 3 *nāḻi* and 1 *uri*, for the sacred offerings (*tiru amartu*) at dawn 5 *nāḻi*, for the sacred offerings at noon 21 *nāḻi* and 1 *uri*, and for the sacred offerings in the evening 5 *nāḻi*—amounting to a total of 48 *nāḻi* of rice.

This 31 *nāḻi* and 1 *uri* of rice used for sacred offerings [at the daily dawn, noon, and evening services] should be taken and given as follows: 5 *nāḻi* of cooked rice to the supervisor (*vārivaṉ*), 4 *nāḻi* of cooked rice to feed the garland [supplier], 3 *nāḻi* of cooked rice to the temple watchman who guards the gate, 2 *nāḻi* of cooked rice to the temple woman (*tevaṭicci*) who pounds the paddy for the sacred offerings and carries the hand-lamps, and 2 *nāḻi* and 1 *uri* of cooked rice for each of the seven drummers (*uvaccakaḷ*) who beat the seven instruments for *śrībali*—totaling, for the seven, 17 *nāḻi* and 1 *uri* of cooked rice.—TAS 5.24 (lines 14–26): this inscription was engraved on copper plates in A.D. 1168; it records a series of endowments to and arrangements made by the Tirupāṟkkaḍal-bhaṭṭāraka temple in Kilimanur, Travancore (Kerala). 11 of the Chola period inscriptions thai describe temple women as temple servants provide only a vague and general notion of the nature of their roles. Two of these inscriptions date from the second subperiod, one from the third, and eight from the last subperiod. Several of the inscriptions of this type—one of which (SII 4.223) is translated here—use the phrase "women who do service" (*paṇiceyya peṇṭukaḷ*) without any further specification of the type of service required.[35] Although this kind of expression is found also in references to male temple service, it is usually obvious from the terms used for the men (e.g., "priest" or "drummer") what the nature of the service was.

In general, in fact, whereas the services to be performed by men are often spelled out in some detail—the names of the hymns to be sung or texts to be recited; the exact ritual occasions when the drummers are to perform and what instruments they are to play—this is relatively rare in the case of temple women, as we have seen. The precise description of the forms of temple service to be rendered by women is found most frequently in inscriptions that record their deals. And detailed specifications for women's services most often concern ranking and order of precedence rather than ritual content. It is evident that the particulars of these arrangements are of much greater concern to the individual temple women involved than they are to the temple.

Out of the 67 inscriptions describing temple women's service functions, seven indicate that they performed more than one *type* of task, of the four types of service that I have described—song and dance, attendance, garland making, and menial tasks. Four of the seven involve a combination of song and dance duties along with attendance functions; we have seen, for example, that temple women might serve as hymn singers and at the same time bear lamps and attend on the deity (IPS 162) or that slave women could be assigned both the task of hymn singing and bearing fly whisks (ARE 149 of 1936–37). One of the translations at the beginning of this section (TAS 5.24) shows that bearing lamps, which I have labeled an attendance function, might be combined with the menial task of pounding paddy. In another inscription translated earlier in this chapter (SII 14.132), lamp bearing is combined with garland making. And finally, in the thirteenth-century inscription from Tirunelvelt district, we have seen a group of temple women assigned tasks of all four types: dancing, applying pastes to the images of the deities, making garlands, and cleaning the floors of the temple compound (ARE 374 of 1972–73).[36]

The total of seven inscriptions that show temple women with multiple roles is not very many—only a tenth of the inscriptions that indicate that temple women had service functions in the temple—but the fact that we find even a small number of such inscriptions is of interest when we consider that there is nothing that parallels them in the case of temple men: we do not encounter Chola period inscriptions that describe men's activity in the temple with reference to a variety of diverse service functions. Men's employment in the temple seems to have been based on a more clearly established and specific professional foundation than was women's.

The vague and diffuse definition of the roles of temple women presents a contrast not only with the specification of distinct functions for many male temple servants but also with the image of the temple woman as a ritual specialist that has been formulated in recent scholarship. Saskia Kersenboom, for example, maintains that the *devadāsī* of South India has been at all times and at all levels of culture and of society a "ritual" person who deals effectively with the divine which is considered dangerously ambivalent. This female ritualist... renders her special power effective in three ways:

1. through her female sexuality that is identified with that of the goddess;
2. through a number of implements of ritual value like the pot, the lamp, coloured water, certain flowers, fruits and unguents;
3. through her art.

Her special qualification is her auspiciousness which earns her the epithet *nityasumaṅgalī*. (1987, 67) Certainly such *nityasumaṅgalīs* have existed in South Indian history—particularly, perhaps, in recent times—but if their defining feature is their role as "ritualists," Chola period temple women should not, it seems to me, be included in their number. The present investigation has shown us, first, that the temple women of the Chola period were not primarily recognized or identified with reference to ritual functions and that, when they did perform services in the temple, their engagement with these tasks—in contrast to men's—frequently seems to have been optional, incidental, and individual. Female temple service in the Chola period was not very organized or well defined, nor was it integrated into the pattern of temple ritual as a whole. Second, there is a lack of fit between the elements of ritual efficacy Kersenboom enumerates and the character of temple women's service in the Chola period temple. We have seen that there is no insistence that the performers of various temple services be female. We have seen very little evidence of temple women's ritual use of pots, lamps, unguents, and so on; the few cases in which such use is in evidence, which we have considered mainly under the category of attendance functions, were less the result of ritual necessity than of the personal efforts of temple women to gain honor and recognition from the temple. And finally, we have seen that the identity of the temple woman was not bound up with the role of singing and dancing; only at the end of the Chola period does she begin to establish a claim to particular rights over or expertise in dance, especially in the context of festivals.

I have suggested that temple women's activities and acquisition of position in the temple occurred in a climate of competition. Temple women's increasing involvement with festival dance seems to have taken place at the expense of men, who had formerly provided this service. Meanwhile, temple women may have been displaced by men in making garlands for the deity and in singing. It appears that in many cases temple service functions were subject to a trend toward greater professionalization and increasingly narrow definitions of eligibility. Temple women's access to various service positions, and the extent of their participation, was from the beginning of the Chola period much more limited than men's, and the changes that occurred in the course of the Chola period in some ways brought about further restrictions on their involvement.

Temple women's roles in the temple were such that their situation was quite different from that of temple men. They were vastly outnumbered by their male counterparts and were entirely or virtually excluded from many of the roles that men fulfilled, including those concerned with the administration of temple affairs. And while there were numerous tasks in the temple and terms for temple functionaries that were exclusively male, the terms and roles assigned to temple women were not exclusively female. We can point to only two sorts of temple service in which women were predominant and in which they became increasingly involved—menial service associated with food preparation and cleaning, and attendance functions. In the former, the tasks were of extremely low status, and in the latter, they were nonessential, occasional, optional, incidental—and perhaps ornamental.

In fact, one or the other of these two characterizations—menial or incidental—can be applied to virtually all of the tasks that were assigned to temple women, most of them of the second type. These activities were not at all central to the ritual life of the temple. With the apparent exception of dance, the services that temple women performed were unskilled and nonprofessional. In many cases, they had more significance in the honor associated with their performance than in the provision of a needed service to the temple. Thus temple women's work had a very different character than that performed by men.

SERVICE, SUPPORT, AND STATUS

In the fifth year of the reign of Tribhuvanaccakkaravattikaḷ Śrī Irācātirājadevar, I, Araiyan̲ Catiran̲ Irācan̲ alias Kulottuṅkacoḷakkiṭāraiyan̲ of Peruvāyilnāṭu in Jayaciṅkakulakālavaḷanāṭu, bought land [which is briefly described] from the Brahman assembly (*sabhaiyār*) of Tirveṅkaivāyil to be a *kāṇi* (property) to support the dancing *of kūttu* on festival days, including the Tiruvātirai festival in the month Vaikāci, for [the deity] Catiraviṭaṅka Nāyakar whom I established in the temple of Tiruveṅkaivāyilāṇṭār.

[The following lines give a detailed description of the boundaries of the land.]

This land is to be enjoyed by the dancer (*cānti kūtti*) Nācci Umaiyāḻvi Catiraviṭankanankai, who is to perform six dances (*kūttu*).

[The next few lines are damaged but indicate that arrangements about the land were made with the *māheśvarar* and the...(?) and that a specified amount of paddy was guaranteed for the person responsible for performing the six dances.]

Thus I, Catiran̲ Irācan̲ alias Kulottuṅkacoḻakkiṭāraiyan̲, give this [land, as an endowment] to last as long as the moon and sun shall shine. May the *pan̲māheśvarar* protect this [endowment].—IPS 139: this inscription was engraved in A.D. 1168 at the Vyāghrapurīśvaram temple in Tiruvengavasal, Tiruchirappalli district (Pudukkottai). Among the advantages of securing a temple position was the possibility that there would be some kind of remuneration. Earlier in this chapter, I have suggested that the performance of responsibility functions might result, indirectly, in obtaining support from the temple, especially in the case of tending arrangements. But many temple servants, including temple women, received support of various kinds directly from the temple. 32, or about half, of the 67 inscriptions that mention women's temple service functions indicate that they received some kind of support. The following table shows that the proportion of female temple servants who received support from the temple was considerably higher in the early Chola period than in the later period.

Chola 1	Chola 2	Chola 3	Chola 4	Total
5/8	7/9	6/19	14/31	32/67
63%	78%	32%	45%	48%

Between the second and third subperiods there was a major change: although in absolute terms the number of inscriptions that refer to women as temple servants more than doubled, the number that describe them as receiving support from the temple actually declined. In the second subperiod service functions were quite securely linked to support, but in the third subperiod this was no longer the case. This detachment of function from support is in part the result of the fact that temple women in this period began to negotiate deals with the temple that did not involve any remuneration: none of the six deals that temple women made in the third subperiod that resulted in temple service roles included arrangements for their support. In the fourth subperiod, when the absolute number of female temple servants again rose, the proportion who received support from the temple remained below 50 percent. This low percentage is in part due to a continuation of the practice of making deals for service functions without pay, but even more to the increase in the numbers of female slaves assigned service functions—almost none of whom were given any property or regular income.[37]

When temple women were given support, a variety of arrangements were made by the temple, ranging from the most well-defined, official, and permanent arrangements—associated with the granting of *kāṇi*—to more ad hoc and informal forms of support.

Kāṇi usually denoted rights over that part of the produce of a piece of land that was not due to be paid in tax. *Kāṇi* was the form of ownership of agricultural land that was most prevalent in the Chola period and that, to a large extent, continued to prevail in Tamilnadu up until the early nineteenth century under the Persian term *mirās*, the land-grants themselves being termed *māṉiyams* or *inārm* in more recent history (see Fuller 1984, 81 and 91; Karashima 1984, 26–31,165–80; Heitzman 1985, 123–47, 163–73). *Kāṇi* implied not only rights but also duties and privileges: *kāṇis*, particularly those linked to responsibilities in the temple, were "positions, around which rights and duties remained balanced" and to which "various perquisites were ancillary" (Heitzman 1985, 140; also 135–37).[38] In the present analysis. I am concerned only with *kāṇis* that were bestowed by the temple or connected to temple tasks. Also, I am categorizing as *kāṇi* other sorts of rights to property, which may not have been identical to *kāṇi* but shared its formal, publicly recognized character; these rights are referred to in Chola period inscriptions by the terms *bhogam*, *jīvitam* or *jivanam*, and *vṛtti* (Ta. *virutti*).[39]

Seven inscriptions refer to temple women as the holders of *kāṇi*. Two date from the early Chola period, one from the first and one from the second subperiod, and both are from South Arcot district. The earlier inscription (SII 26.391) is a record of the granting of a *bhogam* to a woman and her *vaṟkattār* to dance at the time of festivals; this is the only reference to *kāṇi* for temple women that indicates that the rights and responsibilities involved were hereditary. In the other early reference, a person, who seems to be a woman, is given as a slave (*aṭiyāḷ*) to the temple and she (or her son) is provided with a *jivanam* for picking flowers in the temple garden (SII 22.141). One inscription of the third subperiod from Tiruvengavasal in Tiruchirappalli district refers to temple women's *kāṇi* and is translated at the beginning of this section; it records the grant of land as *kaāṇi* to a woman for performing festival dances (IPS 139). Four of the seven inscriptions that mention temple women as holders of *kāṇi* date from the last subperiod. Two record the purchase of *kāṇi* rights from the temple by *tevaraṭiyār* (IPS 367; SI TI 1009), and the other two are grants of *kāṇi* to women (ARE 232 of 1971—72; SII 23.428). In contrast to the three earlier inscriptions, none of these four link the acquisition of *kāṇi* by a temple woman to the performance of any specific function in the temple.

Only a small fraction of temple women had *kāṇi* arrangements, but a somewhat larger number received support from the temple in the form of what I have termed *"kāṇi*-like" arrangements. These are arrangements that are not referred to in the inscriptions by the terms *kāṇi*, *jivitam*, *bhogam*, or *vṛtti* but that involve, like *kāṇi*, the assignment of land to a particular individual. 25 inscriptions mention kāṇi-like arrangements for temple women, and 17, or two-thirds, date from the last subperiod. As in the case of *kāṇi* arrangements, most of the references to *kāṇi*-like arrangements appear in inscriptions from the very end of the Chola period.

Kāṇi and *kāni*-like arrangements for temple women involved the acquisition and possession of property rights by a particular individual. These arrangements are especially characteristic of the last century of the Chola period, when individual identities were increasingly highlighted and when temple women were more and more engaged in making deals with the temple. Another method by which the temple provided support to temple women was by allocating temple resources according to "shares" or "days."[40] While *kāṇi* and kāṇi-like arrangements typically concerned single, named individuals, share arrangements most often involved several different kinds of temple servants, who were frequently referred to as anonymous groups.[41] 26 inscriptions mention temple women as being involved in share arrangements, spread throughout the four subperiods, with somewhat more frequent occurrence in the second and third subperiods. Since the second subperiod is the one in which we find the smallest number of inscriptions that refer to temple women, the eight inscriptions describing share arrangements in this subperiod represent a relatively high proportion—close to half—of all types of support arrangements for temple women.

A comparison of the patterns of support provided to temple women that were typical of the second and of the fourth subperiods indicates that there was a shift in the kinds of relationships that linked temple women to the temple and that connected service, support, and status. In the second subperiod, women were incorporated into temple life as part of a corps of temple servants, who belonged to various groups and were supported by shares in the resources of the temple. But by the last subperiod, the impersonal institutionalized relationship of the share system was much less important for women. Instead, *kāṇi* and kāṇi -like arrangements predominated, in which temples and particular temple women entered into well-defined and formal agreements: the temple would provide support for the temple woman, and the temple woman might—or might not—have to perform services in the temple. In the thirteenth century, unlike the eleventh, women were only rarely integrated into the temple establishment as members of groups; instead they negotiated individual relationships with the temple.

In 53 Chola period inscriptions it is possible to determine the form of support provided to temple women by the temple. Half of these date from the last subperiod, which suggests that the arrangements made by temple women were being increasingly well defined in terms of the details of their support; at the same time, they were less and less specific about the nature of the services to be performed. The forms of support provided to temple women were similar to those given to other temple servants, and consisted primarily of rice or land. The rice used to pay temple servants was almost always in the form of paddy and was only rarely cooked rice.[42] Agricultural lands were granted to temple servants as a source of regular revenue, usually in the form of paddy, or a temple servant might receive a plot of land as a house site. These two forms of support—grants of rice or of land—are represented approximately equally in the inscriptions that indicate support for temple women throughout the whole of the Chola period.

Some of the inscriptions detail the precise amounts of paddy, rice, or land that temple women received. But because the worth and the units of measure of land and of various commodities varied considerably in different times and places.[43] I have considered the value of grants made to temple women in relative rather than absolute terms, by comparing them to those received by other temple servants mentioned in the same inscription or in other inscriptions of the same period and locale. The types of temple personnel who most frequently received support well above the average level are hymn singers and priests, although other types of personnel are also mentioned. Among the lowest paid are drummers, people charged with the task of cleaning and smearing floors, and those responsible for making garlands. Very generally, menial tasks are least well paid, whereas those of ritual importance and those typically held by Brahmans are most well paid, but this pattern is subject to considerable variation. There are several inscriptions, on the one hand, in which the priest's assistants (*māṇis*) receive support well below the standard; drummers, on the other hand, are in some cases among the best paid temple servants. Temple women, for the most part, are on the lower end of the pay scale. 22 inscriptions provide enough information about the support of temple women to allow us to arrive at a rough estimate of its relative value.[44] In only three do temple women receive support at an above-average level. These include a tenth-century inscription from Malabar district (TAS 8,43), which describes the provision of paddy for female singers (*naṅkaimār kāntarpikaḷ*); a twelfth-century inscription from Travancore district which records the provision of paddy for four *tevaṭiccis*, whose functions are not specified (TAS 2.3); and a thirteenth-century record from Kolar district, indicating that land was given to several *taḷiyilār* who were "to serve" (*cevikka*) the deity (EC 1o.kl 121). Of these three inscriptions, only the first provides any clue to the kinds of duties that might have been required of these temple women, and none records the assignment of specific tasks. All three inscriptions are from regions on the periphery of the Tamil country—two from the Kerala region and one from Kolar district in the west. Thus, what we may consider the highest paying jobs for temple women are not very much like actual "jobs" because they are not associated with particular functions; nor are they either very common or at all typical of the central Tamil country.

This pattern holds even for the middle range of support. Only six of the 22 inscriptions can be classified as providing support for temple women at this level. And just one gives the impression that pay was provided in exchange for specific services: this is the thirteenth-century inscription from Tirunelveli district in the far south, which I have referred to several times earlier in ihis chapter and which records the particular tasks—adorning the images of the deities, cleaning and decorating the temple floors, dancing, and making garlands—and precise amounts of paddy assigned to each of 10 temple women. Two inscriptions describing temple women who received an average level of support are from the second subperiod—one (SII 2.66), front the Rājarājeśvara temple in Tanjavur, records the grant of shares to the *taḷicceri peṇṭukaḷ*, and the other (SII 4.223, translated earlier in this chapter), from Chidambaram in South Arcot district, describes the support arranged for a woman who is to bring ihe water vessel and for five women doing service (*paṇiceyya peṇṭukaḷ*). Three other inscriptions date from the thirteenth century and record deals negotiated by temple women at Uttaramerur in Chingle-put district (ALB 8,177; ARE 180 and 183 of 1923). In these three inscriptions, there is an indication that the temple women who had made donations to the temple were entitled to perform certain attendance functions, in addition to receiving support, but these tasks have more the air of privileges than of duties for which the temple women were being paid.

From this discussion, it would appear that the amount of support granted to most temple women was below the level received by the average male temple servant. But it is virtually impossible to demonstrate that temple women received lower pay than men did for equivalent work, for several reasons. First, Chola period inscriptions only infrequently provide information about the tasks performed by temple women—and still less frequently refer also to the amount of support given for the performance of these tasks. Second, temple women did not usually perform the same kinds of tasks that men did.[45] This fact in itself would tend to bring down the level of support that the average temple woman enjoyed, given the exclusion of women from those functions, such as hymn singing or serving as priest, that were most highly remunerated. Even in the realm of menial service, tasks with greater honor—and greater pay—were assigned to men rather than women; this is demonstrated, for example, in the inscription from Chidambaram (SII 4.223), in which the woman assigned to fetch water received two-thirds and each of the five "women who serve" received a quarter of the amount of paddy granted to the male cook.

Temple women, like other temple servants, on occasion received house sites from the temple. I have found 22 references that refer, directly or indirectly, to the housing of temple women. These references include inscriptions that mention in passing the "temple women's street" or that identify temple women in terms of their association with the area around the temple. Seventeen, or over three-quarters, of these inscriptions date from the later Chola period. Most of the 22 references mention the temple women's residence either in the "temple quarter" (*tirumaṭaiviḷākam*) or in the temple streets (*vīti*, *teru*, etc.). Three inscriptions, all from the early Chola period, associate temple women with the temple *ceri*, or "district."[46]

In the few cases in which the exact locations of temple women's residences are specified, there are various arrangements: for example, the *taḷicceri peṇṭukaḷ* of Rājarājeśvara temple in Tanjavur were housed in the streets to the north and south of the temple (SII 2.66), a temple woman of Tiruvarur lived on the south side of the "holy street" (*tiruvīti*) (SII 17.600), and a temple woman of Tiruvannamalai was a resident of the west street (ARE 232 of 1971–72). In recent times, the assignment of areas around the temple to various groups of temple servants became more fixed, with temple women often housed in the "best" areas, defined by proximity to the deity—directly across the street from the temple walls and close to the main gate of the temple, which was typically on the east side.[47] Such a systematic assignment of residences was evidently not a feature of the Chola period temple community.

Another contrast between Chola period temple women and their modern counterparts is related to the issue of whether temple women—or other types of temple servants—were normally provided with places of residence by the temple. This seems to have become a standard feature of the support of female temple servants by the nineteenth century but is relatively rarely found in the Chola period records. In fact, in the Chola period, the exceptional, negotiable, and honorary character of the assignment of houses is indicated by the fact that the most precise specifications of their locations (the "first house" or "corner house") were made in the case of deals (ARE 29 of 1940–41; ARE 471 of 1962–63). It appears that temple women took advantage of the fact that the assignment of places of residence around the temple was not highly formalized in the Chola period, claiming residence in the vicinity of the temple as a mark of status. That such a privileged association with the temple was increasingly acquired by temple women is indicated by the fact that the greatest proportion of references to the housing of temple women comes from the later Chola period.

A final aspect of the support of temple women to be considered is related to the original source of the property that was granted to them. It has been frequently said that, historically, kings have had a special role in the sponsorship of *devadāsīs* and that, in general, *kāṇis* and other temple "service tenures" were originally rights granted by the king.[48] But the evidence of the Chola period inscriptions supports neither of these views. Some of the links between temple women and the temple were established or sanctioned by royal authority, but most came into being by other means: some were created by temple or village officials, some were the result of gifts made by local notables or residents, and some were established through deals—in consequence of a gift made by the temple woman herself. This diversity of sources is demonstrated by the origins of the *kāṇis* held by temple women. Of the seven *kāṇis* acquired by temple women, three were the consequence of gifts made by local residents, two came into being because of deals made by temple women themselves, one was established by the local Brahman assembly (*sabhai*), and only one was the result of a royal order. There was somewhat more royal interest in the creation *of kāṇis* for male temple servants, but even for men the majority derived from sources other than the king.[49]

There were a variety of different kinds of arrangements through which temple women secured support from the temple, and at no time in the course of the Chola period is there evidence that temple women acquired positions through a particular procedure carried out by the temple or that they were predominantly sponsored by a particular type of patron.[50]

Although temple women resembled their male counterparts in receiving support from diverse sources, they were unique among all other types of temple servants in that they, through their deals, became partners with members of the temple establishment in defining the roles they would fulfill in the temple and the remuneration they would receive.

The Chola period temple, dedicated to providing worship for the deities enshrined within, was a focal point for the mobilization of resources, the performance of a wide range of activities, and the participation of many kinds of people. In addition to those who made links to the temple as patrons, many people were employed in the temple in various ways. The patterns of administrative, ritual, and maintenance functions that constituted the life of the temple and defined the temple community were far from fixed; these patterns varied from temple to temple and from region to region and underwent change over time. In this chapter, I have tried to give an idea of the general framework within which these patterns unfolded and of the factors that may have affected the processes of change in order to position temple women within these patterns and processes.

In examining the roles that temple women played in the temple and comparing these with those of their male counterparts, I have attached attributes to the various managerial and service functions that women and men performed and have indicated how the attributes associated with certain functions have shifted over time as different types of people took up these functions. Figure 23.1 gives a schematic view of some of these attributes, representing them as pairs of opposites. Each role in the temple, as fulfilled by a particular type of temple servant at a particular time and place, could in principle be characterized by its location on each of the horizontal lines that join the opposing attributes. The role of temple priest, for example, as it is described in most Chola period inscriptions, would be classified as more "professional" than "honorary," that is, more a job than a privilege, and would also lean toward the left side of the scales in being relatively skilled, well paid, and associated with specification of function; and would be on the far left end of the scales in terms of the essential character of the role and its association with ritual proximity to the temple deity. The role of the women who purchased the rights to dance and sing *Tiruvempāvai* at festivals from the temple at Nallur (ARE 160 and 161 of 1940–41) would be located differently: toward the left, perhaps, with regard to the skill of the role, ritual proximity, and degree of specification; fairly far to the right in the role's being honorary and optional; and all the way to the right for pay, given that these temple women paid the temple to perform these functions rather than vice versa.

I would like to suggest that although temple men's roles might have a wide range of patterns of attributes—including the clustering of attributes on the left side of the scales, as in the case of the temple priest—the variety of temple women's roles would be much more restricted, would scarcely ever resemble the pattern of the male priest's role, and would instead tend toward the clustering of attributes on the right side of the scales. Men's roles, certainly, might slide to the right as well—many men with responsibility functions were engaged in temple

Professional	<—>	honorary
essential	<—>	optional
skilled	<—>	unskilled
ritual proximity	<—>	ritual distance
specification of function	<—>	vagueness of function
high pay	<—>	low pay
		no pay
		negative pay (deal)

Figure 23.1 Attributes of Roles and Functions in the Chola Period Temple

functions that were honorary, optional, not particularly skilled (except, perhaps, in the case of temple accountants), unpaid, and more or less neutral in ritual proximity and specificity of function—but such roles were, typically, not ones that women played.

The attributes on the right side of the chart cannot all be reconciled with one another—it is unlikely, for example, that a role could be regarded as having an honorary character and at the same time involve ritual distance from the divine presence in the temple—but in virtually every type of role that Chola temple women played, it appears that several, if not many, of the right-hand attributes are relevant.[51] The fact that the cluster of characteristics of temple women's roles tend to be located on the right side of this chart does not mean that these roles were, by definition, inferior to the roles played by men. Temple women's roles were, perhaps, more marginal than central to temple life, but we must not assume that those women whose roles were honorary, optional, unpaid, unskilled, and vaguely defined were people who had tried and failed to become highly paid and skilled professional temple servants. Underlying temple women's associations with the temple was a different kind of rationale. Most temple women acquired functions in or support from the temple as a way to enhance a status that was already theirs. A woman's role in the temple was not primarily viewed as a source of livelihood, nor was her role what defined her identity and status—unless, perhaps, she was a slave acquired by the temple specifically to perform menial services. The temple woman's role was, instead, an adjunct or marker of her status.

The identity of the temple woman of the early twentieth century, understood in the context of hereditary, specialized, professional female temple service, seems to be based equally on three carefully defined and interconnected features: ritual tasks and privileges, entitlement to support from the temple, and temple woman status—acquired by birth or adoption into the *devadāsī* community and by a ceremony of dedication to the temple. For Chola period temple woman, we see an entirely different picture. It is the temple woman status that is central to her identity, and temple service roles or support from the temple are accessories to this status. There are only four Chola period inscriptions in which the three aspects—temple service function, support by the temple, and status as denoted by the use of "temple woman" terms—appear in conjunction with one another.[52] If it is the status of being a temple woman that is at the core of her identity—and if, as we begin to suspect rather strongly, this status was acquired and defined very differently for her than it was for the temple woman of the early twentieth century—we must turn now to an examination of its nature.

identifiers add up to more than the figure given for the hometown total because some of the inscriptions name several different types of men using different kinds of identifiers.

NOTES

1. The tending relationship that temple Brahmans entered into was similar to that of temple women, although Brahmans are much more frequently described in this role—being charged with providing a regular return on temple resources entrusted to them (e.g., Heitzman 1985, 137–38; 177, n. 32). The extent to which they may themselves have profited from such arrangements is not clear, but it is possible that both Brahmans and temple women were being provided with support by the temple through this system. The tending relationships of shepherds are of a somewhat different character because these people were not temple men but had simply entered into an investment contract with the temple. It has been suggested, however, that at Tanjavur and elsewhere in South

India this kind of arrangement made shepherds (or agriculturalists) into temple servants, who may in some cases have eventually taken on other temple duties (Spencer 1968, 279 and 292; Talbot 1988b, 184–85, 284; 1991, 331).

2. In the Jain context in medieval Tamilnadu, we find a parallel situation. Of the 104 inscriptions that refer to Jain 'religious men,' 13 (12%) describe them as being in charge of the administration of endowments or of institutions, such as Jain *paḷḷis*. None of the 29 inscriptions that refer to Jain 'religious women' mention their involvement in such responsibility functions (Orr 1998).
3. Although here I am primarily concerned with how temple men—the male counterparts of temple women—secured status through their involvement in responsibility functions, men who had more secular identities were also engaged in temple business, evidently with similar interests in the positive effect on their reputation that this activity might have. In his study of intermediate authorities, or 'lords,' in the Chola period, James Heitzman argues that 'the most important means for determining the relative power or influence of different titled lords was the holding of public ceremonies that become "political contests" for demonstrating the extent and commitment of each lord's following, his gentility and his generosity. The typical style of "administration" in this system was the public meeting or court where resource transfers took place according to stylized ritual prescriptions' (1997, 225). Heitzman (1997, 206–16) provides several concrete examples of individual men whose public activity, 'multidimensional' exercise of influence and 'ramified contacts' included extensive involvement in temple affairs.
4. Saskia Kersenboom's work is particularly noteworthy in this regard. The interest of Frédérique Marglin, of Anne-Marie Gaston and of Avanthi Meduri in the study of *devadāsīs* was inspired by their own experience and training in Indian classical dance. Amrit Srinivasan—although she does not consider the *devadāsī's* dance in terms of its ritual importance, as do Kersenboom and Marglin—focuses her analysis of temple women in recent South Indian history, and the organization of their community, on their professional status as dancers. Khokar (1983), Srinivasan (1983) and Meduri (1996) have documented the evolution of the dance traditions of the *devadāsī* after the advent, early in the twentieth century, of the campaign to prevent the dedication of temple women.
5. Song and dance are occasionally included by the Āgamas and other ritual handbooks among the 6, 16, 21, or 32 *upacāras* ('ways of service' or 'rites of adoration') offered in daily ritual to the deity (Kane 1930–62, 2: 729–30; Brunner-Lachaux 1963, App. VII; Appadurai and Breckenridge 1976, 193; R. Davis 1986, 265–74, 317–18). But none of these sources gives the impression that the performance of song and dance is a ritual necessity; these texts characteristically present a number of different options for the conduct of daily worship, and if song and dance are mentioned at all, it is in the context of worship done in the most elaborate fashion. Most of the references to dance in the Āgamas appear in descriptions of festival celebrations rather than of daily ritual, but even at festivals, dance is not represented as a ritual necessity. Furthermore, the Āgamas provide very little specification of '*what*' dances were to be performed, in either daily or festival worship (cf. V. Subramaniam 1980, 36; Viswanathan n.d.). Were dance performances regarded as ritually significant, they would have been given more detailed treatment; instead, the Āgamas usually refer to dance in only the vaguest terms—as *nṛttagītavādya* ('dance, song and instrumental music') or *śuddhanṛtta* ('pure dance'). (See Orr 1994c; Gorringe 1998.)
6. In discussing the temple arts of the Chola period, Kersenboom mentions the term *cāntikkūttu* but spells it with a short *a* and gives a derivation from Sanskrit *sandhi*; *she speculates that this may be a variant of navasandhi kautvam*, a dance performed by the *devadāsīs* of Tamilnadu in more recent times which honours the deities of the nine cardinal points (*sandhis*) (1987, 29; see also Janaki 1988, 167–175; Meduri 1996, 41–42; Viswanathan n.d.). Although we frequently encounter the word *canti* (with a short *a*) in the Chola period inscriptions, usually designating the three times of day (*sandhyas*)—morning, noon and evening—when worship was offered to the deity, the word *cānti* when combined with *kūttu* is consistently spelled with a long *a*.
7. The interpretation of *kūtti kāl* to mean 'prostitute tax' may be argued on the basis of the fact that the word *kūtti* has the meaning of 'prostitute' in later Tamil usage (MTL, 1071) and the hypothesis that a tax on prostitutes existed in medieval South Indian society. It is, however, difficult to support the idea that in the Chola period inscriptions *kūtti* means 'prostitute.' On the one hand, *kūtti* did not have this meaning in the Cankam and *bhakti* literature of preceding periods, and in inscriptional usage, *kūtti* and the parallel male term *kūttaṉ* appear in contexts in which the meaning of 'dancer' is quite clear. Kūttaṉ, one of the names of Śiva in Tamilnadu, is also very common as a male given name. The idea that there was, in medieval South India, a tax on prostitutes is suggested by T. N. Subramaniam in his glossary in *South Indian Temple Inscriptions*, Volume 3, in reference to the terms

mukampārvai and *kaṇṇāṭi*, which both mean 'looking glass' (1957, xxiv, xxxix; cf. Gopalan and Subbarayalu 1967, 432, who define *mukampārvai* as a 'customary present at the time of seeing a superior person'). Even if Subramaniam's interpretation of these terms is correct, they do not appear in Tamil inscriptions before the fourteenth century, fully three centuries after the references to *kūtti kāl* that are being considered here. A tax on dancers, on the other hand, is quite conceivable: we find parallels in three thirteenth century inscriptions (SII 1.78; SII 17.564; SII 17.568) that refer to taxes on drummers (*uvaccaṉ kāl* or *uvaccaṉ perkkaṭamai*).

8. It is possible that *cāntikkūttar* as professional dancers may have been inheritors of an older bardic or indigenous Tamil tradition (Kersenboom 1987, 57, 151). But professional singers and dancers, male or female, were not generally referred to as *kūttar* or *kūttikaḷ* in the literature of the early Cankam period. The masculine forms *kūttaṉ* and *kūttar* are used in the *Poruḷ* section of the Tamil grammar *Tolkāppiyam* (which may date from around the fifth century A.D.) to refer to bards and minstrels as characters in literature (e.g., *Tolkāppiyam* 88, 148, 191, 491). In *Cilappatikāram* and *Maṇimēkalai* (probably of a still later date), the term *kūttu* is used to refer to the art of dance (e.g., *Cilappatikāram* 3.12,13 and 19), and masculine *kūttar* and feminine *kūttikal* are frequently used to designate dancers, singers, or actors (e.g., *Cilappatikāram* 5.50; 14.156; 26.106 and 228; 28.165; *Maṇimēkalai* 12.51; 18.6 and 35; 28.47). In the devotional poems of the Āḻvārs and Nāyaṉmārs (sixth to ninth centuries), *kūttu* mostly refers to the dance of a god—Kṛṣṇa or, especially, Śiva (Orr and Young 1986, 50–54).

   Another theory is that the term *cāntikkūttu* refers to classical as opposed to popular dance (Khokar 1979, 64; Kothari 1979, 23). In this case, the Chola period *cāntikkūttar* may have been developing new dance forms, perhaps under the influence of northern Indian classical dance and drama traditions. That these influences were present in Tamilnadu in this period is clear from the fact that there are so many reflections of the *Nāṭya Śāstra* in the descriptions of dance in *Cilappatikāram,* a Tamil work composed before Chola times.

   Cāntikkūttu was performed at temple festivals. Other festival dances mentioned in Chola period inscriptions include *cākkaikkūttu,* which was performed by both men and women (ARE 65 of 1914; ARE 120 of 1925; ARE 8 of 1929; ARE 160 of 1941; SII 19.171) and *āriyakkūttu*, performed by men (ARE 120 of 1925; SII 3.202).

9. Singing and dancing at festivals, along with other forms of participation in festival observances, are also the most prominent ritual roles for women sanctioned by the Agamic texts (Orr 1994c). These roles are mentioned with particular frequency in the Pāñcarātra texts *Śrīpraśna Saṃhitā* and *Iśvara Saṃhitā*, both of which reflect practices particular to medieval South India (such as the use of Tamil hymns as part of temple liturgy). I suspect, therefore, that the Agamic imaging of the temple woman as a festival performer has been, at least in part, influenced by the actual increase in the middle of the Chola period in women's involvement with festival dance.

10. These temple women of the later Chola period may be contrasted with a woman mentioned in an earlier (tenth century) inscription (SII 26.391), who did have the capacity to transfer her rights hereditarily. She was granted land by the temple to support her as a festival dancer, and her descendents (*vaṟkattār*) were to continue to serve as dancers and to use the land.

11. Only one of the 13 Chola period references to *naṭṭuvar* that I have found (SII 23.306) explicitly mentions the *naṭṭuvaṉ*'s connection with dance, but the term is clearly derived from Sanskrit *nāṭ*, 'to dance' (MTL 2136–37; MW 525). Terms like this one, related to Sanskrit *naṭa, nāṭya*, or *nṛt*, are not at all common in Tamil inscriptions. Apart from *naṭṭuvaṉ*, the only other term of this type that I have found is *naṭṭiyāṭṭar*, which is probably a compound of Tamil *naṭṭiyam* ('dancing, acting,' from Sanskrit *nāṭya*) and *āṭṭar* ('dancers,' from Tamil *āṭu*). Two early Chola period inscriptions from Tiruchirappalli district (SII 8.659 and 698) mention *naṭṭiyāṭṭar* as owners of land. Terms of this type were much more widely used to refer to dancers outside of Tamilnadu. I have found the terms *naṭa, nartaka, nartakī, nṛtyantī* or *nṛttānganā* in 10 non-Tamil inscriptions, dating before A.D. 1300, from various parts of India including Karnataka and Andhra Pradesh. In 7 of the 10 references, the dancers were women. None of the female performers of dance in Chola period inscriptions is referred to by such terms.

   That we find in the Tamil inscriptions *kūttu*-based terminology for 'dancers' and *naṭa*-based language for 'dance masters' may indicate the presence of two different dance traditions—an indigenous *kūttu* tradition, performed by professionals not linked to the temple and a northern-influenced *nāṭya* tradition (see note 14). Each of these two traditions may have had its own group of professional specialists; if *cāntikkūttu* skills belonged to both women and men (although, as we have seen, *cāntikkūttar* with the title *ācāriya*, 'teacher,' were all men), *nāṭya* expertise seems to have been monopolized by men, by the *naṭṭuvar.*

12. In 6 of the 13 inscriptions that refer to *naṭṭuvar*, they are listed together with temple women and other temple servants and described as receiving support from or acting as functionaries in the temple. But there is no indication of any special connection between *naṭṭuvar* and temple women, unless we consider significant the fact that *naṭṭuvar* and temple women are frequently in close proximity in the lists given in the inscriptions.
13. The renowned Tamil poet Kampaṉ, who lived during the later Chola period, was a member of the *uvaccar* community. His pre-eminent status as the author of the Tamil Rāmāyaṇa contrasts with the obscure and peripheral position of the later Ōcchar.

    Another community of drummers, the *paṟaiyar*—whose anglicized name 'pariah' is synonymous with 'outcaste'—also experienced a drastic decline in status. The *paṟai* (the drum)—which features prominently in Cankam and *bhakti* literature—is frequently mentioned in Chola period inscriptions as an element in temple performances. But *paṟaiyar did not serve as temple drummers. There are three contexts in which we find references to paṟaiyar:* (a) in inscriptions, particularly from Tanjavur district, where there is the mention of *paṟaicceris*, which were evidently separate areas within villages where *paṟaiyar* resided; (b) in the imprecations of later Chola period inscriptions, which sometimes warn that those who overturn the terms of an endowment will have sunk to the level of a man who gives his wife to a *paṟaiyar*; and (c) in at least a handful of inscriptions (all from outside Tanjavur district) in which *paṟaiyar* appear as temple patrons and thus as people with economic resources and a legitimate public presence. I disagree with Heitzman, who considers that in the Chola period *paṟaiyar* 'were practically if not legally attached to the lands and wills of the landowners and cultivators who controlled the land' (1985, 160; see also Jha 1974 and Hanumanthan 1980). *Paṟaiyar* in the Chola period ceased playing the ritual and professional roles they had in an earlier age—having been, perhaps, displaced by the *uvaccar*—but they were not yet entirely identified with the degraded and serflike status they were to acquire in later times (see also Appadorai 1936, 23–24, 313–18; Nilakanta Sastri 1955, 555–57; Arokiaswami 1956–57; K. Swaminathan 1978).
14. *Naṭṭuvar* may have competed with *uvaccar*, as well as with *cāntikkūttar*, for the role of dance teacher in the temple. That drummers and the *uvaccar* themselves, were connected as teachers to temple women is suggested by Thurston's report that in Chingleput district, in the early twentieth century, the Ōcchar 'act as dancing-masters to Devadāsīs, and are sometimes called Naṭṭuvaṉ' (Thurston and Rangachari 1909, 5; 419). In Tamilnadu in the last hundred years, most temple women have been trained in dance by *naṭṭuvaṉār*, men who belonged to the *ciṉṉamēḷam*, the male wing of the *devadāsī* community. The *ciṉṉamēḷam* is one section of the *mēḷakkāraṉ* 'caste' group, which also includes the *periyamēḷam* (*nagaswarant*-players). Male members of the *ciṉṉamēḷam* might remain in their sisters' households and serve as musical accompanists (especially drummers) for the *devadāsīs* or establish themselves as dance teachers to the *devadāsīs* (*naṭṭuvaṉār*) (Thurston and Rangachari 1909, 2: 127–28; 5:59–60; Pillay 1953, 248; A. Srinivasan 1984, 198–226; cf. the *naṭṭuvaṉār* interviewed by Milton Singer 1972,177, who emphatically denied any connection with *devadāsīs).*

    The earliest inscriptional reference to *mēḷakkārar*, *ciṉṉamēḷam* or *periyamēḷam* that I have encountered is an inscription of A.D. 1603 from South Arcot district that mentions *tevaraṭiyār* and *mēḷakkārar* (SIOT 31).
15. Out of the 13 inscriptions that mention *viṇṇappañ ceyvār* that I have located, 6 apply the term to men and none to women.
16. In the preceding discussion of dance, I have considered two inscriptions that refer to groups of 'dancers' (*āṭinār*) and 'singers' (*pāṭiṉār*). The term used for 'singers' is based on the Tamil verb *pāṭu*. We cannot, however, determine whether these singers were male or female.
17. In the 12 inscriptions I have found that referred to the singing of *Tiruvāymoḻi*, this responsibility was assigned to men in four cases, to groups of singers whose sex was not apparent in eight cases, but in no case to singers who were clearly women.
18. On the one hand, we find in a thirteenth century record (SII 7.118) from North Arcot district a list of communities swearing loyalty to their ruler: *pāṇar* are grouped with low-status groups like *paṟaiyar*, *veṭar* (hunters) and *iruḷar* (tribals) at the end of the list (*uvaccar*, interestingly, are listed toward the beginning, together with shepherds and *śivabrāhmaṇas*). On the other hand, in the same period—but much to the south, in Madurai district—we find an inscription (ARE 476 of 1963) that confirms the land rights, (*kārāṇmai*) *of a pāṇaṉ* who is mentioned by name, which suggests a relatively high social and economic standing for this individual. The only other reference to *pāṇar* that I have found is from the second subperiod, in the long inscription from the Rājarājeśvara temple

at Tanjavur (SII 2.66), where three (or perhaps four) *pāṇar* are mentioned by name and were assigned shares as support from the temple. It is impossible to know what roles these *pāṇar* were meant to play in the temple, but it is perhaps significant that they are listed with artisans (carpenters, goldsmiths, etc.) rather than with the musicians mentioned earlier in the inscription. There is no indication of a connection between the *pāṇar* of the Tanjavur temple and the large group of temple women—*taḷicceri peṇṭukal*—named in this inscription.

19. The stories of the recovery, setting to music, and establishment of a professional group for the performance of the hymns are very similar in the Śaiva and Vaiṣṇava traditions, and both refer to events that are supposed to have taken place in the tenth or eleventh century (see Cutler 1987, 44–50). The Śaiva tale is found in Umāpati's *Tirumuṟaikaṇṭa Purāṇam* (fourteenth century), and the story of the Vaiṣṇava canon is told in *KQyil Oḻuku* (which was compiled between the twelfth and the eighteenth centuries). In both traditions, a particular community or family is given the special responsibility of performing the hymns. It seems likely that these stories were used to legitimize the rights of those people who had succeeded in acquiring the role of singing hymns in the course of the Chola period.
20. In the first stanza of the Tamil poem *Tirupporcurṇṇam*, by the ninth century Śaiva poet Māṇikkavācakar, women are called to the temple to make offerings, beautify the temple, sing praises, and take up fly whisks (*kavaris*) (*Tiruvācakam* 9.1; see Orr and Young 1986). In an early Chola pweriod inscription from Tanjavur district, the *cāmarai* is mentioned as one of the marks of nobility bestowed by the king on a feudatory, along with a hereditary title, an army of elephants, palanquin (*civikai*), and so on (SII 3.89).
21. In the only passage in the Āgamas that I have found which specifically refers to the bearing of flywhisks, men perform this activity (*Īśvara Saṃhita* 11.308–9). In the chronicle of the Srirangam temple, *KQyil Oḻuku*, bearing flywhisks is described as a task performed both by male temple servants (*kaikkQḷar*) and by temple women (*emperumāṉaṭiyār*) (*KQyil Oḻuku*, 94).
22. In addition to the three inscriptions considered here that use the term *kava-rippiṇā* for women who perform flywhisk service, four other inscriptions use this term in other contexts (e.g., identifying a female donor as a *kavarippiṇā* or indicating support from the temple for *kavarippiṇās*). All seven inscriptions date from the mid-tenth to the mid-eleventh century; the term falls out of use in the later Chola period.
23. Tewari, in his study of royal attendants, says of *chauri* (*cāmarā*) *bearers, as they are depicted in Sanskrit literature, 'in comparison to the chauris* they were holding and waving over the kings, specific references to them are few and far between'—whereas in artistic representations, 'there is hardly an illustration of a *chauri* bearer in Indian art which does not present her as elegant, seductive and full of youth' (1987, 54–55).
24. There is more emphasis in Agamic texts than in Chola period inscriptions on women's involvement in temple festivals. But frequently the texts describe women as only one type of festival participant, out of several possible candidates. For instance, the *Sanatkumāra Saṃhitā* says that either a *devadāsī* or an *ācārya* ('teacher') should act as leader in the offerings to the directions during the *bhūtabali* ritual preparatory to the celebration of a festival (*Sanatkumāra Saṃhitā* Śivarātra 2.9.42). And in a number of Agamic references, *devadāsīs* are listed with other sorts of people, suggesting that the point of the text is to be inclusive of, rather than insistent on, the participation of such women along with other members of the temple or village community. In a festival procession described by *Īśvara Saṃhitā* (11.207), for example, the participants include not only *gaṇikādevadāsīs* but also townspeople, Brahmans, and so on. The *Parama Saṃhitā* (22.18–19) says that *gaṇikādevadāsikās*, artisans (*śilpins*) and servants (*sevakas*) should be brought together for a festival procession. It seems that functions associated with festival celebrations need not necessarily be performed by women or by a special class of female temple servants (see Orr 1994c).
25. On the basis of her interviews with South Indian informants and her study of recent commentaries on ritual texts, Kersenboom has concluded that 'the most important task of the devadasi ... was to remove evil influences from the deity [through her participation in the daily *dīpārādhanā* ("lamp-worship") ritual]. Her special qualification of being ever-auspicious (*nityasumaṅgalī*) made her more suited to this task than any of the ritual personnel' (1987, 119; see also 60–61 and 112–13).

There is, however, little textual or inscriptional evidence to support the idea that this interpretation is relevant to premodern South India. Although the Āgamas contain more references, than Chola period inscriptions, to temple women's involvement with lamp service, these references are not extremely abundant, nor do they insist that temple women are pre-eminently qualified to perform this ritual function. I have found 8 references in the

Āgamas to temple women performing this function (out of a total of 53 references in the Āgamas to women's involvement in temple ritual), and 3 of these references clearly indicate that the employment of a woman in this ritual task was optional. For instance, the Śaiva text *Ajitāgama* (3.23.6) says that either the temple women of Śiva (*rudrayātanayoṣit*) or male assistants (*paricāraka*) might bring plates for lamps in the daily lamp offering service. We find very similar mentions of alternative ritual performers—to bear lamps in procession or to participate in the daily lamp waving (*nīrājana*) ceremony—in two Vaikhānasa texts, the *Vaikhānasāgama* (29.5) and *Bhṛgu Prakīrṇādhikāra* (Goudriaan 1970, 202; see Orr 1994c).

26. There are many references in the Sanskrit Epics and in Indian Buddhist literature, to enormous numbers of women in the train of kings (Chanana 1960, 123–28). Although this aspect of the kingly persona is not particularly pronounced for kings in the Chola period in South India—less so, I would argue, than Shulman (1985, 303–39) has led us to believe—there is no question that the courts of Chola period kings included many palace women. That some of these women were, at least nominally, associated with personal attendance to the king, is suggested by their identification as belonging in some cases to the *mañcanattār veḷam*, the 'palace of the ceremonial bath' (e.g., SII 8.678; SII 22.27).

27. It is tempting to consider that the term *kambhada suḷeyār*, 'pillar prostitutes,' applied to temple women in medieval inscriptions from Karnataka, may reflect a similar, ornamental function for these temple women, whose roles, in addition to bearing flywhisks on occasion, were unspecified (Parasher and Naik 1986, 67), In a Tamil text of the post-Chola period—*KQyil Oḻuku*, the chronicle of the temple of Srirangam—there is a suggestion of the ornamental character of temple women's services. The first of the duties assigned to temple women (*emper umāṉaṭiyār) in this text seems to involve no ritual action at all but simply standing in the presence of the deity: 'One [of the emperumāṉaṭiyār]* would bathe herself, at dawn, and adorning herself, go to the temple and stand well in sight of the God.' The text goes on to specify other tasks assigned to temple women, which involved bringing plates of incense and pots and dancing (*KQyil Oḻuku*, 95–96).

Marglin (1985b) and Kersenboom (1987) have analyzed in detail the significance of temple women's roles as attendants in temple and palace ceremonies in more recent history. In their view, temple women who performed these services were not merely ornamental but served a critical function as representatives of auspiciousness, whose ritual actions were necessary for the protection and prosperity of temple and palace affairs. Given that in the Chola period temple women were engaged in attendance in the temple only occasionally—and in the king's palace, not at all—it does not seem that this interpretation of their ritual functions is very useful here.

The ornamental may, of course, be auspicious, but the question is whether this ornamental auspiciousness should be considered a ritual necessity or not.

28. The inscriptions do not provide any direct evidence of the character of women's domestic ritual, but there are some hints in Tamil literature. Hardy cites several references to the use of lamps in the worship performed by women in Cankam poems (*Neṭunalvāṭai* and *Maturaikkāñici*) which he dates to the second to fourth centuries A.D.: 'Girls... light the wicks immersed in oil of the "lights made of iron," scatter rice and flowers, and worship'; 'carrying many things, holding bright lamps in front and boiled rice ... women undergoing a difficult pregnancy worship with devotion' (1983, 140). The ninth century work by the Vaiṣṇava poet-saint Aṇṭāḷ, *Nācciyar Tirumoḻi*, describes women's creation of auspicious designs and other preparations that were part of the performance of a vow (*Nācciyār Tirumoḻi* 1.1; see Orr and Young 1986).

29. In the Śaiva devotional poems, there are references to the plaiting of garlands as one of the tasks of the devotees (*Tiruvācakam* 5.14) or of the Brahmans who worship Śiva (*Tēvāram* 7.30.3). The Vaiṣṇava poet-saints Toṇṭaraṭippoṭi and Periyāḻvār, both of whom were Brahmans, tended gardens and supplied garlands to the Lord, according to hagiographical accounts (Govindacharya 1982, 3, 22). Since there appears to be no evidence of their engagement in these activities in the poems themselves, it may be that the hagiographers of these two Āḻvārs were inspired by developments of the late Chola and post-Chola periods.

30. At the Vaiṣṇava temple of Srirangam, where a large number of inscriptions concern arrangements for the provision of flowers to the temple, we find in later Chola period inscriptions the responsibility for gardening assigned not only to labourers (*āḷs*) but also very frequently to *nampis* and *dāsanampis*, *śrīvaiṣṇavas* and even *jīyar* (Orr 1995c). These figures, who are very often referred to by name, were individuals with high status in the corps of temple personnel or the sectarian community. At some temples, however, gardening and garland making continued to be treated as tasks for menial labourers even in the later Chola period. We can see this pattern at the

great Śaiva temple of Chidambaram, where the gardeners mentioned in inscriptions of the twelfth and thirteenth centuries are all anonymous groups of *kuṭikaḷ* (Orr 1995a).

31. The *Bhāgavata Parāṇa* (XI.11.39) exhorts the devotees of Kṛṣṇa to sweep, wash, plaster and decorate the floor of his shrine. We find references in the early Tamil Śaiva text *Tirumantiram* (1444, 1447) to the duty of the devotees to erect temples and to clean them (Narayana Ayyar 1974, 253–54). There are many passages in the Tamil poems of both Śaiva and Vaiṣṇava poet-saints that describe the cleaning of the floor of the temple as an act of worship appropriate to the ideal devotees (see, e.g., *Tiruvācakam* 5.14; *Tiruvāymoḻi* 10.2.7; Dorai Rangaswamy 1958, 1070; Orr and Young 1986).
32. It is interesting that there is no inscriptional evidence from the Chola period for women's involvement in pounding powders and pastes for adorning images, despite the several textual references to women's participation in this activity as part of festival observances. There are two such references in the Sanskrit Āgamas of the Vaiṣṇava Pāñcarātra tradition (*Śrīpraśna Saṃhitā* 34.74–75 and *Aniruddha Saṃhitā* 21.63). In Tamil devotional literature, an entire poem is built around the description of women pounding powder for a festival, the *Tirupporcuṇṇam* ('Gold-dust Song') in *Tiruvācakam*, composed by the ninth century Śaiva poet-saint Māṇikkavācakar (see Orr and Young 1986). K. K. Pillay describes the involvement of temple women in this activity at the Suchindram temple, in the far south, in recent times: as part of festival observances, the ceremonial powdering of gold dust along with turmeric, to be smeared over the images, is done 'by the Otuvar (chorist) and the Devadasi (of the 1st Kudi) together.... The pestle is held both by the Otuvar and the Devadasi during the pounding process... [and] both the persons sing a particular hymn from Manikkavacaga's Tiruvacagam' (1953, 228).
33. Five inscriptions refer to temple women who bear marks (in four cases the *triśūla*, Śiva's trident) indicating that they belong to a temple or a god. In four of the inscriptions (ARE 230 of 1921; ARE 141 of 1922; ARE 94 of 1926; EZ 4.24), these women appear to have been slaves; and in the fifth (ARE 537 of 1922), 'those marked with the trident' seem to be temple servants or devotees in general, rather than temple slaves (ARE para. 19 of 1922; Nilakanta Sastri 1955, 556, 564, n. 43; Balasubrahmanyam 1975, 76; 1979, 53). In three inscriptions, we are able to learn the identity of the person who marked the temple women: in two cases, the person who gave women to the temple, and in one case—in which slaves were purchased to work in a *maṭha*—the temple authorities.

    Because of its association with the status of being, literally, a slave and because of the apparent lack of a ritual context in which the marking or branding ocurred, it is doubtful whether this practice is connected either with the South Indian *bhakti* and the Agamic sectarian traditions of marking, sometimes associated with rites of initiation (Hardy 1978, 134; Kingsbury and Phillips 1921, 39; Jaiswal 1967, 143–44), or with the ceremony of dedication performed by South Indian temple women in recent times, which was called 'branding' (Ta. *muttirai*, from Skt. *mudrā*) and which involved the impression of a sectarian mark on the body of the dedicated *devadāsí* (Kersenboom 1987, 188; Viswanathan n.d., 57–58).
34. 15 of the 22 inscriptions that refer to slaves are from Tanjavur district.
35. The term used for 'work' or 'service' in this expression is *paṇi*, a word with very strong devotional connotations in the earlier Tamil *bhakti* literature. In the poems of both the Āḻvārs and Nāyaṉmārs, we frequently come across descriptions of the ideal devotee as one who performs service (*paṇicey*) *for god (e.g., Māṇikkavācakar's Tiruvācakam* 7.9, 10.12, 13.9, 27.5, 40.10, etc.; Cuntarar's *Tēvāram* 7.77.4; Nammāḻvār's *Tiruvāymoḻi* 1.10.11; Periyāḻvār's *Tirumoḻi* 5.3.3).
36. A much later record, dating from A.D. 1867, from the Suchindram temple at the southern tip of Tamilnadu, mentions three types of roles in outlining the duties of temple women: they were responsible for dancing and singing on various occasions; for the attendance functions of bearing lamps and flywhisks; and for the menial tasks of sweeping and cleaning the temple courtyard and shrines, washing the vessels used in worship and clearing up after the offering of food to Brahmans (Pillay 1953, 283–85).
37. Of the seven inscriptions in the fourth subperiod that record deals made by temple women which resulted in temple service positions, three mention that support was provided by the temple. Of eight inscriptions from this subperiod that mention female slaves with temple service functions, only one describes arrangements for support.
38. The idea that all forms of *kāṇi* involved position, as well as property, is emphasized by Heitzman (1986, 11), who puts forward the notion of the 'conditional nature of all property, dependent on the performance of public, social obligations'; by Karashima (1984, 26–27, 175, 196, n. 33), who stresses the idea that *kāṇi* and *mirāsi* were not only rights to land but also rights to privilege and power; and by Granda (1984, 122, 184), whose analysis

of property relations in the post-Chola period leads him to say that land rights 'adhered to individuals like some personality trait,' involving status as much as property.

39. In my analysis of religious *kāṇis* I am not distinguishing between village service *kāṇis* connected with temple duties (e.g., the grant of a *kāṇi* to a dancer or an artisan for service to the temple) and eleemosynary *kāṇis* (*brahmadeyas* and *devadānas*) that benefited temple servants. The distinction between the service tenure and the eleemosynary tenure was perhaps first made in Anglo-Indian law and does not seem to reflect any real functional division between types of temple service (Presler 1987, 77, 87). In the scholarly literature, Appadorai (1936, 164) and Nilakanta Sastri (1955, 570) make this distinction, and their lead is followed by later historians (Heitzinan 1985, 135–37; Dirks 1987, 426–32).

    Heitzman (personal communication) has suggested that *jivanam,* understood as a revenue grant allocated from public funds ordinarily collected as taxes (the 'upper' share of produce from a piece of land), is different in source from *kāṇi* or *bhogam* (rights to the 'lower' share). He distinguishes *brahmadeyas* and *devadānas* from *kāṇis* on the same basis.

    Peter Granda (1984, 89–110, 219–23) provides a very comprehensive discussion of *kāṇi* and of the transmission of temple rights and land rights in the post-Chola period.

40. The notion of a share was in some instances closely linked to the concept of *kāṇi.* At times the term *paṅku* ('share') seems synonymous with *kāṇi* (e.g., SII 8.644); in other cases a specific service *kāṇi* might be divided into shares or days, distributed through the course of a month. In the present analysis, share arrangements are those in which various temple servants and temple expenses were assigned fixed amounts of income (in paddy or gold) out of the total revenues of the temple. A good example is provided by the long Tanjavur inscription (SII 2.66), in which each of the 400 *taḷicceri peṇṭukal* was assigned one share (*paṅku*), defined as the amount of paddy (100 *kalam*) *that 1 veli* of land would produce; other temple servants were also assigned one share (e.g., the supervisor of the *taḷicceri peṇṭukaḷ*, the conch blower and the goldsmith) or variously assigned a half or three-quarter share (some of the *uvaccar*, singers, carpenters and barbers), two shares (*naṭṭuvar* and temple accountants), and so forth.

41. Every one of the seven inscriptions that refer to the *kāṇi* of a temple woman gives her name, and not one mentions arrangements for the support of other temple servants. Of the 25 inscriptions in which *kāṇi-like* arrangements are made for temple women, only 4 mention arrangements, made with other temple servants and all but 9 refer to the temple women by name. In contrast, 23 of the 26 inscriptions that describe share arrangements for temple women also specify allotments for other temple servants, and 20 of these inscriptions refer to temple women as members of an anonymous group (e.g., as *tevaraṭiyār*, or singing women).

42. In a few cases, temple women and other temple servants were paid with cooked rice (*coṟu*). Although payment in consecrated food (*prasāda*) and honours based on the distribution of consecrated food may have become very important in the post-Chola period, this does not seem to have been the case in the Chola period. See note 24 in chapter 3.

43. In my calculations of the value of the various kinds of property referred to in Chola period inscriptions, I have relied on the analyses of economics and mensuration undertaken by Appadorai (1936, 258–64, 701–32, 769f, 782–85, 796–810), K. Chatterjee (1940, 160–61), Nilakanta Sastri (1955, 557–62, 585–88, 613–24), Pandeya (1984, 144–45) and Heitzman (1985, 241–42, 510–12).

44. Of these 22 inscriptions, 2 are dated in the first subperiod, 6 in the second subperiod, 4 in the third subperiod, and 10 in the fourth subperiod.

45. Ramaswamy (1989, 92, 94, 98) cites several Chola period inscriptions as evidence for her conclusion, that in general women in early South India were paid less than men for domestic and agricultural labour. I have not found such a discrepancy in the case of temple service because women and men were not assigned to the same tasks within a single inscription or within a group of inscriptions from the same locale and period.

46. The term *cēri* has a wide range of meanings in Tamil literary and inscriptional usage. It may mean village, hamlet, suburb, district or street, and it frequently denotes the quarter where a particular caste or professional group, resides (MTL, 1636; SII 2.4 and 2.5; Gros 1968, 204, n. 38; Sethu Pillai 1974, 55; Karashima 1984, 46–48).

47. Amrit Srinivasan (1984, 148–56) describes the spatial organization of the area around the South Indian temple in recent history, highlighting the way in which the assignment of houses to temple women and allied groups near the east side of the temple and near the residences of the temple Brahmans served to demonstrate and enhance

their 'pure' or 'high' status. Studies of the temples at Suchindram and Uttaramerur bear out Srinivasan's account to some degree (Pillay 1953, 10 and plan 2 'Sucindram in the time of Balamartanda Varma, 1729–1758 A.D.'; Gros and Nagaswamy 1970, 124–27 and the map 'Uttaramērūr: la ville moderne'). In the Chola period, however, we see different patterns of habitation and land use around temples: residences were not densely clustered around the temple and much of the agrarian landscape was preserved in the process of 'temple urbanization' (Heitzman 1987b). It appears that it is primarily in the post-Chola period—particularly at a few major temples that were renovated in this period (e.g., the Mīnākṣī temple at Madurai)—that we see the systematic application of the ideal model of the *mandate*, prescribed in Śilpaśāstra texts, to the organization of the streets and residences around the temple; in these cases there is a more orderly pattern of hierarchy 'from the center outward' (J. Smith 1976, 31–36; see also B. Dutt 1925, 142–64; Reiniche 1985, 77–81, 85–91, 109, 112).

There are frequent references in inscriptions from Karnataka, dated in the eleventh to thirteenth centuries, to the housing of temple women, apparently in the vicinity of the temple; these districts are called *sūḷegeris*.

48. For the notion of a close connection between temple women and kings, see note 9 in chapter 3. The idea that *kāṇis* (or in more recent times, *ināms* and *māṉiyams*) have their ultimate source in royal largesse has been argued—or simply assumed—by British administrators, temple personnel and many historians. Karashima (1984, 179–80), for example, has suggested that the *mirāsi* rights that the British attempted to deal with in the nineteenth century had their genesis in royal grants in the Chola period. Stein takes issue with the notion put forward by Nilakanta Sastri and other historians that rights to land rested ultimately in the state and he traces this concept to colonial British interests rather than early South Indian practice: 'Assuming the politic fiction that the government was landlord, the British claimed the right to a substantial portion of produce' (1980,192). Heitzman (1985, 118–19, 144)—although he, like Stein, notes the vested interest of the British in the concept of universal royal possession of land—seems to support the idea that in fact in the Chola period *kāṇi* was understood as having its source in the universal lordship of the ruler, at least 'conceptually,' however irrelevant this 'concept' might have been at the local level (1985, 141–42, 144, 164). Dirks (1987, 125–26, 128–29, 410–11) emphasizes strongly the idea that *ināms* and *kāṇis* were, at least 'in cultural terms' or 'ideally,' grants from the king—just as temple honours ultimately depended on royal prestige and largesse (Dirks 1976, 152; 1987, 289).

I am not persuaded that in the Chola period *kāṇis* 'conceptually' or 'ideally' derived from the king. It is true that in the colonial and modern periods, South Indian temple servants have upheld the view that their rights originated in royal grants (Fuller 1984, 91–92). This claim may not so much reflect ancient historical circumstances (or even 'concepts'), however, as it does more recent changes: it has, for instance, been argued that profound alterations in the definition of *ināms* and in the relations between temple servants and the temple were the consequence of the policies of nineteenth century British administrators (especially those in the Board of Revenue), who took, too literally, the idea that the state was the source of *ināms* (Appadurai 1981, 140–41; Fuller 1984, 94; Presler 1987, 77–81).

49. Neither royal sponsorship nor hereditary temple service arrangements were typical of the Chola period, but there seems to be a correlation between arrangements of support that were established by royal authority and those that were hereditary. This is not the case for temple women—there being so few instances of royal involvement with their support arrangements and, in addition, so few instances when their relationship with the temple were hereditary—but among temple men, it appears that a substantial proportion of royally sanctioned arrangements were hereditary and that a substantial proportion of hereditary arrangements were authorized by the king.

50. The arrangements for the support for temple women in medieval Tamilnadu may be compared with those in the same period in Karnataka, where, according to Parasher and Naik (1986, 70–77), temple women were largely patronized by members of the ruling family and of the top levels of the feudal hierarchy. The analysis of the types of donors responsible for establishing temple women in the temples of Karnataka serves as the starting point for the argument that these temples found both their material and their ideological basis in the feudal, hierarchical political order of the period. The power relations and ethos that were thus absorbed into the temple milieu had, according to Parasher and Naik, its effect on temple women, in their ritual tasks (modeled on royal ceremony), their standing in the hierarchy of temple servants, and the expectation that they were available for the

'enjoyment' of those who held positions at the top of the various power structures—gods, Brahmans, kings or members of the elite. If Parasher and Naik are correct about the sources of support for temple women in medieval Karnataka, the differences from the situation in Tamilnadu are very striking: it would appear that temple women in Tamilnadu depended to a much greater degree on local support—and on their own initiative—in securing their positions as temple servants.

51. The only possible exception that I can discover is that of the female singers (*naṅkaimār kāntarpikaḷ*) mentioned in a tenth century inscription from Malabar district (TAS 8,43), whose role was (presumably) relatively professional, essential, skilled and associated with proximity to the deity, in addition to being well paid. The only right-hand attribute in this case is the inscription's complete lack of specifications of the actual tasks of these singers—an omission that may put in doubt some of the left-hand characteristics we have assumed.

52. These four inscriptions include three from the second subperiod (ARE 128 and 153 of 1912; SII 14.132) and one from the late thirteenth century (ARE 26 of 1928–29). In two of these inscriptions, it is not even entirely clear that the temple women involved did have functions in the temple.

Chapter 24

In the Business of Kama: Prostitution in the Classical Sanskrit Literature from the Seventh to the Thirteenth Centuries*

SHALINI SHAH

Like all other social institutions of our time, prostitution also has to be studied in the context of the overarching patriarchy with which it was intimately linked. The terms *vesya*, *ganika* or any other synonym for it,[1] in the classical literature of the period analysed in this article, are all gendered or gender-specific—they specifically refer to women prostitutes. In none of our sources do we find any term referring to male prostitution.

In Yasodhara's *Jayamangala*, an eleventh century commentary on the *Kamasutra*,[2] we can find references to nine types of prostitutes,[3] viz.

kumbhadasi:	A slave woman who was assigned the duty of fetching water
paricarika:	Female attendant
kulata:	Unchaste woman
svairini:	Sexually promiscuous woman
nati:	A dancing girl, an actress (*rangayosita*) as Yasodhara describes her.
silpakarika:	A female artisan. Yasodhara describes them as wives of dyers and weavers. They too must have worked as such.

* Reproduced with permission from the author. Previously published as 'In the Business of Kama: Prostitution in the Classical Sanskrit Literature from the Seventh to the Thirteenth Centuries' in *Medieval History Journal.*

[1] Ludwick Sternbach, Vesya: *Synonyms and Aphorisms, Bharatiya Vidya*, vols 4 and 5, Bombay, 1942, 1945.

[2] *Jayamangala Commentary on Kamasutra*, (ed. and tr.) Madhavacharya, 2 vols, Bombay, 1995.

[3] Ibid., 6.6.50.

prakasavinasta:	A woman who leaves her family, says Yasodhara, either when the husband dies or even in his lifetime, to become someone's mistress.
rupajiva:	A woman living on her beauty.
ganika:	Regular courtesan.

A mere glance at this list shows that women workers were included in the category of prostitutes. This would reinforce the view that under patriarchy, in historical times, it was not possible for women to enter any profession or work for wages and thereby earn a livelihood, and at the same time maintain the integrity of her body. Not only did women workers get classified as prostitutes, many a prostitute upon the end of her earning phase ended up as a beggar woman who had to perform lowly jobs to subsist. It was thus a two-way traffic. In Ksemendra's *Samayamatrka*,[4] an eleventh century satirical tract on prostitutes, we can observe a significant statement that unlike men who can live on their knowledge and experience, old courtesans (*yauvananase vesya*) can live only on charity (*bhiksa*). The career of bawd Kankali in this text amply illustrates this aphorism. The cycle of the prostitute's existence in this social setup in historical times is also very pithily summed up in a verse from an anthology[5] which says 'courtesans are first servants (*purvam ceti*), then courtesans (*tato beti*), afterwards old procuresses (*paschata bhavati kuttani*) and at the end when they are completely without funds (*sarvopayapariksina*) they end up as ascetic nuns (*vrddha vesya tapasvint*)'

Although the sources of our period put all kinds of women under the category of prostitutes, women who were forced to be sexually available to their masters like *kumbhadasi* and *paricarika* or women who were generous with their sexual favours out of their own free will such as *svairinis*, *kulatas* and *prakasavinasta*, are not objects of analysis in this article. For the sake of clarity we will restrict the definition of the prostitute to those who accept payment in exchange for sexual favours. Otis[6] describes prostitution as an institution in which 'socially identified groups of women earn their living principally or exclusively from the commerce of their bodies'.

I

In classical Sanskrit literature a prostitute is one of the *nayika* type and is discussed as such in all the works of poetics from the time of Bharata's *Natyasastra*[7] onwards (i.e., from the third and fourth centuries). She is variously described as a *bahya* in *Natyasastra,* as *samanya* in Rudraka's *Srngaratilaka* and *srngaraprakasa* of Bhoja. Dhananjaya in *Dasarupaka* describes

---

[4] *Samayamatrka*, (ed. and tr.) Ramshankar Tripathi, Varanasi, 1967: 8.103.

[5] Ludwick Sternbach, *Ganika Vrtta Samgrha*: *Texts on Courtesans in Classical Sanskrit*, Hoshiarpur, 1953: 63.

[6] Leah Otis, *Prostitutes in Medieval Society*: *The History of an Urban Institution in Languedoc*, Chicago, 1987: 2–3.

[7] *Natyasastra*: *A Treatise on Ancient Indian Dramaturgy and Histrionics*, (tr.) Manomohan Ghosh, Calcutta, 1967: ch. XXIV.

her as *sadharana stri.* Since she was a *nayika* who was not exclusive[8] she could not, even if she was genuinely in love (*rakta*), be shown with a king or a noble as a *nayaka* opposite her.[9] In the sources of our period we find her presiding mainly over forms of plays that are called *prahasana* and *bhana.* Here she is depicted stereotypically as bold, cunning and mercenary.[10] In the *prakarana* she did not have to be depraved as in the stereotype, for instance, Vasantasena's character in Sudraka's *Mrcchakatikam.* In the period of our study there is a specific class of works such as Rupa Gosvamin's *Ujjvalanilamani*, datable to 1150 AD in which *samanya* as a *nayika* type did not figure at all. *Ujjvalanilamani* was a leading text on the rhetoric of divine *srngara* which dealt with love towards Krsna as a supreme *nayaka.* According to Rupa Gosvamin there was no *samanya nayika* in *Krsnarati.* Even a low class woman like *sairandhri* was subsumed within the *parakiya* (others' woman) and within Krsnabhakti *parakiya* as a *nayika* was considered superior.[11] The logic in dropping *samanya* as a *nayika* in these rhetorical texts was that anyone in love with Krsna (and no one can love God falsely) was automatically transformed into being uncommon and unique.

Three conclusions can be drawn from the above discussion; First, *vesya nayika* is one who feigns love and sells her sexual favours for material gain. Second, she could be occasionally shown genuinely in love but then she does not remain a prostitute; she either dies (Harlata in Damodaragupta's *Kuttanimatam*) or she gets royal permission to marry her *nayaka* (Vasantasena in *Mrcchakatikam*). Third, if any woman (even if a prostitute) loves God, she could no longer have an appellation of being a common woman.

II

Beyond the routine textual description of the *samanya nayika*, which has been discussed above, we have to examine the social institution of prostitution as depicted in our sources. Was prostitution a 'safety valve' of a patriarchal social life, a mere adjunct that preserved the stability of its family life? We get an interesting verse in Damodaragupta's *Kuttanimatam*[12] which states that 'sex with the wife is necessary for the sake of progeny and intercourse with a prostitute for avoiding sickness (*vyadht*), i.e. excessive sexual desire'. We see in this verse a reiteration of the patriarchal view that treats a prostitute as a 'necessary evil'. It also shows how the prostitutes' sexuality was treated as non-marital and non-procreative, and hence dangerous. We also notice here the patriarchal ideology at work which divided women into virtuous women and whores. Even in *Mrcchakatikam* where *vesya* Vasantasena

[8] In *Mrcchakatikam*, (ed. and tr.), M.R. Kale, Bombay, 1962, vita says to vesya Vasantasena (Act 1.31) that you are as common as the creeper that grows beside the road (*margajata lateva*).

[9] *Natyasastra*: 24.153–54.

[10] *Dasarupaka*, (ed. and tr.) Srinivas Shastri, Meerut, 1969: 2.23: 150.

[11] V.R. Raghavan, *Srngaramanjari of Saint Akbar Shah*, Hyderabad, 1951: 27–28.

[12] *Kuttanimatam*, (ed. and tr.) Atrideva Vidyalankara, Varanasi, 1961: verse 789.

is an object of romantic love rather than a mere erotic object[13] the *nayaka* Carudatta[14] feels shame in admitting that a courtesan is his friend (*mitra*). He finally qualifies his admission of friendship with Vasantasena by saying that it is his youth (*yauvana*) which is at fault and not his character (*caritra*). In the same play[15] we find *vita* (see below) describing a courtesan's profession as one 'which is the birthplace (*janmabhume*) of hypocrisy, deceit, treachery and falsehood, and one which consists of perfidy'.

Not only is there a need to loosen the prostitutes from this castigating and judgemental language in which they are embedded within the hegemonic patriarchal discourse, but also to rescue her from a certain kind of feminist counter-discourse which, too, is a negative construction and reproduction of the prostitute's body and which focuses on the undesirable suffering and oppression bound up with prostitution through the centuries. This approach which tends to view the prostitute as a 'victim' is best illustrated in Bhattacharji's historical survey of prostitution in ancient India.[16] Simone de Beauvoir[17] notwithstanding her perceptive comment that 'of all women they (prostitutes) are the most submissive to the male and yet more able to escape him; this it is that makes them take on so many varied meanings', was unable to pursue this insight further and simply ended up with the 'prostitute as victim' approach. This is evident when she says that 'the greatest misfortune of the hetaira is not only that her independence is the deceptive obverse of a thousand dependencies, but also that this liberty is itself negative'.[18]

A more recent approach to the study of prostitutes/prostitution is represented by scholars like Oldenburg[19] and Shannon Bell.[20] Bell resorts to 'reverse discourse' (which is the discourse of the subjugated subject of the hegemonic discourse) to study the prostitute. In this reverse discourse the meaning and power of the dominant discourse are to some extent challenged. Like Bell, Oldenburg too tends to see prostitutes as social agents acting with relative autonomy within the confines of the male body politic. In fact, Oldenburg[21] on the basis of her survey of the nineteenth century Lucknow courtesans, talks of the 'self-perception of prostitutes' as powerful. Not only do they view themselves as an experienced lot but they even manage to create a counter culture/ideology of their own which both subverts and mocks the existing positions and roles of the patriarchal culture. Oldenburg, therefore, concludes that courtesan tradition far from reinforcing patriarchy represents a circumvention of it. With this approach as a starting point, scholars have tried to recover a prostitute history

[13] Carudatta often addresses her as beloved (*priya*) and not by appellations which describe her physical allure.

[14] *Mrcchakatikam*, Act IX.

[15] Ibid.: Act V.36.

[16] Sukumari Bhattacharji, 'Prostitution in Ancient India', in Kumkum Roy (ed.), *Women in Early Indian Societies,* Delhi, 1999: 196–228.

[17] Simone de Beauvoir, *The Second Sex*, London, 1988: 266.

[18] Ibid.: 585.

[19] Veena Oldenburg, 'Lifestyle as Resistance: The Case of the Courtesans of Lucknow', in D. Haynes and G. Prakash (eds), *Contesting Power: Resistance and Everyday Social Relations in South Asia*, Delhi, 1991: 23–61.

[20] Shannon Bell, *Reading, Writing and Rewriting the Prostitute Body*, Bloomington, 1994: 11.

[21] Oldenburg, *Lifestyle as Resistance*: 23.

which is 'herstory'. Wells[22] argues that the courtesans functioned outside the restrictions that the male state (Greco-Roman antiquity) imposed on its women (i.e., wives and daughters). The hetairae could inhabit the public space, exchanging conversation and sexual interaction for payment. They had the most freedom. They were intelligent, witty, articulate and educated and they were the only women who were allowed to manage their own financial affairs. They were accomplished conversationalists and intellectual equals of the men they ~ entertained. They were poets, artists and herbalists, a truly talented lot. Even de Beauvoir[23] grudgingly acknowledges that

> [P]aradoxically enough those women (hetairae) who exploit their femininity to the hilt, create for themselves a situation almost equivalent to that of a man; beginning with that sex which gives them over to the males as objects, they came to be subjects. Not only do they make their own living like men, b\It they exist in a circle that is almost exclusively masculine, free in behaviour and conversation, and they can attain the rarest intellectual liberty.

III

In order to recover such a prostitute history from our sources we need to first of all analyse the prostitute household organised along lines which were distinct from patriarchal households. The study of the household in writing the history of any social institution is immense, for it is a truism that the household is the arena in which gender relations are structured and maintained. Unlike the patriarchal households surrounding it, the prostitute households were rigorously matrifocal institutions. Our sources allow us to recover some of the characteristics of such households. The gender equation in these households was very different. For one, daughters were highly prized over sons. A bawd says in *Kuttanimatam*[24] that 'the birth of a daughter is desirable (*duhita eva slaghya*) and to be satisfied with the birth of a son is worthy of criticism'. This disregard for sons in the prostitute household is strikingly brought out in the *Mrcchakatikam.* In this play when Maitreya on his visit to a *vesya* household asks his escort *bandhulas* who they are,[25] they respond by saying that 'we are *bandhulas,* that sport about like the cubs of elephants, being reared in other peoples' houses (*paragrhalalita*), fed on others' food (*parannapusta*), begotten by other men upon stranger women (*parapurusearjanita paranganasu*), enjoying other's riches (*paradhananirata*), and possessing no merit to speak of (*gunesvacya*)'.[26]

---

[22] Jess Wells, *A Herstory of Prostitution in Western Europe*, Berkeley, 1982: 6–7.

[23] de Beauvoir, The *Second Sex*: 581.

[24] *Kuttanimatam*, verse 146.

[25] *Mrcchakatikam*, Act IV.28.

[26] Amrit Srinivasan, 'Reform or Conformity? Temple Prostitution and the Community in the Madras Presidency', in Bina Agarwal (ed.), *Structures of Patriarchy*, Delhi, 1988: 187. In his sociological survey of the *devadasi* household, Srinivasan points out that men in the' *devadasi* household stayed as appendages of their sister's or mother's household only on sufferance.

Yet again when Maitreya is introduced to Vasantasena's brother, he remarks:[27] 'I must not (think highly of him) for although he is gaily dressed, gentle and well-perfumed, still he is to be shunned by the people just like a champaka tree growing in the enclosure of a cremation ground, although it may be bright, attractive and sweet-smelling'. In fact children in the prostitute household, unlike the patriarchal household where they belonged to the father's lineage, were completely under their mother's control.[28] This was the reason why lawgivers ignore them completely. Medhatithi,[29] in his commentary on the *Manusmrti*, while describing *samkara* (the progeny of miscegenation) who would have no right to perform *udakakriya*, that is, the ritual offering of water to dead persons, includes the offspring of the *vesya* in it. Evidently, then, such children were not claimed by fathers for ritual needs.

There was also a greater fluidity of domestic arrangements within such households. Srinivasan[30] in her study of the *devadasi* household points out that girls who were dedicated to the deity, i.e. *devadasis*, were not permitted to cook or perform mundane domestic tasks[31] either for the men of their own households or for their *gums.* Oldenburg's[32] data on courtesans also confirms that prostitutes take pride in being able to avoid the drudgery of housework which was the lot of 'respectable' household women. The household division of labour (the sexual division of labour) has an important bearing on the status of women in society/community. Familial relations shape women's access to work and other resources, and also play a key role in producing and maintaining gender ideologies.[33] Within the set-up of the prostitute household their labour/work was not subsumed within the category of housework and, therefore, was not marginalised; in fact, it can be designated as 'the work'.

Within the prostitute household not only was her work 'the work', but also the 'space' was her own. Patriarchy relegated the wives and daughters solely to the sphere of the private which was also a space controlled and regulated by men. In this universe their very identities were defined by their ties to men—mother, wife, daughter and so on. Even if there was some dispersal of power to the suitable age group and category of women, it was according to male-defined rules. So while there could be room for women at every level there was no 'room of her own'. The prostitute, on the other hand, was defined by a space of her own. She had her own place (*vesavasa*) over which she had complete command. It is interesting to note that when Maitreya

---

[27] *Mrcchakatikam*, Act IV 29.

[28] Srinivasan, (*Reform or Conformity*?: 180), points out that in the devadasi's household the young woman did not owe her paramour either any household service or her offspring.

[29] *Manubhasya*, (tr.) Ganganath Jha, vols. 1–5, Calcutta, 1920–26: 5.88.

[30] A. Srinivasan, *Reform or Conformity?*: 186.

[31] *Devadasis* in the sources of our period are essentially treated as *vesyas* or courtesans of God, and it is their sexual service which is emphasised. As Parasher and Naik, 'Temple Girls of Medieval Karnataka', *Indian Economic and Social History Review*, 23(1), 1986: 63–91 have shown from their study of inscriptions from AD 700 to AD 1200 from Karnataka, there was a blurring of the *devadasi/vesya* divide, if at all one existed in the first place. This is also apparent from the story of Rupinika in the *Kathasaritsagara*, (ed. and tr.) Penzer and c.H. Tawney, 10 vols, Delhi, 1968. It refers to *vesya* Rupinika 'who went at the time of worship to the temple to perform her duty'. Ibid. vol. 1: 139.

[32] Oldenburg, *Lifestyle as Resistance*: 40–41.

[33] Henrietta Moore, *Feminism and Anthropology,* Minneapolis, 1988: 42.

visits *ganika* Vasantasena's house[34] her maid introduces Vasantasena's mother and brother in relation to mistress (*arya*) Vasantasena. In *Kathasaritsagara*[35] we read the tale of the *vesya* Kumudika who gives refuge to even a defeated King Vikramasimha. It was this autonomy of the *vesya* household and her subversive potential which made her house be perceived as dangerous. The *Smrti* literature which represents the patriarchal Brahmanical viewpoint underlines this. Manu as well as his commentator Medhatithi[36] agree on the threat that they represent.

It would not be an exaggeration to state that *vesavasa* culture was considered dangerous enough by the patriarchal household and the patriarchal state would not allow any transgression of the boundaries separating the patriarchal domain from that of the prostitute household. Prostitutes as far as patriarchy was concerned were located in the space of the erotic and were denied any familial spaces. The patriarchal household used the mechanism of purity and pollution to achieve this. In *Mrcchakatikam*, *ganika* Vasantasena visits Carudatta's house twice but never gains entry into his inner apartments or meets his wife. Carudatta himself[37] says that even Vasantasena's ornaments cannot be taken inside the inner apartments for safe keeping since they have been worn by a prostitute (*prakasanari*).

From *prakasanari* to a *kulavadhu* of the inner apartment was a Rubicon that could not be crossed over with ease. In Buddhasvamin's *Brhatkathaslokasamgraha*[38] it is said for a prostitute that the blemish of her appellation as a courtesan (*ganikasabdadosastu*) does not leave her even now. Sarvilaka tells Madanika[39] that the title of a bride (*vadhu*) is hard (*durlabha*) to obtain. The prostitute tradition with its evidently subversive potential required the permission of the state which was the upholder of a patriarchal ideology, if an individual prostitute was to achieve a change in her status to that of a wife. In both *Mrcchakatikam*[40] and *Brhatkathaslokasamgraha*[41] the permission for a *ganika* to become a *kulastri* was given by the king himself (*rajadesa*). In Bhoja's *Srngaramanjarikatha*[42] again it is the king who gives *vesya* Asokavati permission to become the wife of Caddalaka who was a feudatory of the king. In *bhana Padmaprabhrtaka*[43] for a particularly loyal *vesya* it is hoped that she soon earns a veil (*avagunthanabhagini*) at the hands of the queen (*mahisi*). It is of course obvious that all these instances of royal permission[44] came after it was made sure that the *vesya* in question had internalised the *pativrata* ideology of the patriarchal household. In

---

[34] *Mrcchakatikam*, Act IV.
[35] *Kathasaritsagara*, vol. V: 16.
[36] *Manubhasya*, 4.85.
[37] *Mrcchakatikam*, Act III.7.
[38] *Brhatkathaslokasamgraha,* (ed. and tr.) R. P. Poddar, Varanasi, 1986: Canto XI.86.
[39] *Mrcchakatikam,* Act IV.24.
[40] Ibid., Act X.
[41] *Brhatkathaslokasamgraha*, canto XII.83, canto XIII.1–2.
[42] *Srngaramanjarikatha,* (tr.) Kalpana Munshi, Singhijain Series No. 30, Bombay, 1959: 78.
[43] *Srngarahata: Caturbhani, A Collection of Four Sanskrit Bhanas,* (ed. and tr.) Morichandra and V.S. Agrawal, Bombay, 1960: 41.
[44] In the sixth tale of *Srngaramanjarikatha* we find a *kulastri – lavanyasundari* – taking to the life of a *vesya* of her own accord in order to make money to free her imprisoned husband. And when her objective of getting 100 elephants was realised she left the life of a *uesya* to once again become the wife of her husband. This is the only exceptional instance in our sources of a crossover twice by a woman at her own initiative of the *kulastri-varastri* divide.

Yasodhara's commentary[45] we are told that a *vesyii* could be given in marriage to one who could provide special musical assistance to the establishment, for such a marriage leads to greater prosperity. The marriage bond here was not governed by patriarchal ideology and marital ties were only notional.

The obverse side of this shutting out of the *vesya*[46] from patriarchal domesticity was that prostitutes could create their own counter-culture with their own value system against the ethics of the dominant patriarchal culture. Their ostracism within this patriarchal universe simultaneously ensured their greater independence and autonomy within their own space. Prostitutes led an independent life (*svadhina*) and though they took others' money they did not become slaves. On the contrary they were clever enough to overpower men (*vasikartum naram*). They had the whole world under their control and were, therefore, proverbial as persons who did not suffer under anybody's authority.[47]

IV

Within the boundary of the prostitute household it was the mother figure who reigned supreme. Her will was law. Yasodhara[48] states that a *vesya* should never disagree with the mother, who could be either real or adopted, and she should seek her advice on everything. Jalhana's *Mugdhopadesa* underlines this advisory role of the bawd (*mantri jaratkuttani*).[49] In Dandin's *Dasakumaracarita*[50] prostitute Kamamanjari's mother talks of *ganikamatu-radhikara.* Even if the younger daughters were the earning stars of the family it was the old bawd/mother, referred to as *kuttani* in the sources, who was the real authority and manager of the *vesya* household. So crucial and indispensable was her role that in her absence[51] it is said that the house becomes a happy hunting ground of all kinds of rogues and penniless men who become difficult to dislodge, and the *vesya*gets no peace by day or night. In *Dhurta-vita Samvada*[52] a *vesya* protected by her mother is described as a river filled by crocodiles from which it is best to stay away. It would not be wrong to conclude that it was the presence of the *kuttani* which prevented the *vesya* from becoming an object of exchange between the pimp and the clients. It was the *kuttani* who ensured wealth for the prostitutes. Thus, we find in the *Samayamatrka* that the bawd Kankali was adopted as mother by *vesya* Kalavati.

---

[45] *Jayamangala Commentary*: 7.1.22–23.

[46] Not only were *vesyas* living in their own household variously described as *ganikakutumba, vesyagrha* (Sternbach, *Vesya: Synonyms and Aphorisms*, 1945: 135–38), but in most cases were in separate areas of the town. We get a reference to *vesyavithi* (*Srngarahata: Caturbhani*: 32) in our sources. *Manasollasa* refers to *vesya* houses on the outskirts of the town [cited in Kumkum Roy (ed), *Women in Early Indian Societies*: 215].

[47] Sternbach, *Ganikavrttasamgraha*: 64.

[48] *Jayamangala Commentary:* 6.2.3–4, 8; 6.2.60–61.

[49] Sternbach, *Ganikavrttasamgraha*: 17

[50] *Dasakumaracarita,* (ed. and tr.) K.N. Sharma, Varanasi, 1965: 132–34.

[51] *Samayamatrka*, (ed. and tr.) Ramashankar Tripathi, Varanasi, 1967: 1.40–49.

[52] *Srngarahata: Caturbhani*: 100.

Sociological data from the colonial period would also support this analysis. Srinivsan[53] referring to the *devadasi* household says that

> The person in charge in the *dasi* establishment—the *taikkizhavi* (old mother)—was the seniormost female member…the strict discipline of this old lady over both the private and the professional lives of her relatives, her control over income, its pooling and expenditure, provided the fundamental source of unity for the *dasi* household. The critical role that she thereby played in the status and prestige of an establishment was appreciable…. Most homes had photographs on the walls, of previous such leading lights of the family, before whom daily worship was offered.

The authority of the mother figure within the *vesyii* household can be appreciated better if we analyse the standing and nature of *kuttani's* relations with different men who populated the courtesan's universe. Apart from the clients (*bhujangas*) there were certain hangers-on and *vita* was perhaps the most important of them. He was a cultured man in the prostitute's gathering. Bharata[54] describes *vita* as 'one who is skilled in pleasuring the prostitute (*vesyopacharakusalo*), sweet (*madhuro*), courteous (*daksina*), poet (*kavi*), proficient in argumentation (*uhapohksamo vagmi*) and is shrewd (*caturasca*), he is *vita*' (*vito bhaveta*). Bhoja in his text *Sarasvatikanthabharana*[55] calls *vita* accomplished (*gunavana*). In Rudraka's *Srngaratilaka*[56] he is described as a master of one art (*ekavidyovita*) while still others like Bhanudatta in his *Rasamanjari*[57] described *vita* as the master of the science of erotics (*kamatantrakalakovidavita*). Although Ksemendra in his satirical works like *Samayamatrka*[58] and *Desopadesa*[59] is dismissive of the *vitas*:

> *sinaya gunahinaya sadosaya kalabhrte*
> *vitaya krsnapaksendukutilaya namo namab*

This criticism has to be placed in its historical context. The time in which Ksemendra was writing (the eleventh century AD in Kashmir), saw the shrinkage of urban centres and the urban economy in many parts of the country. It is only to be expected that those institutions which drew their sustenance from a flourishing urban *nagaraka* culture were also showing signs of degeneration.

Vatsyayana[60] defines a *vita* as a man who has exhausted his wealth in enjoyment (*bhuktavibhavastu*), is endowed with good qualities (*gunavana*), is married and is respected among *vesyas* and in *gosthis,* and earns his livelihood thereby. In fact, Yasodhara[61] explains that by stating that he draws his very sustenance from *vesyas* and *nagarakas* (*vrttimanyamnichan*

[53] Srinivasan, *Reform or Conformity?*: 188.
[54] *Natyasastra*: 35.55.
[55] Cited in *Srngaramanjarikatha*: 52.
[56] Ibid.
[57] Ibid.
[58] *Samayamatrka*: 8.18, 24, 25.
[59] Cited in *Srngaramanjarikatha*: 52.
[60] *Kamasutra,* (ed. and tf.) Madhavacharya: 2 vols, Bombay, 1995: 1.4.32.
[61] *Jayamangala Commentary*: 1.4.32.

vesyajana nagarakajana chopajivati). It is thus clear that the *vita* was no male centre of authority in the prostitute's universe. He was only an intimate and cultured hanger-on. He was an indispensable part of the cultured gathering which higher class prostitutes like *ganikas* were forever having. He also performed the functions of a trusted messenger between the hetaira and her clients[62] and sometimes he acted as an escort.[63] He could also be called upon to mediate between *vesyas* and their clients in quarrels relating to fees etc.[64] No doubt the *vitas* performed a useful function for the *vesya* household, but within the household itself it was the *kuttani* or mother who presided. Neither were the *vitas* male challengers nor did they emerge as alternative centres of authority in the household.

In the *Kuttanimatam*[65] we get a reference to one *Sula-Pala* (keeper of prostitutes). He looked after the arrangements of the theatrical performances given by *vesyas* belonging to his establishment. A verse also refers to him not allowing a *vesya* on stage for she was in her monthly period. An eleventh century AD inscription from Rajasthan[66] also refers to *Sula-Pala* accompanying courtesans to give music and dance performances on religious and festive occasions. However, these descriptions do not give the impression that *Sula-Pala* was in a position of control over the prostitutes. He seems more like a male escort of the prostitute establishment (in a serving capacity) who went with the courtesans whenever they stepped outside their establishment.

Dindikas who were represented as low, vulgar characters in Syamalaka's *bhana Padataditaka* are another set of men referred to in association with prostitutes. *Dindikas* are here described as ugly like monkeys and in their actions they are the devils (*pisaca*) themselves.[67] In Bhoja's *Srngaramanjarikatha*[68] *kuttani* Visamsila is compared to a group of *dindikas* who accumulate wealth by 'draining the purses of others'. It seems, says, Munshi,[69] that these *dindikas* were pickpockets who were adept at taking away money by sleight of hand. To the class of *dindikas* also belonged the *khala* or rogue. In Ksemendra's *Desopadesa*[70] as also in *Kuttanimatam*[71] he is described as a dishonest man without any principles. It is thus obvious that while the more cultured *vitas* were part and parcel of the *ganika's* household, scum like *dindikas*, *khalas* and *dhurtas* (cheats) also surrounded them, particularly the lower level prostitutes like *rupajivas*. This must have certainly contributed to the brutalisation of the *vesya* s environment.

In spite of the presence of these men around *vesyas,* the *kuttani* never allowed them to get the better of her. Bhoja in *Srngaramanjarikatha*[72] while delineating the character of *kuttani* Visamsila, mother of *vesya* Srngaramanjari, states that 'she is never cheated by *vitas*;

[62] *Kuttanimatam*: 339–40.
[63] *Mrcchakatikam,* Act V.
[64] *Kuttanimatam,* verse 342, *Srngarahata: Caturbhani*: 158.
[65] *Kuttanimatam,* verses 68, 796.
[66] Ajay Mitra Shastri, *India as seen in the Kuttanimatam of Damodargupta,* Delhi, 1975: 119.
[67] *Srngarahata: Caturbhani*: 184, 196.
[68] *Srngaramanjarikatha*: 53.
[69] Ibid.
[70] Ibid.
[71] *Kuttanimatam,* verse 114.
[72] *Srngaramanjarikatha*: 20–21.

she is requested by *dhurtas* for deceiving others but is never troubled; she deceives others but is never deceived herself; she stupefies others but does not get stupefied herself'. He further states that 'she is an expert in subduing paramours…she deceives even the clever, unsettles even the steady, makes a fool even of the wise, dances about even the *dhurtas*, makes the clever foolish, renders weak even the daring'. In spite of the exaggerated nature of the description, in Visamsila we get the picture of the power and strength of the *kuttanis*. It was the *kuttani* who had the 'agency', she was never at the command of the others, and could not be manipulated by the various kinds of men who frequented the prostitute household. As Bhoja[73] says for Visamsila 'she has brought the fall of many beast-like men into her various snares like *maya'*.

It was precisely this power of the *kuttani* which made her a figure of dread and also of caricature in the male sources. In all the texts of our period, the *kuttanis* such as Vikrala of *Kuttanimatam*, Kankali of *Samayamatrka* and Visamsila of *Srngaramanjarikatha* are described in identical terms as hideous in physical form, cruel in mind and unscrupulous in their dealings. Their very names like Yamajihva, Vikrala, Bhujangavagura and Makaradamstra invoke a sense of fear and dread in which they were held by the paramours of the *vesyas*.

V

Given the reality of the prostitute's existence in an essentially hostile patriarchal social world outside, with which it was inextricably linked,[74] there was a need to consolidate the position of the *vesyii* household. This consolidation was achieved through an intricate system which, seen from a male perspective, was based on falsehood, deception and deceit. Damodaragupta says in *Kuttanimatam*[75] *vesyas* are deceitful and this is a slander current among people (*vancakavrtta vesya ityapvado janesu yo ruda*). The prostitute functioning is derisively[76] called *Vaisika Tantra* in overwhelmingly male sources. Yasodhara[77] in his *Jayamangala* commentary refers to Svetaketu's treatise on this subject which was condensed into seven chapters, 'Vaisika' of Pancalabhabhravya being one of them. Then at the request of the *ganika* of Pataliputra, one Dattaka undertook to write about the courtesans and their lives. It is indeed surprising that women, who as a class were the only literate group of women in the society, needed male writers to record their lives. Bhoja[78] mentions Dattaka who made the secret knowledge about prostitutes known to others. Yasodhara[79] also refers

73 Ibid.: 23.

74 In *Mrcchakatikam* (Act 1.31) *vita* tells Vasantasena that the courtesan quarter is dependent on young men for help (*tarunajanasahaya*).

75 *Kuttanimatam,* verse 485.

76 Ksemendra in *Kalavilasa* satirises the prostitute strategies as their practice of sixty four arts (cited in *Ganikavrttasamgraha*: 45–47).

77 *Jayamangala Commentary:* 1.1.9–11.

78 *Srgaramanjarikatha*: 47–48.

79 *Jayamangala Commentary*: 6.3.44.

to Dattaka's efforts. Perhaps this organised male attempt to write on the secrets of prostitutes' lives was part of a concentrated attempt to disseminate knowledge about prostitutes from their own standpoint.

In order to study this 'hegemonic discourse' we need to adopt the strategy of 'reverse discourse'[80] and thus critique the hegemonic patriarchal interpretation of the prostitute's functioning. There is a need to recover the prostitute strategy as one which was self-affirming and empowering for the practitioners. In fact, if one views prostitute strategies as the way she organised and conceptualised the rules she invented, it may indicate a pattern of life-choices and values which would suggest an alternative female culture that both subverted and mocked the dominant patriarchal one.

Ksemendra's *Samayamatrka*[81] begins with a salutation to the god *Kama* and goddess *Kali,* an unusual combination in the classical sources of our period. But perhaps there is a logic here, while *Kama* is the presiding deity of love, *Karns* the fearsome goddess who drinks blood. Ksemendra in this work was aiming at warning men against the wiles or strategies of the prostitutes[82] who used all kinds of methods, even false love, to bleed their paramours of their wealth. However, unintentionally Ksemendra's satire on the prostitute's wiles ends in a documentary on the triumph of the *vesya.* Kalavati's adopted mother *kuttani* Kankali, who through her manifold brilliant strategies,[83] was able to secure the maximum gain for Kalavati.

The prostitute strategies were also subversive of the values and norms of the patriarchal social system. The prostitute association was particularly subversive of parental authority. In Isvardatta's *Dhurtavitasamvada*[84] a young man given to keeping a prostitute's company tells the *vita* that fathers are a headache personified (*murtimanasiraroga*) and he even expresses the wish that as Parasurama cleared the earth of all Ksatriyas he would like to make the world free of all fathers. This statement[85] of *pater lese majeste* is virtually unique in the classical Sanskrit sources. The *vesya's* subversion of parental authority was also a topic of lament in Damodargupta's *Kuttanimatam.*[86] Another interesting example which illustrates this analysis comes from the fourth tale of *Srngaramanjarikatha.*[87] The clever courtesan Devadatta had an extraordinary capacity to plan strategy and get results. Through her clever ploys she was able to get her paramour Suradharman to yield his secret. Suradharman, was in the habit of hiding it by always saying that his 'mother' alone knows everything. After Devadatta was successful she asked Suradharman 'Ah, does your mother know or do I know?' Folding his hands Suradharman said 'Mother does not know anything, you know everything'. Devadatta then crisply replied 'If I know everything then out with you', and she kicked him out of her house.

---

80 Bell, *Reading, Writing and Rewriting the Prostitute Body*: 14.

81 *Samayamatrka*: 1.1–2.

82 Ibid.: 1.3 and 8.128.

83 Ibid.: 8.127

84 *Srngarahata: Caturbhani*: 71–73.

85 Ibid.: 71

86 *Kuttanimatam,* verses 411–24.

87 *Srngaramanjarikatha*: 40.

Fritz Blackwell[88] notes about the prostitute strategy that 'perhaps most dangerous about her is the fact that, her *dharma* is not passive, built upon devotion to husband and family like the wife's; it is quite active, designed by its very nature to destroy the man, at least financially, and even his family if necessary'.[89] It was this dangerous and subversive potential of the prostitute strategy which made men warn 'respectable' women of patriarchy against it. Yasodhara[90] quoting Katyayana in his *Jayamangala* commentary talks of acts (*vesa*) which are fit for prostitutes (*vesya*) but not for the women of the household (*kulayosita*). Because of these acts the former are called *vesyas.* It is thus obvious that men feared the self-affirming power of these strategies and were eager to ensure that at least they were not practised by their household women so as to keep the patriarchal authority within the *grha* intact.

Prostitute strategies also militated against many other cherished values of patriarchy. For instance, the prostitute view of pregnancy and childbirth (although it emerged from the prostitute strategy to remain physically attractive for male clients) was completely opposed to the patriarchal view. In K~emendra's *Samayamatrkii*[91] the bawd expresses the view that giving birth (*prasava*) is a curse (*srapa*) for a woman's youth (*yauvana*) and the beauty of her body parts like breasts. But if she is condemnatory of one of the most cherished goals of patriarchy it is because she sees this as something that completely circumscribes woman's personal growth. In fact the bawd contrasts[92] the attractiveness of the *vesya* who knows the art of dressing up and of enlivening the gathering by her smiling (*satatasmitasu*) demeanour. The *kulavadhu* on the other hand are seen as constantly pregnant (*nityaprasuti*) with their youth (*yauvana*) destroyed (*hata*). They have no taste for the pleasures of cultured gatherings (*gosthivilasasarasakeli niradaresu*). Although this different socialisation of the prostitutes did not radicalise their status in the wider society, it did provide a space and platform from which to mock the existing positions, roles and ideologies of patriarchy.

If prostitutes were castigated for their wiles the 'normal' women under patriarchy were not spared either. They were at the receiving end of the male vitriol for their *stri-sva bhava.* The entire range of patriarchal Brahmanical literature has condemned women for being sinful, dishonest, heartless and the root of all evils.[93] This campaign of misogyny against *triya caritra* or womanly character was used by the patriarchs to keep women psychologically subjugated. The prostitutes on the other hand used opprobrium against them to their own advantage to create greater space for themselves. They had little incentive to obey the ethics of the dominant culture to which they were only liminally connected. So they invented their own standards and lived by their own directives to achieve greater economic and social independence for themselves.

[88] Fritz Blackwell, 'Misogyny and Philogyny: Bifurcation and Ambivalence of the Stereotypes of the Courtesan and the Mother in Literary Tradition', *Joumal of South Asian Literature,* vol. XII, nos. 3–4, 1977: 39.
[89] Ibid.
[90] *Jayamangala Commentry*, 6.3.45.
[91] *Samayamatrka*, 8.101.
[92] Ibid.: 8.93–94.
[93] Sternbach, *Ganikavrttasamgraha*: 74–75.

VI

In the hierarchy of '*trivarga*' (i.e., *dharma*, *artha*, *kama*) for the prostitutes, *artha* was the highest goal[94] and this was a goal that they shared with the king of the realm. In Dandin's *Dasakumaracarita*[95] it is said that the *kuladharma* of the *vesya* was to assiduously accumulate riches. In the play *Mrcchakatikam*[96] there is a fairly detailed description of the courtesan Vasantasena's household which was run on a lavish scale. Maitreya while admiring it did not quite know whether to call it *ganikagrha* or *Kuberabhavana*. In the eyes of the contemporary observers, the prostitute's command over her own resources 'masculinised' her. As Carudatta observes in *Mrcchakatikam*[97] 'through (the absence of) money a man becomes a woman; and she who is a woman becomes a man also through (the possession of) money' (*arthata puruso nari ya nari sarthatah pumana*). It was this recognition of the prostitute's status and ownership of wealth that resulted in their acknowledgement as autonomous subjects for the purpose of taxation as well as discipline and punishment. This acknowledgement was also a recognition of the fact that prostitutes had 'agency'. Prostitutes in antiquity were virtually the only group of women who by themselves were dealing with the state without any male mediation. *Nammayasundarikatha,*[98] a twelfth century text, refers to the state receiving 25–30 per cent of the prostitute's income as tax. Since the state was a beneficiary of tax income from to-e prostitute, it had a vested interest in perpetuating the matriarchal feature of the prostitute household.[99] *Narada Smrti*[100] also states that the ornaments of the prostitute cannot be confiscated (they are like the tools of the trade).

If the ownership of resources 'masculinised' the prostitute vis-à-vis the state and ensured her recognition as an autonomous subject, even within the household itself prostitutes were recognised as the breadwinners of the family. Thus, in the absence of the earning of the *vesya* Kamamanjari her entire family (*kutumba*), said her mother in *Dasakumarcarita*[101] would be without support and sustenance. In Bhoja's *Srngaramanjarikatha*[102] Makaradamstra says, 'You (i.e., paramour) have killed my daughter, by whose favour will this family live now? How will I live? You have destroyed the head of the family'. Dominance of women (apart from the fact that sisters/daughters alone inherited) within the prostitute household was in a large measure due to the very nature of its economic base. Household property was largely

[94] *Jayamangala Commentary*: 6.6.5.

[95] *Dasakunaracarita*: 174.

[96] *Mrcchakatikam,* Act IV.

[97] Ibid., Act III.27.

[98] Cited in Kumkum Roy, *Women in Early Indian Societies*: 203.

[99] Thus, we are told in the *Arthasastra,* (ed. and tr.) R.P. Kangle, pt. 2, Delhi, 1992, that a courtesan's establishment could not be inherited by her son. On her death or retirement her daughter or sister alone could take her place. Ibid.: 2.27.2–3. The *Arthasastra* (2.27.11) also says that a prostitute cannot give her ornaments, which was the main form in which the prostitutes owned wealth, to anyone but her mother.

[100] *Narada Smrti,* (tr.) J. Jolly, Bharatiya Publishing House, 1978: XVIII.10.

[101] *Dasakumaracarita*: 137.

[102] *Srngaramanjarikatha*: 40.

earned income acquired in the form of cash, goods and more importantly jewellery, and it was through women that the prostitute household acquired these.

In the *Jayamangala* commentary Yasodhara[103] defined prostitute as always bejewelled (*sadalamkrta*). In *Mrcchakatikam* Vasantasena is depicted as well-ornamented. In the same play Dhiita the *pativrata* wife of Carudatta on the other hand proudly claims[104] that 'my husband alone is my ornament' (*aryaputra eva mamabharana*). This statement is significant not because it tells us about the wife's loyalty to her husband, but because it draws attention to the wife's lack of economic rights. Even their *stridhana* had to be shelled out to the husband in need (Dhuta gives her own precious jewel necklace to her husband in need). Interestingly enough, since the play *Mrcchakatikam* aimed at depicting the transformation of *ganika* Vasantasena into a *kulavadhu,* we see the metamorphosis occurring with Vasantasena giving up her ornaments (i.e., her pride in her ownership of wealth). In the play[105] her lover Carudatta's son refuses to recognise her as 'mother' because his mother does not wear ornaments. Vasantasena not only takes off her jewels, she also fills the toy clay cart of the little boy with them. In that moment of maternal generosity Vasantasena transgresses the *kula dharma* of *ganika.* This act transforms her psychologically and symbolically thus preparing for her entry into the patriarchal household as wife. The significance of this event in the play is evident from the fact that it gives the play its title *Mrcchakatikam* ('the little clay cart').

In Damodaragupta's *Kuttanimatam*[106] *vesya* is described as *ratisilpajivika* ('one who has made a craft of sex and as a form of livelihood'). But In this process of commodifying her desire (*kama*) she, unlike the *kulavadhus,* managed to acquire control over her own *dharma* and *artha.* It is ironical that women whose socio-sexual status was not legitimate were more easily recognisable as economically independent actors. Both textual and epigraphic records attest to the status of a *vesya* as independent owners of resources and this gives them the autonomy to make religious donations in their own capacity. An eighth century epigraph of the Chalukyas of Badami refers to a *vesya* making donations to a temple.[107] In Yasodhara's commentary[108] we get a reference to the *vesya* initiating similar donations.

VII

There is a tendency to view a prostitute merely as an erotic being. But there is more to her than a body on *sale-pa1Jyabhutam sariram*, as *vita* alleges in the *Mrcchakatikam.*[109] The courtesan class (Le., *ga1Jikas*) among the prostitutes were more famous for their cultural

[103] *Jayamangala Commentary*: 6.1.7.
[104] *Mrcchakatikam,* Act VI.
[105] Ibid., Act VI.
[106] *Kuttanimatam,* verse 637.
[107] Cited in L.K. Tripathi (ed.), *Position and Status of Women in Ancient India,* Varanasi, 1988: 339.
[108] *Jayamangala Commentary*: 6.6.22.
[109] *Mrcchakatikam,* Act 1.31

accomplishments than for their erotic appeal. It was intellectual and artistic accomplishments (the proficiency in 64 arts) which made a common prostitute into a courtesan (*ganika*). She became, says Yasodhara in her commentary,[110] worthy of respect from even the king (*rag-yapujita*). The connoisseurs showered praise on her (*gunavadina samstuta kalakausalamiti prasansita*) and she even became a teacher and was idolised by those who wanted to learn from her (*prathaniya kalopadesarthina*). On the other hand a common *vesya* like *rupajiva* was described by Yasodhara[111] as one who was distinguished only by beauty (*rupasya prad-hana*) and not by her skills (*kala*); obviously she was no more than an ordinary streetwalker.

In antiquity prostitutes were those women who played an important role as creators and sustainers of culture. This association of prostitutes with an educated, cultured dispensation was a longstanding one. Rajasekhara in his *Kavyamimamsa*[112] explicitly states that *ganikas* are among those women who are proficient in *sastra* and poetry. Bhoja in *Srngaramanjarikatha*[113] while describing *vesyd* Srngaramanjari states that 'she is faultless in local dialects, civilized in talks, . . . bold in questioning and answering different kinds of riddles... unrivalled in composing stanzas, well-enlightened in essays and treatises, excellent in composing poetry; foremost in composing *gathas*'. Undoubtedly prostitutes were the presiding divas of the cultured world and this fact is acknowledged in Bharata's *Natyasastra*[114] as well, who states that 'one excelling (*visesayet*) in all the arts (*kalii*) is called a gallant (*vaisika*)'. Or he is so called because of his dealings with the courtesans (*vesyopacara*). This association of cultured men with the courtesans is significant. He is *vaisika* for he is cultured, but he is also a cul-tured one for he keeps the company of courtesans, who by implication were themselves the epitome of culture. Srinivasan's[115] sociological study of the *devadasi* household in southern India reveals that *devadasis* were permitted to read and write and pursue vocational skills traditionally denied to all other women in India. And what was most important was that their knowledge was not for private consumption but had a public platform. A fact which gave them both money and prestige. As Devangana Desai[116] also notes, it was to give a public platform to the art of the *devadasis* that structures such as dance halls (*natyamandapas*) and music halls (*sabhamandapas*) were added to the temples in the early medieval period.

Unlike the *kulastri* who had to have a low voice[117] or be altogether silent, the prostitute is marked by an articulate voice. In most works of poetics belonging to our period, in the delineation of the character of *sadharana stri* there is emphasis on her articulate tongue. *Dasarupaka* of Dhananjaya[118] describes her as a *ganika* whose attributes are knowledge and accomplishments (*kala*), chutzpah and eloquence (*pragalbhata*) and a crafty cleverness (*dhurtata*). Although in the sub-classification of the *astanayikas* in the text on the poetics

---

[110] *Jayamangala Commentary*: 1.3.17–18.

[111] Ibid: 6.5.29.

[112] *Kavyamimamsa*, (ed. and tr) Gangasagar Rai, Varanasi, 1977: ch. 10, 138.

[113] *Srngaramanjarikatha*: 15.

[114] *Natyasastra*: 25.1

[115] Amrit Srinivasan, *Reforms or Conformity?*: 190.

[116] Devangana Desai, *Erotic Sculptures of India: A Socio-cultural Study,* Bombay, 1975: 155.

[117] *Kuttanimatam,* verse 848.

[118] *Dasarupaka,* (ed. and tr.) Srinivas Sastry, Meerut, 1969: 2.21: 148.

we get a *pragalbha* type even among the *non-samanya nayikas,* the logic of her delineation is different. This *pragalbha* is one who is at the full development of youth and is, therefore, no longer marked by the restraining force of bashfulness,[119] which is the inherent trait of girls of good families. Eloquence of speech is not her inherent trait, which is that of the *ganikas.* This is evident from the fact that in literary works, the 'clever speech' of the courtesans has a proverbial status even if non-prostitutes were resorting to it. This was how the speech of princess VegavatI was described in Buddhasvamin's *Brhatkathaslokasamgraha*[120] Sternbach[121] also quotes a Sanskrit verse which illustrates this analysis. It says 'In the presence of a sovereign, among scholars and on meeting with the courtesans even an eloquent man is embarrassed for fear intimidates his heart'.

Not only were the prostitutes articulate as a rule, they were in many cases grouped among those women in the classical Sanskrit literature who were entitled to speak the 'masculine language', that is, Sanskrit. In the classical dramas courtesans are those rare female characters who made use of Sanskrit. In Sudraka's *Mrcchakatikam ganika* Vasantasena speaks in Sanskrit. Although in Act III of the play we find Brahmana Maitreya making fun of women who read Sanskrit, in Act IV we get a specific reference to Vasantasena speaking in Sanskrit (*samskrtmasritya*) with Maitreya. Thus, Bharata[122] underlines that 'for the pleasure of all kinds of people, and in connection with the practice of arts, the courtesans are to be assigned Sanskritic recitation which can be easily managed'.

Bhoja in *Sarasvatikanthabharana*[123] described a *ganika* as *ubhaya catuhsastikalavida.* In *Srngaramanjarikatha*[124] the *vesya* Srgaramanjari is described as distinguished in 64 arts. In *Kuttanimatam*[125] we are told about a prostitute's proficiency in 64 arts (*catuhsastikarmakusalanam*). Yasodhara in his *Jayamangala* commentary describes both these groups of 64 arts. The first is the 64 *angavidyas;*[126] while some among these were purely aesthetic arts like dance, singing, painting, others were meant for intellectual development. For instance, accomplishments[127] such as *Kavyasamasyapuranam* (completing the verse from a given single line) *pratimala* (capping verses) *prahelika* (riddles) *duroacakyoga* (expressing that which is difficult in words or sense) *pustakavacanam* (book reading) *malicchitvikalpa* (using synonymous words of the *mlecchabhasa*) *desabhasavigyanam* (using *desya* words to make known that which is unknown) *dharanamatrka* (remembering heard books) *kavyakripa* (composing poems) *abhidhanakosa* (knowledge of dictionaries) *chandogyanam* (knowing the metrical works) *kriyakalpa* (knowing poetics) and *vrksa ayurveda* (arbori horticulture). Their expertise in this branch of *ayurveda* shows *ganikas* as healing women with knowledge

---

119 V.R. Raghavan, *Srngaramanjari of Saint Akbarshah*: 22.
120 *Brhatkathaslokasamgraha,* canto XV.46.
121 Ludwick Sternbach, *Vesya: Synonyms and Aphorisms,* vol. 5: 16.
122 *Natyasastra*, 18.40.
123 Cited in *Srngaramanjarikatha*: 93–94.
124 Ibid.: 15.
125 *Kuttanimatam,* verse 499.
126 *Jayamangala Commentary*: 1.3.17–18.
127 E. Venkatasubbiah and E. Muller, 'The Kalas', *Journal of the Royal Asiatic Society,* 1914: 351–67.

of the medicinal properties of various roots and plants. In Dandin's *Dasakumaracarita*[128] the *vesya* Kamamanjari's mother while listing the subjects in which she carefully trained her daughter from childhood refers to writing and conversation (*lipigyanavacanakausala*) and to some extent in grammar, logic and philosophy. It is thus apparent that there was an intellectual context to a prostitute's formal training. In Hemacandra's *Prabandhacintamani,* a twelfth century text, a prostitute is described as 'a storehouse of intellect' and for whom the king considered 'a kingdom would be too small a present'[129] Interestingly in *Mrcchakatikam* the playwright Sudraka while introducing himself[130] talks of the manifold skills in which he has proficiency. He knows the Vedas, mathematics and *kalavaisiki* which was a reference to the 64 *anga vidyas.* Thus, we see that even if others such as King Sudraka himself refer to their being knowledgeable in that branch they also give it the appellation of *vaisika.* The second group of 64 arts in which prostitutes were trained were the samprayogika which Vatsyayana mentions in the second book of the *Kamasutra.* Prostitutes, by mastering it, gained proficiency in the science of erotics. In fact, it is ironical that women of such learning and accomplishment were given the appellation of *samanya* or *sadharana stri.*

This confluence of knowledge, sexuality and spirituality[131] in the personality of the prostitute in the historical period helps us recover the prostitute from the image of a mere 'sexual body' meant for male satisfaction. The above analysis shows that courtesans functioned outside the restrictions which patriarchy imposed on other women (wives and daughters). The prostitutes could function within those public spaces which were ordinarily preserved for males-teaching, conversation and also freer sexual interaction. It was the power of this well-rounded personality of the prostitutes which was acknowledged even in a rabidly anti-prostitute text like Ksemendra's *Samayamatrka*[132] which states that 'courtesans ravish men just as the sweet speech of poets ravishes people (i.e., they speak beautifully). They are attractive creatures, possess excellent qualities, are carefully anointed, are exciting and well-disposed, give men through their arts the highest pleasure and satisfaction, and offer ever new enjoyment'. The attraction of prostitutes for the paramour was thus much more than sexual; this was the attraction of her personality in which her education played an important role. In Bhoja's *Srngaramanjarikatha*[133] bawd Vi~amsl1a advises *vesya* Srngaramanjari thus: 'Always be careful in propitiating the minds of others. For it is possible to please a person only if his mind has been attracted, and he only whose mind has been propitiated dedicates his wealth and his life'. This would question the whole notion of prostitutes as an 'erotic body' meant for sexual consumption.

---

128 *Dasakumaracarita:* 132–33.

129 Cited in *Kathasaritsagar,* vol. III: 207, fn. 2.

130 *Mrcchakatikam,* Act 1

131 As *devadasis,* prostitutes were particularly auspicious. It is important to remember that in ancient India they were the only class of women who were as near to the deities in the temples as the male priest. Parasher and Naik ('The Temple Girls of Medieval Karnataka': 76) in the context of the early medieval temples of Karnataka point out that an integral and necessary aspect of any ritual to be performed daily in the temples, was that pertaining to the *rang-abhoga* (pleasure of entertainment) and *angabhoga* (physical enjoyment) of the deity. This was performed by the *patras* and *sulas* (i.e., *devadasis*), respectively.

132 *Samayamatrka,* epilogue 1.

133 *Srngaramanjarikatha*: 23.

VIII

The prostitute's sexuality is the most problematised area of scholarly investigation. When we investigate various terms that stand for prostitutes[134] we find appellations like *asati*, *kulata*, *svairini* (all these meaning promiscuous women), *abhisarika* (women on rendezvous), *dhrsta* (impudent one), *lanjika* (adulteress), *lilavati* (flirtatious woman), *didhisu* (twice married), ete. It is thus obvious that patriarchal ideology was intolerant of any form of female sexuality that denoted their 'agency', that is to say, strategy whereby autonomy of desire and behaviour was asserted and maintained. Therefore, all such women under patriarchy were categorised as prostitutes. The *Manusmrti*[135] as also its commentator Medhatithi forbid Brahmanas to accept food from *ganas* and *ganikas*. This homology had a logic. Historically, the *gana* form of state formation was associated with women whose sexuality was not constrained by patriarchal norms.[136] The formation of a patriarchal, Brahmanical, monarchical state not only marginalised *ganas* but its 'free women' too, who ended up as stigmatised *sudras*[137] on the obverse side of the brahmanical social set up. The *ganikas* (women of *ganas,* by now prostitutes) were presented in the Brahmanical-dominated sources as defiled impure ones. In *Kuttanimatam*[138] it is said that for a prostitute the consideration of *varna* (colour) is only for cosmetic purposes (*prasadhana*) and it (i.e., *varna*/caste) is not a consideration for sexual intercourse (*ratiprasangesu*). In other words, the 'caste' of the paramour was of no consequence. Prostitutes were thus those women who were not only sexually promiscuous but whose sexuality could not be harnessed towards procreation in the correct *varIJa* order. For patriarchy the non-marital non-reproductive and libidinous female body was perceived as dangerous. As against this deviant, dangerous 'whore', there was the virtuous woman or *sati* whose sexuality was a reproductive one and it also eschewed any active sexual desire and pleasure. Moreover, for many radical feminists, prostitute sexuality cannot be understood as a free, liberated one. Scholars have argued[139] that prostitution supports 'objectification' of women's sexuality and it is linked to violence against them. Here the prostitute body is seen as an 'abused' body. The sources of our study amply demonstrate violence against prostitutes. In *Mrcchakatikam*, *ganika* Vasantasena was strangled by the king's brother-in-law for repulsing his overtures. On regaining consciousness Vasantasena[140] perceived her state as one that befits the profession of a prostitute (*yatasadrsam vesabhavasya*). In the eleventh tale of Bhoja's *Srngaramanjarikatha, vesya* Malayasundari's paramour Pratapasimha physically abused her, and instead of being punished by the king he got away

[134] Ludwick Sternbach, *Vesya*: *Synonyms and Aphorisms.*

[135] *Manusmrti,* (tr.) Wendy Doniger and Brian K. Smith, Penguin, 1992: 4.209.

[136] Shalini Shah, 'Gender and Sexuality in Ancient Punjab: A Case Study of the *Karna Paroa* in the *Mahabharata'*, paper presented at the Institute of Punjab Studies, Chandigarh, November 1998: 3.

[137] This is the term used for prostitutes in *Kuttanimatam,* verses 440, 797.

[138] *Kuttanimatam,* verse 310.

[139] S. Jackson and S. Scott, *Feminism and Sexuality*: *A Reader,* Edinburgh, 1996: 342.

[140] *Mrcchakatikam,* Act VIII.

scot-free,[141] and it was *vesya* Malayasundari who became an object of ridicule. Prostitutes were also vulnerable because of their movable wealth such as ornaments. *Samayamatrka*[142] refers to prostitutes (*panyangana*) being vulnerable in every city to those who covet their jewels (*bhusanalubdhe*). Although women in general could be at the receiving end of male violence, prostitutes were particularly vulnerable because they were the only women who were visible in the public sphere. Moreover, while men in the private sphere could dominate women's/wife's sexuality, the prostitute's sexuality was only accessible on purchase in the public sphere (i.e., the market).

If in the patriarchal discourse the deviant prostitute sexuality is not 'normal', for radical feminists it is a 'dominated' sexuality and it is therefore to be categorised as negative. Pateman[143] argues that prostitute sexuality is a public recognition of men as sexual masters; it puts submission on sale as a commodity in the market. Prostitution, she states, is an inherently gendered practice in which women are constructed as the sexual servants of men and the buying of sexual service is defined as a benefit for men. Luce Irigaray[144] also sees prostitution as sex which is not one's own and is constructed according to the desire of the other. A prostitute is, in Irigaray's words, merely an 'obliging prop' for the enactment of men's fantasies. Thus, Irigaray explicitly links the prostitute body to 'phallic' (i.e., male defined) female sexuality. For Mackinnon[145] since heterosexuality institutionalised male sexual dominance and female sexual submission there can be no scope for prostitute 'agency' in her commercial sexual encounters. But Mackinnon in her totalising theory[146] tends to ignore the existence of the multiplicity of desires some of which do not conform to the requirements of the masculinist system. Liberal feminists like Gayle Rubin and Carol S. Vance,[147] however, argue against treating any kind of sexual practice as either 'bad' or 'abnormal'. Heterosexual coitus itself cannot be taken as a mark of women's sexual subordination for even their own sexual choices are also often exercised. Both Rubin and Vance have examined the issue of 'pleasure' and 'agency' in sex work.

A careful analysis of the literary sources of our period would reinforce the liberal feminist view regarding prostitute sexuality. If one juxtaposes the socialisation of the *kulavadhu* (a household woman) against the *varavadhu* (a prostitute) the latter appears far removed from 'domination'. The notion of shame (*lajja*) is an important element in controlling female sexuality under patriarchy. Here the female body is controlled and regulated both at the level of the individual and the social body. In fact, patriarchy rests on the foundation of the controlled female body. Along with purity and pollution, honour and shame are two of the most

[141] While *Arthasastra* (2.27.14–17; 4.13.38–39) and also *Narada Smrti* (6.19) do provide for state action against those who rape, disfigure or kill the prostitute, the punishment is never very heavy (mainly in the form of fines). On the other hand, if a prostitute killed a cliem, the *Arthasastra* (2.27.22) states that she was to be awarded the death sentence either by burning or being drowned alive.

[142] *Samayamatrka*: 8.35.

[143] Cited in Christine Overall, 'What's Wrong with Prostitution? Evaluating Sex Work', *SIGNS*: *Journal of Women and Culture in Society,* 17(4), 1992: 722.

144 Cited in Shannon Bell, *Reading, Writing and Rewriting the Prostitute Body*: 74, 88.

[145] Catherine MacKinnon, 'Feminism, Marxism, Method and State: An Agenda for Theory', *SIGNS*, 7(3), 1982: 515–44.

[146] Shannon Bell, *Reading, Writing and Rewriting the Prostitute Body*: 80.

[147] Carol S. Vance, *Pleasure and Danger*: *Exploring Female Sexuality,* London, 1984.

prominent cultural ideologies of brahmanical patriarchy, and have played an important role in controlling women's behaviour and the spaces that they can occupy, as also the limits of their socio-sexual relations. In the *bahya* and the *abhyantara* (a woman of the inner apartment) classification of the *nayikas* we see the operation of the purdah system. Sociologically speaking[148] *purdah* delimits the spheres that women can legitimately occupy. *Kuttanimatam*[149] tells us that the veil (*vadanavrttijalika*) was what distinguished respectable (*arya*) ladies from ordinary (*anarya*) ones. These ordinary women were usually prostitutes. In *Samayamatrka,*[150] Ksemendra refers to a mischievous courtesan who passed herself off as the daughter of a high-ranking royal officer by half-covering her face. In *Dhurtavitasamvada*,[151] a *kulavadhu* s veil is tellingly referred to as *lajja-pata* (i.e., what covers the shame). A woman of a good family not only had to have a veil (*avagunthana*) on their faces but they were also required, says *Kuttanimatam*,[152] to have humility, a low voice and slow movements. The *bahya* on the other hand was without the veil. In *Mrcchakatikam*, Vasantasena was without a veil till the king's announcement declared her to be the bride (*vadhu*) of Carudatta, and immediately[153] upon this announcement Sarvilaka veiled her. The system of the veil also affected the way the sexuality of women was perceived. In the *Natyasastra*[154] it is said about the courtesan[155] that when she goes out to meet her lover she decorates her body with various ornaments and goes forth to meet him with (a display 00 passion and joy. The abhyantara *nayika*[156] on the other hand, walked the street covering her face with a veil, and walked timidly with her limbs contracted, and very often she turned her face away and looked back. According to the *Natyasastra*,[157] a *bahya nayika* could be depicted displaying her love: 'She expresses her passion by casting side-long glances (*kataksa*), touching her ornaments, itching ears, scratching the ground with her toes, revealing the breasts and the navel, cleaning the nails and gathering her hair', whereas in a high-born lady the signs of love are to be depicted differently:[158] 'She looks continuously with blooming eyes, conceals her smile, speaks slowly and with a downcast face, gives a reply with a smile, conceals her sweat and appearance, has throbbing lips and is trembling'. Not only was a prostitute allowed greater freedom of expression of her sentiments, but was also entitled to greater freedom as far as her bodily gestures were concerned. Bharata notes in the *Natyasastra*[159] that higher class women could not be shown using cosmetics (unguents and collyrium), painting the body, coyly handling their breasts and combing their hair. They also could not be shown dressed poorly (*apavrta*) or wearing only one piece of garment (*ekavastra*). They could also not use colours for their

148 Hanna Papanek and Gail Minault (eds), *Separate Worlds*: *Studies of Purdah in South Asia,* Delhi, 1982.
149 *Kuttanimatam,* verse 895.
150 *Samayamatrka*: 2.54.
151 *Srngarahata*: *Caturbhani*: 74.
152 *Kuttanimatam,* verse 848
153 *Mrcchakatikam,* Act X.
154 *Natyasastra*: 24.225–28.
155 Ibid.: 24.226.
156 Ibid.: 24.227.
157 Ibid.: 24.163–65.
158 Ibid.: 24.166–67.
159 Ibid.: 24.240–42.

lips. This was done to distinguish them from women of inferior types who, with a view to exposing their charms, dressed scantily and took pleasure in using cosmetics.

The entire notion of 'shame acquired a totally different meaning for the prostitute'. In the *Kuttanimatam*[160] we are told that 'for a *vesya* covering the lower part (*jaghanavarana*) is not out of "shame" but to arouse desire in others'. Prostitutes were also quite open in discussing their sexual experiences with all types of clients. In one such comic verse[161] a *vesya* tells others how when she closed her eyes in the ecstasy of sexual pleasure her inexperienced paramour ran away from her thinking her to be dead.

The above data would lend itself to the interpretation, that as compared to the circumscribed sexuality of the women in patriarchy, the prostitute enjoyed greater freedom of sexual expression. We get an interesting example of *Madanamancuka* in *Brhatkathaslokasamgraha*[162] who was the daughter of a *vesya.* She took the vow of constancy and thus transformed as an ideal *pativrata*; she guarded any access to her body like a Sita.

Much is said about a prostitute's sexuality being slavishly commanded by the man, who as client, pays for it. But if one contrasts the location of the man's wife in the inner apartment (*antabpura*) and that of the *vesya's* life outside, we observe a binary spatial structure where the former is completely closed and its occupants, the wife/wives, owe complete fidelity to their husband. The husband-wife tie was one which did not necessarily depend on the existence of an erotic relationship in order to constitute itself. The sexual relations between the two were carried on the basis of a statutory relationship that empowered the husband to 'demand' from his wife all services including sexual ones. The *pativrata* ideology ensured their compliance. Within the confines of the *antahpura* the marital partners were also hierarchically placed. While *kulavadhus* were thus relegated to a private sphere and their status was in being *asuryasprsya*, the *ganikas* who were significantly enough called *prakasanan*"[163] were the women par excellence of the public sphere. Vasantasena is appreciatively described as *nagarasyabhusanam* and *nagarsri* in *Mrcchakatikam.*[164] In *Dasakumaracarita,*[165] *vesya* Kamamanjari was similarly described as an ornament of the city of Campa. These *ganikas* and their paramours met in common and open spaces like brothels, gardens or the temples of the God *Kama.* All these were spatially open areas in which everyone moved about freely. Freedom of space also dictated the freedom of choice. One could not in such a case exercise statutory authority. A *ganika* was thus free to accept or reject any proposition. Vasantasena exercised this prerogative quite tellingly when she rejected the king's brother-in-law for the impoverished Carudatta. In order to secure her consent no *pativrata* ideology could come to the rescue. Her favours (which many were in a position to refuse) had to be secured by persuasion and very often this persuasion took the form of gifts that could outshine those offered by the rivals.

---

[160] *Kuttanimatam,* verse 306.

[161] Ibid., verse 399.

[162] *Brhatkathaslokasamgraha,* canto XIV.113.

[163] *Mrcchakatikam,* Act III.7.

[164] Mrcchakatikam, Act VIII.23; VIII.39.

[165] *Dasakumaracarita*: 130.

The prostitute's autonomy introduced an element of male anxiety in the *vesya-client* relationship. It was this precariousness of the relation which was most often used by the *vesya* to milk her clients. Luce Irigaray[166] sees the prostitute as a 'speaking subject' who actively intervenes in the male exchange economy (which had the exchange of women at its foundation). A prostitute took herself to the market and named her price, and in so doing she disrupted the male exchange economy (since she was breaking the silent exchange of women and was thereby no longer a passive participant in the exchange). Although it is true that a prostitute negotiated sexuality only as a commercial exchange inside the male exchange economy, but she did negotiate it. Should the prostitutes then be seen as an empowered lot (her sexuality being used as a bargaining chip), who had the power to set the terms of her sexuality and demand substantial payment for her time and skills?

In the sources of our period the sexual life of the prostitute-the unlimited freedom and the unbounded pleasure of intercourse with any man they like-is often portrayed in a positive light. Ksemendra in *Kalavilasa*,[167] says that because of this independence they (i.e., prostitutes) are envied by some women who think sighing that 'fortunate are courtesans (*vesya dhanyeti*) who enjoy life without restrictions with many young men' (*bahuvidhatarunanirgala sambhoga sukharthabhogini*).

Prostitutes are described as proficient in providing sexual pleasures (*kalakelikusala*) and this quality of theirs became proverbial.[168] We find many aphorisms which state that a good wife is one who behaves in bed like a *vesya* (*sayane tu vesya*). This notion of *vesya* as a seductive woman par excellence does attribute a degree of agency to her. In fact, the free sexual behaviour or sexual experience of the prostitutes is seen as giving greater pleasure than consorting with wives. This is expressed very pithily in Isvardatt's *Dhurtavitasamvada*[169] where a young man tells *vita* that he is about to be married. *Vita* expresses surprise that the young man wants to leave *vesya mahapatha* for *kulavadhu kumargena.* The *vita* further asks how can pleasure be had from consorting with *kulavadhus* who are blind to sexual pleasures (*jatyandham suratesu*), who talk inaudibly (*antaramukhabhasini*), who are so shy that they have never seen their own lower part (*jaghana*), and are no better than a yoked animal (*strirupabadhampasu*)? These descriptions contrast the sexuality of a *sati* and a whore, and the picture that emerges is one that attributes greater agency and even an element of pleasure to the sexuality of the whore. The prostitute sexuality is thus not so much a 'deviant' sexuality; rather she has to be seen as an 'erotic teacher'.

Far from being a mere 'obliging prop' for the enactment of male fantasies we find from our sources that prostitutes were taking pleasure in their sexual encounters. In. *Brhatkathaslokasamgraha*[170] we are told about *vesya* Gangadatta who openly desires and asks for access to the body of the hero Sannudasa. In fact the sexual encounter between Gangadatta and Sannudasa[171] is described as a mutual exchange of bodies (*sariram*) on

---

[166] Cited in Shannon Bell, *Reading, Writing and Rewriting the Prostitute Body*: 89–91.
[167] *Ganikavrttasamgraha*: 65.
[168] Ibid.: 12.
[169] *Srngarahata*: *Caturbhani*: 74.
[170] *Brhatkathaslok*
[171] Ibid.: XVIII.73–75.

equal terms. In *Kuttanimatam*,[172] we see a *vesya* performing *purusayita* or *viparitarata* form of coitus where the woman rides the man. Yasodhara in his *Jayamangala* Commentary[173] refers to many patrons (*vita*) uniting with one *vesya* and this is referred to as *gosthipari-grha*. It is important to note that one woman uniting with many men is not considered by Vatsyayana and his commentator Yasodhara as an acceptable social practice.[174] In book two of the *Kamasutra*[175] where Vatsyayana described various sexual practices including orgies, he attributes such a practice as taking place in a woman's kingdom (*gramanarivisaye* and *strirajya*) and Vahika[176] Yasodhara[177] refers to the men who partner women in these orgies as those who live like kept women of *anta/:lpura* and are not independent.

The above descriptions would put a question mark on the notion of prostitute sexuality as a completely male dominated one, i.e. the view that prostitution caters to and reinforces the idea of male desires and where macho sexual desires are given primacy. One could argue that a feature of the paramour's sexual activity with the prostitute is the opportunity it would provide to men to escape conventional heterosexual roles (*gosthiparigrha* and *purusayita* are examples of this) which places heavy emphasis on masculine prowess and domination. In fact, *vesavasa* or the prostitute quarters were those liminal places where socially dominant sexual relations and socially acceptable sexual practices could be transgressed. Prostitute quarters became privileged spaces for experimentation with censured sexual behaviour.

Irigaray sees prostitute sexuality as 'phallic' (or male defined) sexuality, but prostitutes could at times assert sexual autonomy. In the sources of our period we get one indirect reference to prostitute linkage with lesbian love. The *Mitaksara* commentary on *Yajnavalkyasmrti*,[178] quotes the *Skandapurana* as saying that prostitutes constitute a separate caste springing from the apsara Pancacuda. In the *Anusasana Parva* of the *Mahabharata*[179] it is the self-same Pancacuda *apsara* who talks of sapphic love among women.

IX

Although most writers on poetics talk in terms of the feigned love of the prostitute, Rudrabhana in *Srngaratilaka*, who like his predecessors (Bharata and Vatsyayana) accepted *samanya* as one of the *nayikas*, makes an important observation that though some consider her (*samanya*) interested only in money and not in love, he is of the view that she too as a woman has her love without which hers will become a case of the semblance of sentiment (*rasabhasa*).[180]

---

172 *Kuttanimatam*, verses 389, 575.

173 *Jayamangala Commentary*: 6.6.44; 2.6.48.

174 In none of the narrative or *kavya* texts is this mentioned.

175 *Kamasutra*: 2.6.45.

176 These are the marginal areas of the brahmanical patriarchy where 'normal' practices are suspended. Although sometimes (*Jayamangala Commentary*: 2.6.38, 48) the royal women of *pracya* land indulge in this practice it is done only in secret (*pracchadayanti*).

177 *Jayamangala Commentary*: 2.6.45.

178 Manjushree, *The Position of Women in the Yajnavalkyasmrti*, Delhi, 1990: 52.

179 Shalini Shah, The Making of Womanhood: Gender Relations in the Mahabharata, Delhi, 1995: 56.

180 R. Raghavan, *Srngaramanjari of Saint Akbarshah*: 20.

Visvanatha in his *Sahityadarpana*[181] also attributes occasional real love to a *vesya* (*kvapi satyanuragini*).

In spite of these exceptional views a prostitute's love in the sources is mainly depicted as a false one. *Kuttanimatam*[182] states that 'Prostitutes are adroit in yielding their bodies (*sarvangarpanadaksa*) but not their hearts (*asamarpitahrdaya*)'. It is said for *vesya* Srgaramanjari in Bhoja's *Srngaramanjarikatha*[183] that 'she pleases others, though *not* in love herself, and comes in contact with lovelorn though not attached herself'. The prostitute's love, the sources argue, is rooted in mercenary considerations. As *Kuttanimatam*[184] notes, 'The wealth of the paramour is the barometer on which the prostitute's (*varastri*) attachment (*raga*), love (*prema*) and sexual desire (*madanaruja*) can be measured. All these sentiments are friends of wealth which increase when wealth increases and decrease with the decrease of wealth'.

Insofar as a prostitute herself uses her love as a strategy of material gain the expression of this sentiment is circumscribed. The *vesya* codes also circumscribe it. In *Kuttanimatam* when *vesya* Harlata feels genuine love for Sundarsena she is cautioned against it by her friends. It is said[185] that for a prostitute (*panyanari*) a love that originates in a sense of empathy (*sadbhavajanurakti*) is not good. The *vesya* is advised to shower her love[186] only after ascertaining the wealth of the paramour for her beauty is a means to realising that end. A *vesya*[187] who is attracted only towards handsomeness (*abhirama*) of the paramour and neglects the factor of gain (*vividhalabhanirpeksa*) becomes a laughing stock among the clever courtesans. In *Brhatkathaslokasamgraha*[188] a prostitute bent on constancy (*sativratam*) is described as a bad woman (*duracareva*). In *Mrcchakatikam*,[189] *vita* describes Vasantasena's rejection of paramours like Sakara as *vesavasavirudha.* In another such verse referred to in Rajasekhara's *Kavyamimamsa*,[190] an old bawd tells her daughter who was bent on constancy to her lover that 'for us marriage means to love boys in childhood, young men in youth and old men in advanced age. On which road you want to travel, O daughter! For in our family no one has ever been abused of being a *sati* (*satilanchana*)'. In Bhoja's *Srngaramanjarikatha*,[191] another bawd tells her daughter that 'the secret of the profession of harlotry is that one's own self should always be protected from love as from a tiger'.

Vesya Ragamanjari in Dandin's *Dasakumaracarita*[192] declares that she is *gunasulka* and not *dhanasulka,* i.e. she is attracted to the merit and not the wealth of the paramour, and further asserts that her sexual favours (*bhogyayauvanam*) will be granted only to the one who marries her (*panigrahana*). This insistence by Ragamanjari is seen by her mother as acting

[181] *Sahitya Darpana,* (ed. and tr.) Satyavrata Singh, Varanasi, 1970: III.71.
[182] *Kuttanimatam,* verse 313.
[183] *Srngaramanjarikatha*: 15.
[184] *Kuttanimatam,* verse 303.
[185] Ibid., verse 277.
[186] Ibid., verse 278.
[187] Ibid., verse 279.
[188] *Brhatkathaslokasamgraha*: XVIII. 103.
[189] *Mrcchakatikam,* Act 1.31.
[190] *Kavyamimamsa,* eh. VI: 71.
[191] *Srngaramanjarikatha*: 25.
[192] *Dasakumaracarita*: 174.

against *svakuladharma*, that is, *vesya* codes, and as a desire on the part of Ragamanjari to enact the role of a household woman (*kulastrivrta*). The certitude of the bawd that 'love' was a sentiment fit for the household women needs to be problematised. Can one say that *kulastris* were more 'free to love'? If the *vesyas* love was circumscribed by the *vesavasa* code, the *kulavadhu* s love was circumscribed by the patriarchal *pativrata* ideology. A wife was not required so much to love as to show devotion to her husband. It needed that penetrating eyes of the old bawd *Visamsila* in Bhoja's *Srngaramanjarikatha*[193] to expose this myth of love for women. The bawd tells her daughter that love is three-fold—once born on hearing, once on sight and the third on union. All the three, says Visamsila, 'should be abandoned from a distance for by these even family women are made objects of contempt'. We thus see that love as an autonomous emotion was something which women could not or dared not experience under patriarchy. The prostitute commodified her love for material gain, and the *kulastri* erased hers or bartered it to accommodate herself in the patriarchal household.

But even if a prostitute used her love as a strategy she alone was in a position to choose to display this emotion fearlessly. Vasantasena shows such an affection for Carudatta in *Mrcchakatikam.* She knew that Carudatta was poor (*daridra*) yet she was in love with his virtues (*gunanuraktaganika*). It is significant that in the play Vasantasena did not see her involvement with Carudatta in the light of a prostitute–client relationship at any point of time. In Act II when Vasantasena's maid Madanika asked her who it was that had to be served (by Vasantasena), Vasantasena replied that she wanted to enjoy, sport and not serve (*rantumichami na sevitum*). Yet again in Act IV when Vasantasena prepared to pay a visit to Carudatta of her own accord she again used the terms sporting and enjoying (*carudattam-abhirantum gacchava*). This tie of genuine love between *ganika* Vasantasena and Carudatta is also recognised by Vasantasena's mother. In Act IX when she was called upon to give testimony in the court and the judge asked her about the whereabouts of her daughter, she too replied that her daughter was enjoying the pleasures of youth with her friend (*mitra*) Carudatta (*tatra me darika yauvanasukhanubhavatt*).

X

In the classical Sanskrit sources of our period, prostitutes were one of the *nayika* types referred to as the *bahya* or *sadharanastri* They were also the central figures in the entire business of *kama*. It was their conscious commodification of *kama* which enabled them to gain autonomy over both *artha* and *dharma*, the other two ends of human life.

Nonetheless, the *vesavasa* or prostitute quarter cannot be treated as a space of complete equality. It had its own hierarchy. A *ganika* was the presiding diva of these quarters in a way a *rupajiva* could not be. The lesser status of the latter also made her more dependent on the generosity of her male clients.

A close scrutiny of the textual evidence allows us to jettison the prostitute-as-victim image and to recover the 'prostitutes as social agents with relative autonomy within the confines of the patriarchal system'.

[193] *Srngaramanjarikatha*: 88.

Chapter 25 Prostitution in Ancient India*

SUKUMARI BHATTACHARJI

The earliest mention of prostitution occurs in the *Ṛgveda*, the most ancient literary work of India. At first however we hear of the illicit lover, *jāra* and *jāriṇī*—male and female lover of married spouses. What distinguished such an illicit lover from the professional prostitute or her client is the regular payment for favours received. When we merely hear of an illicit lover there may or may not have been an exchange of gift; in a case of mutual consent, gifts must have been optional. In the remote days of barter economy when money or currency was yet unknown, such gifts were equivalent to payment in cash. We have oblique references to women being given gifts for their favours, but the contexts leave us guessing whether the woman was a willing partner or whether she agreed to oblige in return for the gifts she received. But clearly, even in the earliest Vedic age, love outside wedlock was a familiar phenomenon and unions promoted by mere lust are mentioned in quite an uninhibited manner.

Prostitution as a profession appears in the literature of a few centuries after the *Vedas* although it must have been common in society much earlier. After the earliest Vedic literature between the twelfth and the ninth centuries BC (i.e., *Ṛgveda*, Books II-VII), we have a vast literature which covers the period between the eighth and the fifth centuries BC. In this literature, too, we hear of the woman of easy virtue, of the wife's illicit love affairs.[1]

Extra-marital love may have been voluntary and unpaid but there is the possibility of it being regarded by the male partner as a form of service for which he was obliged to pay in some form. But as long as it was confined to a particular person, it was a temporary contract and was not regarded as a profession. The later Pali term *muhuttiā* (lasting for an instant), or its Sanskrit equivalent *Muhūrtikā* signified such purely temporary unions with no lasting relationship or obligation. Such affairs may have been voluntary or professional, depending on the attitude of the partners.

*Reproduced with permission from Tanika Sarkar. Previously published in *Social Scientist*, V. 15, No. 165, Feb. 1987, pp. 62–97.

Gradually, there arose a section of women who, either because they could not find suitable husbands, or because of early widowhood, unsatisfactory married life or other social pressures especially if they had been violated, abducted or forcibly enjoyed and so denied an honourable status in society, or had been given away as gifts in religious or secular events—such women were frequently forced to take up prostitution as a profession. And when they did so, they found themselves in a unique position: they constituted the only section of women who had to be their own bread-winners and guardians. All the others—maiden daughters, sisters, wives, widows and maidservants—were wards of men: fathers, brothers, husbands, masters or sons.[2] So, women who took up prostitution had to be reasonably sure of an independent livelihood; their customers had to make it a viable proposition for them.

ECONOMIC STATUS

It is easy to see that all avenues to prostitution did not offer the same kind of economic security. A raped woman had little chance of an honourable marriage and social rehabilitation; so, reduced to prostitution, she had to accept whatever came her way. This also held true for the old maid turned prostitute. But a young widow or a pretty wanton maid or an unhappily married attractive woman could perhaps choose her partner and name her price, at least in the beginning of her career while she still enjoyed the protection of her father's, husband's in-laws' home. We have absolutely no way of knowing prostitution in India arose as a recognizable profession or how much the prostitute received by way of payment. Its emergence and recognition as a profession was presumably concomitant with the institution of strict marriage rules, especially monandry, and the wife being regarded as the private property of her husband. The terms *sādhāraṇī* or *sāmānyā* (common), synonyms for prostitute, distinguish her as a woman not possessed by one man; this is the desideratum. When a woman does not belong to one man but obliges many, as the terms *vārāṅganā*, *varastrī, vāravadhū and vāramukhyā*[3] signify, since she is not the responsibility of any one man, she looks after herself. She does so by accepting payment from each of the men she obliges; she then becomes *paṇyastrī*, one whose favours can be bought with money.

The process of the emergence of prostitution must have been slow, varying from region to region and from age to age. By the later Vedic age, that is, around the eighth or seventh centuries BC, we have references to a more regularised form of prostitution recognised as a social institution. Early Buddhist literature, especially the Jātakas, bear testimony to the existence of different categories of prostitutes, and incidentally provides some information about their fees as also of their financial position.

Professional prostitution presupposes an economic condition in which surplus was produced, a surplus which also earned prosperity from abroad through trade and commerce. It also presupposes the rise of petty principalities, the breakdown of tribal society, the rise of the joint or extended family and the social subjugation of women in general. In a settled agricultural community, the woman gradually lost social mobility and a measure of freedom that she had been enjoying before. She became man's ward, possession, object of enjoyment. Also, with the accumulation of private property, the wife was more zealously guarded and jealously watched over. Society was now polygamous; polyandry disappeared except in some small pockets.

Whether as an unmarried girl, a wife or a widow, she *belonged* to some man; as other men could not approach her without trespassing on the owner's property rights. Pleasure outside the home, therefore, had to be paid for, hence prostitution had to be institutionalised so that there was an assurance of a steady supply for ready payment. It must have been a long and tortuous process for women of this profession to congregate in a 'red light area', away from the village—and later also from towns—where men could go and seek their company. Social ostracism on the one hand and professional solidarity of the guild type of association on the other, ensured their security and prosperity.

Although the later Vedic literature tacitly assumes and sometimes even overtly mentions prostitutes, it is in the Buddhist texts that we see them first as professionals. In Vedic literature, especially in the *Aitareya* and *Śaṅkhāyana* Āraṇyakas, the prostitute is mentioned in an apparently obscene altercation with the neophyte (*brahmacārin*). In the Vrātyasūkta of the *Atharvaveda*, she follows the Māgadha. These are clearly part of a fertility ritual. It is in this role that she has persisted in ritual and literature down the ages.

There are various myths and legends regarding the origin of prostitution. The *Mahābhārata* account of the destruction of the Yādavas and Vṛṣṇis[4] ends with the women of these tribes being abducted by barbarian brigands. In the Kuru and Pāñcāla regions[5] inhabited by the Madras and the Sindhu-Sauvīras, the Brahmin sages Dālbhya Caikitāyana and Śvetaketu's nephew Aṣṭāvakra were said to be associated with the teaching of erotics in which prostitution constitutes a section. In the *Mahābhārata*[6] and the *Matsya Purāṇa*[7] we are given fictitious accounts of the origin of prostitution. Kṣemendra says that wicked mothers give their daughters, enjoyed and abandoned by men, to others.[8] Vātsyāyana in his *Kāmasūtra* gives detailed instructions on how a chaste girl should be seduced cleverly until she yields to a man's lust.[9] Presumably, when such a man abandoned her she was forced to adopt prostitution as a profession. We also hear of the *jāyopajīvins* or *jāyājīvins*, husbands who lived on the wife's income which she earned by selling herself. This itself was regarded as a minor sin on the husband's part, an *upapātaka* which could be expiated by taking the comparatively mild *cāndrāyaṇa* vow.[10] All these texts reveal to us some of the channels by which women came to prostitution. Another old channel of the supply of prostitutes was young virgins given away as gifts on special religious and secular occasions. The number of such girls given away to brahmins, guests, priests, sons-in-law is staggering. In later Vedic times we hear of *dakṣiṇās*, sacrificial fees to officiating priests. Such fees included horses, cattle, gold and also women of various categories—unmarried, married without children and married with children. One wonders what a priest did with hundreds of such women. Some he could marry, others he would enjoy and abandon, still others he would employ as maidservants. Many of these would later find their way to brothels or to slave markets. Yet another source of supply was the royal palace. A king could summon pretty maids to his palace, enjoy them for some days and then send them away. In the Vatsagulma region, ministers' wives had to oblige the king by paying visits (on being summoned) to the palace. In Vidarbha, pretty maids were enjoyed by the king for a month and then sent away. When such women came out of the palace, one obvious solution for their future life was prostitution. Of course, courtiers would sometimes marry some of them but the rest had few alternative courses open to them. Kauṭilya says that prostitutes were recruited from four sources: either they were born as prostitutes' daughters, or they were purchased,[11] or captured in war,[12] or they were women who had been punished for adultery.[13]

Finally, a totally abhorrent manner of procuring women for temple prostitution was buying women and giving them to the temples. Such donors were said to grow rich in this life and live in heaven for a long time. We hear that he who gave a host of prostitutes to the Sun god went to the region of the sun after death.[14]

Temple dancers do not appear before the last few centuries BC, and are mentioned frequently in the early centuries AD in some regions. The *Jātakas* do not know them, Greek visitors after Alexander do not mention them. Even Kauṭilya does not associate professional dancers with temple prostitution. Evidently, the institution arose in the troubled period of foreign invasion before and after the early centuries AD Kālidāsa, in the fifth century AD, assumes their existence and function as an established tradition.[15] From the sixth century AD onwards, literature and epigraphy bear many evidences of its existence. As townships and cities arose along the trade routes in northern India around the sixth century BC internal and maritime trade flourished along these, and towns and cities became centres where courtesans plied their trade and attracted money from travellers, merchants, soldiers and men of various trades. These courtesans were trained in many arts and if they were young and pretty they could amass a fortune, but evidently only the exceptionally beautiful, young and accomplished among them were so fortunate. Since entertainment was their primary function, they had to provide song, dance, music and various other kinds of pleasure; they had to keep a troupe of artistes in the different fields in readiness for the cultivated customer. To the upper class of courtesans sometimes came men of refined aesthetic sensibilities and intellectual ability; hence they were obliged to provide entertainment like the hostesses of the French salons of the last century or the Japanese *geisha* girls. They themselves were trained in the various arts including literature, for their training was quite lengthy and elaborate. We hear of texts composed for such training; these are called *Vaiśikatantra.* But every courtesan could not herself provide all kinds of aesthetic pleasure, so they had to make an initial and also recurring investment for training and maintaining a troupe of artistes. Occasionally, the royal treasury came to her aid.

Chief courtesans of prosperous cities and towns maintained their own train of singers and dancing girls. Royal courts also patronised such singers and dancers who could be enjoyed by the king and his favourities and who could also be employed as spies.

From the earliest times we have many different names for courtesans. The *Ṛgveda* knows the *hasrā*, a frivolous woman the *agrū,*[16] and the *sādhāraṇī*. The *Atharvaveda* knows the[17] *pumścalī*, she who walks among men,[18] the *mahānagnī*, she of great nakedness (i.e., who bares herself to many) is mentioned in the *Atharvaveda,*[19] *atiskadvarī* and *apaskadvarī*, women with fancy dress and bare bosoms are mentioned in the *Taittirīya Brāhmaṇa.*[20] *Rajayitrī*, she who entertains and is given to sensuality, also figures in some texts.[21] *Sāmānyā* and *sādhāraṇī* are generic terms for the common woman.[22] In the Mahāvrata rite the *pumścalī*, a prostitute pairs ritually with a *brahmacārin.*[23] The *kāmasūtra* in the second or first century BC mentions the *Kumbhadāsī* and *paricārikā* maidservants who could also be enjoyed at will. *Kulaṭā* and *svairiṇī*, wanton women, *naṭī*, the actress, *śilpakārikā*, she who is engaged in arts and crafts, *prakāśavinaṣṭā*, the openly defiled one, *rūpājīvā* and *gaṇikās*, are courtesans with different social ranks.

The *Jātakas* mention *vannadāsī, veṣī nāriyo*, *gāmaniyo*, and *nagarasobhinī itthī,*[24] *muhuttiā*[25] and *janapadakalyāṇī* are mentioned in several Buddhist texts in the sense of the most beautiful women who can be enjoyed, by an entire *janapada*. The *gaṇikā* must initially have connoted a woman at the disposal of all the members of a *gaṇa*, a tribe, and later of the political unit, or constituent of a confederacy. Some later names include *sālabhañjikā*, who is no other than a prostitute in *Jaṭādhara's* dictionary.

VARIATIONS IN STATUS AND FUNCTIONS

This profusion of synonyms cannot be explained by regional or temporal variations only, it also signifies the social and financial status of the various categories of courtesans.[26] The numerous synonyms also testify to the widespread presence of the institution through the ages.

The *rūpājīvā* was not accomplished in the arts like the *gaṇikā*; her only stock in trade as the name signifies was her beauty and charm. She owed the state two days' income for a month. If a man forcibly enjoyed her, he was fined 12 *paṇas*, but in times of crisis half her monthly income could be forfeited to the state.[27] She could also belong to the royal harem[28] and could also be exclusively kept by one man; in which case another enjoying her was fined 48 *paṇas*.[29] Disguised as a wife she could help a man escape and could also be employed by the state as a spy.[30] Vātsyāyana also mentions the *rūpājīvā*.[31] Another name of the mistress of one individual man is *avaruddhā*. The *rūpadāsī* was unaccomplished and was employed in the personal attendance of a wealthy man. Like the *vannadāsī* mentioned in the *Jātakas* she could entertain customers on her own or serve under some other person.[32] The *gaṇikādāsī* was a female slave of the *gaṇikā* who could also become independent and set up her own establishment. The *Sāmājataka* mentions *Sāmā*, a courtesan of Kasi who had a retinue of 500 *gaṇikādāsīs*.[33] Other common and late names are *vārāṇganā, vārabadhū, vāramukhyā,* all of which stand for a prostitute while *vṛṣalī*, which originally meant a Śūdra woman later came to mean a harlot; *pāṃśulā* and *lañjikā* are later synonyms of harlots. *Kulaṭā* was a married woman who left home to become a public woman and *vandhakī* was a housewife turned loose; her husband was known as *vandhakīpoṣā*, maintaining or being maintained by a *vandhakī*. A *vandhakī* too had to pay part of her income to the state coffers in times of national crisis. The *raṇḍā* was a low common woman, a mistress to *viṭa,* usually an old hag who pretended to be engaged in penance but was actually out to catch customers.

The *gaṇikā* and sometimes the *rūpājīvā* too, received free training in the various arts and those who teach prostitutes, female slaves and actresses arts such as singing, playing on musical instruments, reading, dancing, acting, writing, painting, playing on instruments such as *vīṇā* (lyre), pipe and drum, reading the thoughts of others, manufacture of scents and garlands, shampooing and the art of attracting and captivating the mind of others shall be endowed with maintenance from the state. They, the teachers shall train the sons of prostitutes to be chief actors (*raṅgopajīvin*) on the stage. The wives of actors and others of similar profession who have been taught various languages and the use of signals (*saṃjñā*) shall, along with their relatives be made use of in detecting the wicked and murdering and deluding foreign spies.[34]

In a sixth century Jain work we have an exhaustive list of the prostitute's attainments—writing, arithmetic, the arts, singing, playing on musical instruments, drums, chess, dice, eight board chess, instant verse making, Prakrit and Apabhraṃśa poetry, proficiency in the science of perfume making, jewellery, dressing up, knowledge of the signs of good or bad men and women, horses, elephants, cocks, rams, umbrellas, rods, swords, jewels, gems which antidote poison, architecture, camps and canopies, phalanx arrangement, fighting, fencing, shooting arrows, ability to interpret omens, etc. Altogether seventy-two arts and sciences were to be mastered by her.[35]

It is clear that the prostitute especially *gaṇikā*, the most accomplished among them, offered men something which by the early centuries AD had become absolutely rare among the women of the gentry, namely accomplishment. We read in the *Manusaṃhitā*: 'The sacrament of marriage is to a female what initiation with the sacred thread is to a male. Serving the husband is for the wife what residence in the preceptor's house is to the man and household duty is to the woman, what offering sacrifices is to the man.'[36] This series of neat equations deprive the woman of education, dooming her to household chores only, especially the service of her husband and in-laws, but also thereby indirectly doom her to the loss of her husband's attention. With an unaccomplished wife at home, the man who cared for cultured female company went to the brothel for it. Manu belongs to the early centuries AD;[37] a steady deterioration in the status of the woman and the śūdra followed his codification of the social norm and the brothel flourished because it catered to the cultured man-about-the-town's (*nāgaraka*) tastes in women.

The *gaṇikā* because of her youth, beauty, training and accomplishment belonged to a superior social status. With an extensive, elaborate, and apparently expensive education she could frequently name her price, which, as Buddhist texts testify was often prohibitive. She was patronised by the king who visited her sometimes, as also by wealthy merchants. Because of her high fees none but the most wealthy could approach her. She alone enjoyed a position where as long as her youth and beauty lasted she could not be exploited.

TAXES TO THE STATE

We have seen that the *gaṇikā, rūpājīvā, veśyā* and *vandhakī* had to pay taxes to the state but a careful study leads to the conclusion that almost all categories had an actual or potential obligation for paying taxes; the collection, however, depended on the degree and nature of the organisation. Organised red light areas paid taxes regularly, at a fixed rate, while it was much more difficult to ascertain the income of the women 'kept' in seclusion by a man or of the unorganised individual women plying the trade in isolated pockets or even, like the *vandhakī*, at home. Similarly, organised brothels enjoyed greater security from the state in lieu of the taxes they paid while individuals who paid 'hush-money' to extortionist officers could hardly demand any protection from injustice, manhandling, coercion and cheating. The *Nammayasundarīkathā*, a twelfth century text says that the state received 25% to 30% of the prostitute's income.

We hear of the extremely high fees of some famous gaṇikās in the Buddhist texts. *Bhaṭṭi*[38] and *parivvayam*[39] denote two different types of fees. Vāsadavattā of Mathura charged very high rates per night.[40] Sālāvatī of Rajagraha charged a hundred *karṣāpaṇas* per night while Ambapālī's fees led to a dispute between the cities Rajagṛha and Vaiśālī. A Jain text[41] says that a courtesan who had a faultless body and whose attainments were complete may charge 1000 *karṣāpaṇas* per night. Evidently, only the richest merchants could pay such fees. The play *Mṛcchakaṭika* mentions a thousand gold coins and ornaments being sent in advance to lure a *gaṇikā* to a paramour's house. The *gaṇikā*, says Kauṭilya, was also paid a monthly salary from the royal treasury and the *pratigaṇikā*, her short-time substitute, received half the amount. The *gaṇikā*, however, did not enjoy property rights. 'There is every likelihood that their palatial establishments and gardens were state property with life interest.'[42] On her death, her daughter inherited her property but only for use; she could not sell, mortgage, exchange or donate them. This, of course, is true of the ordinary prostitute living in an organised brothel; many outstanding *gaṇikās* were mistresses of their own property. Hence in Buddhist literature we have many instances where she gave away her property. A *gaṇikā* could be bought out by a sympathetic customer; her redemption money (*niṣkraya*) was 24,000 *paṇas*, a very high sum in view of the fact that her annual salary paid by the state was between 1000 and 3000 *paṇas.* A *rūpājīvā's* fees were 48 *paṇas*, she usually lived with actors, wine-sellers, meat-sellers, people who sold cooked rice and vaiśyas generally. It is obvious that she kept company with people who controlled ready cash.

A man who forcibly attacked a *gaṇikā's* daughter paid a fine of 54 *paṇas* plus a fine (*śulka*) of 16 times her mother's fees, presumably to the mother herself.[43] The second fine may also be a hush-money paid to the bridegroom at the daughter's wedding. Foreign customers had to pay 5 *paṇas* extra tariff duty to the state apart from the courtesan's regular fees. The *pumścalī* (a common whore) did not have any fixed fees; she could only demand fees on marks of cohabitation, if she tried to extort money from her customers her fees were liable to be forfeited to the state—also if she threw temper tantrums or refused to oblige the customer in any way. The *Kuṭṭanīmmata* says that the temple prostitute (*tridaśālayajīvikā*) got paid by the temple authorities and that her income was fixed by tradition. Kṣemendra's *Samayamātṛkā* says that they were paid in grain as remuneration and that they were employed in rotation.

If after receiving her fees a prostitute refused to oblige her customer she paid a fine of double her fees; if she refused him before accepting the fees she paid her fees as fine.[44] Apparently it is a fair business deal where the defaulter pays. a fine but if we pause and think that a sensible person would not ruin the prospects of gain or income unless she had some serious reason for disobliging her customer, it becomes clear that she did not have the option to refusing to sell herself. In other words, society refused to look upon her as a human being; she was just a commodity, nothing more. If a price had been accepted the commodity was the customer's for use.

Regarding her customers Vātsyāyana is very clear. The ideal one is young, rich, without having to earn his wealth (i.e., born to wealth), proud, a minister to the king, one who can afford to disregard his elders' commands, preferably an only son of a rich father. Born in an aristocratic family, he should be learned, a poet, proficient in tales, an orator, accomplished in the various arts, not malicious, lively, given to drinks, friendly, a ladies' man but not under their power, independent, not cruel, not jealous, not apprehensive.[45] The courtesan is advised not to stick to one visitor when she has offers from many. She should go to the person who can offer the gifts she covets.[46] Since money can buy everything she should oblige him who can afford the highest sum—this, says the text, is what the teachers instruct. When she wants to bring her paramour back from a rival she should be extra nice to him and be satisfied with less payment temporarily. This is to ensure her future...she should leave the impoverished lover and never invest in one from whom there is no hope of return.[47] She should be able to read the signs of his disaffection; a long list of such signs are given.[48] Above all, a courtesan should never encourage or entertain a suitor of reduced means. When she has squeezed her customer dry, she should remorselessly leave him and search for a rich one. Normally, a *gaṇikā* chose her own customer except when the king forced one on her. Then, if she refused she was whipped with 1000 lashes or was fined 5000 *paṇas*. She did not have any right over her own body where the royal wish was concerned.[49] The punishment for forcing an unwilling *gaṇikā* was 1000 *paṇas* or more. Once she admits a client into her own house to share it with her she could not throw him out. If she did, the fine was eight times her fees. She could only refuse if he was diseased. When the client cheated her of her fees he had to pay eight times the fees.

The prostitute could own ornaments, money, her fees, servants, maidservants who could be concubines. But other texts indicate that this ownership was not real or ultimate; but merely a right of use. The concubine, however, was obliged to pay the mistress for her own upkeep, plus one *paṇa* per month.

Prostitution in ancient India existed both overtly and covertly. In other words, besides brothels or open establishments run by and for one or more prostitutes, ancient texts give a list of many professions for girls where she could potentially be enjoyed by her employer with impunity. She could act as a substitute for the wife. In the Jain text *Vasudevahiṇḍi* we read of Bharata, a leader of his clan having another woman besides the wife. All the feudatories under him sent their daughters who arrived at the same time. The queen threatened to leave, so it was decided that they would serve him in the outer court and that later they would be handed over to the *gaṇa*, the tribe, to become *gaṇikās*, the text thus explains the origin of the term *gaṇikā*. The *Mahābhārata* tells us that the Pāṇḍava army was followed by a host of prostitutes who went in the rear of the army on baggage carts.[50] Yudhiṣṭhira on the eve of the war sent his greetings to the prostitutes.[51] In the train of the Paṇḍavas when they left for the forest there were "chariots, traders' goods and brothels", presumably to entertain the army.[52] King Virta after his victory ordered young girls to dress well, come out[53] and entertain the assembled men. Such a command could only be given to public women. When Kṛṣṇa went on a peace mission to the Kauravas, Duryodhana's entertainment of the former included a rest house with women; Dhṛtarāṣṭra ordered fair harlots to go with his sons to meet Kṛṣṇa. The later didactic interpolations of the *Mahābhārata*, however, are full of imprecations and stigma against prostitutes.[54] The *Rāmāyaṇa* mentions *gaṇikās* and *veśyās* in the list of comforts, luxuries and status symbols. It is quite clear that prostitutes became a symbol of the prosperity concomitant with urban civilisation. Like gold and jewellery, like corn and cattle, a rich man desired prosperity and plenty in the number of women he could enjoy freely.

WOMEN AS COMMODITY

The concept of women as chattel or commodity for man's enjoyment is borne out by the inclusion of women—pretty and young—in large numbers in any list of gifts given to a man in return for a favour or as a mark of respect. Thus she is a part of *dakṣiṇā*, fees to the sacrificial priest. At Yudhiṣṭhira's horse-sacrifice women were sent by other kings as a donation to make up a necessary part of the entertainment.[55] Yudhiṣṭhira himself gives away pretty maids to guest kings;[56] he is even said to have given away hundreds of thousands of pretty girls as did King Saśabindu of old at his horse sacrifice.[57] Pretty maids as part of *dakṣiṇā* are also mentioned when King Bhagīratha gave hundreds of thousands of lovely maids, well decked out with gold ornaments.[58] Even at a *srāddha* ceremony Brahmins received thousands of pretty maidens as gifts.[59] These girls could sometimes find husbands but presumably, since prostitution was being looked down upon more and more and maidenhood became an essential prerequisite for marriage in the *Smṛti* texts, most of them were forced to become prostitutes.

In heaven heroes are rewarded with a large number of beautiful girls.[60] The same idea is also seen in classical Sanskrit literature. In the *Kumārasambhava,*[61] *Raghuvaṃśa*,[62] *Kirātārjunīya*,[63] and in *Śiśupalvadha*,[64] in Subandhu and Bāṇa we have references to courtesans as a prestigious decoration of a royal palace and an indispensable part of city life. Bhāguri calls her *puramaṇḍana* an ornament of the city. Thus her status was that of an inanimate decorative object, an object of enjoyment; it was sub-human.

Courtesans sometimes did perform several other functions. In the *Mahābhārata* they participated in the victory celebrations.[65] They even played a political role as spies whose duty it was to seduce important men who were potential sources of vital political information, to collect such information and supply it to the relevant officers through the superintendent (*gaṇikādhyakṣa*). Their role as temptress is emphasised in the *Vaṭṭaka Jātaka.* The names of various types of courtesans gives us an inkling of their roles. Thus the *devaveśyā* was the temple dancer, something like the Greek *hierodoules*; the *rājaveśyā* served the king; while the *Brahmaveśyā* or *tīrthagā* visited holy places or pilgrimages. In the *Brahmapurāṇa* we have the description of *Ekāmratīrtha*, where lived many prostitutes[66] presumably to cater to the pilgrims and visitors. In the *samāja* public functions there used to be a separate gallery where sat the courtesans who gave musical performance for the *samāja.* Kauṭilya assigns them the duties of common maidservants at the palace. We hear of a prostitute serving Dhṛtarāṣṭra when Gāndhārī was pregnant.[67] Uddyotana Sūri in his *Kuvalayamālā* describes nymphs in Indra's heaven who carried water vessels, fans, fly-whisks, parasols, mirrors, kettledrums, harps, ordinary drums, clothes and ornaments. In the *Rāmāyāṇa* and the *Mahābhārata* such women followed the king in the palace and served him in his train. The *Lalitavistara* mentions women who carried full pitchers, garlands, jewellery and ornaments, the throne, the fan, jars full of perfumed water, etc. Evidently in all these instances, as also in many references in the *Purāṇas* and later literature the pretty damsels giving light personal service to the king are projected to heaven where the earthly prostitutes figure as celestial nymphs serving the gods. Whether on earth or in heaven monarchs or wealthy potentates used such women to enhance their glory and pleasure.

The retired temple prostitute was employed by the state for spinning cotton, wool and flax. The *nāgaraka*, man-about-the-town, in his love-intrigues could have assistance from widows, Buddhist nuns, and old courtesans who acted as go-betweens. In the palace the courtesan held positions as the royal umbrella-bearer, masseuse in charge of the king's (also of the royal family's) toilet, dress and ornaments, and as the king's bath attendant. They also had a place in the royal entourage in hunting and military expeditions, and on occasion entertained royal guests. What is true of their function with regard to the king is also true of the rich courtier merchants and nobles described as nāgaraka in the Kāmasūtra. In the non-monarchical gaṇa states the chiefs gambled and indulged themselves in the company of prostitutes. The keepers of brothels procured pretty women from their establishment for these chiefs' entertainment. These aged women the brothel keepers were adept in bringing about and resolving quarrels between rival suitors as and when needed by them or by political agents of the state. Courtesans belonged to kings or wealthy citizens' trains in their amusements and festivals, their garden parties, boat trips, musical soirées, and bathing and drinking sprees. The *Kāmasūtra* describes the different sports and festivals of rich barons to each of which courtesans were invited.

At-homes could be held in a courtesan's salon where assembled men of the same age, intellect, wealth who would hold discussions with courtesans. This was called *goṣṭhī*; there they talked about the problems of poetry and art. They shifted the venue to the different members' houses where they indulged in food and various drinks. Courtesans were to be served first, then the men should eat and drink. These men-about-the-town rode out to an appointed place together with the courtesans in the forenoon, and having spent the day in various kinds of sports and entertainments such as cockfights, ramfights, theatrical performances, etc., they should return in the evening. In summer they should indulge in water-sports.[68]

The text goes on to name twenty different sports and festivals[69] which depended on the seasons, the moon and auspicious days or the year. 'Villagers should learn of these sports of the townsmen, describe and imitate them.'[70]

No doubt the prostitutes occasionally enjoyed themselves at such times, but whether they spied, massaged, bathed, dressed or carried the umbrella we do not hear of any extra payment for these additional duties to which they were certainly entitled because their main task as prostitutes only earned them a place in the king's or rich man's establishment. In a sense in the organised brothel prostitutes were better off, because normally they were not expected to do other chores although when with their customers, they sometimes entertained them with minor services. It all depended on the social and economic status of the prostitute. The city's chief courtesan was a wealthy person of a high rank who had a host of servants and maidservants for the menial chores; she herself was too accomplished, rich and respectable to do the chores herself; whereas a poor and common strumpet had to cater to many customers, also indigent and therefore, each able to pay very little. Hence she had to do all the menial chores for herself and her customer for bare subsistence.[71] The *avaruddhā*, a woman 'kept' by a man, enjoyed freedom from manual labour only if her patron was rich; otherwise she had to work for herself and for him. Hers was like a 'contract marriage' and, as in marriage, the status of the woman depended on the man's income.

SOCIAL STATUS

At this distance of time it is difficult to form an adequate idea of the social status of prostitutes. We have seen that not all prostitutes belong to the same category. The accomplished young beauty could name her price, sometimes at an apparently exorbitant rate, because she was in great demand. Speaking of the ranks of royal attendants the *Kurudhamma Jātaka* says that the lowest of the courtiers was the door-keeper, the *dvārika*; he occupies the last place but one, for he is above the public woman, the *gaṇikā*. Every city had a chief courtesan who was 'an ornament to the city'.[72] The *janapadakalyāṇī* for the *sādhāraṇī* of the non-monarchichal state of the Licchavis were in great demand and were often looked up to because of their beauty and culture and so could ask any price for their favours. And they got it as many Buddhist texts testify. The word *janapadakalyāṇī* literally meant the most beautiful woman in a country. The *Dīgha Nikāya*,[73] the *Majjhima Nikāya*,[74] *and the Saṃyutta Nikāya*[75] refer to her, Buddhist texts mention many affluent and powerful courtesans who fed the Buddha and his train and gave gifts to the order. We thus hear of Ambāpālī giving such a feast to the Lord and his hundred thousand followers. She also gave away her big mango grove to the order.[76]'Śālavatī's daughter Sirimā received 1,000 *kāhāpaṇas* per night.[77] We hear of a banker's daughter who chose to become a prostitute. Her father set too high a price; few customers came; she reduced it to half and was called *ardhakāśī*.[78]

As looks, age and accomplishments came down the price and social prestige also came down so that middle aged, unaccomplished or plain-looking women had to agree to mere subsistence rales or even less. Even that they did not always get as many texts on erotics tell us. The *Kuṭṭanīmata*, a major text on prostitution, describes the plight of such discarded prostitutes who were reduced to begging, stealing, and various other tricks. They had no guarantee of the next meal or shelter, no provision against old age, disease and penury. The heart-rending description of an abandoned, unattractive prostitute who takes recourse to becoming a confidence trickster and is pursued by society is occasionally rendered ludicrous by the very comicality of her various moves and the invariable failure of each move. But beyond this comic portrait is the tragic situation of a woman who, after having provided pleasure to many men's lust all through her life, has to fend for herself at a time when she is worst equipped for such a lone battle. In many texts we hear of such retired harlots begging.[79] The classic example is Kaṅkālī, an inn-keeper's daughter, sold at seven as a slave in the market place, who started as an ordinary prostitute and in time lost her youth and whatever charm she had earlier had. So she tried her hand at different professions but since she had no training in any she could not earn a livelihood through them. Then she tried to seduce people at pilgrimages, dressing up and disguising her age and loss of looks, but was eventually caught and summarily dropped. She changed roles frequently, was even imprisoned; in a bid to escape she murdered the warder. She then fled to a monastery where she could not stick it for very long. Later she begged openly until there was a famine and she could not get alms. So she became a nurse to a child whose gold chain she stole one night and escaped. When that money was exhausted she took to selling loaded dice. Then she returned to begging as a profession. But the strain and poor returns prompted her to steal food offered to idols. She next became a wine-seller, a fortune-teller and an actress in turn and finally she went about pretending to be insane. For a time she enjoyed royal hospitality because she gave out that she could paralyse a hostile army. But quite naturally she had to take to her heels before the actual encounter took place. Finally, she returned to her native place and became a procuress for a pretty young prostitute, Kalāvatī.[80] This tale, evidently a concatenation of many disparate episodes epitomises the fate of old prostitutes. Their tragedy was not only the lack of social security but also their lack of proficiency in any alternative profession through which they could earn a livelihood. Besides, having known better days they could not slick to any mean profession which did not provide comfort. Hence they flitted from one profession to another with cunning and the ability to cheat through play-acting—arts they had mastered as prostitutes—as the only stock-in-trade. In the *Deśopadeśa* we hear of a sixty-year old woman making herself up as a young girl in the hope of catching a customer.[81]

Institutionalised prostitution, however, offered somewhat better prospects for old and retired courtesans. Kauṭilya lays down the rule that *gaṇikās, pratigaṇikās*, (short term substitutes for the *gaṇikās*), *rūpājīvās, veśyās, dāsīs, devadāsīs, pumścalīs, śilpakārikās, kauśikastrī* (woman artisan) are to be given pension by the state in old age. Since Kauṭilya was writing for a prince it is to be assumed that these women were employed by the state and had earlier paid taxes to the state which the state regarded partially as provident fund contributions against old age, disability, retirement and penury. We are not told what the pension was in terms of money, whether it was adequate for sustenance. But a steady income, however small, must have meant some measure of security to elderly women who would otherwise be wholly destitute. But since women and their labour was exploited in most spheres of life, we may assume that this rule was not strictly observed, because such women were totally powerless to sue the slate for non-payment. Yet the few who actually received some pension were lucky to have it. Retired prostitutes were employed as cooks, store-keepers, cotton, wool and flax spinners, and in various other manual jobs, so the state did not have to pay the pension until they were too old and weak to work anymore. In old age some prostitutes became *mātṛkās*, that is, matrons-in-charge of a brothel.

We hear of prostitutes' *anvaya*, family: their mothers, sisters, daughters and sons. The mother looked after her personal possessions, like dress and ornaments; she could not deposit her ornaments anywhere else; the daughter inherited them on her mother's retirement or death. But only for use. The sister could act as her substitute in a commission and the son was trained as a musical artist or an actor. He became a property of the state, almost a slave, and was obliged to hold musical performances for the stage for eight years. The manumission fees for him was higher than that for the prostitute. But in the play *Mṛcchakaṭika* we hear of *bandhulas* 'who are begotten by unknown clients of the prostitutes'. Without any social identity these boys lived in a brothel until they could eke out a livelihood for themselves. The pathetic tone of the verse tells us how these hoys were looked upon as waste products, like slag in a factory.

A prostitute was obliged to keep the brothel superintendent posted about her income and expenses and he could stop her from being extravagant. She could not sell or mortgage her property at will; for doing so she paid a fine: fifty and a quarter *paṇas*.

Occasionally a prostitute was married. Vātsyāyana lays down a provision whereby a *vcśyā* could be given in marriage to one who could provide special musical assistance to the establishment; such a marriage leads to greater prosperity.[82] Otherwise we hear of a notional sort of marriage which was more in the nature of initiation. The man did not have any exclusive claim on her person or services. The *avaruddhā* belonged to her patron exclusively and the law-givers say that his exclusive right to her should be respected.[83] Nārada has no objection to a man having sexual relations with a non-Brahmin *svairiṇī veśyā, dāsī* and *nikāśinī* (one who did not live a secluded life) of a lower caste if she was not another's wife.

That even a prostitute can fall in love is admitted theoretically by Vātsyāyana even though he says that they are and should always be after money.[84] A prostitute, according to the *Skandapurāṇa*, belongs to a separate caste: if a man of the same or a superior caste enjoys her he is not to be punished, provided she is not another's concubine. If she is, then he simply performs the *prājāpatya* (a light) penance[85] and gets away with it. In literature we have a few instances of the prostitute falling in love.[86]

VILIFICATION IN LITERATURE

Both institutionally and individually prostitutes depended upon certain categories of middlemen and procurers. Chief among these was the *kuṭṭanī* or *sambhalī*. Now, in a brothel the mother of the chief prostitute was the person-in-charge who watched over her daughter's and the other girl's interests. Her duties included checking the payments, protecting the girl's health and wealth, driving away undesirable customers (i.e., those with depleted coffers), using deceit and delay tactics to spare the girl as much as possible, bargaining for greater emoluments by pretending that other, richer customers are making bigger offers, varying custom, that is, to deprive an eager one for a time in order to extort better fees from him.[87] No wonder she was vilified in literature. 'She is like a blood-thirsty tigress, only where she is absent does the client appear as a fox'. 'The *kuṭṭanī* with her ear glued to the door in greedy expectation of money becomes eager even when a blade of grass drops'.[88] The *Kāmasūtra* mentions these procuresses together with beggar women, cultivated women, female mendicants with shaven heads, *caṇḍāla* women and old prostitutes.[89] Apparently she is an old hag with the nature of a vampire. But if one pauses to think, then it becomes clear that she was the prostitute's only guarantee of safety and fair payment. Without her, if the prostitute had to deal with the customer directly, she could be cheated, robbed, insulted, maimed, even killed with impunity. The basis of this surmise is offered by Kauṭilya in his *Arthaśāstra* where we read that the fine for defamation of a courtesan was 24 *paṇas*; for assault 48 *paṇas* and for lopping off her ears 51 ¾ *paṇas* and forced confinement. The *Yājñavalkya Smṛti* says that the fine for molesting a prostitute is 50 *paṇas*; and if she is gang-raped each assailant had to pay 24 *paṇas* to her.[90] For the safety of her person some laws had to be framed and for graver crimes the penalty varied between 1000 and 48,000 *paṇas* according to the degree of the heinousness of the crime and the status of the injured courtesan. On the other hand, later religious and law books have nothing but contempt for courtesans, and hold them solely responsible for the institution. They go to the length of saying that the murder of a prostitute is no crime.[91] Manu believes that all prostitutes were thieves and swindlers.[92] It is true that the erotic text *Kalāvilāsa* lists 64 specified modes in which a courtesan could deceive her customer. It also tells us the story of King Vikramāditya, who when he fell on hard days became the prostitute Vilāsavatī's guest. She showered her own wealth on him and when he gave himself out to be dead, threw herself on his pyre. With her help he regained his kingdom and made her the chief queen. Then she confessed to him her love for a young man who was arrested as a thief. With the king's help he was freed and the lovers were united. Then the king remembered his minister's warning: they are not to be trusted. This innate deceitfulness of prostitutes is a recurring note in all literature. But in this instance the text ignores her contribution: the re-instatement of the king as sovereign, and betrays only a sneer, shared no doubt by the entire community, for, the possibility of a prostitute being in love so deeply that she treads a dangerous and tortuous path to gain her lover appeared totally absurd to them. The text condemns the woman for everything, and more so the prostitute, wholly ignoring her client's role, and her own contribution to his career.

We have just seen that their clients also maltreated and manhandled them and these were not isolated incidents or exceptions or there would be no need to frame laws against crimes and stipulate the exact amount of fines for the several kinds of assault. She was often used and then cheated, robbed, thrashed, mutilated and murdered. If the institution was for society a necessary evil, and the state had a vested interest in extracting revenue and epion age service from this 'evil', then it could not afford to ignore a situation when the source of such revenue was harmed so that she could not multiply the revenue. Hence the laws. But the attitude of society was clearly against the prostitute and not against her client.

The procuress, the matron of the brothel or the mother of the chief courtesan sought to safeguard her physical, social and financial well-being.

The *viṭa* was the middleman and/or companion of the courtesan. Because the *viṭa* was a man he could procure custom for her. Technically, a *viṭa* was a worthy spendthrift who, reduced to penury, takes shelter (sometimes with his wife) in a brothel or in similar pleasure resorts.[93] The *viṭas* are counsellors of both the courtesans and their clients and could bring about misunderstandings between them and also reconcile them to each other. The *pīṭhamarda*, on the other hand, was a teacher of the prostitute as also an associate of the *nāgaraka*, the man-about-the-town, who helped his friend achieve his ends.[94] Both, but especially, the *viṭa*, looked after the courtesan's interests where she needed a man to help her. In the *Mṛcchakaṭika* he escorts her in a dark night, instructs her when she goes to seek pleasure, has no illusion about the profession but has respect for her as a person. In the four famous Bhāṇas of the late classical period the *viṭas* are helpers, peace-makers, go-betweens, procurers and counsellors of the partners. Evidently, the courtesan was also helpless against certain situations so that she shared her income with a male go-between for protecting her own interests. This and the services of the *kuṭṭanī* already signify that the courtesan was liable to be exploited, cheated, insulted and physically injured. The *viṭa*, apparently a parasite, gave valuable service to her where her sex and social position rendered her vulnerable.

What was the prostitute's social status? Strangely enough, prostitution is recognised as a profession with laws to regulate it because it served its specific purpose by catering to men's needs of extramarital sexual gratification and also the state's needs by bringing in considerable revenues and secret political information through espionage. As townships sprang up along trade routes and as rich men a long away from home frequented these brothels, these became a regular feature with the chief courtesans, beauty queens, being regarded as ornaments of the town or city, *nagaraśobhinī* or *nagaramaṇḍanā*. Because she was in high demand and because she would fetch a rich revenue if she was accomplished and attractive, the state undertook to supervise her education (with quite a heavy and rigorous syllabus) at its own expense, provided she remitted part of her income to the state. Not only was she obliged to pay revenue to the state, she often undertook some works for public welfare. Thus we read in the *Bṛhatkalpasūtrabhāṣya*, a Jain text, of a picture gallery set up by a courtesan. The Buddhist texts record Āmrapālī as also giving similar services.

Other courtesans fed the hungry during a famine, gave away money, land, and property for the Buddhist cause. Many treated the Buddha and monks to sumptuous feasts. Frequently, when the courtesans amassed wealth they set up works of public utility: they sank wells, constructed bridges, temple gardens, *caityas* (sacred mounds), donated money to the needy, gave gifts, *and* generally served the community through such works for public utility. yet we read in the *Mahābhārata* that the prostitutes' quarters should be situated in the south because that is the direction of Yama, the god of death. In the *Mānasollāsa*, a medieval text, we read that houses of ill-fame should be situated on the outskirts of the town. But in Greece the courtesans had a different status; one of the most beautiful sections of any Grecian city was where the richest of the courtesans built their houses. The lyric poem *Pavanadūta* of Dhoyī describing the temple prostitutes says that it seemed that Lakṣmī, the goddess of beauty has herself descended there. Kalhaṇa in his *Rājataraṅgiṇī* mentions an extremely qualified *devadāsī* by the name of Kamalā. In some *Purāṇas* we read of the *anaṅgavrata,* a rite which signified temple prostitution.[95] The *Kāmasūtra* lays down that she should always be decked out with jewellery and without being fully visible should streetwalk discreetly 'because she is a commodity'.[96] The same text defines her conduct: 'without really getting attached to her client she should act as if she were; she should submit to her cruel and mendacious mother and if the mother is not there she should submit to the matron of the house. She has the right of use of her ornaments, food and drinks, garlands, perfumes, etc.'[97] 'She should pretend the loss of her own and her client's ornaments, should engage in a mock quarrel with her mother on the subject of excessive expenses and having to incur debts, should make the client pay her bills, should pretend to be obliged to sell her ornaments in order to make both ends meet, should report about her rivals. 'greater income, etc. etc.'[98] If this long list of deceptions is any index of how society expected her to conduct herself in her profession, one fails to understand the bitter censure society meted out to her when she complied. The *Rājataraṅgiṇī*, a poetical chronicle of Kashmir, records that King Lalitāpīḍa gave out that anyone proficient in courtesan lore and clever at jokes would become his friend. Later literature has no inhibition in mentioning or describing courtesans attached to the palace, to the manor houses of the nobility, especially of merchants, and to temples as well as those who lived in brothels. Such descriptions in Kālidāsa, Bhāravi, Daṇḍin, Bhaṭṭi, Subandhu, Bāṇabhaṭṭa, Śrīharṣa (*Naiṣadhacarita*) are totally uninhibited and done with great gusto and skill. Yet other didactic texts are full of imprecations against prostitutes. The *Viṣṇu Saṃhitā* lays down that he who associates with a courtesan should perform the *prājāpatya* penance.[99] The vituperation against prostitutes begins in the didactic sections of the *Mahābhārata*, the *Dharmasūtras* (many of which belong to the age of the Brahmanical interpolation of the *Mahābhārata*), and continue through the *Purāṇas* and *Smṛti* texts. Such texts choose to ignore the fact that courtesans are not born but made; they can only exist as long as society has a demand for them. Therefore, since a section of society calls courtesans into being to cater to their need, the condemnation should be shared by that section as well. But apart from mild half-hearted penalties—more in the nature of not-too-obvious strictures and threats of notional ostracism—the male clients go morally scot-free.

This double standard is not an isolated phenomenon, it is the product of a rooted ambivalence in society's consciousness. Since the designation of *gaṇikā* was the highest and had to be earned through beauty, charm and accomplishments,[100] it signified the highest social class among prostitutes. Kauṭilya says that the superintendent of prostitutes conferred the title of *gaṇikā* to the pretty, young and cultured hetaira;[101] she drew 1000 *paṇas* from the state presumably for her establishment, and her teachers in the various arts were also paid by the state. She had a measure of social security in the sense that those who harmed her physically, financially and socially were liable to be punished heavily by the state. Needless to say, such a coveted position was not accorded to many; only a handful of prostitutes were made *gaṇikās* whose favours were enjoyed by kings, princes and the richest of the merchants. It can be guessed that pretty young women with real cultivated taste and accomplishments flocked to well-governed towns and cities where they could not be molested by rakes and ruffians with impunity and where trade and commerce thrived. Even in such townships as well as in prosperous villages women with less beauty and culture and presumably older in age plied their trade as *rūpājīvās* and *veśyās* depending on their age, accomplishments and charm. The very name of the *rūpājīvā* clearly distinguishes her from the *gaṇikā,* for, while the latter was an educated person the *rūpājīvā* had only her beauty as her stock-in-trade. The veśyā may have lacked even that and relied on her clothes and jewellery (veśa) for attracting customers. The *avaruddhā* as we have seen was the mistress of an individual in the role of a concubine; the relationship was temporary but while it lasted, society respected its rights. The *pumścalī vāravilāsiṇī, svairiṇī, Kulaṭā*, etc. were free agents who were out to turn whatever charm they had to the best financial capital. Sometimes they employed middlemen to attract custom and sometimes they hawked themselves. From all accounts they had less to offer and, therefore, earned much less. The *devadāsīs* were a class by themselves who, because they were attached to institutions (i.e., temples) governed directly or indirectly by the state, enjoyed some degree of protection.

It is common knowledge that in most centres of ancient urban civilisation temple prostitution was a common feature. Whether in ancient Greece, Rome, Egypt, Babylon in temples of Baal and Astarte, or in Chaldea, Phoenicia or India and in the Far East, it flourished under the dual patronage of the state and the church. Temple priests frequently got paid from the royal treasury, the temple prostitute was an extra allowance to them. Of course, the financial and social status of the temple varied from place to place. City temples enjoying royal patronage were entirely different from poor village temples subsisting on local contributions. Hence the status and prosperity of the temple prostitutes too differed according to the kind of patronage the temple received.

Just what the social background of these unfortunate girls was is far from clear. Apart from the parents making a devotional gift of their daughters to the temple,[102] there must have been the daughters of *devadāsīs*, or distress sales of girls to the temple, recruitment of local beauties under moral pressure, or girls abducted from helpless parents, girls won as war booty or recruited through superstitious practices. However they came in, it is quite clear that it was an all-India and age-long phenomenon. Even though the Madras Legislative Assembly banned it by a law in 1929, it persisted there and in the rest of India and still persists in many pockets after it was banned all over India by a legislation in 1947. The overt duty of the *devadāsīs* was to dance at the time of the evening worship in the temple, but they were also treated as concubines by the temple priests. Kālidāsa refers to them as *veśyās* and describes them as enjoying the first drops of monsoon rain as a welcome relief to their tired limbs.

Once inside the temple and under the thumb of the priests they became like slaves with no clear definition of their rights and duties. The *Kuṭṭanīmata* does mention payment from temple authorities but this evidently did not mean anything more than subsistence and clothes and ornaments for them as temple dancers. In the *Samayamātṛkā*[103] we hear of grains being given to *devadāsīs* who danced in rotation. In the third century BC in the Jogimara inscription we hear of Devadatta's love for the *devadāsī* Sutanukā. Many other cave inscriptions[104] mention of the music and dance provided by courtesans and *devadāsīs*. Since major treatises are nearly all silent on the duties and rights of the *devadāsīs,* it appears that they were completely at the mercy of the temple priests, a specially privileged section in Indian society who enjoyed immunity from the penal code and were thus free to exploit these girls as they pleased. Evidently, here, too, the more talented beauties coming from the upper rung of society enjoyed somewhat fairer treatment than those born to temple prostitutes or recruited from destitute parents or as rich men's gifts or war booty. But because the masters of these prostitutes, the priests, enjoyed privilege both through their sacerdotal office and through royal patronage, the *devadāsīs*' position was more abject than presumably of those organised in the brothels regarding whose rights and privileges some rules had been clearly enunciated. The very helplessness of the *devadāsīs* must have led to the widespread distribution of the institution and its prolonged continuation in the name of religion. The violent resistance and opposition of the hieratic section, esp. in South India when its abolition was proposed, testifies to the nature and measure of the priests' vested interest in the institution.

What happened to the *devadāsī* when she grew old? Presumably not all of them enjoyed royal patronage. Those who did were employed in the state textile factory as we find in the solitary mention of the *devadāsī* in Kauṭilya.[105] Dancing was the only art she had learned and she could not practice it in old age, so that if she was one of those who did not enjoy royal care she would be reduced to destitution. Her profession prevented her from having a family and her long stay in the temple isolated her from society; therefore, even if she worked in a textile factory for a time she would face penury in real old age when both the temple and the community cast her off as wholly redundant. Thus at the end of a long career of double exploitation—as a temple dancer and as the priests' concubine—she faced complete destitution, for neither the state nor the temple had any obligation to look after her.

It is both rewarding and revealing to turn the pages of dictionaries on the subject of prostitution. Apart from older, that is, Vedic and later Vedic terms like *agrū, hasrā, aliskadvarī,* and *vṛṣalī*, each of which emphasised one aspect of the public women, we have a host of later synonyms which varied with time and place. The standard Sanskrit lexicon *Amarakoṣa* says that *veśyā, varastrī, gaṇikā* and *rūpājīvā* are synonyms. Jaṭādhara adds *Kṣudrā* and *śālabhañjikā*; the *Sabdarātnabalī* has a few more entries: *jharjharā, śulā, vāravilāsinī vāravanī, bhaṇḍahāsinī*, while the *Śabdamālā* adds *lañjikā, vandhurā, kuntā, kāmarekhā* and *varvaṭī.* The standard dictionary of Hemacandra has *sādhāraṇastrī, paṇyāṅganā, bhuñjikā* and *vāravadhū* to which the *Rājanirghanṭa* (lexicon) adds *bhogyā* and *smaravīthikā*. Even a cursory glance at these names tells us that while some signify the profession itself, others (like *kṣudrā, śūlā, kuntā, bhaṇḍahāsinī, bhuñjikā, bhogyā* or *smaravīthikā*) express society's sneer and contempt.

In the *Brahmavaivarta Purāṇa* we read that a woman loyal to her husband is *ekapatnī* (wife to one), if she goes to another she is a *kulaṭā.*[106] If she goes to three she is a *vṛśalī,* a *pumścalī* with a fourth, a *veśyā* with a fifth and sixth, a *yungī* with a seventh and eighth. Above that she becomes a *mahāveśyā* whom no one of any caste may touch.[107] Although it appears that all except the *mahāveśyā* may be touched that is not true. The *Dharmaśāstras* generally lay down that visiting a prostitute is a crime but since they also prescribe mild expiatory rites, it appears that society did not look upon it as either a heinous crime, or an irremediable sin.

As we have seen, there is an evident ambivalence regarding the profession. The *Samayapradīpa*, a late ritual text mentions the sight of a prostitute as an auspicious sign; a man gains his desire if he sees her on setting out on a journey. Other such items are obviously auspicious—like a cow with its calf, a bull, horse or a chariot, fire with its flame turning to the right, a goddess, a full pitcher, garlands, banners, white rice, etc. The only apparently inauspicious item in the catalogue is the prostitute; yet a sight of her is regarded as a good omen. Similarly, soil from near a prostitute's house is an essential item for fashioning the image of Durgā, the goddess of cardinal importance in Bengal. The mystery is solved when we remember the role of the prostitute in the earlier rituals where she had to copulate with a man or engage in a mock altercation with a neophyte, the *brahmacārin*, in an exchange of obscenities. In all of these instances the same incentive is noticeable, namely fertility. Her very profession involved repeated sexual relations with many men and so potentially symbolised fertility and the power of reproduction. For a community whose prosperity and wealth depended on ensuring fertility of the field and of cattle, she symbolised the fertility principle. Hence her place in rituals. This association of fertility of field and cattle with the sexual act, especially magnified in the prostitute's profession, is not unique to India. In all primitive societies this ritual association can be noticed. And since this has come down from a much older age, society did not dare to ignore it. Such beliefs die hard and in a primarily agricultural country like India the need to ensure fertility was too urgent to disregard. Besides, the unacknowledged awareness that the prostitute offered services indispensable to the society led to this ambivalence.

But apart from this aspect society unambiguously looked down upon the profession. All its efforts at segregation of the rest of the community from contagion through the prostitute's proximity, the rule of allocating an area in the south, Yama's direction, outside the common habitat, for the brothel, the prohibition against eating food offered by her, the rule against touching or associating with her signify this contempt. But this is obviously a later development, for the *Kāmasūtra* describes kings, courtiers, and the mercantile nobility of the cities and towns (and also of villages) as indulging in the company of courtesans. The attitude there is totally uninhibited. The *Arthaśāstra*, too, presupposes the existence of prostitution as an institution and has no value judgement regarding them. Underlying both of these texts is the assumption that this institution has been brought into existence not by the perversity of certain women or by an aberration in any section but by a social need. A society which practically forbade female education and relegated the woman to virtual subordination under the husband and in-laws reduced her to a chattel who could serve and for a time cater to the man's sexual needs but after children started coming and she became sorely taxed in her strenuous household obligations, nursing and bringing up the children, she was no 'fun' any more. Altekar says: 'courtesans had a peculiar position in ancient India. As persons who had sacrificed what was regarded as specially honourable in a woman, they were held in low estimation. But society treated them with a certain amount of consideration as the custodians of fine arts which had ceased to be cultivated elsewhere in society. Men who had a liking or love for music and dancing could not delight in the company of their own wives who ceased to possess these accomplishments from C. 400 BC. Though despised in one sense, courtesans began to be respected for their achievements in fine arts.'[108] Apart from this man must have desired companionship in his intellectual and aesthetic pursuits from men friends as well from women. This entirely normal and healthy desire could in no way be satisfied by the wife who, encumbered with household duties and children, soon lost youth and charm and whose husbands were therefore driven to prostitutes. But evidently not all men did so, and those who did, did it in a surreptitious manner. All that charmed a man in a prostitute was forbidden for the wife, who should be uneducated, demure and plainly dressed except on ritual occasions. She was primarily a house-wife, busy with her chores, children and in-laws which left her little leisure for the cultivation of either her looks, dress or mental faculties. Society expected her to be good, hard working, devoted and obedient. This was bound to make her less attractive to her husband who craved for charm and companionship in a woman. This very need of combining sexual pleasure with intellectual-aesthetic companionship or simply with the charm of a good-looking, youthful person tastefully decked out in clothes, and jewellery attracted men to a prostitute. And repelled them, precisely because she could not be exclusively possessed, for she was enjoyed by many. In a society where women became a personal possession, a woman who could not be possessed individually provoked this ambivalence.

WOMEN AS CHATTEL

Woman has been a chattel in India ever since the later Vedic times when she was included in the list of *dakṣiṇā* along with items like cattle, horses, chariots, etc. Such gifts were given to priests. Evidently they were enjoyed and then sold as slaves or prostitutes. Later in the epics we have references to women as gifts.[109] Heroes are said to be rewarded with hosts of beautiful women in heaven; undoubtedly this is a reflection of earthly prizes given to heroes and eminent men. In classical literature, too, we meet prostitutes as a decoration to courts, as part of the entourage in military and hunting expeditions.[110] Women also came with victories as booty and after serving the victorious generals and eminent military personages they would find their way to brothels. Thus Arjuna brought over the women of the enemy as booty;[111] King Virāṭa also expressed his pleasure at Arjuna's prowess by giving him pretty maidens.[112] In the battlefield Karṇa declared that whoever pointed out Arjuna to him would receive a hundred well-dressed maidens from him.[113] A king who does not give such gifts is branded with the epithet *rājakali* (a *kali*, i.e., evil spirit of a king).[114] At Draupadi's wedding a hundred slave girls in the early bloom of their youth were given away.[115] Krsna entertained guests with pretty maidens.[116] Also at Subhadrā's wedding no less than a thousand girls were offered to guests for enjoyment in the drinking and bathing sports.[117] Yudhiṣṭhira received 10,000 slave girls.[118] King Śaśabindu at his horse sacrifice gave away to priests hundreds of thousands of pretty girls,[119] so did Bhagīratha.[120] We also hear of thousands of beautiful girls as gifts in *śrāddhas*.[121] Instances can be multiplied.[122] We are told that pretty young girls are natural gifts to brahmins[123] and that whoever gives this gift lavishly on this earth receives plentiful fruits in heaven, that is, is rewarded with many nymphs there for his enjoyment.[124] In the *Mahābhārata* and in the *Purāṇas* we have numerous instances where the host entertains his guest by sending his own wife to him at night and/or other pretty women. In the *Sanastujātīya* section of the *Mahābhārata* five marks of true friendship are enumerated; one of these is to share one's wife with a friend. Pretty girls also formed part of the dowry. Two things are clear from these references. First, there must have been an easily available source of pretty young girls, a steady supply for instant enjoyment, or for giving away. One wonders where such girls could be found. Prostitutes, daughters is a ready answer. The Mahābhārata has an episode: King Yayāti's daughter Mādhavī was given to Gālava; the father lent her in lieu of money so that she could be hired out to three kings in turn for a year each. The kings gave Gālava handsome rewards with which he paid his school-leaving fees to his preceptor. Clearly here Mādhavī is a money-earner to her father and the latter satisfies Gālava by prostituting her to three different kings. Apart from this kind of distress sale in times of crisis, women as war-booty was another big source of supply. Wives caught in certain cases of adultery were also driven out; such unwanted women drifted towards the brothel, as also women who could be bought and kept in palaces as occasional gifts. In the royal courts and rich households where many abducted women were kept for service and as status symbol, these proliferated and became yet another source of supply.

The second point that strikes us is that these women were regarded as inanimate objects of enjoyment. They figure in lists of material gifts, sacrificial fees, donations, entertainment, prizes, rewards, and dowry. And after the temporary enjoyment the recipient or donée could not but turn them loose; at least in most cases they did so. Thus there were hosts of women who eventually ended up in the brothel where they catered commercially to men. All along this dismal history we notice that women had very little initiative or choice about their destiny. They were pawned, lost or gained in battles, given as gifts at sacrifices and weddings, were relegated to the position of slaves and chattel in palaces and rich households, sexually enjoyed whenever their owners so desired and discarded when the desire abated.

They got paid only in brothels; in other instances they were only fed, clothed and decked out with jewellery so that their masters would find them attractive. Even in brothels their labour could, and frequently was, exploited, as many rules in the scriptures testify. Vātsyāyana has a long section on how the harlots could play-act, feign, seduce, cheat and deceive their customers with or without the help of middlemen and procuresses. So does Dāmodaragupta teach novices how to make the best use of youth and charm and extort money from customers by hook or by crook. Other texts also teach similar lessons. None of these texts is authored by women. When after being trained in the art of deception, the prostitutes practised these arts, they are given foul names by the entire community. The very nature of the profession entailed a degree of deceit and the entire social set-up and its attitude encouraged it. Instead of accepting responsibility for it and admitting that prostitutes act as men force them to act and that they exist because they render a service that society needs, the entire blame is loaded on the prostitutes themselves. The situation was very different in Greece and Rome as Aristophanes, Menander or Terence's plays testify. Here in India the exploitation is redoubled because male customers frequently sought to cheat prostitutes of their rightful wages as the law books bring out clearly. And on top of this they tried to rob them of their rightful place in society. But when literature does not seek to be respectable but truthful as Kauṭilya and Vātsyāyana's works or the Bhāṇas (which decidedly belong to a lower, less respectable genre), prostitutes come into their own. The customer looks upon them if not with positive respect yet not with contempt and society betrays its awareness of the necessity and significance of their role and profession. But the major, respectable literary tradition is that which reflects the upper class reaction to the institution, a class which is not a bit averse to use their services but is yet too respectable to regard them as human beings. Once this attitude is fostered and becomes prevalent, depriving prostitutes of their fees, manhandling or insulting them is condoned. But this was only true of the common harlot with little charm and no accomplishment. The well-trained and well-preserved beauty, the *gaṇikā*, who belonged to the upper class enjoyed the patronage of royalty or nobility and was comparatively secure and comfortable.

Since the prostitute's labour was regarded as a necessary evil—the evil being much more magnified than the necessity—male society seemed to bear her a grudge born of its fundamental ambivalence and this seems to have given it the right to exploit the victim, the common prostitute.

Another proof of the double standard is that although associating with prostitutes or accepting their food was punishable, there is no rule against accepting benefits from them. Thus Ardhakaśī gave away her vast wealth to various charitable institutions, and laid a vast sum at the Buddha's feet. In the Jain text *Bṛhatkalpasūtrabhāṣya*[125] we hear of many good and generous courtesans. One ran a picture gallery (as did Amrapālī in Buddhist literature), others gave vast sums to the poor and to the order. 'When the courtesans grew rich they often set up works of public utility such as wells, temples, tanks, gardens, groves, bridges, *chaityas* and provided perfumes and rice.'[126] Records in the Tiruvarriyur temple show that the *devadāsīs* there made rich endowments. Evidently such works of public utility were enjoyed by all, that is, by the community for whom it was a sin to touch a prostitute or to eat her food. Thus society had no hesitation in using the fruits of her labour while looking down upon her. Presumably, by enjoying such charitable institutions set up by her, society was kindly deigning to offer her an opportunity to expiate for the sins of her profession, a profession which could not flourish without the patronage of a section of the male population. This section was punished only notionally.[127]

Society thus created situations in which many women were deprived of the right to remain respectable and be regarded so, so that such women were pushed to this profession. And they could live as prostitutes because a steady supply of male customers was ensured. These men found their wives dull as companions and so flocked to the prostitutes. In return society ostracised the prostitutes, but not their customers. Whether in the palace, or in the temples or in brothels they served men with an uncertainty regarding payment and the fear of molestation, mutilation, torture and death. They had scant provision for old age and infirmity. Their bodies, accomplishments, and gifts and charily were enjoyed by the community which otherwise treated them as untouchables and showered curses and imprecation on the profession itself, as if prostitutes alone could make prostitution viable as a profession. Penalty for maltreatment or deceit is mentioned, but one wonders how few wronged prostitutes could actually sue the state for their flouted rights and dues. Such was the precarious existence of prostitutes who could, with a few exceptions of really upper class or outstanding individuals, be exploited by men at will and with impunity.

NOTES

1. Cf. the sacrificer's wife being publicly questioned by the officiating priest regarding her secret lovers at the Varuṇapraghāsa sacrifice: 'with whom (plural) hast thou had secret affairs?' But though she confessed we hear of no penalty for her transgression.
2. Cf. the terms *svatantrā*, independent, or *svādhīnayauvanā*, she who can freely enjoy her youth, as synonyms for the prostitute. Scriptures lay down that women are wards of their fathers in childhood, of their husbands in youth and of sons at old age.
3. A woman with whom men lake turns (*vāra*), that is, one who can be possessed or enjoyed by different men in turns.
4. Described in the Mauṣalaparvan.
5. Eastern Punjab and western U.P.
6. VIII: 27, 30, 57–59.
7. ch. 70.
8. *Samayamātṛkā* III: 18.
9. III: 5: 14–26.
10. *Viṣṇupurāṇa*, ch. 37; *Yājñavalkya Smṛti* 240.
11. Megasthenes also bears this out in his account.
12. Women of the vanquished side.
13. *Arthaśāstra* II: 27, X: 1–3.
14. *Padma-Purāṇa,* Sṛṣṭikhaṇḍa 52: 97.
15. Cf. the *Meghadūta,* verse 35.
16. IV: 19, 9: 16, 19, 30.
17. I: 167, 4; II: 13, 12, 15, 17.
18. XV: e; Also the *Pañcaviṃśa Brāhmaṇa* VIII: 1: 10: Kauṣītaki Br. XXVII: 1; *Lāṭyāyana Srautasūtra* IV: 3: 11; *Vājasaneyī Saṃhitā* XXX: 22.
19. XIV: 1: 36; XX: 136: 5 Also *Aitareya Brāhmaṇa* 1: 27: 2.
20. III: 4: 11: I.
21. *Vāja, Sam.* XXX: 12, *Tait, Br.* III: 4: 7: 1.
22. *Vāja Sam.* XXX: 12: *Tait Br.* III: 4: 7.
23. *Jaim. Br.* II: 404 ff, *Kat. Gr. S.* XII: 3: 6.
24. I: 43.
25. *Vinaya Piṭaka* III: 138.
26. Cf. the English synonyms: courtesan, prostitute, harlot, strumpet, hetaira, whore, trollop, slut etc, bearing different connotations and also signifying the social strata to which they belong.
27. *Artha*: V: 2.
28. *Ibid.*, I; 20.
29. *Ibid.*, III: 20.
30. *Ibid.*, VIII: 17.
31. *Kāmasūtra* VI: 6: 54.
32. *Arthasastra* II: 27; *Jātakas* mention the *vannadāsī* in II: 380; III: 59–63, 69–72; 475: 8.
33. *Jātaka* III: 59–63.
34. R. Shamasastry (ed.): *Kauṭilya's Arthaśāstra*, Mysore, 1st edn., 1915, 6th edn. 1960, section on the *gaṇikādhyakṣa*, superintendent of prostitutes.
35. *Bṛhatkalpasūtrabhāṣya*, (ed.) by Punyavijayaji, Bhavnayar, 1933–38. Kauṭilya includes reading and writing, Vātsyāyana mentions reading and composing poems, and deciphering code words in her syllabus.
36. *Manusaṃhitā* II: 67.
37. Probably to the first century AD.
38. From Sanskrit word *bhṛti*, fees.
39. Sanskrit *parivyayam*, expenses.

40. Cf. *Diyāvadāna* ed. by P.L. Vaidya, p. 218.
41. *Jñātadharmakathā* I.
42. Moti Chandra: *The World of Courtesans*, Vikash, 1973, p. 48.
43. *Arthaśāstra* IV: 12.
44. *Yājñavalkyasaṃhitā* II: 295.
45. *Kāmasūtra* VI: 1: 10, 12.
46. *Ibid* VI: 5: 1–6.
47. *Ibid* VI: 6: 31.
48. *Ibid* VI: 3: 28–31.
49. *Arthaśāstra* IV: 13.
50. V: 195: 18–19.
51. V: 15: 51–58.
52. III: 238 ff.
53. IV: 64: 24–29.
54. XII: 88: 14, 15; XIII: 125: 9 et al.
55. *Mahābhārata* XIV: 85: 18.
56. *Ibid* XIV: 80: 32.
57. *Ibid* VII: 65: 6.
58. *Ibid* VII: 60: 1,2, XII: 29: 65.
59. *Ibid* XV: 14: 4: 39: 20: XVII: 1: 4, XVIII: 6: 12, 13.
60. *Mahābhārata* III: 186–87, VIII: 49: 76–78, XII: 64: 17; 30; XII: 96: 18, 19, 83, 85–86, 88; 106: 6ff. Also in the *Rāmāyaṇa* II: 71: 22, 25, 26; VV: 20: 13.
61. XVI: 36, 48.
62. VII: 50.
63. IX: 51.
64. XVIII: 60, 61.
65. IV: 34: 17, 18.
66. XI: 30–35.
67. *Mahābhārata I*: 115; 39.
68. I: 4: 34–41.
69. I: 4: 42.
70. I: 4: 49.
71. The *synonyms vārāṅganā, vāravilāsinī, vārastrī, vāramukhyā*, etc., for the prostitute: the word vāra, means 'turn'. This was true of the socially lower class of prostitutes.
72. Cf. the important drama *Mṛcchakaṭika* where the heroine is a beautiful courtesan, accomplished in the various arts; she is described as 'an ornament to the city'.
73. Rahula Sankrityayana's Hindi tr., Benares 1936, pp. 73–88.
74. By the same translator, Benares 1964, pp. 321–325.
75. 47: 20: 23.
76. Sacred Books of the East, Vol, XVII, pp. 106–7, 171–72.
77. *Dhammapada* commentary, Pali Text socy. London, 1906–14, pp. 308–9.
78. *Vinayapiṭaka*: Sacred Books of the East, Vol. XX. pp. 360–61.
79. *Cf. Samayamātṛkā* VIII: 102, 103, 112, *Kuṭṭanīmata* 532. *Śārṅgadharapaddhati*, 4052.
80. *Samayamātṛkā* II: 28–80.
81. III: 33.
82. *Kāmasūtra* VII: 23, 24.
83. *Yājñavalkya Smṛti* II: 290, *Narada*. 78, 79.
84. *Kāmasūtra* I: 62–65.
85. II: 290.
86. Esp. in Aśvaghoṣ a and Śūdraka's dramas.

87. All this and much more are taught in the *Kuṭṭanīmata* of Dāmodaragupta and also in the *Deśopadeśa* IV: 12, 19, 30, 36.
88. *Samayamātṛkā* I: 40, 45. *Kāmasūtra* VII: I: 13–17; See also *Daśarūpaka* II: 34.
89. II: 4: 48.
90. II: 293.
91. Gautama, *Dharmasūtra* XXII: 2.
92. IX: 259–60.
93. *Kāmasūtra* I: 4: 5.
94. *Daśarūpaka* II: 8.
95. Cf. *Viṣṇupurāṇa*, ch. 70.
96. VI: 1: 4.
97. A woman in any case, like a child or a slave, was not allowed to own property. *Mahābhārata* I: 82; 22, II: 71: 1; V: 33: 64.
98. VI: 2; 3–23.
99. 103: 4; also in *Atri Saṃhitā* 267 *Saṃvarta S.* 161: *Parāśara* S. 10: 15, *et al.*
100. *Kāmasūtra* I: 3: 20.
101. *Arthaśāstra* II: 27.
102. As a mark of gratitude fo divine favours received or as a gift given in faith for favours expected from the temple deity.
103. Ch. VIII.
104. Like those at Nasik, Kuda, Mahada, Junagad sitabenga, Ratnagiri.
105. *Arthaśāstra* II: 23.
106. The term may have a secondary reference to tarnishing the family's (kula) prestige. However, the etymology is not clear.
107. Prakṛtikhaṇda, ch. XXVI & XXVII.
108. *The Position of Woman in Hindu Civilization*. Motilal Banarasidas, 1st edn. 1938, pp. 181–82.
109. Cf. *Rāmāyana* II: 11, 22, 25, 26; IV: 20: 13: 24: 34, *Mahābhārata* III: 186: 7; VIII: 49: 76–78; XII: 98: 46, XIII; 96:18: 19, 82.
110. Cf. *Kumārasambhava* XVI: 36, 48; *Raghuvamsa* VII: 50.
111. *Mahābhārata* III: 8: 27.
112. *Ibid*, IV: 34: 5.
113. *Ibid*, VIII: 38: 4ff.
114. *Ibid*, XII: 12: 366.
115. *Ibid*, I: 198: 16.
116. *Ibid*, IV: 72: 16.
117. *Ibid*, I: 221: 49, 50.
118. *Ibid*, II: 51: 8, 9; 52: 11, 29.
119. *Ibid*, VII: 65 6.
120. *Ibid*, VII: 60: 1, 2, XII: 29: 65.
121. *Ibid*, XV: 11: 4; 39: 20; XVII: 1: XVIII: 6; 12, 13.
122. Cf. Sagara's gifts Brahmins: Vainya's to the sage Atri, etc.
123. *Op. cit.*, III: 315: 2, 6; 233; IV: 18 21; XII: 68: 33, 171: 5, 173: 16ff.
124. *Op. cit.*, XIII: 15: 2.
125. Ed. Punyavijayaji, Bhavnagar, 1933–38.
126. Moti Chandra: *The World of Courtesans*. Vikash, 1973, 9.72.
127. The *prājāpatya* expiatory rite was seldom honoured by actual performance as is borne out by a vast amount of literature.

About the Editor and Contributors

EDITOR

Vijaya Ramaswamy is Professor and Chairperson, Centre for Historical Studies, Jawaharlal Nehru University. She is an alumni of the School of Oriental and African Studies, University of London, and was a Fulbright Fellow at the University of California, Berkeley, California, in 1988–1989. She was a teacher-fellow on an Indo-Canadian Fellowship at York University, Ontario, Canada, in 1998. She was also a Fellow at the Indian Institute of Advanced Study between 1992 and 1995. She was also a Senior Fellow at the Nehru Memorial Museum and Library, Teen Murti House, New Delhi from 2012 to 2014.

Vijaya Ramaswamy is the author of 10 books amongst which the best known are: *Textiles and Weavers in Medieval South India* (1985, 2nd ed. 2006), *Divinity and Deviance: Women in Virasaivism* (1996); *Walking Naked: Women, Society, Spirituality in South India* (1997, 2007), *Historical Dictionary of the Tamils* (2007), *Song of the Loom* (2013) and *Migrations in Medieval and Early Colonial India* (2016). Vijaya has been the President of the Medieval India Section of the 63rd Indian History Congress Session at Mysore, 2003. She also won the 'Professor Hiralal Gupta Research Award' for the Best Book by a Woman Historian for the years 1996–2001, Indian History Congress, 60th Session, Bhopal, 2001.

CONTRIBUTORS

Aparna Basu, PhD (Cantab), was Professor of History, University of Delhi. She is the UGC Convenor of the national subject panel on History and Archaeology. She is also the Chairperson of the Gandhi Museum Board. She is the author of several books including *Growth of Education and Political Development in India Women's Struggle: A History of All India Women's Conference, Rebel with a Cause: Biography of Mridula Srabhai, From Independence to Freedom: Women and Fifty Years of India's independence* and *A History of Delhi University* on the occasion of its Platinum Jubilee. She is on the Editorial Advisory Board of *Gender and History, Indian Economic and Social History Review, Indian Journal of Gender Studies* and *Women's History*.

Uma Chakravarti is a feminist historian who taught at Miranda House, University College for Women, Delhi, from 1966 to 1998. She writes on Buddhism, early Indian social history and on contemporary issues. She is the author of *Social Dimensions of Early Buddhism* (1987); *Rewriting History: The Life and Times of Pandita Ramabai* (1998); *Gendering Caste through a Feminist Lens* (2002); and *Everyday Lives, Everyday Histories: Beyond the Kings and Brahmanas of Ancient India* (2006). She has also co-authored *Delhi Riots: Three Days in the Life of a Nation* (1987); *Shadow Lives: Writings on Widowhood* (2006) and *From Myths to Markets: Essays on Gender* (1999).

Upasana Dhankhar has been engaged in understanding the nuances of ancient Indian legal systems within the specific context of gender studies. She is also researching on the social history of Early India and has been writing on various socio-jurisprudential questions pertaining to socio-economic, legal and gender history. She has been teaching undergraduate students since 2011. Presently, she is teaching at Department of History, Miranda House (University of Delhi).

Kavita Gaur is presently an Assistant Professor in Department of History at Shyama Prasad Mukherji College, University of Delhi. She has received her doctorate degree on the following topic—Understanding the Household: Norms and Everyday Lives in Textual Traditions (c. 3rd century BCE to 5th century CE) from Jawaharlal Nehru University. Her research interest includes social history, history of caste and class, gender relations, marriage practices, sexuality and conjugal relations in early India.

Shireen Moosvi had been Professor and Dean at the Centre for Advanced Studies in History, Aligarh Muslim University. Apart from holding a PhD in Medieval Indian History, she also has an MSc in Math and is known for her application of the statistical method to historical data. She is Secretary of the Aligarh Historians Society and is currently the National Fellow of The Indian Council of Historical Research. She has authored many books and innumerable articles. Her books include *People, Taxation and Trade in Mughal India*, Oxford University Press, 2008, *Economy of the Mughal Empire—A Statistical Study*, Oxford University Press, 1987 and *Episodes in the Life of Akbar* published by the National Book Trust.

Kanakalatha Mukund is an economic historian who is now retired from the Centre for Economic and Social Studies, Hyderabad. She is the author of four books and many research papers and reports. Her main interests are trade and merchants in early colonial south India, textiles and handloom weaving. She has also worked on women's traditional property rights.

Leslie Orr joined the Department of Religion at Concordia in Canada in 1991. Her research interests include the religious and social history of medieval Tamil Nadu; women in precolonial South Asia; devadasis; temple architecture, iconography and epigraphy. Her current research project is on 'Renovation, replication, recovery, and revival: Building temples and building histories in South India'. She is the author of the book *Donors, Devotees and Daughters of God: Temple Women in Medieval Tamilnadu* (NY: Oxford University Press, 2000) and co-editor with A. Luithle-Hardenberg and J. Cort of *Co-operation, Contribution* *and Contestation: The Jaina community, British Rule and Occidental Scholarship from the 18th to early 20th century* (Berlin: EB Verlag, forthcoming).

A. Padma has done post-graduation in Ancient Indian History, Culture and Archaeology from Osmania University. Her book *Socio-cultural World of Women in Medieval Andhra* was published in 2000. Additionally she brought out another book, *Women in Medieval Times (11th to 14th Centuries A.D.)*. Padma joined in Mahila Samakhya programme of GoI (Ministry of HRD) and worked as Coordinator, Resource Centre. Empowerment of Women through Education, capacity building, advocacy and implementation of innovative initiatives for mainstreaming gender in development is the principal objective of the programme.

Shalini Shah teaches in the department of history, University of Delhi. She has authored *The Making of Womanhood: Gender Relations in the Mahabharata* (1995; second revised edition 2012), *Mahabharata: A Book of Quotes* (2014), and *Love, Eroticism and Female Sexuality in Classical Sanskrit Literature: 7th–13th Centuries* (2009). She has published widely on gender issues in prestigious journals.

Jaya Tyagi is Professor of Ancient Indian History in Delhi University. Her areas of specialisation are: Social History, Household and Society, Religion and Its Social Context and Gender. Her major publications are: *Contestation and Compliance: Retrieving Women's agency from Puranic Traditions*, 2014, monograph published by Oxford University Press and *Engendering the Early Indian Household, Brahmanical Precepts in the Gṛhyasūtras*, 2008, published by Orient Longman Publishers.

Anna Varghese has done her PhD on 'Temple Functionaries in Medieval Kerala: A Study of Their Evolution from the Sixth to the Sixteenth Centuries'. She has won the Award for the best essay twice from the Indian History Congress for her contribution on temple women of Kerala and on the service groups in Medieval Kerala. She is currently Senior PGT teacher at the Carmel convent, Delhi.

BRIEF PROFILES OF THE PIONEERING SCHOLARS AND CONTRIBUTORS WHO ARE NO MORE

Anant Sadashiv Altekar (1898–1960)
He was a prolific scholar, a historian, archaeologist, and numismatist from Maharashtra, India. He was the Professor and Head of the Department of Ancient Indian History and Culture at Banaras Hindu University in Varanasi, India, and later the director of the Kashi Prasad Jayaswal Research Institute and Professor of Ancient Indian History and Culture at the University of Patna. Though he has written on varied range of issues, his book *The Position of Women in Hindu Civilization from Prehistoric Times to the Present Day* (1938) is considered as the first historical survey of the status of women in India.

Sukumari Bhattacharji (12 July 1921–30 May 2014)
Primarily a Sanskritist and Indologist, she began her career as a lecturer in English at Lady Brabourne College in Kolkata. She joined Jadavpur University's Comparative Literature department in 1957 and later shifted to the Sanskrit department. Professor Bhattacharji was known for her work on diverse range of issues related to Sanskrit language and literature, comparative analysis of country's mythology from Vedas to Puranas, study and analysis of various Vedas, and women's role in the family as defined in the ancient Indian texts to modern-day prose. Her pioneering work includes *Women and Society in Ancient India* which highlights women's relationship with society. Professor Tanika Sarkar, the celebrated feminist historian who retired as Professor of Modern Indian History from Jawaharlal Nehru University is her daughter.

N. N. Bhattacharyya
Narendra Nath Bhattacharyya taught religious and social history in the department of Ancient Indian History and Culture at Calcutta University. He was a prolific author. Some of his best publications include *Buddhism in the History of Indian Ideas* which looked at Buddhism as a part of the stream of Indian intellectual history. His *Encyclopaedia of Ancient Indian Culture* attempts a panoramic survey of aspect of art and material culture. His books *History of Tantric Religion* and *The Indian Mother Goddess* are both pioneering contributions in the domain of religious studies.

I. B. Horner (30 March 1896–25 April 1981)
She was an English Indologist and a leading scholar of Pali literature. In 1930, she published her first book, *Women under Primitive Buddhism*. In 1933, she edited her first volume of Pali text, the third volume of the *Papancasudani* (Majjhima Nikaya commentary). In 1934, Horner was awarded the title of an M.A. from Cambridge. From 1939 to 1949, she served on Cambridge's Governing Body.

M. A. Indra
Indra is known for her book *Legal Rights of Women in Ancient India.*

Julia Leslie (23 January 1948–24 September 2004)
She obtained an Oxford MPhil in Classical Indian Religions and the Oxford DPhil thesis which later on emerged as her celebrated monograph titled *The Perfect Wife: The Orthodox Hindu Woman according to the Stridharmapaddhati of Tryambakayajvan* (1989). Her famous edited work included *Roles and Rituals for Women* (1991) which provides an insight to normative images of an ideal woman in textual sources.